OXFORD WORLD'S CLASSICS

ROMAN LIVES

PLUTARCH was born about AD 45, and lived most of his life in the small town of Chaeronea in central Greece, dying some time after 120. In the first decades of the second century AD, when he did much of his writing, the Roman Empire was in its most prosperous and peaceful period. Plutarch wrote a large number of dialogues, treatises, and essays covering diverse subjects, such as the oracle at Delphi, vegetarianism, and the nature of love, which are loosely classified as his *Moralia* or *Moral Essays*. Alongside these essays, Plutarch created a collection of 46 biographies of ancient Greek and Roman statesmen, arranged in pairs ('parallel'), a Roman matching a Greek. These *Parallel Lives* were written when he was at the height of his powers, and are his major and enduring achievement. Drawing upon earlier histories, anecdotes, inscriptions, and his own researches and broad acquaintance, he shaped masterful portraits of the most famous figures of the classical world. The value of the *Lives* as a historical source, questioned in the nineteenth century, has been reaffirmed by recent scholarship.

ROBIN WATERFIELD was born in 1952. After graduating from Manchester University, he went on to research ancient Greek philosophy at King's College, Cambridge. He has been a university lecturer (at Newcastle upon Tyne and St Andrews), and an editor and publisher. Currently, however, he is a self-employed consultant editor and writer, whose books range from philosophy to children's fiction. He has previously translated, for Oxford World's Classics, Plato's *Republic*, *Symposium*, and *Gorgias*, Aristotle's *Physics*, Herodotus' *Histories*, and Plutarch's *Greek Lives*.

PHILIP A. STADTER, Falk Professor in the Humanities at the University of North Carolina at Chapel Hill, is the author of *A Commentary on Plutarch's Pericles* (Chapel Hill, 1989) and editor of *Plutarch and the Historical Tradition* (London, 1992). He has written *The Public Library of Renaissance Florence: Niccolò Niccoli, Cosimo de' Medici and the Library of San Marco* (Padua, 1972, with B. L. Ullman) and *Arrian of Nicomedia* (Chapel Hill, 1980), as well as numerous articles and reviews on Plutarch and other ancient historians, including Herodotus, Thucydides, Xenophon, and Arrian.

OXFORD WORLD'S CLASSICS

For over 100 years Oxford World's Classics have brought readers closer to the world's great literature. Now with over 700 titles—from the 4,000-year-old myths of Mesopotamia to the twentieth century's greatest novels—the series makes available lesser-known as well as celebrated writing.

The pocket-sized hardbacks of the early years contained introductions by Virginia Woolf, T. S. Eliot, Graham Greene, and other literary figures which enriched the experience of reading. Today the series is recognized for its fine scholarship and reliability in texts that span world literature, drama and poetry, religion, philosophy and politics. Each edition includes perceptive commentary and essential background information to meet the changing needs of readers.

OXFORD WORLD'S CLASSICS

PLUTARCH

Roman Lives

A selection of eight Roman Lives

Translated by
ROBIN WATERFIELD

With Introductions and Notes by
PHILIP A. STADTER

OXFORD
UNIVERSITY PRESS

Great Clarendon Street, Oxford OX2 6DP

Oxford University Press is a department of the University of Oxford.
It furthers the University's objective of excellence in research, scholarship,
and education by publishing worldwide in

Oxford New York

Athens Auckland Bangkok Bogotá Buenos Aires Calcutta
Cape Town Chennai Dar es Salaam Delhi Florence Hong Kong Istanbul
Karachi Kuala Lumpur Madrid Melbourne Mexico City Mumbai
Nairobi Paris São Paulo Singapore Taipei Tokyo Toronto Warsaw

with associated companies in Berlin Ibadan

Oxford is a registered trade mark of Oxford University Press
in the UK and in certain other countries

Published in the United States
by Oxford University Press Inc., New York

First published as an Oxford World's Classics paperback 1999

British Library Cataloguing in Publication Data
Data available

Library of Congress Cataloging in Publication Data
Data available

ISBN-13: 978-0-19-282502-5

13

Typeset by RefineCatch Limited, Bungay, Suffolk
Printed in Great Britain by
Clays Ltd, St Ives plc

For Henryk and Juanita

CONTENTS

General Introduction ix
Translator's Note xxix
Select Bibliography xxx
Chronology xxxiii
Maps xxxv

ROMAN LIVES 1
Cato the Elder 3
Aemilius Paullus 36
Tiberius and Gaius Gracchus 77
Marius 116
Sulla 169
Pompey 216
Caesar 297
Antony 360

Roman Money and Measures 431
Special Terms 432
Note on Roman Names 434
Explanatory Notes 435
Textual Notes 533
Index of Literary and Historical Sources Cited by Plutarch 535
Index of Proper Names 537

GENERAL INTRODUCTION

Of all the ancient writers, Plutarch is in many ways the most accessible. Readers as diverse as Beethoven, Rousseau, and Harry Truman have admired the vividness of his narrative and the immediacy of his anecdotes in the *Parallel Lives*. When he wrote in the first decades of thc second century AD, the Roman empire was in its most prosperous and peaceful period. While the emperor Trajan drove back the barbarian tribes of eastern Europe and the Parthians in Asia, expanding the empire to its greatest extent, Plutarch and his friends in Athens, Corinth, and his home town of Chaeronea met, dined, discussed philosophy, and considered the lessons of history. Yet the edge of chaos was not far off. Plutarch was about 23 in 68, when insurrection and civil war ended the reign of Nero: three emperors whirled on and off stage in one year before Vespasian established himself upon the throne. Plutarch later toured the battlefield of Bedriacum in northern Italy with a Roman friend who had fought there, and was told of piles of corpses higher than the tops of the eagle standards: in civil wars no prisoners are taken (*Otho* 14). Some twenty years later, the emperor Domitian became afraid that philosophers teaching in Rome might encourage tyrannicides, and expelled them all from the city. Plutarch may well have been among their number. Domitian raged against senators, authors, and others who might oppose him, until he was assassinated in 96. The short reign of Nerva which followed prepared for the twenty-year rule of Trajan (98–118).

In this time of recently acquired and still insecure serenity Plutarch lived in Chaeronea and Athens (of which he was also a citizen), teaching philosophy to a small group of young men and writing an enormous volume of work, of which we possess perhaps half. His family wealth and education set him among the élite of Greece, and he regularly entertained powerful and cultured friends, both Greeks and Romans. Since his youth he had served on commissions to meet with the Roman governor, and he was on good terms with Romans of the highest rank. His culture and heritage was fully and proudly Greek, but he like other members of his class accepted the Roman imperial system and worked within it. The nearby sanctuary of Apollo at Delphi, of which he was priest for many years, gave him another occasion to meet important visitors, as well as to investigate both historical and theological questions tied to this venerable site. His cosmopolitan interests did not stop him from serving even in small ways at Chaeronea: he mentions supervising stones and mortar being transported. Living in a small town, which lacked the books and learned discussion which could be found in a large city, he chose 'to cling to his town, lest it become smaller' (*Dem.* 2).

The Parallel Lives*: Scope and Purpose*

His major work, a series of parallel biographies which gradually grew to 48, of which we possess 46,[1] probably was begun early in the reign of Trajan, and continued until Plutarch's death *c.*120–5.[2] Prior to the biographies, and continuing alongside them, Plutarch wrote a large number of short essays and some larger collections, which we now subsume under the title of *Moralia*, or *Moral Essays*. The title is indeed appropriate to some, such as *Control of Anger*, *Quiet of Mind*, *Brotherly Love*, and *Talkativeness*, which present philosophical and ethical truths in a charming and thoughtful format.[3] Others explore religious and theological topics dear to the author: several 'Pythian' dialogues on the sanctuary at Delphi and its oracles, and others on *Superstition*, *Isis and Osiris*, the *Face in the Moon*, and *Socrates' Sign*. A third category encompasses contemporary politics and the role of the philosopher in them. Most interesting of these is the *Advice on Public Life*, addressed to a young aristocrat of Sardis who wished to play a major role in the life of his city, and perhaps beyond. The nine books of *Table Talk* show the philosopher chatting with his friends at dinner, on topics ranging from the effect of old age on sight to the

[1] The first two Lives, *Scipio* and *Epaminondas*, have been lost. Four other extant Lives do not belong to the *Parallel Lives*: *Galba* and *Otho*, part of a series of Lives of the emperors, and *Aratus* and *Artaxerxes*, were written independently, as were other lost Lives.

[2] Cf. C. P. Jones, 'Towards a Chronology of Plutarch's Works', *Journal of Roman Studies*, 56 (1966), 61–74, repr. in B. Scardigli (ed.), *Essays on Plutarch's Lives* (Oxford: Clarendon Press, 1995), 95–123.

[3] I use the English titles given by D. A. Russell in his listing of the *Moralia* in *Plutarch* (London: Duckworth, 1973), 164–72 and *Plutarch: Selected Essays and Dialogues* (Oxford: Oxford University Press, 1973), pp. xxiii–xxix. The titles vary slightly among translators. Russell's *Plutarch* provides an excellent general introduction to Plutarch.

proper time for sex, with special attention to the best customs for a dinner party. Such a list is only a sampling of the riches to be found in this marvellously varied collection, a delight and inspiration for Montaigne and Emerson.[4]

The *Parallel Lives* represent a new initiative, which nevertheless grows naturally out of the earlier essays. A major feature of the essays had been Plutarch's effort to encourage his readers to allow the effect of philosophy to penetrate their daily lives and their way of thinking about the world, whether in shaping their own character and behaviour, or in considering the workings of the gods and the afterlife. Over time, however, he seems to have become dissatisfied with this format, and decided to turn to biography. In the series of Lives of the Roman emperors from Augustus to Vitellius, written perhaps shortly after Domitian's death, of which only *Galba* and *Otho* survive, he seems to have tested his skill at writing historical narrative from a philosophical perspective.[5] With the *Parallel Lives* he undertakes a grand project to explore, in the lives of famous statesmen and commanders, all major historical figures, the interplay of character and political action. In the proem to his Life of Nicias, whose defeat in Sicily had been the focus of some of the most memorable pages of Thucydides' history, Plutarch writes,

> I have touched briefly on the essentials [from Thucydides and Philistus, another historian]—enough to avoid gaining a reputation for carelessness and indolence—while trying to collect the facts which may have been mentioned here and there by other writers or which can be found recorded on ancient votive offerings or in decrees, but are unnoticed by most people. My purpose was not to gather meaningless historical data, but to record data which promote the understanding of character and personality.
> (*Nic.* 1)

In *Alexander*, in a frequently quoted passage, he asserts,

> I am not writing history but biography, and the most outstanding exploits do not always have the property of revealing the goodness or badness of the agent; often in fact, a casual action, the odd phrase, or a jest reveals

[4] See the essays translated in the World's Classics by Russell, *Plutarch: Selected Essays and Dialogues* and by Robin Waterfield, *Plutarch: Essays* (Harmondsworth: Penguin, 1992).

[5] Cf. A. Georgiadou, 'The Lives of the Caesars and Plutarch's Other Lives', *Illinois Classical Studies*, 13 (1988), 349–56.

character better than battles involving the loss of thousands upon thousands of lives, huge troop movements, and whole cities besieged . . . I must be allowed to devote more time to those aspects which indicate a person's mind and to use these to portray the life of each of my subjects. (*Alex.* 1)

Exactly this focus on character sets the *Lives* apart from military and political histories and gives them their interest, charm, and usefulness.

Nevertheless, a tension exists between Plutarch's professed aim—to treat character—and the subjects he chose for his biographies, all of whom are statesmen, and most are generals who commanded large armies and won or lost great battles. Earlier authors interested in ethics had written the Lives of philosophers or lawgivers. By turning to Lives of statesmen, Plutarch changes the nature of the enquiry, which becomes not what is the best way to live, but how have real men of influence, acting in real situations, brought their lives to a successful conclusion, or failed to do so. Once it was believed that Plutarch regularly depended on earlier biographies for his *Lives*: now it has been established that his major sources for most if not all of the *Lives* were histories. Plutarch's project thus involved a massive rethinking of this historical material in terms of his philosophical understanding of character and moral behaviour.

The *Parallel Lives* set a Greek and a Roman biography side by side, each pair making a single unit. The modern practice of dividing the *Lives* into two series, one Greek and one Roman—followed also in the present collection—is based on our historical interests, a natural result of our distance from the ancient world. Since the *Lives* are such an important source for our knowledge of leaders and of events, it is useful, clearer, and more accessible to treat the course of Greek and Roman history separately. Plutarch, who presumed that his readers would be familiar with their own history and would have access to full histories of both countries, found several advantages in a parallel presentation. First of all, the comparison between Greek and Roman statesmen, at a time when Greece itself was under Roman rule, asserted the dignity and long tradition of Greece, and suggested the idea of a close collaboration in government based on that tradition. Second, Plutarch knew from his rhetorical training that comparison was a powerful means of analysis and instruction.

Comparison of the lives of two men would reveal the underlying qualities of each, and highlight their similarities and differences.[6] One of the most important results of the scholarship of the last twenty-five years has been the recognition that Plutarch thought of each pair as a single work, developing a single overall impression, and linking the two lives not only in external features or accidents, but in many small ways regarding both events and traits of character. Thus, while the modern reader will usually approach each Life individually, it is useful to keep the other member of the pair constantly in mind, as an aid to recognizing the features which Plutarch finds significant in the life. For this reason, in the introductions to the individual Lives in this book, special attention is given to the relation of each to its pair.

The individual books of the *Parallel Lives* (i.e. each pair of biographies) follow a standard pattern. Most often there is a proem, which serves as introduction to the pair. This may discuss the reasons for coupling these two men, or Plutarch's sentiments behind writing these biographies, or other features of interest. Where a clearly defined proem is lacking, the function of the proem is served by the opening chapters of the first Life (e.g. in *Lycurgus* or *Solon*, where Plutarch's discussion of problems of chronology and sources leads into the pair).[7] The two biographies follow, first the Greek, then the Roman, with three exceptions.[8] Finally, most of the pairs add on a *synkrisis* or 'Comparison' which reviews certain major elements of the two lives in an overtly comparative form, often drawing conclusions or expressing opinions different from the narratives themselves.[9] Since the two Lives form one book, there is often a development of thought and analysis not only within each Life, but

[6] Cf. *Virtues in Women* 243b–d: 'There is no way of understanding the similarities and differences between virtue in women and virtue in men, other than by comparing life with life, action with action, as works of a great craft . . . Virtues do, of course, acquire differences—peculiar colours, as it were—because of the nature of the persons, and are assimilated to their underlying habits, physical temperaments, diet, and way of life. Achilles was brave in a different way from Ajax. Odysseus' wisdom was not like Nestor's. Cato and Agesilaus were not just in the same way.' (Trans. Russell, *Plutarch: Selected Essays and Dialogues*, 307.)

[7] See in general P. A. Stadter, 'The Proems of Plutarch's Lives', *Illinois Classical Studies*, 13 (1988), 275–95; for a different approach, T. G. Rosenmeyer, 'Beginnings in Plutarch's Lives', *Yale Classical Studies*, 29 (1992), 205–30.

[8] *Coriolanus-Alcibiades*, *Aemilius Paullus-Timoleon*, *Sertorius-Eumenes*. Some editions reverse these to make the Romans follow.

[9] There are no comparisons for four pairs, *Themistocles–Camillus*, *Pyrrhus–Marius*, *Phocion–Cato Minor*, and *Alexander–Caesar*.

from one Life to another, so that the first Life regularly serves as a kind of introduction to the second.[10] As a result, the Greek Lives sometimes present in a simpler fashion character traits which appear more complex or extreme in the Roman Lives, many of which are significantly longer than their Greek counterparts. In *Agesilaus*, for example, we see a leader both friendly and able to relate well with others, yet aggressive in pursuing his own honour and military success, to the extent that he creates enemies for Sparta and ultimately presides over its collapse as a major power. The corresponding Life, *Pompey*, is almost twice as long, and shows a man of similar characteristics, whose pursuit of his honour and susceptibility to his friends leads to civil war at Rome, and finally to his own death and the end of the Roman republic.

Plutarch expected both his readers and himself to benefit from the *Parallel Lives*. In the proem of *Aemilius*, he writes:

> Although I originally took up the writing of Lives for others, I find that the task has grown on me and I continue with it for my own sake too, in the sense that I treat the narrative as a kind of mirror and try to find a way to arrange my life and assimilate it to the virtues of my subjects. The experience is like nothing so much as spending time in their company and living with them: I receive and welcome each of them in turn as my guest so to speak, observe 'his stature and his qualities', and choose from his achievements those which it is particularly important and valuable for me to know. 'And oh, what greater delight could one find than this?' And could one find a more effective means of moral improvement either?
>
> (*Aem*. 1. 1–3)

It is worth exploring more exactly how Plutarch expected this 'moral improvement' to occur. Plutarch's readership most likely was that same circle of Greek and Roman friends to whom he dedicated his other works and whom we meet in the conversations of *Table Talk* and other dialogues. Comments in Plutarch's works and inscriptional and literary evidence allow us to identify many of these people as members of the ruling class in Greece and in the Roman empire.[11]

[10] Cf. C. Pelling, 'Syncrisis in Plutarch's Lives', in F. Brenk and I. Gallo (eds.), *Miscellanea Plutarchea* (*Quaderni del giornale filologico ferrarese*, 8; Ferrara, 1986), 83–96. This feature seems to explain why in certain pairs Plutarch has the Roman Life precede the Greek.

[11] See B. Puech, 'Prosopographie des amis de Plutarque', *ANRW* II.33.6 (1992), 4831–93, and C. P. Jones, *Plutarch and Rome* (Oxford: Clarendon Press, 1971), 39–64.

The Greeks were among the wealthiest in the province, and held major offices in Athens, Sparta, and elsewhere. Among the Romans, no less than nine had held the consulship, a mark of special honour even at this time.

Sosius Senecio, the close friend to whom he dedicated the *Parallel Lives*, *Table Talk*, and *Progress in Virtue*, was a lead consul (*consul ordinarius*) in 99, the first full year of Trajan's reign, and again in 107, and held a high command during Trajan's wars in Dacia (modern Romania), for which he was awarded special honours and a public statue by Trajan. He clearly was a close associate of the emperor. Other friends held the important posts of proconsul in Asia or Africa. One friend, Antiochus Philopappus, grandson of the last king of Commagene, was consul in 109 (the first Athenian to become consul) as well as a fellow citizen of Athens: his grandiose monument stands opposite the Acropolis on the hill of the Muses. Plutarch's friends and readers, then, were not apolitical provincials, dabbling in philosophy or history to while away their time, but men with responsibilities and obligations, active in imperial and provincial politics, some of them in close contact with the emperor.

Plutarch's biography project needs to be seen in the context of this audience. The conversations which Plutarch reports show that these men were trained in basic philosophy and history. The *Moral Essays* of Plutarch were written to give them more specific guidance on particular points, often in response to a request of a friend. But the *Parallel Lives* reveal that Plutarch found these works unsatisfactory in responding to the ethical needs of men active in public life, and sought a different solution. A century and a half before, Cicero had complained that philosophers did not provide clear guidelines on making choices in business or political contexts. When the stakes were high, many respectable men chose something advantageous to themselves over a higher good. He cites as examples the actions of Pompey and Caesar, each fighting for his own honour rather than the good of Rome.[12] Plutarch's *Parallel Lives* are an attempt to fill that gap, and to provide the material which will allow men in power, statesmen and commanders themselves, to become aware of results of personal choices, and the moral decisions—and often ambiguities—inherent in political action.

12 See Cicero, *On Duties*, book 3, esp. 3. 73–88.

In aiming at this audience of politically involved readers, Plutarch follows his own advice in such works as *Philosophers and Princes* and *Old Men in Politics*, that a philosopher should not hold back from attempting to influence public affairs. Throughout the *Parallel Lives*, Plutarch is fascinated by the figure of the wise adviser in politics, of which the model might be Solon, advising successively the Athenian people, Croesus and other foreign kings, and the tyrant Pisistratus. Legislators, such as Lycurgus and Numa, fit this role, and the very limited number of philosopher-statesmen who are protagonists of Lives: Dion, Phocion, Cato the Younger, Brutus. More often the adviser is an important influence on the protagonist: Anaxagoras for Pericles, Socrates for Alcibiades, Aristotle for Alexander. Romans tend to be influenced by Greek culture and philosophy in general, not a particular adviser, as in the case of Aemilius Paullus, Cicero, or Caesar. Plutarch undoubtedly saw himself in the role of adviser to his political friends and readers, helping them take a philosophical view of their situations and actions.[13]

In perusing one of Plutarch's *Lives*, the reader encounters a major statesman, one well known in history and admired for his achievements, seen not through a single witty anecdote, or a short speech in a history book, but through the whole course of his life. In the beginning the reader is introduced to the subject's family, major personality traits, and intellectual influences, as far as they are known. Then he or she is led through the statesman's life, with a focus on major turning points and crises, until his death. Along the way Plutarch offers comments, interpretations, and especially anecdotes which can suggest the character (*ēthos*) which underlies the statesman's actions.

Plutarch, although generally a Platonist, took his basic philosophy of ethics from Aristotle. He believed that it was possible by constant practice to progress step by step in virtue. In *Control of Anger*, he presents one of his friends, Minucius Fundanus, explaining how he learned to control his temper. Fundanus describes himself as actively taking command of his temper, first by making himself sensitive to

[13] Cf. A. Wardman, *Plutarch's Lives* (London: Elek, 1974), 211–20; S. Swain, 'Hellenic Culture and the Roman Heroes of Plutarch', *Journal of Hellenic Studies*, 110 (1990), 126–45 (= Scardigli, *Essays on Plutarch's Lives*, 229–64); and C. Pelling, 'Plutarch: Roman Heroes and Greek Culture', in M. Griffin and J. Barnes (eds.), *Philosophia Togata: Essays on Philosophy and Roman Society* (Oxford: Clarendon Press, 1989), 199–232.

its effects, then by conscious, well-prepared effort to subject it more and more to his rational control. Little is said about rules or precepts: rather the emphasis is on sensitizing oneself to the nature of anger, its effects, and the circumstances which produce it, then working carefully to strengthen oneself in these areas. Of major importance is the observation in others of the fault you are trying to correct, noting especially the effects of the fault on their friends, wives, and families, and the subsequent realization that the same thing is happening to you. Such observation, Fundanus affirms, is like having someone hold up a mirror to you during your moments of rage.[14] Observation also allows us to understand the general nature of vice and virtue, and of the emotions and passions which lead to vice—knowledge learned only abstractly in philosophy lessons. The same is true of good qualities as of bad, of virtue as of vice. We can learn by observing in others not only given qualities, but the effects that they have on the men involved, their families, and their states.

When in *Aemilius* Plutarch speaks of meeting the men whose biographies he writes, of inviting them into his house, and considering them at close range, he describes exactly this process of observation. Like Fundanus, he compares such inspection to holding up a mirror before oneself. A mirror enables us to see ourselves as others see us, and to approve or correct our appearance as needed. Plutarch wished his *Parallel Lives* to serve this function, not in some abstract forum, but for men who wished and were able, like his statesmen and commanders, to have some effect in the larger affairs of Greece and of the Roman empire. The statesmen of the *Lives*, then, are not simply models to be imitated, or paradigms of virtue—many in fact are unsavoury types, or at the best unsatisfactory models—but case studies in political behaviour, set out to be considered and evaluated by the reader. Although Plutarch often points the way to the interpretation of an action which he considers preferable, the reader is encouraged to work actively in evaluating the behaviour and choices of the heroes, forming his own judgement as to their value and effect. Plutarch invites his readers to observe, then fashion their own lives based on what they have learned.

Furthermore, as Plutarch notes elsewhere, observation of behaviour in one area can be applied in other contexts. In the last

[14] *Control of Anger* 455e–456b.

book of the *Iliad*, Achilles receives Priam in his tent, has pity on him, and determines to give back Hector's body to his father. But he wisely decides not to bring the mutilated and disfigured body into Priam's sight before carefully washing and preparing it, lest Priam become angry, and Achilles end up killing him. Plutarch approves of Achilles' foresight concerning his own emotions, and the use of reason to guard against his irrational passion. But Plutarch goes on to assert that this lesson can be generalized, and be applied in different contexts: in the same way, one who is given to drink should be wary of drunkenness, or one given to love be wary of love, as was Agesilaus with the kiss of the beautiful boy.[15]

Each individual Life, while presenting a vivid portrait of an ancient statesman in action, invites moral reflection. As has been noted, this process is enriched by the technique of presenting the Lives in pairs: the reader is induced to shift focus back and forth between the two, comparing, changing perspective, re-evaluating. The formal syncrisis repeats this process, again shifting perspective, refocusing the elements of comparison. Both techniques prepare readers to use the pair as a double mirror for their own lives. The *Lives* acts as a powerful imaginative tool, recreating with extraordinary vividness the characteristics of statesmen of the past, and bringing them alive in the readers' minds.

The understanding of the human self implied in Plutarch's biographies differs from that of many modern thinkers. Although he treats major historical figures, his general rule is not to glorify them as independent spirits, breaking away from their social world by an act of will to create an autonomous self. Nor does he see them as unique personalities, unparalleled in the particular conglomeration of environmental influences and personal drives at the basis of their personality, which create strong tensions pulling them in different directions. Greek thinkers thought of the human person first of all as a rational animal, able to act on the basis of reasoning which was generally available to other humans as well. This thinking, as developed by Plato, Aristotle, and the Stoics in different ways, argued that it was theoretically possible for a person, in active co-operation with other persons, to arrive at '(*a*) objective knowledge of what constitutes the best in human life and (*b*) a corresponding

[15] *On Reading the Poets* 31bc, referring to Homer, *Iliad* 24. 560–86. The story of Agesilaus and the kiss is found in *Ages.* 11.

character and way of life'.[16] In addition, an individual who was acting like a human being (i.e. reasonably) would attempt to shape his life according to that knowledge. In this conception, the individual could and would want to form his own life according to objective criteria of behaviour, rather than follow spontaneous responses to the situation of the moment, or a set of moral principles established solely by oneself, and subject to change based on new experience. This is the basis for the moral thinking which pervades the *Lives*, and which modern readers sometimes find intrusive or gratuitous. Plutarch as a Platonist accepts that there are moral truths which, at least in theory, can be established by reason, to which any sensible person would wish to subscribe, and according to which he would shape his behaviour. From this standpoint Plutarch is able to evaluate the behaviour of his heroes, offer judgements and criticisms, and suggest alternative behaviour. Moreover, this is precisely the perspective from which Plutarch is able to use his heroes as mirrors for himself and his readers, presuming that they, like him, wish to shape their lives by reason in the most suitable way.

However, Plutarch's Platonism was strongly tinged with scepticism, the philosophical notion that many truths were in fact not knowable, so that one may have to hold back from a final decision in individual cases. This awareness of the difficulty of certitude allows Plutarch to be unusually flexible and even tolerant in his judgements, or to leave questions in abeyance. To take an example: Pericles' refusal to back down from a confrontation with Sparta precipitated the Peloponnesian War, a war between Greeks of which Plutarch could not approve. The decision could be a major black mark against Pericles, and Plutarch initially treats it that way. As his discussion proceeds, however, and he examines various reasons Pericles may have had, he ends up withholding judgement: 'So these are the reasons given by my sources to explain why he did not allow the people to yield to the Spartans; the truth is, however, uncertain.'[17] For this reason also the formal comparison often presents a different evaluation of an action from the narrative, or there are different evaluations in different Lives. While moralist in theory, Plutarch's sensitivity to human motives and circumstances creates a vivid

[16] The formulation is that of C. Gill, *Personality in Greek Epic, Tragedy, and Philosophy: The Self in Dialogue* (Oxford: Clarendon Press, 1996), 12.

[17] *Per.* 32. The whole discussion is at 30–2.

picture of the dynamics of moral decision, and in the last resort transfers to the reader the final judgement on his hero's behaviour.

Another aspect of the ancient view of character was that a number of traits tend to cluster in one type of character: an early philosophical example is Plato's descriptions of the different kinds of lives associated with different regimes in *Republic* books 8 and 9. Whereas moderns tend to emphasize the complexity of character, looking for those unexpected traits or quirks which make each individual unique, Plutarch tends to search for unifying factors. This results in what have been called 'integrated' characters:

> a man's qualities are brought into some sort of relation with one another, and every trait goes closely with the next. We are unsurprised if Antony is simple, passive, ingenuous, susceptible, soldierly, boisterous, yet also noble and often brilliant; or the younger Cato is high-principled and determined, rigid in his philosophy, scruffy (as philosophical beings often are), strange but bizarrely logical in the way he treats his women, and disablingly inflexible and insensitive in public life.[18]

In this kind of integrated character-portrayal, the different traits of character are seen as naturally cohering facets of a given combination of inborn qualities, education, and mind-set. Antony's or Cato's characters are unique, yet in a certain sense expected, because the different elements which might seem contradictory in fact complement each other so well. Thus the deceptive simplicity of Plutarchan character-drawing hides an exceptional sensitivity to the variety and complexity of human behaviour. The reader is not shocked by startling quirks or unexplained outbursts of genius, but gradually led to see, in the course of the biography, the complex and often surprising results of traits already visible in childhood or at the beginning of a political career.

Biographical Method

Plutarch's method is generally to set out at the beginning basic features of his subject's nature and the influences which affected

[18] C. Pelling, 'Aspects of Plutarch's Characterization', *Illinois Classical Studies*, 13 (1988), 256–74 at 262; cf. also his 'Childhood and Personality in Greek Biography', in Pelling (ed.), *Characterization and Individuality in Greek Literature* (Oxford: Clarendon Press, 1990), 213–44.

it: thus we learn in the first chapters of the respective Lives of Agesilaus' training in the Spartan educational system and his ambitious competitiveness, and of Antony's tendency to let others set his agenda and susceptibility to women. Physical appearance, when it is reported, often provides a clue to character: Sulla's blotched face and intimidating eyes point to the harshness of the later tyrant. This preliminary sketch prepares for the statesman's political career, which usually proceeds in a series of stages, with one or two major peaks. The Life ends with the subject's death, though often Plutarch chooses to follow out some narrative thread—the fate of his children, or of his murderers, or his successors—to reach an effective closure.

This basic outline, which implies that the structure is straightforwardly chronological, is deceptive. Writing in an age when rhetoric formed the basis of education, Plutarch carefully shapes his presentation for maximum effectiveness. Each Life is thought out in terms of the problems which it presents, the features which Plutarch wishes to highlight, and the material available. The resulting organization therefore combines chronological, thematic, and rhetorical principles. While maintaining for clarity a basic chronological scheme, Plutarch uses flashbacks and future references to call attention to continuing traits or explain particular incidents. Moreover, he regularly introduces anecdotal material from all periods of the life to exemplify traits which he treats in connection with a given event.

Anecdotes are frequently clustered at major points in the subject's life, e.g. in *Themistocles* 18, just after the victory at Salamis; in *Alexander* 21–3, after the victory at Issus. The first sixteen chapters of *Alcibiades* are almost continuous anecdotes, which gradually lead from Alcibiades' youth to his relations with his lovers and with Socrates to the beginnings of his political career.[19] The anecdotes may be taken from every sort of source, historical, philosophical, or rhetorical, and can be combined in different lengths and degree of elaboration. 'They need not be correctly placed in date in relation to their neighbours,'[20] so that extreme caution is needed in trying to fit them into a chronological sequence. While all anecdotes assist in

[19] See D. A. Russell, 'Plutarch Alcibiades 1–16', *Proceedings of the Cambridge Philological Society* (1966), 37–47 (=Scardigli, *Essays on Plutarch's Lives*, 191–207).

[20] Russell in Scardigli (above n. 19), 206.

portraying *ēthos*, Plutarch's method of employment can be extremely flexible. *Alexander* provides numerous examples. Alexander's taming of Bucephelas (*Alex*. 6) seems to be especially significant, raising the question of mastery and training of genius. The sequence which forms the account of naphtha in *Alex*. 35 falls immediately after the battle of Gaugamela and is often considered a digression, but in fact comments on *ēthos*, exploring Alexander's own dangerous fieriness. Sequences of anecdotes build up a larger picture: after Alexander wins the battle of Issus, three chapters of anecdotes show his idea of kingship and his self-restraint (*Alex*. 21–3). They can also create a sense of false continuity, when a series of anecdotes serves in place of historical narrative, as at *Alex*. 25–6 and 45–56. Finally, Plutarch can use a sequence of anecdotes as a technique to comment on and interpret his subject's behaviour, as he does in *Alex*. 45–56. In presenting the most scandalous actions of Alexander's career, anecdotes are able to suggest that Alexander was not completely guilty and that the Macedonians also had some responsibility in the events.[21]

The whole is united by a remarkably facile style: 'learned and allusive, imaginative and metaphorical, exuberant and abundant.'[22] Strongly influenced by classical models, he fashioned a literary language for his own day, a varied and rich instrument to express his thinking on everything from philosophy and medicine to vegetarianism and astronomy. His style tends to be generous rather than spare: he regularly doubles synonyms, and employs amplification, in the form of examples, general thoughts, and anecdotes, to enlarge on a topic. Frequent poetic quotations give authoritative support to an argument as well as a cultured flavour. When he wishes a higher style, the sentences can become quite long, built up carefully from subordinate clauses, creating luxuriant accumulation of words and ideas. Throughout, the range and aptness of examples and metaphors delights and instructs, while the vividness of the narrative charms the imagination.

[21] Cf. P. A. Stadter, 'Anecdotes and the Thematic Structure of Plutarchean Biography', in J. A. Fernández Delgado and F. Pordomingo Pardo (eds.), *Estudios sobre Plutarco: Aspectos formales* (Madrid: Ediciones Clásicas, 1996), 291–303.

[22] Russell, *Plutarch*, 20. The whole chapter, 18–41, is an excellent study of his style, to which this paragraph is indebted.

Historical Value

The *Parallel Lives*, however, are most often read as historical sources for the periods which he treats. They are in fact extraordinarily valuable as sources, both because they give us Plutarch's insight into the men he treats and because they preserve a vast spectrum of evidence which otherwise would have been lost, collected in the course of Plutarch's omnivorous reading and his special research for the *Lives*. His historical contribution came under severe scrutiny from positivist historians in the nineteenth century, but in the latter half of the twentieth century, as we have learned more of his method and his purpose, a clearer picture has emerged of his value to the historian.

Although he famously protests that he is a biographer, not a historian (*Alex.* 1), historical narratives provide the base for his biographies. Political biography before Plutarch was not a common genre. The only example we possess is a Latin writer and contemporary of Cicero, Cornelius Nepos, and his biographies, though they treat many of the same Greek figures as Plutarch, have a much more limited scope.[23] There do not seem to have been biographies in any way similar to Plutarch's before he wrote the *Lives*.

Plutarch was one of the most educated men of antiquity. His reading from childhood on provided him a comfortable background in the history of Greece. Latin, however, he admits to learning late and imperfectly (*Dem.* 2). He cites many fewer Latin authors than Greek, and does not cite passages from Latin poets, though he frequently quotes from Greek poets. He knows and quotes all the major Greek historians—Herodotus, Thucydides, Xenophon, Polybius—and many historians and antiquarians now lost to us. But these historical narratives are supplemented with information from contemporary letters and poetry, inscriptions and public documents, philosophical authors, and his own autopsy and conversations with knowledgeable friends.[24]

A clearer idea of Plutarch's method of using these sources

[23] Cf. J. Geiger, *Cornelius Nepos and Ancient Political Biography* (*Historia* Einzelschriften, 47; Stuttgart, 1985).

[24] Cf. e.g. B. X. de Wet, 'Plutarch's Use of the Poets', *Acta Classica*, 31 (1988), 13–25; F. Frost, 'Some documents in Plutarch's Lives', *Classica et mediaevalia*, 22 (1961), 182–94; P. Desideri, 'I documenti di Plutarco', *ANRW* II.33.6 (1992), 4536–67; J. Buckler, 'Plutarch and Autopsy', *ANRW* II.33.6 (1992), 4788–830.

emerges when we compare his account against an extant source, as we can in many Lives, or when we compare two accounts of the same events in two Lives. Particularly instructive are the Lives of the late republic at Rome, six of which apparently were written at about the same time and used many of the same sources (*Crassus*, *Pompey*, *Caesar*, *Cato*, *Brutus*, *Antony*).[25] For these lives he used first-hand sources, probably Pollio for the Civil Wars and Dellius for the Parthian War of Antony, memoirs, Cicero's *Second Philippic*, Livy, Sallust, and other writers. In addition he used oral tradition, both Greek and Roman. We can identify two stages of composition, an initial reading of sources (undoubtedly less necessary for the Greek lives than for the Roman) and preparation of detailed notes, before the final draft or drafts.

In adapting the historical material, Plutarch took several steps to focus attention on his protagonist. Thus he may abridge his source by simplifying it, either conflating several similar incidents into one (e.g. meetings of the senate), by chronological compression (making two items seem to follow closely which in fact were separated by a period of time), or reorganizing events in non-chronological order, especially to bring out causal or logical connections. Occasionally he may even transfer an item from one character to another, whether consciously or not. More commonly, he may attribute to his protagonist an action which might be generally ascribed to a group (the senate, the city) in his source, personalizing an impersonal action. On the other hand, he will expand inadequate material, not by free invention but by a visualization of what must have been the case, what antecedents would naturally precede an action, or what context seems to be implied by a historical notice.[26]

His interpretations of his characters' motives are not fixed, but can vary depending on the biography in which they are given. Naturally, more complex motives are likely to appear when the actor is protagonist of a Life. Moreover, generally Plutarch tends to view his protagonist more favourably than other characters in a Life, and to

[25] Cf C. Pelling, 'Plutarch's Method of Work in the Roman Lives', *Journal of Hellenic Studies*, 99 (1979), 74–96 and 'Plutarch's Adaptation of his Source Material', *Journal of Hellenic Studies*, 100 (1980), 127–40 (=Scardigli, *Essays on Plutarch's Lives*, 265–318 (with postscript) and 125–54 respectively), to which the following paragraph is indebted. *Cicero* and *Lucullus* were written earlier.

[26] Cf. C. Pelling, 'Truth and Fiction in Plutarch's Lives', in D. A. Russell (ed.), *Antonine Literature* (Oxford: Clarendon Press, 1990), 19–52.

adopt the protagonist's perspective on the events of which he takes part. This focalization via the protagonist of a Life, and therefore on multiple protagonists in several Lives dealing with the same events, is a significant aspect of Plutarch's metamorphosis of history into biography, and supported his philosophical purpose by permitting his readers to identify individually with each protagonist, moving, for instance, from Pompey to Cato to Caesar in different pairs of Lives. Again, different Lives will emphasize different aspects of the protagonist: some will concentrate on historical incident (e.g. *Caesar*), others will be more philosophical or personal, such as *Cato the Younger* or *Pompey*.

Of course, the effort to bring out parallel aspects of Lives which form a pair has a significant effect on choice of detail and overall presentation, and sometimes on the interpretation of particular incidents. Plutarch might have passed over as insignificant Pericles' offer to give his land to the city if it were not ravaged in the war, though it is recorded in Thucydides, if he had not known that Hannibal caused difficulties at Rome to Pericles' parallel figure, Fabius, by sparing Fabius' land.[27]

Viewed from a historical perspective, Plutarch's work has a number of limitations, many tied to his biographical purpose, others reflecting the views of his class and his society, others still his Platonism. Although more familiar than most men of his time with the society of classical Greece, he is not always able to abandon a somewhat idealized picture of the great age of Greece. His basic political scheme, seen again and again in both Greek and Roman Lives, is set in terms of a conflict between élite and populace, where the élite may be land-owning Athenians, leading Spartans, or the Roman senate. Within the élite struggles will occur, and some men will appeal to the emotions of the crowd. This scheme glides over the marked differences between different systems of government, and the nature of practical politics at different times. Plutarch rarely takes a larger view of his protagonist's actions, and generally refrains from commenting on their effect in the history of their city or of world affairs:

[27] *Per.* 33, cf. *Fab.* 7. On such parallels, see e.g. P. Stadter, 'Plutarch's Comparison of Pericles and Fabius Maximus', *Greek, Roman and Byzantine Studies*, 16 (1975), 77–85 (=Scardigli, *Essays on Plutarch's Lives*, 155–64), and id., 'Paradoxical Paradigms: Lysander and Sulla' and A. B. Bosworth, 'History and Artifice in Plutarch's Eumenes', in P. Stadter (ed.), *Plutarch and the Historical Tradition* (London: Routledge, 1992), 41–55 and 56–89.

he clearly expects his readers already to have some idea of the importance of these figures on the stage of history. Finally, given the fact that our historical sources are often so meagre, the potential misunderstandings and distortions introduced by Plutarch's biographical technique can offer frustrating barriers to modern efforts at historical reconstruction and interpretation. Nevertheless, it is hard for the historian to imagine ancient history without him: his contribution to our understanding is invaluable.

Plutarch encapsulates the greatness of Greece and Rome, and brings alive the great moments of history as lived by their protagonists. The range of his sources is immense, and he regularly uses contemporary materials otherwise not available to us. To these he adds his own narrative gift and insight into the dynamics of character,[28] which bring alive in a uniquely vivid presentation scores of figures from classical antiquity. It was this drama of living which Shakespeare recognized in Plutarch, from whom he drew not just the plot, but many of the scenes and the dynamics of action for *Coriolanus*, *Julius Caesar*, and *Antony and Cleopatra*. The liveliness, intimacy, and imagination of Plutarch's vision of his heroes has moulded our modern understanding of classical antiquity.

This Selection of Roman Lives

The eight Lives in this collection illustrate the variety of Roman statesmen in the second and first centuries BC and the path which the republic followed from a strong senatorial oligarchy to a monarchy based on the loyalty of the military and the realization by all that one-man rule was preferable to anarchy. Each figure is of interest in his own right, but each also plays a significant part in the changes, often violent, which reshaped the Roman empire. The first two figures are a study in contrasts. Cato the Elder (234–149), gruff, unyielding, a figure of old-fashioned integrity in a Rome flooded with the wealth of Macedonia and Carthage, insisted in his eighties that Carthage should be destroyed. Aemilius Paullus (*c.*228–160), a patrician and philhellene, ended the Third Macedonian War by his defeat of King Perseus of Macedon in 168, but the glory of his

[28] Cf. e.g. C. Pelling, 'Plutarch and Thucydides', in *Plutarch and the Historical Tradition* (London: Routledge, 1992), 10–40, noting that Plutarch's comments on character can be more perceptive than Thucydides'.

triumph was shadowed by the death of his two sons. The lives of Tiberius Gracchus (*c*.164–133) and his brother Gaius (153–121) mark the beginning of the Roman revolution, as each in turn tried to use his position as the tribune of the people to force the senatorial oligarchy of which they were a part to share some of its newly acquired wealth and power with a larger segment of citizens and allies. Both died in the streets of Rome, introducing a hundred years of civic violence. There follow two outstanding generals, who locked in a vicious battle to control the city. Gaius Marius (*c*.157–86) made his fame and was elected consul by denouncing the nobility, then won five more consulships when it seemed that he was the only man who could defeat the Germanic tribes threatening to invade Italy. Not content, he attempted to usurp the command against Mithridates, was outlawed, and returned to soak the city in blood. Cornelius Sulla (138–79) won his reputation under Marius in 107, but the rivalry engendered early came to a head in 88, when Marius attempted to deprive him of his command. He seized the city once in 88, then, after a victorious campaign against Mithridates, returned again in 82. Made dictator with the intention of upholding senatorial government, his proscriptions and executions terrified the city. Out of this carnage emerged two outstanding generals and statesmen, Pompey the Great (106–48) and Julius Caesar (100–44)—at first reluctant allies, so that each could pursue his own goals, then bitter foes in a new civil war. When Caesar defeated Pompey at Pharsalus it seemed that the end of strife had come, and he was made perpetual dictator, only to be assassinated by senators who could not accept his domination. Mark Antony (83–30) attempted to pick up the mantle of Caesar, pursuing and defeating the Liberators, Brutus and Cassius, at Philippi with the help of Caesar's young heir, Octavian. Soon, however, these two divided the empire into two halves, East and West. Antony, distracted more than aided by his alliance with Cleopatra, the Egyptian queen, was defeated at Actium, finally leaving Octavian to consolidate his position and emerge as undisputed monarch. Again and again, these Lives put before us the dynamic relation between power and character, examining from every side the nature of ambition, of compromise, of friendship, of integrity, as manifested in these outstanding individuals. Always present is Plutarch's own world of the second century AD, when the imperial monarchy seemed strong and fair with Trajan as emperor. But the biographer had lived through times of civil war and assassination, and he writes with insight on the drives and tensions which can destroy individuals and republics.

TRANSLATOR'S NOTE

THE Greek text used as the basis for these translations (with one exception) is the Teubner edition. Any places where I have adopted a different text have been marked in the translation with an obelus, which refers the interested reader to a note in the Textual Notes section at the back of the book. The Teubner editions of Plutarch's Lives are currently (1998) in the process of being updated, but this process is not complete. To be precise, therefore, I have used the following editions:

For Cato the Elder: *Plutarchus, Vitae Parallelae*, I.1, ed. K. Ziegler (1969).
For Aemilius Paullus: *Plutarchus, Vitae Parallelae*, II.1, ed. K. Ziegler, addenda by H. Gärtner (1993).
For Caesar: *Plutarchus, Vitae Parallelae*, II.2, ed. K. Ziegler, addenda by H. Gärtner (1994).
For Marius and the Gracchi: *Plutarchus, Vitae Parallelae*, III.1, ed. K. Ziegler, addenda by H. Gärtner (1996).
For Sulla and Pompey: *Plutarchus, Vitae Parallelae*, III.2, ed. K. Ziegler (1973).
For Antony: *Plutarch: Life of Antony*, ed. C. B. R. Pelling (Cambridge: Cambridge University Press, 1988).

SELECT BIBLIOGRAPHY

(Further reading on the individual lives will be found after the introductions to each Life.)

Background and Criticism

ANRW = Haase, W., and Temporini, H. (eds.), *Aufstieg und Niedergang der römischen Welt*, Pt. II, vol. 33.6 (Berlin and New York, 1992), has many articles on Plutarch in English and other languages.

Brenk, F. E., Hershbell, J. P., and Stadter, P. A. (eds.), *Illinois Classical Studies*, 13: 2 (1988), special volume devoted to Plutarch.

Jones, C. P., *Plutarch and Rome* (Oxford: Clarendon Press, 1971).

Mossman, J. (ed.), *Plutarch and his Intellectual World: Essays on Plutarch* (London: Duckworth, 1997).

Russell, D. A., *Plutarch* (London: Duckworth, 1973).

Scardigli, B. (ed.), *Essays on Plutarch's Lives* (Oxford: Clarendon Press, 1995).

Stadter, P. A. (ed.), *Plutarch and the Historical Tradition* (London: Routledge, 1992).

Wardman, A., *Plutarch's Lives* (London: Elek, 1974).

Articles

Bosworth, A. B., 'History and Artifice in Plutarch's Eumenes', in Stadter, *Plutarch and the Historical Tradition*, 56–89.

Buckler, J., 'Plutarch and Autopsy', *ANRW* II.33.6 (1992), 4788–830.

Desideri, P., 'I documenti di Plutarco', *ANRW* II.33.6 (1992), 4536–67.

Frost, F., 'Some Documents in Plutarch's Lives', *Classica et mediaevalia*, 22 (1961), 182–94.

Geiger, J., 'Plutarch's Parallel Lives: The Choice of Heroes', *Hermes*, 109 (1981), 85–104.

Georgiadou, A., 'The Lives of the Caesars and Plutarch's Other Lives', *Illinois Classical Studies*, 13 (1988), 349–56.

Jones, C. P., 'Towards a Chronology of Plutarch's Works', *Journal of Roman Studies*, 56 (1966), 61–74 (repr. in Scardigli, *Essays*, 95–123).

Pelling, C., 'Plutarch's Method of Work in the Roman Lives', *Journal of Hellenic Studies*, 99 (1979), 74–96 (repr. in Scardigli, *Essays*, 265–318, with postscript).

—— 'Plutarch's Adaptation of his Source Material', *Journal of Hellenic Studies*, 100 (1980), 127–40 (repr. in Scardigli, *Essays*, 125–54).

—— 'Syncrisis in Plutarch's Lives', in F. Brenk and I. Gallo (eds.), *Miscellanea Plutarchea* (*Quaderni del giornale filologico ferrarese*, 8; Ferrara, 1986), 83–96.

—— 'Aspects of Plutarch's Characterization', *Illinois Classical Studies*, 13 (1988), 256–74.

—— 'Plutarch: Roman Heroes and Greek Culture', in M. Griffin and J. Barnes (eds.), *Philosophia Togata: Essays on Philosophy and Roman Society* (Oxford: Clarendon Press, 1989), 199–232.

—— 'Childhood and Personality in Greek Biography', in C. Pelling (ed.), *Characterization and Individuality in Greek Literature* (Oxford: Clarendon Press, 1990), 213–44.

—— 'Plutarch and Thucydides', in Stadter, *Plutarch and the Historical Tradition*, 10–40.

Puech, B., 'Prosopographie des amis de Plutarque', *ANRW* II.33.6 (1992), 4831–93.

Russell, D. A., 'On Reading Plutarch's Lives', *Greece and Rome*, 13 (1966), 139–54.

Stadter, P. A., 'Plutarch's Comparison of Pericles and Fabius Maximus', *Greek, Roman and Byzantine Studies*, 16 (1975), 77–85 (repr. in Scardigli, *Essays*, 155–64).

—— 'The Proems of Plutarch's Lives', *Illinois Classical Studies*, 13 (1988), 275–95.

—— 'Paradoxical Paradigms: Lysander and Sulla', in Stadter, *Plutarch and the Historical Tradition*, 41–55.

—— 'Anecdotes and the Thematic Structure of Plutarchean Biography', in J. A. Fernández Delgado and F. Pordomingo Pardo (eds.), *Estudios sobre Plutarco: Aspectos formales* (Madrid: Ediciones Clásicas, 1997), 291–303.

Swain, S., 'Hellenic Culture and the Roman Heroes of Plutarch', *Journal of Hellenic Studies*, 110 (1990), 126–45 (repr. in Scardigli, *Essays*, 229–64).

—— 'Plutarch, Plato, Athens, and Rome', in J. Barnes and M. Griffin (eds.), *Philosophia Togata II: Plato and Aristotle at Rome* (Oxford: Clarendon Press, 1997), 165–87.

Wet, B. X. de, 'Plutarch's Use of the Poets', *Acta Classica*, 31 (1988), 13–25.

Translations

Lives:

A companion volume to this, R. Waterfield and P. A. Stadter, *Plutarch: Greek Lives* (Oxford: Oxford University Press, Oxford World's Classics, 1998), contains *Lycurgus*, *Solon*, *Themistocles*, *Cimon*, *Pericles*, *Nicias*, *Alcibiades*, *Agesilaus*, and *Alexander*.

The complete *Lives*, in Greek with facing English translation by B. Perrin, are in *Plutarch's Lives*, 11 vols. (Loeb Classical Library; Cambridge, Mass.: Harvard University Press, 1917–51).

Selected Lives have been translated in the following volumes:

Warner, R., *Plutarch. The Fall of the Roman Republic* (Harmondsworth: Penguin, 1958).

Scott-Kilvert, I., *Plutarch. The Rise and Fall of Athens* (Harmondsworth: Penguin, 1960).

—— *Plutarch. Makers of Rome* (Harmondsworth: Penguin, 1965).

—— *Plutarch. The Age of Alexander* (Harmondsworth: Penguin, 1973).

Talbert, R., *Plutarch on Sparta* (Harmondsworth: Penguin, 1988).

Moralia:

The complete *Moralia* are translated in the Loeb Classical Library, *Plutarch Moralia* (Cambridge, Mass., and London, 1927–76, 14 vols. (with facing Greek)) and W. W. Goodwin, a revision of an eighteenth-century version 'by many hands' (Boston, 1874–8). There are three recent translations of selected essays:

Russell, D. A., *Plutarch: Selected Essays and Dialogues* (Oxford: Oxford University Press, Oxford World's Classics, 1993).

Waterfield, R., *Plutarch: Essays* (Harmondsworth: Penguin, 1992).

CHRONOLOGY

754 BC	Legendary foundation of Rome
509	Establishment of the Roman republic
220–202	The Second Punic War; Scipio defeats Carthage
197	Philip V of Macedon defeated at Cynoscephalae; end of Second Macedonian War
191	Antiochus III defeated at Thermopylae
184	Cato the Elder is censor
168	Aemilius Paullus defeats Perseus at Pydna; end of Third Macedonian War
146	Scipio Aemilianus ends Third Punic War; Carthage destroyed
133	Tribunate of Tiberius Gracchus
122–121	Tribunates of Gaius Gracchus
107	First consulship of Marius
105	Jugurtha surrendered to Sulla; end of Jugurthine War
104–100	Marius consul for five successive years
91–87	The Social or Italic War
88	Consulship of Sulla; Marius outlawed
87	Consulship of Cinna; return of Marius
82	Sulla invades Italy, seizes Rome, is named dictator
79	Death of Sulla
70	First consulship of Crassus and Pompey
63	Cicero consul; conspiracy of Catiline
60	Agreement ('first triumvirate') of Pompey, Crassus, and Caesar
59	Caesar consul
58–51	Caesar proconsul in Gaul
55	Pompey and Crassus consuls
54	Crassus killed in invasion of Parthia
49	Caesar crosses the Rubicon; civil war with Pompey
48	Caesar defeats Pompey at Pharsalus; Pompey killed in Egypt
46	Caesar defeats Cato at Thapsus; Cato commits suicide
44	15 March: Caesar assassinated by Brutus and Cassius

44	May: Caesar Octavianus (Octavian) arrives in Rome
	November: Antony fights Decimus Brutus at Mutina
43	November: Antony, Octavian, and Lepidus take office as triumvirs 'to establish the republic' ('second triumvirate')
42	October: Antony and Octavian defeat Brutus and Cassius at Philippi
41	Cleopatra meets Antony in Tarsus
40	Agreement of Antony and Octavian at Brundisium; Antony marries Octavia
39	Agreement of Antony, Sextus Pompey, and Octavian at Misenum
36	Antony's Parthian campaign ends in failure
32	Break between Antony and Octavian; Antony divorces Octavia
31	2 September: battle of Actium, Octavian defeats Antony and Cleopatra
30	August: death of Antony and Cleopatra in Alexandria
28	Caesar Octavianus assumes title of Augustus
AD 14	Death of Augustus

MAPS

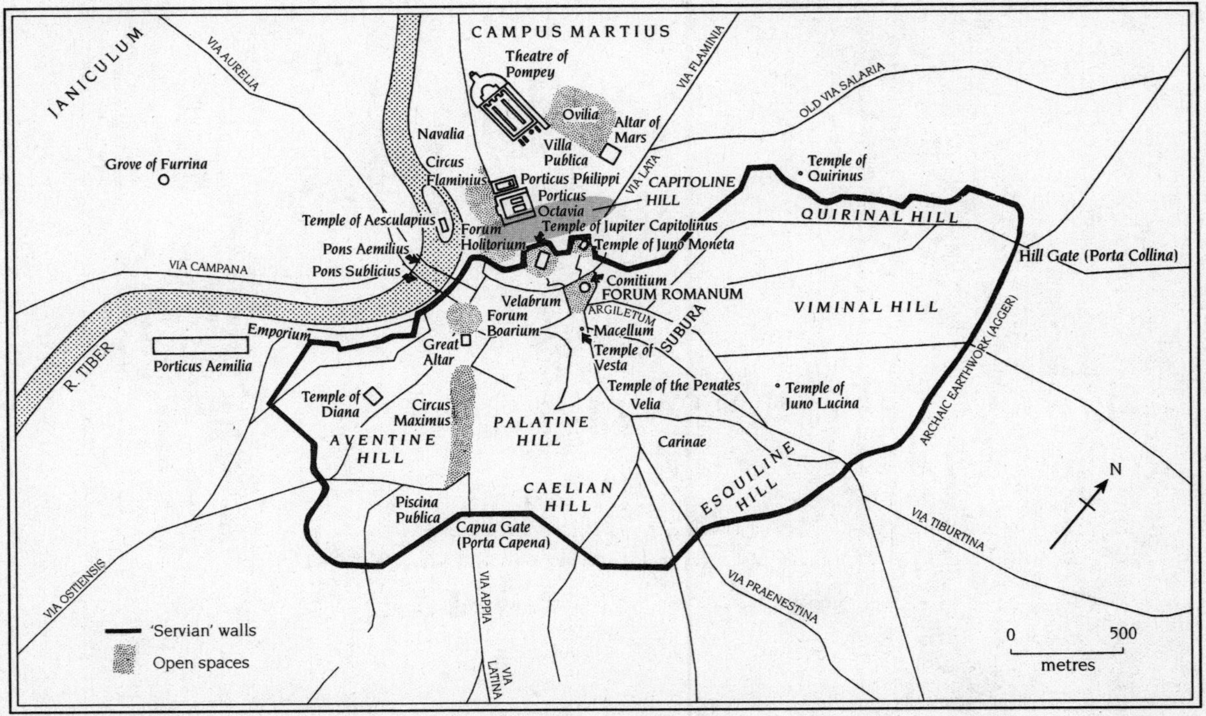

CAMPUS MARTIUS
JANICULUM
VIA AURELIA
VIA FLAMINIA
OLD VIA SALARIA
Theatre of Pompey
Ovilia
Altar of Mars
Villa Publica
Navalia
Grove of Furrina
Circus Flaminius
Porticus Philippi
Porticus Octavia
VIA LATA
CAPITOLINE HILL
Temple of Quirinus
QUIRINAL HILL
Temple of Aesculapius
Forum Holitorium
Temple of Jupiter Capitolinus
Temple of Juno Moneta
Pons Aemilius
Pons Sublicius
VIA CAMPANA
Hill Gate (Porta Collina)
Comitium
FORUM ROMANUM
Velabrum
ARGILETUM
VIMINAL HILL
Forum Boarium
Macellum
SUBURA
Emporium
Great Altar
Temple of Vesta
Porticus Aemilia
R. TIBER
ARCHAIC EARTHWORK (AGGER)
Temple of the Penates
Temple of Juno Lucina
Temple of Diana
Velia
Circus Maximus
PALATINE HILL
AVENTINE HILL
Carinae
ESQUILINE HILL
N
CAELIAN HILL
Piscina Publica
Capua Gate (Porta Capena)
VIA TIBURTINA
VIA OSTIENSIS
VIA APPIA
VIA PRAENESTINA
VIA LATINA
'Servian' walls
Open spaces
0
500
metres

MAP I. ROME

Virunum
R. ATESIS
R. DANUBE
Aquileia
Mediolanum
GALLIA
Sirmio
Verona
Patavium
Tergeste
PANNONIA
ISTRIA
Cremona
Mantua
Bedriacum
Placentia
Vercellae?
R. PADUS
Parma
Pola
DALMATIA
ILLYRICUM
Mutina
Genua
CISALPINA
Bononia
Ravenna
R. RUBICON
Ariminum
Carrara
Luca
Pisa
Faesulae
R. ARNUS
Florentia
Ancona
UMBRIA
Salonae (Split)
Volterra
Arretium
ETRURIA
Iguvium
Cortona
PICENUM
Perusia
Populonia
Vetulonia
Clusium
Asculum
Volsinii
Spoletium
SABINES
Volci
Cosa
Falerii
R. TIBER
Tarquinii
Alba Fucens
Aleria
Corfinium
Veii
LATIUM
R. LIRIS
CORSICA
Rome
SAMNIUM
Ostia
Praeneste
Luceria
Sipontum
Arpinum
Velitrae
Fregellae
Antium
CAMPANIA
APULIA
Cales
Cannae
Barium
Minturnae
Beneventum
Olbia
Capua
Nola
TYRRHENIAN SEA
Neapolis
Cumae
MT. VESUVIUS
Brundisium
PITHECUSAE
Pompeii
Puteoli
Herculaneum
CALABRIA
Tarentum
SARDINIA
Paestum
Metapontum
LUCANIA
Heraclea
Velia
Laus
Thurii
Sybaris
IONIAN SEA
Caralis
BRUTTIUM
Croton
Terina
N
Hipponium
Lipara
Medma
Messana
Locri
Rhegium
Panormus
Tyndaris
Segesta
Himera
MT. ETNA
Tauromenium
Lilybaeum
Motya
Naxos
SICILY
Centuripae
Altitude in metres
Over 1000
200–1000
0–200
Selinus
Enna
Catana
Agrigentum
Leontini
Utica
Syracuse
Carthage
Gela
0 25 50 75 100 miles
Camarina
0 50 100 150 km

MAP 2. ITALY

THRACE
R. AXIUS
R. STRYMON
Philippi
Abdera
Amphipolis
THASOS
Pella
MACEDONIA
Levkadia
Therme (Salonica)
Stageira
Aegae (Vergina)
Pydna
CHALCIDICE
Olynthus
Potidaea
Dion
Mende
Torone
MT. OLYMPUS
LEMNOS
EPIRUS
M. OSSA
Dodona
Tricca
Larissa
MT. PINDUS
MT. PELIUM
THESSALY
Pagasae
CORCYRA
Pherae
Pharsalus
Ambracia
Nicopolis
Actium
ACARNANIA
LEUCAS
Stratus
Thermopylae
EUBOEA
SCYROS
MT. PARNASSUS
PHOCIS
AETOLIA
Delphi
Orchomenus
Chalcis
ITHACA
Chaeronea
LAKE COPAIS
Lefkandi
Eretria
MT. HELICON
BOEOTIA
Delium
Patrae
Aegium
Leuctra
Thebes
Tanagra
Plataea
CEPHALLENIA
ACHAEA
Marathon
ATTICA
Megara
MT. PENTELICUM
Elis
Sicyon
Corinth
Athens
ELIS
SALAMIS
Piraeus
ANDROS
Cleonae
Mycenae
AEGINA
ARCADIA
ARGOLIS
Laurium
CEOS
Mantinea
ZACYNTHOS
Olympia
Argos
Tiryns
Epidaurus
Sunium
TENOS
Bassae
Troezen
Calauria
Tegea
Megalopolis
CYTHNOS
DELOS
N
MESSENIA
Messene
SERIPHOS
PAROS
Sparta
LACONIA
Pylos
SIPHNOS
Methone
Gythium
MELOS
Altitude in metres
over 1000
200–1000
0–200
CYTHERA
0
20
40
60
80
100 miles
0
40
80
120
160 km

MAP 3. GREECE

BRITANNIA
TRINOVANTES
THAMES
English Channel
MENAPII
SUGAMBRI
SUEBI
UBII
EBURONES
NERVII
MORINI
ATREBATES
BELGAE
AMBIANI
SAMBRE
TREVERI
BELLOVACI
VIROMANDUI
REMI
MOSELLE
Vosges Mts
SEINE
AISNE
MEUSE
AREMORICAE CIVITATES
PARISII
SUESSIONES
RHINE
VENETI
CARNUTES
SENONES
Agedincum
Quiberon Bay
Cenabum
LINGONES
MANDURII
LOIRE
SEQUANI
Alesia
Vesontio
Avaricum
SAONE
DOUBS
PICTONES
CELTAE
BITURIGES
Noviodunum
(Nevers)
AEDUI
Bibracte
Jura Mts
HELVETII
Bay of
Biscay
ALLIER
Gergovia
Geneva
ARVERNI
ALLOBROGES
Uxellodunum
Gt St Bernard
pass
DORDOGNE
Cevennes Mts
VOCONTII
NITIOBRIGES
RHONE
AQUITANI
GARONNE
Arausio
GALLIA TRANSALPINA
RUTENI
NARBONENSIS
Aquae Sextiae
Pyrenees Mts
SALLUVII
Narbo
Massilia
N
High land
0
200
400 km
0
250 miles

MAP 4. GAUL

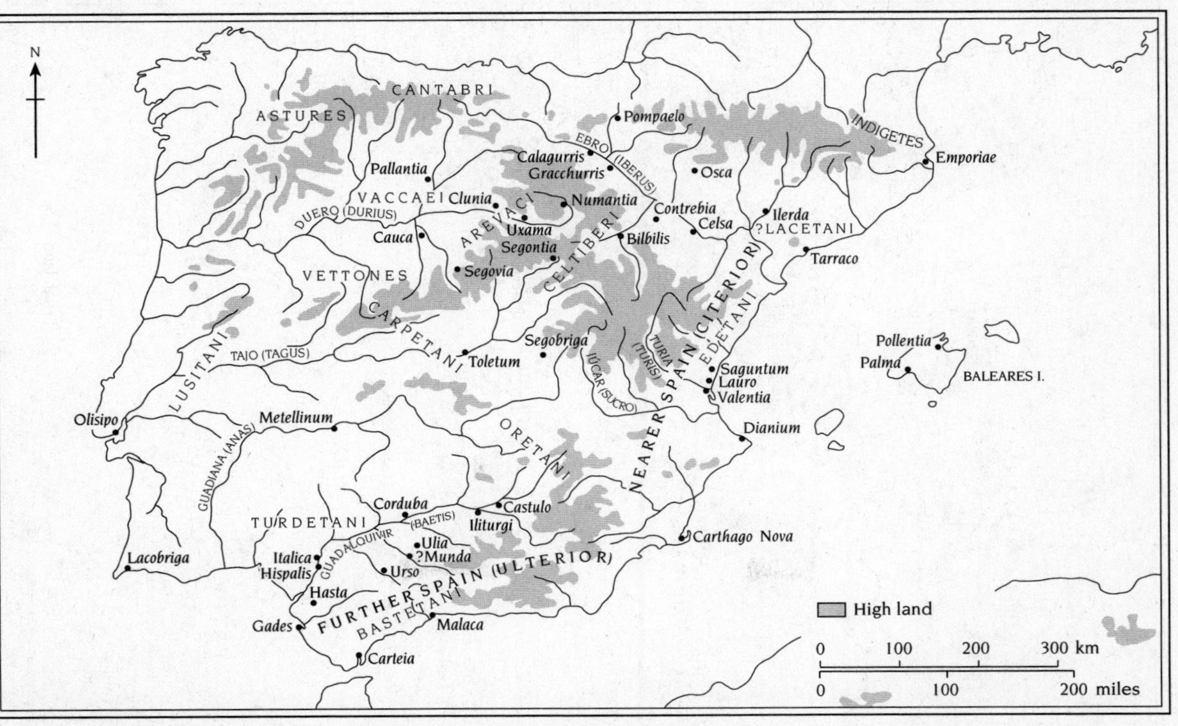
N
CANTABRI
ASTURES
Pompaelo
INDIGETES
Emporiae
EBRO (IBERUS)
Calagurris
Gracchurris
Osca
Pallantia
VACCAEI
Clunia
Numantia
AREVACI
Contrebia
Ilerda
?LACETANI
DUERO (DURIUS)
Uxama
Celsa
Cauca
Segontia
Bilbilis
Tarraco
CELTIBERI
Segovia
VETTONES
NEARER SPAIN (CITERIOR)
EDETANI
CARPETANI
Segobriga
Pollentia
Palma
BALEARES I.
TAJO (TAGUS)
Toletum
TURIA (TURIS)
JÚCAR (SUCRO)
Saguntum
Lauro
Valentia
LUSITANI
Olisipo
Metellinum
Dianium
GUADIANA (ANAS)
ORETANI
Corduba
Castulo
TURDETANI
(BAETIS)
Iliturgi
GUADALQUIVIR
Ulia
?Munda
Carthago Nova
Lacobriga
Italica
Hispalis
Urso
FURTHER SPAIN (ULTERIOR)
Hasta
BASTETANI
Gades
Malaca
Carteia
High land
0
100
200
300 km
0
100
200 miles

MAP 5. SPAIN

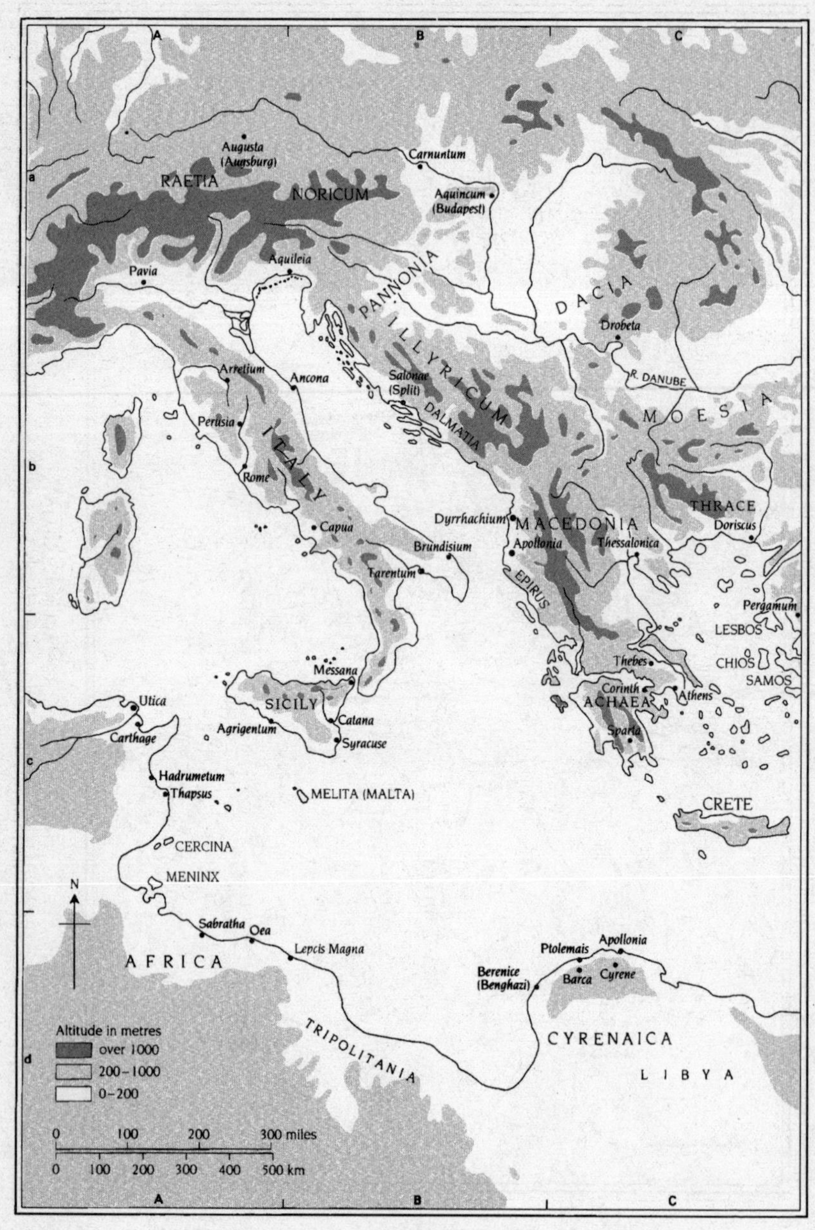

MAP 6. THE ROMAN EMPIRE, CENTRAL PORTION

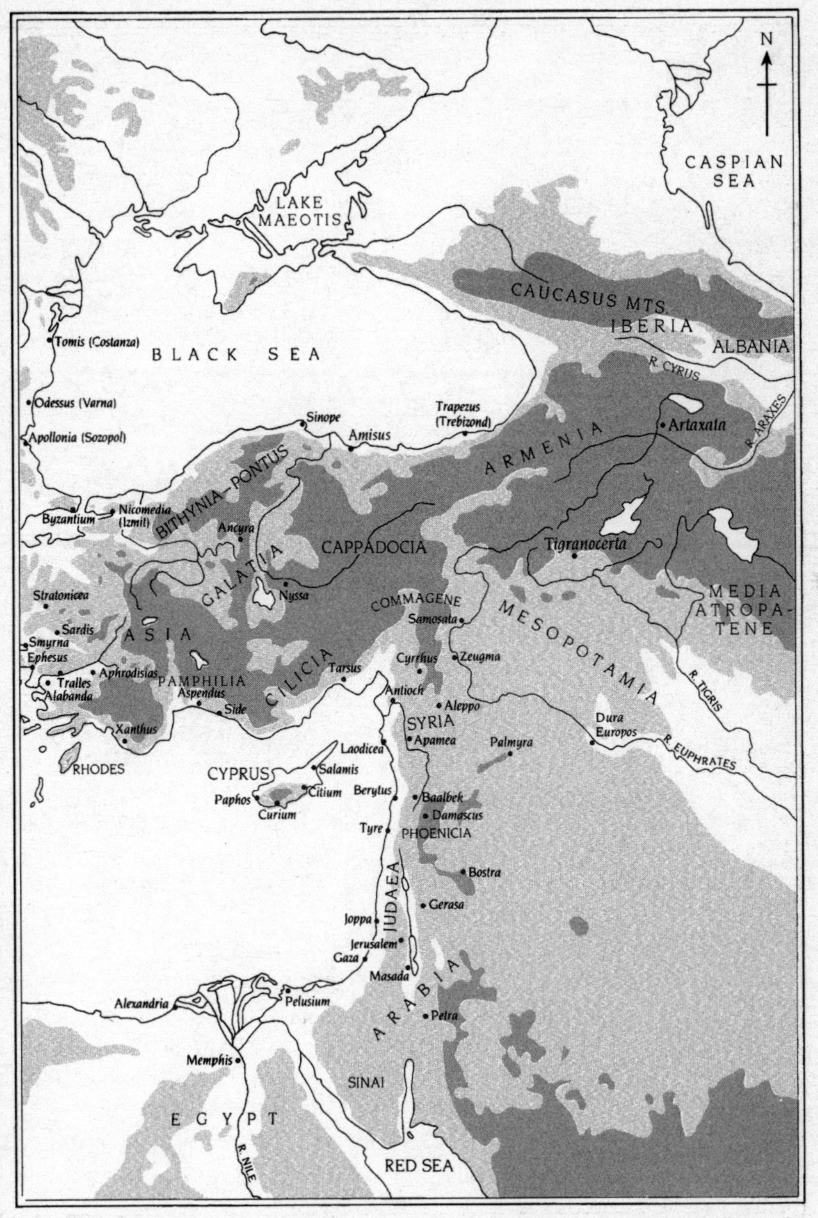

MAP 7. THE ROMAN EMPIRE, EASTERN PORTION

ROMAN LIVES

CATO THE ELDER

INTRODUCTION

Cato the Elder[1] was the very epitome of the old Roman: raised in the Sabine country, tough, parsimonious, outstanding in war, continuously active in politics. Born in 234 BC, he made a name for himself as a soldier during the Second Punic War, and although his family had never before even been senators, was able to win election as consul in 195. He commanded brilliantly in Spain, for which he was awarded a triumph, then played a major role in the defeat of Antiochus in Greece in 191. The high point of his long career was his term as censor in 184, when he took severe steps, challenging members of the old senatorial families and his rivals the Scipios and Flamininus. His skill at law and oratory was both legendary and necessary, since he was constantly prosecuting others or defending himself. The historian Livy describes him as harsh in disposition and bitter and frank in speaking, 'but his character was absolute proof against the assault of appetites; he was marked by a rigid integrity and a contempt for popularity and riches' (39. 40).[2] His fame lived after him, aided by the literary works which survived him: the texts of his much admired speeches, his *Origins*, which was the first history of Rome in Latin, and other works. Cicero in his *On Old Age* created a portrait of him as a grandfatherly old man, at a time when his great-grandson Cato was causing as much trouble for Caesar and Pompey as the censor had made for the Scipios.

Plutarch had a different vision, of a man hardworking yet litigious, independent but extremely competitive, who lived as austerely as a philosopher, but sold aged slaves to save money and took a young wife in advanced age to satisfy his sexual needs. He pairs Cato with Aristides, a leading Athenian general during the Persian Wars, so noted for his honesty that he received the nickname 'the Just'. Both men represent a type of ancient simplicity, which in Plutarch's day might be associated with Cynic philosophers or Socrates. In fact the figure of Socrates recurs regularly in this pair of Lives (*Arist.* 1, 27; *Cato* 7, 20, 23). Both emerge as teachers in a pre-philosophical mode. That is, in their political lives they try to instruct their fellow citizens in honesty and other traditional virtues. But

[1] M. Porcius Cato is called the Elder or the Censor to distinguish him from his great-grandson and namesake, the Cato who opposed Caesar and committed suicide at Utica in 46 BC (cf. *Caes.* 54), whose Life was also written by Plutarch.

[2] Trans. by H. Bettenson (Harmondsworth: Penguin, 1976).

whereas Aristides is honest because he is uninterested in money, Cato's thriftiness is coupled with a desire to build his estate. Aristides dies so poor that his daughters must be supplied dowries by the city; Cato dies a wealthy man, who has established his family for generations. Aristides' lack of ambition allows him to reconcile himself with Themistocles for the good of Athens; Cato's competitiveness drives him to fight with his leading contemporaries in the senate and in the courts. Both are great men, but their austere simplicity springs from different roots, and has different outcomes, which Plutarch explores in the two Lives and in the paradoxical Comparison which follows them.

After beginning with Cato's origins and early life in the Sabine country outside Rome, Plutarch describes Cato's temperament and two major influences on him: Manius Curius, the great general who preferred his dinner of boiled turnips to the gold offered by the enemy, and the Pythagorean teaching he learned while campaigning at Tarentum (c. 2). The early chapters run through his career down to his consulate (cc. 3–9), but the emphasis is on his character rather than on offices: his simplicity, his litigiousness, his skill in oratory, miserliness, and self-discipline. Brief anecdotes are both scattered in the narrative and accumulated in a mass, quoting many of his own sayings (8–9). The following chapters narrate his military successes, as consul in Spain (10–11) and as a subordinate officer fighting against Antiochus in Greece (12–14). The battle of Thermopylae, in which Cato played a prominent role, is parallel to the battle of Plataea in which Aristides starred. Plutarch then shifts to the political arena, first with examples of Cato's prosecutions of fellow senators (15), then his term as censor (16–19).

The censorship, the most prestigious though not the most powerful Roman magistracy, was the highest rank of the *cursus honorum* (cf. Appendix, p. 433). The two censors, elected every five years almost exclusively from among ex-consuls to serve for eighteen months, made a census of Roman citizens (and thus of the city's military manpower), reviewed the ranks of the senate and of those who had the privilege of a state-supplied horse, let out contracts for public construction, leased public lands and tax contracts, and attended to other duties (16). For the biographer, Cato's role as censor is that of a doctor and teacher, healing the state of its excesses and training it in sobriety and good health practices. In reviewing the citizen and senatorial lists, censors were allowed to remove those whose behaviour or physical condition was not suitable. This gave them some power to regulate morals, which they occasionally exercised. But the powerful image of cutting off the Hydra's heads and cauterizing the scar to prevent regrowth which Plutarch uses of Cato (16) aptly conveys the violence and abruptness of Cato's methods. He expelled distinguished men from the senate and deprived others of honours, forced businessmen to pay more for state contracts on building and taxes, and otherwise attacked the entrenched prerogatives of the nobility. His censorship made him hated by many, but also won him praise and fame (19).

Plutarch sets the censorship against his personal life, which he treats in the following chapters (20–5). Cato's devotion to his family led him to teach his son himself, thus educating his family as well as the state. His management of his estates, like his treatment of his slaves, was idiosyncratic, but showed the same parsimony and respect for the value of work he urged for the city. He rejected Greek philosophy, as represented by an embassy of leading philosophers from Athens, fearing that 'the young men of the city . . . might find a reputation for eloquence more desirable than one gained from practical and military achievements' (22). However, Plutarch is rather shocked by his decision to take a young wife of lower social standing when he already had a grown son (24). The Life ends with his relentless opposition to Carthage, which finally led to war and the destruction of the city. Even the last battle of his life, his often repeated demand that Carthage be destroyed (26–7), Plutarch places in the context of the education of the city. Although Scipio Nasica argued that an external enemy would 'curb the rashness of the masses', Cato insisted that external enemies must be destroyed before domestic faults were attacked.

Although Cornelius Nepos had written a biography of Cato in the first century BC (now lost, though a much shorter Life by Nepos survives), Plutarch does not seem to have used Nepos' or another biography as a source for this Life. Polybius, the major historian of this period, whom Plutarch cites at chapter 10, probably provided the basic historical outline and many of the individual items. Polybius not only wrote in Greek, but from 167 BC was for many years confined in Rome and became intimate with leading political figures, including Scipio Aemilianus, so that Plutarch would have respected his thorough narrative and the fact that he was a contemporary witness to Cato's activity in his later years.[3] Much of the text of Polybius for the years after the Second Punic War is now lost, however, and we must rely on Livy, who lived under Augustus and used Polybius as well as Roman sources. Livy wrote a history of Rome from its foundation to 9 BC in 142 books of which thirty-five survive, including books 31–45 treating 202–167 BC.[4] His account frequently

[3] Plutarch cites Polybius in *Aemilius* 15, 16, and 19 and in *Tiberius and Gaius Gracchus* 4 in this collection, as well as in *Pelopidas*, *Aratus*, *Agis and Cleomenes*, *Marcellus*, *Philopoemen*, *Virtues in Women* 258e–f, *Fortune of Rome* 325f, and *Old Men in Politics* 791f.

[4] Plutarch cites Livy also in *Sulla* 6 and *Caesar* 47 and 63 in this collection, as well as in *Camillus*, *Marcellus*, *Flamininus*, *Roman Questions* 269e, and *Fortune of Rome* 326a.

highlights Cato's role in politics, and he offers a masterly sketch of him at 39. 40. 4–12. Plutarch certainly used Livy also, though it is not clear how much. In chapter 17, he refers both to Livy and to Cicero's *Cato, or On Old Age*, a charming dialogue in which Cato is the major figure. Several items of the Life seem to be drawn from this dialogue, which he mentions also in *Flamininus* 18.

Plutarch's most important source, however, was Cato's own speeches and writings, which he refers to some thirty-four times. Plutarch preferred to employ contemporary sources for his *Lives* when they were available, and Cato's speeches and books gave him excellent material. Cato was the earliest Roman known to have left written copies of his speeches: Cicero knew more than 150, and we know of some 80 titles. There is no doubt that Plutarch had access to a collection of some sort. Many of the anecdotes in chapters 8–9 and elsewhere in the Life derive from them. He also refers to Cato's letter to his son (20), which is frequently quoted by Roman writers, to a treatise or notebook on medicine (23), and to *On Agriculture*, the only work of Cato's to survive (25). Plutarch may also have used the *Origins*, which, with his speeches, may be said to give Cato the title of founder of Latin prose. Earlier literary Roman historians had written in Greek; Cato chose to write in Latin, emphasizing the early history of the Italic communities and bringing his history down to his own day. Never modest, he included texts of at least two of his own speeches.

The quotations from the speeches give the Life an unusual vividness and charm. Nevertheless there are stories which may owe more to Cicero's imaginative dialogue than to the historical record, some intriguing gaps, and a few errors in names in Plutarch's account. Probably the most difficult part of Roman republican history for Plutarch to master was the host of persons in the Roman aristocracy. Since the politically active families were relatively few, and tended to use the same names even among members of the same generation, it was very easy to confuse one individual with another. In this Life, Plutarch speaks of Scipio Africanus once when the elder Scipio Nasica must be meant, and at one point confuses Cato's two sons and their relation to the younger Cato (cf. the notes to cc. 11 and 27). Plutarch omits events in Cato's career which we know from other sources, such as his outstanding contribution at the battle of the Metaurus in 207 or his being plebeian aedile in 199, both reported by Cornelius Nepos. Nepos also notes that he was responsible for bringing the major poet Ennius to Rome from Sardinia. This seems an unlikely story, but has been accepted by many scholars. Plutarch and our other sources are silent. Two political events which are dramatically presented by Livy are also omitted: his opposition as consul to the repeal of the Oppian law on spending by women (Livy 34. 1–8), and his first campaign for the censorship in 189 (Livy 37. 57. 13–15). Plutarch alludes only briefly to the series of court battles that occupied Cato after his consulship. Unlike Livy or Polybius, he does not trace the currents of Roman politics year by year, but gives an overall view of Cato as a highly competitive politician and a man of rigid old-fashioned principles.

Astin, A. E., *Cato the Censor* (Oxford: Clarendon Press, 1978).

Linderski, J., 'Cato Maior in Aetolia', in R. W. Wallace and E. M. Harris (eds.), *Transitions to Empire: Essays in Greco-Roman History, 360–146 BC, in Honor of E. Badian* (Norman and London: University of Oklahoma Press, 1996), 376–408.

Malcovati, H. (ed.), *Oratorum Romanorum Fragmenta liberae rei publicae*, 4th edn., i (Turin: Paravia, 1976), 12–97. The standard Latin edition of Cato's speeches.

Pelling, C. B. R., 'Plutarch: Roman Heroes and Greek Culture', in M. Griffin and J. Barnes (eds.), *Philosophia Togata: Essays on Philosophy and Roman Society* (Oxford: Clarendon Press, 1989), 199–232.

Sansone, D., *Plutarch: The Lives of Aristides and Cato* (Warminster: Aris and Phillips, 1989). Greek text, translation, and commentary.

Scullard, H. H., *Roman Politics 220–150 BC*, 2nd edn. (Oxford: Oxford University Press, 1973). Appendix II, 256–72, gives a summary account of Cato's speeches.

Swain, S. C. R., 'Hellenic Culture and the Roman Lives of Plutarch', *Journal of Hellenic Studies*, 11 (1990), 126–45; reprinted in B. Scardigli (ed.), *Essays on Plutarch's Lives* (Oxford: Clarendon Press, 1995), 229–64.

CATO THE ELDER

[1] Marcus Cato's family came originally from Tusculum, they say, although before embarking on his military and political career he lived on ancestral estates in the territory of the Sabines.* His forebears seem to have been altogether unremarkable people, but Cato himself praises the excellence and military skills of his father Marcus and claims that Cato, his great-grandfather, was often awarded prizes for valour, and after losing five war-horses in various battles was paid back for them out of the public treasury in honour of his courage.* The Romans traditionally refer to men who come from an undistinguished family, but begin to gain prominence by their own merits, as 'new men',* and they certainly used this expression of Cato, but he himself used to say that although he was new in terms of high office and fame, his ancestors' exploits and virtues made him truly ancient. His third name was originally Priscus rather than Cato, but then he gained the nickname 'Cato' from his abilities—*catus* being the Roman word for someone astute.*

In appearance, he had reddish hair and grey eyes, as we know from the author of the following rather barbed epigram:

> With his red hair, his habit of snapping at everyone, and his grey eyes,
> Even in death Porcius is rejected by Persephone.*

Since from his early days he was familiar with manual labour, a modest lifestyle, and military campaigning, he was physically fit, with his body an effective instrument, made for both strength and health, and he developed and equipped himself with an eloquent style of speech as if it were a second body—a tool that is virtually indispensable if a man is to avoid a life of obscurity and failure. He was often to be found in the courts of the towns and villages near where he lived, helping people who needed assistance, and so he acquired a reputation at first as someone who would commit himself to a cause, and then later as a good public speaker. After this, people who had dealings with him increasingly came to see that he was a man of substance and self-esteem, destined for great achievements and political leadership. Apparently, not only did he provide his services for lawsuits and court cases without sullying himself by demanding fees, but he also gave people the impression that he did not even regard as particularly important the reputation he gained from this kind of attitude towards court cases. He much preferred to shine in the military sphere, when fighting enemy troops, and even as a young adult he was wounded time and again on the front of his body. He himself says that he was 17 years old when he first saw military service, at the time when Hannibal was setting Italy ablaze with his success.*

His hand in battle was fierce, his foot steady and reliable, his face exultant. He would use a threatening and savage tone of voice on his enemies, since he correctly recognized, and taught others, that this often strikes more terror into an opponent than a sword. On the march he carried his own arms and armour, while a single attendant would follow with his provisions, and it is said that Cato never lost his temper with this man or found fault with the way he served his meals, but would even lend a hand himself and help him prepare most of the meals, once he had finished with his military duties. Out on campaign he used to drink water, unless he had a raging thirst, when he would call for vinegar,* or was feeling weak, when he would add a little wine to his water.

[2] A favourite walk of Cato's used to take him to the villa, near his farm, which had once belonged to Manius Curius,* a man who had celebrated three triumphs. When he saw how small the estate was and how simple the house was, he would reflect that although the man had become the greatest Roman of his time, although he had subdued the most belligerent tribes and driven Pyrrhus out of Italy, he used to turn the soil of this little estate with his own hands and live in this villa even after three triumphs. This was the house where a delegation of Samnites had once found him sitting by the fire and boiling turnips; they offered him a great deal of money, but he sent them packing, saying that anyone who was content with the kind of meal he was cooking had no need of gold, and that he found defeating those who possessed gold more attractive than possessing it himself. Cato would return home with his mind filled with these things; they made him see his own house, land, slaves, and lifestyle in a new light, and he would increase the amount of manual labour he put into his farm and do away with luxuries.

Cato was a young man at the time when Fabius Maximus* took Tarentum, and he served under him during the campaign. He happened to be staying with a man called Nearchus,* a Pythagorean, and he expressed an interest in hearing something of Pythagorean doctrine. As the man spoke, Cato heard from him notions which had been central to Plato as well: that there is no greater temptation to evil than pleasure, which is therefore to be avoided; that the mind's worst misfortune is the body; and that freedom and purification come about particularly when the mind detaches and distances itself from bodily sensations by making use of its rational faculty. This teaching made Cato even more attracted to a life of simplicity and self-discipline. Other than this, however, it is said that contact with Greek culture came to him late in life, and that he was really quite old when he took up Greek books and had his rhetorical style improved by Demosthenes, and to a lesser extent by Thucydides. But Greek ideas and stories are fairly well scattered throughout his writings, and a number of literal translations from the Greek are deployed among his maxims and aphorisms.

[3] There was a man, as well born and powerful as anyone in Rome, who had the ability to perceive budding excellence, and the kindly inclination to nourish it and bring it forth into the light of general approbation. His name was Valerius Flaccus.* His estate bordered Cato's and he heard from his slaves how Cato lived and how he laboured on his own land. He was impressed to hear that Cato walked to the forum in the morning and helped those who needed his assistance, before returning to his estate, where he worked alongside his slaves, wearing in the wintertime a labourer's toga and in the summertime no more than his underclothes; after work, they said, he sat down with his slaves, eating the same bread and drinking the same wine. After hearing further examples of Cato's decency and lack of pretension from his slaves, who even mentioned some of his aphorisms, he had Cato invited to dinner. He came to like him and to recognize that his humane and refined character was like a plant which needed cultivation and room to gain distinction, and so with encouraging words he persuaded him to take up a public career in Rome. On arriving in the city it did not take Cato long to acquire a number of admirers and friends on his own merits as a result of the cases he pleaded in court, and his prestige and influence also grew thanks to Valerius. The first office he obtained was that of military tribune, and then later a quaestorship. By now he was well known in Rome, a man of distinction, and along with Valerius himself he

sallied forth after the highest offices, so that they served together as consuls and then as censors.

Among the elder Romans, Cato attached himself to Fabius Maximus, a man whose reputation and power in the city were second to none, but Cato was more interested in having his character and his lifestyle before him as outstanding examples. That is why he did not hesitate to quarrel with Scipio the Great,* still a young man then, who was a political opponent of Fabius and was generally thought to be resented by him. He was sent out along with Scipio as his quaestor for the war in Africa, but when he saw him indulging in his usual extravagance and wasting money in a profligate way on his campaigns, he spoke his mind to him, saying that the worst aspect was not the sheer expense, but the fact that he was corrupting the traditional frugality of his men, who turned to hedonism and self-indulgence when they had more than they needed. Scipio replied that, with the wind behind him as he sailed for war, the last thing he wanted was a pernickety quaestor, since Rome would require from him an account of his achievements, not of his costs. So Cato left Sicily, and he and Fabius joined forces in the senate to denounce Scipio's incredible expenditure and the way he spent his time on childish pursuits in the wrestling-schools and theatres, as if he were celebrating a festival rather than commanding an army. The upshot was that the tribunes were sent to bring Scipio back to Rome, to see if the charges were valid. Scipio argued that in war victory depended on the preparations, convinced the senate that, however pleasant he was with friends in his free time, his social life did not make him sluggish when it came to serious and important business, and then sailed back to the war.

[4] Cato owed his vastly increased power to his eloquence—in fact, most Romans called him a second Demosthenes—but his way of life was more famous and celebrated. After all, the young men of Rome had already made skill at public speaking a universally desired prize, whereas it was a rare man who endured manual labour as his ancestors had, who was content with a plain evening meal, an uncooked breakfast, simple clothing, and an unpretentious house, and who was less impressed by the possession of luxuries than he was by the ability to do without them. By that time Rome had grown too big to preserve its integrity; so many lands and people were under its control that it was in contact with a variety of practices and

was influenced by all kinds of customs. It is hardly surprising, then, that they admired Cato: all around them they could see people collapsing in the face of hard work and becoming enfeebled by a life of hedonism, whereas he was impervious to both. This was the case not only while he was young and ambitious, but also when he was quite elderly and had already held the consulship and celebrated a triumph; like a victorious athlete he maintained his training schedule consistently right up to the end of his life. He says that he never wore any item of clothing that cost more than a hundred drachmas; that even during his periods of office as praetor or consul he drank the same wine as his rowers;*† that he used to spend thirty asses in the forum on the savouries for his evening meal, and did so for Rome's sake, so that he would be physically fit for his campaigns; that when he inherited an embroidered Babylonian rug he sold it straight away; that none of his villas ever had plastered walls; and that he never bought a slave for more than fifteen hundred drachmas, since he did not want delicately handsome young men, but sturdy workmen who could serve as grooms, for instance, or as ox-herders (and his policy when even these slaves became too old to give him useful service was to sell them rather than support them).* Basically, he used to say, the term 'cheap' did not apply to something inessential: even if something cost only an as, you should regard it as expensive if it was not something you needed. And he said that he bought land to sow grain and graze cattle, not to sprinkle lawns and sweep up debris.

[5] Some people interpreted this as evidence of a streak of miserliness in Cato, but others took it as the sign of a man whose purpose was to discipline others and show them the right way to behave by keeping within his own means. In my personal opinion, however, to banish slaves and sell them when they get old is to treat them like yoke-animals and indicates excessive callousness and a belief that the only bond between one human being and another is utility. It is obvious, however, that kindness has a wider scope than justice, because we naturally apply law and justice only to men, but benevolence and compassion sometimes flow from the rich spring of our humane side and reach even irrational animals. For instance, a kind owner continues to maintain his horses when they are past their prime, and does not keep dogs only for breeding purposes, but also looks after them in their old age. When the Athenian people were building the Parthenon, they set free all the mules they noticed were

particularly hard-working, and let them graze free and unrestricted. Apparently, one of these mules used to go down of its own accord to the work-site and run alongside the yoke-animals which were pulling the carts to the Acropolis, showing them the way, as if it were encouraging them and urging them on. The Athenians passed a decree to the effect that the mule was to be fed at state expense for the rest of its life. Then there were the horses with which Cimon won three victories at the Olympic Games, which are buried near his own tomb. Among a large number of cases involving dogs which were brought up along with people and became their close companions there is the story from long ago of how the dog which swam beside Xanthippus' trireme to Salamis, during the Athenian abandonment of the city, was buried by him on the headland which is still called Houndsgrave even today.* We should not treat any living creature as we do our footwear or utensils, and just discard them once they become tired and worn down by the uses to which we put them. No, even if only in order to practise kindness, we should use animals to acquire the habit of being gentle and tender. For my part, I would not sell even a draught ox because it was old, let alone an elderly human being; I would not take a few coins to uproot a man from the place where he has long lived and his familiar way of life—to banish him from his homeland, so to speak—when he is going to be just as useless to the buyer as he was to the seller. Cato, however, seems to revel in this kind of behaviour when he says that he left behind in Spain even the horse which he used on his campaigns during the year of his consulship,* to save the state the cost of transporting it by boat. But anyway, it could plausibly be argued either that this behaviour of his stemmed from high principle or that it was due to miserliness.

[6] On the whole, however, his self-discipline was unusually admirable. As commander, he would take for himself and his men rations of no more than three Attic medimni of wheat per month, and less than one and a half medimni of barley per day for the yoke-animals. As praetor, he was assigned the province of Sardinia,* and the contrast between him and his predecessors was incredible. They had invariably been housed, fed, and clothed at state expense, and had oppressed the islanders with the size of their retinue, the number of their friends, and the cost and burden of preparing their meals, but Cato made no extra demands on the public purse, and

visited the island's communities in person, without taking a chariot and with a single servant in attendance, provided by the state, who carried the clothing and libation-bowl Cato would need to perform sacrifices. His subjects found him an undemanding and unpretentious praetor, and yet he restored the dignity and solemnity of the position by being uncompromising in his administration of justice, and by adhering in a direct and forthright manner to the edicts issued on behalf of the government, with the result that for the islanders Roman rule was simultaneously more formidable and more congenial than it ever had been.

[7] Much the same kind of description applies to Cato's public speaking as well, which was simultaneously graceful and forceful, pleasing and terrifying, humorous and stern, aphoristic and argumentative. One is reminded of how Plato says* that on the outside Socrates appeared to his acquaintances to be a rude, satyr-like bully, whereas on the inside he was deeply serious and filled with issues which could move his followers to tears and wrench their hearts. I have no idea, then, why some people claim that Cato's style of speaking was very similar to that of Lysias.* Still, there are others better equipped than I to recognize the different styles of Roman oratory, and they will decide this matter, while I will briefly record some of Cato's sayings, since I maintain that men's character is revealed far more clearly by their speech than it is, as some believe, by their faces.

[8] Once, when the Roman people were planning to distribute and dole out an inordinate amount of grain and Cato wanted to try to dissuade them, he began his speech by saying, 'My fellow citizens, it is hard to argue with the stomach, which has no ears.' As part of a denunciation of extravagance he said that a city was well on the way to ruin when a fish cost more than an ox.* Once he compared the Romans to sheep, on the grounds that even when individual sheep had no reason for compliance, the whole herd still all followed their leaders: 'The same goes for you too,' he said. 'When you all meet together, you let yourselves be led by people whose advice you wouldn't deign to listen to in private.'

On the subject of the power of women he said, 'Men rule their wives, yet we, who rule all men, are ruled by our wives.' But this, at any rate, is a version of one of Themistocles' sayings. His son kept using his mother to tell him what to do, so Themistocles said, 'Woman, the Athenians rule the Greeks, I rule the Athenians, you rule me, and our son rules you. For all his immaturity, then, he is the most powerful person in Greece; he had better not abuse this position.'*

Cato said that the Roman people regulated the price not only of purple-dyed material but also of behaviour. 'Dyers', he explained, 'make a particular point of using whatever dye they see people like, and in the same way our young men learn and emulate whatever behaviour attracts your praise.' He used to tell them that there was no need for them to change if they owed their importance to moral and virtuous conduct, since any change would only be for the worse, but that if they owed it to vicious and immoral conduct, they should change for the better, since it was enough that they had become as great as they were by relying on that kind of conduct.

He described men who wanted to hold high office over and over again as people who did not know where they were going and needed lictors* to show them every step of the way forward and stop them from getting lost. And he used to criticize his fellow citizens for electing the same people over and over again: 'You will make people think', he said, 'that in your opinion either high office is virtually worthless, or there are virtually no people who are worthy of high office.'

One of his opponents had the reputation of living a disgraceful and degrading life, and Cato said, 'The prospect of leaving him alive after her death is not something his mother asks the gods to guarantee, but to avert.' Pointing to a man who had sold his ancestral farm by the coast, he pretended to be much impressed by how much stronger he was than the sea: 'He had no difficulty in gulping down what the sea hardly lapped at,' he said.*

On a visit to Rome, King Eumenes* was received by the senate with extraordinary pomp and ceremony, and the leading citizens were eagerly trying to outdo one another in lavishing attention on him, but Cato made no secret of the fact that he was keeping a wary and suspicious eye on him. When someone remarked, 'But he is a good man, and pro-Roman', Cato replied, 'That may be, but it is the nature of the beast to eat meat.' He once said that none of the kings who were objects of admiration then could stand comparison with Epaminondas or Pericles or Themistocles or Manius Curius or Hamilcar, surnamed Barca.

He used to claim that his opponents resented the fact that every day he got up while it was still dark, paid no attention to his own private affairs, and occupied himself with state business. He used to say that he would prefer not to be thanked for doing good than not to be punished for doing bad, and he said that he could forgive everyone's wrongs except his own.

[9] When the Romans chose three ambassadors to send to Bithynia, of whom one suffered from gout, another had a dent in his head as a result of having been operated on with a trepan, and the third was generally held to be an imbecile, Cato said with a mocking laugh that the Romans were sending a delegation which lacked feet, head, and heart.*

The question whether or not Rome should allow the Achaean exiles to return to their homeland came to be the topic of a great deal of discussion in the senate, with opinions divided on either side. Cato (to whom Scipio had, at Polybius' instigation, made an appeal) got to his feet and said, 'Here we sit all day long, as if we had nothing better to do, debating whether some elderly Greeks should be buried by the undertakers here or in Achaea.' Then a few days later, after the senate had voted to repatriate them, Polybius tried to gain entry into the senate again, this time to help the exiles regain the rights and privileges they had formerly held in Achaea. When he tried to find out how Cato felt about the matter, Cato smiled and said that Polybius was behaving like Odysseus, wanting to return to the Cyclops' cave because he had accidentally left his cap and his belt there.*

He used to say that intelligent men profited more from fools than the other way round, because they were wary of fools' errors, whereas fools failed to imitate the achievements of intelligent men.

He said that he preferred to see young men go red in the face than turn pale, and that he had no need for a soldier who moved his hands on the march and his feet in battle,* or one whose snore was louder than his battle-cry. Once, when he was abusing someone who was overweight, he said, 'What possible good is a body like that to Rome? The whole region from gullet to groin is nothing but belly.' When a hedonist suggested that they get acquainted, he refused, saying that he could not spend time with a man whose palate was more sensitive than his heart. He used to say that a lover's mind lives in someone else's body.

He said that he had only three regrets in his whole life: that he had once trusted a woman with a secret, that on one occasion he had taken a ship when he could have gone by foot, and that he had spent a particular day intestate.

To a wicked old man he said, 'Sir, old age has degradations enough without your adding the disgrace of depravity.' Once a tribune who had been accused of administering poison was trying to force the passage of a pernicious law, and Cato said, 'Young man, I don't know which is worse: to drink your potion or to ratify your proposal.' When he was being insulted by a man who had lived a coarse and foul life, he said, 'You have the advantage over me in this battle: it doesn't bother you to be abused and you have a facility at abusing others, but I find both giving and receiving insults distasteful.' This is a representative sample of his sayings.

[10] He was appointed to the consulate with Valerius Flaccus, his close friend, as his colleague, and was assigned the province which the Romans call 'Nearer Spain'.* In the course of subduing some of the native tribes and winning others over by diplomacy, he was attacked by a huge enemy army. He was close to being driven ignominiously out of the province, so he asked the neighbouring Celtiberians for reinforcements. They replied that their assistance would cost two hundred talents. Everyone else regarded it as out of the question for Romans to agree to pay foreigners for help, but Cato argued that nothing terrible would come of it: if they won they would get the money from their enemies rather than pay themselves, and if they lost there would be nobody left to issue or receive the demand. However, he overwhelmed the enemy in the battle, and made outstanding progress on all fronts. In fact, Polybius says* that on his orders all the fortifications of the towns on this side of the river Baetis—and there was a very large number of towns, filled with warlike men—were demolished in a single day. Cato himself says that he captured more than one town for every day he spent in Spain, which is no idle boast, if there really were four hundred of them.

Despite the fact that his troops had enriched themselves during the campaign, he still gave a pound of silver more to each man, with the remark that it was better for many Romans to come back home with silver than for a few to do so with gold. As for himself, he says that all he gained from the booty was his food and drink. 'It's not that I find anything wrong with people seeking to enrich themselves from warfare,' he says, 'but my goal is to excel in virtue, not in wealth or avarice.' He tried to keep those close to him free from the slightest stigma of profiteering, as well as himself. There were five men who attended to him while he was on campaign, and one of them, called Paccius, bought three boys from among the prisoners of war. When Cato found out, Paccius hanged himself before he could be brought to face him. Cato sold the boys and gave the money to the public treasury.

[11] Scipio the Great,* who was a political opponent of Cato, wanted to curb his successes and take over the command of Spanish operations. So while Cato was still in Spain, Scipio got himself appointed as his successor in the province, hurried there as fast as he could, and relieved Cato of his command. But taking a detachment of five cohorts of legionaries, with an escort of five hundred cavalrymen, Cato subdued the tribe of the Lacetani and recaptured six hundred deserters, whom he executed.* When Scipio complained,* Cato ironically said that this was a good example of how Rome would achieve true greatness when the eminent notables of the city refused to yield the prize for virtue to less distinguished members of society, and when plebeians like himself set themselves up as rivals in the domain of excellence of those who owed their prominence to their families and their reputations. In any case, the senate decreed that none of Cato's provisions should be altered or interfered with, and meanwhile Scipio's administration did more harm to his own reputation than to Cato's, since he wasted his time there in inactivity and indolence, and Cato was awarded a triumph. Now, most people who attain the highest honours, hold a consulship, and celebrate a triumph, then go on to abandon public life and make sure that they see out their days in pleasure and idleness, because their sights had been set on fame rather than excellence. Cato, however, did no such thing. Rather than letting the freshness and vigour go out of his commitment to excellence, he behaved more like someone just embarking on a political career and still hungry for honour and fame. He summoned up his energies for a fresh start and made himself available to both his friends and his fellow citizens, never turning down either a court case or a military campaign.

[12] So he acted as legate to the consul Tiberius Sempronius* and shared his achievements in Thrace and around the Danube, and as military tribune he joined Manius Acilius on his campaign abroad in Greece against Antiochus the Great,* who was making the Romans more anxious than anyone had since Hannibal. He had retaken

almost as much of Asia as Seleucus Nicator had controlled, and with very many warlike eastern peoples under his dominion he felt strong enough to take on the Romans, who were the only ones, in his opinion, who might be able to resist him. Claiming that he was going to war in order to free the Greeks (even though this was entirely unnecessary since thanks to the Romans they had recently gained their freedom and independence from Philip and the Macedonians*), he crossed over with his army. Greece was immediately thrown into a state of turmoil and uncertainty, with the popular leaders corrupting the Greeks' resolve with optimistic talk of what being ruled by a king might hold for them. Manius therefore sent delegates to the Greek cities, and while it was Titus Flamininus, as I described in my account of his life,* who kept most of the states which were inclined to rebel calm and peaceful, Cato placated the people of Corinth and Patrae, and also won over the people of Aegium. He spent a long time in Athens, and it is said that a speech of his is extant which he delivered in Greek to the Athenian people, to the effect that he admired the noble qualities of the ancient Athenians and was glad to have seen such a beautiful and great city. But this is not true, since he spoke to the Athenians through a translator. He could have made the speech on his own, but he was a staunch traditionalist and used to mock those who admired Greek ways. For example, he made fun of Postumius Albinus, who wrote a *History* in Greek and begged his readers to excuse him for doing so, by saying that his behaviour was excusable only if the job had been forced on him by Amphictyonic decree.* He says that the Athenians were impressed by how quickly and concisely he spoke, since the translator had to use lengthy circumlocutions to express what took him only a few words. And he says that in his opinion the Greeks speak from the mouth and the Romans from the heart.

[13] Antiochus barricaded the pass at Thermopylae with his army, enhanced the natural defences of the place with palisades and fortifications, and sat back, thinking that he had precluded the possibility of war. The Romans were beginning to lose all hope of forcing their way in by the direct route when Cato recalled the famous Persian outflanking and encircling manoeuvre* and set out under cover of darkness with a portion of the army. They made their way up to the heights, but then the prisoner who was guiding them lost his way and started wandering aimlessly over impossible, craggy terrain,

which disheartened and terrified the troops. When Cato saw how dangerous the situation was, he ordered the whole army to stay calm and wait, while he went on ahead himself, with an expert mountaineer called Lucius Mallius. It was hard and perilous work, since it was the middle of a moonless night, and there were so many wild olive-trees and rocks that they often had their view blocked or obscured, but at last they struck a path which they thought went down to the enemy camp, so they marked some rocks which jutted out over Callidromum and would be easy to find again, and made their way back to the army. Once they had picked up the rest of the army, they led the way back towards their marks, found the path, and started forward. They had gone only a short way, however, when the path gave out and a ravine suddenly greeted them. Once again, they were filled with confusion and fear, since they could not know or see that they were in fact close to the enemy.

By now day was beginning to break. One of the men thought he could hear voices, and before long a Greek palisade and a guard-post became visible at the foot of the cliffs. Cato therefore halted the army there and told the Firmans,* whose reliability and commitment he constantly used to depend on, to detach themselves from the rest and come to him. When they were standing around him in a group, after running over, he said, 'Well, I need to capture one of the enemy alive and to find out from him which troops are manning this guard-post, how many of them there are, how the rest of the enemy army has been arranged and deployed, and what preparations they have made to meet us. Success has to be snatched by the speed and daring with which unarmed lions boldly move against nervous creatures.' At these words of Cato's, the Firmans immediately dashed without hesitation down the mountain and raced for the outpost. The enemy were thrown into confusion by this unexpected assault and scattered, but the Firmans captured one of them, weapons and all, and handed him over to Cato. From this man Cato learnt that the main army, along with the king himself, had taken up a position in the pass, and that these men, who were guarding the mountain paths, were an élite unit of six hundred Aetolians. Seeing how pitifully few there were and how easily they neglected their duty, Cato drew his sword, followed by his men, and then lost no time in leading them into the attack to the sound of trumpets and war-cries. When the enemy saw men bearing down on them from the cliffs, they turned tail and fled back to the main camp, where they spread terror throughout the army.

[14] At this point, while Manius was forcing a passage down towards the fortifications in a massed attack on the pass, Antiochus was struck on the mouth with a stone, which knocked out his teeth. In his agony he turned his horse around, and then his army gave way all along the line before the Roman assault. The only escape-routes they could find lay over awkward and impossible terrain, through deep marshes and over sheer cliffs where there was a good chance of slipping and falling, but they still poured through the pass on to these paths, jostling and pushing at one another until, terrified by the prospect of feeling the blow of enemy weapons, they brought about their own destruction. Now, although Cato was apparently never the kind of person to hold back when it came to self-praise, and he did not even shun outright boasting, which he saw merely as the corollary of great exploits, this was the achievement on which he prided himself most. He says that those who saw him then, as he harried and struck at the enemy, felt that the debt Cato owed the Roman people was nothing compared to the debt the Roman people owed Cato; and he also says that when he and the consul, Manius, were both still flushed with victory, Manius threw his arms around him and hugged him for a long time, shouting out in his joy that there was no way either he or the whole Roman people could repay Cato for his services. Immediately after the battle he was sent to Rome to give a firsthand report of the result of the conflict. He had a trouble-free crossing to Brundisium, and from there it took him only a day to cross over to Tarentum and then four further days of travel, so that he reached Rome on the fifth day after landing in Italy and was the first to bring news of the victory. Everywhere in the city could be seen the smiling faces of people performing sacrifices of thanks, and Roman self-esteem increased until they felt that there was nowhere on land or sea over which they could not gain control.

[15] These are pretty much the most famous of Cato's military exploits, and in the sphere of politics he makes it clear that he regarded as very important the aspect of his public life which was concerned with the impeachment and conviction of criminals.† Not only did he prosecute plenty of them himself, but he supported other prosecutors by arguing on their behalf and generally by making sure that they had everything they needed for their cases. So, for

instance, he supported Petillius against Scipio,* but Scipio used the resources of his great lineage and genuine self-assurance to trample down the charges that were brought against him. Having failed to secure his execution, Cato ignored him, joined forces instead with the accusers of Scipio's brother Lucius, and got him sentenced to pay a large fine into the public treasury. It was too much for Lucius to pay, however, and he was in danger of being imprisoned, but he just managed to secure a pardon by appealing to the tribunes. There is also a story that when a young man managed to get an enemy of his dead father's disenfranchised, Cato went up to him after the court case as he was walking through the forum, greeted him warmly, and said, 'Yes, exactly! The offerings dead parents require from us are not young sheep or goats, but the tears and convictions of their enemies.'

At the same time he did not survive political life unscathed himself, but was constantly being taken to court and in danger of being convicted, whenever he gave his enemies the opportunity to prosecute him. In fact, it is said that he was the defendant in just under fifty cases,* the last of which took place when he was 86 years old. It was during this trial that he made the memorable remark that it was hard for someone who had lived his life among one kind of people to defend himself in front of people of another kind. Even then he did not bring his legal activities to an end, but four years later, when he was 90 years old, he brought a suit against Servius Galba.* Like Nestor, he seems to have lived an active life for three generations, because, as I have mentioned, he often took sides against Scipio the Great in the public arena, and he lasted right down to the time of the younger Scipio, who was the grandson by adoption of Scipio the Great, but the natural son of Paullus, the conqueror of Perseus and the Macedonians.*

[16] Ten years after his consulship he announced his candidacy for the censorship.* This office is one of the crowning honours and is, in a sense, the consummation of political life, since a censor wields a great deal of power, especially when it comes to assessing people's moral conduct. For the Romans thought that various aspects of a person's life should be subject to examination and scrutiny—his marriage, his procreation, his habits, his social life—to see what each man's desires and inclinations are, because they believed that these are much better indicators of a man's character than his visible,

public behaviour. So to stop people being tempted by personal whims to contravene the traditional and normal way of life, and to chastise and punish those who did, they used to appoint one of the so-called patricians and one of the plebeians. They called them 'censors', and they had the power to confiscate a man's horse* and to expel from the senate anyone whose conduct was loose and immoral. They also received and supervised property valuations, kept the definitive list of every citizen's family and age in the registers, and had a number of other important powers.

Because the office was so powerful, a number of notable senators close to the top of the hierarchy resisted and opposed Cato's candidacy. The patricians deeply resented what they saw as the terrible insult being offered to nobility of birth by the fact that men of humble origins were attaining the highest status and power, and those who knew perfectly well how immoral their behaviour was and how far they had departed from traditional ways were afraid that a position of power would make Cato's severity inexorable and ruthless. And so these two factions joined forces, made their plans, and put up, to rival Cato, seven candidates who proceeded to ingratiate themselves with the masses by raising their hopes, since they assumed that the Roman people wanted a soft and indulgent government. Cato, on the contrary, offered no compromises at all. He openly threatened wrongdoers from the rostra, cried out that the city needed a thorough cleansing, and insisted that if they were sensible the people of Rome would choose the most forceful doctor rather than the most amenable one—in other words, that they should choose himself and, among the patrician candidates, Valerius Flaccus, who was the only man with whose help he thought he could make progress in cutting out and cauterizing the Hydra-like diseases of luxury and effeminacy.* As for the other candidates, he said, it was obviously fear of the office being used well that was making each of them try to force his way into a position he would use badly. However, the Roman people proved their true greatness and showed that they deserved great leaders: instead of being put off by Cato's inflexibility and authoritarianism, they rejected those amenable candidates who gave the impression that they would do everything to please them, and chose Cato and Flaccus. So they obeyed Cato as if his recommendations came from someone who was already in office, rather than someone who was merely a candidate for office.

[17] Cato named as leader of the senate his colleague and friend Lucius Valerius Flaccus, and he expelled a large number of men from the senate, including Lucius Quinctius,* who had been consul seven years previously, but whose claim to fame depended less on his consulship than on the fact that his brother was Titus Flamininus, the conqueror of Philip. The grounds for the expulsion were as follows. A constant companion of Lucius' was a young man he had taken on because of his youthful charms. This young man accompanied Lucius when he took up his military command and was given more prestige and authority than any of his closest friends and relatives. Now, at a particular symposium, during Lucius' term as governor of his consular province, the young man was, as usual, lying on the couch next to him. Lucius was very susceptible to flattery when he had been drinking, and the young man started to lay it on in various ways; at one point he said that he loved him so much that although he had never seen a gladiatorial display before and there had been one on in Rome, he had rushed away to join Lucius, even though he wanted to see a man being killed. Lucius too professed his love for the young man and then said, 'But I don't want to have you lying there upset about this. I'll make you feel better.' He gave orders that a man who was facing the death penalty was to be brought in to the symposium and he had his lictor stand by him with a battleaxe. Then he asked his beloved again whether he wanted to watch a fatal blow being struck, and when he said he did, Lucius ordered the man's head cut off. This is the most common version of the story, and in his *On Old Age*, which is in dialogue form, Cicero actually puts the story into Cato's mouth.* Livy, however, says that the man who was killed was a Gallic deserter and that Lucius did not have him killed by his lictor but did it himself, and cites a speech of Cato's as the source of the story.* Lucius' brother, who was angry at Lucius' expulsion from the senate by Cato, resorted to the people and demanded an explanation from Cato. When Cato gave him his reasons and told the story of the symposium, Lucius tried to call him a liar, but when Cato challenged him to prove it, or accept the consequences, Lucius backed down. At the time there was general recognition that Lucius had got what he deserved, but later there was a show on in the theatre, and when Lucius walked past the senatorial section and took a seat as far away from it as he could get, the people felt sorry for him and loudly insisted that he change seats, which

rectified and alleviated the situation. Another man Cato expelled from the senate was someone who had been a promising future consul, Manilius,* for kissing his wife in broad daylight with his daughter looking on. Cato claimed that for his part he never embraced his wife except after a loud clap of thunder, and he said as a joke that Jupiter's thunder made him a happy man.

[18] However, when Cato confiscated the horse of Scipio's brother, Lucius, a man who had celebrated a triumph,* he came in for a certain amount of hostile criticism, since it looked as though he was motivated by a desire to humiliate the now dead Scipio Africanus. A great many people were particularly irritated by his attempt to curtail extravagance. There was no way that he could eradicate it altogether, since by then most people had been infected and corrupted by it, so he tried to come at it from an oblique angle: he ruled that any items of clothing, vehicles, women's jewellery, and household utensils that were worth more than 1,500 drachmas each were to be reassessed at ten times the value. The idea was that the increase in valuation would lead to people having to pay more tax as well, and he added a further penalty of three asses per 1,000 drachmas, hoping that the burden of these penalties and the sight of others paying less into the public treasury despite the fact that their incomes were the same, simply because they lived modest and simple lives, would make people change their ways. The upshot was that he annoyed not only those who had to endure the burden of these taxes as a result of their luxurious lifestyle, but also those who went without their luxuries in order to avoid the taxes, because most people see no difference between being prevented from displaying their wealth and being robbed of it, since display makes use of inessential items, not necessities. This is precisely what apparently puzzled the philosopher Ariston—that those who own inessential things are thought to be better off than those who have plenty of useful necessities. And when Scopas of Thessaly was asked by one of his friends for something which was not particularly useful to him, with the friend assuring him that he would not ask him for anything essential and useful, Scopas replied, 'But these useless and inessential items are the source of my prosperity and wealth.'* This goes to show that admiration of wealth is not related to any naturally arising feeling, but is an imposition caused by vulgar and alien opinion.

[19] So far from paying any attention to his critics, however, Cato

increased the stringency of his measures. He cut off pipes which people had been using to divert the flow of public water into their own houses and allotments, he pulled down and demolished any buildings which encroached on public land, he reduced payments for public-works contracts, and drove up to the highest limit the cost of winning at auction tax-farming contracts. All of this led to his being the target for a great deal of hatred, until Titus* and his supporters made a concerted effort to resist him. They succeeded in getting the senate to repeal the measures that had been taken concerning the hiring and farming out of contracts for the construction of sanctuaries and public works, on the grounds that they had not proved profitable to the state, and they encouraged the most defiant of the tribunes to summon Cato before the Roman people and fine him two talents. They also took a number of steps to oppose the construction of the basilica which Cato built at public expense next to the forum, under the senate-house, and called the Basilica Porcia.*

However, the people made it perfectly clear that they were incredibly pleased with his censorship. At any rate, the inscription on the statue of Cato they put up in the temple of Health did not mention his military achievements or his triumph, but may be translated as follows: 'When the Roman constitution was in a state of collapse and decline he became censor and set it straight again by effective guidance, sound training, and sensible instruction.' And yet there had been a time when he himself used to mock people who were pleased by this kind of thing, and say that they seemed not to realize that they were taking pride in the work of metalworkers and portrait-painters, while perfect images of him were carried around in the minds of his fellow citizens. When people expressed surprise that there were no statues of him while there were plenty around of undistinguished men, he said, 'I'd prefer people to ask why there are no statues of me than why there is one.' And in general he thought it the mark of a good citizen to be reluctant to hear himself praised unless the state benefited from it. Despite all this, however, there is no one who has ever praised himself more than Cato. It is he who says that when people were caught in some misdemeanour they used to say, 'You shouldn't blame us: we're not Catos.' He also says that people who bungled an attempt to imitate some of his achievements were known as 'left-handed Catos', that in desperate situations the senate used to look to him as passengers on a boat would look to a helmsman, and that the senate used to postpone especially important business if he was not there. But other writers confirm the truth of all this. He was in fact held in high regard in Rome thanks to his behaviour, his eloquence, and his great age.

[20] He was also a good father and a kind husband, and when it came to providing for his family he did not set about the job in a half-hearted fashion, as if it were something trivial and unimportant. So I think I should go into all the excellent aspects of his life in these respects as well. He married a woman from a noble rather than an especially rich family,* because he believed that while dignity and assurance may be attributes equally of well-born or wealthy women, those from noble families are more likely to obey their husbands' precepts about virtue, since they detest disgrace. He used to say that anyone who hit his wife or child was laying hands on the most sacred of objects, and a man gained more credit in his view for being a good husband than an important senator. He even used to say that the only thing he found impressive about Socrates from the old days was that he constantly treated his difficult wife and idiot sons with decency and civility. After the birth of Cato's son no business, unless it was for the state, was urgent enough to keep him away from his wife when she was bathing the baby and wrapping it in swaddling clothes. She breastfed the baby herself,* and often let even the children of her slaves suckle at her breast, as a way of ensuring that they would be loyal to her son, in view of the fact that they had been nursed together.

As soon as the boy had reached the age of understanding, Cato took him over and began to teach him to read and write. As a matter of fact, he did have an accomplished slave called Chilo who had taught plenty of children reading and writing, but, as he himself says, if his son was slow on the uptake, he did not want him to be told off or have his ear pulled by a slave, and he did not think it right for his son to be indebted to a slave for such important information. So he undertook his son's education himself: he taught him reading and writing, instructed him in the law, and acted as his physical trainer; in addition to teaching him how to throw a javelin, fight in armour, and ride a horse, he also taught him how to box and endure heat and cold, and made him a good enough swimmer to be able to force his way across even the turbulent and rough parts of the river.* He also says that he wrote out his history books by himself in large letters, so that his son would have the chance to profit, in his own home, from familiarity with the history of his ancestors. He claims to have avoided bad language when his son was around just as carefully as he did in the presence of the virgin priestesses they call the Vestal Virgins, and says that he never bathed with his son. This seems to have been normal in Rome: even fathers-in-law used to avoid bathing with their sons-in-law, since they were embarrassed to undress and go naked in front of them. Later, however, they acquired the habit from the Greeks, and then in their turn reinfected the Greeks with the practice of going naked even in the presence of women.

In the course of moulding and shaping his son in this way into a product with an exemplary attitude towards virtue, Cato found that the boy's enthusiasm left nothing to be desired and that thanks to his natural aptitude his mind was inclined towards obedience, but that his body was not tough enough to endure hard work, and so he relaxed the over-strenuous and punishing aspects of the regime. Despite this, he proved his prowess in military contexts, and played an outstanding part serving under Paullus in the battle against Perseus.* Later in the battle, however, his sword was knocked out of his grasp, or perhaps he lost his grip on it because his hand was damp; in irritation he appealed to some of his friends for help, and with them by his side hurled himself back against the enemy. After a fierce fight and a terrible struggle he cleared the field, and at last found his sword under a blanket of weapons among the heaped corpses of friends and enemies together. This exploit earned the young man the congratulations of his commander, Paullus, and there is in existence a letter written by Cato himself to his son in which he praises his son to the skies for his diligence and determination over the sword. Subsequently, in fact, the young man married Paullus' daughter, Tertia, the sister of Scipio,* and it was due to his own merits as much as to those of his father that he gained an alliance with such an important family. So the trouble Cato took over his son paid appropriate dividends.

[21] He owned a lot of slaves,* and bought especially prisoners of war who were still young enough to be reared and trained, as young hounds and horses are. None of his slaves entered anyone else's house unless he had been sent there on an errand by Cato or his wife. If any of them were asked what Cato was doing, their only response was to say that they did not know. A slave in Cato's house had to be

either busy or asleep, and Cato did not at all mind if they slept, because he believed that would make them more docile than if they stayed awake, and that if they were rested they would be better at their chores than if they were short of sleep. He believed that the most common reason for slaves to neglect their duties was sex, and so on his instructions they could sleep with his female slaves for a stipulated amount of money,* but were forbidden from having intercourse with any other women.

At first, while he was still poor, he was not at all fussy about any aspect of his meals when he was serving in the army, and in fact made it clear that he thought there was nothing more demeaning than to have one's belly provoke a quarrel with a slave. Later, however, when he was better off and he entertained friends and colleagues, as soon as the meal was over he would punish any of his slaves whose service had been in any way slipshod or whose preparations had been at all careless by beating them with a leather strap. He was continually finding ways to make sure that there was some kind of feud and dispute going on among his slaves, since their unanimity made him anxious and afraid. If any of them were suspected of having committed a capital crime it made sense, in his opinion, to try them and put them to death, if they were found guilty, in front of all their fellow slaves.

When he began to put more effort into making money, since he regarded farming as recreational rather than profitable and wanted to invest his capital in safe and secure businesses, he acquired sites which would make him a lot of money without, as he himself says, being liable to be harmed by Jupiter—things like ponds, warm springs, places dedicated to fulling cloth, undeveloped land† with natural pasturage and copses. He also engaged in the most disreputable form of money-lending, bottomry. This is what he would do. He used to tell those who owed him money to encourage plenty of others to club together, and when there were fifty partners and the same number of ships, he himself would hold a single share in the name of his freedman Quintio, who would sail with the debtors and help them with the business side of things. In this way he did not take on the whole risk, but only a fraction of it, with the possibility of massive profits.* He also used to lend money to any of his house-slaves who wanted it, so that they could buy boys, train and educate them at Cato's expense, and then sell them a year later. Cato actually kept quite a few of these boys himself, but in that case he would credit the slave's account with an amount equal to the highest offer he had received from another bidder. He used to recommend these practices to his son, saying that decreasing the value of one's estate was something a widow would do, not a man. But he surely went too far when in a rash moment he said that any man whose account-books show that he added to his estate more than he inherited deserves to be admired and revered as a god.

[22] Cato was an old man when Carneades the Academic and Diogenes the Stoic philosopher*† came to Rome as members of a delegation seeking to overturn a fine of five hundred talents which had been imposed on the people of Athens *in absentia* by the Sicyonians in a case brought by the Oropians. All the young Roman intellectuals immediately rushed to meet them, and became their admiring followers. Carneades was highly charismatic, no less impressive in reality than in reputation, and it was he in particular who won large and sympathetic audiences. Like a wind, his presence filled the city with noise, as the word spread about a Greek with an extraordinary ability to amaze his audiences. People spoke of how nothing could resist his charm and his authority, and said that he had instilled in the young men of the city a fierce passion which caused them to banish all their other pleasures and pastimes, and succumb to love of knowledge. No one else in Rome had any objection to what was happening; they were glad to see the younger generation acquiring some Greek culture and spending time with such impressive men. But right from the start Cato disliked the aspiration for intellectual pursuits which was flooding into Rome, since he worried that the young men of the city might divert their energies there and find a reputation for eloquence more desirable than one gained from practical and military achievements. So as the philosophers' reputation grew in the city, and when no less a person than the eminent Gaius Acilius* eagerly offered his services and translated their first speeches to the senate, Cato decided to find a polite way to remove all the philosophers from the city. So he stood up in the senate and told the authorities that it was wrong for them to have kept the delegation waiting so long, when it consisted of men who could easily convince them of anything they wanted. There was therefore no need, he said, for the senate to waste any further time in deciding what to do about the delegation and in putting it to the vote, so that these men could

return to their schools, where they could hold discussions with Greek boys, while young Romans could rediscover their former obedience to the laws and their rulers.

[23] This action of his was not motivated by dislike of Carneades, as some people believe, but by a general disapproval of philosophy and a desire to denigrate Greek culture and learning as a whole. After all, this is the man who goes so far as to say that Socrates was a babbling bully who tried his utmost to set himself up as a tyrant in his homeland by subverting tradition and by enticing his fellow citizens to adopt unconventional views instead of their usual ones. He also mocks Isocrates' teaching,* saying that the reason pupils of his were still studying under him in their old age was so that they could try out the techniques he taught them in Hades as they pleaded their causes before Minos. In the course of trying to turn his son against Greek ways, he uses a tone of voice that is too presumptuous for an old man when he predicts, in an almost oracular fashion, that Rome will be destroyed when it has become infected by Greek learning. But now we can see that this slander of his is hollow, since we live at a time when Rome is at a pinnacle of political success and has appropriated Greek learning and culture. As well as hating Greek philosophers, he was suspicious of those Greeks who practised medicine in Rome. He had apparently heard how Hippocrates had said, when the king of Persia tried to lure him to his court with an offer of many talents, that he would never work for Greece's foreign enemies. Cato used to say that all doctors took this oath, and he told his son to have nothing to do with any of them. He also says that he himself had written a treatise which he used as the basis for treatments and regimens when people in his household fell ill. He never put anyone on a starvation diet, but fed them vegetables and morsels of duck, pigeon, or hare (which was not a heavy meat, in his view, and so was suited to invalids, but had the drawback that eating it made one dream a lot). He says that this is the treatment and diet he used to keep both himself and members of his household healthy.

[24] However, it looks as though he met with divine retribution in this regard, because he lost both his wife and his son. Since he himself had a solid foundation of physical fitness and strength he resisted debility for a very long time, remained sexually active even when he was really quite old, and even got married at an inappropriate age. Here is how this second marriage came about. After the

death of his wife he arranged for his son to marry one of Paullus' daughters (whose brother, then, was Scipio*), while he himself, now a widower, resorted to a prostitute, who used to come to him secretly. But it could not remain a secret in such a small house, especially with his son's new bride there, and once, when the woman stalked past the young man's bedroom rather too brazenly for his taste, he gave her a hostile look and turned away from her in such a way as to make his feelings perfectly clear to his father without saying a word. Despite now being well aware of their anger at the situation, Cato did not reproach them or find fault with them. One day, however, on his usual trip down to the forum with a group of friends, he called out to Salonius, a former secretary of his, who was there among his retinue, and asked him whether he had yet matched his young daughter up with a husband. Salonius replied that he would not even think of doing so without consulting him first, and then Cato said, 'Well, I've found a suitable son-in-law for you, as long as age doesn't put you off. You couldn't fault him in other respects, but he is rather old.' When Salonius put the matter in his hands and asked him to arrange the marriage to the man he had in mind, since she was his dependant and relied on his consideration, Cato stopped prevaricating and explained that he was asking for the girl for himself. At first, of course, the man was shocked by what Cato had said, since he had assumed that the possibility of Cato remarrying was as remote as the possibility of himself making an alliance with a household of consular rank and gaining a relation who had celebrated a triumph. But when he saw that Cato was serious, he said that he was delighted and had no objections at all, and they immediately went down to the forum to formalize the betrothal.

While arrangements for the marriage were in progress, Cato's son, accompanied by some of his friends for support, asked his father if it was because his conduct had displeased or upset him at all that he was bringing a stepmother into the house. With a cry of protest Cato said, 'Don't even think it, my boy! You've done nothing wrong as far as I'm concerned. I have no complaints with your behaviour. In fact I want to leave my house more sons like you and my country more citizens like you.' Apparently this was in imitation of a sentiment expressed by Pisistratus, the Athenian tyrant,* on his marriage to Timonassa of Argos when his sons were already grown up.

Timonassa is the woman who is said to have borne Pisistratus Iophon and Thessalus.

Cato gained another son from this new marriage, whom he named Salonius* after his mother, but his elder son died while serving as praetor. Cato often mentions him in his books as having been a fine man, but it is said that he bore the tragedy with philosophical equanimity and that it did not make him any less enthusiastic about political life. In later years Lucius Lucullus and Metellus Pius came to regard public service as an oppressive duty and retired from public life when they got old, while, before Cato, Scipio Africanus had turned his back on the Roman people as a result of envious challenges to his reputation and made apolitical inactivity the goal of his remaining years. Cato's attitude was quite different. Reminiscent of how Dionysius was persuaded that a man could have no finer shroud than tyranny, Cato considered that a man could put his declining years to no finer use than public service, and in his spare time he used writing books and farming his estates as his means of rest and relaxation.

[25] As well as speeches on all sorts of subjects, he also wrote books of history.* Where farming is concerned, he took it seriously when he was young and had no choice in the matter—for, as he himself says, he had only two means of income, farming and thrift—but it was now of merely recreational and theoretical interest to him. Indeed, he wrote a book on farming,* and he was so anxious to display his thorough and erudite grasp of the subject that he even included instructions for cooking flat cakes and preserving fruit. The dinners he used to give when he was on his country estate were also particularly lavish. He would always invite his neighbours and other close friends from the district, and they used to have a fine time together. Young people as well as those his own age used to find his company a delightful treat, because he had been through so much and had read so many important books and treatises. There was no better way to make friends, in his opinion, than over dinner, and the extent to which tributes were paid there to fine and excellent members of society was matched by the extent to which bad and worthless men were ignored, since Cato refused to allow either praise or criticism to gain them entry into the symposium.

[26] His final act as a politician is regarded as having been the destruction of Carthage, since although it was the younger Scipio

who actually brought the task to completion, it was Cato above all who urged and recommended the Romans to undertake the war in the first place. This is how it all came about. When war broke out between the Carthaginians and Masinissa of Numidia,* Cato was sent on a mission to discover what reasons each side was giving for the hostilities, because Masinissa had always been on good terms with the Roman people, and ever since the defeat of the Carthaginians by Scipio there had been a treaty between them and Rome, which had deprived the Carthaginians of their empire and imposed a heavy tribute on them, so as to keep them under control. The Romans therefore assumed that Carthage was in a miserable and humiliated state, but Cato found that this was not the case at all: the city was teeming with young men of military age, overflowing with money, bristling with all kinds of weapons and military equipment, and therefore far from unconfident in itself. He believed that it would be a waste of time for the Romans simply to settle and administer the affairs of Masinissa and the Numidians; he thought that if they did not check the incredible growth of a city which had shown its malignant hostility in the past, they would face just as much danger as they had before. So he quickly returned to Rome and explained the situation to the senate. He told them that the Carthaginians' earlier defeats and setbacks had pruned their ignorance rather than their power—that is, had probably improved their military expertise rather than weakened them—and that in his opinion they were now using the Numidians to warm themselves up for conflict with the Romans. The words 'peace' and 'treaty', he said, were for the Carthaginians just alternative ways of describing the postponement of the war that they were waiting for the opportunity to launch.

[27] There is also a story that Cato deliberately dropped an African fig in the senate when he was rearranging his toga, and then, when people admired its size and beauty, pointed out that the land where these figs grew was only three days away from Rome by sea. But he surely went too far in adding to any statement he made on any subject whatsoever, 'It seems to me that Carthage should cease to exist.'* At this Publius Scipio, surnamed Nasica,* would always take up the opposite position and declare: 'It seems to me that Carthage should continue to exist.' Nasica had apparently noticed the offensive insolence that characterized the Roman people by this time—how they were becoming so assertive as a result of their successes

that they were proving difficult for the senate to restrain, and were powerful enough to drag the whole city by brute force in whichever direction their latest whims took them. So he wanted to use fear of Carthage as a bridle to curb the rashness of the masses, since he believed that although the Carthaginians were too weak to defeat Rome, they were too strong to be ignored. But this was precisely what made Cato afraid—that at a time when the Roman people were intoxicated by power and in frequent danger of falling they were being threatened by a city which had always been great, and which now had also been sobered up and chastened by calamity. He thought they should completely eliminate any threats to their supremacy from abroad, and thereby leave themselves the opportunity to deal with their domestic faults. This is said to be the reason why Cato instigated the third and final war against the Carthaginians. Soon after the beginning of the war, however, he died—but not before he had delivered a prophetic assessment about the man who would bring the war to a conclusion. He was still a young man at the time, but during his period of office as military tribune, while out on active service, he gave concrete evidence of his sound judgement and bravery in combat. Reports about him found their way back to Rome, and when Cato heard them he is supposed to have said: 'He alone has intelligence, while the rest are flitting shades.'* And before long Scipio's achievements had confirmed the correctness of this pronouncement.*

Cato was survived by one son, the child of his second marriage, who as I have already said was called Salonius, and one grandson, the son of the son of his who had died. Salonius died during his term of office as praetor, but his son Marcus became consul, and was the grandfather of Cato the philosopher,* a man of outstanding virtue whose fame was unrivalled in his time.

AEMILIUS PAULLUS

INTRODUCTION

Lucius Aemilius Paullus crushed the forces of the Macedonian king Perseus at the battle of Pydna in 168 BC. With this defeat Rome asserted its absolute authority over the Greek peninsula, already sufficiently demonstrated by the victory of Flamininus over Philip V at Cynoscephalae in 197 and the settlement which had followed. Aemilius' victory brought to an end a major phase of Rome's eastward expansion, and these two wars against Philip V and Perseus have become our most fascinating case study for the process of Roman imperialism and the causes, social, economic, and political, which lead to conquest.

Plutarch's introduction to his Life of Aemilius, however, points in a different direction: to a personal vision of moral behaviour. In this first chapter Plutarch reveals his own use of his *Lives* as a moral mirror. The work of researching and writing up a Life, he tells us, is equivalent to inviting a famous statesman into his house, where he can 'receive and welcome each of them in turn as my guest'. In getting to know them, he studies their admirable qualities, and uses these as a means of self-improvement. The notion of the mirror takes the simple idea of using a mirror to adjust our clothing and comb our hair and applies it to the moral realm. As he writes elsewhere, good men should always be before our eyes, and we should ask ourselves, 'What would Epaminondas have said, how would Lycurgus or Agesilaus have conducted himself?' In this way these good men 'are like a mirror, before which one puts oneself in order, adjusts one's stance, refrains from a petty saying, or resists some emotion' (*Progress in Virtue*, 85a–b). The lives of good men call to our attention our weaknesses and areas to improve, as well as encouraging us in what we do well. The self-examination which is necessary for moral growth is facilitated by observing the effects of virtues in others, thus being stimulated to emulate them. The notion is similar to that enunciated in *Pericles* (1–2), that seeing the good works of great men inspires the individual to emulate their fine actions in his own life. Although the method can work with both good and bad exemplars, since even from seeing bad behaviour one can come to recognize it in oneself and learn why and how to avoid it, for this pair of Lives Plutarch chooses two men outstanding for their moral behaviour, Aemilius Paullus and Timoleon, who will furnish 'congenial, beneficial images' to his mind, and his readers'.[1]

[1] See also the more extensive discussion of Plutarch's purposes in his biographies in the General Introduction (pp. x–xx).

The two statesmen are united not only by their excellence as generals and politicians, but by the special role which fortune has played in their lives. In both cases, fortune was almost completely favourable, but gave them one moment of great pain which tested their resolve. The concept of fortune as a way of understanding historical action varies somewhat in Plutarch's works. In *Aemilius* fortune is a power which guides Aemilius to success through the virtues which he demonstrates. To a degree this conforms to Plutarch's overall view that fortune in history is always working towards harmony and order in the world, especially through the establishment of Roman rule and the Roman monarchy under which he lived. In *Aemilius*, however, fortune's major function is to reveal how Aemilius reacted nobly to its caprice, that is, to the death of his two sons following his great victory, at the very time of his triumphal entrance to the city. This juxtaposition of glory and grief maximizes the effect of fortune on Aemilius' life, and his own heroic ability to confront it.

Unusually, the Roman Life is the first in this pair, and the Greek Life, *Timoleon*, the second. Timoleon, a member of the ruling oligarchy of Corinth, after being invited to Sicily in 344 BC by forces hostile to Dionysius II, the tyrant of Syracuse, found that his leading opponent would be Hicetas, the tyrant of Leontini who wished to rule Syracuse. When Dionysius II fled into exile, Timoleon went on to defeat Hicetas, some tyrants in other Sicilian cities, and the Carthaginians who had been supporting them. In the following years, until his death in the middle or late 330s, he introduced a new constitution in Syracuse, invited as many as sixty thousand new settlers from mainland Greece, and initiated an economic revival for the island. Plutarch presents the great victory over Hicetas as parallel to Aemilius' victory over Perseus. Timoleon's extraordinary success in this endeavour, after arriving in Sicily with only seven hundred mercenaries, justifies the emphasis in the Life on fortune, which supported Timoleon's own military and political genius at every turn: 'not the work of fortune, but of virtue supported by good fortune' (*Tim.* 36). In addition, Timoleon's actions brought order and prosperity to a Sicily oppressed by tyrants. Unlike so many glorious actions in classical Greece, in which Greeks had fought one another in a kind of civil war, Timoleon fought Carthaginians and tyrants, so that he could say that a god had brought him to save Sicily. Whereas *Aemilius* focuses on the effect of fortune on one individual, *Timoleon* concentrates on the larger effect on the cities of Sicily. It is probably this broader and more complex view which explains the Greek Life's position in the pair. *Aemilius* reveals the caprice of fortune, *Timoleon* its providential quality, and allows the reader to read this same quality back into *Aemilius*. Other themes which unite the pair include the great familial misfortunes (Aemilius lost his children at the end of his career, Timoleon as a young man acquiesced in the assassination of his brother) and the idea of bringing peace to Greek territory, in mainland Greece or in Sicily. In both cases, this peace requires that tyrannical leaders be defeated, Perseus and Hicetas.

After the introduction holding up these men as exemplars, Plutarch runs rapidly through Aemilius' earlier career, including his proconsulship in Spain and his first consulship in 182 (cc. 2–6). Apparently he had very little information concerning Aemilius' career before his second consulship, although he clearly had a distinguished career.[2] The major segment of the Life begins when the hero was about 60 years old.[3] The preliminaries to the war with Perseus occupy chapters 7–17, the battle itself 18–22, the flight and surrender of Perseus, with various digressions, 23–7. There follow in chapters 28–30 Aemilius' actions in Greece, and particularly his vicious slaughter and plunder in Epirus, ordered by the senate and carried out with tactical skill, though 'completely contrary to his decent and honest nature' (30). After reporting the debate at Rome on whether he should be granted a triumph, which serves to increase rather than diminish Aemilius' glory (31), Plutarch describes the triumph itself at extraordinary length (32–4), and contrasts it to the sorrow brought by the death of his two sons (35–6). The remaining chapters round off the Life with an account of the fate of Perseus and his family, and Aemilius' censorship and death in 160 (37–9).

The central and dominating event of *Aemilius* is the battle of Pydna, Aemilius' greatest military action, the glory of which is made visible in the abundance of his triumphal procession. Two techniques give focus to the relation of fortune to virtue in Aemilius' victory and in his politics: the series of speeches Plutarch ascribes to Aemilius, and an internal comparison set up between Aemilius and the conquered King Perseus. The figure of Perseus, avaricious, cowardly, abject and cringing in defeat, serves as foil to Aemilius' traditional Roman firmness and courage in adversity. This first appears when Perseus' miserliness and lack of faith in paying his mercenaries is contrasted with Aemilius' careful preparations

[2] The full career is preserved on an inscription: 'L. Aemilius Paullus, son of Lucius, twice consul, censor, interrex, praetor, curule aedile, quaestor, military tribune for the third time, augur. He triumphed in first consulship over the Liguri. Made consul a second time to wage war against King Perseus, he was elected [. . .]; he destroyed the forces of the king [within ten days] of arriving in Macedon; he cap[tured the king with his children]' (*Inscriptiones Italiae*, xiii. 3, *Elogia* (Rome: Libreria dello stato, 1937), ed. A. Degrassi, no. 81).

[3] *Timoleon* is also silent on much of the hero's life, with a long gap between Timoleon's participation in the assassination of his tyrant brother in the mid-360s and his expedition to Sicily in 344.

(13). His pathetic flight from Samothrace and grovelling before Aemilius reveal his demeaning fear of death (26). Finally, although he begged Aemilius not to parade him at the triumph, his cowardice kept him from removing himself by suicide (34). Aemilius' own attitude towards fortune is apparent from the speeches which Plutarch quotes. The first Aemilius directs at Perseus, reproaching him for his inability to bear his reversal of fortune (26). This is followed by a longer speech to his sons, sons-in-law, and officers, reproaching their pride in their victory, and giving a lesson on the variability of fortune: 'What occasion can there possibly be for men to take heart, when victory over others is precisely the time when we are most compelled to be afraid of fortune, and when a happy man can be plunged into the depths of depression by the realization that fate follows a cyclical course and attaches itself to different people at different times?' Finally, after the death of his sons, he addresses the Roman people, thankful that the change of fortune which he had feared following his great victory had struck him and his family, and not the Roman state (36): 'Fortune is content to have made use of me and my troubles, since just as clear an instance of human frailty is provided by the person celebrating a triumph as by the person who is the victim of the triumph. The only difference is that even in defeat Perseus has his sons, whereas Aemilius, the conqueror, has lost his.' Speeches in general are rather rare in Plutarch's *Lives*, so carry special weight here. The first seems invented by Plutarch; the second and third are similar to speeches reported more briefly in Livy (45. 8. 41), which themselves probably derived from Polybius. Unlike Livy, Plutarch focuses especially on Aemilius' awareness of fortune and his firm resolution in accepting both the good and the bad. Significantly, Plutarch traces his ability to do this to the training in virtue rather than the law which he pursued in his youth (2), which seems to reflect the training in Greek philosophy received by his ancestor, the first Aemilius, and the Greek training he gave to his sons (2 and 6, and cf. 28).

Polybius, who is cited at chapters 15, 16, and 19, was most likely Plutarch's major source for this Life.[4] Polybius' account is now preserved only in fragments, but there are several close parallels to the extant fragments both in this Life and that of Flamininus, the victor over Philip V. In addition, there are correspondences to Livy, who is also known to have used Polybius. And Plutarch may have used Livy directly, as he does in other Lives. Some have suggested also that Valerius Antias, a Roman annalist whom Livy cites for Aemilius' triumph (45. 40. 1) may have been a source,

[4] The suggestion of R. E. Smith, 'Plutarch's Biographical Sources in the Roman Lives', *Classical Quarterly*, 34 (1940), 1–10, that this Life, like those of Cato and Flamininus, derives from a single biographical source is unfounded.

but the evidence is inconclusive. Polybius, who was one of the Greek leaders brought to Rome as part of Aemilius' settlement of Greece and kept there for many years, was both a contemporary of the events and a very interested party. He shared much of Plutarch's moral outlook.[5] In addition, he became a close friend of Aemilius' two sons, Fabius and Scipio Aemilianus. Plutarch supplements his account with those of two other contemporaries. The first of these is Scipio Nasica Corculum, who played an important part in the battle of Pydna as a lieutenant of Aemilius (15–18). Plutarch corrects Polybius' account of the troops assigned him from 'a note about this business to one of the kings' written by Nasica himself, and quotes Nasica several more times for details of the action (15 with note, 16, 18, 21). Nasica may also be behind the reference to Perseus' confidence in Nasica at 26. The other contemporary source is a certain Posidonius, 'who claims to have been alive at the time and to have taken part in these events' (19); he provided Plutarch with an account favourable to Perseus, to which he refers several times (19 and note, 20, 21). It is an indication of Plutarch's research and recognition of the importance of contemporary sources that these two writers are cited only by him. The extremely detailed account of the triumph (32–4) must derive from a contemporary source, but unless Polybius reported it (there is nothing in the fragments), Plutarch probably got it at second hand.

The biography is also enriched by several digressions. In chapter 14, Aemilius drills wells at the foot of Mount Olympus and obtains a plentiful supply of water. This fact is also found in Livy (44. 33), but Plutarch goes on to discuss physical theories explaining the phenomenon, preferring that of Aemilius, that the water from the mountain flowed underground to the base. In chapter 15, he calls attention to the calculation made by a certain Xenagoras of the height of Olympus. Finally, he again notes Aemilius' scientific understanding of the natural world in reference to the lunar eclipse which preceded the battle (17).

In *Aemilius*, Plutarch has combined excellent contemporary sources with a strong ethical focus, giving his reader both a dynamic account of a major moment in Rome's imperialist expansion into Greece and a stirring tale of the ability of a noble mind to meet the shifts of fortune, keeping a level head in both enormous success and drastic loss.

Hammond, N. G. L., 'The Battle of Pydna', *Journal of Hellenic Studies*, 104 (1984), 31–47.

—— *A History of Macedonia*, iii (Oxford: Clarendon Press, 1988).

[5] Cf. in general A. M. Eckstein, *Moral Vision in the Histories of Polybius* (Berkeley and Los Angeles: University of California Press, 1995).

Reiter, W., *Aemilius Paullus, Conqueror of Greece* (London: Croom Helm, 1988).

Scullard, H. H., *Roman Politics, 220–150 BC*, 2nd edn. (Oxford: Oxford University Press, 1973). See especially chapter 12, 'The Achievement of Aemilius Paullus'.

Swain, S., 'Plutarch's Aemilius and Timoleon', *Historia*, 38 (1989), 314–34. An extremely useful study of the structure, theme, and content of the pair.

AEMILIUS PAULLUS

[1] Although I originally took up the writing of Lives for others, I find that the task has grown on me and I continue with it for my own sake too, in the sense that I treat the narrative as a kind of mirror and try to find a way to arrange my life and assimilate it to the virtues of my subjects. The experience is like nothing so much as spending time in their company and living with them: I receive and welcome each of them in turn as my guest, so to speak, observe 'his stature and his qualities',* and choose from his achievements those which it is particularly important and valuable for me to know. 'And oh, what greater delight could one find than this?'* And could one find a more effective means of moral improvement either? According to Democritus, we ought to pray that we meet favourable images—in other words, that from the air around us we encounter congenial, beneficial images rather than pernicious, disagreeable ones;* but this introduces into philosophy a doctrine which is not only false, but which also leads people astray into the path of endless superstition. In my case, however, the study of history and the familiarity with it that my writing breeds equip me, as my mind is always welcoming the records of the best and most illustrious men, to repel and keep at bay anything pernicious or malicious or contemptible my inevitable association with those I deal with may bring, because I calmly and composedly turn my thoughts away from such aspects towards exemplars of unparalleled worth. Two such admirable cases are the Lives I have now chosen for you—those of Timoleon of Corinth and Aemilius Paullus, men who were alike not only in their principles, but also in the good fortune their actions enjoyed, and who will make it hard for you to decide whether they owed their greatest achievements to luck or to intelligence.*

[2] Most writers agree that the house of the Aemilii was one of the ancient patrician houses in Rome, and some of those who attribute the education of King Numa to Pythagoras add that the first of the Aemilii, the one who gave his name to the family, was Mamercus, whose father was the philosopher Pythagoras, and who was surnamed Aemilius because of the subtlety (*haimulia*) and charm of his speech.* Most of the members of this household who became famous

thanks to their aspiration for excellence enjoyed good fortune, with the exception of Lucius Paullus;* but despite his defeat at Cannae, the misfortune showed him to be a man of intelligence and courage. He could not dissuade his colleague from giving battle and so he reluctantly joined him in engaging the enemy, but then he refused to join him in running away. Despite being deserted by his colleague, who was responsible for the danger in the first place, he stood his ground and died fighting the enemy. This Aemilius had a daughter, Aemilia, whose husband was Scipio the Great, and a son, Aemilius Paullus, the subject of this Life.

Aemilius Paullus came of age at a time when there were so many great and outstanding men that glory and virtue were thick on the ground. Nevertheless, he made his mark, and did so without being attracted to the pursuits followed by other eminent young men of the time and without pursuing the same course as them at all. That is, he did not practise forensic oratory, and he completely avoided the cries of greeting and the friendly gestures which most of his peers used to wheedle their way into the good graces of the general populace, whose enthusiastic servants they had made themselves. It was not that he was incapable of either of these courses of action, but rather that he set out to secure for himself something better than either of them, namely the glory that accrues from courage and fairness and integrity, and in these respects he was very soon the outstanding man of his generation.

[3] At any rate, when he first set out to win one of the curule offices, the aedileship,* he was elected over twelve rival candidates, every single one of whom is said to have become consul later. And when he became a priest (one of the augurs, as they are called, whom the Romans appoint to survey and watch over divination by birds and celestial portents), he was so attentive to tradition, and so thoroughly understood the religious scruple evinced by the ancients, that the priesthood, which had been taken to be something of an honorific, sought merely for its prestige, was shown to be one of the most exalted professions and testified in favour of those philosophers who define piety as knowledge of how to serve the gods.* For he performed all his functions skilfully and diligently, and made sure that he had no other business to attend to when he was engaged with the priesthood. He left nothing out and made no innovations either, but he was constantly at odds with his colleagues even about matters of

detail, and tried to teach them that even if one regarded the gods as easygoing and disinclined to find fault with neglect, still a lenient and casual attitude towards these things could do considerable harm to the city, at any rate, since anarchy is not the result of the commitment, all at once, of a serious crime, but people who fail to be strict about minor matters also destroy the guard that protects more serious concerns.

He showed himself to be the same kind of person when it came to learning and protecting traditional military practices. He did not use military command as a means of winning popular favour, nor did he use his first command as an opportunity to court appointment to a second, as almost all his contemporaries used to do, by gratifying his men and being gentle with them. Instead, like a priest of other formidable rites, he would explain each aspect of their ritual practices, and was an object of terror to anyone who disobeyed him or broke the rules. In this way he restored his country's honour, because he regarded defeating the enemy as a mere accessory to educating his fellow citizens.

[4] Rome's most competent commanders were busy with the war against Antiochus the Great when another war broke out in the west, in Spain, where there had been serious disturbances. Aemilius was dispatched there with the rank of praetor, but he had six extra lictors over and above the usual six praetorian lictors, with the result that his office was equivalent in dignity to that of a consul.* He won two pitched battles against the local tribesmen, who lost about thirty thousand men, and apparently it was plain to see that his success was due to his tactical skill, since he made victory easy for his troops by ensuring that they fought on favourable ground, on the far side of a certain river. He also subdued 250 towns, which were happy to open their gates to him. Then he returned to Rome, leaving behind a province which was united in peace and mutual trust, without having made himself one drachma richer as a result of the campaign. Generally speaking he was not particularly concerned about making money, while at the same time being open-handed and generous with what he had. His estate was not large, however, and in fact after his death it was only just enough to cover the dowry owed to his wife.*

[5] He married Papiria, whose father, Maso, was an ex-consul,* but he divorced her after they had lived together for many years, even though he could not have asked for better children than the ones she

had borne him, since she was the mother of Scipio, the one whom everyone has heard of, and of Fabius Maximus. No grounds for the separation have come down to us in official documentary form, but there is a story told about divorce which has the ring of truth about it. A Roman who dismissed his wife was being told off by one of his friends. 'Isn't she well behaved?' he said. 'Isn't she beautiful? Isn't she fertile?' The man held out his shoe (the kind the Romans call a *calceus*) and replied: 'Isn't it smart? Isn't it new? But not one of you can know where it rubs my foot.' And in fact serious, blatant flaws rarely cause husbands and wives to break up,† whereas it is the slight, often-repeated irritation of petty annoyances and incompatibilities that is responsible for irreparable estrangement in marriages, for all that it may go unnoticed by everyone else.*

In any case, once he had divorced Papiria, Aemilius took another wife, who gave birth to two male children. He kept these sons at home, but he arranged for his sons by Papiria to be adopted by two of the most important houses and most illustrious families in Rome. The older son joined the house of Fabius Maximus, who had been consul five times, while the younger one was taken in by his cousin, the son of Scipio Africanus, who gave him the surname Scipio.* As for Aemilius' daughters, one became the wife of the son of Cato, and the other of Aelius Tubero,* a man of the highest calibre whose attitude towards poverty was unrivalled in Rome for its nobility and magnificence. For sixteen Aelii, all relatives, with only a tiny little house and a single small plot of land between them, occupied a single hearth with their wives and numerous children. One of these wives was the daughter of our Aemilius, who was consul twice and celebrated two triumphs. Rather than feeling ashamed about her husband's poverty, though, she admired his goodness, which is what kept him poor. Nowadays, however, brothers and relatives who share property have to mark it with mounds, rivers, and walls, and leave wide open spaces between one another, if they are to stop their constant squabbling. History allows anyone who is prepared to keep the facts in mind to take a look at them and come to this kind of conclusion.

[6] After being elected consul,* Aemilius led an army against the Ligurians (or Ligustini, as they are sometimes known), whose territory ran alongside the Alps. The Ligurians were a warlike and courageous people who were having their military skills honed by the

Romans, whose neighbours they were. The Ligurians live in the far north of Italy, all the way up to the Alps, and, along with Gauls and coastal Spaniards, also inhabit those parts of the Alps themselves that face Africa and are washed by the Tyrrhenian Sea. At the time in question they had taken to the sea and were using their vessels for acts of piracy, stealing and destroying merchandise on expeditions as far as the Pillars of Heracles. Aemilius' advance was met by a force of forty thousand, five times the number of his eight thousand men, but he engaged them in battle, forced them back, and pinned them inside their strongholds. However, he let it be known that he was prepared to be lenient and come to terms with them; after all, the complete eradication of the Ligurians would not suit the Romans at all, since they formed a kind of shield or bulwark between them and the forays of the Gauls, who were always hovering threateningly on the border of Italy. The Ligurians trusted Aemilius and surrendered both their ships and their settlements to him. He restored their settlements to them unharmed, or at the most with their walls demolished, but he confiscated all their ships and left them no vessel larger than a three-oared boat. He also rescued all the people who had been captured by the Ligurians on land or sea, and there turned out to be a lot of them, both Romans and non-Romans. These were the notable things he achieved in this consulship.

Later, he often made it clear that he would like to be consul again, and once he went so far as to announce his candidacy,* but he failed to get elected and was passed over in favour of others, so he made no further efforts in this regard, but attended to his priestly duties and his sons' education. He made sure that they received a Greek education, as well as the native, traditional training which he had undergone. This was so important to him that not only did he provide Greeks to teach the boys language, philosophy, and rhetoric, but the sculptors and painters they made use of were Greeks as well, and so were the men in charge of their foals and puppies, and the men who taught them hunting. And provided public business did not stop him doing so, their father was also present as the boys trained and exercised; there was no fonder parent in Rome.*

[7] Where Rome's affairs are concerned, this was the time when, during the war with King Perseus of Macedonia, the Romans accused their military commanders of being so unskilled and timid that they had prosecuted the war in a disgraceful and embarrassing

fashion, and had incurred heavier losses than they inflicted. Not many years previously they had forced Antiochus, who had been called 'the Great', to pull back from most of Asia, driven him across the Taurus mountains, and confined him to Syria, where he had been glad to buy a truce for fifteen thousand talents; a short while before that they had crushed Philip in Thessaly and so freed the Greeks from Macedonian rule; and they had defeated Hannibal, unrivalled by any king for his daring and resources. Because of all these recent past events, they found it intolerable that they were merely holding their own in a long drawn-out war with Perseus, as if he were a match for Rome, when he was fighting them with an army consisting of remnants left over after his father's defeat; they were unaware that after his defeat Philip had considerably strengthened the Macedonian army and made it a far more effective fighting force than before. I will go back to the beginning and give a brief explanation of the whole affair.*

[8] Antigonus, the most powerful of Alexander's successors and military commanders, who acquired for himself and his descendants the right to be called 'king', had a son, Demetrius, whose son was Antigonus, surnamed Gonatas. The son of this Antigonus, Demetrius, died after a brief reign, leaving a son called Philip, who was still a child. The leading Macedonians were alarmed at the prospect of there being no effective rule in the country, so they called for Antigonus, a cousin of the dead man, and got him to marry Philip's mother. Initially, they gave him the titles 'regent' and 'general', but later, once they had found him to be a moderate and public-spirited man, they called him 'king'. He was given the surname Doson, with the implication that he tended to make promises, but then failed to carry them out.* Philip succeeded to the throne after him and although he was still only a young adult he displayed an abundance of kingly qualities. People began to think that he would restore Macedonia to its former greatness and that he would be the only one, among all the possibilities, who would check the power of Rome, which was then on the increase. But defeat at the hands of Titus Flamininus in a major engagement at Scotussa broke his spirit: he surrendered all his power to the Romans and was glad to get off with a moderate fine. Later, however, he came to resent his subservient condition and to believe that ruling with the Romans' permission made him a captive slave, content with a life of luxury,

rather than a man of pride and spirit. So he began to plan for war and, with great secrecy and cunning, to make his arrangements. He let the towns situated on the roads and the coast become weak and somewhat abandoned, so that he would become an object of contempt, while up in the hills he was gathering a sizeable army. Once he had stocked the inland villages, fortresses, and towns with weapons, money, and prime troops, war was like an athlete he was training and yet keeping cloaked in secrecy. Thirty thousand sets of weapons lay idle in storage, and eight million medimni of grain were shut up in his strongholds, along with enough money to maintain ten thousand mercenaries for a ten-year defence of the country.

However, Philip died of grief and misery before he could mobilize these resources and put them to work, when he realized that he had wrongly killed one of his two sons, Demetrius, as a result of lies told by his other son, the inferior one.* His surviving son, Perseus, inherited his hostility towards the Romans along with his kingdom, but lacked the strength to bear the burden of the war. He did not have the requisite largeness and nobility of character, but was riddled with all kinds of weaknesses and flaws, chiefly avarice. In fact, he might not have been a true son of Philip's: it is said that Philip's wife got him when he was a new-born infant from his mother, who was an Argive seamstress called Gnathaenius, and passed him off as her own. This is supposed to be the main reason why he did away with Demetrius: he was afraid that if the house had a legitimate heir his own bastardy would be revealed.

[9] Nevertheless, despite being small-minded and second-rate, he was propelled by the tide of affairs towards warfare. He maintained a firm and prolonged resistance, in the course of which he beat off successive Roman leaders of consular rank with their armies and huge fleets, and actually defeated some of them. For instance, he routed the first Roman commander to invade Macedonia, Publius Licinius, in a cavalry battle, killing 2,500 good men and taking another 600 alive. Then he fell unexpectedly on the fleet which was lying at anchor at Oreus, captured twenty transport ships with their cargoes intact, sank the remaining ships, whose holds were filled with grain, and seized four quinqueremes as well.† He repelled Hostilius, the second of the consuls, when he tried to force his way into the country at Elimiae, and after Hostilius had sneaked in via Thessaly Perseus offered battle, but Hostilius was too scared to meet him.* As

an adjunct to the main war Perseus launched a campaign against the Dardanians, as if to say that he had nothing but contempt for the Romans and did not feel under any pressure; in the course of this campaign he slaughtered ten thousand Dardanians and gained a great deal of booty. He also stirred up the Basternae, a warlike Gallic tribe of horsemen living on the Danube, and invited the Illyrians, through their king, Genthius, to join him in the war against Rome. There was a widespread rumour, in fact, to the effect that he had bribed the Illyrians to march through lower Gaul along the Adriatic and invade Italy.*

[10] When the Romans found out what Perseus was up to, they decided to have no more to do with the promises and ingratiating ways of their would-be military commanders, and instead to invite a man of intelligence, with the experience to cope with important matters, to take charge of the war. The man they chose was Aemilius Paullus, who, at about 60 years of age, was no longer a young man, but was still in prime physical condition, and was surrounded by young sons-in-law and sons, and by a host of powerful friends and relatives, all of whom set about persuading him to obey the summons to the consulate the people had issued him. At first he demurred when addressing the masses, and tried to avert their importunate enthusiasm, saying that he did not want the post; but when they kept coming to his house every day, insisting that he come to the forum and shouting down his objections, he gave in. As soon as he came down to the Campus Martius* and presented himself as one of the candidates for the consulship, he gave the impression that he was there bringing gifts for the people—gifts of victory and dominion—rather than because he wanted to win the position. That was how high everyone's hopes were, and the warmth with which they welcomed him and made him consul for the second time was commensurate with their hopes. They waived the usual system whereby provinces were chosen by lot, and wasted no time in voting him the command of the war in Macedonia. There is a story that after he had officially been given command of the war against Perseus and had been escorted home with great pomp by the entire body of the Roman people, he found his daughter Tertia, who was still a young child, in tears. 'Hello,' he said. 'Why are you upset?' She threw her arms around him, gave him a kiss, and said: 'Don't you know, father? Our Perseus has died.' She was talking about a pet dog of hers which

she had called by that name. Aemilius said, 'What a stroke of luck, my dear! I welcome the omen.' The orator Cicero has recorded this story in his work on divination.*

[11] Traditionally, the new consular appointees used to say thank you in return, as it were, in a courteous speech delivered before the people from the rostra. But when Aemilius convened his fellow citizens in assembly, he told them that although he had gone after his first consulship because he wanted high office, he had gone after the second because *they* wanted a military commander, and so he was under no obligation to them. If they thought that someone else would do a better job in the war, he went on, he would resign his command; but if they put their trust in him, he asked them not to interfere with his strategies or even to address the war in their speeches, but just quietly to get on with doing what they had to do to support the war effort. Otherwise, he said, if they tried to command the commander, they would make even worse fools of themselves in their campaigns than they already were. These words of his inspired the Romans with a great deal of respect for Aemilius, and with high hopes for the future; everyone was delighted that they had avoided the flatterers and chosen a proud and candid commander. This shows how the Roman people subjected themselves to virtue and goodness in order to gain power and dominion over the rest of the world.*

[12] I attribute to the gods the fact that when Aemilius Paullus set out on his campaign he met with good luck on his voyage, had an easy journey overland, and reached the army's encampment quickly and safely; but when I consider that the successful conclusion of the war and his command was due partly to bold and rapid strikes, partly to good planning, partly to the willing service of friends, and partly to a combination of courage and appropriate decisions in the face of danger, I find myself incapable of attributing the brilliance and sheer perfection of the achievement to the man's famous good fortune, as one might in the case of other military commanders. Would one really ascribe Perseus' avarice to Aemilius' good luck in the business? For it was Perseus' avarice and cowardly refusal to commit his money that brought the Macedonians' prospects for the war crashing and tumbling down from the great and glorious heights to which they had been raised by their hopes. At Perseus' request a force of Basternae came to help, consisting of 10,000 horsemen and 10,000

light infantry, all professional mercenaries; they were men with no experience of farming or sailing or living as shepherds, men who specialized in just one job and had just one skill, which they were constantly honing—the ability to fight and to overcome whichever troops they faced at the time. Once they had pitched camp at Maedica, they began to mingle with Perseus' troops.* The height of the men, their incredible training, and their haughty and conspicuous disdain for the enemies' threats raised the Macedonians' morale and made them think that the Romans would be too terrified by the mere sight of these men, with their alien and horrifying gestures, to stand their ground. But then Perseus—who was, after all, responsible for his men's mood and had filled them with these hopes—was asked to pay each mercenary officer a thousand pieces of gold. The enormous quantity of gold involved made his head swirl and his meanness robbed him of his judgement: he refused to pay up, and he dissolved the alliance. It was as if he were the Romans' accountant rather than their opponent, and would be giving his enemies an exact statement of everything he had spent on the war. And yet he had only to look at the Romans to learn his lesson, since, not counting all the rest of their equipment, they had a hundred thousand men mustered and ready to see to their needs.† But despite the fact that he was up against such an enormous force and was involved in such an important war—a war for which he had huge reserves—he measured out his gold, watched over it in person, and was as afraid to touch it as if it belonged to others. And this was a man with no Lydian or Phoenician blood in him, but one who by right of kinship shared in the nobility of Alexander and Philip, who conquered all their enemies thanks to their belief that money was to be spent on acquiring power, not the other way round. It was said, for instance, that the Greek cities fell not to Philip, but to Philip's money; and when, at the start of his expedition to India, Alexander noticed that his Macedonians were heaving along all the bulk and weight of the Persian valuables they had taken, he first set fire to his own royal wagons and then persuaded everyone else to do the same to theirs, so that they set out for the war in an unencumbered state, like men who had been freed from chains. Perseus, however, who had lavished money on himself, his children, and his kingdom, refused to buy their safety for a small amount of money, but preferred to be taken to Rome as a wealthy captive, surrounded by plenty, and to show the Romans all the wealth he had guarded for them.*

[13] Apart from the fact that he dismissed the Gauls after misleading them, there was also his treatment of Genthius the Illyrian, whose support in the war he won with an offer of three hundred talents—money which he showed all counted out to Genthius' agents, and even allowed them to store in their own sealed caskets. Genthius, secure in the conviction that his requirements had been met, then committed a sacrilegious and terrible deed: he seized the members of a delegation which had come to him from Rome and threw them into prison. At this point Perseus thought that the money was no longer needed to make Genthius an enemy of Rome, since with this awful crime Genthius had already given absolute guarantees of his hostility and committed himself to the war, so he robbed the poor man of his three hundred talents, and then a little later sat by and watched as Lucius Anicius, the Roman commander who had been sent at the head of an army to deal with Genthius, flung Genthius out of his kingdom, along with his children and his wife, like birds ousted from their nest.

This was the opponent Aemilius came to take on. He found Perseus himself contemptible, but was impressed by the men at his command—the 4,000 horsemen and about 40,000 foot soldiers who made up his army—and by his preparations. He had taken up a position at the foot of Mount Olympus on terrain which was unassailable from all directions, since he had the sea behind him and had blocked off all possible approaches with wooden barricades and fortifications. There was no doubt in his mind that time and Aemilius' expenses were on his side and that he would win the war of attrition. Now, Aemilius had an active mind and left no plans or military possibilities unconsidered, but he could see that his men's earlier confidence had made them impatient and that they were inclined to suggest a number of unfeasible strategies. He sharply warned them not to interfere in his job, and told them that their sole concerns were their physical condition and the state of their arms and armour, so that they could wield their swords in an effective fashion, like true Romans, when their commander gave them the opportunity to do so. He also told the sentries during the night watches to do their guarding without spears, the idea being that if they were incapable of defending themselves against an enemy attack, they would be more alert and would resist sleep better.*

[14] The worst thing about their situation as far as his men were concerned was the shortage of drinkable water: there was only a trickle of unwholesome water which formed a pool right on the seashore. Aemilius could see near by the thickly wooded heights of Mount Olympus, and he deduced from the greenness of the foliage that there were sources of water flowing down the slope deep under the ground, so he dug plenty of wells at the foot of the mountain to let the water escape. The wells immediately filled with clean running water, as the compressed water rushed in towards the empty space under the impetus of its downward motion.*

Some people, however, deny that there are sources of water lying ready made within the places from where they flow, and that their emergence is no more than the uncovering or the bursting forth of these reservoirs. They say instead that springs are formed and created by the liquefaction of matter on the spot, and that moist vapour is liquefied and becomes fluid by a process of condensation and cooling when it is compressed deep underground. Just as a woman's breasts are not like vessels—that is, they are not full of ready-made milk in a fluid state—but produce milk by transforming food within themselves, and then percolate it through, so, the argument goes, places which are cool and full of springs do not have water hidden away, and there are no such things as basins capable of emitting streams and deep and mighty rivers from a ready-made and pre-existent source. What happens, they say, is that these places subject air and mist to pressure and condensation, and so turn them into water. For example, it is when ground is being dug up that it lets water emerge and flow through more, as a result of this kind of manipulation (just as a woman's breasts do as a result of being sucked), because it moistens and softens the vapour; however, ground which is unworked and tightly packed has no opportunity to create water, since it has not been subjected to the movement which produces the liquid. But those who come up with this theory leave it open to attack from the sceptics, who might say that creatures have no blood either, but that blood is created as a result of wounds by the transformation in some sense of air or flesh, a transformation which produces fluidity and liquefaction. The theory is also refuted by the fact that people come across rivers deep underground when they are digging tunnels and mines, and these rivers do not gradually collect, as they presumably would if they were created at the precise moment when the ground is moved, but they pour out in a flood. It is also observable that† when a rock is split open a torrent of water gushes out and then stops. But that is enough on this topic.

[15] Aemilius made no move for a few days, and they say that never before had there been such deep quiet when two vast armies were encamped as close to each other as these two were.* But he continued to probe and explore every possibility, and he found out that there was still a single means of approach which had been left unguarded, the route through Perrhaebia past the Pythium and Petra. The hopes raised in him by the fact that the place was unguarded outweighed his worries about the difficulty and harshness of the terrain, which was why it had been left unguarded, and so he called a meeting to decide on a plan of action. Among those present Scipio Nasica (the son-in-law of Scipio Africanus*), who was later one of the most powerful men in the senate, was the first to volunteer for the job of taking a force in to surround the enemy, and next, to Aemilius' delight, his eldest son, Fabius Maximus, who was still a young adult, leapt to his feet and committed himself to the task. Aemilius gave them a force whose size Polybius got wrong:* the actual numbers were as Nasica himself wrote in a note about this business to one of the kings*—that is, 3,000 Italian auxiliaries, and 5,000 men for the left wing. Nasica attached to this force 120 cavalrymen and a 200-strong unit of both Thracians and Cretans under Harpalus, and then he set out on the seaward road and set up camp by the Heracleum, as if he were intending to sail around the coast and come at the enemy from the rear. After the men had eaten their evening meal, however, and night had fallen, he told his officers the truth and led them under cover of darkness in the opposite direction, away from the coast, and stopped under the Pythium, where he pitched camp. At this point Olympus rises to a height of more than ten stades, as is shown on the following inscription by the man who measured it:

> As found by perpendicular measure,† the height of the peak
> Of the sacred mountain Olympus, at Apollo's Pythium,
> Is a full ten stades, plus four feet short of a plethron.
> Xenagoras, Eumelus' son, measured the distance.
> Greetings, Lord Apollo! May you be generous and merciful!

Now, geometers claim that ten stades is the limit of the height of any mountain and of the depth of the sea too; but it looks as though Xenagoras took his measurements carefully and systematically, using instruments.*

[16] Anyway, this is where Nasica spent the night. Perseus saw that Aemilius was staying put and had no idea what was going on, until a Cretan deserter who had run away from the army while it was on the march came to him and told him about the circuitous route the Romans had taken. Perseus was deeply disturbed at the news, but rather than move his army from its position, he dispatched Milo with 10,000 foreign mercenaries and 2,000 Macedonians, with instructions to make their way quickly to the passes and occupy them. According to Polybius, these men were still asleep when the Romans fell on them, but Nasica says that a fierce and close-fought battle took place for possession of the heights, and tells how he brought down a Thracian mercenary, who had charged up to him, by plunging his spear into his chest. Finally the enemy was pushed back and Milo was forced into ignominious flight, without his weapons or armour; then, Nasica goes on, he followed the retreating enemy troops in safety and brought his army down into Macedonia.

Under these circumstances, Perseus hastily broke camp and pulled back, overcome by terror and with his hopes dashed. All the same, he was caught on the horns of a dilemma: he could either make a stand in front of Pydna and risk battle, or scatter his troops here and there among the towns and cities and wait for war to come to them, since now that it had reached Macedonia he would not be able to drive it out again without a great deal of bloodshed and loss of life. His friends tried to raise his morale, arguing that as things were he had numerical superiority, and his men were wholly committed, since they were fighting in defence of their children and wives, and since the king was watching over everything and was himself in the forefront of the danger. And so Perseus struck camp and deployed his troops for battle: he surveyed the terrain and gave his officers their commands, since he planned to meet the Romans as soon as they made their first assault. The place seemed very suitable, because† there was a plain for the heavy-armed troops, who needed level footing and even terrain, and there was a continuous range of hills, one after another, with places where his skirmishers and light-armed troops could take refuge and launch their attacks from. There were also rivers flowing through the middle of the plain—the Aeson and Leucus—which were not very deep at that time of year, the end of summer, but still looked as though they might make things difficult for the Romans.

[17] Aemilius joined up with Nasica and came down in formation to meet the enemy, but the sight of their disposition and their numbers so astounded him that he halted his advance and began to think things over. His young officers—especially Nasica, who was still high on his success at Olympus—were all for fighting, and they rode up and begged him to press on, but Aemilius smiled and said, 'Of course, if I was as young as you! But all the foes I've defeated have taught me by their mistakes, and I refuse to come straight out of a march and engage an enemy whose troops are already drawn up in close battle order.' Next, he ordered the vanguard, who were visible to the enemy, to make up cohorts and create the illusion of a battle formation, while he had the men in the rear wheel round, build a fence of stakes, and construct a camp. Then he gradually peeled the forward troops off, line by line, starting with the ones nearest the back, so that before the enemy knew it he had broken up his battle formation and brought all his men in due order back within the palisade.

That night the men were relaxing after their evening meal and getting ready for sleep, when suddenly the moon, which was full and high in the sky, grew dark. As its light was fading it kept changing colour, until after a variety of colours it finally vanished.* The Romans followed their usual practice and tried to call its light back by clashing metal together and by holding out towards the sky the flames of numerous brands and torches. The Macedonians' behaviour was quite different, however: fear and trembling gripped the camp, and a rumour quietly reached the ears of most of the men that the portent indicated the eclipse of a king. Aemilius had studied and learnt something of the odd phenomena connected with lunar eclipses, and how they occur at regular intervals when the moon in its orbit falls under the shadow of the earth and is hidden, until it has passed through the darkened region of the sky and once again reflects the light of the sun; however, he was very observant of religious custom, and much given to sacrifices and divination, so as soon as he saw the moon re-emerging from the darkness, he sacrificed eleven cows to it, and at dawn the next day he kept sacrificing oxen to Heracles, but by the time he had slaughtered twenty of them he still had not received favourable omens. The twenty-first brought the correct signs, however, which indicated that victory would go to the side that remained on the defensive. He vowed to sacrifice a hundred oxen to the god and to put on a contest in his honour, and then ordered his officers to arrange the troops in battle formation. He did not want his men to fight with the morning light of the sun in their faces, so he waited for the sun to pass overhead and begin to go down, and passed the time sitting in his tent, which faced the plain and the enemy encampment.

[18] In the mid-afternoon, the enemy attacked. According to some writers it was Aemilius himself who found a way to get them to do this: the Romans drove an unbridled horse out of their lines and came into contact with the enemy, and it was the pursuit of this horse that triggered the battle. Others, however, say that some Thracians under Alexander's command attacked a Roman baggage-train which was bringing in fodder, that seven hundred Ligurians hastily sallied forth to help the baggage-train, and that each side in this skirmish received more and more reinforcements, until both armies were engaged in a full battle. Like a good helmsman, Aemilius judged the size of the impending conflict from the swell and surge taking place within the two camps, so he left his tent and circulated among the ranks of his legionaries, giving them words of encouragement.

Nasica rode out to the skirmishers and saw that almost all the enemy troops were committed. First came the Thracians, who Nasica says were terrifying to see—tall men, with the armour of their shields and greaves gleaming white over the black tunics they wore, wielding in their right hands their heavy broadswords held vertically at shoulder height. Alongside the Thracians the mercenary troops advanced into the attack, with their assorted equipment and Paeonians mingled among them.† Next to the mercenaries came a third division consisting of the élite troops, the pick of the Macedonians themselves, chosen for their prowess and their youth, with their gilded armour and new red cloaks flashing in the sun. As they were taking their places in the battle array the phalanxes of the Bronze Shields* emerged from the encampment and filled the plain with the gleam of iron and the glitter of bronze, while the hills re-echoed with their shouts and the sound of their rallying cries. The

Macedonian troops advanced with such daring and swiftness that the first casualties fell only two stades from the Roman camp.

[19] So the onslaught began. Aemilius found on arriving at the battlefield that the Macedonian divisions had already thrust the tips of their pikes against the Romans' shields, making it impossible for the Romans to reach them with their short swords, while the rest of the Macedonian forces had removed their light shields from their shoulders and, at a single word of command, had angled their pikes upwards to resist his heavy-armed troops. When Aemilius saw how solid a line the Macedonians formed with their interlocking shields and how fiercely they attacked, he was astounded and filled with fear; he had never seen a more terrifying spectacle, and often in later years he used to recall the sight and the feelings it aroused in him.* At the time in question, however, he put on a happy, smiling face for the sake of his troops, and rode past them on horseback without a helmet or a breastplate. But the Macedonian king, according to Polybius, took fright at the start of the battle and rode back to the city of Pydna on the pretext that he was going to sacrifice to Heracles.* But Heracles does not accept cowardly offerings from cowards and does not answer their unlawful prayers. For just as it violates law for anyone to hit the target without making a shot, or to win a battle without standing his ground, so in general it is unlawful for success to follow inactivity or for good fortune to come to a bad man. The god hearkened to Aemilius' prayers, however, since he prayed for victory with his spear in his hands, and from the thick of battle called on the god to fight alongside him.

However, there is a history of Perseus in several books, written by a man called Posidonius,* who claims to have been alive at the time and to have taken part in these events, in which he says that Perseus left the battlefield not out of cowardice or on the pretext of having a sacrifice to make, but because the day before the battle he had been kicked on the leg. He also says that during the battle, despite his pain and the protests of his friends, Perseus ordered a pack-horse to be brought to him and, mounted on this horse and without the protection of a breastplate, he joined his men in the line of battle. Various missiles were flying all around him, and he was actually struck by an iron javelin—not by its head, however, but by its shaft, which ran along his left side. The force of its passage tore his tunic, but did not break his skin, and only left a livid red weal, which remained for a long time. This is what Posidonius has to say in Perseus' defence.

[20] Although the Romans could not make an impression on the Macedonians, they stood their ground, until Salvius, who was in command of the Pelignians,* seized his men's standard and threw it into the midst of the enemy—whereupon the Pelignians, who, like all Italians, regard it as unlawful and sacrilegious to abandon a standard, charged after it. In the ensuing conflict both sides took terrible losses. The Romans tried everything, deflecting the Macedonians' pikes with their swords, thrusting at the enemy with their shields, and even using their bare hands to grab hold of men and hurl them out of the way. But the Macedonians gripped their weapons firmly with both hands, impaled their attackers armour and all, since there is no shield or breastplate which can offer protection against the Macedonian pike, and tossed over their heads the bodies of the Pelignians and Marrucinians, who hurled themselves with irrational, bestial fury towards the enemy's blows and certain death. After the front line had been cut down, the ranks behind them were beaten back, and although they did not turn and flee, they withdrew to the mountain called Olocrus—and at the sight even Aemilius rent his tunic, according to Posidonius. Some of his men were pulling back, while the rest were trying to turn aside the Macedonian infantry, who left the Romans no means of approach, but met their assaults with a wall of pikes as solid and as completely impregnable as a palisade.

However, the ground was too uneven and the line of battle too long for shields to remain firmly interlocked. When Aemilius noticed that the Macedonian phalanx was beginning to gape and break up in many places, since—as is likely in any large army where the combatants are under a variety of different stresses—in some places it was hard pressed, while in others it was pushing forward, he rushed up, divided his troops into cohorts, and ordered them to penetrate the gaps and openings in the Macedonian lines and engage the enemy as separate units, so that they were not fighting the whole enemy army in a single battle, but were fighting a number of separate battles all at once. Aemilius gave these orders to his officers, and the officers passed them on to the troops. As soon as his men inserted themselves into the gaps and prevented the Macedonians from closing them up again, they were either able to attack them in the flank, where they were unprotected, or come round behind them and take them in the rear. The Macedonian phalanx fell apart and immediately lost the strength it had gained from the fact that all the men had been working together. Men fought as individuals or in small groups, and in this situation the Macedonians could only stab with short daggers at solid shields which covered their enemies from head to feet, and protect themselves with small, light shields against their enemies' swords, which were brought down on them with such force that they penetrated through all their armour to their bodies. So Macedonian resistance crumbled and they were put to flight.

[21] They put up a fierce fight, however. During the struggle Marcus, the son of Cato and son-in-law of Aemilius, lost his sword while fighting with unrivalled heroism.* Now, he was a young man who had been inculcated with all the finest precepts, and he owed his noble father proof of his own noble valour; moreover, it was more than he could bear to let his weapon fall into enemy hands while he was still alive. So he ran here and there over the battlefield, telling every friend and acquaintance he spotted of his misfortune and asking for their help. In the end a sizeable body of valiant men forced a passage through the rest, placed themselves under his leadership, and attacked the enemy. A fierce fight followed, with considerable loss of life and many casualties, but Cato and his men swept their opponents off the field, took possession of an area of ground that was undefended and bare of enemy troops, and began to search for the sword. When at last it was found buried in a pile of weapons and corpses, they were delighted and, with victory cries on their lips, they threw themselves with renewed energy upon those of the enemy who still held together. Eventually every single one of the élite three thousand, who kept their formation and fought on, was cut down. All the rest turned and fled, but were massacred as they ran, until the plain and the foothills were covered with corpses, and the waters of the river Leucus were still red with blood when the Romans crossed it the day after the battle. For it is said that over twenty-five thousand of the enemy lost their lives, whereas the Romans sustained losses of one hundred men, according to Posidonius, or eighty, according to Nasica.*

[22] Never has a battle of such importance been so speedily resolved: fighting began at the ninth hour, and victory was decided before the tenth.* The rest of the day was given over to pursuit,

which the Romans carried on for 120 stades, so that it was late in the evening when they turned back. On their return, servants carrying torches met them and took them with exclamations of joy back to their tents, which were brightly lit and decorated with garlands of ivy and laurel. This was the experience of everyone except the commander himself, who was consumed by grief because, of the two sons of his who had joined him on this campaign, the younger one, who was his particular favourite and who was, in his opinion, far more gifted than his brothers, was nowhere to be found. He had a passionate and ambitious nature, and was still little more than a child, so his father inevitably supposed that inexperience had led him to get caught up among the enemy during the battle and lose his life. Soon everyone in the army came to realize that Aemilius was beside himself with grief, and they interrupted their meals, leapt up, and ran about with torches, either to Aemilius' tent or to the outside of the encampment, searching among the first bodies. Gloom filled the camp, and the plain was filled with the sound of people calling out the name of Scipio, since he was universally popular, and from childhood had been temperamentally better suited than any of his relatives for high office in both military and civil capacities. Anyway, when it was late and people had more or less given up hope of finding him alive, he returned from the chase with two or three companions, covered in enemy blood and gore: like a young pedigree hound overcome by sheer pleasure, he had been carried away by the victory. This is the Scipio who in later years devastated Carthage and Numantia, and became the outstanding Roman of his day by far for his excellence, and by far the most powerful too. So fortune postponed the retribution due to Aemilius for his success, and on this occasion let him feel nothing but pleasure in his victory.*

[23] Perseus fled back from Pydna to Pella with his cavalry, which had survived the battle almost intact. Later, however, when infantrymen caught up with the cavalry contingent, they began to curse them as cowardly traitors, pull them off their horses, and beat them up. This unruly behaviour made Perseus afraid for his life, so he turned his horse off the road, removed his purple cloak and laid it on the horse's back in front of him, so that he would not be conspicuous, and carried his diadem in his hands. He also dismounted and led the horse behind him, in order to be able to talk to his companions as he made his way along the road, but one of them

pretended to fasten a loose shoe, while another said he had to water his horse, and a third that he needed a drink, and so gradually they all fell behind and ran away. They were more afraid of his cruel temper than they were of the enemy, because he had been cut to the quick by the disaster and was looking for a way to divert responsibility for the defeat away from himself and on to everyone else.

It was dark when he entered Pella.* He was met by Euctus and Eulaeus, the ministers in charge of his finances, but partly because they blamed him for what had happened and partly because they tactlessly chose this inopportune moment to offer him outspoken advice, he lost his temper and killed them both himself with his sword. After that the only people to stay with him were Evander of Crete, Archedamus of Aetolia, and Neon of Boeotia. All his troops deserted except for the Cretans, who remained by his side not out of loyalty, but because they were as partial to his wealth as bees are to honey, since he had let them steal from the huge amount of valuables he had with him about fifty talents' worth of cups, bowls, and other gold and silver implements. His first stop after Pella was Amphipolis, and then from there he went to Galepsus.* By now he was feeling a little less afraid, and he gradually succumbed once more to the familiar chronic disease of meanness; he began to tell his friends how sorry he was that he had stupidly squandered some of the treasure of Alexander the Great on the Cretans, and to beg and beseech those who had the treasure to accept money in exchange for it. It was obvious to those who knew him well that he was lying like a Cretan to the Cretans,* and indeed those who believed him, and gave back what they had, lost everything. Not only did he not pay them the money, but he raised thirty talents from his friends—money which before long would be in his enemies' hands—and sailed across with it to Samothrace, where he took refuge as a suppliant at the temple of the Cabiri.*

[24] Now, the Macedonians are said to have never failed in their loyalty to their kings, but on this occasion they felt that there was nothing secure left for them to rely on, and they surrendered to Aemilius and in two days made him master of all Macedonia. This seems to support those who claim that his achievements were due to good luck, and then there was the extraordinary incident at the sacrifice. Aemilius was performing a sacrificial ritual in Amphipolis and the proceedings had begun, when a thunderbolt struck the altar,

set it alight, and burnt up the sacrifical offering. But never did the gods and good fortune play a greater part in his life than in the episode of the rumour. Three days after Perseus' defeat at Pydna, there were horse-races on in Rome, which were open to the public. Suddenly, a rumour arose in the front seats of the arena that Aemilius had conquered the whole of Macedonia after defeating Perseus in a great battle. From there, the rumour rapidly spread to the general populace, who clapped and cheered in a spontaneous expression of the joy they felt. This remained the prevalent mood in the city the whole day, but when people found that the story could not be traced back to any identifiable starting-point, and that it just seemed to occur everywhere equally, the rumour dissipated and evaporated. A few days later, however, when reliable information reached the city, people were astonished at how there was truth in the lie.*

[25] Other famous stories along the same lines concern news of the battle fought against the Greeks on the river Sagra reaching the Peloponnese, and the Plataeans hearing about the battle fought against the Persians at Mycale: in both cases the news is said to have arrived on the actual day of the battle.* Then there was the battle at which the Romans defeated the army of the Tarquins and their Latin allies, when two tall and handsome men were seen shortly afterwards bringing an eyewitness report straight from the army.* The Romans tentatively identified them as Castor and Pollux. The first man to meet them, as they were cooling down their heavily sweating horses at the spring in the forum, found it hard to believe their account of the victory. But then, the story goes, they calmly smiled and touched the man's beard with their hands, and the hairs immediately changed colour from black to red, which gave their report credibility and the man his name of Ahenobarbus or 'bronze-beard'. All these stories become more plausible in the light of an event from my own lifetime, dating from Antonius' rebellion against Domitian.* Terrible war was expected any day from Germany, and Rome was in a state of turmoil, when suddenly the people of Rome started a rumour of victory, which arose by spontaneous generation out of the masses themselves. The story rapidly spread throughout Rome that Antonius himself had been killed and his army had been completely eliminated in the defeat. Belief in this story became so strong and vigorous that many of the city officials actually offered sacrifices to the gods in gratitude. However, when it became clear, on

investigation, that the story had not started with any particular person, and that its traces, as it sought places of safety, could be followed only so far from person to person until it finally plunged into the abysmal sea of the endless masses, without any identifiable starting-point, the rumour soon disappeared from the city, and it was only when Domitian and his army were on their way, marching off to war, that they were met by letters containing news of the victory. And the day of the victory was also the day of the rumour, even though the distance between the two places was more than twenty thousand stades.* These facts are known by everyone my age.

[26] Gnaeus Octavius, the commander of Aemilius' fleet, anchored off Samothrace, and although for the gods' sake he honoured Perseus' right to sanctuary, he tried to make sure that he could not take a boat off the island and escape. Nevertheless, Perseus somehow managed secretly to persuade a Cretan called Oroandes, who owned a small boat, to pick up him and his valuables. Oroandes, in true Cretan fashion,* took his money on board one night, and told Perseus to come the following night to the harbour by the temple of Demeter along with his children and any attendants he could not do without—but then sailed off just before nightfall. Perseus suffered terribly, first in squeezing out through a narrow window and along the town wall with his children and his wife, who were unused to hardship and homelessness, but this was nothing compared to the suffering he expressed in a groan when he was wandering about on the sea-shore and someone told him that he had seen Oroandes—day was beginning to break—in his boat out at sea. Perseus retreated in utter despair back towards the town, but not before the Romans spotted him. He and his wife eluded their pursuers and got back within the walls, but a man called Ion, who many years previously had been Perseus' beloved, but now became his betrayer, caught his children and handed them over to the Romans. And so, thanks to Ion, Perseus had the most compelling reason—a reason which governs the behaviour even of a wild animal whose young ones have been captured—to surrender and hand himself over to those who were holding his children prisoner. The person he trusted most, Nasica, was not there, so he asked for him in vain. He wept at this misfortune, but then, seeing no way out wherever he looked, he put himself into Gnaeus' hands.

Perseus now revealed that avarice was not his most demeaning trait, but fear of death, which made him throw away the only blessing fortune leaves those who have been brought low, namely pity. At his request he was taken to Aemilius, who treated him as a great man brought low by the anger of the gods and the hostility of fortune. He stood up and came forward to meet him, with his friends by his side and tears in his eyes. Perseus, however, made a disgraceful spectacle of himself: he threw himself on the floor and clasped Aemilius' knees, whimpering and pleading in a most demeaning fashion. Aemilius could not stand it and refused to listen to his pleas. He looked at Perseus with a pained and distressed expression, and said, 'You poor fool, why are you robbing fortune of the most serious charge you could bring against it? If you behave like this people will think you deserve your misfortune. Instead of thinking that your present condition is undeserved, they will think that of your past state. And why are you undermining my victory and denying my success its significance, by showing that in you the Romans found a mean and unworthy opponent? Courage in those who meet with misfortune goes a long way towards enabling them to win the respect even of their enemies, but for Romans there is nothing more dishonourable than cowardice, even if the coward prospers.'*

[27] Despite his displeasure, Aemilius raised Perseus to his feet, gave him his right hand, and entrusted him to Tubero.* Then he convened a meeting in his tent of his sons, sons-in-law, and other officers, particularly the younger ones, but at first, to everyone's surprise, he sat in silent reflection for a long time. Then he began to talk about fortune and human affairs. 'Is there really any point', he said, 'in a man taking heart from a moment of success, or feeling proud at having conquered a race or a city or a kingdom? Shouldn't a military man rather see the reversal in Perseus' life as an illustration offered him by fortune of the weakness we all share, and learn to regard nothing as stable and secure? What occasion can there possibly be for men to take heart, when victory over others is precisely the time when we are most compelled to be afraid of fortune, and when a happy man can be plunged into the depths of depression by the realization that fate follows a cyclical course and attaches itself to different people at different times? When you consider that it took just one hour for the heritage of Alexander, the man who scaled the greatest heights of power and won the mightiest empire ever, to come tumbling down to where you have it now, under your feet, and

when you see kings who a short while ago were protected by horsemen in their thousands and foot soldiers in their ten thousands now receiving their daily food and drink from the hands of their enemies, can you suppose that fortune holds out for our affairs any guarantee that they will survive over time? So won't you young men shed this empty whinnying and prancing over victory? You should cower in abject humility in the face of the future, ever watchful for the end, whatever it may be, that the gods will cause to strike each and every one of you in retribution for your current success.' It is said that Aemilius went on in this vein for some time before dismissing the young men, with their vain and insolent pride well and truly curbed by the bridle of his trenchant words.

[28] Aemilius next gave his men a period of rest and himself a period of travel around Greece, seeing the sights and passing his time with activities that combined prestige and kindness, in the sense that wherever he went he not only restored democratic government and re-established the rights of citizens, but also handed out gifts of grain or oil, drawing on the royal stores. According to my sources, so many provisions were found in reserve that they ran out of petitioners and people to give them to before they had used up all they had found.

At Delphi he saw a tall square pillar made out of blocks of white stone, on top of which a statue of Perseus was to have stood; he gave orders that a statue of himself was to be placed there instead, on the grounds that it was only appropriate for the conquered to make way for the conquerors.* In Olympia he is said to have made the famous and often-repeated statement that Phidias had sculpted Homer's Zeus.*

When the ten commissioners arrived from Rome,* he gave the Macedonians back their country and their towns for them to live in as free and independent citizens, on payment to Rome of a hundred talents, whereas they used to pay more than double this amount as tribute to their kings. The many different contests he put on as public shows, and the sacrifices he performed to the gods, were accompanied by feasts and banquets, lavishly funded by the royal treasuries. In managing and arranging these feasts, and in seating and greeting the guests and discerning what degree of respect and consideration was due to each of them, he displayed a high degree of precision and care. The Greeks were impressed to see a man with so much important business to conduct not belittling these amusements, but paying appropriate attention even to trivial details.* But these things gave him pleasure, as also did the fact that, though surrounded by splendour, his guests found nothing more enjoyable there than him, and could not take their eyes off him. If anyone expressed amazement at the care with which he prepared these feasts, he used to tell him that the same mental faculty was involved in taking charge of a military formation and a symposium; the only difference was that you had to make one strike as much fear as possible into the enemy, and the other give as much pleasure as possible to the guests.* But the qualities which people found most impressive were his generosity and detachment, as displayed by his refusal even to look at all the silver and gold which had been gathered together out of the royal treasuries, rather than just handing it all over to his quaestors for depositing in the public treasury. At the most he allowed his sons, who were devoted to literature, to pick and choose among the king's books, and when he was handing out prizes for valour in the battle he gave his son-in-law, Aelius Tubero, a bowl weighing five pounds. This is the Tubero who, as I have said,* lived with sixteen relatives, with one small farm to support them all. This bowl is said to have been the first silver object to have entered the house of the Aelii, and it owed its introduction to virtue and the recognition of virtue, but up until then neither they nor their wives had ever used implements of silver or gold.

[29] Everything was sorted out under his skilful management. Then, after saying farewell to the Greeks and encouraging the Macedonians to reflect on the liberty which Rome had bestowed upon them and to preserve it by keeping the peace and avoiding dissension, he broke camp and marched to Epirus, with a senatorial decree to the effect that he should enrich the soldiers who had fought with him against Perseus from the communities there. He wanted to make a surprise attack, when no one was expecting it, on all the communities at once, so he sent for the ten leading men from each community and ordered them to bring him, on a stated day, all the silver and gold they had in their homes and temples. He sent back with each of them a garrison of soldiers with an officer in charge, ostensibly just to look for and take possession of the valuables. But when the appointed day arrived, at precisely the same time these men all set about overwhelming and looting the communities,

and in the space of just one hour 150,000 people were enslaved and seventy communities were sacked. Despite all this destruction and mayhem, however, each soldier received no more than eleven drachmas as his ration, and men all over the world shuddered in abhorrence at the outcome of the war, in which the crushing of a whole people resulted in so little profit and gain for each man.*

[30] After discharging this duty, which ran completely contrary to his decent and honest nature, Aemilius went down to Oricum, from where he crossed over to Italy with his troops, and sailed up the river Tiber in the royal galley, with its sixteen banks of oars. The ship was adorned on the outside with arms and armour captured during the war, and with red and purple cloth, in such a splendid and festive fashion† that in a sense the Romans enjoyed all the pomp of a triumphal procession before one had actually taken place, as they walked along the banks, keeping pace with the splashing of the oars as they gently propelled the ship upstream.

Aemilius' soldiers, however, had cast covetous glances at the royal treasure and come to the conclusion that they had not received their due. This made them, under the surface, seethe with discontent and resentment against Aemilius. They openly accused him of having been a heavy-handed and tyrannical leader, and were no more than half-hearted supporters of his desire for a triumph. Now, Servius Galba, despite having been made a military tribune under Aemilius, was a political enemy of his, so when the soldiers' discontent came to his attention, he found the courage to deliver a public speech, arguing that Aemilius should not be awarded a triumph. He put a number of false accusations against their commander into the mouths of the army rabble, fanned the flames of their anger, and then asked the tribunes of the people for another day to debate the issues, on the grounds that there was not enough time remaining that day for him to formulate his charges, even though there were still four hours of daylight left. The tribunes ordered him to say his piece then and there, so he embarked on a long speech filled with all kinds of slanders, which used up the rest of the day. When darkness fell the tribunes of the people dissolved the assembly, but the soldiers, who had by now become more defiant, flocked to Galba, organized themselves into a body, and at dawn once again occupied the Capitol, which was where the tribunes planned to hold the assembly.*

[31] Voting began at daybreak, and the first tribe voted against the

triumph. News of what was happening began to reach the rest of the people and the senate down in the city. The general populace was incensed at the way Aemilius was being insulted, but they could do no more than shout out their disapproval; however, the most notable senators loudly denounced what was going on and thus encouraged one another to take steps against the lawless defiance of the troops, which would escalate to total anarchy and violence if nothing was done to stop them from depriving Aemilius of his victory honours. They pushed their way through the crowd, climbed in a body up the hill, and told the tribunes of the people to stop the voting until they had spoken their minds to the masses. The tribunes complied, silence fell, and up stepped Marcus Servilius, an ex-consul who had killed twenty-three opponents in single combat.* He said that now more than ever he knew how great a commander Aemilius Paullus was, when he saw how unruly and bad the army was with which he had won such noble victories and achieved such important results. He said that he was surprised to find the people delighting in triumphs over Illyrians and Africans*† and then cheating themselves of the sight of a live Macedonian king and of the glory of Alexander and Philip being carried as booty, subject to Roman arms. 'I find it quite inexplicable', he went on, 'that some time ago, when an unreliable rumour of victory reached the city, you sacrificed to the gods and prayed for early visual confirmation of the news, and yet now, when the commander has come with the victory verified, you deprive the gods of the honour owed to them and yourselves of the pleasure of a triumph, as if you were afraid to view the enormity of his achievements or wanted to spare the feelings of the enemy king. It is true, though, that pity for the king would make a better reason for dispensing with the triumph than resentment of the commander. You have allowed malice to grow so strong that a man unscarred by wounds, a man with a body all sleek and smooth from indoor living, has the effrontery to talk to us about leadership and triumphs, when we have learnt the hard way to assess how good or bad military leaders are—by our wounds!' And with these words he tore aside his clothing and revealed a chest covered with an incredible number of scars. Then he twisted and uncovered parts of his body that it is normally considered impolite to expose in a crowd. He turned to Galba and said, 'You may laugh, but I find no reason to be embarrassed about these scars before my fellow citizens, in whose defence I gained them, from constant service day and night in the cavalry. Go ahead! Take these people off to vote. I shall come down too: I shall stand by all their sides and see which of them are ungrateful villains who in time of war prefer a demagogue to a leader.'

[32] They say that the troops were stopped short by this speech and changed course so completely that Aemilius' triumph was ratified by every single tribe. Here is a description of the procession, taken from my sources.* The people built benches in the circuses (which is what the Romans call the arenas used for horse-races) and the forum, lined all the other parts of the city which afforded a view of the procession, and changed into clean clothes to watch the spectacle. Every temple was opened, with garlands and clouds of incense everywhere; large numbers of adjutants and lictors held back the crowds, which surged uncontrollably into the middle of the route and ran from one place to another, and tried to keep the roads open and clear. Three days were set aside for the procession. The first day—and it was only just enough—was given over to the spectacle of all the statuettes, paintings, and statues taken during the war, which were transported on 250 wagons. On the next day the most beautiful and valuable of the Macedonian arms and armour were carried through the streets on large numbers of carts. The bronze and iron parts of the weapons had been polished until they shone, and all the objects had been artfully and aesthetically positioned, so as to look as much as possible as though they had fallen into random heaps of their own accord: there were helmets lying next to shields, breastplates on top of greaves, Cretan targes and Thracian wicker shields and quivers all jumbled up with horses' bridles; the piles bristled with unsheathed swords, and pikes had been planted among them. The arms and armour were somewhat loosely arranged, so that as they were carried along they struck against one another and gave out a harsh and fearsome sound, and even though they had belonged to the losers in the war their appearance was not without its terrors. After the wagons with the arms and armour came three thousand men carrying coined silver money in 750 boxes; each box held three talents' worth of money and was carried by four men. Then came more men carrying silver mixing-bowls, drinking-horns, drinking-bowls, and cups, each shown off to its best advantage and each remarkable for its size and for the depth of the chased work on it.

[33] Early in the morning of the third day trumpeters made their

way through the streets, but the music they played was unusual for a procession or an exhibition: it was the kind with which the Romans used to rouse themselves in battle. Behind the trumpeters 120 stall-fed oxen, with their horns gilded, and arrayed with head-bands and chaplets were being led to sacrifice by young men dressed in ceremonial aprons with purple borders, and boys went with them, carrying silver and gold libation cups. Next came the men carrying the gold coinage, which had been divided up, like the silver money, into vessels with a capacity of three talents, and there were seventy-seven such vessels altogether. They were followed by men carrying the sacred bowl, which had been made, on Aemilius' instructions, out of ten talents of gold and studded with gems. Next came men displaying the Antigonid, Seleucid, and Thericlean goblets,* and all the golden table-ware Perseus had used. They were followed by Perseus' chariot, which carried his arms and armour with his diadem lying on top of them. Not far behind the chariot Perseus' children were led along as slaves, accompanied by a throng of weeping nurses, teachers, and tutors, who stretched out their hands in supplication to the spectators and taught the children to beg and plead. There were two boys and one girl, too young to comprehend the magnitude of the disaster—and this made people feel so much more sad for them, considering the fact that one day this incomprehension would end, that Perseus walked by almost unnoticed by the Romans, who were just staring at the children in pity. Many people started crying, and in all of them the spectacle aroused a mixture of pleasure and pain, until the children had passed by.

[34] Behind the children and their retinue came Perseus. He wore a grey cloak and Macedonian boots, and looked as though he was utterly astounded and bewildered by the magnitude of the disaster that had happened to him. He too was accompanied by a crowd of associates and friends; their faces were heavy with grief, but because they were constantly glancing at Perseus and weeping they gave the spectators to understand that they were mourning his fate and did not care in the slightest for their own. Perseus had written to Aemilius, asking not to be paraded through the streets and included in the triumph, but Aemilius, apparently in mockery of Perseus' cowardice and fear of death, remarked: 'The situation is no different now from what it was before: he could grant his own request, if he wanted.' He meant that he could always choose death instead of

dishonour, but the coward could not bring himself to do that. Instead, unmanned by hope, he became a part of his own spoils.

After Perseus and his retinue, four hundred golden garlands were carried along, which had been brought and presented to Aemilius by representatives from the various cities in recognition of his valour. Then came the man himself, mounted on a magnificently decorated chariot. He would have made a remarkable sight even without all these trappings of power; he wore a cloak dyed with purple and shot through with gold, and held in his right hand a spray of laurel. Every single soldier likewise carried laurel. The army marched behind their commander's chariot in their units and divisions, with the men singing partly traditional songs with an element of humour in them, and partly hymns of victory and praise for Aemilius' achievements. No one could keep their eyes off him; he was an object of universal admiration, and there was no good man in the world who wished him ill. But perhaps there is some deity whose job it is to prune immoderately great success and make human life a mixture, so that every life might be tempered and tainted with trouble and, as Homer says, we might regard as best off those whose fortunes alternate from one side of the scales to the other.*

[35] Aemilius had four sons, two of whom—Scipio and Fabius, as I have already said—had been adopted by other families,* and two of whom, the children of his second wife, who were still boys, he kept at home. One of these two boys died, aged 14, five days before Aemilius celebrated his triumph, and the other, who was 12, died three days after the end of the triumph. Everyone in Rome was affected by this and was horrified at the savagery of fortune, seeing that it had no qualms about introducing such terrible sorrow into a house that was filled with pride and joy and grateful sacrifices, and blending hymns of victory and triumph with tears of grief.

[36] Aemilius, however, concluded correctly that men need bravery and courage not only when faced with arms and Macedonian pikes, but also to deal with each and every retaliatory strike that fortune may make, and he adapted and arranged the constitution of his life in such a way that the bad was obscured by the good and the private by the public, and he could avoid debasing the importance or impairing the dignity of his victory. He buried the first of the two sons who died just before celebrating his triumph, as I have said. When the second died after the triumph, he convened an assembly

of the Roman people and addressed them not as a man who needed to be consoled, but rather as one who wanted to console his fellow citizens in their grief at his misfortune. He said that he had never been afraid of anything mortal men could do, but that in the realm of the gods he had always regarded fortune as a particularly fickle and variable thing, something to fear. In this recent war, he said, fortune had attended his exploits like a favourable wind, and so he had been expecting some change for the worse. 'After all,' he said, 'it took me one day to cross the Ionian Sea from Brundisium and land at Corcyra; five days later I had already sacrificed to the god in Delphi, and then in another five days I took over the army in Macedonia. As soon as I had performed the customary expiatory rites, I got the operation started, and only fifteen days later I had brought the war to an admirable conclusion. Things had gone so well for me that I was mistrustful of fortune, and now that there really was nothing to fear or be alarmed about from the enemy, I was deeply concerned, during my voyage home, about the possibility of a change in my luck after all my good fortune, since I was transporting a huge, victorious army, spoils, and royal prisoners. In fact, though, I got back safe to you, but even so, when I saw the city filled with delight and pride and grateful sacrifices, I was still suspicious of fortune, since I knew that, though we may benefit enormously from it, the favours it grants are never straightforward, and some payment is always required. And my mind continued to suffer from this fear and to be filled with anxiety about what the future might bring for Rome, until I experienced this terrible misfortune in my own house and spent holy days seeing to the successive burials of two noble sons, who were the only heirs remaining to me. Now, then, I am no longer threatened by any serious danger, and I feel confident that fortune will stand by you and that you can trust it to do you no harm. As far as retribution for our successes is concerned, fortune is content to have made use of me and my troubles, since just as clear an instance of human frailty is provided by the person celebrating a triumph as by the person who is the victim of the triumph. The only difference is that even in defeat Perseus has his sons, whereas Aemilius, the conqueror, has lost his.'*

[37] This is the noble and high-minded speech we are told that Aemilius delivered, in all sincerity, to the people of Rome. Although he pitied Perseus' downfall and had a strong desire to help him,

the best he could do was to arrange for him to be moved from prison—the Roman word is *carcer*—to somewhere clean where he could live more like a human being. Despite being guarded in these new quarters, Perseus managed to starve himself to death—at least, that is what most writers say, but some record that he died in a peculiar and unusual way. They say that his guards got angry with him for something he did that they disapproved of, and since there was nothing else they could do to hurt him and do him harm, they did not allow him to sleep. They used to watch carefully for when he was falling asleep and then stop him doing so, and they came up with all sorts of ways to keep him awake, until eventually, worn out by this treatment, he died. Two of his children died as well, but the third, Alexander, is said to have become an expert at chasing and fine engraving; also, once he had learnt to write and speak the Roman language, he used to act as secretary to people in office, a job which he was found to perform in a skilful and accomplished manner.

[38] My sources attribute Aemilius' enormous popularity with the masses to his achievements in Macedonia, since he filled the public treasury with so much money that the people were exempt from taxes until the consulate of Hirtius and Pansa, at the time of the first war between Antony and Caesar.* However, a peculiar and remarkable feature of Aemilius was that despite the extraordinary support and acclaim he received from the people, he remained loyal to the aristocratic party: he never said or did anything to court favour with the masses, and in political matters was always counted as one of the powerful Roman élite. Some years later this was used by Appius to disparage Scipio Africanus. These two, the most important men in Rome at the time, were rival candidates for the office of censor.* Appius, in keeping with the traditional political position of his family, had the support of the senate and the aristocrats, while Scipio was not only a great man in his own right, but was also always a popular favourite with the common people. Once, then, when Appius saw at Scipio's side as he entered the forum a crowd of low-born ex-slaves, vulgar manipulators who knew how to convene a mob and force any issue through with their solicitations and shrill talk, he said in a deliberately loud voice, 'Aemilius Paullus, you may well groan in your grave! See how your son is assisted to the censorship by Aemilius the town-crier and Licinius Philonicus!' But Scipio won the loyalty of the people by invariably increasing their power,

whereas Aemilius Paullus, despite belonging to the aristocratic party, could not have been more popular with the masses if they had thought that he was going out of his way to win their support and was seeking their favour in all his dealings with them. Apart from all the other honours he received, they demonstrated this by electing him to the censorship, which is the most sacred of all the offices at Rome.* Moreover, the censors wield a great deal of power, especially when it comes to assessing people's conduct, because they have the right to expel from the senate anyone whose way of life is inappropriate, to name the leader of the senate, and to disenfranchise a young man of loose conduct by confiscating his horse. They also supervise property valuation and the registers. In Aemilius' time 337,452 men were registered as citizens, and he named as leader of the senate Marcus Aemilius Lepidus, who had already enjoyed this privileged position four times previously. He also expelled three senators, but they were men of no particular eminence, and he and his colleague, Marcius Philippus, exercised a similar degree of moderation when it came to assessing the knights.

[39] He saw to all the most important things that needed to be done, but then fell ill. At first he was critically ill, and though after a while the threat to his life passed, the illness still lingered and proved troublesome, so on his doctors' advice he sailed to Velia in Italy, where he spent quite a bit of time resting in the country by the sea. The Romans missed him, however, and in the theatres they often gave voice to what seemed to be prayers and appeals to see him. And so, when a sacrifice was to take place which required his presence, and his health seemed up to it, he returned to Rome. He performed the sacrifice along with his fellow priests,* surrounded by a crowd of visibly happy Romans, and then the next day made another sacrifice, in private, asking the gods to keep him in good health. When the sacrifice had been performed in the prescribed manner, he returned home and lay down, but suddenly, before he had time to notice and comprehend the change, he became delirious and deranged, and two days later he died.*

He lacked for nothing that is traditionally held to contribute to happiness. His funeral was accompanied by a remarkable and enviable procession, and the distinction and solemnity of the rites were a fitting tribute to the man's virtue—which is not to say that they involved gold, ivory, and all the usual expensive and extravagant paraphernalia, but that they were an opportunity for a display of goodwill, respect, and gratitude even from enemies, let alone his fellow citizens. At any rate, there happened to be some Spaniards, Ligurians, and Macedonians in town.* and they all took turns to carry the bier on their shoulders, if they were fit and young enough to do so, while the older ones followed in the train, calling on Aemilius as the benefactor and saviour of their countries. It was not just that on the various occasions when he had conquered them he had treated them all leniently and decently, but also that throughout the rest of his life, up to the time of his death, he had always done them some good and cared for them as if they had been members of his own household or family.

It is said that his estate amounted to a mere 370,000 drachmas. He bequeathed it to his two sons, but since the younger one, Scipio, had been adopted by Africanus, who was rather wealthy, he let his brother have the whole estate.* So much for the character and life of Aemilius Paullus; this is what they are said to have been like.

TIBERIUS AND GAIUS GRACCHUS

INTRODUCTION

The tribunates of Tiberius and Gaius Sempronius Gracchus mark the beginning of an era of civil turmoil and violence at Rome which would end when Octavian, later Augustus, emerged as sole leader and introduced the principate, the imperial system under which Plutarch lived. In the centuries before the Gracchi, the senatorial aristocracy had ruled with a firm hand, making accommodations when necessary, but never losing control. Then, at the time of the Gracchi, the opposition of obstinate senators and aggressive reformers led to a refusal to compromise, and ultimately to the murder of both brothers and of thousands of their followers. The brothers were seen as *populares*, men who sought the support of the Roman plebs for themselves and their programmes, but themselves were of an excellent senatorial family, as Plutarch makes clear. Their father, who died early, had been extremely distinguished, twice consul, a censor, and augur; their mother, Cornelia, was the daughter of Scipio Africanus. Both young men served on the staff of the younger Scipio, their cousin and brother-in-law, Tiberius in Africa in 147–146 BC, Gaius at Numantia in 134.

Despite numerous personal and family ties to other senators, Tiberius, as tribune of the people in 133, undertook with the help of other leading Romans to challenge the leaders of the senate, including Scipio, with an agrarian law which would end the illegal but long customary control of public land by the wealthy, and distribute land to poor citizens. Senatorial opposition to this reform led to an escalating series of conflicts, ending with Tiberius' death. Gaius, who was hardly 20 when his brother was killed, stayed quiet for a while, but as tribune in 123 and 122 undertook a much further-reaching programme of legislation, which the senate took as revolution, and crushed with brutal force. The senate won for the moment, but related issues soon erupted once more, often framed in terms of political tendencies which became apparent with the Gracchi: the *optimates*, those defending the traditional senatorial oligarchy, against the *populares*, those who for various reasons chose to challenge the system, especially through the tribunes or by appealing to the popular assembly. These tendencies, when coupled with intense personal ambition, led to the violence which Plutarch depicts in other Lives: *Marius*, *Sulla*, *Pompey*, *Caesar*, *Antony*, all of which follow in this collection. Finally, after a century of violence, Romans eagerly embraced the new monarchical regime of Augustus.

Plutarch sees the two Gracchi as major figures in the emergence of the Roman state as he knew it. Yet, as with the Lives that follow, his admiration, though genuine, is ambivalent: civil war, for Plutarch, was not a desirable outcome. The Gracchi appear in a unique double biography, set parallel to the third-century BC reforming Spartan kings, Agis (king *c*.244–241) and Cleomenes (king 235–222). These kings took power legitimately, but wished to overthrow the current constitution and restore their conception of the Lycurgan constitution of centuries before. As at Rome, the wealthy opposed them, and civil war resulted. In the double pair, Plutarch explores the motivations for reform in the two cities, and the character flaws which aided the opposition and prevented the efforts of the reformers. In each case, the two lives are treated as one, and are properly given continuous numeration, although in many editions the second Life is numbered separately.

The figure of Ixion in the proem to *Agis and Cleomenes* introduces both sets of Lives:

> The fable of Ixion, who, embracing a cloud instead of Hera, begot the Centaurs, has been ingeniously supposed to have been invented to represent to us ambitious men, whose minds, doting on glory, which is a mere image of virtue, produce nothing that is genuine or uniform, but only, as might be expected of such a conjunction, misshapen and unnatural actions. (*Ag.Cl* 1)

Ixion, a mortal, had attempted to rape Hera, but was deceived by a false image: those who pursue glory, and especially the adulation of the people, are also deceived, and fall equally short of their goal. In the paragraphs which follow, Plutarch delineates the fundamental error for a politician, to substitute this adulation for what is truly good for the state, allowing himself to be led by the multitude rather than leading it. He thus becomes like the serpent in the fable, whose tail insisted that it should lead for a while instead of the head, with disastrous results for both head and tail. These thoughts are provoked by the fate of the Gracchi,

> men of noble nature, and whose generous natural dispositions were improved by the best of educations, and who came to the administration of affairs with the most laudable intentions; yet they were ruined, I cannot say by an immoderate desire for glory, but by a more excusable fear of disgrace. For being excessively loved and favoured by the people, they thought it a discredit to them not to make full repayment, endeavouring by new public acts to outdo the honours they had received, and again, because of these new kindnesses, incurring yet further distinctions; till the people and they, mutually inflamed,

> without noticing it, became involved in actions which permitted no good continuation, but were shameful to abandon. (*Ag.Cl* 2)

Ixion was punished by being placed on a spinning wheel: Plutarch suggests that the fate of the Gracchi was similar, falling into a perpetual circle of honours and benefactions, with no way to stop. Thus the problem for the politician: good nature, good training, good intentions—but, with no limit, an all too easy slide from doing what is right to doing what is gratifying. The people, irrational and fickle, draw the noble soul into a self-destructive tailspin. This vision, twice repeated, makes *Tiberius and Gaius Gracchus* one of the most moving, even tragic, of the *Lives*: the noble promise and the unhappy end are artfully juxtaposed.

Plutarch's sympathy for his protagonists is palpable. His analysis of the moral situation of the Gracchi does not diminish his admiration for their noble courage and dedication. The last two chapters (39–40) are clear: Opimius, the consul who led the attack on Gaius, is shamefully condemned for accepting bribes, and grows old amid the hate and insults of the people, while the people erect statues in the two brothers' honour, and their nobility, in the memory of their mother Cornelia, is like that of the heroes of old.

Revolutionaries are always hard to evaluate, especially unsuccessful ones, and modern scholarship has taken various positions on the Gracchi. The problem is exacerbated by the fact that we have only two major sources, Plutarch and the first book of Appian's *Civil Wars*, both from the second century AD, supplemented by comments in Cicero, Sallust, and other Latin authors. Often historians have set the problem in terms of accepting either Plutarch's narrative or Appian's, but this is unsatisfactory, not least because Plutarch is not writing a narrative history, and wishes to bring out the moral implications of his subjects' behaviour. More recently scholars have attempted to understand the cultural and social setting of the Gracchi, exploring the interaction of a number of variables which were in the process of change at this time: the rise of immense fortunes, the influence of senatorial dynasts who were able to claim kings and peoples as clients, the ambitions of the non-Roman inhabitants of Italy, the changing nature of the army, and so on. Yet even so, no convincing synthesis has emerged.

Plutarch and Appian clearly shared some sources, but frequently disagree: we cannot establish what their sources were. Plutarch quite frequently gives general references (e.g. 'so the story goes', c. 1), and we can only presume he used standard works of history available to him. But he often used contemporary sources too, citing the speeches of both Gracchi (cc. 9, 15, 23, 24), the letters of Cornelia (34), and the *Annals* of Gaius

Fannius, who was a contemporary of Tiberius and served with him in Africa (4). No doubt Fannius was used for other information besides the attack on Carthage. Cicero (in his *Brutus* 21. 81) cites Fannius for a speech of Metellus against Tiberius, so his text may have reported some of the speeches found in Plutarch. We know, however, that Gaius' speeches were preserved separately and studied (cf. Cicero, *Brutus* 33. 126), and Plutarch may have had direct access to them. The fragments of his speeches are collected in *Oratorum Romanorum Fragmenta*, 4th edn., H. Malcovati (Turin, 1976), 174–98 and by D. Stockton in *The Gracchi* (Oxford, 1979), 217–25. Plutarch also cites (c. 8) a book written by Gaius, probably a political pamphlet, which described Tiberius' impressions on travelling through Etruria; this may be the work addressed to a friend, Pomponius, cited by Cicero (*On Divination* 2. 29. 62) for the omen of the two snakes reported in chapter 1. The letters of Cornelia were known to Cicero (*Brutus*. 58. 211) and Quintilian (1. 1. 6). Besides these contemporary sources, Plutarch cites Cornelius Nepos, who wrote Lives of the two Gracchi (21). He refers to Polybius, who did not treat the Gracchan period, for the marriage of Cornelia (4), and to Cicero's *On Divination* 1. 26. 56 for the dream of Gaius (22). The Lives of the Gracchi reveal particularly well the opposition of senate and people which is such a prominent feature of Plutarch's political analysis.[1] His historical value lies in his use of contemporary sources, and in his own vision of the dangers facing a reforming politician.

The two Lives are distinctive for focusing on a very small part of the protagonists' short lives. The structure is chronological, but the emphasis is on the years of their tribunates (133 BC = cc. 8–21; 122–121 BC = cc. 24–38), with practically no early life.

1–3	Early life; similarities and differences of the Gracchi
4–7	Tiberius' service in Africa (147 BC?) and Numantia (137)
8–9	Tiberius begins his reforms: the agrarian law (133)
10–12	The opposition of Octavius; Tiberius deposes him
13–15	The land commission; Tiberius' defence to the people
16	Campaign for re-election; new laws to win votes
17–19	Election day; Tiberius and supporters killed
20–1	Aftermath: the land commission, ignominy of Nasica
22–3	Gaius' initial withdrawal; senate keeps him as quaestor in Sardinia (126–124)

[1] See C. B. R. Pelling, 'Plutarch and Roman Politics', in B. Scardigli (ed.), *Essays on Plutarch's Lives* (Oxford: Clarendon Press, 1995), 319–56, esp. 331–7.

24–8	Election as tribune; legislation (123)
29–31	More legislation; the tribune Drusus opposes him; Gaius re-elected (122)
32–3	Difficulties in Carthage and rejection by voters
34–8	Opimius consul (121); matters come to a head, Gaius and three thousand supporters killed
39–40	Fate of Opimius; Cornelia recalls her children

In each case there is a turning-point after the initial legislation. Tiberius is put on the defensive after his completely untraditional deposition of his fellow tribune Octavius, and thereafter needs to run for re-election to keep his influence. Plutarch reproaches him, pointing out that the legislation proposed during his re-election campaign was 'motivated by anger and dissension rather than considerations of right and expediency' (16). Gaius too, after his position was attacked by Drusus, another tribune working for the senate (9), never recovered the initiative, and had to keep promising more to retain his support.

Cornelia, the mother of Tiberius and Gaius, plays a special role in the anecdotes that frame their lives. She is seen first as a beloved wife, who after the premature death of her husband raised her children alone. She instilled in them virtues of courage, self-restraint, liberality, eloquence, and nobility (1), but also incited them to pre-eminence in the political arena (8). She trained them well, but also instilled that love of glory which was to be their undoing. When her sons were murdered, she remained stoically calm, and refused to lament their loss, instead recalling 'the stories of their deeds and fates without grief or tears, as if narrating the story of some ancient heroes'. Plutarch insists that her behaviour reflected neither insensibility nor excessive grief, but the dominance of reason over fortune (40). In presenting Cornelia, Plutarch focuses not on her powerful social position and the political influence that she wielded, though he is aware of both, but on her role as mother, first training her sons, then rationally controlling her grief at their violent deaths, showing the same kind of philosophically grounded self-possession that he expected of his wife Timoxena, in *Consolation*. As in other cases (such as Cratesicleia in *Agis and Cleomenes*), he does not expect a woman to have her own agenda, to which a husband or strong and noble males should be subordinate, but to support the male statesman.

Badian, E., 'From the Gracchi to Sulla (1940–1959)', *Historia*, 11 (1962) 197–245.

—— 'Tiberius Gracchus and the Beginning of the Roman Revolution', in W. Haase and H. Temporini (eds.) *Aufstieg und Niedergang der römischen Welt*, I. 1 (Berlin, 1972), 668–731.

Bernstein, A. H., *Tiberius Sempronius Gracchus* (Ithaca: Cornell University Press, 1978).

Boren, H., *The Gracchi* (New York: Twayne, 1968).

Brunt, P. A., *Social Conflicts in the Roman Republic* (London: Norton, 1971).

Earl, D. C., *Tiberius Gracchus: A Study in Politics* (Brussels: Latomus, 1963).

Gruen, E., *Roman Politics and the Criminal Courts, 149–78* (Cambridge Mass.: Harvard, 1968), 45–105.

Pelling, C. B. R., 'Plutarch and Roman Politics', in B. Scardigli (ed.), *Essays on Plutarch's Lives* (Oxford: Clarendon Press, 1995), 319–56.

Stockton, D., *The Gracchi* (Oxford: Clarendon Press, 1979).

TIBERIUS AND GAIUS GRACCHUS

[1] Having completed the first part of this narrative,* we turn now to the Roman pair. We will be able to contemplate just as much suffering there as we found in the lives of Agis and Cleomenes, since the parallel lives in this case will be those of Tiberius and Gaius. They were the sons of Tiberius Gracchus, a man who owed his eminence more to his moral goodness than he did even to the fact that he had held the office of censor at Rome, had twice been consul, and had celebrated two triumphs.* This explains why, even though he had been no friend of Scipio (the one who defeated Hannibal), but had actually been on bad terms with him, he was given permission after Scipio's death to marry his daughter, Cornelia. Once, so the story goes, he caught a pair of snakes on his couch and the diviners he consulted about the portent told him that he should not kill both the snakes or let both of them go either, but gave him a choice in their interpretation, and said that the death of the male snake would bring death to him and the death of the female snake would bring death to Cornelia.* Now, Tiberius was fond of his wife, and also thought it more appropriate for him to die, since he was getting on in age while she was still a young woman, so he killed the male snake and let the female go—and not long afterwards he died. He was survived by twelve children, borne him by Cornelia, who inherited the responsibility of looking after both the children and the household. She proved to be so proper in her behaviour, and such a good and principled mother, that Tiberius was generally held to have made the right decision in choosing to die instead of such a woman. In fact, when King Ptolemy* proposed marriage to her and invited her to be his queen, she turned him down and remained a widow. She lost all her children except one of her daughters, who married the younger Scipio,* and the two sons who are the subject of this book. She brought up these two boys, Tiberius and Gaius, with such devotion that although they were, by common consent, the most gifted young men of their generation in Rome, their education was generally held to have played a more important part than nature in forming their excellent qualities.

[2] When sculptors and painters portray the Dioscuri, they make

them basically alike but also different in certain respects, since they give one the physique of a boxer and the other that of a runner.* In the same way, these two young men were remarkably similar in terms of their courage and self-restraint—and also their generosity, eloquence, and high principles—but at the same time enormous differences erupted, so to speak, and appeared in their public careers and achievements, and I think it would be as well for me to begin with these.

In the first place, then, Tiberius' features, expression, and bearing were calm and unassuming, whereas Gaius was lively and intense. One result of this was that when they spoke in public Tiberius stayed standing in a decorous fashion in the same place, but Gaius was the first person in Rome to pace around on the rostra and to pull his toga off his shoulder while speaking—in other words, to behave like Cleon of Athens, who is said to have been the first public speaker to pull his cloak open and slap his thigh.* In the second place, the way Gaius spoke was emotive and designed to provoke indignation in his audience, whereas Tiberius was less harsh and aimed more at arousing pity. Also, Tiberius' style was simple and carefully worked out, while Gaius' was persuasive and flamboyant.*

Their lifestyles and eating habits reflected the same kinds of differences. Tiberius lived a frugal and simple life, but although Gaius' life was moderate and restricted compared with what could be found all around him, in contrast to his brother's it was fancy and elaborate. In fact, Drusus* used to take him to task for buying silver dolphins which cost 1,250 drachmas per pound. In keeping with their styles of speaking, Tiberius was a decent and mild-mannered kind of person, while Gaius was blunt and passionate. In fact, without meaning to, Gaius often got so carried away by anger in the middle of a speech that his voice would become shrill, and he would lapse into abusive language and lose track of what he was saying. To remedy this habit of digressing he got an intelligent slave of his called Licinius to stand behind him while he was speaking, holding the kind of voice-training instrument that singers use to practise their scales, and whenever he noticed that Gaius' voice was becoming strident and was starting to crack with anger, he would sound a gentle keynote, which immediately alerted Gaius to moderate his emotions and his voice, calm down, and make himself obedient to the call to rein himself in.

[3] While the two of them were different in these respects, they were indistinguishable when it came to showing courage in battle, treating subject peoples fairly, taking their official duties seriously, and demonstrating self-control about pleasure. Tiberius, however, was nine years older than Gaius,* which meant that their public careers were separated in time and was the main reason for their failure: they did not achieve prominence at the same time, so they could not combine and realize the potential the two of them together had for being an irresistibly powerful force. And so I should discuss each of them separately, starting with the older one.

[4] Soon after reaching maturity his fame was great enough to earn him entry into the so-called priesthood of augurs, an honour he owed to his excellence rather than to his noble birth.* This was evident from the behaviour of the former consul and censor Appius Claudius, a person of such importance that he had been named leader of the Roman senate, who was by far the most dignified man of his day.* For during the communal banquet for the priests he made friendly overtures to Tiberius and asked him if he would consider marrying his daughter. Tiberius accepted gladly and the betrothal was agreed upon there and then. Later, as soon as he got home, Appius shouted out the news to his wife from the doorway at the top of his voice: 'Antistia,' he said, 'I've engaged our Claudia to someone!' The news took her aback and she said, 'Why the hurry? There was no need to rush, unless† you've got Tiberius Gracchus to be her husband.' I am well aware that some people have Tiberius, the father of the Gracchi, and Scipio Africanus as the protagonists of this story, but the majority tell the version I have written here, and Polybius says that after the death of Scipio Africanus his relatives chose Tiberius out of all possible candidates to be Cornelia's husband, which shows that her father died without having betrothed her or made arrangements for her marriage.*

Anyway, his son, our Tiberius, saw active service in Africa under the command of the younger Scipio,* who had married his sister. Since he shared a tent with Scipio, he soon got to know him well and to appreciate in how many important ways he inspired people by his actions to emulate and imitate his virtue. He also soon showed himself to be the most disciplined and courageous young man of his generation. In fact, he was the first to scale the enemy's walls, according to Fannius,* who adds that he was right behind Tiberius and joined him in this feat of bravery. While he was with the army many of his comrades came to feel affection for him, and when he left they missed him.

[5] After this campaign he was elected quaestor,* and was assigned to serve in the war against Numantia under the consul Gaius Mancinus, who was not a bad man, but was the unluckiest Roman commander ever. But this meant that, surrounded as he was by mishap and adversity, Tiberius' intelligence and courage were even more evident than they would normally have been; moreover, it was also clear—and surprising—that he had the highest respect and regard for his leader, despite his habit, in difficult circumstances, of forgetting that he was a military commander. For instance, after losing several major engagements he tried to break camp and pull his troops out under cover of darkness. As soon as the Numantians noticed what was going on they seized the camp, and then fell on the Romans as they were retreating. After slaughtering the tail-enders, they surrounded the entire army and drove them on to difficult ground from which there was no escape. Mancinus gave up the idea of winning safety by main force, and sent heralds to the Numantians to solicit a truce and an end to the hostilities. They replied that the only Roman they trusted was Tiberius and insisted on his being sent to them. The young man was held in very high esteem in their camp, and they trusted him not only for his own sake, but also because they remembered his father, who after conquering numerous tribes during his war against the Spanish had entered into a peace treaty with the Numantians and had always made sure that the Roman people observed the treaty with scrupulous fairness.* So Tiberius was sent to meet with them. With a combination of coercion and concession he negotiated a truce which clearly saved the lives of twenty thousand Roman citizens, not counting slaves and camp followers.

[6] However, the Numantians kept all the valuables that had been abandoned in the camp and distributed them among themselves as spoils of war. The booty included Tiberius' ledgers, containing statements and accounts of his official expenses as quaestor, which he was very anxious to recover.* So, when the army was already well on its way, he turned back towards the Numantian capital with three or four companions. He invited the Numantian leaders to a meeting outside the town, and asked them to return his tablets, so that he could forestall any criticism that might arise from his political

enemies in Rome if he was unable to give an account of his term of office. The Numantians were delighted to find that they had an opportunity to do him a favour, and they invited him to join them inside the town. Tiberius did not know what to do, but as he stood there they came up to him, grasped his hands, and implored him to stop regarding them as enemies; instead, they said, he should treat them as his friends and trust them. Tiberius decided to do as they suggested, partly because he wanted to protect his tablets, and partly because he did not want to offend the Numantians by appearing to mistrust them. When he entered the town the Numantians first served their morning meal and did everything they could to persuade him to sit down and share their food with them, and then they gave him back his tablets and told him he could also take any of the valuables he wanted. However, he took nothing except the incense he used for his public sacrifices. Then with expressions of friendship he bid them farewell and left.

[7] Back in Rome, although the operation as a whole was being denounced and condemned as a disaster and an embarrassment for Rome, the relatives and friends of the soldiers, who made up a sizeable portion of the population, flocked to Tiberius. They were inclined to attribute all the embarrassing aspects of the matter to the commanding officer and to maintain that Tiberius was the reason so many men were still alive. However, some people were so angry at the affair that they were urging the Romans to follow the example of their ancestors, when they took the commanders who had been content to have the Samnites release them and hurled them back at the enemy, stripped of their weapons.* They also did the same to everyone who had played any part in arranging the treaty, such as the quaestors and the military tribunes, as a way of making sure that when the agreement was broken the responsibility and the perjury fell on their heads. But this was the occasion, more than any other, when the Roman people demonstrated their affection and liking for Tiberius. For although they voted to strip the consul of his weapons and surrender him in chains to the Numantians, for Tiberius' sake they spared all the other officers. It is generally held that this lenient attitude was also due to Scipio, who was then the most important and powerful man in Rome.* Nevertheless, Scipio came to be criticized for his failure to save Mancinus and for not ensuring that the treaty with the Numantians was ratified, when it had been negotiated by

his relative and friend, Tiberius. Apparently, the two men fell out largely as a result of Tiberius' personal ambition and at the instigation of the friends and sophists who egged him on; but on this occasion, at any rate, there was no danger of a permanent and bitter disagreement between them. And it is my opinion that the disasters that later overwhelmed Tiberius would never have happened if Scipio Africanus had been in Rome at the time of his political activity. As it turned out, however, Scipio was in charge of the war in Numantia when Tiberius introduced his reforms, the background to which is as follows.

[8] Whenever the Romans annexed land by military means from one of the nations whose territory bordered theirs, they used to sell some of it and keep the rest in state ownership. This common land was given to the most impoverished and needy members of the citizen body, and it was theirs to cultivate on payment of a small rent to the public treasury.* But the rich began to drive the poor off the land by offering higher rents, until a law was passed forbidding anyone from owning more than five hundred plethra of land. For a short time this edict did check greed and help the poor, and they stayed on the land they had rented, with each person occupying the plot of land he had originally held. Later, however, their rich neighbours began to transfer the leases to themselves under fictitious names, and then ended up by blatantly owning most of the land in their own names. The dispossessed poor lost any interest they might have had in performing military service, and could not even be bothered to raise children, with the result that before long all over Italy there was a noticeable shortage of free men for hire, while the place was teeming with gangs of foreign slaves, whom the rich used to cultivate their estates instead of the citizens they had driven away. Scipio's friend Gaius Laelius* took on the job of rectifying the situation, but faced with powerful opposition he became worried about the disruption his measures might cause and put an end to his programme of reform. This earned him the nickname 'the wise' or 'the sensible'—the word *sapiens* can bear either meaning, apparently.

No sooner had Tiberius been appointed tribune,* however, than he made a determined assault on the heart of the problem, at the urging, according to the majority of my sources, of Diophanes the orator and the philosopher Blossius. Diophanes was an exile from Mytilene, while Blossius was a native Italian, from Cumae, who had become a close friend of Antipater of Tarsus in Rome, and had received the signal honour of having Antipater address his philosophical writings to him.* Some people also claim that Cornelia was at least partly responsible, because she often told her sons off for the fact that she was known in Rome as Scipio's mother-in-law, but not yet as the mother of the Gracchi. Others blame a man called Spurius Postumius, a contemporary of Tiberius who was determined to use his work in the law courts to become more famous than him.* So when Tiberius returned from military service and found that Spurius had left him far behind in terms of both reputation and influence, and was now an object of general admiration, he apparently initiated his risky measures, which promised so much, as a means of beating him into second place. However, according to a pamphlet written by Tiberius' brother Gaius,* while Tiberius was travelling to Numantia through Etruria he saw how the land had been abandoned, and how the only people farming or cultivating the land were slaves introduced from abroad, and it was then that he first conceived the idea of the policies which would cause him and his brother such endless trouble. But in fact it was the general populace who did the most to kindle his resolve and determination, by calling on him in graffiti written on colonnades and walls and monuments* to recover the common land for the poor.

[9] Still, he did not draft the law by himself, but consulted the best and most eminent men in Rome, including Crassus the pontifex maximus, Mucius Scaevola, a legal expert who was consul at the time, and Appius Claudius, who was Tiberius' father-in-law.* And it is generally held that, especially considering the extent of the injustice and rapacity it was designed to combat, no law was ever more moderately or mildly worded.* Those who should have been punished for breaking the law, and should have incurred an additional financial penalty over and above the necessity of giving up the land from which they were illegally profiting, were to be compensated, under the provisions of this law, for quitting the land they had unjustly acquired, and were merely required to tolerate the presence of those of their fellow citizens who needed assistance. The people were content to forget the past as long as there would be no more injustice in the future, but despite the remarkable leniency of these reforms the wealthy landowners were too greedy to tolerate the law, and too angry and aggressive to tolerate the person who introduced

it, so they tried to turn the Roman people against Tiberius by claiming that his land-redistribution proposals and his radical programme of reform were designed to subvert the constitution. This got them nowhere, however, because Tiberius was fighting for a noble and just cause with an eloquence that might have enhanced even a less worthy issue. Whenever he mounted the rostra, with the people crowding around him, and addressed the subject of poverty, he was so formidable that no one could make a stand against him. 'The wild animals of our Italian countryside have their dens,' he would say. 'Each of them has a place of rest and refuge, but those who fight and die for Italy have nothing—nothing except the air and the light. Houseless and homeless they roam the land with their children and wives. And they make liars of our military commanders: "The enemy must not be allowed near our tombs and temples," our leaders say, to inspire their troops in battle, but none of all these Romans has an ancestral altar or a family tomb. No, they fight and die to protect the rich and luxurious lifestyle enjoyed by others. These so-called masters of the world have not one clod of earth that they can call their own.'*

[10] Tiberius' opponents found themselves helpless in the face of these words which, prompted by dignified self-assurance and genuine feeling, found a sympathetic hearing among the Roman people, who shared his passion and his reforming zeal. So they abandoned any attempt to raise objections and turned to Marcus Octavius, one of the tribunes.* He was a young man of sober and self-disciplined character, who was an associate and close friend of Tiberius. At first he hesitated, therefore, out of regard for his friend, but the earnest entreaties of large numbers of powerful men eventually dislodged him from his position, so to speak, and he set himself up in opposition to Tiberius and obstructed the passage of the law. Power lies with whichever of the tribunes exercises his right of veto; despite being in the majority the rest can get nothing done if just one of their number opposes their wishes. In frustration, Tiberius withdrew his lenient law and instead introduced one which was more pleasing to the masses and harder on the wrongdoers in that this time he made provision only for their vacating the land they had acquired in contravention of the earlier laws. Almost every day he and Octavius came into conflict on the rostra, but although each of them was fully committed to these arguments and did his very best to win, it is said

that neither of them ever resorted to personal abuse or in the heat of anger spoke rudely to the other. It is not just during Bacchic rites, it seems, but also in situations where ambitions and tempers flare, that a good natural disposition and a sound education controls and regulates the mind.*

When it came to Tiberius' attention that Octavius was liable to the law, since he was in possession of large tracts of common land, he begged him to back down, and offered to recompense him out of his own resources, even though they were not exceptional. Octavius refused to comply, however, and then Tiberius issued an edict forbidding any other city official from transacting any public business until his law had been put to the vote. He also placed his personal seal on the temple of Saturn, to stop the quaestors making any withdrawals or deposits, and announced that any of the praetors who disobeyed his edict would be fined.* The upshot of this was that all the officials were too frightened to carry out their duties. In response, the landowners wore mourning clothes and went about in the forum with forlorn and pitiful looks, but also began secretly to intrigue against Tiberius and to organize a gang of men to murder him, which in turn meant that he took to carrying a dagger concealed under his toga—although everyone knew about it—of the kind favoured by robbers, which is called a *dolon*.*

[11] On the appointed day Tiberius was summoning the people to cast their votes when the voting-urns were stolen by the wealthy faction, and events began to get chaotic. But Tiberius and his supporters were numerous enough to force the issue, and they were grouping themselves together to do just that when two ex-consuls, Mallius and Fulvius, fell on their knees before Tiberius, seized his hands, and begged him in tears to desist. He realized that things were poised to turn very nasty, and out of respect for the two men he asked them what they would have him do. They told him they did not feel capable of advising him on such a crucial matter, and strongly recommended that he submit the whole problem to the senate, a suggestion with which Tiberius agreed.

The meeting of the senate, however, was rendered completely ineffective by the dominance of the wealthy members of society there,* and so Tiberius resorted to an action which was both illegal and extreme: he removed Octavius from his office,* because there was no other way for him to put his proposal to the vote. First, however, he took Octavius by the hands and asked him politely and kindly, in front of witnesses, to give in and to grant the Roman people what they wanted, since their demands were fair and they would receive hardly anything in return for all the efforts they had made and risks they had taken. But when Octavius rejected his appeal, Tiberius explained that since the issues over which they had fallen out were crucial, and since they were both office-holders with equal power, it was impossible for them to complete their term of office without there being an outbreak of war. He said that the only solution he could see was that one or the other of them would have to resign his position. He asked Octavius to put the vote about his own future to the people first, and promised to resign his post there and then, before descending from the rostra, if that was what his fellow citizens wanted. But Octavius refused to do this, and so Tiberius said that, unless Octavius had further thoughts and changed his mind, he would ask the people to vote about him.

[12] Under these circumstances he dissolved the assembly for that day, and when the people convened the next day he mounted the rostra and resumed his efforts to win Octavius over. Octavius remained uncooperative, however, so Tiberius proposed a bill to remove him from his tribuneship, and put it to the people's vote straight away. There were thirty-five tribes, and when seventeen of them had cast their votes and it needed only one more for Octavius to become an ordinary citizen, with no official position, Tiberius called a temporary halt to the proceedings and renewed his appeal to Octavius. He flung his arms around him in a public embrace, in full view of the people, and implored him, 'Don't let yourself lose your office, and don't lay on me the burden of responsibility for such a serious and ominous measure!'

It is said that Octavius was not altogether unmoved and unaffected by this appeal. His eyes filled with tears and he said nothing for a long time. But then he looked over at the assembled landowners and members of the wealthy faction, and, apparently because he was overawed by them and did not want to risk losing the high regard they had for him, he plucked up his courage to face whatever dire consequences might follow, and told Tiberius to do as he wished. So the motion was passed, and Tiberius told one of his freedmen to drag Octavius off the rostra. He regularly used his own freedmen as his deputies, and this made the sight of Octavius being ignominiously dragged away even more pitiful. A crowd of people surged towards Octavius, and he only just managed to escape them and get safely away because some of the rich flocked to his side and kept the mob at bay with their hands; but a loyal slave of his, who stood in front of his master to afford him some protection, was blinded, much to the distress of Tiberius, who had sprinted over to see what could be done about the riot as soon as he had noticed what was going on.*

[13] After this, Tiberius' agrarian law was passed, and a committee of three* was formed to oversee the setting of boundaries and the distribution of land. The three men chosen were Tiberius himself, his father-in-law, Appius Claudius, and his brother, Gaius Gracchus, who was not actually in Rome at the time, but was serving under Scipio in the war against the Numantians. Tiberius succeeded in getting these measures through without any rioting or opposition, and he also found a replacement tribune called Mucius, who was not a person of distinction, just one of his clients.* But the powerful men of Rome were deeply concerned about all these measures and were afraid of Tiberius' growing influence, and so they constantly insulted him in the senate. For instance, when he asked for a tent, which would usually be provided at public expense, to live in while he went about the business of distributing land, they refused, despite the fact that plenty of other people had been given one for less important tasks; or again, they fixed his daily allowance for expenses at nine obols.* The instigator of these insults was Publius Nasica,* who now indulged wholeheartedly in his hostility towards Tiberius, since he owned very large amounts of public land and was angry at being forced to leave it. But the common people were even more enraged, and when one of Tiberius' friends suddenly died, and was found to have suspicious marks all over his body, they cried out that he had been poisoned; they flocked to his funeral, carried the bier on their shoulders, and crowded around as the body was receiving its last rites. And in this case their suspicions are generally held to have been right, because the body burst open on the pyre and so much foul liquid matter gushed out that the flames were extinguished and when people tried to rekindle the pyre it would not catch light. They had to take the body elsewhere, and even then it was by no means easy to get it to burn. At this Tiberius, who wanted to arouse the anger of the people even more, made it seem as though he had given

up any hope of survival: he changed into mourning clothes, brought his sons into the popular assembly, and asked the people to look after them and their mother.

[14] After the death of Attalus Philometor, his will was brought to Rome by Eudemus of Pergamum, and it named the Roman people as the king's heirs.* Tiberius lost no time in introducing a popular bill to the effect that the king's money should be fetched and presented to all the Roman citizens who were being given allotments of land, to help them start and equip their farms. As for the towns and cities within Attalus' kingdom, he said that it was not the senate's job to decide what to do about them, but that he would put a proposal to the people. The senate hated him more for this than for anything else he did, and Pompeius formally stated in the senate that as a neighbour of Tiberius he knew that Eudemus of Pergamum had given him a kingly diadem and a purple cloak, on the assumption that he would soon be king of Rome.* Meanwhile, Quintus Metellus cast aspersions against Tiberius by saying that during his father's period of office as censor, the citizens of Rome doused their torches when they went home after a banquet, because they did not want people to think they spent an inordinate amount of time drinking at parties, whereas Tiberius' way was lit† at night by the most defiant and impoverished of the common people.* And Titus Annius, who was a rather dubious and immoral character, but had the reputation of being irresistible when it came to the give and take of dialogue and argument, challenged Tiberius to prove, or accept the consequences, that he had not dishonoured the person of his colleague, which was sacred and inviolable under the law.* This proposal was warmly applauded, but Tiberius stormed out of the senate, convened an assembly of the people, and ordered Annius to be brought before him to answer certain charges he wished to bring against him. Since he was no match at all for Tiberius either in eloquence or in popularity, Annius took refuge in his strong point and invited Tiberius to answer a few questions before the speeches began. Tiberius gave him permission to put his questions, and silence fell. Then Annius said, 'Let's imagine that you want to expel me from my office and insult me. Now, suppose I call on one of your fellow tribunes, and suppose he mounts the rostra to defend me, which makes you angry: would this make you remove him from office?' It is said that Tiberius, who normally had more of a way with words than anyone, and was the last

person to be cowed, was so disconcerted by this question that he made no reply.

[15] So he dissolved the assembly for the time being. He was aware, however, that among his measures the business with Octavius had not only offended the powerful men of Rome, but was also pretty unpopular with the masses, since it was felt that the gravity of the tribunate, which had until then remained intact in its high and noble position, had been besmirched and destroyed. He therefore delivered a long speech before the people, and it does not seem out of place to display a few of his arguments, in order to give some idea of the man's persuasiveness and skill.*

'A tribune', he said, 'is sacred and inviolable, in so far as he is a dedicated champion of the people. But if he changes, if instead he injures you, the Roman people, checks your strength, and reduces the power of your vote, he has deprived himself of his office by failing to do the job he was appointed to do. Otherwise, we might as well let a tribune demolish the temples on the Capitol and set fire to the shipyards. This, however, is just the behaviour of a bad tribune; but if a tribune sabotages the people, he is no tribune. What a strange situation it would be, then, if a tribune may imprison a consul, but the Roman people cannot deprive a tribune of his power when he uses it to harm those who gave it to him in the first place! After all, it is the Roman people who elect both a consul and a tribune. Next, consider kingship: not only does it encompass and contain within itself all political authority, but it is also dedicated to the divine in virtue of the fact that it performs the most important ceremonies. Yet the city expelled Tarquin when he did it wrong, and the traditional form of government, which had laid the foundations of Rome, was abolished because of the arrogant brutality of just one man. Or again, is there anything in Rome as sacred and holy as the virgins who attend and guard the undying fire? But if one of them does wrong, she is buried alive, since if they sin against the gods they lose their right to inviolability, which was theirs only because of their service to the gods. So too in the case of a tribune: it is wrong for him to keep the inviolability he gains thanks to his service to the people of Rome if he wrongs the people of Rome, since the power he destroys is precisely the source of his strength. Moreover, if it is fair for him to gain the tribunate by a majority vote of the tribes, surely it is even more fair for him to lose it by the unanimous vote of all the tribes. Then again, nothing is as sacred and inviolable as the offerings that have been dedicated to the gods, and yet no one has made it illegal for you to make use of these offerings, or tamper with them, or move them around as you want. So you have the right to transfer the tribunate too from one person to another, just as you might move an offering. Besides, the fact that people in office have often resigned their positions or asked to be excused on their own initiative shows that political office is not something inviolable or the kind of thing that cannot be taken from a person.'

[16] These were the main kinds of arguments Tiberius employed in his defence. Nevertheless, in view of the threats and the alliance against him, his supporters believed that it would be best if he had the protection of another term of office as tribune in the future, and so he once more set out to win the masses over to his side with further laws.* He reduced the length of military service, granted to those sentenced in the lawcourts the right of appeal to the people, tempered the juries, which were made up at the time entirely of senators, with an equal number of knights, and did everything he could to curb the power of the senate. But these reforms were motivated by anger and dissension rather than by considerations of right and expediency. However, it became obvious to his supporters, while the voting was still in progress, that their enemies were winning, thanks to the fact that the people were not there in full strength, and so they first delivered filibusterous speeches denouncing Tiberius' colleagues, and then dissolved the assembly, with instructions to reconvene the following day. Immediately after this Tiberius went down to the forum and begged people, with misery on his face and tears in his eyes, to vote for him, and then he claimed to be afraid that at night his enemies would break into his house and kill him. These words of his worried the people so much that large numbers of them camped outside his house and spent the night there on guard.

[17] At daybreak the man in charge of the birds which the Romans use for divination arrived. He threw some food down for them, but only one of them emerged, even though the man gave the basket a vigorous shake. Also, the bird which left the basket ignored the food; all it did was raise its left wing, stretch out its leg, and then return to the safety of the basket.* This omen reminded Tiberius of an earlier portent, when some snakes hid in his helmet—the one he used in battle, a splendidly ornate piece of work—and laid and hatched eggs

there before anyone had spotted them. This made him all the more disconcerted by what had happened with the birds. Nevertheless, when news arrived that the people had gathered on the Capitol, he got ready to go out. On his way out, however, he tripped over the threshold with enough force to break the nail of his big toe, and blood trickled out through the gaps in his sandal. A short distance further on, crows were seen on his left, fighting on the roof of a house, and, although the street was of course crowded with passers-by, a tile dislodged by one or the other of the crows fell close to Tiberius, right by his foot. This made even the most defiant of his supporters hesitate. But Blossius of Cumae was there, and he said it would be a scandalous disgrace if Tiberius, the champion of the Roman people, the son of Gracchus and grandson of Scipio Africanus, were to let fear of a crow make him disregard a direct appeal from his fellow citizens. Moreover, he said, his enemies would not regard the scandal as a laughing matter, but would denounce him to the people and argue that he was now showing all the signs of a fickle tyrant.* Just then a group of his friends from the Capitol ran up to Tiberius and told him to hurry because everything there was going well. And indeed things did look outstandingly good for him at first. As soon as he appeared at the foot of the Capitol the crowd raised a welcoming cheer, and as he climbed up the hill they greeted him warmly and formed a protective shield around him to stop any strangers approaching.

[18] However, when Mucius began to summon the tribes again to cast their votes, the usual procedure was disrupted by a commotion at the far edge of the crowd, where some pushing and shoving was going on between Tiberius' supporters and their opponents, who were trying to force their way in and mingle with the crowd. And then Fulvius Flaccus, a senator,* stood up where he could be seen, and since it was impossible for him to make himself heard, he gesticulated with his hand to let Tiberius know that he wanted to have a private word with him. Tiberius told the crowd to let him through, and he struggled up to Tiberius and delivered his message: in the senate, which was in session, the rich had tried and failed to persuade the consul to have Tiberius killed,* and so they were planning to kill Tiberius themselves, and had armed a large number of their slaves and supporters for this purpose.

[19] As soon as Tiberius passed this news on to the people around

him, they girded up their togas, broke up the quarterstaffs with which, in their capacity as Tiberius' deputies, they had been keeping the crowd at bay, and handed out the bits of wood to use as weapons to stave off an attack. People further away did not know what to make of this. When they tried to find out what was going on, Tiberius put his hand on his head, in an attempt to communicate the danger by visual means, since they could not hear what he was saying. But when his enemies saw him do this, they ran and told the senators that Tiberius was asking for a diadem*—that this is what his touching his head had meant. Cries of outrage swept through the senate, and Nasica demanded that, for the sake of Rome, the consul must put down the tyrant. The consul, however, replied in a reasonable tone of voice that he would not initiate any violence and refused to kill any of his fellow citizens without a trial. On the other hand, he went on, if Tiberius persuaded or forced the Roman people to pass any illegal resolutions, he would not regard such a vote as binding. At this Nasica leapt to his feet and said, 'Since the consul is a traitor to Rome, if any of you want to protect the constitution, follow me.' With these words he covered his head with the end of his toga* and set off for the Capitol. Behind him others, each with his toga wrapped around his left arm, pushed past anyone who stood in their way. They were such exalted members of society that no one dared to stop them; everyone gave way before them and trampled his fellows underfoot in the stampede. Their supporters went to fetch clubs and sticks from their homes, while the senators themselves picked up legs and other pieces of wood from the seats which were being smashed by the crowd as it fell back, and made their way up the hill towards Tiberius, clubbing his bodyguards to death or driving them to flight. Tiberius himself tried to escape, but someone grabbed hold of his toga. He let it fall, but as he fled in his undergarments, he tripped over some of the bodies lying in his way and fell to the ground. As he was getting to his feet, the first blow to his head came, as is well known, from a chair-leg wielded by Publius Satyreius, one of his fellow tribunes, while Lucius Rufus claimed to have struck the second blow, and used to boast about it as if he had done something fine and admirable. Besides Tiberius, over three hundred people lost their lives. They were clubbed or stoned to death; not one was killed by a sword.*

[20] This is said to have been the first time since the revolution

against the monarchy that civil strife in Rome ended in bloodshed and the loss of citizens' lives. All other major disputes on important issues ended in compromise, thanks to the fact that the men of power were afraid of the masses and the people held some respect for the senate. And even at the time it was generally agreed that Tiberius would readily have yielded to persuasion, and would have been even more inclined to back down if his attackers had not resorted to killing and injuring people, because he had only three thousand supporters at the most. It looks as though the rich ganged up against him out of anger and hatred rather than for any of the plausible reasons they gave. This is strongly suggested by the savage, illegal, and disrespectful treatment of his corpse. They refused his brother permission to collect the body and bury it at night, and instead threw it, along with all the other corpses, into the river. Even this was not the end of the matter. Some of his friends were banished without a trial, while others were arrested and put to death. This is how Diophanes the orator lost his life, and they killed a man called Gaius Villius by shutting him up in a large jar and then putting vipers and other snakes in there with him.* As for Blossius of Cumae, when he was brought before the consuls and was questioned about his part in the events, he replied that he had done nothing except on Tiberius' orders. Then Nasica asked him what he would have done if Tiberius had ordered him to set fire to the Capitol. Blossius' first response was to insist that Tiberius would never have given any such orders, but once the same question had been put to him over and over again by various people, he said, 'Yes, if he had told me to do it, it would have been right for me to obey, because Tiberius would never have ordered anything which wasn't in the best interests of the Roman people.' Anyway, Blossius was acquitted. Later he went and joined Aristonicus in Asia, and killed himself when that enterprise came to nothing.*

[21] As a sop to the people under the circumstances, the senate dropped its opposition to the distribution of the land and allowed the masses to choose a new committee member to replace Tiberius. They took a vote and chose Publius Crassus,* who was already within the family circle of the Gracchi, in that his daughter, Licinia, was married to Gaius Gracchus. Cornelius Nepos* says that it was not Crassus, but Brutus (the one who celebrated a triumph after his defeat of the Lusitani) whose daughter married Gaius, but most

writers give the version I have written. The Roman people were furious at the death of Tiberius and were obviously just waiting for an opportunity to take revenge. Nasica was already being threatened with prosecutions, so the senate voted to send him to Asia—not that there was anything for him to do there, but they were worried about what might happen to him in Rome. People made no secret of their loathing for him when they saw him in the streets: they shouted enraged insults at him, vilifying him as an accursed tyrant who had polluted the most holy and solemn of the city's sanctuaries with the murder of a man whose body was sacred and inviolable. So Nasica surreptitiously left Italy, despite being duty-bound to remain, since as pontifex maximus he had vital religious rites to carry out. He wandered aimlessly here and there in foreign lands, living an undistinguished and unsettled life, and not long afterwards died in Pergamum.* It is not surprising that the Roman people should have hated Nasica so much, given that even Scipio Africanus, who was quite rightly more popular than anyone else, came very close to losing the people's favour. There were two reasons for this. First, when he was in Numantia and heard about Tiberius' death, he declaimed, after Homer, 'So may all die who do such deeds as he.'* And secondly, when Gaius and Fulvius* asked him before the assembled people what he thought about Tiberius' death, he gave an answer which showed his disapproval of Tiberius' reforms. At this, the people shouted him down while he was still speaking, which they had never done before, and he himself was stung into abusing them in return. But I have given the details of this episode in my *Life of Scipio*.*

[22(1)] At first, Gaius Gracchus withdrew from public life and lived the quiet life of an ordinary citizen, perhaps because he was afraid of his enemies, or perhaps because he wanted to aggravate people's feelings against them. He gave so clear an impression of a man who was not only concerned with humble matters for the time being, but would also continue to live that kind of non-political life in the future, that the suggestion even arose in some quarters that he was expressing disapproval of and hostility towards Tiberius' political programme. Besides, he was only just out of childhood; he was nine years younger than his brother, who had died before reaching 30. But as time went on he gradually revealed his character and showed that a life of feeble inactivity, filled with parties and commerce, was quite alien to him. In fact, by developing rhetorical skills and making them the wings that would bear him into public life, he made it clear that he was not going to remain idle. When he defended a friend of his called Vettius in court, the people reacted to his speech with ecstatic euphoria and he made the other speakers look like mere children. This reawakened the fear of the powerful men of Rome, and there was a great deal of talk in their circles about how they had to stop Gaius attaining the rank of tribune. It so happened, however, entirely fortuitously, that he was assigned to go to Sardinia as quaestor to the consul Orestes.* This delighted his enemies, and did not displease Gaius either, because he was a skilled fighter and had trained for the battlefield just as thoroughly as he had for the lawcourt. Besides, although politics and the rostra still made him nervous, he was finding the appeals of the Roman people and his friends increasingly impossible to resist, so he was perfectly content to spend some time abroad. The dominant view, however, is that he was an out-and-out demagogue, far more illustrious† in the eyes of the masses than Tiberius was. But this is not true. On the contrary, it looks as though Gaius' involvement in politics came about through a kind of necessity, rather than through choice. And the orator Cicero also records the story that Gaius was not seeking election to any office and had chosen to live the quiet life of an ordinary citizen, when his brother appeared to him in a dream and said, 'Why are you hesitating, Gaius? There's no escape. Both of us are destined to live the same kind of life, and to die the same kind of death, as champions of the people'.*

[23(2)] In Sardinia Gaius gave clear evidence of all-round excellence. No one else his age could come close to him when it came to bravery in confronting the enemy, or to fairness in dealing with subject peoples, or to loyalty and respect for the proconsul, and he surpassed even his elders in self-restraint, frugality, and diligent determination. Winter in Sardinia turned out to be severe and unhealthy, but when Orestes asked the island communities to provide clothing for his men, the islanders petitioned Rome to be let off this requisition, and the senate approved their petition and told the proconsul that he would have to get clothing for his troops from elsewhere, which was impossible. The men were in a bad way, so Gaius visited the island communities and persuaded each of them to come to the Romans' assistance and send clothing out of their own resources. When a report of what he had done reached Rome the senate became worried all over again, since it seemed to constitute the preliminary stages of a bid for popular leadership.* In the first place, then, when a delegation arrived from the African king, Micipsa, to announce that as a favour to Gaius Gracchus the king had sent grain to the Roman commander in Sardinia, the senators took offence and refused to receive the delegates.* In the second place, they passed a decree to the effect that replacement troops should be sent to Sardinia, but that Orestes should stay on there, the idea being that Gaius too would have to stay behind in order to fulfil the terms of his office. This news infuriated Gaius and he sailed off to Rome, but not only was his unexpected appearance there criticized by his enemies, but the masses too found it strange that a quaestor should leave the province before the proconsul.* However, at the hearing before the censors, he asked permission to speak and changed the minds of his audience so thoroughly that by the time he left it was generally believed that he had been terribly wronged. He argued that he had served in the army for twelve years, whereas the normal mandatory term of service was ten years, and that he had stayed on as quaestor to the proconsul for a third year, whereas he was legally entitled to return after one year. He also claimed that he was the only man in the army who had gone out with a full purse and brought it back empty,† while everyone else had drunk the wine they had taken and had come back to Rome with the amphoras stuffed with silver and gold.*

[24(3)] After this, further charges and lawsuits were brought against him. He was accused of encouraging the allies to revolt and, as a result of information received, of having been party to the conspiracy at Fregellae.* As soon as he had cleared himself of every trace of suspicion and established his innocence, he set his sights on the tribunate. Every single one of the notables of Rome opposed his election, but such a vast crowd of Italians* flooded into the city to help him get elected that in many cases there was nowhere for them to stay, and their voices rang out in unison from the roofs and the tiles of the houses, since they could not all fit into the Campus Martius. However, the men of power did manage to prevail over the people of Rome and dash Gaius' hopes, at least to the extent that when the results were announced he did not come first, but a disappointing fourth.* Nevertheless, as soon as he took up office, he left all his colleagues behind, since no one could rival his powerful rhetoric, and his pain made it possible for him to speak his mind whenever he mourned the fate of his brother. He used to seize every opportunity to introduce this topic when addressing the assembled people. He would remind them of what had happened, and compare their behaviour with that of previous generations of Romans, who had declared war on the inhabitants of Falerii because of the insulting way they had treated the tribune Genucius,* and had condemned Gaius Veturius to death for failing to make way, as everyone else did, for a tribune who was walking through the forum. 'But right before your eyes,' he said, 'these men clubbed Tiberius to death, and his body was dragged from the Capitol through the middle of the city, to be thrown into the river. Then those of his friends who were caught were put to death without trial. And yet in Roman tradition, whenever a person charged with a capital crime fails to appear in court, a trumpeter goes to his front door in the morning and uses his trumpet to summon him forth, and the jurors do not vote on his case until this has happened. This is just an example of the kinds of precautions and safeguards our ancestors employed in capital cases.'

[25(4)] Once he had the Roman people worked up with this kind of speech—and he had a very loud and strong speaking voice—he introduced two bills. The first prohibited any man who had been removed from office by the Roman people from holding office on a subsequent occasion; and the second gave the people the right to prosecute any city official who banished a Roman citizen without trial.* The first of these laws was a blatant attempt to disqualify Marcus Octavius from holding office, because he had been stripped of his tribuneship by Tiberius; and the second was relevant to Popillius, who, as consul, had banished Tiberius' friends.* Popillius fled Italy into exile before his case came to court, but Gaius himself withdrew the other bill, claiming that he was sparing Octavius at the request of his mother, Cornelia. The people gladly let him get away with this, because they had a very high regard for Cornelia, as much on her sons' account as on her father's. Later, in fact, they put up a bronze statue of her, with the inscription 'Cornelia, mother of the Gracchi'.* Quite a few of the things Gaius said about her in the course of a speech against one of his enemies have been preserved, in the low rhetorical style he favoured. 'Are you insulting Cornelia, the mother of Tiberius?' he said. And since the man who had insulted her was suspected of being homosexual, he went on: 'What gives you the right to compare yourself with Cornelia? Have you given birth to children as she has? I mean, everyone in Rome knows that despite being a man you have slept with a man far more recently than she has!' This is just one example out of many from his speeches of the caustic quality they had.

[26(5)] He proposed a number of laws designed to gratify the people and sabotage the senate. One, on land-settlement, distributed the common land among the poor.* Another, on the army, ruled that soldiers were to be supplied with clothing at state expense and were not to have any of the cost deducted from their pay, and that no one under the age of 17 was to be conscripted into the army. A third, on the allies, gave the Italians the same voting rights as those of Roman citizens.* A fourth, on grain, reduced the price at which it was to be sold to the poor. A fifth, on the lawcourts, severely limited the powers of the senate. Cases had previously been judged by senators alone, and this had kept both the common people and the knights intimidated; but Gaius added to the list of three hundred senators a further three hundred knights, and gave all six hundred equally the privilege of deciding court cases.* When introducing this bill, Gaius is said to have shown in various ways how exceptionally seriously he took it, including the fact that while all public speakers before him had faced the senate and the *comitium*, as it is called, he created a precedent by turning outwards, towards the forum, when he addressed the people—a practice he continued from then on, after this first occasion. By means of this slight change of angle and posture he raised some critical questions, and in a sense, with the implication that speakers should address the masses rather than the senate, shifted the whole constitution from an aristocratic to a democratic basis.*

[27(6)] The people not only approved this law, but also entrusted him with the decision as to which knights were to have the right to judge cases. This gave him almost autocratic powers, with the result that even the senate paid respectful attention to his recommendations. The suggestions he made to the senate, however, were always appropriate for that body. For example, there was the admirably fair senatorial decree on the subject of the grain which Fabius, the propraetor, sent from Spain. It was Gaius who persuaded the senate to sell the grain and return the money to the Spanish, and also to have Fabius censured for making Roman rule intolerably oppressive to the people.* As well as a considerable amount of fame, this decree won him many loyal adherents in the provinces. Further legislation saw to the founding of colonies abroad, the construction of roads, and the establishment of granaries. He put himself in charge of seeing all these measures put into effect, and never flagged, despite their importance and complexity; on the contrary, he saw each enterprise through to completion with amazing speed and energy, as if it were the only item on his agenda,† with the result that even those who hated and feared him most could not help being astounded by the efficiency and industry he brought to all his tasks. And the mere sight of him was enough to amaze the masses, as he went around with a crowd of contractors, craftsmen, legates, city officials, soldiers, and scholars in close attendance. He conversed easily with all of them, and had the ability to preserve his dignity while displaying kindness and to dispense this blend of kindness and dignity properly, in ways adjusted to suit each individual. He made it clear, then, to everyone he met that to describe him as a threat, or a thorough manipulator, or a man of violence, was just cruel slander. In this way he proved to be a more effective popular leader in his personal dealings with people than he did in the speeches he delivered from the rostra.*

[28(7)] The project into which he put the most effort was the road-building programme, and he made sure that the roads were not only functional, but also aesthetically pleasing and attractive. They were to run perfectly straight through the countryside, with a surface of quarried stone firmly bedded in compressed sand. Depressions were filled up, bridges were thrown across every watercourse or ravine which intersected the route, and from one side to the other the roads were made flat and level, so that the finished products presented an even and beautiful appearance all along their length. Gaius also measured every road in miles (a mile being a little less than eight stades) and set up stone columns to mark the distances. At smaller intervals he also placed further blocks of stone on both sides of the road, to make it easy for people to mount their horses without needing a leg-up.*

[29(8)] These projects raised him so high in the people's estimation that they would gladly have done anything to demonstrate their affection for him. Under these circumstances, he once said in a speech to them that he had a favour to ask, and that while it meant more to him than anything else in the world, he would quite understand if they did not feel they could do it for him. Everyone took this to be a request for a consulship and assumed that he was expressing an interest in holding a consulship at the same time as a tribuneship. And when the time came for the nomination of consular candidates, with everyone in a high state of suspense, he did indeed put in an appearance—but he escorted Gaius Fannius down to the Campus Martius and joined Fannius' supporters in canvassing on his behalf. This tipped the scales considerably in Fannius' favour; he was appointed consul, and even though Gaius did not announce his candidature or express an interest in the position, he was elected tribune for the second time, at the people's insistence.* And so, when he was faced with the outright hostility of the senate and the cooling of Fannius' goodwill towards him, he bound the masses to him even more securely with a fresh round of legislation. He introduced proposals for colonies at Tarentum and Capua,* and for bringing the Latins into the community of Roman citizenship. The senate was terrified that Gaius might become completely invincible, and they found an unusual new way of trying to drive a wedge between him and the people, which was to take Gaius on at his own game and curry the favour of the Roman people by gratifying their desires even when they ran contrary to the best interests of the state. One of Gaius' colleagues was a man called Livius Drusus,* who was at least the equal of anyone in Rome in terms of birth and upbringing, and who in virtue of his character, eloquence, and wealth was a match for those who owed their high status and great power to such qualities. This was the man, then, to whom the most eminent members of Roman society turned with the invitation to take Gaius on. They wanted him to join them in attacking Gaius, but without resorting to violent methods or to direct conflict with the masses; instead, they suggested, he should use his position as tribune to gratify them and to let them have their way even when the best course would have been to risk incurring their hatred.

[30(9)] Livius put his tribuneship at the service of the senate for this purpose and then proceeded to propose laws without taking into consideration factors such as right and wrong, or the public good. Just like rival demagogues in comedy,* the only thing he was concerned about was doing more than Gaius to gratify the whims of the masses. In this way the senate made it perfectly clear that it did not disapprove of Gaius' measures *per se*, but wanted to destroy him or, failing that, to humiliate him utterly. So, for instance, when he proposed a bill to found two colonies and to man them with perfectly respectable members of society, they accused him of currying favour with the people, but they backed Livius' initiative to found twelve colonies and to send to each of them three thousand of the country's poor.* And when Gaius distributed land to the poor on the condition that each man was to pay rent into the public treasury, they raged at him for trying to ingratiate himself with the masses, but they approved of Livius' plan to let the tenants off this rent. Moreover, while they found Gaius' scheme to give equal voting rights to the Latins offensive, they supported Livius' bill to outlaw the beating of any Latin with rods, even during military service. Besides, when Livius addressed the people he always pointed out that these bills of his had the approval of the senate, in its concern for the welfare of the masses. In fact, this was the only useful aspect of his measures: the Roman people were reconciled to a certain extent with the senate, and whereas earlier they had regarded the men of distinction in Rome with suspicion and loathing, Livius did succeed in dispelling their memories of past grievances and toning down this bitterness by claiming that he had embarked on his career as a popular leader with the backing of the senate, which approved of his conciliatory measures.

[31(10)] The main reason why Drusus' actions were thought to stem from goodwill for the people and a sense of justice was that his proposals clearly never involved his own advantage or benefit. He sent out other men to look after the founding of colonies and he had no part in the management of funds, whereas Gaius gave himself the majority and the most important of such jobs. When one of his fellow tribunes, Rubrius, introduced a bill providing for the colonization of Carthage, which had been destroyed by Scipio,* and Gaius was chosen by lot to sail out to Africa to supervise the establishment of the new colony, Drusus took advantage of his absence to make further inroads against him, and he proceeded to cultivate the masses and to win them over to his side, above all by casting aspersions on Fulvius, who was a friend of Gaius and had been chosen along with him as a member of the committee responsible for the distribution of land.* He was a disruptive influence, however, and as well as being openly hated by the senate he was also widely suspected of fuelling allied discontent and of secretly fomenting revolt among the Italians. Although there was no evidence or proof to support these claims, Fulvius himself gave them plausibility by his insane and revolutionary policies. He was the chief cause of Gaius' undoing, since Gaius reaped the reward of the hatred people felt for him. So, for instance, when Scipio Africanus died for no apparent reason and, as I have written in my account of his life, his body was found to be covered in certain marks indicative of blows and violence,* most people thought that Fulvius was responsible, because he was a political opponent of Scipio and had been berating him from the rostra on the actual day of his death, but some suspicion came Gaius' way too. In fact, even though the victim of such a terrible and audacious deed was the first and foremost man of Rome, the case never came to court, and was not even the subject of an inquiry either, because the masses were so afraid of Gaius being implicated in the charge if the murder was investigated that they opposed a trial and made sure that it did not happen. But this took place some years earlier.

[32(11)] Gaius was in Africa seeing to the establishment of a new colony on the site of Carthage. He called the new town Junonia (or 'Heraea' in Greek*), but the work was often disrupted, and they say that this was the gods' doing. For instance, the standard that was leading the procession was caught in a gust of wind, and when the bearer held on to it with all his strength, it broke into pieces; the entrails lying on the altars were scattered by a wind-storm and carried here and there beyond the stakes marking the new city's boundaries, which had already been traced; and the markers themselves were attacked, uprooted, and carried a long way off by wolves. Nevertheless, Gaius got everything settled and sorted out within a total period of seventy days and returned to Rome, since he had heard of the pressure Drusus was bringing to bear on Fulvius, and there were also other factors making his presence there necessary. Lucius Opimius, a powerful senator with oligarchic principles, had previously failed in a bid for the consulship because Gaius had cheated him of election by bringing forward Fannius as his favoured candidate.* But this time he had powerful support, and it looked as though he would become consul and would then destroy Gaius. And in a sense Gaius' influence was already on the wane, because the people had become glutted with the kind of measures he was offering, since there were now plenty of politicians courting their favour and even the senate was prepared to compromise.

[33(12)] The first thing Gaius did back in Rome was move house from the Palatine hill to the district around the forum, on the grounds that it was more in keeping with his democratic principles for him to live where most of Rome's lower-class and poorest inhabitants had their homes. He next published details of his future legislation, with a view to putting these proposals to the vote. A horde of people flocked to his side from all over Italy, but the senate persuaded the consul, Fannius, to expel from the city everyone who was not a Roman citizen. So the unusual, not to say extraordinary proclamation went out, forbidding any of Rome's allies and friends from showing their faces in Rome for the relevant period of time.* Gaius responded with a counter-edict condemning the senate and promising the allies his support if they stayed in the city. However, he did not keep this promise: when he saw a guest-friend of his, with whom he was on very good terms, being dragged away by Fannius' lictors,* he walked on by and did not come to his defence, perhaps because he was afraid of a trial of strength, now that his power was on the decline, or perhaps because, as he used to say, he was reluctant to be the one to give his enemies the excuse they were looking for to initiate open conflict and confrontation.*

Now, coincidentally he had also offended his fellow tribunes. How this happened was that there was a public gladiatorial show planned in the forum, and most of the city officials† had built seats around the forum and were hiring them out.* Gaius ordered them to remove the seating, so that the poor could use the places occupied by the seats to watch the show for free. No one paid the slightest attention, however, so he waited until the night before the show and then took all the craftsmen who were working for him under contract and dismantled the seats, so that the next day the common people found the space all cleared for them. To the masses this was the action of a true man, but his fellow tribunes were furious with him and regarded him as a hooligan and a ruffian. This was widely held to be the reason why he failed to gain a third term as tribune. Although he won a majority of the votes, his colleagues criminally falsified the returns and the declaration of the result. A dispute arose over the results, and Gaius was terribly upset at his failure. In fact, it is said that in a fit of excessive recklessness he told his enemies, who were exultant at his defeat, that they were laughing Sardinian laughter,* because they did not realize how much darkness would overwhelm them as a result of his measures.

[34(13)] After securing Opimius' election as consul, Gaius' enemies set about repealing much of his legislation and tried to disrupt the arrangements at Carthage, as a way of annoying him, to see if he might get angry enough to give them a reason for killing him. For a while Gaius put up with this, but his friends, especially Fulvius, stirred him into activity and he set out to gather a fresh body of supporters together to oppose the consul. This was the occasion, they say, when his mother too joined his side in the dispute, by secretly hiring men from abroad and sending them to Rome disguised as casual labourers for the harvest. She is also supposed to have sent her son coded letters telling him what she had done. However, others say that Cornelia strongly disapproved of what Gaius was up to.

Be that as it may, the day when Opimius was intending to repeal Gaius' laws began with the Capitol being occupied early in the morning by both parties. After the consul had performed the sacrificial ritual, Quintus Antyllius, one of his lictors, was carrying the entrails away and he said to Fulvius' supporters, 'Make way, scum, for good Romans.' Some sources say that as he spoke these words he also waved them away with his bare arm in a rude gesture. Anyway, Antyllius died there and then, stabbed to death with long writing-styluses, which are said to have been new ones, made especially for this purpose.* The murder threw the crowd into chaos, but it affected the two leaders in opposite ways. In a rage, Gaius rebuked his supporters for having given his enemies the pretext to get at them which they had been after for so long. Opimius, however, reacted as if he had been given a signal and, in an exultant mood, he urged the people to avenge Antyllius' death.

[35(14)] Just then it started raining, and the assembly was adjourned. Early the next day, however, while the senate were carrying on their business indoors, having been convened by the consul, others laid out Antyllius' body unadorned on a couch, and carried it through the forum to the senate-house, with cries of grief and mourning. This had all been pre-arranged. Although Opimius knew what was going on, he pretended to be surprised, and the upshot was that the senators followed him outside, where they found that the couch had been put down where everyone could see it. The senators started to decry what they described as a terrible and disastrous tragedy, but the masses responded with expressions of hatred and hostility for the oligarchs. They were the ones, they said, who had with their own hands murdered Tiberius Gracchus, a tribune of the people, on the Capitol and had casually disposed of his body; even if the lictor Antyllius had met a worse fate than he deserved, they said, the responsibility for it was more or less entirely his own, and yet he was laid out in the forum with the Roman senate in attendance, mourning and assisting at the funeral of a hired servant because they wanted to destroy the one man still alive who cared for the common people.*

At this, the senators returned to the senate-house and passed a decree ordering the consul, Opimius, to use all the means at his disposal to preserve the city and put down the tyrants.* He warned his fellow senators that they should arm themselves, and he gave notice that every one of the knights was to assemble the next morning and bring two armed slaves with him. Fulvius responded by mustering and organizing a mob, but Gaius stopped on his way out of the forum by his father's statue† and looked at it for a long time in silence, weeping and sighing, before continuing on his way home. Quite a few of the witnesses to this felt sorry for Gaius, cursed themselves for abandoning and betraying the man, and ended up going to his house and spending the night watching his front door. The behaviour of Fulvius' guards, however, was quite different. They spent a rowdy night drinking and boasting in loud voices of what they would do, and no one there got more drunk than Fulvius himself, who spoke and acted in a coarse fashion quite unbecoming in someone his age. Gaius' supporters, on the other hand, were aware of the general catastrophe facing their country and passed a quiet night worrying about the future and taking turns to watch or rest.

[36(15)] At daybreak Fulvius was eventually woken up from his drunken stupor by his men, who then equipped themselves with the arms and armour they found in his house, which he had brought back as spoils of war after his victory over the Gauls when he was consul.* Once they were armed, they set out to occupy the Aventine hill, calling out loud threats as they went. Gaius, however, refused to wear armour, and left his house dressed only in his toga, as if he were just going to the forum as usual, except that he wore a small dagger under his clothing. As he was leaving the house his wife embraced him, with one arm wrapped around Gaius himself and the other around their young son, and said, 'When I see you off today, Gaius, it won't be like it was before. You won't be going to the rostra as a tribune with political business to take care of, and you won't be setting out for some glorious war where even if you were to suffer the common lot of mortal men you would leave me, if nothing else, honour to console my grief. No, you are offering yourself up to Tiberius' murderers, and you are taking the moral high ground by going unarmed, so that you will be the victim rather than the perpetrator of wrong. But Rome will not gain from your death: corruption already has the upper hand here, and people resort to weapons and violence to settle their disputes. If your brother had died in Numantia his body would have been returned to us under a truce. But now I too will probably have to beg some river or sea to cast up your body some time from the prison of its depths. For Tiberius' murderers also destroyed our ability to trust the laws and the gods.'* In the course of this plaintive speech by Licinia, Gaius gently freed himself from her embrace and left without saying a word, accompanied by his friends. She reached out to grasp his toga, but sank to the ground and lay there for a long time in silence, until her slaves picked up her unconscious body and took her to her brother, Crassus.*

[37(16)] When everyone had gathered, at Gaius' insistence Fulvius sent his youngest son to the forum with a herald's staff in his hand. He was a particularly attractive young man, and he now presented himself politely and deferentially, and with tears in his eyes offered a reconciliation to the consul and the senate. Most of the people there were favourably disposed towards a settlement, but Opimius argued that it was wrong of Gaius and Fulvius to use a messenger to try to win the senate over, and that instead they should come down to the forum in person and give themselves up, like honest citizens, for trial. That was the way, he said, for them to avert his anger, and he told the young man either to come back on these conditions or not to come back at all. Now, Gaius was apparently inclined to go there and convince the senate to accept their terms, but no one else agreed with him, and so Fulvius sent his son back again with pretty much the same message as before. Opimius, who was now interested only in armed conflict, immediately arrested the young man and put him under guard. Then he set out into the attack with a large force of legionaries and Cretan archers, whose arrows rained down on Fulvius and his men. Large numbers of men were injured, and eventually they panicked and ran. Fulvius hid in an abandoned bath-house, but before long he was discovered and slaughtered along with the older of his two sons. Gaius conspicuously took no part in the fighting, but withdrew to the sanctuary of Diana,* stricken with grief at the turn of events. He wanted to commit suicide on the spot, but he was stopped by his faithful companions, Pomponius and Licinius, who were there with him.* They took his sword away from him and insisted that he continue running. At this point, it is said, he fell to his knees and, with hands outstretched towards the goddess, prayed that the Roman people might pay for their ingratitude and treachery with continual slavery, since it was clear that most of them were taking advantage of the amnesty that had been declared to change sides.

[38(17)] So Gaius fled, but his enemies were close behind—so close that they almost caught him at the wooden bridge.* His two friends, however, told him to carry on, and turned to make a stand against their pursuers. They died fighting, and it was only then that anyone got past them on to the bridge. Gaius now had only a single companion on his flight, a slave called Philocrates.* Everyone was urging him on as if he was in a race, but no one helped him or was prepared to give him the horse he was asking for. His pursuers were now hot on his heels. He just managed to reach the shelter of the sacred grove of the Furies* ahead of them, and there he died at the hands of Philocrates, who killed first his master and then himself as well. Some say that both of them were found alive by their enemies, and that the slave threw his arms around his master so securely that Gaius could not be hit until Philocrates had fallen dead under a hail of blows. It is said that someone cut off Gaius' head and was carrying it along when a friend of Opimius called Septimuleius snatched it away from him, because at the start of the fighting the proclamation had gone out that anyone who came back with the head of Gaius or Fulvius would receive the weight of the head in gold. When Gaius' head was brought back to Opimius by Septimuleius impaled on a spear, scales were fetched, and it was found to weigh seventeen and two-thirds pounds! Septimuleius had committed a further vile and criminal act: he had extracted the brain from the skull and poured in melted lead instead.* The men who brought in Fulvius' head, though, were men of no distinction, and so received nothing. All the bodies, including those of Gaius and Fulvius, were thrown into the river.* Three thousand men lost their lives, and their estates were made state property. Moreover, none of the wives was allowed to mourn, and Licinia, Gaius' wife, was also not allowed to keep her dowry.* But what they did to Fulvius' younger son was horribly cruel, considering that he had neither raised a hand against them nor taken part in the fighting. He came to them as part of a peace effort before any fighting broke out, and they arrested him and put him to death after it was all over. But the thing that particularly annoyed the masses, more than what happened to Fulvius' son or anything else, was the fact that Opimius built a sanctuary to Concord. They felt that he was making the murder of so many of his fellow citizens an occasion for proud boasting, and in a sense was celebrating a triumph over it. And so one night some people added to the temple's inscription the following line: 'This temple to Concord is the product of an act of insanity.'*

[39(18)] Despite being the first man to take on the powers of a dictator during his consulship, and despite killing without trial not only three thousand Roman citizens but also Gaius Gracchus and Fulvius Flaccus, one of whom was an ex-consul who had celebrated a triumph, while the other was the best and most eminent man in Rome of his generation, Opimius was not averse to dishonest gain. During an official mission to Numidia he was corrupted by an offer of money from the king, Jugurtha.* After his conviction and utter humiliation for having accepted a bribe, he lived out his old age in dishonour, surrounded by the hatred and insults of the Roman people, who may have been cowed and oppressed at the time of the actual events, but who shortly afterwards showed how much they missed and longed for the Gracchi. They began to erect statues of them and to display them in prominent places; they consecrated the places where they were murdered and used to offer there the first-fruits of all the seasonal sacrifices; and many people even sacrificed to the Gracchi on a daily basis, and bowed down before their statues as if they were visiting sanctuaries dedicated to gods.

[40(19)] Furthermore, Cornelia, who is said to have endured all her misfortunes in a noble and principled manner, apparently remarked, on the consecration of the sites of her sons' murders, that now their bodies had the tombs they deserved. She stayed in her house at Misenum,* but without changing the way she lived. She had a wide circle of friends and her hospitality meant that she was never short of dinner guests. She surrounded herself with Greeks and scholars, and used to exchange gifts with kings from all over the world. Her guests and visitors used particularly to enjoy the stories she told of the life and habits of her father, Africanus, and were most impressed by how she could mention her sons without sadness or tears, and would answer questions about all they did and suffered as if she were talking about people from long ago. This made some people think that she had become senile, or had become desensitized by the enormity of her troubles and misfortunes; but in fact the insensitivity lies in these people, because they fail to see the extent to which pain can be alleviated in people's lives by a combination of inherent quality, noble birth, and a good upbringing, and fail to understand that although fortune often overcomes the attempts of virtue to shield us from trouble, it cannot remove our ability to endure times of hardship rationally.

MARIUS

INTRODUCTION

The upheavals of the Gracchan period revealed the deep divisions in the Roman governing classes, and began an era of bloodshed which reached its first, astonishing climax in the civil wars of Marius and Sulla. The lives of the two generals, so different in ideology, so similar in viciousness, are among the most powerful and frightening that Plutarch wrote. Here there is little to admire, much to condemn. In composing these Lives, Plutarch forces his readers to face unpleasant truths, filling his pages not with 'favourable images' (cf. *Aem.* 1) in his usual fashion, but those which are 'pernicious or malicious or contemptible'.

Marius, the outstanding general and seven-times consul (157–86 BC), is paired with Pyrrhus of Epirus (319–272), a dynamic but relatively minor actor in the wars of succession which followed the death of Alexander the Great in 323. Using as a base his hereditary kingdom of Epirus on the Adriatic Sea, Pyrrhus succeeded for a short time in winning half of ancient Macedonia from Demetrius Poliorcetes. In 280 he invaded Italy to fight the Romans on behalf of the city of Tarentum, and had some success, until he suffered his famous Pyrrhic victory at Ausculum, winning with severe losses. He attempted an invasion of Sicily, but was forced to retire to Epirus. In a new attempt against the king of Macedonia, he made an attack on the Peloponnese, but was killed in street fighting in Argos in 272.

Never content with what he has, constantly hopeful of acquiring territory and fame by force of arms, Pyrrhus trusts in each new occasion to bring him the fulfilment he wishes. Gaius Marius shares the same ambition, but reveals a darker side when his ambition is thwarted, especially after he is driven into exile by Sulla. Marius was not a 'noble', one of the old families whose members had already held the consulship. Although he must have had substantial support from noble families, he presented himself as a man of the people, winning the consulship against the wishes of his noble patron, Metellus. His first great successes came in 107–105 BC when, as consul and proconsul, he defeated and led in triumph the Numidian king, Jugurtha. He then profited from the threat of a Germanic invasion, the incompetence of other senators, and his own skill as a military organizer to be elected consul for four successive years, 104–101. Even after victories at Aquae Sextiae and Vercellae had ended the crisis, an alliance with the radical politician Saturninus won him a sixth consulship in 100. Without a war, however, Marius' claims to political power became irrelevant, and he passed the following decade in relative obscurity, hoping for a new command. The opportunity presented itself in the sharp rise of King Mithridates of Pontus in Asia Minor. Marius lobbied to be appointed commander of a war against the king, but the position went to his former subordinate in the Jugurthine War, Lucius Cornelius Sulla. The no-holds-barred fight between these two men for this command and for control of Rome lasted until Marius' death in 86 and beyond, to Sulla's dictatorship of 82–79.

No preface or formal Comparison to the Pyrrhus–Marius pair survives to explain the biographer's rationale for pairing these men or to focus the reader's attention. Rather, as with many of the pairs, Plutarch allows the beginning of his narrative of Pyrrhus' ancestry to set the tone.[1] The history of the kings of Epirus begins with the Deluge,[2] then proceeds through Achilles' son Neoptolemus to Pyrrhus' own day. Pyrrhus himself, as an infant, was forced to flee from murderous relatives, and was only saved when his protectors were able to cross a raging river with the help of peasants to whom they revealed the child's identity. Thus the narrative opens with two references to the forces of nature, and an allusion to the martial valour of Achilles and his son, Pyrrhus' ancestors. In the course of the pair of Lives, the reader discovers that both subjects share both valour and a resemblance to an elemental force: frightening, irrational, uncontrolled, like the Deluge or the raging river. In *Marius* 2, Plutarch continues the image, but transforms it to Marius' inner life: Marius was 'driven by the winds of rage, an inordinate love of power, and insatiable greed to founder on the reefs of a particularly brutal and savage old age'. At the end of his life (c. 45), Plutarch comments again on Marius' insatiable ambition: 'Although he had lived for seventy years, was the first man ever to have been elected consul seven times, and had acquired enough property and wealth for many kingdoms at once, he still lamented his fate, and felt that he was dying without having attained and achieved all that he desired.' Ambition, violence, and the power of fortune prove to be themes that run through the two Lives, and shape their interpretation. *Pyrrhus* is the simpler Life, dominated by Pyrrhus' heroic fighting, single combats, and emulation of Alexander the Great. *Marius* explores similar yet darker behaviour, revealing the flaws that in the next generation would destroy republican Rome.

[1] Cf. P. A. Stadter, 'The Proems of Plutarch's Lives', *Illinois Classical Studies*, 13 (1988), 275–95.

[2] Like the Hebrews, the Greeks had a myth which recounted the destruction of humanity in a deluge, to be replaced by the descendants of the sole survivors, Deucalion and Pyrrha.

Marius follows a chronological scheme, clearly marked by the stages of his military/political career at Rome.[3] Within this framework, Plutarch marks major moments for special treatment. Pride of place goes to Marius' great triumph, the defeat of the Teutones and Ambrones at Aquae Sextiae (modern Aix-en-Provence) in 102 BC (cc. 15–22). A second battle against the Cimbri was a Roman victory (in 101), but Marius on this occasion had to share the glory with Lutatius Catulus and Sulla (cc. 23–7). In 88 he was declared an outlaw by Sulla, and Plutarch recounts the melodramatic adventures of Marius' desperate flight through Italy to Africa with novelistic detail (35–40). Finally, the ferocity evident even in Marius' statue (2), which his troops had found so reassuring against the Germanic invaders (14), turns to brutal savagery when Marius, back in Rome, takes vengeance on Sulla's partisans, and any Roman who crossed his path (41–4).

Marius' significance in Roman political history cannot be underestimated. Not a member of one of the hereditary consular families, he rose to the top by combining adroit use of support from aristocratic houses such as the Metelli with populist, anti-aristocratic rhetoric. A soldier who recalled the ancient farmer-heroes of the early republic, he became the man of the hour in the war against the Germans. As commander, he created a semi-professional army by recruiting soldiers without the old property qualification and changing its tactical dispositions. He was the first to demonstrate the political power available to someone with a military command and a loyal army, dependent upon its commander for rewards of land and money at the end of service. He and Sulla together taught the Romans that the army could be used against Romans, even in the city itself.

The biographer invites us to consider what sort of man Marius was: both an excellent general and a vicious politician, tough and Spartan on campaign, but uncontrolled in his rage against his fellow citizens. In his Life, Plutarch suggests several interlocking traits of character and training: a passionate nature, ambition, a trust in fortune, and the lack of a philosophical education. By nature, Marius was courageous and suited for war, and his training too was military, not political, so that he exercised his

[3] Thus he is a soldier with Scipio in Numantia (Spain) (c. 3, 134 BC); tribune of the people (c. 4, 119), praetor (cc. 5–6, 115); lieutenant of Metellus in Africa, fighting Jugurtha (cc. 7–8, 109–108); consul I (cc. 9–10, 107); consul II (cc. 12–14, 104); consul III (c. 14, 103); consul IV (cc. 15–21, 102); consul V (cc. 22–8, 101); consul VI (cc. 29–30, 100); travels in Asia Minor (c. 31, 98); commands in the Social War (c. 33, 90); is driven from Rome by Sulla (cc. 35–40, 88); returns to Rome with the support of Cinna and is made proconsul (cc. 41–3, 87) and consul VII (cc. 45–6, 86). He died 13 or 17 January 86.

spirit without restraint when he had the power. Plutarch explains that he showed no experience of or interest in Greek education, the training in rhetoric and philosophy which we have seen attracted Aemilus Paullus. Plutarch does not speak of a particular programme, but of learning to view one's life from a philosophical and, especially, ethical perspective.[4]

In the early part of the Life, though there are suggestions of less satisfactory traits, we see the good features of his character: his fine behaviour with Scipio Aemilianus, his courageous conduct as tribune of the people, his drive as commander in Africa, his outstanding victory against the Teutones. This is the period when fortune favours him: when he is awarded the command against the Germans, they become less aggressive, while the Roman people rely on his good luck (14). At the very moment of the festive celebration of the victory over the Teutones, Marius learns of his election to his fifth consulship (22).

But fortune can turn, as Plutarch notes in the very next chapter: there is something which makes life various, a mixture of good and bad, and never undiluted good. The following battle, against the Cimbri, Plutarch sees as already poisoned: Marius does not directly engage with the enemy, but is lost in a dust-cloud; the glory goes to Catulus and his former subordinate and future enemy, Sulla. In sharing his triumph with Catulus, Plutarch notes, Marius wished to show himself moderate in good fortune. In fact, his good fortune has moderated. With the German threat removed, he can only hold power by more and more outrageous action at Rome, in league with the revolutionary tribune Saturninus. Yet his ambition and passion do not allow him to hold back. He must try to stay in command, and finally he fixes on leading a war against Mithridates. It is now the mid-90s, he is over 65 years old. Still, he exercises with the young men, riding and using his weapons. The 'better people', whose voices regularly express Plutarchan moral judgement, pitied him for his greediness and hunger for fame: 'He thought his good fortune should go on and on.' (34).

Marius' ambition and passion demanded that he succeed constantly. In political terms, this went contrary to the aristocratic ethic of the senatorial government of the Roman republic, in which members of the oligarchy would each have limited power in their turn. In personal terms, it expressed a lack of awareness of the realities of the human situation and of the resources which protect one from changes in fortune and give meaning to one's life apart from them. The story of Metellus' deception and

[4] See S. Swain, 'Hellenic Culture and the Roman Heroes of Plutarch', *Journal of Hellenic Studies*, 110 (1990), 126–45 (repr. in B. Scardigli (ed.), *Essays on Plutarch's Lives* (Oxford: Clarendon Press, 1995), 229–64) and C. Pelling, 'Plutarch: Roman Heroes and Greek Culture', in M. Griffin and J. Barnes (eds.), *Philosophia Togata: Essays on Philosophy and Roman Society* (Oxford: Clarendon Press, 1989), 199–232.

banishment (29) provides a paradigm of the qualities Marius lacks. By an adroit and deceitful shifting of his position, Marius puts Metellus in the wrong with the people. Metellus refuses to change his own position, and is forced to remove himself to Rhodes, where, however, he lived quietly and philosophically, until the people changed their hearts and recalled him. Marius could not do this, but forced a confrontation with Sulla. Sulla triumphed, and Marius, outlawed, in humiliating flight, several times barely escaped death. His experiences did not teach him to restrain himself, but brought out all the savagery of his temper. Even in victory, he is frustrated, and the blood of his enemies cannot give him peace. At the end, Plutarch's thoughts return to philosophy, as he recalls Plato, who died in peace, thanking his good fortune, and remembers the similar contentment of the Stoic Antipater of Tarsus (46).

The Life of Marius is meant to provide exactly the kind of philosophical education that Marius himself lacked. Marius was one of the great figures of Roman history, a general and *popularis* who inspired Cicero, Sallust, and Caesar. Plutarch acknowledges this, but goes further, to explore the elemental power of his ambition. In *Pyrrhus*, ambition led to useless warfare in Greece, Italy, and Sicily; in *Marius*, it led to a terrifying eruption of bloodshed and civil war in Rome itself, and the descent of a Roman farmer-hero into the viciousness of a wild beast.

We know of three contemporaries of Marius who would have described many events of his life in their works: Quintus Lutatius Catulus, Rutilius Rufus, and Sulla, Marius' bitter enemy. All of these had reason to be hostile to Marius. Catulus, his consular colleague in 101, at the time of the battle with the Cimbri at Vercellae, wrote a memoir on his consulship and the famous battle, in which he accused Marius of trying to take all the honour for the victory; it is cited indirectly in chapters 25–7. Rutilius would have met Marius early, since both were at Numantia with Scipio, and later they both served under Metellus in Africa. After an active but not smooth political career, Rutilius won the consulship in 105, and helped to reconstruct the Roman army which had been demoralized by the defeat at Aurasio (cf. note to c. 16). In 92 Marius supported the prosecution of Rutilius for extortion. In exile after his condemnation Rutilius wrote a history with a strong autobiographical interest, and an anti-Marian slant. He is cited as truthful, but a political enemy at *Marius* 28. Sulla, who tried to have Marius killed in 88, in his later years composed *Memoirs*, which Plutarch quotes frequently in *Sulla*, and in *Marius* at chapters 25, 26, and 35. Unsurprisingly, they glorify their author and attack Marius: see p. 172 below. It is disputed whether Plutarch used Rutilius and Sulla directly, but his interest in using contemporary sources is well known, and the heavy use of Sulla's *Memoirs* in his Life indicates that he was familiar with them. Furthermore, in his citations he clearly states that he is using Catulus' account indirectly.

A fourth author, the Greek philosopher-historian Posidonius of Apamea, who continued the history of Polybius down into the first century BC, is cited at *Marius* 1 and 45. He was both a contemporary—Plutarch notes that he personally met Marius at the end of his life (c. 45)—and may have provided important narrative continuity and synthesis.[5] Posidonius' account would have been detailed (fifty-two books from 146 to the mid-80s), though much space was given to ethnographic and geographical digressions: Plutarch seems to have used one on the German tribes in his chapter 11.[6] Plutarch probably also used Sallust's *Jugurthine War*, which has Marius as its protagonist. Sallust supported Julius Caesar in the Civil War, and in 46 was made governor of Africa Nova, Jugurtha's old kingdom. His monograph, written about 40, depicts the arrogance of the nobility, and the ambition of the 'new man' Marius. His use of contemporary sources, despite their biases, makes Plutarch's Life a valuable supplement to our other sources for the period, the most important of which are Appian's *Civil Wars* book 1, the epitomes of the lost books of Livy (the *Periochae*), and innumerable notices in the speeches and essays of Cicero. Source criticism has attempted to divide Plutarch's (and Appian's) sources neatly between pro- and anti-Marian, but Marius was too complex a figure, and Plutarch's own interests and skills as a biographer too sophisticated, for this analysis to give convincing results.

With all the names and stories that he provides for the historian, Plutarch is silent or unsatisfying on many issues of this poorly documented period. He exaggerates Marius' poverty and early isolation, without explaining his equestrian background and the nobles, especially the Metelli, who supported his early rise. He does little to illuminate the turbulent politics and vacuum in the senatorial ranks which allowed Marius not only to win a consulship but add four more with apparently little effort. His alliance with Saturninus is painted in the blackest colours, but Plutarch gives little idea of Marius' own programme, or why he might have been forced to look to Saturninus for support, and the same problem

[5] F. Jacoby, *Die Fragmente der griechischen Historiker*, iiA (Berlin: Weidman, 1926), no. 87; L. Edelstein and I. G. Kidd, *Posidonius*, i: *The Fragments* (Cambridge: Cambridge University Press: 1972) and ii: *The Commentary*, 2 vols. (1988). Cf. I. G. Kidd, 'Posidonius as Philosopher-Historian', in Griffin and Barnes, *Philosophia Togata*, 38–50. He also met Pompey (Plutarch, *Pomp.* 42) and Cicero asked him to write an account of his consulate (*Letters to Atticus* 2. 1. 2).

[6] Another might be the excursus on pirates in *Pompey* 24. Besides the references in *Marius*, Plutarch cites Posidonius in *Fabius*, *Marcellus*, and *Brutus*, and in *Philosophers and Princes* 777a.

recurs with the intrigues of 88. As regularly in the Roman Lives, Plutarch sees the matter in terms of the 'better people' and the 'people', failing to clarify the roles of equestrians, Italian allies, veteran soldiers, rabble-rousing tribunes (some from aristocratic families), and other groups. Yet his eye for vivid detail, his use of excellent eyewitness sources as well as standard works, and especially his own reading of Marius' character, with all its strengths and flaws, breaks down the wall between our time and Marius', allowing the reader to step into a different age.

Badian, E., *Foreign Clientelae* (Oxford: Clarendon Press, 1958), 192–225.

—— 'From the Gracchi to Sulla', *Historia*, 11 (1962), 197–245 (repr. in Seager, R. (ed.), *The Crisis of the Roman Republic* (Cambridge and New York: Cambridge University Press, 1969).

—— 'Marius and the Nobles', *Durham University Journal*, 36 (1964), 141–54.

Carney, T. F., 'Cicero's Picture of Marius', *Wiener Studien*, 73 (1960), 90–122.

—— 'Plutarch's Style in the Marius', *Journal of Hellenic Studies*, 80 (1960), 24–31.

—— *A Biography of Gaius Marius* (Chicago: Argonaut, 1970) (repr. of *Proceedings of the African Classical Association*. Suppl. 1; Assen, 1961).

Evans, R. J., *Gaius Marius: A Political Biography* (Praetoria: University of South Africa, 1994).

Gruen, E., *Roman Politics and the Criminal Courts, 149–78* (Cambridge, Mass.: Harvard, 1968), 106–247.

Luce, T. J., 'Marius and the Mithridatic Command', *Historia*, 19 (1970), 161–94.

MARIUS

[1] We do not know Gaius Marius' third name. We are in the same position with him as we are with Quintus Sertorius, who conquered Spain, and Lucius Mummius, who captured Corinth, since Mummius was surnamed 'Achaicus' in honour of his achievements, just as Scipio was called 'Africanus' and Metellus 'Macedonicus'.* This is the chief evidence Posidonius* relies on in his attempt to disprove the view that for Romans the third name—Camillus, for example, or Marcellus, or Cato—is the main name. If this were so, he argues, people with only two names would really be nameless. Instead, he supposes that the first name is the main name for Romans, but what he fails to consider is that if this were the case women would be nameless, since women are never given one of these first names.* Where the other two names are concerned, one is a shared, family-based name, and so there are Pompeii and Mallii and Cornelii, just as in Greek there are Heraclidae or Pelopidae;* and the other is an extra, adjectival name, which refers to achievements or physical features and characteristics. Examples of these are Macrinus, Torquatus, and Sulla, just as in Greek there are Mnemon, Grypus, and Callinicus.* However, there is no single practice, fixed by custom, and so no theory is completely unassailable.

[2] As for Marius' appearance, there is a stone statue of him in Ravenna, in Gaul, which I have seen, and which perfectly matches what one reads about his harsh and bitter character.* He was a virile and warlike person, trained for the battlefield rather than for public life, and short-tempered when wielding authority. It is said that he never learnt to read and write Greek and never spoke Greek on any important occasion, since he regarded it as ridiculous to learn to read and write a language whose teachers were other men's slaves.* And when after his second triumph he laid on a Greek-style show for the consecration of some temple or other, he came to the theatre, but had scarcely sat down before he got up and left. Plato often used to say to the philosopher Xenocrates, who apparently had a rather dour temperament, 'My dear Xenocrates, go and make a sacrifice to the Graces!' Likewise, if Marius had been persuaded to sacrifice to the Muses and Graces of Greece, he would not have brought his

outstanding military and political achievements to such an ugly <conclusion>,† and been driven by the winds of rage, an inordinate love of power, and insatiable greed to founder on the reefs of a particularly brutal and savage old age, as we shall shortly see from his career.

[3] Marius came from extremely humble origins. His parents—his father was also called Marius, and his mother's name was Fulcinia—were poor smallholders, so throughout his childhood he never saw the city or experienced city life, but lived in a village called Ceraetae, in the district of Arpinum. His life there was fairly crude by comparison with the sophistication and refinement of the city, but it involved self-restraint and conformed to traditional Roman methods of upbringing.* He first saw active service against the Celtiberians, when Scipio Africanus was besieging Numantia,* and he came to his commander's attention as a young man of exceptional courage, and as someone who was perfectly happy to accept the changes in lifestyle which Scipio was imposing on an army corrupted by luxury and extravagance. There is also a story that he encountered and killed one of the enemy before Scipio's eyes. As a result of all this, he was singled out by Scipio for a number of honours, and there was one particular occasion when the after-dinner conversation turned to military commanders, and someone there asked Scipio, either as a genuine question or as an act of flattery, where the Roman people would find a man of sufficient calibre to lead them and champion them after he was gone, and Scipio gently patted Marius (who had the couch next to his) on the shoulder and said, 'Perhaps this is the man.' It was a tribute to Marius' talents that from such an early age his potential for greatness could be recognized, and to Scipio's that he could see the end in the beginning.

[4] It is said that Marius' entry into public life was prompted above all by this remark of Scipio's, which he regarded as an omen, inspired by the gods, and which filled him with high hopes. With the support of Caecilius Metellus—the Metelli had always been patrons of his family—he was elected tribune.* As tribune he introduced a proposal to change the way votes were cast, which was interpreted as a threat to the control the men of power exerted over legal cases, and so Cotta, who was consul at the time, spoke out against the proposal.* He persuaded the senate to contest it and to summon Marius to explain himself. The senate voted to do so, but when Marius

appeared before them he did not behave like a young man who had just emerged from obscurity to a role in Rome's political life. He already allowed himself the kind of proud assurance his subsequent achievements sanctioned; in fact, he threatened to have Cotta removed and thrown into prison if he did not repeal the resolution. Cotta turned to Metellus and asked him for his views, and when Metellus got up and said that he thought the consul was right, Marius sent for the lictor from outside and told him to take Metellus himself off to prison. Metellus appealed to the rest of the tribunes, but none of them supported him, and so the senate gave in and retracted the resolution. Marius marched smartly out of the senate to the popular assembly and got his law passed. People now thought of him as a man who could not be cowed by fear or diverted from his path by respect for his superiors, and as a formidable champion of the interests of the masses in opposition to the senate. A little later, however, another political action of his made people change their minds about him: a law on the distribution of grain came up for ratification, and he argued extremely forcefully against the common people and carried the day. This made both parties look up to him with equal respect, as someone who would gratify neither side if that meant going against the interests of Rome.

[5] After he had been tribune, he announced his candidacy for the more important kind of aedileship. (There are two ranks of aediles, one named after the curule seats on which they sit to carry out their duties, and the lesser one which they call 'plebeian'.*) Now, voting takes place to elect the lesser aediles as soon as the more prestigious aediles have been chosen, so when it became clear that Marius was not going to make it in the first round of voting, he quickly changed and put his name forward for the second kind of aedileship. But this was regarded as presumptuous and insubordinate, and so he was not elected. He was in the unique position of having met with failure twice on a single day, but this did not dent his self-assurance in the slightest, and not long afterwards he tried for a praetorship. He did succeed this time, but only just: he was the last on the list and was prosecuted for bribery.*

What particularly attracted suspicion towards him was the fact that a slave belonging to Cassius Sabaco, who was a very close friend of Marius, had been seen inside the railings, mingling with the voters. Sabaco was summoned to appear before the judges, and he said that he had sent his slave to go and get him some cold water, because the heat had made him thirsty, and that he left immediately after drinking the water the slave brought him in a cup. (In any case, Sabaco was expelled from the senate by the following year's censors, and was generally held to have deserved this punishment, either for lying in court or for his general misconduct.) Gaius Herennius was also summoned to testify against Marius, but he said that there was no precedent for a patron to testify against his clients, and in fact that the law let patrons off any such obligation ('patron' being the Roman word for champion), the point being that Marius' parents and Marius himself had been clients of the Herennii all their lives.* The judges accepted the validity of this reason not to testify, but Marius himself argued against Herennius, claiming that from the moment he had been elected to an official position he had ceased to be a client. This was not perfectly true: it is not election to every official position which releases the incumbent and his descendants from cultivating a patron, but only election to those to which the law grants a curule seat.* However, although the first few days of the trial went badly for Marius, and he found the judges disinclined to exercise leniency, at the end he was unexpectedly acquitted on a tied vote.

[6] As a praetor, then, Marius earned himself only a moderate amount of praise. For his propraetorship, however, he was allocated Further Spain,* and it is said that he swept the whole province clear of brigands, which needed doing because people there still lived a wild and bestial life, and at that time the Spanish had yet to learn not to regard robbery as a highly commendable activity. But his political career was hampered by his lack of wealth and eloquence, which were the resources employed in those days by the most eminent men in Roman society to influence the common people. However, the very intensity of his self-assurance, his perseverance in the face of hard work, and his unpretentious lifestyle did win him a certain amount of support from his fellow citizens, and his standing in society began to increase his power. The upshot of this was that he married into the illustrious house of the Caesars by taking as his wife Julia, whose nephew was the Caesar who in later years became the greatest man in Rome and who, as I have written in his Life,* was motivated by the fact that they were related to take Marius as his role model to a certain extent.

His self-restraint and endurance are confirmed by the sources. One example of his endurance is the famous episode of the surgical operation. Both his legs, apparently, became riddled with large varicose veins and he decided to go to a doctor, because he thought they were unsightly. He refused to be strapped down, but just presented one of his legs to the doctor. Throughout the operation, he did not flinch or groan, but put up with the terrible agony with a composed face and in perfect silence. However, when the doctor made a move towards the other leg, Marius pulled back, and said that he could now see that the cure was not worth the pain.

[7] When Caecilius Metellus, the consul at the time, was appointed to take charge of the war against Jugurtha, he took Marius to Africa with him as his legate.* In this situation, Marius had within his grasp great achievements and glorious battles. Whereas everyone else was concerned to enhance Metellus' reputation and had Metellus in mind as he performed his duties, that did not concern Marius at all; in his opinion, the invitation to become legate had not come from Metellus so much as fortune, which had offered him this wonderful opportunity and brought him to a great theatre where achievements could be shown. So he put on a display of consummate courage. The war often involved adversity, but no task was so great that he shrank from it, or so small that he thought it beneath his dignity. He stood out among his fellow officers for the soundness of his suggestions and his skill at foreseeing profitable courses of action, and he won considerable affection and loyalty among the troops by showing that he was as capable as they were of enduring meagre rations and hardship. In general it does seem to be the case that everyone finds his own discomfort eased when someone else voluntarily shares it: it begins to seem less of a burden laid on one by an external agency. And there is nothing a Roman soldier enjoys more than the sight of his commanding officer openly eating the same bread as him, or lying on a plain straw mattress, or lending a hand to dig a ditch or raise a palisade. What they admire in a leader is the willingness to share their danger and hardship, rather than the ability to win them honour and wealth, and they are more fond of officers who are prepared to make efforts alongside them than they are of those who let them take things easy. As a result of this kind of behaviour and approach, Marius became a popular favourite with the troops, and his name and reputation soon spread throughout Africa,

and then through the streets of Rome, as the soldiers wrote letters home saying that the only way the African war would be brought to a successful conclusion was if Gaius Marius were elected consul.

[8] Metellus was visibly displeased by all this, but it was the Turpilius affair that caused him the most aggravation. Turpilius was a guest-friend of Metellus, as their fathers had been before them, and at the time in question he was serving along with Metellus as the officer in charge of the engineers. He was in command of the garrison at the large city of Vaga, but his policy of treating the inhabitants in an even-handed and kindly fashion rather than oppressing them enabled the enemy to regain control, and before he realized what was going on they had restored the city to Jugurtha. So far from hurting Turpilius in any way, however, the inhabitants of Vaga obtained permission to release him unharmed. This meant that he was accused of treachery and brought before a committee, one of whose members was Marius. Now, Marius' bitter attack on Turpilius swayed most of the rest of the committee, and in the end Metellus had no choice but to condemn him to death. A little later, however, it became clear that the charge had been unfounded, but whereas everyone else sympathized with Metellus in his grief, Marius was delighted. He claimed that the outcome of the trial had been his doing, and he went around brazenly saying that he had inflicted on Metellus an avenging spirit who would punish him for killing a guest-friend.* After this, Metellus and Marius made no secret of their hostility. In fact, there is a story that on one occasion Metellus said in front of Marius, as if he meant to humiliate him, 'So, Marius, you're leaving us, are you? You're planning to sail home and announce your candidacy for the consulship. What about you and my son here being consuls together? Would you like that?' At the time, though, Metellus' son was still no more than a young adult.*

Nevertheless, Marius pushed for permission to leave and eventually, after constantly putting it off, Metellus let him go just twelve days before the consular elections.* He made short work of the lengthy journey from the camp to the coast, taking just two days and a night to reach Utica. He offered up a sacrifice before setting sail, and apparently the diviner told him that the signs from heaven indicated that the future held incredible success for him, beyond his wildest dreams. He therefore set sail in a highly optimistic mood, and a favourable wind carried him across the open sea in three days.

On his arrival in Rome the people realized how much they had missed him, and he was presented to the popular assembly by one of the tribunes. After a thorough denunciation of Metellus he asked for the consulship, promising either to kill Jugurtha or to capture him alive.

[9] His election went ahead without a hitch, and he immediately began to raise an army.* Contrary to law and custom he enrolled a large number of paupers, and even slaves, when previously commanders had refused to take such men, but used to dispense arms, on the same principle as they dispensed any other honour, only to those who deserved them by virtue of their standing in society, since it was believed that a person's wealth was a token of his commitment.* But this was not the chief thing people found offensive about Marius; even more irritating to the leading men in Rome were the speeches he delivered, shot through with arrogant and abusive disrespect. He used to cry out that he had carried off the consulship as booty snatched from the effete high-born and wealthy members of society, and that if he wanted to show off to the people of Rome, he would display the wounds on his own body rather than the tombs of corpses and the portraits of other people.* He would often mention the military commanders who had met defeat in Africa—namely, Bestia and Albinus*—and describe them as men who, for all the eminence of their families, had no talent for war and had come to grief because of sheer ignorance. Then he would ask his audience if they did not think that he was closer to the kind of descendant even the ancestors of these unfortunate commanders would have prayed for, seeing that it was not nobility of birth that brought them distinction, but their courage and splendid achievements. These speeches of his were not mere empty posturing; there was a definite purpose to his desire to make himself hated by the men of power, because the enjoyment the common people took in hearing insults hurled at the senate, and the way they invariably took the boastfulness of a person's words to be a measure of his self-assurance, kept inspiring him and encouraging him not to spare the notables of Rome, if he wanted to be popular.*

[10] Marius sailed back to Africa to find Metellus overcome by resentment. Metellus was furious at the thought that although he had effectively brought the war to a successful conclusion and there was nothing left to do except to take Jugurtha into actual custody,

Marius—a man who had risen to power on the basis of ingratitude towards him—had come to claim the garland and the triumph. So he refused to meet him, and slipped out of the country, leaving his legate, Rutilius, to hand the army over to Marius. In the end, however, Marius did suffer some kind of divine retribution for his actions, in the sense that he was robbed of the glory of the victory by Sulla, just as Metellus had been by him. I will just briefly describe how this happened, since a more detailed account can be found in my *Life of Sulla*.*

Bocchus, the king of the inland Africans, who was Jugurtha's father-in-law, had apparently given him little support in the war, on the grounds that Jugurtha was not to be trusted and because he was alarmed at the growth of his power, but now that he was a homeless fugitive Jugurtha turned to him as a last resort and found a safe haven with him. Bocchus took him in and kept him safe more out of deference to his position as a suppliant than because he felt loyalty towards him. To keep up appearances, he asked Marius in a letter to forget about Jugurtha and forcefully assured him that he would never give him up, but at the same time he was secretly plotting to betray him, and in this context he sent for Marius' quaestor, Lucius Sulla, who had done him a favour during the war. Sulla took him at his word and made the journey inland to him, but then in a fit of remorse Bocchus began to have second thoughts, and for quite a few days he could not make up his mind whether to give Jugurtha up or to hold on to Sulla. In the end he decided to put his original plan of betrayal into effect, and he handed Jugurtha alive over to Sulla. This was the original seed which came to fruition in that terrible and irreconcilable feud which almost destroyed Rome. For plenty of people hated Marius enough to want credit for the affair to go to Sulla, and Sulla himself used to wear a signet ring he had made, on which was engraved a picture of Jugurtha being handed over to him by Bocchus. Sulla's constant use of this seal irritated Marius, who was too ambitious and irascible a man to tolerate the idea of sharing glory, and meanwhile Marius' enemies stirred things up by attributing the most important achievements of the first phase of the war to Metellus and the final concluding stages to Sulla, with the intention of bringing the unique position Marius occupied in the hearts and minds of the Roman people to an end.

[11] But all the resentment, hatred, and criticism of Marius was

dispersed and dissipated by the danger threatening Italy from the west, as soon as the city felt the need of a great military leader and hunted around for a helmsman to save it from the impending deluge of war.* At the consular elections no one was interested in the candidates from noble or wealthy houses, but they elected Marius in his absence.* Rumours about the Teutones and Cimbri had begun to circulate not long after the news of the capture of Jugurtha had arrived, and although at first people had been disinclined to believe what they were hearing about the size and strength of the armies that were bearing down on them, they later found that the stories had erred on the side of conservatism. Three hundred thousand armed warriors were on their way, accompanied by hordes of children and women, who by all accounts far outnumbered the fighting men.* They were in search of land which could support their huge numbers, and cities where they could settle and live, much as in times past the Gauls, they had discovered, had taken over the most fertile part of Italy from the Etruscans.*

Because they had never had dealings with other peoples, and because of the vast distance they had already travelled, no one knew who they were or where this thundercloud which was descending on Gaul and Italy had come from. The most widespread conjecture, based on their enormous stature, their blue eyes, and the fact that the German word for robbers was *cimbri*, was that they were German peoples, whose territory extends up to the northern part of the Ocean.* However, there are some who say that the territory inhabited by Gauls or Celts was so wide and extensive that it reached as far west as the regions under the Bear on the outer sea, and as far east as Lake Maeotis, where it bordered Pontic Scythia.* Further east, they say, there was considerable intermingling of tribes, and on this theory these mixed peoples left their homeland in successive waves, rather than all at once, and every year in the summer battled their way further westward, until eventually, after many years, they had crossed the whole continent. That is why, although they have various names according to which part of the continent they are to be found in, those who propound this theory refer to the army as a whole as Celtoscythians. Another view is that the Cimmerians who were first identified by the ancient Greeks did not constitute a large part of the whole people, but were a body of refugees or a splinter group forced by the Scythians to cross over from Lake Maeotis into Asia under the leadership of Lygdamis, while the bulk of this extremely warlike people lived at the ends of the earth, on the shores of the outer sea, in a gloomy, thickly wooded land, which was so entirely covered in huge, dense forests (which extend as far as Hercynia)* that the sun never shone on it. Over this land is the part of the sky where, thanks to the inclination of the parallels, the pole seems to stand so high in the heavens that, with respect to this region, it is situated little short of the zenith, and where time seems to be distributed equally into days and nights which take turns in each being short and long. This, they say, provided the material for the story in Homer of Odysseus and the ghosts of the dead.* It was from this part of the world, they say, that these invaders came to attack Italy, and they were originally called 'Cimmerians' and then, with good reason, 'Cimbri'. But these theories are the product of conjecture rather than reliable research.

Quite a few writers claim that the invading army was larger than I have suggested, and certainly no smaller. They attacked with irresistible fierceness and courage and, when it came to fighting, they joined battle with the speed and violence of fire. No one could stand up to them; everyone they came across was carried away as plunder, and they inflicted thorough and humiliating defeats on a number of sizeable Roman armies and their commanding officers, who had been deployed to protect Transalpine Gaul. In fact, it was the military ineffectiveness of these commanders which was particularly responsible for drawing the invaders on against Rome. Flushed by their defeat of everyone they met and by the vast wealth they were accumulating, they decided not to settle anywhere until they had destroyed Rome and devastated Italy.

[12] Reports about the invasion began to reach Rome from all quarters. In response, then, they invited Marius to take command of the army and appointed him consul for the second time, even though it was illegal for a man to be chosen in his absence or to be elected for a further term before a certain definite period of time had elapsed. However, if anyone raised these objections, the people threw him out of the assembly. This would not be the first time, they reckoned, that considerations of legality had given way before considerations of what was good for Rome, and the reasons for doing so now were certainly no less compelling than when they had illegally appointed Scipio consul, since the issue then had not been fear of losing their own city, but the desire to destroy the city of the Carthaginians.* So

the decision was taken, and Marius crossed over from Africa with his army.

On 1 January, which is the first day of the year for the Romans, he not only took up his consulship, but also entered the city in triumphal mode, displaying Jugurtha in chains. This was a sight the Romans had despaired of ever seeing; none of them would even have expected to defeat the enemy while Jugurtha remained alive, since he adapted himself so well to the winds of change and combined courage with a distinct lack of principles. But they say that after the procession he went mad. Once the triumph was over he was thrown into prison, where some of his guards tore the clothes off his back and others were so eager to grab his golden earring that they tore off a piece of his ear-lobe at the same time. Afterwards he was shoved naked down into the dungeon. His head filled with confusion, and with a mad grin on his face, he said, 'God, what a cold bath-house you have!' For six days he struggled against the pangs of hunger. He never lost his will to live until the last moment, when with his death he paid the penalty for his sacrilegious crimes.*

It is said that the triumphal wagons carried 3,007 pounds of gold, 5,775 pounds of uncoined silver, and 287,000 drachmas of coined money. Immediately after the procession Marius convened the senate on the Capitol, and entered the meeting still wearing his triumphal robes.* This may have been sheer absent-mindedness, or he may have been vulgarly flaunting his good fortune, but he soon realized that it was offensive to the senators, and he left and changed into his purple-bordered toga before returning to the meeting.

[13] So the campaign got under way. *En route* Marius toughened up his men by getting them to run in all kinds of conditions and to undertake forced marches, and making each of them carry his own supplies and prepare his own meals. This was the origin of the later practice of calling men who were hard-working, and who carried out their orders cheerfully and silently, 'Marian mules'. But some people believe that the phrase has a different origin. They say that during the siege of Numantia* Scipio wanted to make a thorough inspection, including the mules and the carts as well as the weapons and the cavalry horses, to check up on the condition and the state of readiness the men had them in. Marius, the story goes, produced for his inspection not only a horse of which he had taken excellent care, but also a mule which was far fitter, sleeker, and healthier than any of the

others. Scipio often mentioned Marius' animals, which had caused him great pleasure, and so as a joke people began to praise industrious, patient, hard-working soldiers by calling them 'Marian mules'.

[14] Now, the current of the foreign invasion was diverted—by an eddy, so to speak—against Spain,* and this is generally held to have been a great stroke of luck for Marius. It gave him the time to train his men physically, to recharge their morale, and most importantly to get them to understand what kind of man he was. Once his men had acquired the habit of conformity and obedience, his severity in command and his intransigence in punishment came to seem not merely fair, but valuable, while as a result of familiarity they gradually began to regard his terrible temper, harsh voice, and scowl as things that boded no good for his enemies, but had no such implication for themselves. The soldiers particularly liked his impartiality when it came to meting out justice, and the following story illustrates it well.

His nephew Gaius Lusius, who had been commissioned into this campaign as an officer, was basically not a bad man, by all accounts, but had a weakness for attractive young men. He conceived a passion for a young man serving under him called Trebonius, but all his efforts to seduce him came to nothing. Eventually he sent a servant one night to summon Trebonius to his tent, and the young man had no choice but to go, since he could not disobey the summons. Once he was inside the tent, however, Lusius tried to rape him, whereupon Trebonius drew his sword and killed him. Now, this happened when Marius was away from the army, but when he returned he arranged for Trebonius to be brought to trial. At the trial Trebonius faced plenty of accusers, but found no one to speak in his defence, so he boldly stepped up himself. He explained what had happened and provided witnesses to testify how often he had resisted Lusius' advances and to show that none of Lusius' generous offers had induced him to let him have his way with his body. Marius was so impressed and pleased with the young man that he ordered the garland to be fetched which was traditionally used as a prize for valour. He took it and with his own hands placed it on Trebonius' head, on the grounds that he had performed a noble deed at a time when noble deeds were needed to show others how to behave.*

News of what Marius had done reached Rome and helped him immensely when it came to gaining his third consulship, along with the fact that the invaders were expected to arrive in the summer and he was the only military commander they wanted in the face of that threat.* However, the invasion did not happen as quickly as they had expected, and the period of Marius' consulship again expired. Since the election was imminent and his fellow consul had died, he left Manius Aquillius in charge of the army while he went to Rome. There were a number of fine candidates for the consulship that year, but Lucius Saturninus, the tribune with the most influence over the general populace, was won over by Marius and used to tell the people, in his speeches before the assembly, to elect him consul. Marius disingenuously claimed to refuse the position, pretending that he did not want it, but Saturninus said that he would betray his country if he avoided command at a time of such critical danger.* It was obvious that Saturninus was just helping Marius maintain the pretence, and he was not very convincing in the role either, but all the same the masses realized that the situation required Marius' skills and luck, and so they voted him consul for the fourth time. They appointed as his colleague Lutatius Catulus, a man who was simultaneously respected by the upper classes and not disliked by the masses.*

[15] As soon as he learnt that the enemy were near, Marius crossed the Alps and built a fortified camp on the banks of the Rhône,* which he used to store a vast quantity of supplies, so that he would never be forced by lack of provisions to give battle against his better judgement. He also increased the speed and ease of the transport of supplies to the army by sea, which had previously been a long and costly process. Where the waters of the Rhône met the sea, the waves had caused its mouths to become silted up so much that banks of deep, packed mud had formed, which made it difficult, arduous, and laborious for the transport ships to enter the river. His men had nothing else to do, so he put them to work there digging out a huge canal. He then diverted a considerable proportion of the river into this canal and so brought the river round to a suitable part of the coast, where the water was deep enough for even large ships to ride at anchor, and the river could issue into a calm, waveless part of the sea. Even today this canal is named after him.*

The invaders divided their army into two parts, with the Cimbri detailed to march inland through Noricum against Catulus and to force a passage there,*† while the Teutones and Ambrones were to take the coast road through Ligurian territory and attack Marius. Now, the Cimbri encountered quite a few obstacles and delays, but the Teutones and Ambrones lost no time in setting out. The land separating the two armies was soon traversed, and the Romans caught sight of them. Their numbers were limitless, they were hideous to look at, and their speech and war-cries were unique. They occupied a substantial portion† of the plain, built their camp, and challenged Marius to battle.

[16] Marius paid no attention to these challenges. He kept his soldiers within the palisade and bitterly attacked all signs of recklessness, calling those who got carried away by their enthusiasm, and wanted to fight, traitors to their country. He said that their object should not be to gain triumphs and trophies, but to find a way to turn back this vast storm-cloud of war and keep Italy safe. This was the message he repeated to his officers and colleagues in his private meetings with them, while he got the soldiers to take turns at standing on the fortifications and observing the enemy, until they stopped being alarmed by the appearance of their adversaries, or their outlandish and primitive speech, and studied their equipment and manoeuvres. The eventual outcome was that through the agency of the sense of sight things that had once seemed frightening became tolerable to his men's minds. For it was Marius' opinion that daunting objects gain a large number of extra and unreal attributes when they are unfamiliar, while familiarity strips the power to terrify from even inherently frightening things. But in fact there was another result too, on top of the fact that the the daily sight of the enemy went some way towards removing the Romans' stupefaction. Faced with the invaders' boastful threats, which soon reached intolerable levels, the Romans' anger rose and their minds were filled with the heat and fire of indignation. Not only did the enemy ravage and plunder all the surrounding countryside, but with supreme insolence and impertinence they used to charge right up to the Roman camp. In the end Marius came to hear his troops' mutterings and complaints: 'Does Marius take us to be cowards or something? Why does he refuse to let us join battle? We're no better off than women, locked and bolted into their apartments. Why don't we behave like free men and ask him whether he's waiting for others to come and fight to prevent the enslavement of Italy, while he continues to use us as workmen on the state's payroll whenever he needs canals digging,

or mud clearing out of the way, or rivers diverted? It looks as though these were the tasks he put us through all that rigorous training for, and as though they'll remain the sole achievements he has to show for his consulships when he returns to Rome. Perhaps he's afraid of suffering defeat at the hand of the enemy, as Carbo and Caepio did.* But compared with them Marius is a giant, renowned for his excellence, and the armies they commanded were far inferior to ours. In any case, it's better to do something, even if it means suffering their fate, than to sit here watching the devastation of our allies' land.'

[17] Marius was delighted to hear the soldiers' complaints. He proceeded to calm their restless anger by telling them that it was not that he had no faith in them, but that he was waiting for the right time and place for victory to be theirs, as foretold in certain prophecies. For everywhere he went he did in fact take a Syrian woman called Martha, who was said to have the gift of prophecy. She travelled in his retinue reclining in high style in a litter, and Marius used to offer up sacrifices at her suggestion. Some time earlier she had asked for an audience with the senate to tell them how to achieve victory, and had begun to foretell the future, but they had evicted her. But she was welcomed by the senators' wives and gave them proof of her abilities, most importantly when she sat near Marius' wife at a gladiatorial contest and successfully predicted the winners. Marius' wife sent her to see her husband, and he was impressed by her. She was usually carried around in a litter, but for sacrificial ceremonies she got down and put in an appearance dressed in a purple mantle of double thickness which was fastened with a brooch, and carrying a spear festooned with wreaths and garlands. This was so theatrical that it made a lot of people wonder whether Marius was showing the woman off because he really believed in her, or whether he was making it all up and playing a role along with her.*

However, the business with the vultures, recorded by Alexander of Myndus, is quite remarkable.* What happened was that two vultures always used to appear near the army before their victories and follow it from place to place. They knew it was the same pair of vultures because of the bronze collars they wore: the soldiers had captured the birds, put the collars on them, and then released them. After this they could always identify the vultures. The men used to greet them as their allies, and when they appeared as the army was setting out for somewhere new, the Romans were glad and felt that they would do well.

There were also a large number of portents, most of which were of the normal kind. However, news arrived from the Italian towns of Ameria and Tuder* that at night flaming spears had been seen in the sky, and shields which first drew apart and then came together, in a way that made them look and move just like the shields of men in battle. Eventually some of these fiery shields gave way before the onslaught of the others, and they all rushed away in a westerly direction. At much the same time Bataces, the priest of the Great Mother, also arrived from Pessinous, with the news that he had heard the voice of the goddess issuing from her shrine, saying that the Romans would win the war.* The senate welcomed the prophecy and voted to build a temple to the goddess to commemorate their victory, but when Bataces came before the popular assembly with the intention of telling them what he had told the senate, one of the tribunes, Aulus Pompeius, stopped him, calling him an impostor and driving him ignominiously from the rostra. In actual fact, though, it was this more than anything that made people believe Bataces' story, because hardly had the assembly broken up for that day than Aulus went home and came down with a fever of such severity that he was dead within seven days—which became the talk of the town and everybody got to hear about it.*

[18] Since Marius was remaining inactive, the Teutones made an attempt to storm the Roman camp, but the hail of missiles they met from the palisade and the loss of some of their number made them decide just to carry straight on, since they expected to cross the Alps without meeting any opposition. So they packed up their gear and proceeded to bypass the Roman camp. The length of their column and the time involved now made it clearer than it had been before just how many of them there were, since it apparently took them six days of continuous marching to pass Marius' camp. They kept close to the camp, and amused themselves by taunting the Romans. 'Do you have any messages for your wives?' they asked. 'After all, we'll soon be with them!' But once the invaders had passed the camp and were on their way, Marius broke camp too and calmly set out after them. He always halted only a short distance away, right on their heels, but fortified his camps strongly and made sure there was awkward terrain between him and the enemy, so that his men could pass

the night in safety. And so the two armies proceeded on their way, until they reached the place called Aquae Sextiae,* from where they would have to travel no great distance to find themselves in the Alps, and so this was where Marius prepared to give battle. As a location for his camp he chose a place that was strong, but poorly supplied with water, and they say that the reason for this was that he wanted to motivate his troops. At any rate, when they grumbled, as a lot of them did, and said that they were going to be thirsty, he pointed to a river which flowed near the invaders' camp and told them that they could get water to drink there, though they would have to pay for it in blood. 'Why, then,' they said, 'don't you lead us against them straight away, while our blood is still moist?' To this Marius calmly replied, 'We must first fortify the camp.'

[19] His men carried out his orders, though with some reluctance, but most of the slaves, who had nothing to drink themselves and nothing to give the yoke-animals either, grabbed hatchets, axes, and even swords and spears, and went down *en masse* to the river with their water-bottles, determined to get water even if they had to fight for it. Few of the enemy came out to fight them at first, since the majority were either eating their morning meal after bathing, or still bathing in the warm springs which rise out of the ground there. In fact, to a certain extent the Romans caught the invaders relaxing in the streams and making the most of the delights and wonders the place afforded. But then more of them ran over, attracted by the shouting, and it became difficult for Marius to keep his troops under control, since they were afraid of what might happen to their slaves. Finally, the most warlike division of the enemy, the ones who had previously defeated the Romans under Mallius and Caepio* (they were called the Ambrones, and there were thirty thousand just of them alone), ran to arm themselves. Although their stomachs were heavy with food and their minds were unfocused and befuddled by neat wine, there was nothing confused or crazy about the way they rushed around, nor were their voices slurred as they shouted out their war-cry. They clashed their weapons together in a rhythmic fashion, leapt into the air, and chanted their name over and over again, all together in unison—'Ambrones'—perhaps as a way of encouraging one another, or perhaps to unnerve their opponents by giving them advance notice of who they were facing. The first of the Italians to go down to face them were the Ligurians, and when they

could make out what they were shouting, as well as hear them, they responded that that was *their* ancestral name, for the Ligurians call themselves 'Ambrones' by descent.* So before battle was joined the air was filled on both sides with the sound of the rallying cry, and since—first on one side, then on the other—the soldiers joined in with their comrades and made it the first contest of the battle to see who could shout the loudest, their spirits were inflamed and aroused by all the noise.

Now, the Ambrones became separated by the river, because the Ligurians ran up and fell on the first ones to reach the other bank as soon as they could, and so hand-to-hand fighting had started before the rest had crossed and formed up in ranks. Then the Romans charged down from the high ground to help the Ligurians and forced the invaders back. Most of the Ambrones were slaughtered on the actual battlefield near the river, where they were crushed against one another, until the river became clogged with their corpses and flowed red with their blood. Then the Romans crossed the river and cut down the rest, who lacked the courage to regroup, as they fled all the way back to the camp and their wagons. At this point, however, the womenfolk came out against the Romans armed with swords and axes, and with terrible screams of fury tried to keep both the fugitives and their pursuers at bay, since they did not want either traitors or enemies to enter the camp. They hurled themselves into the thick of the fighting, and used their bare hands to tear at the Romans' shields and grasp their swords; whatever the cost in wounds and injuries, their courage remained unvanquished to the end. And so, they say, this riverside battle happened by accident rather than by Marius' design.*

[20] After inflicting heavy losses on the Ambrones the Romans pulled back and darkness fell. Despite their resounding success no hymns of victory greeted the returning army, and there was no drinking in the tents or cheerful feasting. They could not even get a good night's rest, which is what men who have fought and won enjoy most; instead, the night that followed was more frightening and disturbed than any other throughout the campaign, because their camp was unprotected by palisade or fortifications, and there were still thousands upon thousands of the enemy left undefeated. They had been joined by the surviving Ambrones, and all night long an inhuman keening—unlike any sound that comes from men who are

grieving and mourning, but rather a compound of bestial howls and grunts, along with curses and expressions of grief—rose up from the vast multitude and echoed around the surrounding mountains and the river valley. The plain was filled with a hideous noise, the Romans were gripped by fear, and even Marius was worried about the prospect of a chaotic and confusing night battle. But in fact the enemy did not attack that night or the following day, but spent the time getting organized and ready.

At this point Marius sent Claudius Marcellus to the sloping glades and thickly wooded glens on the heights above the enemy, along with three thousand legionaries, with orders to secrete himself there until battle was joined, and then to put in an appearance in the enemy's rear. Meanwhile, the rest of the men had their evening meal at the usual time and slept through the night. Early in the morning Marius led them out in front of the camp and deployed them for battle, while he sent the cavalry ahead into the plain. The Teutones could not restrain themselves at the sight. Rather than waiting for the Romans to come down to them where battle could be joined on equal terms, they hurriedly armed themselves in the heat of the moment and charged up the hill. Marius sent his officers to every part of the line, to pass on his orders that the men were to stand firm, to release their javelins when the enemy had come within range, and then to use their swords and shields to resist their onslaught and force them back. The terrain would be treacherous for the enemy, he explained; their blows would lack force and they would not be able to present a solid line of shields, since they would constantly be diverted and upset by the unevenness of the ground. As well as giving this advice to his men, he was manifestly the first to put it into practice, drawing on his physical fitness, which was the equal of anyone's, and his courage, in which he left everyone else far behind.

[21] The Romans' methods of defence and engagement checked the uphill charge, and then they gradually forced them back down on to the plain. The front ranks of the enemy set about regrouping on the level ground, but at the same time there was uproar and chaos in the rear. Marcellus had seen his opportunity, and when the sounds of battle had reached him up in the hills, he had ordered his men to their feet and they had charged down to take the enemy from behind, yelling as they went. They killed the men in the rearmost ranks, who then infected those in front of them with confusion, until soon the

whole army was in complete chaos; unable to maintain resistance for long against this two-pronged attack, they abandoned their battle-lines and fled, with the Romans in hot pursuit. The Romans killed or captured over a hundred thousand of the enemy,* and took possession of their tents, wagons, and valuables, all of which, with the exception of what was lost to looters, the troops voted to give to Marius. Despite the magnificence of this donation, it was generally held that it fell short of what he deserved for his leadership in the war, given the enormity of the danger Rome had faced. This donation of the spoils is denied by some writers,* and there are different versions of the numbers of the dead, but it is said that the people of Massalia used the bones as supports for their vines, and that after the bodies had disintegrated in the soil and the winter rains had fallen, the earth became so rich and so thoroughly permeated by decayed matter throughout its depth that in subsequent seasons it produced unusually plentiful harvests, and confirmed Archilochus' saying that this is how fields are fattened.* In fact, people say that extraordinarily heavy rain is quite normal after great battles. Perhaps this is some deity purifying and drenching the soil with clean, heaven-sent water, or perhaps the air, which is unstable and can easily be radically altered by the slightest of factors, is condensed by a moist, heavy vapour emitted by all the blood and decaying matter.

[22] After the battle Marius selected from among the foreign weaponry and spoils everything of outstanding quality that was unbroken and was capable of enhancing the splendid show he wanted for his triumph,* and then he piled all the other objects on a huge pyre and carried out a magnificent sacrifice. With his men standing around the pyre garlanded and under arms, Marius himself, wearing his purple-edged toga girt up in the manner traditional for such occasions,* took a blazing torch, raised it up to the sky with both hands, and was just about to use it to light the pyre when some friends of his came into sight, riding hard in his direction. There was total silence: everyone was waiting to see what was happening. The riders drew near, leapt off their horses, and saluted Marius. The news they brought was good—that he had been elected consul for the fifth time*—and they gave him letters to this effect. The victory celebrations were now supplemented with great joy, and the men shouted out their delight with one voice, while crashing and banging their weapons together. His officers once again crowned Marius

with a laurel garland, and then he lit the pyre and finished the sacrifice.

[23] Yet there is something which refuses to let any great success be attended by pure, unalloyed pleasure, but sprinkles human life with a mixture of bad and good. Whatever it is—it may be fortune, or divine retribution, or the way things are necessarily constituted—within a few days it delivered to Marius the news about his fellow consul, Catulus, and once more brought a storm of fear to Rome, like a thunderhead gathering in a clear, calm sky. Catulus, whose job it was to resist the Cimbri, decided against guarding the Alpine passes, because that would involve splitting his army into numerous smaller divisions and might make him weak. He immediately left the mountains for Italy, where he put the river Adige† between him and the enemy, fortified both banks strongly against the possibility of a crossing, and bridged the crossing-point, so that he could come to the assistance of his men on the other side if the invaders forced their way through the passes and attacked the fortresses.* But the Cimbri were so full of contempt for the Romans, and had so much confidence in their own abilities, that even though it was unnecessary, and was really only a way of showing how tough and brave they were, they first endured snowstorms with no extra clothing and made their way through frost and deep snow to the peaks of the mountains, and then sat on their broad shields and let themselves hurtle down the craggy mountains, despite all the landslips and the immense cliffs. They camped near the Romans and, after inspecting the crossing, began to construct a dam. As if they were giants, they broke up the surrounding hills and dumped in the river whole uprooted trees, boulders torn from cliffs, and piles of earth, in order to stem the flow of the river. They also let the current of the river sweep large, heavy objects downstream against the struts supporting the bridge with sufficient force to make the bridge totter when they collided with it. These tactics unnerved the Roman soldiers, until most of them abandoned the main camp and fled.

At this point Catulus behaved as a good and accomplished leader should, and showed that he considered his own reputation less important than that of his fellow citizens. Once he realized that there was nothing he could do to persuade his men to stand their ground and that they were too terrified to do anything but break camp, he ordered his standard-bearer to take up the eagle and he ran to the front of the retreating troops. So he led the way, to take the disgrace on himself rather than let it be attached to his country, and to make it seem as though his men were not fleeing back to Rome, but were following their commanding officer there. The invaders attacked and took the fortress on the far bank of the Adige, but they were so impressed with the Romans there, who proved their courage and formed a worthy first line in defence of their country, that they let them go under a truce sworn on a bronze bull (which, they say, was subsequently captured after the eventual battle, and was taken to Catulus' house as the pick of the victory spoils). And so the invaders poured in and devastated the now defenceless land.*

[24] Under these circumstances, Marius was recalled to Rome, and when he got there, everyone expected that he would celebrate the triumph which the senate had overwhelmingly voted him. He refused, however, either because he did not want to deprive the men who had fought alongside him of their share in the honour,* or, taking into account the dire situation, because he wanted to raise the morale of the masses by entrusting to the fortune of the city the glory of his first successes, in anticipation of the time when it could be returned to him in an enhanced condition, during a second round of successes. So, after saying the kinds of things required by the occasion, he set out to join Catulus. Once he had revived his spirit, he sent for his own troops from Gaul and, when they arrived, he crossed the Po in an attempt to keep the invaders from reaching central Italy.* The Cimbri, however, kept postponing the battle, on the grounds that they were expecting the Teutones, and could not understand why they were taking so long. Perhaps they really did not know about their annihilation, or perhaps they wanted to make it clear that they did not believe what they had heard. The latter hypothesis is also suggested by their cruel treatment of anyone who brought them news of what had happened to the Teutones, and by their constant messages to Marius demanding land and enough towns for them and their brothers to live in. When Marius asked their heralds who they meant by 'their brothers', they said that they were referring to the Teutones. All the other Romans burst out laughing, and Marius jokingly said, 'In that case, you needn't worry about your brothers. They already have land, and they'll keep it for ever; it was a gift from us.' The heralds did not understand his irony and they brusquely told him that the beating the Cimbri would give him in the near future

would be supplemented by one from the Teutones whenever they arrived. 'But they're already here,' Marius said. 'You really shouldn't leave before saying hello to your brothers.' With these words he had the kings of the Teutones brought forward in chains, since they had been captured by the Sequani while fleeing through the Alps.*

[25] This news immediately provoked the Cimbri to march once more against Marius, who made no response except to defend his camp. It was for this battle, we hear, that Marius introduced an innovation in the design of the javelin. Previously, the part of the wooden shaft which was slotted into the iron head had been held in place by two iron pins, but now Marius removed one of these iron pins—leaving the other as it was—and replaced it with an easily breakable wooden dowel. The idea of this new design was that after striking an enemy's shield the javelin would not stay upright, but that the snapping of the wooden dowel would cause the shaft to bend around the iron head and to be dragged along, while still remaining fixed in the shield by the bent point.*

Boeorix, the king of the Cimbri, rode with a small retinue up to the Roman camp and challenged Marius to come out and fight for possession of the land, on a day and at a place of his choosing. Marius replied that Romans had never relied on an enemy to recommend battle plans to them, but that just this once he would gratify the Cimbri. He settled on two days' time as the appointed day and named as the place the plain by Vercellae,* which would suit the Roman cavalry and was large enough to accommodate the huge numbers of Cimbri.

On the appointed day, the Romans drew up their forces opposite the Cimbri, Catulus with 20,300 men under his command, and Marius with 32,000. Marius' troops were divided between the two wings, with Catulus in between them in the middle, as Sulla, who fought in this battle, reports.* He also accuses Marius of deploying the forces in this way because he hoped that the main brunt of the fighting would take place at the ends of the line, on the wings, so that he might claim victory for his own troops and prevent Catulus from playing any part in the battle or even engaging the enemy at all, since the middle of a greatly extended battle-line usually forms a recess. And it is also recorded that Catulus himself produced the same argument when he was asked to explain his conduct in this battle, and accused Marius of acting with extreme malice towards him.*

The Cimbrian infantry gradually advanced from behind their fortifications, and their line was as deep as it was long, with each side of the formation extending thirty stades. The 15,000-strong cavalry unit rode smartly out, wearing helmets made to look like the gaping jaws of fearsome wild beasts or the heads of fantastic creatures which, when topped with feathered crests, made the wearers look taller. They were also equipped with iron breastplates, and white shields which gleamed in the light. For throwing, each man had a javelin sharpened at both ends, and for fighting at close quarters they wielded large, heavy swords.

[26] In the first instance, however, the Cimbrian cavalry did not charge the Romans head on, but veered to the right in an attempt to draw them gradually in that direction, so that they could trap them between themselves and their infantry, who had been posted on the left. The Roman commanders saw through the trick, but were not quick enough to restrain their men: one man shouted out that the enemy was in flight, and then they all set out in eager pursuit. Meanwhile the foreign infantry surged forward into the attack like a vast sea. At this point Marius washed his hands, raised them to heaven, and solemnly committed himself to sacrifice a hecatomb to the gods in the event of victory; Catulus likewise raised his hands and made a vow that he would consecrate a temple to the fortune of that day.* There is also a story that when the entrails were shown to Marius after he had performed the sacrifice he cried out in a loud voice, 'Victory is mine!'

Something that happened to Marius after the attack had started was, according to Sulla, an act of divine retribution. It was only to be expected that an immense dust-cloud would be raised, but this one hid the two armies from each other, so that when Marius first set out in pursuit of the enemy, drawing his forces after him, he failed to locate them and, having swept past their line of battle, he wandered about here and there on the plain looking for them for a long time. However, the invaders did happen to encounter Catulus, and he and his soldiers (one of whom was Sulla, he says) bore the brunt of the fighting. Sulla also records that the heat and the sunlight, which dazzled the Cimbri, favoured the Romans in the fight. Although cold meant nothing to them—they were, after all, native to cold, shady places, as I have said*—the heat created problems for them: they sweated profusely, they were short of breath, and they had to hold their shields in front of their faces. For the battle took place just after the summer solstice, which falls, in the Roman calendar, three days before the Calends of the month which was called Sextilis in those days, but which is now known as August.* The dust-cloud too helped the Romans by obscuring the enemy: because from a distance they could not tell how many of the enemy there were, they did not lose confidence, and each group simply ran up to the men opposite them and engaged them in hand-to-hand combat without being terrified by the sight of the whole army. And, as Catulus himself is said to have reported in commendation of his men, they were physically so fit and tough that not a single Roman was seen sweating or short of breath, despite the heat and the fact that they ran into the attack.

[27] The majority of the enemy, and certainly the most warlike part, were cut down on the battlefield, since in order to prevent gaps opening up in their formation the élite fighters were joined to one another by long chains which were tied through their belts. The rest, the ones who turned and fled, were forced back towards their camp. At the camp the Romans were faced with a terrible and tragic spectacle. The women, standing by the wagons dressed in black, killed the fugitives—killed their own husbands, brothers, and fathers—and then strangled their babies, and threw them under the wheels of the wagons and the hoofs of the yoke-animals, before cutting their own throats. They say that one woman was suspended from the end of a cart-pole, where she had hanged herself with her children attached by nooses to her ankles, one on each side. Because there were no trees the men tied themselves by their necks to the horns or legs of their cattle, and then goaded them into motion and were dragged or trampled to death when the creatures started forward. Nevertheless, despite all these suicides, the Romans took over sixty thousand prisoners, and twice that number are said to have been killed.

Marius' men seized the valuables for themselves, but the spoils of war, the standards, and the trumpets are said to have been taken to Catulus' camp, and this was the most important piece of evidence supporting Catulus' argument that the victory was due to him. Moreover, a dispute apparently arose among the soldiers too about who was responsible for the victory, and the members of a delegation from Parma who happened to be there were chosen to act as arbitrators. Catulus' men took them on a tour of the battlefield and showed them all the enemy bodies with their javelins sticking in them—the javelins could be identified by the fact that the shafts had been inscribed, at Catulus' orders, with his name. Nevertheless, Marius got the credit for the overall achievement, because of his earlier victory and thanks to the dignity of his rank.* Most exceptionally, the masses proclaimed him the third founder of Rome, on the grounds that the danger he had averted was no less than at the time of the Gallic invasion.* and in their domestic celebrations with their families they would make offerings of food and wine to the gods and Marius at the same time. They wanted him to have the honour of both triumphs all by himself, but this is not what happened: he shared his triumph with Catulus, since he wanted to demonstrate that all this good fortune had not gone to his head. Besides, he was probably also concerned about the soldiers, who had been drawn up in battle array with orders to stop him celebrating a triumph if Catulus was denied the honour.

[28] Marius was in the middle of his fifth consulship, but he was as hungry for a sixth as anyone else would be for a first, if not more so. He therefore set about endearing himself to the Roman people by doing them favours and by letting the masses have their way, which ran contrary not only to the gravity and normal dignity of his office, but also to his own nature, in so far as he was trying to be acquiescent and plebeian, when he was not really like that at all. However, we hear that in a political context, when faced with uproar from the mob, his desire to be well thought of made him extremely timid, and that in public meetings the imperturbable resoluteness he showed in battle deserted him, so that he was knocked off balance by random expressions of praise or criticism. And yet there is a story that when he bestowed citizenship on about a thousand men from Camerinum to reward them for conspicuous bravery in the war, and some people voiced the general belief and accused him of acting illegally, he replied that the noise of fighting had prevented him from hearing the law.* But it does look as though he was more easily disturbed and frightened by shouting at public meetings. In a military context his status and power were based on the fact that he was needed, but in political life his pre-eminence was curtailed, and so he took refuge in the goodwill and favour of the masses, and abandoned any attempt to be the best man in Rome, as long as he could be the most powerful.

This brought him into conflict with the aristocrats, and Metellus was a particular cause of concern to him.* Metellus had been treated with considerable discourtesy by Marius, and was naturally inclined, because of his true goodness, to take sides against those who insinuated themselves into the favour of the masses when it was not in the best interests of the state, and who won popular favour by pandering to the whims of the common people. Marius therefore tried to find a way to banish the man from Rome. To this end he enlisted the help of Glaucia and Saturninus,* the worst troublemakers in the city, who commanded the loyalty of a mob of the poor and unruly. Through their agency he introduced various bits of legislation, and by stirring up the army and getting his troops to infiltrate public meetings, he acquired a following which was more powerful than Metellus'. Now, Rutilius, who is basically an honest and reliable source,* but admits that he had a personal difference of opinion with Marius, reports that Marius gained his sixth consulship by distributing a lot of money among the tribes, which bought him the votes to deny Metellus the post, and got him Valerius Flaccus as his colleague (although he was a deputy rather than a colleague*). There was no precedent for the Roman people giving one man so many consulships, except in the case of Valerius Corvinus; but that was different because, we hear, he spread his consulships out over a 45-year period, whereas after Marius' first one a single burst of good fortune carried him through the other five.*

[29] A great deal of resentment built up against him during this last consulship of his, because he shared responsibility with Saturninus for a lot of the crimes that were committed. One of these was the murder of Nonius, killed by Saturninus because he was a rival candidate for the tribuneship. Then, when he was tribune, Saturninus introduced his agrarian legislation,* with a rider to the effect that the senate had to come forward and swear to abide without opposition by the decisions of the people. In the senate Marius made a show of objecting to this part of the bill. He said that he found the oath intolerable and saw no reason why anyone in his right mind would accept it, since even if the law were harmless, it was an insult for the senate to make such concessions under compulsion, rather than of its own free will, after listening to convincing arguments. He said this not because it was what he really thought, but in order to snare Metellus in an inescapable trap.* For since he personally counted the ability to lie as a mark of virtue and skill, he had no plans to do anything other than disregard his agreements with the senate, but

Metellus, as he knew, was a man of principle who regarded 'truth as the prerequisite of virtue', as Pindar puts it.* Marius therefore wanted to lay a trap for him by getting him to voice his protest to the senate, and then, once he had actually refused to let the people administer the oath to him, Marius would turn the full force of the people's uncompromising antagonism on to him.

Everything went according to Marius' plan, and Metellus said that he would refuse to take the oath. The session of the senate ended, but then a few days later Saturninus summoned the senators to the rostra and tried to force them to swear the oath. When Marius stepped forward silence fell and everyone gazed expectantly at him. He wished a hearty farewell to the presumptuous statements he had voiced in the senate, and said that his throat was not wide enough to express a premature opinion, once and for all, on such an important matter; he declared that he would take the oath and would obey the law, if it was a law.* This final subtlety was added to disguise the disgrace of what he was doing. The people were delighted, and clapped and cheered when he swore the oath, but the aristocrats were cast into deep despair at Marius' treachery, which utterly condemned him in their eyes. So out of fear of the common people they all swore the oath, one after another, until it was Metellus' turn. Although his friends were begging and imploring him to take the oath so as to avoid bringing down on himself the irreversible penalties which Saturninus was proposing for anyone who refused to do so, Metellus stayed true to his principles and was prepared to put up with any fate, however terrible, as long as he avoided doing anything shameful. So he left the forum, telling his friends that while doing wrong was demeaning, and doing good when there was no risk involved was unexceptional, it was an indication of true virtue to do good when there was a risk involved.

Saturninus next got a proposal ratified to the effect that the consuls should officially proclaim Metellus an outcast from fire, water, and shelter, and the worst elements among the masses supported the consuls by showing their willingness to kill the man. The best members of society flocked to Metellus' side out of sympathy with his plight, but he refused to be responsible for civil strife breaking out. Instead, he acted in a clear-headed and intelligent manner, and left the city, explaining, 'Either matters will improve until the people change their mind and call me back, in which case I shall return, or things will stay the same, in which case it's better for me to be away from here.' But his own Life will make a more appropriate place for the story of all the loyalty and honour Metellus won during his exile, and how he spent the time studying philosophy in Rhodes.*

[30] In return for Saturninus' help in this business, Marius had to stand by and watch while he proceeded to push back the limits of presumptuous abuse of power. As a result, although he never intended this consequence, he became the cause of intolerable evil, which led straight to the use of weaponry and murder to establish tyranny and to overthrow the state. And since he was torn between respect for the men of power and courting the favour of the masses, he had no qualms about behaving in a way worthy of the meanest and most unreliable slave. For when one night the leading men of Rome came to visit him in an attempt to enlist his support against Saturninus, he let Saturninus in by another entrance without the others' knowledge, and then, using a pretended attack of diarrhoea to explain his behaviour to both parties, he ran to and fro in the house, from them to him and back again in turns, trying to stir up hostility between the two sides. Later, however, when the senate and the knights joined forces and began to express their irritation, he brought armed men into the forum, chased the offenders on to the Capitol, and parched them into submission by cutting off their water supply.* They gave up, asked for Marius' help, and surrendered by the process known as 'public faith'.* Marius did everything he could to save the men, but it was no good, and they were killed as they came down into the forum.* This affair brought him into conflict with the men of power as well as the ordinary people, and contrary to expectations he did not stand for the censorship when the time for the election came, but let others be elected, even though they were men of less eminence than himself, because he was afraid of not securing enough votes. In any case, he used to justify himself by saying that a bitter investigation of people's lives and habits* would make him thoroughly unpopular, and that was something he wanted to avoid.

[31] When it was formally proposed that Metellus should be recalled from exile, Marius strenuously argued against the idea and did all he could to prevent it, but it was no good: the common people wholeheartedly welcomed the proposal, and in the end he had to give up the fight. However, he could not bear the thought of seeing

Metellus returning, so he sailed away to Cappadocia and Galatia.* The ostensible purpose of his journey was that he had to fulfil his solemn promise and make the sacrifices he owed to the Mother of the Gods,* but in actual fact there was another reason, one that most people did not realize. He had no aptitude for peace or life as a private citizen; he owed his prominence to war, and it seemed to him that his power and prestige were now being gradually worn away by idleness and inactivity, so he was looking for openings for new ventures. He thought there was a good chance that if he stirred up the Asian royal houses and provoked Mithridates, who was on the verge of declaring war on Rome anyway, he would be chosen to lead the army against him, and would fill the city with fresh triumphs and his house with spoils from Pontus and a king's riches. And so, although Mithridates was unfailingly polite and respectful to him, Marius refused to bend or give way, and only said, 'You have a choice, my lord: you can try to be stronger than Rome, or you can keep quiet and do what you're told.' Mithridates was taken aback, because although he had often heard Romans speak, this was the first time he had been addressed so bluntly.*

[32] When Marius returned to Rome he had a house built for himself near the forum. His stated reason for doing this was so that people who wanted to pay their respects to him would not have all the bother of a long walk, but perhaps it was because he thought the long walk was the reason he did not have more visitors than other people. In fact, though, that had nothing to do with it; he simply lacked the social graces, and did not know as well as others how to do people politically useful favours. That was why he was neglected, like a weapon of war in peacetime. He was not particularly annoyed at being eclipsed by most people, but it really galled him to see Sulla's fame overtaking his own, since Sulla's rise was based on the hostility of the men of power towards Marius, and he used the personal animosity he felt for Marius as his means of entry into politics. To mark the occasion of his formal declaration as an ally of Rome, Bocchus of Numidia set up on the Capitol statues of Victory bearing trophies, with a golden frieze running alongside the statues depicting his surrender of Jugurtha to Sulla.* Marius became obsessed with the idea that Sulla was stealing the glory of his achievements, and he was so furious and jealous that he was planning to demolish the votive offerings by force. But Sulla was just as furious himself, and

it was only the sudden outbreak of the Social War against Rome that prevented the feud between Marius and Sulla spreading and infecting the wider populace. In this war the largest and fiercest Italian peoples joined forces against Rome and almost put an end to its hegemony, because as well as being fit and well armed, they had military commanders whose incredible skill and daring made them a match for the Romans.*

[33] The Social War, littered with tragic events and frequent reversals of fortune, saw Sulla's prestige and power wax exactly as much as Marius' waned. Marius seemed reluctant to attack, and hesitant and slow in every sphere. Perhaps old age was extinguishing his famous energy and heat (after all, he was now over 65 years old), or perhaps, as he himself used to say, despite his painful sinews and the fact that his body was not functioning as well as it might, he was driven by a sense of shame to endure campaigns which were actually beyond his abilities. But even so, he was victorious in an important battle, in which six thousand of the enemy died and he never gave them the slightest chance of success.* Even when they dug a trench around his position he held on, and when they taunted him and tried to provoke him into fighting he remained unperturbed. It is said that Pompaedius Silo, the most impressive and powerful of his opponents, said to him, 'If you are a great commander, Marius, come out and fight.' To this Marius replied, 'If *you* are a great commander, make me fight even though I don't want to.' On another occasion, when the enemy had left themselves open to attack but the Romans had lost their nerve, and both sides had withdrawn, he convened a general meeting of his troops and said, 'I don't know whether to call you or the enemy the greater cowards. They could no more abide the sight of your backs than you could the sight of their napes.' Eventually, however, he felt that he was too incapacitated by his ill health to continue, and he gave up his command.*

[34] After the Italians' surrender, however, when quite a few people in Rome were canvassing, through the agency of the tribunes, for the command of the Mithridatic War, much to everyone's surprise Sulpicius—a tribune, and the worst kind of troublemaker—backed Marius for appointment as proconsul in command of the army against Mithridates.* The people were in two minds: some wanted to choose Marius, while others called for Sulla and suggested that Marius should go to the warm springs at Baiae and cosset

himself now that he was, by his own admission, worn out with old age and fluxes. The point was that at Baiae, near Misenum, Marius owned an expensive house, designed for the kind of luxurious life-style which would be more suited to a woman than a man who had been personally involved in so many wars and campaigns. It is said that Cornelia paid 75,000 drachmas for the house, and that only a short while later Lucius Lucullus bought it for 2,500,000—which shows how quickly extravagance spread and the extent to which luxury gained a hold on Roman life.*

Marius, however, committed himself wholeheartedly and with youthful enthusiasm to the project, cast off his old age and ill health, and went down to the Campus Martius every day to exercise with the young men. He demonstrated that he was still agile under arms and a fine horseman, even though in his old age he was no longer a trim figure, but tended towards obesity and was rather heavy. Some people liked what he was doing, and they used to go down to the Campus Martius and watch him competing with determination, but the sight moved the best men of Rome to pity him for his greedy desire for status. From poor and humble origins, he had become fabulously wealthy and reached a pinnacle of power, but he thought his good fortune should go on and on. He could not be content with the admiration that already came his way; he was incapable of just quietly enjoying what he had. Despite all the triumphs and glory he had won in the past, he was setting out for Cappadocia and the Euxine Sea as if he had everything to prove, and carrying his advanced years ashore with the intention of fighting it out with Archelaus and Neoptolemus, the satraps of Mithridates. And the way Marius justified his behaviour was obviously just plain nonsense: he said he wanted to take part personally in the campaign in order to train his son.

[35] For many years there had been a festering sickness beneath the surface of Rome, but now the present situation caused it to erupt. Marius had found the perfect tool for the destruction of the state in the militancy of Sulpicius, who was essentially an admirer and imitator of Saturninus, except that he found him too timid and hesitant in the political arena! So far from being hesitant himself, he not only had a personal guard of six hundred knights—the 'anti-senate', as he called them—to protect him, but he also invaded a public meeting called by the consuls with a gang of armed men. When one of the

consuls fled the forum, Sulpicius grabbed his son and murdered him.* Meanwhile Sulla, who was being chased past Marius' house, dashed inside, which was the last thing anyone would have expected him to do. In this way he shook off his pursuers, who ran past the house, and it is said that Marius himself let him safely out of the house by another door, so that he escaped to where his troops were stationed. However, in his *Memoirs* Sulla denies that he took refuge in Marius' house, but says that Sulpicius got men with drawn swords to surround him and drive him to Marius' house as a way of forcing him, against his will, to enact certain measures, which he was allowed to go and talk over with Marius. After this, according to Sulla, he left Marius' house and returned to the forum, where he rescinded the decree suspending public business, which is what Sulpicius and his men had wanted him to do.

The upshot of all this was that Sulpicius was now the effective master of Rome, and he got the popular assembly to give Marius command of the war against Mithridates. As part of his preparations for the expedition, Marius sent two military tribunes off to take charge of Sulla's army, but Sulla aroused his troops' anger—he had at least thirty-five thousand legionaries—and marched on Rome. His men fell on the tribunes Marius had sent and killed them, while in Rome Marius put to death many of Sulla's friends and issued a proclamation to the effect that any slaves who joined his army would be freed—an offer which is said to have been taken up by only three slaves, however. And before long, having hardly impeded Sulla's entry into Rome, Marius was forced into exile.* At first, with his friends scattered in the aftermath of his expulsion from the city, he took refuge under cover of darkness in one of his villas, called Solonium.* He sent his son to get supplies from the estate of his father-in-law, Mucius,* which was not far away, while he went down to the coast at Ostia, where a friend of his, called Numerius, had got a boat ready for him. Without waiting for his son, however, he went on board with his stepson Granius and set sail. Meanwhile, on Mucius' estate, day found the young man still in the process of collecting things and packing them up, and, since he had not quite shaken off his enemies, some horsemen rode up to investigate the place, just on the off chance that something might be going on. But when the foreman of the farm saw them coming, he hid Marius in a cart-load of beans. Then he hitched up his oxen and drove the cart off to the city, right under the noses of the horsemen. This was the way Marius travelled to his wife's house, where he got all the supplies he needed. He journeyed to the coast under cover of darkness, boarded a ship bound for Africa, and crossed the sea.

[36] As for the elder Marius, after putting to sea he sailed on a favourable wind along the coast of Italy, but he was afraid of a man called Geminius, a political opponent of his who was one of the men of power in Terracina, and he told the sailors to steer clear of Terracina.* They wanted to do as he said, but a landward wind arose and brought heavy waves down on them. For a while the boat was in danger of being swamped, and Marius was also suffering badly from seasickness, but they did manage to reach the shore near Circeium. The storm was getting worse, and they were low on provisions, so they went ashore and roamed about. Not that they had anywhere to go, but it is typical of times of thorough confusion that people try to escape from their current situation, since they can imagine nothing worse, and pin their hopes on an uncertain future. So, for Marius and his men, there was nothing hospitable about either the land or the sea; the prospect of meeting people was frightening, but so was the prospect of not meeting people, since they badly needed to stock up on supplies. But in the evening they did meet a few ox-herds, who had nothing to give them to satisfy their needs, but recognized Marius and told him to get away from there as quickly as he could, because a little earlier in the day a large body of horsemen had been seen in the area scouring the countryside for him. In total despair, and not helped in the slightest by the fact that his companions were faint from hunger, he left the road for the time being and plunged deep into a wood, where he spent a miserable night. The next day, in a terrible state of deprivation, and wanting to make use of his strength before it failed him altogether, he walked along the coast, trying to lighten his companions' mood and asking them not to give up yet; there was still one final cause for hope, he said—an omen he had received years before, which he had no reason to doubt and for whose fulfilment he kept himself in readiness. Once, when he was still very young and lived in the countryside, he had caught in his cloak an eagle's nest which had fallen from its eyrie with seven chicks in it. His parents were astonished at the sight and asked the diviners what it meant. They said that he would become the most eminent man in the world and was destined to hold the highest and

most powerful office seven times.* Some writers claim that this really happened to Marius, while others say that the story was completely fictitious, but was written down by those who heard it then and on other occasions during his period of exile, and who believed it. As evidence for its falsity they cite the fact that eagles do not lay more than two eggs at a time. In fact, they say that Musaeus was wrong* when he described an eagle as 'the bird which lays three eggs, hatches two, and rears one'. But it is generally agreed that during his exile, when things were particularly desperate, Marius often said that he would gain a seventh consulship.

[37] When they were twenty stades* from the Italian city of Minturnae, they saw in the distance a squadron of horsemen riding in their direction—but at the same time, by coincidence, they also saw two merchantmen out at sea. Summoning up all their speed and strength, they ran down to the sea, dived in, and started to swim out towards the ships. Granius reached one of the ships and crossed over to the island off the coast, which was called Aenaria.* But two slaves had to struggle to keep Marius afloat, because he was heavy and awkward, and they only just managed to get him aboard the other boat, with the horsemen now halted and calling out orders to the sailors from the land, telling them either to come ashore or to throw Marius back into the sea and then sail away wherever they wanted. Marius begged them with tears in his eyes, and after considerable vacillation in a short space of time between the two options the boat's owners told the horsemen they would not give Marius up. Bitterly frustrated, the horsemen rode away—but then the sailors changed their mind again and took him ashore after all. They anchored near where the river Liris expands into a marshy lake and told Marius to take some food and go ashore; he should recuperate, they said, after all the terrible experiences he had been through, while they waited for a favourable wind to arise, which would happen at the usual time, when the wind from the sea died down and the marshes gave off a reasonably strong breeze. Marius thought this was good advice, and he did what they suggested. The sailors took him ashore and he lay down on some grass without the slightest inkling of what was to happen—whereupon they immediately returned to their boat, weighed anchor, and left as fast as they could. They did not think it was right to hand Marius over to his enemies, but at the same time they did not think it was safe for them to be the ones to rescue him.

And so he was abandoned with no companions. For a long time he lay dumbfounded on the shore, but then at last he pulled himself together and set out in utter misery through the trackless land, through deep marshes and across ditches filled with water and mud. Eventually he stumbled across a cabin belonging to an old fisherman. Marius threw himself to the ground at his feet and begged him to rescue and help a man who, as long as he escaped his present danger, would repay him with wealth beyond his wildest dreams. Perhaps the man recognized Marius from before, or perhaps he saw in him something impressive, indicating his greatness, but at any rate he told him that if he needed to rest his hut would be fine, but that if the reason he was roaming around was that he was trying to evade capture he would hide him in a place where he was far less likely to be disturbed. Marius asked him to do just that, and the old man took him into the marshes and told him to crouch down in a dip in the ground beside the river. Then he brought armfuls of reeds and other plants which were light enough to cover him without hurting him, and threw them on top of him.

[38] A short while later, however, Marius heard the sounds of some kind of commotion coming from the hut. A detachment from the large body of men Geminius had sent from Terracina to hunt Marius down had chanced upon the hut and were now engaged in yelling at the old man and terrifying him out of his wits with the accusation that he had taken in and concealed an enemy of Rome. Marius therefore burst out of his hiding-place, stripped naked, and jumped into the thick, muddy water of the lake. But this did him no good and he was spotted by his pursuers. They dragged him out all covered with mud, took him naked back to Minturnae, and handed him over to the authorities. Now, the announcement had by this time already gone out to every town and city in the area that Marius was to be hunted down at public expense, and that whoever caught him was to kill him. Nevertheless, the authorities in Minturnae wanted to talk things over first, and they left Marius for safe keeping in the house of a woman called Fannia, who was generally held to have a long-standing grudge against Marius, for the following reason. When she divorced her husband, Titinnius, she asked for her dowry back, which was a considerable sum. Titinnius, however, accused her of adultery, and during his sixth consulship Marius had to judge the case. It turned out during the trial that Fannia had indeed been a

woman of loose morals, but that her husband had known what she was like when he married her, and had still lived with her for a long time. This made Marius disgusted with them both, and as well as ordering the husband to return the dowry, he imposed a fine on Fannia of four copper coins as a mark of her disgrace. Despite this, at the time in question Fannia did not behave like a woman who felt herself to have been wronged. So far from holding a grudge against him, the sight of Marius was enough to make her look after him as best she could under the circumstances and to try to boost his morale. He thanked her for her consideration and told her that he was not worried, because he had received a very positive portent, as follows. Just as he reached Fannia's house, when he was being taken there by his guards, the doors opened and a donkey ran out from inside, to get a drink from a nearby stream. With a cheeky look at Marius, as if glad to see him, it paused opposite him before giving a loud bray and bounding past him with head held high. To Marius' way of thinking, he told her, the gods were showing that he would find safety by sea rather than by land, because the donkey showed no interest in its dry fodder, but turned instead to the water. After explaining this to Fannia, he asked her to close the door of his room and leave him alone to rest.*

[39] The officials and councillors of Minturnae decided, after deliberation, to put Marius to death without further delay. However, none of the townsmen was prepared to do the deed, so a horseman—different versions have him as a Gaul or a Cimbrian*—took a sword and went in to find him. Now, the story goes that the room where Marius was lying was gloomy and dimly lit, and that the soldier saw flames shoot out from Marius' eyes and heard a loud voice from the deep shadows, which said, 'Sir, do you dare to kill Gaius Marius?' At this the foreigner fled from the room, and as he passed through the doorway of the house he threw the sword down on the ground in front of everybody, but said nothing except to shout out loud, 'I cannot kill Gaius Marius.'*

Once they had got over their astonishment, they started to feel sorry for Marius, and before long they changed their minds and felt bad for the criminal ingratitude they had displayed in coming to such a decision in the case of a man who had been the saviour of Italy, and who therefore deserved their help. 'Let him go into exile wherever he wants,' they said. 'Let him suffer his allotted fate elsewhere. And as for us, let us pray that the gods will not punish us for throwing Marius out of our city unclothed and in his hour of need.' Prompted by these considerations, they rushed in a crowd into the room, surrounded him, and set out to take him down to the sea. But despite the fact that everyone was anxious to make things easy for him in some way or other, and that no one was wasting any time, there was still a delay. For their route down to the sea was blocked by the grove of Marica, as it is called, which was a sacred place for them, and which nothing was allowed to be taken out of, once it had been taken in.* They would have had to spend time going all the way round the outside of the grove, but then one of the town elders cried out in a loud voice that no way which helped Marius to safety could be sacrosanct and impassable, and he was the first to take up some of the supplies that were being carried to Marius' ship and walk through the place.

[40] This is just one example of the kind of purposefulness that made short work of the job of gathering supplies. Marius' ship was provided by Belaeus, who later commissioned a painting of these events and dedicated it in the sanctuary at the place where Marius embarked and put to sea.* As chance would have it, the wind made fair sailing for the island of Aenaria, where Marius picked up Granius and the rest of his friends, and set sail for Africa.* However, lack of drinking-water forced them to put in at the territory of Eryx in Sicily, where the Roman quaestor happened to be on the lookout for Marius,* and came very close to capturing him after he had gone ashore; in fact, he did succeed in killing about sixteen of the men who had gone to collect water. Marius hurriedly put to sea again and sailed across the open sea to the island of Meninx, where he first learnt that his son had escaped alive with Cethegus and was on his way to Hiempsal, the king of Numidia, to ask for help.* This news restored Marius' spirits a little, and gave him the confidence to set out from the island for Carthage.

The praetor in charge of Africa at the time was Sextilius, a Roman whom Marius had neither benefited nor injured in the past, but who might be expected to help him out of pity, at least. However, Marius had only just landed with a few companions when he was met by one of Sextilius' deputies who stood in front of him and said, 'In his capacity as praetor, Sextilius forbids you, Marius, to set foot in Africa. If you disobey, he warns you that he will uphold the decrees of the senate and regard you as an enemy of Rome.' When he first heard this Marius was too upset and depressed to be able to make any kind of reply, and for a long time he did nothing except stare in horror at the deputy. But when the man asked what message or response he should take to the praetor, Marius sighed heavily and said, 'All right, tell him you have seen Gaius Marius in exile from Rome, sitting among the ruins of Carthage'—thus neatly comparing his own fall with the fate of Carthage.

Meanwhile, Hiempsal, the king of Numidia, was in two minds. On the one hand, he was treating the younger Marius and his companions with perfect politeness, but on the other hand whenever they wanted to leave he found some reason for keeping them there, and it was clear that in doing so he was up to no good. But events conspired in an unusual fashion to bring about their safety. The younger Marius was a good-looking man and it offended one of the king's concubines to see him being treated in such a humiliating fashion—a feeling of pity that developed and grew into one of love. At first he spurned the woman's advances, but when he realized that it was his last chance to escape and that her actions were motivated by more than mere lust, he accepted her kindness. With her help he fled the country with his friends and they escaped to Marius. After greeting each other, father and son were walking along the sea-shore when they saw a battle going on between some scorpions, which Marius interpreted as a bad omen. They immediately boarded a fishing-boat and set sail for the island of Cercina, which lies close to the mainland—and they had only just put to sea when some of the king's horsemen came into view, riding towards the place they had just left. This was generally held to be as narrow an escape as Marius ever experienced.*

[41] The news from Rome was that Sulla was fighting Mithridates' forces in Boeotia,* and the consuls had fallen out and resorted to open warfare. Octavius had won the battle, and then expelled Cinna, who had been trying to set himself up as a tyrant, and made Cornelius Merula consul instead. Cinna, however, had mustered an army from all over Italy and renewed the war against them.* When Marius heard this, he decided to sail there as quickly as possible. In Africa he raised a force, about a thousand strong at the most, consisting of Moorish cavalrymen and Italians who had found their way to that part of the world, and set sail. They reached land at Telamon in

Etruria,* where he disembarked and proclaimed the slaves free. The free farmers and herdsmen of the district also flocked down to the coast, attracted by his reputation, and he recruited the fittest of them too, until in a few days he had gathered together a sizeable army and manned forty ships. He knew that Octavius was an excellent man, who wanted to hold power in strict conformity with the law, while Cinna was distrusted by Sulla and wanted to overthrow the established constitution, so he decided to put himself and his forces at the disposal of Cinna, and to that end he sent a letter to Cinna, recognizing him as consul and promising to obey all his commands.* Cinna accepted the offer, gave him the rank of proconsul, and sent him the fasces and other insignia of office. Marius, however, declared that these adornments ill became his misfortunes, and dressed in shabby clothing, with his hair uncut since the day he was exiled from Rome, and now over 70 years of age, he slowly advanced to meet Cinna. He wanted people to feel sorry for him, but mingled in with his pitiful demeanour was the familiar predominant aspect of his appearance, his fearsomeness, so that his dejection was framed by a spirit that did not just remain uncowed, but had been made fiercer by his downfall.

[42] As soon as he had greeted Cinna and met his troops, he set to work and drastically altered the state of affairs. First, by using his fleet to intercept the enemy's grain-ships and to plunder merchant vessels, he gained control of the city's supplies; then he sailed against the coastal towns and captured them; and finally Ostia itself was betrayed to him.* At Ostia he ransacked property, killed most of the inhabitants, and bridged the river so as to cut off the enemy's last chance of being supplied by sea. Then he set out with his army, marched on Rome, and occupied the hill called the Janiculum.* If Octavius harmed his own cause, this was due not so much to inexperience as to his strict adherence to the laws, in the sense that it was not in his best interests to neglect the demands of necessity and refuse, despite all the advice he was receiving, to recruit the slaves with a promise of freedom. However, he said that he would not give slaves a share in Rome when it was precisely in order to defend the laws of Rome that he was trying to keep Gaius Marius out of it. But when Metellus came to Rome—this was the son of the Metellus who had commanded the Roman forces in Africa and had been exiled thanks to Marius—he seemed to be a far better commander than Octavius, and some of the troops transferred their allegiance from

Octavius to him.* They asked him to take charge and told him that he would be the saviour of the state, because all they needed to fight and win was an experienced and effective leader. And when Metellus angrily told them to return to the consul, they went over to the enemy, while Metellus too left Rome, since he thought the situation hopeless.

Octavius, however, was persuaded by certain Chaldean soothsayers, readers of sacrificial entrails, and interpreters of the Sibylline books to remain in Rome, since they held out the prospect of eventual success.* In other respects Octavius showed more common sense than any of his fellow citizens, and he took special care to make sure that the dignity of the consulship was not liable to be swayed by external influences, in accordance with the customs and laws he had received from past generations, which he regarded as immutable directives. But in this sphere he did display vulnerability, and he spent more time with beggar-priests and diviners than he did with expert statesmen and strategists. Anyway, Marius paved the way for his entry into the city by sending assassins on ahead, who pulled Octavius down from the rostra and butchered him;* and it is said that a Chaldean horoscope was found in the folds of his toga* after he had been murdered. And it is a strange fact that the high regard in which both these outstanding leaders held divination saved the life of Marius and cost Octavius his.

[43] Under the circumstances, the senate met and sent envoys to Cinna and Marius, inviting them to enter Rome, and asking them to spare their fellow citizens. As consul, Cinna received the envoys while seated on the chair of office, and he responded in friendly terms to their petition. Marius, however, stood by the side of the chair, and although he said nothing, it was clear throughout, from the severity of his expression and the grim looks he gave, that he was going to lose no time in making the city run with blood. After the meeting, they set out and made their way to the city. Cinna entered with a squad of personal guards, but Marius stopped by the gates and pointed out, with feigned anger, that he was an exile, barred by official decree from his homeland, and so if anyone wanted him there, they would have to pass a further law rescinding the decree of banishment—as if he were the kind of person who cared for laws, and as if the city to which he was returning was free to make its own decisions! So a general meeting of the Roman people was convened

in the forum, but after only two or three tribes had cast their votes Marius gave up the pretence and all the legalistic talk of being an exile, and entered the city with a personal guard of slaves picked from among those who had joined his forces, whom he called the Bardyaei.* They killed many people at Marius' word of command, and many more at a mere nod from him; eventually things got so bad that when Ancharius, a senator of praetorian rank, met Marius, but failed to receive a greeting from him, the Bardyaei struck him down with their swords, while Marius looked on. After this, if anyone greeted Marius, but received no word or greeting in return, this in itself was the signal for him to be murdered right there in the street, until even his friends were riddled with anxiety and terror every time they came up to Marius to greet him. After large numbers had been killed, Cinna became sated and lost his appetite for further slaughter, but Marius' anger and thirst for blood grew stronger every day, and he carried on killing everyone he had ever doubted at all. Every street and every city was filled with people chasing and hunting down others, who were trying to escape or who had gone into hiding, and trust in the ties of guest-friendship and loyalty was found to offer no more security than fortune might have brought anyway, because there were extremely few who did not betray those who had taken refuge with them. This makes the behaviour of Cornutus' slaves all the more commendable and impressive: after hiding their master in his house, they got hold of one of the many corpses, put a gold ring on its finger, strung it up by the neck, and showed it to Marius' personal guards. Then they dressed it up in finery and buried it as if they were burying Cornutus. No one suspected anything, and so Cornutus was surreptitiously smuggled across the border into Gaul by his slaves.

[44] The orator Marcus Antonius also met with kindness from a friend, but with unfortunate consequences.* The man was a poor plebeian, but he wanted to do all he could to make his guest, one of the leading men of Rome, feel welcome and comfortable, so he sent a slave to a nearby innkeeper to get some wine. After tasting the wine more carefully than usual, the slave asked the innkeeper for a draught of a better wine, and so the innkeeper asked him why he was buying good, expensive wine rather than the ordinary new wine he normally bought. The slave, knowing that he was talking to a familiar acquaintance, naïvely told him that his master was

entertaining Marcus Antonius, who was lying low in his house. As soon as the slave had left, the innkeeper, a vile and nasty piece of work, dashed off to Marius.

Marius was busy with his evening meal, but when the innkeeper was brought before him and promised to betray Antonius to him, it is said that Marius greeted the news with a great shout and clapped his hands for joy. He was on the point of going to the place himself, but his friends restrained him, so he sent Annius instead, along with some armed men, with orders to hurry back with Antonius' head. When they reached the house, Annius waited by the door while the soldiers climbed the stairs to the room. But when they saw Antonius, each of them hung back and tried to get one of the others to do the killing instead of himself. Apparently, in fact, Antonius was so bewitchingly charismatic and eloquent that once he had begun to speak and to plead for his life, the soldiers could not even meet his eyes, let alone summon up the courage to lay hands on him, but they all hung their heads and wept. Puzzled by the delay, Annius went upstairs, to be faced with the sight of Antonius talking and his men overwhelmed and spellbound by him. Hurling curses at his men, he himself ran over and cut off Antonius' head. As for Lutatius Catulus, who had been Marius' fellow consul and had shared his triumph over the Cimbri,* the only reply Marius made to those who were pleading for his life and asking him for mercy was, 'He has to die.' Catulus therefore locked himself in a room, relit the charcoal left over from a large fire, and died of suffocation.

Headless bodies were tossed into the streets and trampled underfoot, but no one felt pity at the sight, only frissons of horror and fear. What particularly irritated the people was the sickening behaviour of the so-called Bardyaei, who butchered householders in their homes, did appalling things to their children, and raped their wives. Their orgy of pillage and murder continued unchecked until Cinna and Sertorius joined forces, attacked them as they were sleeping in their quarters, and killed them all with repeated volleys of javelins.*

[45] Meanwhile, however, the wind was beginning to change. Messengers started to arrive from all quarters with the news that Sulla had brought the war against Mithridates to an end, recovered the provinces, and was sailing for Italy with a substantial army.* This news caused a brief halt and respite to the unspeakable horrors, since people believed that war was imminent. So Marius was elected

consul for the seventh time, and immediately after assuming office on the first of January, the first day of the new year,* he executed a man called Sextus Licinius by having him hurled from the Tarpeian Rock, which was generally held to be a crucial indication of the renewed trouble that was to plague Marius and the city.

However, by now Marius had been ground down by a lifetime of hardship. Swamped, so to speak, by his cares and utterly worn out, his experience of danger and exhaustion made his mind shrink from the monstrous prospect of yet another war, with fresh struggles and fears. He also realized that this was not going to be a contest against the likes of Octavius and Merula, at the head of a ramshackle mob and a disunited rabble. No, Sulla was coming—Sulla who had once before expelled him from Rome, and who had just finished driving Mithridates back to the Euxine Sea. These thoughts broke his spirit. The long days he had spent lost in the wilderness, his time in exile, the dangers he had faced as he was hounded over land and sea—all this was constantly before his eyes. He fell into a state of utter helplessness, plagued by fears every night and disturbing dreams in which he seemed to hear a voice saying: 'Fearsome is the lair even when the lion is gone.'* What he feared most of all were the sleepless nights, so he resorted to bouts of excessive drinking, and used to get far more drunk than a man his age should, as a means of inducing sleep and so escaping from his anxieties. Eventually, with the arrival of a messenger from the coast, fresh terrors crowded in on him. With the future looking grim and the present consisting of nothing but the burden of over-indulgence, the precarious balance of his health tilted just a little way and he contracted pleurisy. At least, that is what the philosopher Posidonius says,* adding that he personally visited Marius when he was ill and discussed the official business that had brought him to Rome. However, the historian Gaius Piso says that Marius took a walk one day after dinner with some friends and reminisced about all the things he had achieved, from his earliest days onwards; after recounting all the changes that had occurred in his life, from a good state to a bad one and vice versa, he concluded that no one with any intelligence should entrust himself to fortune. Then he bade farewell to his companions and took to his bed, where he stayed and died seven days later.

Some people say that during his illness his longing for recognition reasserted itself and induced in him the strange delusion that he was in command of the Mithridatic War, and that he then proceeded to behave just as he had during actual battles, with all the appropriate gestures and movements, accompanied by impetuous cries and frequent shouts of command. This shows how fiercely and permanently ambition and jealousy had embedded in his mind a passion for that kind of activity. As a result of this passion, although he had lived for seventy years, was the first man ever to have been elected consul seven times, and had acquired enough property and wealth for many kingdoms at once, he still lamented his fate and felt that he was dying without having attained and achieved all that he desired.

[46] When Plato was on his death-bed, however, he offered up thanks to his guardian spirit and to fortune, in the first place because he had been born a man rather than an irrational beast, in the second place because he had been born a Greek rather than a foreigner, and in the third place because his birth had coincided with the time when Socrates had been alive. Then of course there is the story of how when Antipater of Tarsus was likewise close to death, he added up all the good things that had happened to him, and included even the easy voyage he had had from his home to Athens.* This shows how deeply grateful he was for every gift given by benevolent fortune and how he preserved them all his life in his memory, which is the most secure storehouse we have for all the good things that happen to us. Over time, events trickle out of the minds of forgetful, thoughtless people, and so, since they retain and conserve nothing, the empty space within them that should be filled with good things is filled instead with hopes, so that they neglect the present and look to the future, despite the fact that fortune may yet foil the future, whereas the present cannot be taken away. Nevertheless, these people eject the present from their minds as something foreign to them, while they dream of the future despite all its uncertainties. Nor is it surprising that they do this: after all, they accumulate and hoard all the blessings of life before reason and education have had a chance to build a solid foundation on which to preserve these blessings, and this makes it impossible for them to satisfy the insatiable appetites of their minds.

Be that as it may, Marius died seventeen days after taking up his seventh consulship.* Rome was immediately swept by a feeling of intense joy and relief, as if it had been freed from a harsh tyranny.

But after a few days they realized that they had merely exchanged an old master for a young, vigorous one, as the younger Marius revealed the extent of his savagery and brutality in the continued slaughter of the best and most distinguished men of Rome. His daring disregard of danger in battle had gained him quite a reputation, so that at first he was called 'the son of Mars'; but soon his true nature was revealed by his actions and he was called 'the son of Venus' instead. In the end he was trapped by Sulla in Praeneste, and after a number of vain attempts to save his life, when the city fell and there was no hope of escape, he committed suicide.*

SULLA

INTRODUCTION

Sulla was for the Romans and is for us incomprehensible, in the fundamental sense that we have no scheme that can grasp and hold together what he did. Twice he captured Rome with his army; he established himself as a new kind of dictator, one to reconstitute the state; he defeated not only Mithridates, who commanded all the forces of Asia Minor, but also several consular armies defending Italy. Blessed by the gods, cursed by his enemies, his reforming legislation came after the slaughter of thousands in cold blood. Sulla, a champion of order and tradition, brought chaos and revolution such as Rome had never seen.

Born in 138 BC to an impoverished patrician family, Lucius Cornelius Sulla had a knack for being in the right place at the right time: his friendship with King Bocchus of Mauretania allowed him to take into custody the rebellious King Jugurtha in 105, in the 90s he was the first Roman magistrate to deal directly with the Parthians, and in 88, as consul, he was given the command of the war against Mithridates.

Exactly these anomalies attracted Plutarch to him. The absolute power which he wielded made him a model for future dynasts, and then for the emperors. But power in Sulla's hands had proved a two-edged sword. The biographer found a parallel in the life of Lysander, the Spartan commander who conquered Athens and ended the Peloponnesian War. Lysander shared with Sulla ambition and ruthlessness, and the willingness to pander to those he could not control, until his turn came. His victory over Athens also brought empire and riches to his country, which finally subverted the Spartan way of life. He even, like Sulla, had plans to change his country's political structure, but died before he could attempt his revolution. Sulla's character was similar to Lysander's, but his passions were deeper, his skill greater, and his stage larger: not the Aegean but Rome's world empire.

Plutarch creates a richly textured portrait of the man and his world, amazing for its variety of scene, content, and tone. The action moves from cheap Roman apartments to conversations with kings, from massacres to pleasant strolls at a seaside spa, from drunken parties with actors to triumphal processions. In all this diversity, Plutarch isolates a number of themes. First, ambition and rivalry. Sulla began as that saddest of figures, a poor patrician. His brilliant beginning as quaestor for Marius, augmented by his own vanity, led to a rivalry with the older and equally competitive Marius (cc. 4, 6). Expelled by Marius from his command,

Sulla ruthlessly reclaims it (9), and outlaws his enemy. We may contrast the behaviour of Themistocles, Camillus, Cimon, and Lucullus, who preferred to abandon the struggle rather than tear apart their cities. This demand for recognition of his own prerogatives at any cost finally led to the Civil War of 82 and the evils that it brought. His ambition was fuelled by his military and diplomatic successes. Sulla took risks, and was a winner. He entrusted himself to Bocchus, not knowing whether he would betray Sulla to Jugurtha, or Jugurtha to Sulla: and he won (3). He asserted Rome's role on the Euphrates, setting himself between the king of Cappadocia and the Parthian ambassador (5). Deposed from his command by Marius, he seized Rome and sent his rival fleeing for his life (9–10). He captured Athens (12–14), and annihilated the armies of Mithridates at Chaeronea and Orchomenus (18–19, 21). Back in Italy, he shrewdly subverted the consul Scipio's soldiers, destroyed the army of the other consul, young Marius (28), and annihilated a third force in the battle of the Colline Gate (29). Sulla, however, attributed his success to his good fortune and asked that he be granted the title Felix, 'Fortunate' (34). Plutarch follows this theme throughout the Life,[1] profiting from the frequent references in Sulla's own *Memoirs*. For this reason, too, the Life teems with omens and prodigies promising Sulla success, and Plutarch twice reports the predictions of Chaldean diviners (5, 37) whom he scorns in *Marius* 42.

Brilliantly successful, favoured by the gods—and savage. Blood flows in *Sulla* as in no other Life. The blood of Athenians, measured by the quarters of the city which its flood covered (14), blood on the battlefield of Orchomenus (21: 'the marshes ran with the blood of the dead, and the lake was choked with corpses'), blood on the temples, hearths, and homes of Italy (31). Sulla is by nature harsh (6), and the best enemy is a dead enemy. Condemning Marius to death we might understand (10), but what of Ofella run through before his eyes (33), or six thousand prisoners after the battle of the Colline Gate, cut down in the Circus as Sulla addressed the senate (30), or twelve thousand taken and slaughtered at Praeneste (32)? Then there is the thoughtless cruelty of the proscription lists: 'He was proscribing everyone who came to mind, and if there were people he forgot about for the time being, he would get around to proscribing them later' (31). What sort of a man is this?

Sulla is a man of contradictions for Plutarch (cf. 6), though at first he had seemed to use his fortune well. But his behaviour in 82 showed no sign of the 'rule of the best' which was the philosopher's ideal. Sulla showed himself a tyrant, and challenged the very notion of a just monarchy: power must render the ruler 'capricious, vain, and cruel' (30). Sulla is attacked

[1] Cf. cc. 1, 5, 6, 19, 27, 30, 35, 37, 38.

even more strongly in the Comparison with Lysander which follows the Life. Unlike Lysander, he was not chosen freely by the citizens, but once given command, he continued for ten years: 'He made himself sometimes consul, sometimes proconsul, and sometimes dictator, but always remained a tyrant' (Comparison, c. 1). Sulla struck in Plutarch a resonant chord: this is what monarchical power could be. He had seen emperors misuse power; he had seen the excesses of Nero and Domitian. Sulla was a warning against civil war and one man's ambition never to yield.

And yet—he was so favoured by the gods. 'It is the gods' fault that Sulla was fortunate,' writes Seneca in his *Consolation to Marcia* (12. 6). For Plutarch, Sulla was a stage in that providential process by which Rome ruled the world and the monarchy was established under which he and his readers lived.[2] His greatness chastened the ambitions of Mithridates and the lawlessness of Marius, Cinna, and Carbo. One could not imagine Rome without him.

The organization of the Life is chronological, punctuated by Plutarch's comments (e.g. on political rivalry, 4; Sulla's character, 6; the nature of his rule, 30).

1–2	Family, character, habits
3–6	Capture of Bocchus; rivalry with Marius; Cappadocia
7–10	The year 88 BC at Rome; outlawing of Marius
11–14	Sulla in Greece; the siege of Athens (87–86)
15–19	The campaign and battle of Chaeronea (86)
20–1	The battle of Orchomenus (86)
22–4	The treaty with Mithridates (85)
25–6	Sulla in Asia and Greece (84)
27–9	Sulla's march through Italy; battle of the Colline Gate (83–82)
30–5	Sulla master of Rome (82–80)
36–8	Retirement and death

No one as controversial as Sulla can have a simple history. Roman writers of his generation down to the end of the republic viewed him through partisan eyes, from the perspective of the *optimates* or *populares* (cf. p. 77). These biases affected both the primary and secondary sources which Plutarch used. However, although identifying pro- or anti-Sullan sections of the Life was once a popular scholarly activity, our current sense of Plutarch's control of his presentation removes much of its

[2] See in general on Plutarch's idea of providence in Roman history, S. Swain, 'Plutarch: Chance, Providence, and History', *American Journal of Philology*, 110 (1989), 272–302.

purpose. In general, we may assume that both negative and positive material have been included because Plutarch considered them true to his idea of the man, itself formed by his reading, contact with Roman friends, philosophical views, and preoccupation with imperial governance.

Sulla's *Memoirs*, written in twenty-two books, right down to the day before he died, were a gold-mine for a biographer who appreciated contemporary sources, and Plutarch refers to them frequently.[3] He is especially interested in Sulla's comments on his own experiences, and his reports of prodigies or dreams, which must have been numerous in the *Memoirs*, calling attention to the care the gods showed him. Sulla was not hesitant to praise his own achievements. One corollary is that his casualty figures are regularly minuscule for his army and enormously exaggerated for his opponents. The book was no doubt meant also as a defence of his actions, as can be seen in the fragment (not quoted in the Life) where he speaks of 'cleansing Italy of its civil wars'. A rigorous cleansing indeed.[4]

Otherwise, Plutarch gives us little help in identifying his sources. He names five authors one time each: Fenestella (28), Juba (16), Strabo (26), and Livy (6), as well as Sallust in the Comparison (3). All are authors he cites elsewhere and probably used directly; none are contemporary (see p. xxiv in the General Introduction). The first three wrote under Augustus. Fenestella composed Roman annals; he is cited also in Plutarch's *Crassus* 5 and *Roman Questions*. Juba, a Mauretanian prince, wrote numerous learned works in Greek; here, he is cited for a minor point in Sulla's Boeotian campaign.[5] Strabo, whose *Geography* of the Roman empire is extant, also wrote a lost historical work, cited by Plutarch here, in *Lucullus* 28, and in *Caesar* 63. The citation of Sallust[6] comes from the lost *Histories*,

[3] In cc. 4, 5, 6, 14, 16, 17, 19, 23, 24–5, 27, 28, and 37. They were also used in 8 (Sulla escapes to Marius' house), as can be seen by comparison with the citation in *Marius* 35. He is also cited at *Luc.* 1 (the dedication of his Memoirs) and 23 (=*Sull.* 6), *Marius* 25 and 26 (the battle of Vercellae) and *Old Men in Politics* 786e. The last is particularly interesting, because it gives an impression of Sulla not found in the Life: 'Sulla, when he first arrived at Rome after cleansing Italy of its civil wars, did not sleep a wink that night, he was so borne aloft by great joy and gladness as by a gust of wind. Sulla said this about himself in his *Memoirs*.'

[4] For a brief account of Sulla's *Memoirs*, see T. C. Brennan, 'Sulla's Career in the 90's: Some Reconsiderations', *Chiron*, 22 (1992), 103–58, at 106–11.

[5] Plutarch admired Juba's work (cf. *Caes.* 55. 3) and cites him for Roman antiquities in *Romulus*, *Numa*, and the *Roman Questions*, and concerning elephants in *Intelligence of Animals* 972b–c, 977e, but only one other time for a historical point (*Marc.* 31. 8). Juba married Antony's daughter by Cleopatra (*Ant.* 87).

[6] Comparison, c. 3: 'Poverty did not limit Sulla's passions when he was young, nor old age when he was old, but he prescribed laws for the citizens on marriage and chastity, while continuing as a lover and adulterer, says Sallust.' Sallust is also cited at *Luc.* 11 and 33,

which begin after Sulla's death, but Plutarch perhaps already knew the *Jugurthine War*, which he would use again in *Marius* for the Bocchus episode.[7] For Livy, see p. xxiv above. In *Marius* he also used the account by Quintus Lutatius Catulus of the battle of Vercellae, at which Sulla was present (cf. c. 4). Other writers for this period whom he may have known directly or indirectly include: Publius Rutilius Rufus, cited in *Marius*. 28; Lucius Cornelius Sisenna, a supporter of the senatorial nobility, who gave a detailed account of the Social War and the years down to 82, or perhaps Sulla's death; and the anti-Marian annalist Quintus Claudius Quadrigarius, as well as the *popularis* Quintus Licinius Macer.

Especially valuable notices derive from Plutarch's own experience and knowledge of local tradition in Boeotia, Delphi, and Athens. As a resident of Chaeronea and priest at Delphi, he knew the region well, and describes it as one who has walked over the terrain, naming villages, streams, and hills, and referring to the weapons which still turn up in the marshes in his own time, after almost two hundred years (21). He knows the role of local residents such as the two men named Caphis (12 and 15). His notice of the fighting which took place on the hill called Thurium overlooking Chaeronea (17) and the trophy erected there (19) have now been confirmed by discovery of the trophy inscription. At Athens he is familiar with the tale of the gossiping men (though this may be from Sulla's Memoirs) and how far the blood ran in the Cerameicus (14).[8]

Nevertheless, there are notable omissions. Some clearly derive from an effort to move the narrative along, such as the vague reference to the battle of Vercellae (4), or the suppression of Sulla's first presence in Rome and march into Etruria (c. 28 note, *sailed off to Africa*). Of special interest is his silence in chapter 33 on Sulla's reform of the constitution: increasing the senate and ensuring a steady flow of new senators, increasing the number of quaestors and praetors, setting strict limits on the order and intervals between the magistracies, severely limiting the influence of the tribunate, restructuring the courts, and augmenting the number of priests. This should not be a problem of information: Sulla's reforms were well known, and were mentioned in sources Plutarch used. He had discussed at length the legal codes of Solon and Lycurgus: but he saw these as efforts to create a well-run, even 'philosophical' state; those laws could be discussed in terms of the philosophy of civic education. Clearly Plutarch saw no such

[7] See p. xxiv above.

[8] Cf. J. Buckler, 'Plutarch and Autopsy', in W. Haase and H. Temporini (eds.), *Aufstieg und Nierdergang der römischen Welt*, II. 33. 6 (Berlin and New York, 1992), 4788–830, esp. 4801–8 on Boeotia.

possibility in Sulla's legislation. The author of the proscriptions had little to teach about good citizenship.[9]

Angeli Bertinelli, M. G., Manfredini, M., Piccirilli, L., and Pisani, G. (eds.), *Plutarco: Le Vite di Lisandro e di Silla* (Milan: Mondadori, 1997). Although in Italian, it is the most thorough commentary, with full and up-to-date bibliography.

Badian, E., 'Lucius Sulla: The Deadly Reformer', *Seventh Todd Memorial Lecture* (Sydney: Sydney University Press, 1970), repr. in A. J. Dunston (ed.), *Essays on Roman Culture: The Todd Memorial Lectures* (Sarasota, Fla.: Hakkert, 1976), 35–74.

Brennan, T. C., 'Sulla's Career in the 90's: Some Reconsiderations', *Chiron*, 22 (1992), 103–58.

Holden, H. A., *Plutarch's Life of Lucius Cornelius Sulla* (Cambridge: University Press, 1886).

Keaveney, A., *Sulla, the Last Republican* (London and Canberra: Croom Helm, 1982).

Stadter, P. A., 'Paradoxical Paradigms: Plutarch's Lysander and Sulla', in P. A. Stadter (ed.), *Plutarch and the Historical Tradition* (London: Routledge, 1992), 41–55.

[9] For Plutarch's ideal of reconciliation rather than rivalry at a time of civic crisis, cf. *Arist.* 8; *Them.* 11–12; *Cim*; 11, and *Per.* 10.

SULLA

[1] Lucius Cornelius Sulla was of patrician (which is to say, noble) stock, and we hear that one of his ancestors, Rufinus, served as consul, although he is more famous for his demotion than for his promotion to that office. What happened was that he was found to possess more than ten pounds of silver plate, which was illegal, and he was expelled from the senate for this.* Rufinus' descendants achieved nothing important and remained in relative obscurity, and Sulla himself was hardly brought up with plentiful family resources. When he was a young adult he lived in cheap rented accommodation —a fact which was later used to cast aspersions on his apparently undeserved good fortune. For instance, there is a story that once, when he was puffed up with boastful pride after the war in Africa, one of the aristocrats of Rome said, 'How can you possibly be a man of integrity? Your father left you nothing, but look how rich you are!' For although the Roman way of life was no longer as upright and unblemished as it once had been—although people had changed for the worse and now found nothing wrong with aspiring towards a luxurious and extravagant lifestyle—nevertheless they were still just as shocked by those who abandoned their family's traditional poverty as they were by those who lost inherited fortunes. And on a later occasion, when he had power in Rome and was engaged on an extensive programme of executions, a freedman who was suspected of hiding one of the people he had proscribed, and was therefore about to be hurled from the Tarpeian Rock, sneered at Sulla and claimed that for a number of years they had shared a lodging-house, in which he had rented the upper rooms for 2,000 sesterces and Sulla the lower rooms for 3,000, making the difference between their circumstances only 1,000 sesterces, or 250 Attic drachmas. So much for our information about Sulla's original circumstances.*

[2] His basic appearance is clear from his statues, but mention should also be made of the terrible piercing ferocity of his grey eyes. His complexion made his eyes even more terrifying to see, since his face was covered with rough red blotches in between patches of pale skin. In fact, they say that this feature of his complexion gained him his name,* and an Athenian satirist mocked him for it by making up

the following line of verse: 'Sulla is a mulberry splattered with porridge.'

In fact, it is not inappropriate to make use of this kind of evidence in the case of a man who was apparently so fond of coarse humour that not only did he go around with actors and comedians when he was a young man, before becoming famous, and share their dissolute lifestyle, but even after he had gained absolute power he surrounded himself with the worst hooligans from the theatrical world, and every day he would drink and swap rude jokes with them. As well as being regarded as unsuitable behaviour for someone his age, this brought the dignity of his office into disrepute and caused him to neglect a great deal of business that required his attention, because it was not Sulla's way to engage in anything serious once he had taken his place for dinner. Although at other times he was efficient and rather severe, a sudden and complete change came over him as soon as he gave himself over to conviviality and drinking, which meant that singers and dancers found him congenial, and he was submissive and prepared to accommodate every petition that was brought forward. This unhealthy laxity also manifested itself in his susceptibility to love and his powerful sensuality, which continued even into old age, and he never lost his love for an actor called Metrobius.* While he was still a young man < . . . >† and he had the following experience. He fell in love with a common but wealthy woman called Nicopolis, and although at first it was he who pursued her, in the end, once she had become used to his company, she was won over by his youthful charms and fell in love with him. In fact, when she died she bequeathed her property to him. He also inherited the estate of his stepmother, who loved him as if he were her own son, and as a result of these two bequests he became moderately well off.

[3] In Marius' first consulship Sulla was appointed his quaestor and sailed to Africa with him to make war on Jugurtha.* After reaching the camp, he made a name for himself above all by making good use of an opportunity that came his way and getting on good terms with Bocchus, the king of the Numidians. What happened was that he took in some of the king's envoys who had escaped from a band of Numidian brigands, made them feel welcome, and then sent them on their way after presenting them with gifts and providing them with a safe escort. Now, Bocchus had for a long time loathed and feared his son-in-law, Jugurtha, and when Jugurtha took refuge with him after

the Roman victory he proceeded to devise schemes to bring about his downfall. In the end he sent for Sulla, since he wanted Jugurtha's capture and surrender to the Romans to be seen as Sulla's act rather than his own. After telling Marius what was going on, Sulla took a few soldiers with him and placed himself in an extremely hazardous situation. After all, he was trusting a foreigner who was prepared to betray even his closest kin, and was giving himself up in order to secure someone else's surrender. Bocchus now had both men in his power and had committed himself to the inevitability of breaking faith with one or the other of them, but after a lengthy period of equivocation he finally settled on his original betrayal and handed Jugurtha over to Sulla. Although it was Marius who celebrated a triumph for this, credit for the victory went to Sulla, out of resentment of Marius, and this irritated Marius, although he kept his anger to himself.* Now, Sulla was a vain man, and this was the first time he had emerged from the insignificance and obscurity of his past life to a position of some standing in Rome and had tasted prestige. This went to his head so much that he had a picture of the event engraved on a signet ring which he wore and used constantly afterwards. The picture showed Bocchus handing Jugurtha over into Sulla's charge.

[4] Marius was annoyed by this, but he still considered Sulla too insignificant for envy, and so he continued to make use of him on his campaigns—as a legate during his second consulship, and as a military tribune during his third—and through his agency achieved a number of valuable successes. For instance, while serving as legate Sulla captured Copillus, the leader of the Tectosages, and as military tribune he persuaded the important and numerous tribe of the Marsi to enter into a treaty of friendship and alliance with Rome.* However, when he realized that Marius was angry with him for these exploits and was no longer happy to give him opportunities for achievement, but was hindering his advancement, he attached himself to Marius' fellow consul, Catulus—a man of integrity, who unfortunately lacked the verve to make a great military commander.* Catulus entrusted Sulla with tasks of critical importance, and so both his power and his fame began to grow. He not only conquered the majority of the Alpine tribes, but also took on the job of managing the supplies when they were low, and created such a surplus that Catulus' troops lived in plenty and he had some to spare for Marius'

men as well—which, as Sulla himself says,* irritated Marius a great deal. This shows the triviality and childishness of the original pretexts they found for their mutual enmity, which subsequently progressed through civil bloodshed and incurable discord to tyranny and the total overthrow of the constitution, and revealed how well Euripides understood the diseases that can afflict a state when he warned us to beware of ambition, on the grounds that there is no worse or more lethal deity for its devotees.*

[5] Sulla thought that the reputation he had acquired from military exploits would stand him in good stead in the public domain and, turning straight from army life to political activity, he put himself forward as a candidate for the city praetorship, which he failed to secure.* He blames the masses for this defeat: they knew he was on good terms with Bocchus, and so, he says, they wanted to see him serve as aedile before becoming praetor, in the expectation that they would be treated to wonderful hunting shows and contests involving wild animals from Africa. According to him, then, they appointed others to act as praetors in order to force him to become an aedile.* But subsequent events make it look as though Sulla was wrong in attributing his failure to this, because he succeeded in gaining a praetorship the next year, after winning the people round by a combination of concessions and bribery. That is why during his praetorship, when he angrily told Caesar that he would use his own power against him, Caesar laughed and said, 'You're right to consider the post your own, because you bought it.'*

After his praetorship he was sent on a mission to Cappadocia.* The pretext for the campaign was to reinstate Ariobarzanes, but the real reason was to check Mithridates, whose interventionist policies were in the process of at least doubling the empire and resources he had inherited. Sulla did not take out a large army of his own, but made use of the allies, who were glad to help. After inflicting heavy casualties on the Cappadocians themselves, and even heavier casualties on the Armenians, who came to help the Cappadocians, he drove Gordius into exile and made Ariobarzanes king.*

While he was on the banks of the Euphrates, he was paid an official visit by a Parthian called Orobazus, representing King Arsaces. This was the first time the two nations had come into contact, and it is generally held to be another sign of Sulla's considerable good fortune that he should have been the first Roman the Parthians approached when they wanted to discuss the possibility of entering into a treaty of friendship and alliance.* It is also said that on this occasion Sulla put out three chairs, one for Ariobarzanes, one for Orobazus, and one for himself, and negotiated while seated between the other two. The Parthian king later put Orobazus to death for this, and while Sulla was praised in some quarters for the airs he assumed with the foreigners, others charged him with vulgarity and a tactless display of ambition.

We are told that one of the people who came down with Orobazus from inland was a Chaldean* who, after studying Sulla's features and making a careful investigation of the way his mind and body worked, employing the principles of his art to shed light on his nature, declared that he would inevitably become the greatest man in the world, and expressed his surprise that even now he could put up with occupying any position less than absolute supremacy. But when Sulla returned to Rome he found himself accused of accepting bribes. Censorinus, who brought the charge, alleged that he had illegally obtained a great deal of money from a kingdom which was allied to the Roman cause. However, Censorinus failed to appear in court and withdrew the accusation.*

[6] Sulla's feud with Marius was rekindled, taking as its excuse this time the grandiosity of Bocchus, who wanted to court the favour of the people and at the same time to gratify Sulla, and so he set up on the Capitol statues of Victory bearing trophies, with a golden frieze running alongside the statues depicting his surrender of Jugurtha to Sulla.* Marius was furious at this and tried to demolish the statues, while others supported Sulla, and the two of them brought Rome to the very brink of conflagration when the Social War, whose smouldering embers had for a long time been threatening Rome, burst into flames and checked the feud between the two men. The Social War turned out to be a major conflict, full of changes of fortune, which brought terrible suffering and the utmost danger to Rome.* During the war, Marius proved incapable of achieving anything important, and demonstrated that military excellence requires a man to be at the peak of his physical and mental powers, but Sulla gained such remarkable successes that he came to be regarded by his fellow citizens as a great leader, by his friends as the greatest of leaders, and by his enemies as the most fortunate of leaders. But he did not behave like Timotheus the son of Conon.*

When Timotheus' enemies attributed his successes to good fortune and had a picture painted of him sleeping while Fortune captured their cities in her net, he churlishly and angrily claimed that the people who had commissioned the painting were robbing him of the glory of his achievements. And once, on his return from a campaign which was generally held to have gone well, he said to the assembled people, 'At least *this* campaign owes nothing to Fortune, men of Athens.'

Anyway, the story goes that the goddess played a sneaky trick on Timotheus, after he had revealed the extent of his desire for public recognition, so that from then on he never achieved anything glorious, but failed in all his enterprises, fell foul of the people, and was ultimately exiled from Athens. Sulla, however, not only enjoyed being congratulated and admired on these terms, but even contributed to it by exaggerating the part divine intervention had played in his achievements and attributing them to Fortune, either as a form of self-aggrandizement or perhaps because he did genuinely have this attitude towards the gods. For in his *Memoirs* he writes that he had more success acting boldly on the spur of the moment than after long deliberation, even when his achievements were assumed to have been the result of sound planning on his part. Besides, to judge by what he says about his being endowed by his nature for good fortune rather than for warfare, he seems to attribute more to Fortune than to his natural abilities, and to make himself entirely the product of this deity. He even describes his friendship with Metellus, a man of the same rank in society and a relative by marriage, as a piece of divine good fortune, in the sense that although he was expected to make a lot of trouble for him, he could not have found a more amenable colleague.* Moreover, in the dedication of his *Memoirs* to Lucullus,* he advises him not to consider anything so secure as the instructions he receives at night from the gods. And by his own account once when he was dispatched at the head of an army to the Social War a huge chasm opened up in the ground near Laverna* and billowed forth fire, and a bright flame shot up to the sky. The diviners interpreted this as meaning that a brave man, of striking appearance and superior qualities, would take power and relieve Rome of its present troubles, and Sulla claims to be that man, because his golden hair gave him a unique appearance, and he felt no qualms in testifying to his own bravery after all his excellent and important achievements. But so much for his attitude towards the gods.

In other respects he seems to have been an inconsistent kind of person, at odds with himself: he stole a great deal, but gave even more as gifts; he bestowed either honours or insults in an erratic fashion; he acted obsequiously towards those he needed and arrogantly towards those who needed him, so that it was impossible to tell whether he was temperamentally more disdainful or deferential. Consider the inconsistency of his behaviour in regard to punishing others, for instance. At the slightest pretext he might have a man crucified, but on another occasion would make light of the most appalling crimes; or he might happily forgive the most unpardonable offences and then punish trivial, insignificant misdemeanours with death and the confiscation of property. It might be possible to conclude that he was naturally inclined to be short-tempered and vengeful, but was prepared to let considerations of self-interest override his brutality. For instance, to take an example from the Social War with which we are currently concerned, when his soldiers clubbed and stoned to death a man of consular rank called Albinus,* a legate, he connived at the atrocity and did nothing about it; in fact, he even solemnly started a rumour that this crime would increase the commitment with which his men fought, in the sense that they would try to make amends for their guilt by their courage. He took no notice of anyone who found fault with what had happened, but because it was his intention to overthrow Marius and to be given the command of the war against Mithridates,* now that the Social War was generally considered to be over, he courted the favour of his men.

When he returned to Rome, aged 50, he was elected consul along with Quintus Pompeius and entered into a very prestigious marriage with Caecilia, the daughter of Metellus, who was the pontifex maximus.* This marriage was the occasion for a lot of scurrilous verses sung by the plebeians, while, as Titus says,* large numbers of the leading men of Rome were affronted at it, since they did not think he was good enough for her, even though they had found him good enough for the consulship. This was not the only wife he had: first, when he was just a young adult, he married Ilia, who bore him a daughter; then there was Aelia; and his third wife was Cloelia, whom he divorced on the grounds of her inability to have children.* Throughout the divorce proceedings he treated her with politeness, spoke well of her, and even gave her gifts as well, but when a few days later he married Metella people became suspicious about the charges he had brought against Cloelia. However, he was always prepared to gratify Metella—so much so that when the Roman people wanted to bring the Marian exiles back to Rome and Sulla refused their request, they loudly applied to Metella for help. It was also believed that after the capture of Athens he treated the Athenians with undue harshness because they had stood on the city walls and satirized Metella in insulting terms; but this happened later.*

[7] At the time in question, since he viewed the consulship as a trivial matter compared with what the future held for him, he was fired up with enthusiasm about the Mithridatic War. But under the influence of ambition and the lust for glory—passions that have no regard for a person's age—Marius set himself up as a rival to Sulla. Despite the fact that he was now overweight and had chosen not to take part in recent campaigns because of his age, Marius had set his sights on wars abroad and over the seas.* When Sulla set out to join his army to complete some unfinished business,* Marius stayed at home and nurtured that fatal feud which did Rome more harm than all the other wars the city had engaged in put together. The gods did forewarn them of the danger: for no apparent reason some of the poles carrying military standards burst into flames and the fire proved hard to extinguish; three crows brought their young into the street and ate them there, and then took the remains back to their nests; when the attendants of a sanctuary where mice had been chewing some of the gold that was stored there caught one of them, a female, in a trap, she gave birth to five babies right there in the trap, but ate three of them. But the most important omen was that, from a clear, cloudless sky, there came a long, shrill, mournful trumpet blast which was so loud that everyone was terrified out of their wits. Learned Etruscans declared that the portent signified the advent of a new age and a new cosmic order. They said that there are eight ages altogether,† each with different customs and ways of life, and that the god has assigned each of these ages a definite number of years, which is accomplished by the revolution of a great year. Whenever one great year ends and another begins, they said, a remarkable portent appears either on earth or in the sky, to make it clear immediately to those who have studied and looked into such matters that men of a different kind, with different modes of life,

have been born into the world and to show whether this new race of men will be of more or less concern to the gods than their predecessors. They said that divination is particularly affected by the widespread radical changes that take place as one age succeeds another, so that at one time its prestige rises and its predictions come true, since the gods send clear and unmistakable portents, while in another age it does poorly, since it invariably has to rely on guesswork and tries to grasp the future with senses that have become faint and dim. Anyway, this was the tale told by the most learned Etruscans, the ones with a reputation for exceptional knowledge.* And while the senate was occupied with the diviners on these matters, meeting in the temple of Bellona,* a sparrow flew in, in plain view of everyone, with a cicada in its beak, dropped part of the cicada and left it there on the ground, and flew away with the rest. The diviners interpreted this as signifying conflict and dissent between the landowners and the common urban masses, on the grounds that the masses were noisy, like a cicada, while the landowners were rustic country folk.

[8] Marius joined forces with the tribune Sulpicius, a man whose consummate villainy was second to none.* Rather than asking whether there was anyone who displayed a greater lack of morality, people tended to ask under what circumstances he himself displayed a greater lack of morality than usual. He was brutal, presumptuous, and rapacious—and yet entirely untroubled by a sense of shame or wrong. After all, he sold Roman citizenship to the likes of freedmen and resident aliens, and blatantly counted out the price on a table set up in the forum. He maintained a troop of three thousand swordsmen and surrounded himself with a body of young knights who would stop at nothing, and whom he called the anti-senate. Although he got a law passed forbidding any senator from being more than two thousand drachmas in debt, after his death he left debts to the value of three hundred thousand drachmas. This is the man who was now let loose upon the Roman people by Marius. His violent and armed methods threw everything into chaos, and among the pernicious measures he proposed was one giving Marius command of the Mithridatic War. At this the consuls passed a decree suspending all public business,* but Sulpicius attacked them with a mob as they were holding an assembly by the temple of Castor and Pollux, and cut down large numbers of them in the forum, including the young son of the

consul Pompeius, although Pompeius himself managed to get away and escape. Sulla was chased to Marius' house* and was then forced to come out and rescind the decree suspending public business. Sulpicius therefore deprived Pompeius of his assigned command, but let Sulla keep his consulship, and did no more than transfer the expedition against Mithridates to Marius' command. He also lost no time in sending military tribunes to Nola to assume command of the army and take it to Marius.*

[9] Sulla escaped from Rome, however, and reached the camp before the tribunes got there. When his men found out what was going on they stoned the tribunes to death, whereupon Marius and his associates in Rome set about killing Sulla's friends and stealing their property in requital. People began to flee and change sides, with some making their way from camp to city, others from Rome to the camp. The senate was not its own master, but was governed by the commands of Marius and Sulpicius, and when it found out that Sulla was marching on Rome it sent two of the praetors, Brutus and Servilius, to order him to halt. They addressed Sulla rather too brusquely for the liking of his soldiers, who were quite prepared to kill them, but just broke their fasces, stripped them of their purple-bordered togas, and sent them on their way with insults ringing in their ears. Widespread gloom gripped Rome at the sight of them stripped of their praetorian insignia and reporting that there was now no way to prevent the conflict—that war was inevitable.*

While Marius was busy preparing for war, Sulla and his colleague took six legions, which were at full strength, and set out from Nola. Sulla was aware that his army wanted to move against Rome straight away, but he himself was undecided and thought it was still too dangerous an option.* However, after studying the omens indicated by the victims of a sacrificial offering Sulla had made, the diviner Postumius held out both his hands to Sulla and asked to be tied up and kept under guard until the battle. If the whole business was not over soon, he said, and in Sulla's favour, he was prepared to submit to any kind of punishment, even execution. There is also a story that Sulla himself had a dream in which he saw the goddess whom the Romans worship after learning about her from the Cappadocians, who may be Semele or Minerva or Bellona.* In the dream she came up to him and gave him a thunderbolt, with which she told him to strike his enemies, whom she named one by one, and as they were struck they fell and vanished. With his confidence restored by the vision, he told his colleague about it and the very next day continued on his way towards Rome.

At Pictae,* however, he was met by a delegation from Rome who asked him not to plunge straight into the attack, since the senate had voted that all his fair demands should be met. After promising to stay where he was, he ordered his officers to set about measuring out the ground for a camp as usual, and so the delegates returned believing that he was doing as they wished. But no sooner had they left than he sent Lucius Basilus and Gaius Mummius on a mission to seize the gate and the walls near the Esquiline hill,* and once they had done so for him he set out with all speed to join them. Basilus burst into the city and gained control of his objectives, but was prevented from advancing any further by a large crowd of unarmed people who pelted him from the roof-tops with tiles and stones and drove him back to the city wall. Before long, however, Sulla arrived. When he saw what was happening he shouted out that his men were to set fire to the houses, and he grabbed a burning torch and led the way forward himself. He also ordered his archers to use their inflammable arrows and to aim them at the roofs. He did not stop to think before issuing these commands, but in the heat of the moment he let anger dictate events: all he could see were his enemies, and he spared no thought or pity for friends and family and relations, but used fire as the agent of his return to Rome—fire, which made no distinction between the guilty and the innocent. Under these circumstances Marius fell back to the temple of the goddess Earth,* where by public proclamation he appealed for help to the slaves of Rome, offering them freedom in return. Overwhelmed by the enemy's advance, however, he was driven out of the city.*

[10] Sulla convened the senate and had the death sentence passed on Marius and a few others, including Sulpicius, the tribune. But Sulpicius was killed after being betrayed by a slave (whom Sulla first freed and then had hurled from the Tarpeian Rock), while Sulla set a price on Marius' head, which was both unfair and undiplomatic, given that he had been at Marius' mercy only a short while previously in his house and had been released unharmed. And yet if Marius had not let Sulla go then, but had handed him over to be killed by Sulpicius, he would have become the absolute ruler

of Rome. Despite this, he spared his life—only to meet with the opposite treatment a few days later when he offered his enemy the same opportunity. By behaving in this way Sulla antagonized the senate, although they did not show it, but the people made no secret of their hatred and indignation and showed it by their actions. For instance, when his nephew Nonius and Servilius were candidates for office they rejected them in a thoroughly humiliating fashion and elected instead people whose preferment they thought would particularly irritate him. But he pretended to be happy with the candidates they chose, arguing that in doing what they wanted the Roman people were making use of the freedom he had won them; and in order to appease the hatred of the masses he let a political opponent of his, Lucius Cinna, be elected consul,* although he first safeguarded his own policies by getting Cinna to swear an oath of loyalty towards them. Cinna went up into the Capitol and took the oath with a stone in his hand. He prayed that if he did not maintain his loyalty towards Sulla he would be cast out of the city as the stone was from his hand—and so saying he threw the stone on to the ground, in front of plenty of witnesses. But as soon as he assumed office he tried to institute a revolution, prepared a lawsuit against Sulla, and arranged for a tribune called Vergilius† to prosecute the case. Sulla, however, dismissed both Vergilius and the court from his mind and set out to fight Mithridates.*

[11] It is said that while Sulla was busy moving his forces out of Italy, Mithridates, who was in Pergamum at the time, was visited by a number of portents, including the following: a statue of crowned Victory, which the people of Pergamum were lowering by machine into place near Mithridates, broke just as it was almost grazing his head, and the crown fell off on to the ground in the theatre and shattered. Everyone trembled at the sight, and Mithridates became deeply depressed, even though at the time things were going better for him than he could have expected, since he had taken Asia from the Romans, and Bithynia and Cappadocia from their respective kings, and had now settled in Pergamum, where he was distributing fortunes and principalities and kingdoms to his friends.* Moreover, one of his sons was in undisturbed possession of the ancient empire in Pontus and Bosporus all the way up to the uninhabited lands beyond Lake Maeotis, and another son, Ariarathes, was in the process of attacking Thrace and Macedonia with a huge army in order

to try to win them over, while various other places were being subdued by the armies of his commanders. The greatest of these commanders of his was Archelaus: at sea (where his fleet had gained him virtually total mastery) he was in the process of enslaving the Cyclades and all the other islands east of Cape Malea, and had even occupied Euboea, and on land, from his base in Athens, he was encouraging all the peoples up to Thessaly to rebel against Rome. He had, however, received a slight setback at Chaeronea, where he encountered Braetius Sura, an exceptionally daring and intelligent man who was a legate of Sentius, the praetorian governor of Macedonia. Braetius successfully checked the flood of Archelaus' progress through Boeotia, and after fighting three battles with him near Chaeronea forced him back to the coast. However, Sulla was on his way and Lucius Lucullus ordered Braetius to make way for him—to leave the war to the man who had been put in charge of it by senatorial decree—so he left Boeotia straight away and marched back to Sentius, despite the fact that things were going better for him than he could have expected and that, thanks to his true goodness, Greece was inclining towards changing sides. But this was the climax of Braetius' career.*

[12] Sulla immediately gained control of most of the Greek cities, which sent envoys to him and appealed for his help, but Athens was forced by the tyrant Aristion to side with Mithridates, so Sulla brought his entire force to bear against it.* He surrounded Piraeus and began to besiege it, making use of every kind of siege-engine and trying every military means at his disposal in his attempt to take the place. If he had waited just a short time, however, he would have been able to take the upper city in complete safety, since they were already so short of provisions that they were completely desperate and near to starvation. But he was in a hurry to get back to Rome, since he was worried about the revolutionary changes that were going on there, so he forced the pace of the war by taking numerous risks, fighting many battles, and spending vast sums of money. For instance, even apart from all the rest of his equipment, the operation of the siege-engines required the deployment of ten thousand pairs of mules, which were used every day for just this job. And when he began to run out of wood, since most of the engines buckled under their own weight and broke down, or sustained fire damage under the constant hail of missiles from the enemy, he turned to the sacred

groves, and chopped down all the trees in the Academy (which was the most wooded of the city's parks) and the Lyceum.*

The vast amounts of money he also needed for the war led him to lay hands on the sacrosanct treasures of Greece, and he sent for the most beautiful and valuable offerings from both Epidaurus and Olympia. He wrote a letter to the Amphictyons at Delphi as well, in which he said that it would be better for the god's treasure to be sent to him, since he would either look after it more securely than they could, or, if he used it, would later repay them with goods of at least the same value.* He entrusted this letter to one of his friends, Caphis of Phocis, and told him to take note of the weight of each item he received. So Caphis went to Delphi, but he was reluctant to lay hands on the sacred treasures, and faced with the passionate pleas of the Amphictyons he burst into tears at the thought of what he had to do. Some people there said that they could hear the sound of a lyre playing in the shrine, and perhaps because he believed them, or perhaps because he wanted to make Sulla fear the gods, Caphis wrote and told him about it. But Sulla wrote a mocking letter in reply, expressing surprise that Caphis should fail to appreciate that singing was a sign of pleasure, not anger, and telling him therefore to go ahead and take the treasures without worrying, since the god was gladly offering them to him.

Most of the Greeks, at any rate, did not know about the removal of the bulk of the treasures, but the silver jar, which was all that was left of the royal gifts,* was too heavy and large for the yoke-animals to carry, and so the Amphictyons were forced to cut it up. As they did so they called to mind Titus Flamininus and Manius Acilius, the conquerors of the Macedonian kings, and Aemilius Paullus, who had driven Antiochus out of Greece.* Not only had they kept their hands off the Greek sanctuaries, but by their generosity had even considerably increased the prestige and dignity of the shrines.* But they had been the legally appointed commanders of troops who knew self-restraint and who had learnt to carry out their duties in silent obedience; they had been kingly characters who lacked expensive habits and so had kept their costs moderate and within their allowances, since they would have been more ashamed to pander to their troops' desires than to show fear of the enemy. The commanders of this later period, however, won their prominence by force rather than earning it by merit, and needed weaponry to fight one another rather than

Rome's enemies. They therefore had to be popular leaders as well as military commanders, and then, as a result of buying their troops' efforts with the money which they spent on their gratification, they gradually put a price tag on the whole country, and in order to gain authority over their betters they enslaved themselves to the worst elements of society. This was the trend that banished Marius and then brought him back again to combat Sulla; this was what made Cinna murder Octavius and Fimbria kill Flaccus.* And it was Sulla more than anyone else who started this trend, since in order to seduce and win over others' troops he squandered money on his own men. The combination of trying to seduce others into treachery and his own men into self-indulgence meant that he needed a great deal of money, and the siege of Athens was particularly costly.

[13] For Sulla was in the grip of a terrible, overwhelming desire to capture Athens, perhaps because he was driven by a kind of rivalry to pit himself against the shadow of the city's past glory, or perhaps because he was angry at the jokes and sarcastic comments which the tyrant Aristion occasionally used to taunt him, as he jeered at him and Metella from the city walls with his scornful remarks and the mocking dances he performed. Aristion's character was a compound of coarseness and brutality. He had allowed all that was worst and most rotten about Mithridates to pour into himself, and in these desperate times had latched like a fatal disease on to the city which had previously survived countless wars, and numerous tyrants and schisms. At a time when a medimnus of wheat cost a thousand drachmas in Athens, when people were subsisting on the feverfew which grew on the Acropolis and were boiling up and eating the leather from their shoes and oil-flasks, this man spent all his time partying and gadding about in broad daylight, dancing victory dances and making fun of his enemies. He did not care that the sacred lamp of the goddess had gone out through lack of oil, and when the high priestess asked him for a twelfth of a medimnus of wheat, he sent her that much pepper instead.* When members of the Council and the college of priests came and begged him to come to terms with Sulla out of pity for Athens, he scattered them with a volley of arrows. At last, when it was almost too late, he sent two or three of his drinking companions to sue for peace, but instead of coming up with any terms that might save the city they went on and on in a pompous vein about Theseus and Eumolpus and the Persian

Wars,* until Sulla said, 'Go away, sirs, and take these speeches of yours with you. I was not sent to Athens by the Romans to learn its history, but to subdue its rebels.'

[14] Shortly afterwards, it is said, Sulla was told about a conversation some old men were overheard having in Cerameicus, in the course of which they cursed the tyrant for failing to protect the approaches to the wall near the Heptachalcum, which made it the only place where it was still both possible and easy for the enemy to scale the walls. Sulla took the report seriously enough to go there at night, and when he saw that the place was vulnerable, he got right down to business. In his *Memoirs* Sulla himself tells how Marcus Ateius, who was the first to mount the wall, did not give way, but stayed put and stood his ground when his sword broke as he brought it down on the helmet of an enemy soldier who had confronted him. In any case, as aged Athenians used to recall, the city's fall began at that point.*

After demolishing and razing the wall between Piraeus and the Sacred Gates,* Sulla himself marched into the city at midnight. He was a figure to inspire terror, accompanied as he was by the blasts of numerous trumpets and horns, and the cries and shouts of his men, who now had his permission to turn to plunder and slaughter and were pouring through the streets with drawn swords. There was no telling how many people were slaughtered; even now people estimate the numbers by means of how much ground was covered with blood. Leaving aside those who were killed elsewhere in the city, the blood of the dead in the main square spread throughout the part of Cerameicus that lies on the city side of the Double Gate, and a lot is said to have flooded into the suburb outside the gates as well. But although huge numbers of people died like this at the hands of Sulla's soldiers, just as many killed themselves out of grief, unable to face the future without the city of their birth, which they were certain was going to be destroyed. The best men of Athens could see no point in staying alive and facing an uncertain future with their city lost, since they had no reason to hope for the slightest spark of human decency or moderation from Sulla. But partly because of the appeals of Midias and Calliphon, Athenian exiles who threw themselves on the ground at his feet, partly because all the senators who had accompanied him on the expedition begged him to have mercy, and also because he himself had drunk his fill of vengeance, after a few words in praise of the Athenians of old he told them that he would spare the few for the sake of the many, the living for the sake of the dead. By his own account in his *Memoirs* he took Athens on 1 March, a day which usually corresponds with the beginning of the month of Anthesterion, when, coincidentally, the people of Athens perform a number of rites in commemoration of the mayhem and destruction caused by the Flood, since they believe that it was round about then that the Deluge occurred.*

After the fall of Athens the tyrant held out for a long time on the Acropolis, where he had taken refuge and was being besieged by Curio, on Sulla's orders. Eventually, however, shortage of water forced him to surrender, and the gods lost no time in signifying their approval. For at precisely the time, on precisely the day, that Curio brought him down from the Acropolis, clouds suddenly gathered in a clear sky and there was such a heavy rainfall that the whole Acropolis was running with water. Not long after the fall of Athens Sulla also took Piraeus and put most of it to the torch, including the arsenal of Philo, which was an architectural masterpiece.*

[15] Meanwhile Mithridates' military commander, Taxiles, had moved south from Thrace and Macedonia with his army of 100,000 infantry, 10,000 cavalry, and 90 four-horse chariots equipped with scythes on their wheels. He asked Archelaus, whose fleet was still lying at anchor off Munychia,* to join him, but Archelaus had no intention of abandoning the sea and meeting the Romans in battle; his plan was to fight a gradual war of attrition and cut off their supplies. But Sulla outwitted Archelaus by moving his army to Boeotia, away from unfertile land which was too barren to support its inhabitants even in peacetime. It was widely held that he had made a mistake in exchanging the rough terrain of Attica, which was unsuitable for cavalry, for the plains and open terrain of Boeotia, when he could see that the invaders' main strength lay in their chariots and cavalry. But, as I have already said, if he was to escape starvation and shortage of supplies, he was compelled to seek out the risks of battle. Besides, he was also concerned about the fact that the invaders were guarding the passes and watching out for Hortensius, a sound tactician and a daring fighter, who was bringing Sulla an army of reinforcements from Thessaly.* These, then, were the reasons why Sulla moved his army to Boeotia.

Hortensius was saved by Caphis, a countryman of mine, who

sneaked him past the invaders by an alternative route, across Parnassus and down to a spot just below Tithora. In those days Tithora was not as large a town as it is today, but was no more than a stronghold cut into a sheer cliff. Once, a long time ago, it was used as a place of refuge by some Phocians, who saved themselves by packing up their belongings and retreating there in the face of Xerxes' invasion. This is where Hortensius took up his position, and after beating off an enemy attack in the daytime, with the help of the rough terrain, at night he brought his men down to Patronis and joined up with Sulla, who came to meet him with his army.*

[16] The combined forces occupied and pitched camp on the hill called Philoboeotus which rises in the middle of the plains of Elateia.* It has good, rich soil, is thickly wooded, and has a source of water at its foot; Sulla lavishes praise on its natural advantages and its position. The Roman army seemed to the enemy to be very small, since there were no more than 1,500 cavalrymen, and fewer than 15,000 foot soldiers, and so the other commanders overruled Archelaus and drew up their forces for battle, until there was nothing to be seen on the plain apart from horses, chariots, shields, and bucklers. The air was rent with the cries and shouts of all the different peoples as they formed their battle-lines, and at the same time the spectacular flamboyance of their costly equipment played a not unimportant part in creating a fearsome impression. In fact, as the ranks surged back and forth the flashing of their armour, which was magnificently embellished with gold and silver, and the colours of their Median and Scythian clothes mingling with gleaming bronze and iron, presented a radiant and formidable appearance. The upshot was that the Romans cowered behind their palisade, and since Sulla found it impossible to remove their fear by any rational argument, and did not want to force them into a fight from which they would be inclined to run away, he had to keep quiet and watch the foreigners taunting and mocking him—which only made him angry. However, his enforced inactivity was in fact more helpful to him than anything else. For even under normal conditions the enemy soldiers were inclined to disobey their leaders, since there were too many officers set over them, and now their contempt for the Romans made them relax all forms of discipline. Only a few of them remained in their camp, while the bulk of the army was enticed out by the prospect of plunder and booty, and ended up scattered several days' journey

away from the camp. They are said to have destroyed the town of Panopeus and to have sacked Lebadea and plundered the oracular shrine there, even though none of their commanding officers had given them the order to do so.*

It annoyed Sulla intensely to have towns destroyed before his eyes, and he did not let his men remain idle, but took them out and got them to divert the course of the Cephisus and dig ditches. None of them was allowed to rest, and he watched over them and mercilessly punished any shirkers, the idea being that once they had had enough of all the hard work these projects entailed they would welcome the danger of battle. And this is exactly what happened. After two days of work the soldiers called out to Sulla as he passed by and begged him to lead them against the enemy. He replied that their words showed only that they did not want to face hard work, not that they wanted to fight. If they were really feeling like a fight, he said, they should arm themselves and go over there—and he pointed to what had once been the acropolis of Parapotamii, but which was then, since the town had been destroyed,* just a rocky and precipitous hill. This hill was separated from Mount Hedylium by the breadth of the river Assus, which then joined the Cephisus at the very foot of the hill, so that the turbulence of the combined waters made the peak a secure place for a military camp. That is why, when he saw the enemy regiment called the Bronze Shields struggling towards the peak, Sulla wanted to get there before them and occupy it—and the wholehearted commitment of the men at his command meant that he did in fact succeed in occupying the place. As soon as he had been beaten off from there, Archelaus set out to attack Chaeronea. The Chaeroneans in Sulla's army begged him not to abandon the town, so he sent one of his military tribunes, a man called Gabinius, off there with a single legion. He also gave permission for the Chaeroneans to leave, but for all their determination they were unable to get there before Gabinius, which shows what an excellent soldier he was, and how he was more committed to saving the city than those who had asked for it to be saved. Juba, however, says that it was not Gabinius who was sent on this mission, but Erucius. Be that as it may, my native town had the narrowest of escapes from danger.*

[17] Favourable predictions and oracles suggesting victory began to reach the Romans from the shrine of Trophonius at Lebadea. The local inhabitants go into quite a bit of detail about these oracles, but

Sulla has personally described in the tenth book of his *Memoirs* how Quintus Titius, a prominent Roman businessman in Greece, came to him immediately after his victory at Chaeronea to tell him that Trophonius had foretold a second battle there within a few days, which he would also win.* And later an ordinary soldier called Salvenius brought him the god's predictions as to how events in Italy would turn out. Both these two men gave the same description of the god's appearance: they said that he was almost as attractive and as tall as Olympian Zeus.

Sulla now crossed the Assus, advanced to the foot of Hedylium, and established himself not far from Archelaus, who had built a strong camp between Acontium and Hedylium, close to the Assian plains, as they are generally known, although the place where he established his camp is even now called Archelaus after him. Two days later, leaving Murena* with a legion and two cohorts to make things difficult for the enemy if they made any attempt to form up for battle, Sulla first sacrificed by the Cephisus and then, when the omens were favourable, set out for Chaeronea, to pick up the army that was stationed there and to reconnoitre the place called Thurium which had already been occupied by the enemy. Thurium is the craggy, rounded high point of a range of hills we call Orthopagus, at the foot of which is the stream called Morius and a temple of Apollo Thurius. (The name 'Thurius' is derived from Thuro the mother of Chaeron, the legendary founder of Chaeronea, though there is also an alternative version which claims that Cadmus found a cow there, which had been given him by Apollo to be his guide, and—*thor* being the Phoenician word for 'cow'—that the place is named after this cow.*) As Sulla approached Chaeronea, the tribune who had been put in charge of the town led his men out to meet him, all armed and ready for battle, and greeted him with a garland of laurel. After accepting the garland Sulla gave a speech in which he welcomed the soldiers and motivated them for the coming battle. Then two Chaeroneans, Homoloïchus and Anaxidamus, obtained an audience with him and told him that if he gave them a few men they could cut off the troops who had occupied Thurium, since unknown to the invaders there was a path running from the place called Petrachus past the shrine of the Muses to a part of Thurium which was above the enemy position. If they took this path, they said, it would be a simple matter either to stone the enemy from above or fall on them and push them down on to the plain. Once Gabinius had vouched for the men's courage and loyalty, Sulla gave them the go-ahead. He then drew up his legionaries in line of battle and divided the cavalry between the two wings, taking the right wing himself and putting Murena in charge of the left. The legates, Galba and Hortensius, took the reserve cohorts and deployed them in the rear on the heights, to guard against the possibility of the enemy coming round behind them. For it was clear from the concentration of horsemen and nimble light-armed troops in the wing that the enemy were making it flexible and light enough to wheel around, and were planning to extend their line and outflank the Romans.*

[18] Meanwhile the Chaeroneans, who had been given Erucius as their leader by Sulla, had made their way round Thurium without being spotted. When they revealed themselves, the invaders were thrown into confusion and turned to flee. Most of the casualties were self-inflicted, however, and were a result of their rushing downhill rather than standing their ground, because as they did so they fell on their own spears and pushed one another off the edges of cliffs. And at the same time their opponents were attacking them from above and striking at the unprotected parts of their bodies. In the end, there were three thousand casualties at Thurium, while some of the fugitives were killed by Murena, who met them with his men already drawn up in battle formation and cut off their line of retreat, and others, after struggling towards their side's camp, reached their lines in such complete disarray that they infected most of the rest of the army with panic and confusion, and forced their commanders to slow down. This delay was particularly damaging, because Sulla promptly charged them while they were still in chaos, and the speed with which he narrowed the gap between the two armies meant that he deprived the scythe-bearing chariots of their effectiveness. This kind of chariot really comes into its own after covering a lot of ground and building up the speed and impetus required for breaking through enemy lines, but a short start makes them weak and ineffective, like missiles thrown without enough force. And this is exactly what happened to the invaders on the occasion in question. The first of their chariots picked up no speed as they were driven forward and made hardly any impact on the Roman lines. After beating them off, the Romans laughed and clapped and called for more, as if they were attending a chariot race in the Circus. Next the infantry forces

clashed. The foreigners held their pikes out in front of them and tried to preserve an unbroken line by locking their shields together, while the Romans immediately discarded their javelins and drew their swords to deflect the pikes and force a way through to the enemy as quickly as possible. The heat of their anger was increased when they saw that the front ranks of the enemy's forces consisted of fifteen thousand slaves, who had been freed by Mithridates' military commanders by public proclamation throughout the Greek cities, and then distributed among the regiments of heavy-armed troops. In fact, a Roman centurion is supposed to have said that the only other time he had seen slaves behaving with such freedom was during the Saturnalia.* Because of the depth and density of their lines, the Roman legionaries found it hard to repulse them, and they held their ground with extraordinary courage, but at last the constant hail of fire-bombs and javelins from the Romans in the rear ranks turned them back in disarray.

[19] Archelaus now extended his right wing to outflank the Romans, and Hortensius launched his cohorts at the double against this threat. But Archelaus quickly diverted two thousand cavalrymen under his personal command against Hortensius, who was driven back by sheer weight of numbers hard against the hills, and was gradually becoming separated from the main phalanx, with the enemy threatening to surround him. When Sulla found out what was happening, he hurriedly set out to help him from the right wing, which had not yet engaged the enemy. However, the dust-cloud raised by Sulla's men alerted Archelaus to what was going on, and he left Hortensius alone, wheeled his men round, and led them towards the Roman right wing, from which Sulla had just set out, hoping to find it leaderless. Just then Taxiles led the Bronze Shields into the attack against Murena, and with the din of battle coming from two directions, and the mountains re-echoing the cries, Sulla paused, uncertain which of the two parts of the battlefield needed his presence, but soon decided to resume his original position. He sent Hortensius with four cohorts to help Murena, while he hurried back to the right wing, ordering the fifth cohort to accompany him. The right wing was already proving a match for Archelaus on its own, but with the arrival of Sulla they thoroughly overwhelmed and overpowered the enemy, who fled headlong back towards the river and Mount Acontium with Sulla's men in hot pursuit. However, Sulla

did not forget the danger Murena was facing and he set off to help the troops in that part of the battlefield. But when he saw that they had already defeated Taxiles, he allowed himself to join in the pursuit.

Although the foreigners lost a great many men in the plain, the majority were cut down as they were making for their camp. In the end only ten thousand out of such a huge army managed to escape to Chalcis,* whereas according to Sulla only fourteen of his soldiers were missing, and two of these reappeared in the evening. That is why he inscribed on his victory trophies the names of Mars, Victory, and Venus, since he believed that his success was due as much to good fortune as to skill and military superiority. This trophy, commemorating the battle in the plain, stands by the stream called Molus, at the point where Archelaus' troops first gave way, but there is another one on the top of Thurium to commemorate the surrounding of the foreigners, with a Greek inscription naming Homoloïchus and Anaxidamus as the heroes of this manoeuvre.* Sulla celebrated the festival in honour of his victory in this battle in Thebes, and had a stage set up for the purpose near the spring of Oedipus. However, the dramas were judged by Greeks from other cities, who were invited to attend, since Sulla had an implacable hatred for the Thebans.* He also annexed half of their territory and dedicated it to Apollo and Zeus, with orders that some of the income from the land should be used towards reimbursing the gods for what he had taken from them.*

[20] After this, he heard that Flaccus, a political opponent of his, had been elected consul and was crossing the Ionian Sea with an army, ostensibly to fight Mithridates, but actually to be used against him.* He therefore set out for Thessaly to meet Flaccus. By the time he reached Meliteia,* however, reports were arriving from all quarters that behind him the land was again being devastated by another invading army, just as large as the previous one, since Dorylaeus had put in at Chalcis with a sizeable fleet, on which he had transported eighty thousand of the best trained and disciplined troops in Mithridates' army, and had immediately invaded and occupied Boeotia. Dorylaeus wanted to tempt Sulla to fight. He had no time for Archelaus' warnings and in fact spread a rumour around that treachery must have played a part in the earlier battle, otherwise so many thousands of men could not have lost their lives. Sulla lost little time

in turning his army round, however, and showing Dorylaeus that Archelaus was a man of intelligence who was well acquainted with Roman fighting skills. In fact, after a slight skirmish with Sulla at Tilphossium,* Dorylaeus argued more forcefully than anyone for the view that the war should not be decided on the battlefield, but that they should enlist the help of time and their financial resources to wear the enemy down. Nevertheless, Archelaus' confidence was raised a bit by the nature of the place near Orchomenus where they had made their camp, since there could be no better spot for people with cavalry superiority to engage an enemy force. There is no larger or more beautiful plain in Boeotia than this one, which spreads out in a level and treeless expanse from Orchomenus to the marshes where the river Melas is absorbed. The Melas rises near Orchomenus and is the only river in Greece which is deep and navigable from its source. Moreover, its volume increases at the time of the summer solstice, just like the Nile, and similar plants grow in it to those on the Nile, except that they do not bear fruit or grow to any great size. It is not a very long river, however: its course becomes lost after a very short time in choked and muddy lakes, and only a trickle joins the Cephisus, somewhere near the marshes where the reeds out of which musical pipes are made are supposed to grow.*

[21] Once the two armies had taken up their positions near each other, Archelaus let his men relax, but Sulla set about digging trenches on both sides of the enemy camp. His plan was to cut the enemy off from the hard ground where the going was good for horses, if he could, and force them into the boggy areas. However, the invaders could not let them get away with this, and as soon as they were given permission to go by their commanding officers, they charged out into the attack in large numbers. Not only were Sulla's labourers scattered, but most of the soldiers who had been deployed to protect them were also thrown into confusion as they fled.† At this Sulla himself leapt off his horse, grabbed a standard, and pushed his way through the fugitives into the ranks of the enemy, shouting as he went, 'Were I to die here, Romans, it would be a noble death; but as for you, when men ask you where you betrayed your commander, remember to tell them it was at Orchomenus.'

These words of his made the fugitives turn back to face the enemy, and when two cohorts from the right wing came to his assistance he led them in a charge and routed the enemy. Then he withdrew a short way and let his men eat their morning meal, before resuming his attempt to circumscribe the enemy camp with trenches. But the invaders attacked again, and this time with more discipline than before. Diogenes, Archelaus' stepson, distinguished himself in the battle and died a glorious death on the right wing, and the archers were too hard pressed by the Roman soldiers even to withdraw, so they used handfuls of arrows like swords as weapons with which to stab at the Romans at close quarters. Eventually the invaders were driven back and pinned inside their camp, where fear and their wounds made them spend a miserable night. The next day Sulla again brought his troops up to the camp and resumed work on the trenches. Most of the invaders came out to give him battle, but Sulla took them on and scattered them. This time they were too afraid to offer him any resistance, and he took their camp by storm. The marshes ran with the blood of the dead and the lake was choked with corpses. Even today, almost two hundred years after the battle, large numbers of foreign bows, helmets, bits of iron breastplates, and swords are found sticking out of the marshes.* Anyway, that is how the battles of Chaeronea and Orchomenus are said to have gone.

[22] In Rome the lawless thuggery with which Cinna and Carbo were treating the most eminent members of society was forcing a lot of them to flee this place of tyranny and make their way to the haven of Sulla's camp.* Before long, in fact, he was surrounded by what was to all intents and purposes a senate. Metella too just managed to steal away with her children, and she brought the news that his town house and country villas had been burnt down by his enemies. She begged him to come to the aid of those who were still in Rome. Sulla did not know what to do. On the one hand, he could not stand the thought of ignoring his fatherland in its time of trouble, but on the other hand he could not see how he could just go away and leave something as important as the Mithridatic War unfinished. While he was in this quandary, a merchant from Delos, called Archelaus, arrived with a secret message from Archelaus, the king's commander, which held out a certain amount of hope. This was such a relief for Sulla that he swiftly arranged a meeting with Archelaus. The meeting took place near Delium, at the place on the coast where the temple of Apollo is situated.* Archelaus spoke first and proposed that Sulla should forget about Asia and Pontus, and sail off to the war in Rome, with money and triremes and as many men as he

wanted from the king. At this point Sulla interrupted and suggested that Archelaus should leave Mithridates out of it—in fact, that he should usurp Mithridates' throne, after entering into an alliance with Rome and surrendering his fleet. When Archelaus professed his abhorrence of such an act of treachery, Sulla went on: 'So this is the situation, is it, Archelaus? Cappadocian that you are,* and the slave of a foreign king—or, as you would rather put it, his "friend"—you cannot abide the thought of disgrace even when such great benefits are attached to it, but you still have the effrontery to suggest treachery to me, Sulla, the commander of the Roman forces. You talk as if you were not the Archelaus who fled from Chaeronea with a tiny remnant of your 120,000-strong army, hid in the marshes of Orchomenus for two days, and left Boeotia clogged with the massed bodies of your dead.' At this Archelaus changed his tone to that of a humble suppliant, and begged Sulla to put an end to the war and come to terms with Mithridates. Sulla approved of this proposition and entered into an agreement, according to which Mithridates was to abandon Asia* and Paphlagonia, leave Bithynia to Nicomedes and Cappadocia to Ariobarzanes, pay an indemnity to Rome of two thousand talents, and hand over seventy bronze-beaked ships with all their proper fittings, while Sulla was to recognize Mithridates as the ruler of the rest of his empire and get him voted an ally of Rome.

[23] With this agreement in place, Sulla turned back and marched through Thessaly and Macedonia to the Hellespont, with Archelaus as an honoured companion. In fact, when Archelaus fell dangerously ill at Larissa, Sulla halted his troops and looked after him as well as if he had been one of the officers on his staff. This raised suspicions that there might have been some underhand dealings going on at the battle of Chaeronea, and these doubts were increased by the fact that Aristion the tyrant, who was on bad terms with Archelaus, was the only one of all the friends of Mithridates captured by Sulla that he did not release, but put to death (he had him poisoned). But the most suspicious things of all were the ten thousand plethra of land in Euboea granted to the Cappadocian, and the fact that thanks to Sulla he was enrolled among the friends and allies of Rome. At any rate, in his *Memoirs* Sulla argues that all these favours were perfectly innocent.

A delegation now arrived from Mithridates with the news that most of the terms of the agreement were acceptable, but that he insisted on keeping Paphlagonia and wanted the ships to be excluded from the agreement altogether. Sulla lost his temper and said, 'What? Mithridates wants to keep Paphlagonia and refuses to hand over the ships? I'd have thought he'd have come and prostrated himself before me in gratitude if I had just left him his right hand, with which he killed so many Romans. But he'll change his tune quickly enough once I've crossed over into Asia. At the moment all he's doing is sitting in Pergamum and suggesting strategies for a war he's never seen.'

The delegates were too frightened to say anything, but Archelaus pleaded with Sulla, took hold of his right hand, and, with tears in his eyes, tried to calm him down. Eventually, he persuaded Sulla to let him go to Mithridates himself by saying that he would either obtain peace on the terms Sulla wanted, or, if he failed to win Mithridates round, would kill himself. Under these circumstances, Sulla gave him permission to go, while he himself invaded Maedica, inflicted a very great deal of damage,* and then returned to Macedonia, where he received Archelaus at Philippi. Archelaus' news was that all was well, but that Mithridates urgently wanted to meet him. This was chiefly due to Fimbria: after doing away with Flaccus, the commander from the opposing faction, he had defeated Mithridates' generals and was now marching against the king himself. Mithridates did not like this turn of events at all, and saw his best option as getting on good terms with Sulla.*

[24] The meeting took place at Dardanus in the Troad.* Mithridates brought there with him a fleet of 200 oared ships and from his land forces 20,000 heavy-armed infantry, 6,000 cavalry, and a lot of scythe-bearing chariots, while Sulla had four cohorts* and 200 cavalrymen. Mithridates came up to Sulla and held out his right hand in friendship, whereupon Sulla asked him if he would put an end to the war on the terms to which Archelaus had agreed. The king made no reply, so Sulla said, 'Surely it is up to those who need a favour to speak first. It is the victors who can be content with silence.' Mithridates then began to try to exonerate himself, by arguing that the war was partly due to the gods and partly the responsibility of the Romans themselves. At this point Sulla interrupted him and said that he had been told a while ago about Mithridates' skills as an orator, and could now see for himself that his informants were

right, since Mithridates had found no difficulty in coming up with plausible arguments to gloss over such terrible crimes. Then, after a savage denunciation and condemnation of Mithridates' actions, he asked him again whether he would abide by the contract entered into by Archelaus, and this time Mithridates said that he would. Sulla greeted his words with an embrace and a kiss. Later he brought Ariobarzanes and Nicomedes in, and brokered an agreement between these two kings and Mithridates. After handing over seventy ships and five hundred archers, Mithridates sailed back to Pontus. Sulla was aware that the treaty had made his troops very unhappy. There was no king they detested more, and they found it very hard to see the man who had arranged for the massacre of 150,000 Romans in Asia on a single day* sailing away from Asia with his valuables and his booty intact, after four solid years of plundering and taxing the country. But Sulla defended his actions to them by explaining that he would have found it impossible to take on both Fimbria and Mithridates at once, if they had joined forces against him.

[25] Sulla next left the Troad and encamped close to where Fimbria had pitched his camp, which was near Thyateira.* He dug a trench around the enemy camp, but Fimbria's soldiers emerged from it unarmed, greeted Sulla's men, and began to help them in their labours. Faced with this mass desertion, and terrified of Sulla's implacable hostility towards him, Fimbria committed suicide in his camp.*

In the public domain, Sulla imposed a fine on Asia of twenty thousand talents, and in the private domain he utterly ruined whole households by the abusive and greedy behaviour of the men billeted on them. For the instructions were that every day the host should give his guest four tetradrachms and should lay on an evening meal for him and for however many of his friends he wished to invite; and if the person billeted there was an officer, he was to be given fifty drachmas a day and two sets of clothing, one to wear at home and the other for when he went into town.

[26] He put to sea with his whole fleet from Ephesus, and two days later landed in Piraeus. After being initiated into the mysteries,* he appropriated for himself the library of Apellicon of Teos, which included most of the works of Aristotle and Theophrastus (which were at that time still largely unknown).* It is said that after the

library had been taken to Rome, the scholar Tyrannion prepared most of the books for publication, and that Andronicus of Rhodes was supplied with copies by him, published the books, and also wrote down the catalogues which are now in circulation.* The older Peripatetics certainly seem to have been accomplished and scholarly men in their own right, but they had not read many of Aristotle's and Theophrastus' works, and those they had read were inaccurate copies,† because the estate of Neleus of Scepsis (to whom Theophrastus bequeathed his books) devolved on to people who were careless and uneducated.*

While Sulla was in Athens, his feet were afflicted by a tingling pain and a feeling of heaviness, which Strabo says indicates incipient gout. He therefore sailed across to Aedepsus and availed himself of the hot springs there, while relaxing at the same time and spending time with craftsmen in the arts sacred to Dionysus.* One day, when he was walking by the sea, some fishermen brought him some excellent fish. He was very pleased with the gift and when he found out that they were from Halae he said, 'Are there really still people from Halae alive?' The point is that during his pursuit of the enemy after his victory in the battle of Orchomenus, he destroyed three Boeotian towns—Anthedon, Darymna, and Halae. The men were speechless with fear, but he smiled, gave them permission to leave, and told them not to worry, since they had come with such outstanding mediators, the kind that had to be taken seriously. The people of Halae say that it was as a result of this incident that they summoned up the courage to repopulate their town.*

[27] Sulla went down to the coast via Thessaly and Macedonia and got ready to cross over from Dyrrhachium to Brundisium with a fleet of twelve hundred ships.* Not far from Dyrrhachium is Apollonia, and near Apollonia is the Nymphaeum, a sacred place whose green dell and meadows here and there emit streams of ever-flowing fire. There is a story that a satyr was caught while sleeping in the Nymphaeum. He looked just like the portraits of satyrs made by sculptors and artists, and when he was brought to Sulla translators tried to ask him about himself in a number of different languages. At last the satyr spoke, but it was a harsh and incomprehensible sound, a cross between the neighing of a horse and the bleating of a goat. In horror, Sulla ordered the thing to be taken away out of his sight.*

His troops were all ready to be transported across to Italy, but

Sulla was afraid that they might disband and return to their various home towns once they landed there. In the first place, however, they voluntarily swore an oath that they would stay with him and would wait for his orders before doing any harm to Italy; and then, when they realized how desperately short of funds he was, they each contributed a proportion of their own money, according to their means. Sulla thanked them, but refused to accept the offer, and after rousing their morale the crossing began—a crossing which, as he himself says, was taking him to face fifteen hostile commanders with four hundred and fifty cohorts.* But the god gave him unmistakable indications of future good fortune. For instance, as soon as he had crossed over to Tarentum he offered up a sacrifice, and the lobe of the victim's liver was found to be shaped like a garland of laurel with two ribbons hanging off it.* Or again, not long before the crossing, for several days in succession† people in Campania, near Tifata, saw two huge armies fighting and giving a perfectly realistic demonstration of all that people do and experience in a battle. But this turned out to be an apparition, which gradually rose up off the ground and dispersed like insubstantial phantoms here and there in the air before vanishing. And this was the very spot where not long afterwards Sulla was attacked in force by the combined armies of the younger Marius and Norbanus the consul, and without getting his troops to form up in their battle-lines or separate into companies, but merely by taking advantage of the intensity of commitment that gripped his whole army and the force of their courage, he overpowered the enemy, inflicted seven thousand casualties on them, and trapped Norbanus inside the city of Capua.* This victory, he says, was the reason why instead of dispersing to their various home towns, his soldiers remained together and felt nothing but contempt for the enemy, despite the fact that they were heavily outnumbered. As a third example, Sulla says that in Silvium a slave belonging to Pontius obtained an audience with him, went into a trance, and said that he brought from Bellona assurances of military success and victory, but added that he would have to hurry, otherwise he would find that the Capitol had been burnt. And this actually happened, Sulla says, on the day the man foretold—on the sixth day of Quintilis, or July as it is now known.* Fourthly, Marcus Lucullus, who was one of Sulla's commanders, had sixteen cohorts drawn up ready for battle opposite fifty enemy cohorts at Fidentia, and although he felt confident about his men's commitment, most of them were unarmed and so he was reluctant to join battle. He held back, while wondering what it would be best for him to do, and as he did so a gentle breeze blew from the direction of the nearby plain with its meadows. On the breeze came a lot of flowers, which landed of their own accord like scattered seeds on his men, and stayed and ringed their shields and helmets, so that they looked to the enemy as though they were wearing victory garlands. They engaged the enemy with their morale raised even higher because of this incident, won the battle, killed eighteen thousand of the enemy, and captured their encampment. This Lucullus was the brother of Lucius Lucullus who subsequently defeated Mithridates and Tigranes.*

[28] However, Sulla found himself still surrounded on all sides by enemies with large armies and considerable resources at their disposal, so he employed guile as well as force in order to keep himself safe. What he did was hold out the prospect of a peace agreement to Scipio, the other consul. Scipio welcomed the idea, and several meetings and discussions took place, but Sulla kept prevaricating and making excuses, while he got his men to try to suborn Scipio's troops. His men proved themselves the equal of their leader in expertise at every kind of deception and illusion: once they were inside the enemy camp and could mingle with Scipio's soldiers, they wasted no time in winning them over to Sulla's side by bribery or promises or persuasion laced with flattery. The upshot was that when Sulla approached the camp with twenty cohorts his men greeted Scipio's, and Scipio's men returned the greeting and went over to them. Deserted by his men, Scipio was abandoned in his tent and left to his own devices, while Sulla, who had used his twenty cohorts as a hunter uses domestic birds, as a decoy to trap the forty enemy cohorts, took all sixty back to his camp.* This was also the occasion when Carbo is supposed to have said that Sulla had a fox and a lion living in his mind, and that in fighting the man he found the fox more troublesome.*

Next Marius, with eighty-five cohorts, challenged Sulla to battle at Signia.* Now, Sulla was in fact very keen to have the issue decided that day, because of a dream in which he dreamt that the elder Marius (who had died many years earlier) warned his son to beware of the following day, since it would bring him great misfortune. This made Sulla face the prospect of battle with confidence, and he was trying to get Dolabella, who was encamped some way off, to join him, but the roads were held and closed by the enemy, and Sulla's men were tired of fighting to try to open them up. Then they were caught in the middle of their operations in a heavy fall of rain, which made them feel even worse. The officers came to Sulla to ask him to put off the battle, and pointed out how exhausted the men were by their exertions and how they had leaned their shields on the ground and were propping themselves up on them. He reluctantly agreed and gave the order to pitch camp, but just as they were beginning to construct a palisade and dig a ditch in front of the site, Marius rode confidently up, expecting to scatter Sulla's men while they were in this disordered and confused state. And now the gods began to fulfil the statement Sulla had heard in his dream, as the anger he felt communicated itself to his men. They stopped what they were doing, planted their javelins in the ditch, drew their swords, and with a yell hurled themselves at the enemy. Before long Marius' men fell back, and in the ensuing rout huge numbers of them were killed. Marius fled to Praeneste, where he found the gates already closed, but when a rope was let down for him, he tied it around his waist and was hauled up the wall. Others, however, including Fenestella,* say that Marius did not even know that the battle was taking place—that he needed so badly to catch up on lost sleep and recover from exhaustion that he lay down on the ground in a shady spot and succumbed to sleep just as the signal for battle was given, and was then only just woken up during the rout. Sulla says that he lost only twenty-three men in this battle, while killing twenty thousand of the enemy and taking eight thousand prisoners. He was just as fortunate elsewhere through the agency of his generals—Pompey, Crassus, Metellus, and Servilius—who suffered almost no setbacks as they annihilated huge enemy forces. Eventually, Carbo, the main focus of the opposing party, ran away one night from his army and sailed off to Africa.*

[29] In the final battle, however, Telesinus the Samnite, like a fresh wrestler who takes on an exhausted opponent, came close to throwing Sulla and giving him a fall at the gates of Rome. Along with Lamponius the Lucanian he had gathered together a sizeable army and hurried to relieve Marius, who was besieged in Praeneste, but he found himself squeezed to the front and rear, with Sulla racing to meet him head on and Pompey closing in behind him. He

was a pugnacious warrior, however, seasoned by many major battles, and he broke camp under cover of darkness and marched with his whole army on Rome itself. He came very close to finding it unprotected. He pitched camp close to the city, only ten stades from the Colline Gate, filled with pride at having outmanoeuvred so many excellent commanders and facing the future with confidence.* At daybreak the pick of the young men of Rome rode out to meet him, and he struck them down. Among the many casualties was Appius Claudius, a brave man from an excellent family. There was, of course, turmoil in the city, with women shrieking and people running to and fro in expectation of being overrun. Then the first of Sulla's forces showed up, seven hundred horsemen under the command of Balbus riding up at speed. Balbus waited just long enough for the horses' sweat to dry, then† bridled them again and hastened to engage the enemy. Meanwhile, Sulla's forces began to appear as well. He lost no time in ordering his vanguard to eat their morning meal, and then proceeded to deploy them for battle. Dolabella and Torquatus* repeatedly asked him to wait and not risk all with troops who were already exhausted, and reminded him that the battle would not be against Carbo and Marius, but the Samnites and Lucanians, implacable enemies of Rome who were highly skilled at warfare. But Sulla rejected their pleas and, although it was by now getting late in the afternoon, he ordered the trumpets to sound the signal for the advance to begin.

The battle that followed was the toughest of the whole campaign. The right wing, where Crassus was posted,* had a clear advantage, but the left wing was struggling and suffering badly, and so Sulla came to its help, riding a spirited and swift white charger. Two of the enemy recognized him by this horse and drew back their spears to throw them. Although Sulla himself did not notice them doing this, his groom lashed the horse and it just got out of the way by the narrowest of margins: the spears came down and stuck in the ground right by the horse's tail. Now, Sulla apparently always used to carry around with him during battles, in the folds of his clothes, a golden statuette of Apollo from Delphi, but there is a story that on this occasion he kissed it and said, 'Pythian Apollo, in battle after battle you have granted success to Cornelius Sulla, the Fortunate, and raised him to greatness: are you now going to hurl him to the ground after bringing him to the doorway of his homeland, and let him die a degrading death along with his fellow citizens?' After he had called on the god with these words, it is said that he did the rounds of his men: some he begged, others he threatened, and still others felt the touch of his hand, but in the end his left wing was shattered and he retreated among the rest of the fugitives to the safety of his camp.

The casualties included many of his friends and acquaintances, and quite a few of those who had emerged from Rome to watch the battle had also been killed and trampled underfoot. In fact, it was widely believed that the city was lost and that it would not take much for the siege of Marius to be lifted. A lot of the survivors of the rout made their way to Praeneste and advised Lucretius Ofella, who had been left in charge of the siege, to break camp as soon as he possibly could, since Sulla was dead and Rome had fallen to the enemy.*

[30] In the middle of the night, however, men arrived at Sulla's camp who had been sent by Crassus to fetch food for him and his troops, since after defeating the enemy he had chased them inside the town of Antemnae and was now encamped there.* Under these circumstances, and since he now knew that most of the enemy army had been wiped out, Sulla moved his troops at daybreak to Antemnae. A delegation representing three thousand of the men pinned inside the town came to sue for peace, and he guaranteed the safety of the three thousand provided they hurt the rest in some way before coming over to him. They took him at his word and attacked the others, which resulted in a terrible massacre as the two sides fought it out. But despite their help Sulla herded both them and the survivors of the other side, about six thousand men in all, into the Circus, and then called a meeting of the senate at the sanctuary of Bellona.* At precisely the same time that he began to address the senate, picked men began to butcher the six thousand prisoners. As was only to be expected, the screams of so many men being slaughtered in a confined space reached the ears of the senators and filled them with fear, but Sulla continued speaking with the same unmoved, calm expression on his face as before, and told them to listen to what he was saying and not pay any attention to what was going on outside, which was just some criminals being punished on his orders.

As a result of this even the densest person in Rome came to understand that they had merely exchanged one monstrous tyranny for another, not escaped tyranny altogether. Marius had always been cruel, and power had only intensified, not altered his character. Sulla, however, had at first enjoyed his good fortune in a moderate and statesmanlike manner, and people had come to expect that as a leader he would combine aristocratic principles with concern for the interests of the general populace.* Besides, from his youth onwards he had shown that he had a good sense of humour and could readily sympathize with others, so much so that he was prone to burst into tears. Naturally, then, his conduct brought discredit on positions of great power, on the grounds that they made it impossible for people to retain their original characteristics, but were bound to make them capricious, vain, and cruel instead.* However, whether a person's change of circumstances causes an actual change and alteration in his nature, or whether power allows evil tendencies that had previously lain hidden to emerge, is a question that would more properly be settled by another treatise.

[31] With Sulla engaged on the business of butchery and filling the city with more murders than anyone could count or determine, a great many people also lost their lives as the result of private feuds. These were people who had nothing to do with Sulla, but he let their murders go ahead to gratify his supporters. At last one of the young men of the city, Gaius Metellus,* had the courage to ask Sulla in the senate when these evils were going to end and how much further they could expect him to go before these events were finished with. 'We are not asking you to absolve from punishment those you have decided to kill,' he said, 'but to absolve from uncertainty those you have decided to keep alive.' Sulla replied that he did not yet know whom he was going to spare, whereupon Metellus said, 'In that case, tell us whom you are planning to punish'—and Sulla agreed to do so! Some people, however, attribute this last saying to one of Sulla's fawning followers, a man called Fufidius, rather than to Metellus. Be that as it may, before long Sulla proscribed eighty men,* without first discussing his plans with any of those who held positions of authority. Despite the general outrage this provoked, a day later he proscribed another 220 people, and then the next day the same number again. He stated in a public speech on the matter that he was proscribing everyone who came to mind, and that if there were people he forgot about for the time being, he would get around to proscribing them later. He also proscribed anyone who sheltered and saved the life of a proscribed person, and set death as the penalty for

such an act of kindness. Not even brothers, sons, or parents were exempt from this ruling. On the other hand, anyone who killed a proscribed person was to receive two talents as his reward for this act of murder, even if it was a slave who killed his master, or a son his father. But the harshest measure of all, to people's minds, was that he disenfranchised the sons and grandsons of those who had been proscribed, and all of them had their property confiscated. Lists of proscribed people were posted not only in Rome, but in every city in Italy. There was nowhere that remained free from the stain of bloodshed—no god's temple, no guest-friend's hearth, no family home. Husbands were butchered in the arms of their wives, sons in the arms of their mothers.* Only a tiny proportion of the dead were killed because they had angered or made an enemy of someone; far more were killed for their property, and even the executioners tended to say that this man was killed by his large house, this one by his garden, that one by his warm springs. Quintus Aurelius, a man who had never played any part in public life, thought that the sympathy he felt for others' misfortunes would be the only effect the troubles would have on him. One day he went to the forum and read the list of proscribed men. Finding his own name there, he said, 'Alas, I am undone! My Alban estate wants to see me dead.' And before he had gone much further he was murdered by someone who had been following him.

[32] Meanwhile, Marius had committed suicide just as he was about to be captured.* Sulla went to Praeneste, and at first he gave every man his own individual trial before punishing him, but then found that this was taking too long, so he herded them all together into one place, all twelve thousand of them, and gave orders that they were to be butchered. The only one he granted immunity was his guest-friend, but in an act of great nobility this man told Sulla that he refused, now or at any time in the future, to be obliged for his life to the murderer of his home town, and of his own accord he went to join his fellow citizens and was killed along with them. But the most shocking episode, by common consent, was the one involving Lucius Catilina. He had murdered his brother while the conflict was still in progress, and now he asked Sulla to proscribe the man as if he were still alive. Sulla did so, and Catilina paid Sulla back for the favour by killing a political opponent of his called Marcus Marius. After bringing his head to him as he was sitting in the forum, he went to

the nearby stoup in front of the temple of Apollo and rinsed his hands.*

[33] Leaving aside all the carnage, everything else he did fuelled people's indignation as well. For instance, he revived a type of office that had not been used for 120 years and proclaimed himself dictator.* And a decree was passed giving him immunity from all his past deeds and for the future the power to condemn people to death, to confiscate property, found colonies, raze towns, and overthrow kings at whim. He managed the sale of confiscated estates from a chair on the rostra in such an arrogant and tyrannical manner that his gifts came to arouse more abhorrence than his thefts. The territories of whole peoples and the revenues of cities were given to women for their beauty, to transvestite singers, actors, and the worst kind of freed slaves, and women were sometimes forced against their wills to marry his favourites. At any rate, when he wanted to bring Pompey the Great into his fold, he ordered him to divorce his wife and instead marry Aemilia (the daughter of Scaurus and his own wife Metella), whom he forced to leave Manius Glabrio, despite the fact that she was pregnant. Later, the young woman died in childbirth in Pompey's house.* Then again, Sulla first tried to block the attempt of Lucretius Ofella, the man who was responsible for defeating Marius in the siege of Praeneste,* to present himself as a candidate for the consulship, but when Ofella came into the forum with a crowd of enthusiastic supporters, Sulla had one of the centurions in his retinue kill the man, while he sat on the rostra in the temple of Castor and watched the murder taking place below. People seized hold of the centurion and brought him before the rostra, but Sulla told them to stop making such a fuss, admitted that he had ordered the killing, and commanded them to release the centurion.*

[34] His triumph, however, which was impressive enough just because of the value of the Mithridatic spoils and their unusual nature, was greatly enhanced and made an even more striking spectacle by the exiles.* Romans of the utmost eminence and power followed in his train, wearing garlands on their heads and calling on Sulla as their saviour and father, since without him they would never have been able to return to their homeland with their children and wives. When the ceremony was over he gave an account of his achievements to the assembled people and in listing them he laid just as much stress on instances of good fortune as he did on instances of

bravery. In conclusion, he said that in view of his achievements he should be given the surname 'Fortunate', which is pretty much what the word *Felix* means. However, in his letters and dealings with Greeks he used to call himself 'Epaphroditus', 'the favourite of Aphrodite', and on his trophies here in Greece his name is inscribed as 'Lucius Cornelius Sulla Epaphroditus'. And when Metella gave birth to twins, he called the boy Faustus and the girl Fausta—*faustum* being the Roman word for something fortunate and festive.

He was, in fact, so confident that his good fortune outweighed his actions that, despite all the huge numbers of men who had been killed by him, and despite the enormity of the reforms and changes he had made to Roman political life, he laid down his dictatorship and restored the people's right to elect consuls.* He did not put himself forward during these elections, but walked around in the forum, as open as any other private citizen to anyone who wanted to call him to account for what he had done. Contrary to his wishes, however, a dangerous man and an enemy of his, Marcus Lepidus, looked likely to be elected consul, not on his own merits, but because the people were prepared to gratify Pompey, who had supported Lepidus' candidacy and canvassed on his behalf. So when Sulla saw Pompey leaving the forum flushed with victory, he called him over and said, 'An outstanding piece of politics, young man! You've elected Lepidus, the most capricious man in Rome, with more votes than that paragon of virtue, Catulus. But you'd better not be caught napping, now that you've created a stronger rival for yourself.' There was something prophetic about this remark of Sulla's, because before long Lepidus got violently out of control and made war on Pompey.*

[35] As a way of giving up a tenth of all his property as an offering to Heracles,* Sulla arranged extravagant feasts for the Roman people. Supplies so far outstripped demand that every day vast quantities of savoury dishes were thrown into the river. The wine they drank was never less than forty years old. The celebrations lasted for many days, and in the middle of them Metella was taken fatally ill. The priests would not allow Sulla to go near her and reminded him that his house could not be polluted by a funeral,* so he sent her official notice of divorce and ordered her to move to another house while she was still alive. In this respect, then, he did exactly what the law prescribed, out of fear of the gods, but he spared no expense on her

funeral, and so broke the law he himself had introduced earlier, which restricted the cost of funerals.* He also contravened his own regulations limiting the cost of entertaining, as he tried to drown his grief in drinking and banqueting parties where extravagance and crude humour were the order of the day.

A few months later there was a gladiatorial show. Now, in those days men and women could still mingle in the theatres and were not segregated into different areas,* and there happened to be sitting near Sulla a good-looking, high-born woman called Valeria, who was the daughter of Messala and sister of the orator Hortensius. Coincidentally, she had just been divorced from her husband. As she walked past Sulla, on the row behind him, she rested her hand on him and pulled a piece of fluff off his toga, before carrying on to her own seat. Sulla looked at her in surprise, and she said, 'Don't worry, Imperator.* I just want to have a little bit of your good fortune for myself.' Sulla liked her remark, and was clearly intrigued, since he sent someone off to make discreet enquiries about who she was, and he tried to find out what family she was from and what kind of a life she had lived. After this they kept glancing at each other and were constantly turning their heads to look at each other and exchanging smiles. In the end, they became formally betrothed, which was perhaps innocent on her part, but however pure and respectable she might have been, Sulla's motives in marrying her were not pure and virtuous: he proved as vulnerable as a young man to good looks and a flirtatious manner, which tend to provoke the most disgraceful and shameless kinds of feelings.*

[36] However, despite having her as his wife at home, he still consorted with actresses, female lyre-players, and theatrical people, and would lie drinking with them on couches all day long. The people who had the most influence with him at this time were the actors Roscius (who played comic roles), Sorex (who played leading men), and Metrobius (who specialized in camp transvestite roles).* Although Metrobius was past the age of youthful bloom, Sulla remained to the end of his life in love with him, and made no secret of the fact. This dissipated lifestyle aggravated the ailment he was suffering from, which originally had such slight symptoms that for a long time he was unaware that he had an intestinal ulcer. The affliction caused all his flesh to rot and to change into lice—to change so rapidly that although teams of people were employed day and night

in picking them off him, the ever-increasing numbers made what they removed totally insignificant. Gradually the flux and corruption spread so much that it infected all his clothes, his bath and basin, and his food. Sulla therefore used to take a bath several times a day, and thoroughly wash and scrub his body, but it was no good. The change was too quick to be brought under control, and there were too many lice to be killed off by any amount of washing.*

It is said that in ancient times Acastus the son of Pelias died like this from phthiriasis, and that later so did Alcman the lyric poet, Pherecydes, who wrote about the gods, Callisthenes of Olynthus, while he was being kept under close guard in prison, and also Mucius the jurist. And, to mention a man who is infamous rather than famous for any good qualities, we hear that Eunus, the leader of the Servile War in Sicily, was brought to Rome after his capture and died there of phthiriasis.*

[37] Not only did Sulla foresee his own death, but in a sense he wrote about it too. He stopped writing the twenty-second book of his *Memoirs* two days before his death, and he says that the Chaldeans had told him that he would die, after a glorious life, when he was at the height of his good fortune. He also says that he had a dream in which his son, who had died shortly before Metella, came up to him, dressed in shabby clothes, and said, 'Father, why don't you lay aside your cares? Come with me to my mother Metella, and live with her a peaceful life of inactivity.' However, he did not put an end to his political activities. Ten days before his death, after getting the rival parties in Dicaearchia to make peace with each other, he drafted a new constitution for them.* And on the day before he died, when he found out that Granius, the mayor of Dicaearchia, owed the town some money, but was waiting for Sulla to die so that he could avoid paying the debt, he called the man into his room, surrounded him with his slaves, and told them to strangle him. But in doing so he strained his voice and his body, which caused the ulcer to burst, and he lost a great deal of blood. He became extremely weak and died the next day, after passing a miserable night. He was survived by two young children, borne him by Metella; it was only after his death that Valeria gave birth to a daughter, who was called Postuma—the traditional Roman name for children born after their father's death.

[38] A lot of people formed a coalition with Lepidus for the purpose of preventing Sulla's corpse from receiving the normal

funeral arrangements,* but Pompey laid aside the grudge he held against Sulla for mentioning all his friends except him in his will and changed their minds, partly by begging them to do so as a favour to him, and partly by threatening them. Then he brought the body to Rome and saw that it received a safe and honourable burial. It is said that the women of Rome brought such a large quantity of spices for the body that it took 210 litters to carry it all in the procession, and there was still enough good-quality frankincense and cinnamon left over to make a fair-sized image of Sulla himself, and another of a lictor.* Since the day started overcast with the prospect of rain, the corpse was not laid on the pyre until the middle of the afternoon, but then a strong wind howled down on the pyre and whipped the flames up to a considerable height. There was only just enough time, with the pyre still smouldering and the flames dying down, to collect the remains of the body before rain began to pour down and washed out the rest of the day. This made it look as though Sulla's Fortune was still with him, and played a part in the funeral.* His monument stands in the Campus Martius. They say that he drafted the inscription himself and left instructions about what was to be written on the monument, the gist of which is that no one ever did more good than he to his friends, or more harm to his enemies.*

POMPEY

INTRODUCTION

Pompeius Magnus—Pompey the Great—earned his name early, thanks to his brilliant organization, tactical skill, and initiative. His three triumphs celebrated victories on three continents, and the wealth and popularity that they brought him set him above most of the Roman senate like an oak over shrubs. His military success as a youth, and the extent of his conquests, recalled Alexander the Great. His defeat by Julius Caesar in one great battle, leaving him abandoned and vulnerable, seemed inexplicable, the stroke of some capricious fortune. Plutarch, in his longest and perhaps most ambitious life, shapes a portrait and searches for an explanation: what was it in the man which brought him to such greatness, and left him so vulnerable? As regularly, he does not look at larger trends outside his protagonist, but examines the man's interaction with those around him, the facets of character and choice which made him what he was, and perhaps can give the reader insight into a great man.

Sulla had tried to set the senate back on its feet, strengthening it and weakening the tribunes of the people whom he held responsible for bringing down the system. But he could not attack underlying causes, and within ten years the tribunate had regained its old strength, and the senate was showing itself as unable as before to govern the empire. Out of Sulla's shadow emerged ambitious men, the last generation of the republic, whose struggles for power and fame would destroy the state. Plutarch undertook to write the Lives of the most important: Caesar, Pompey, Crassus, Lucullus, Cicero, the younger Cato, Brutus, and Antony, pairing each with a Greek statesman.[1] *Pompey* and *Caesar*, along with four others,[2] seem to have been composed at roughly the same time, using many of the same sources.[3] The two Lives complement each other. Each man had to be first in their society, and would rather die than take second place.

Plutarch chose to pair Pompey with King Agesilaus of Sparta,[4] not

[1] Respectively, Alexander, Agesilaus, Nicias, Cimon, Phocion, Demetrius, and Demosthenes. All but two, Nicias and Cimon, are chosen from the fourth century.

[2] *Crassus*, *Cato*, *Brutus*, and *Antony*.

[3] C. B. R. Pelling, 'Plutarch's Method of Work in the Roman Lives', *Journal of Hellenic Studies*, 99 (1979), 74–96; repr. in B. Scardigli (ed.), *Essays on Plutarch's Lives* (Oxford: Clarendon Press, 1995), 265–318, with 'Postscript (1994)'.

[4] Cf. the *Life of Agesilaus* in *Plutarch: Greek Lives* (Oxford: Oxford University Press, Oxford World's Classics, 1998).

perhaps the most obvious parallel: Pompey himself would have preferred Alexander, but Plutarch destined *him* for Caesar. Agesilaus too led an expedition to Asia Minor, fought innumerable battles, helped his city survive crises, and finally died in Egypt. Although, unlike Pompey, he came to power late, like Pompey his career once he became king had a brilliant beginning, then did not fulfil its promise. Plutarch's Agesilaus is charming, friendly, and ruthlessly ambitious. He supports his friends even when they are in the wrong, and finally forces the showdown with Thebes and its leader Epaminondas which lost Sparta half its territory and destroyed its hopes to dominate Greece. Minor parallels in *Pompey* recall *Agesilaus*, such as his burning of Perperna's letters (c. 20), as Agesilaus did Lysander's plans, his calculated insults to Lucullus (31), similar to Agesilaus' to Lysander, and the emphasis on love relationships (Julia, 53; Cornelia, 55), comparable to Agesilaus' interest in young men. Pompey's relation to the senate is alternately obedient and independent, as Agesilaus' is to the ephors, and finally his conflict with Caesar parallels that of Agesilaus with Epaminondas, since Plutarch sees wars among the Greek states as a kind of factional strife within Greece.

For Pompey, as for Agesilaus, dynamic generalship was the source of his reputation, and his campaigns occupy a significant portion of the Life. Names of cities, countries, and kings race by the reader's eyes, as victory follows victory in the first half of the Life. Pompey is cheered by throngs who welcome him back from every campaign, and praised by older men like Sulla and Philippus. *Pompey*, however, offers a more complex view of its protagonist. His thrust for recognition has a price: he angers men like Metellus, Crassus, and Lucullus, who see him claiming the victories they have won. At home, in his personal life, he is loving and faithful to his wives. In the political arena, he is less successful: the friends he chooses to protect his interests, especially Clodius and Caesar, use him to their own advantage. His caution in evaluating the military situation becomes in the tumultuous political life of the 50s a kind of passivity, so that he is swept along by others' agendas. Nowhere is this truer than when the Civil War breaks out. The senators, aiming each at their own safety and advancement, will not obey orders, but second-guess Pompey's every move. Their demands persuade him to fight at Pharsalus, when time was on his side. He risks all, and loses. It seems strange that Plutarch sees passivity in a general so dynamic as Pompey, as he does also in Antony. But the quality that Plutarch senses is an inner malleability, a feature of that very ambition which is at the basis of Pompey's character. Desiring men's respect and admiration above all, he places himself in their control, and surrenders his own judgement. A first indication is found in the second chapter, immediately after he is compared with Alexander. Pompey surrenders his mistress Flora to a friend, even though he loves her. A generous act, to be sure, but one which suggests a lack of knowledge of oneself.

Yet Pompey is great, and Plutarch will not let us forget it. His weakness is built into the very nature of his greatness, and is what it means to be human. The biography takes on the movement and force of a tragedy, as we watch Pompey move towards his end. While visiting Athens, Pompey saw these words inscribed on the gate: 'To the extent that you are aware of your mortality, you are divine' (27). Fortune, the Greek *tyche*, recurs as a motif in this Life. Being mortal means that fortune always gives bad as well as good. Taking a broad view of history, we cannot know what is best, or what fortune will bring. In flight from Caesar, Pompey confronted the philosopher Cratippus, and complained about Providence. Plutarch answers with the words Cratippus was too polite to say: 'How are we to be convinced, Pompey, that you would have made a better use of fortune than Caesar if it had been you who won? Where is your evidence for this? No, the divine ordering of things must be left as it is' (75).

The Life is built around the major campaigns, which Plutarch interrupts occasionally for digressions and meditative asides.

1–5	Pompey's father, Strabo; Pompey's character; first service under his father
6–9	Commander of an army supporting Sulla's return
10–15	Campaigns in Sicily and Africa; first triumph
16–21	Campaign against Sertorius in Spain; second triumph (71 BC)
22–3	First consulship (70)
24–9	Command against the pirates
30–3	Command in the East against Mithridates, who is driven out of Asia Minor to the Crimea
34–7	Expedition into the Caucasus and return
38–41	Campaign against Syria, Judaea, and Arabia
42–5	Return and third triumph (61)
46–50	The pact of Pompey, Crassus, and Caesar; Caesar's consulate (59); Clodius' opposition and Pompey's recovery
51–5	The consulship with Crassus (54); breakup of the triumvirate, Pompey sole consul (52)
56–9	Caesar's demands refused; plans for war
60–72	The Civil War (49); Pompey's defeat at Pharsalus (48)
73–80	Pompey's flight and death

Before and after the notice of his third triumph, Plutarch inserts comments on Pompey's situation. First he recalls that the gods always mix adversity in with blessings (42: a reference to Achilles' famous words to

Priam, *Iliad* 24. 527–30). After describing the triumph and comparing Pompey with Alexander, he adds, 'What a boon it would have been for him to have died at this point in his life, since so far he had enjoyed the luck of Alexander! In the future his successes would make men hate him and his failures would be beyond redemption' (46). The third triumph is the turning-point of Pompey's career, coinciding with his abandonment of military commands and immersion in politics at Rome. Fortune no longer favours him, but Pompey also is responsible, Plutarch explains, because he 'bent rules for other people' (46), especially for Caesar, and weakened himself while helping them. Other comments follow. After the death of Julia and Crassus, Pompey and Caesar moved rapidly from political wrangling to open war. Now, Plutarch notes, it is not the fault of Fortune, who had been so generous to both, but of their own passion to be first (53). This theme of competition had already been stated early in *Agesilaus*. Writing on the competitiveness of Spartan society, the biographer comments, 'excessive rivalry is not just bad, but extremely risky for states' (*Ages.* 5). At Pharsalus, Plutarch notes the attacks of his supposed friends—and even their thought of ousting him, once Caesar was defeated—before considering Pompey's own character. He was 'a man who was swayed by what people thought of him' (67). For Plutarch, Pompey had always sought the adulation, not just of the people, but of the senate. Thus on other commands he could excel, but not when leading the senate itself in his army. A poor doctor, 'he yielded to the unhealthy elements of his army because he was afraid to pay for their safety with his unpopularity'.

Pompey's career and possible patronage attracted a host of writers. In addition, the sources for *Pompey* differ for the different campaigns and periods. Therefore we cannot be too confident in identifying the authors Plutarch used. However, the Sullan years probably used the same sources as *Sulla* itself, notably Sulla's own *Memoirs* (cf. p. 172 above). The single citation of Gaius Oppius in chapter 10 for Pompey's treatment of Valerius is clearly a detail added to Plutarch's primary account. Oppius wrote a biography of Caesar which Plutarch found strongly biased,[5] but which he used for *Caesar*.[6] The Sertorian War probably depends chiefly on Sallust's lost *Histories*, as does Plutarch's *Life of Sertorius*. Sallust was a Caesarian and had little love for Pompey, but created a good narrative. His work went down to at least 67 BC. The philosopher and historian Posidonius wrote, as well as many other studies, a Roman history which continued

[5] He notes that one must be careful 'about believing anything Oppius says about Caesar's friends or enemies'.

[6] See also p. 300 below.

Polybius, and himself met Pompey on Rhodes. His work may lie behind the digression on the pirates in chapter 24, and the theory of the relation of behaviour to environment in 28. He may have written a book on Pompey, but no trace remains.[7]

Theophanes of Mytilene was an honoured member of Pompey's entourage, and won from him not only Roman citizenship for himself but liberty for his native city (*Pomp*. 42).[8] He wrote a book about his expedition in Asia, in which he made Pompey's campaigns in the Caucasus recall those of Alexander in India. He appears also to have been used by Livy. Plutarch had little respect for him (49, 76), but since Theophanes had the advantage of being an eyewitness on the campaign, he probably used him as his chief source, perhaps alongside Livy or Posidonius.

For events following Pompey's return, beginning with 60 BC, Pelling has shown that Asinius Pollio is the major narrative source for all six Roman lives of this group, and was probably used directly.[9] Pollio, who fought with Caesar in the Civil War and was consul in 40, began with the pact of Pompey, Crassus, and Caesar in 60 and continued at least to the battle of Philippi in 42. While favouring Caesar, he pointed out weaknesses on both sides. He is cited only once in *Pompey* (72, for casualties at Pharsalus) and in *Caesar* (46), though he is mentioned at *Caesar* 32 and 58. He was a contemporary and an eyewitness, though he would have been only 16 in 60 BC. Comparison with Appian and Cassius Dio shows his influence in Plutarch's account of Caesar's first consulate and of Pompey's death. Plutarch, however, presents Pollio's material differently, depending on the particular focus of each Life. The differences allow us to see some of the ways he works with his sources.[10] Thus Pompey's enemy Lucullus is prominent in chapters 46–8, but omitted from the parallel passage in *Caesar* 13–14. At *Caesar* 35, Plutarch correctly places Caesar's stay in Rome after his march to Brundisium; at *Pompey* 62, he displaces it before Brundisium, perhaps to make an account more centred on Pompey's flight.[11] In *Pompey* 58–9, *Caesar* 30–1, and *Antony* 5, Plutarch simplified the senate debates at the outbreak of the war, but simplified in different ways: see

[7] See also p. 121 above.

[8] Cf. B. K. Gold, 'Pompey and Theophanes of Mytilene', *American Journal of Philology*, 106 (1985), 312–27.

[9] The frequent parallels with Appian, and others with Cassius Dio and Suetonius, make this certain.

[10] Cf. C. B. R. Pelling, 'Plutarch's Adaptation of his Source Material', *Journal of Hellenic Studies*, 100 (1980) 127–40; repr. in B. Scardigli (ed.), *Essays on Plutarch's Lives* (Oxford: Clarendon Press, 1995), 125–54.

[11] Other displacements, though less confusing, are found at *Pomp*. 64, Labienus' inclusion with new arrivals (cf. *Caes*. 34), and *Pomp*. 48, Clodius' taunting in 56 BC.

notes to *Pompey* 59 and *Caesar* 30–1. Naturally, interpretations shift as well, as can be seen by contrasting *Pompey* 46 on Clodius's tribunate and Cicero's exile with *Caesar* 14: the former gives Clodius the initiative, the latter speaks of Caesar as the agent behind Clodius.[12] In general, Pompey in his Life is made to seem more passive, more manipulated by his friends.

Cicero is cited twice in *Pompey* (42, on the divorce of Mucia; 63, on Pompey's desertion of Italy, both from letters) and in other Lives as well. Plutarch clearly knew some of his works, including some which do not survive, though it is uncertain whether he had read *On the Manilian Law* urging Pompey's appointment to the Mithridatic command. Caesar's *Civil War* is cited once for his criticism of Pompey's instructions at Pharsalus (69), and the description of Pompey's camp after the battle (72) echoes Caesar. However, Pollio, cited also in 72, would have reproduced much of Caesar's account.

Plutarch refers in passing to Timagenes (49), a rhetorician and historian who arrived in Rome as a prisoner in 55. His name reminds us of the many historians who were available to Plutarch but whose work we no longer possess. Josephus, for example, mentions that the histories of Nicolaus of Damascus, Strabo, and Livy dealt with Pompey's campaign in Judaea (*Jewish Antiquities* 14. 104). All three were contemporaries of Augustus, and Plutarch quotes them elsewhere.

Pompey frequently supplements our other sources, especially for the early years. Its major contribution, however, is its dramatic re-creation of moments in Pompey's life: the young man, freshly back from Africa, facing down Sulla, demanding a triumph; the great crowds pouring out to greet him; the conqueror of Mithridates reading the dead man's private letters; Pompey in court, bewildered by the hate-filled taunts of Clodius' mob; Pompey at Pharsalus, watching his cavalry run away from Caesar's hardened soldiers, and thinking—what thoughts? After it all, Plutarch allows an old veteran to have the final word (80): 'the greatest Roman imperator there has ever been.'

De Wet, B. X., 'Aspects of Plutarch's Portrayal of Pompey', *Acta Classica*, 24 (1981), 119–32.

Gold, B. K., 'Pompey and Theophanes of Mytilene', *American Journal of Philology*, 106 (1985), 312–27.

Greenhalgh, P. A. L., *Pompey the Republican Prince* (London: Weidenfeld and Nicolson, 1981).

Gruen, E. S., *The Last Generation of the Roman Republic* (Berkeley, Los Angeles, and London: University of California Press, 1974).

[12] *CMin.* 33 presents Clodius as the agent of the triumvirs.

Hillman, T. P., 'Plutarch and the First Consulship of Pompeius and Crassus', *Phoenix*, 46 (1992), 124–37.

—— 'Authorial Statements, Narrative, and Character in Plutarch's Agesilaus–Pompey', *Greek, Roman, and Byzantine Studies*, 35 (1994), 255–80.

Leach, J., *Pompey the Great* (London: Croom Helm, 1978).

Pelling, C. B. R., 'Plutarch's Method of Work in the Roman Lives', *Journal of Hellenic Studies*, 99 (1979), 74–96; repr. in B. Scardigli (ed.), *Essays on Plutarch's Lives* (Oxford: Clarendon Press, 1995), 265–318, with 'Postscript (1994)'.

—— 'Plutarch's Adaptation of his Source Material,' *Journal of Hellenic Studies*, 100 (1980), 127–40; repr. in B. Scardigli (ed.), *Essays on Plutarch's Lives* (Oxford: Clarendon Press, 1995), 125–54.

Seager, R., *Pompey: A Political Biography* (Oxford: Blackwell, 1979).

POMPEY

[1] How the Roman people felt about Pompey right from his early days seems to be perfectly encapsulated by what Aeschylus' Prometheus says to Heracles after being rescued by him: 'I hate the father, but dearly love this son of his.'* For no Roman commander ever met with so much bitter hatred from the Romans as Pompey's father, Strabo. While he was alive they were apprehensive about his military might (and he was certainly an expert soldier), and after his death—he was struck by a thunderbolt—as his body was being taken to the funeral they dragged it off the bier and abused it.* On the other hand, no Roman ever met with such fierce loyalty as Pompey did: it started unusually early in his life, rose to an extraordinary pitch of intensity while his fortune was good, and endured surprisingly well after his downfall. And although there was only the one reason why they hated the father—namely, his insatiable appetite for money—there were many reasons for their affection for the son: the modesty of his lifestyle, his honed military skills, the persuasiveness of his public speaking, his trustworthiness, and his easy manner with acquaintances, which was such that no one ever gave less offence when asking a favour, or more pleasure when granting one. For one of his many appealing features was that he could give without seeming harsh and receive with dignity.

[2] At first, his appearance also contributed quite a bit towards his popularity, and made people sympathetic to him before he had even opened his mouth to speak. The blend of dignity and kindness in it was attractive, and at a very early age its freshness and charm revealed the nobility and kingliness of his character. The slight upturn of his hair and the mobility of his features about the eyes made his face resemble that of King Alexander, as portrayed in his statues, though this was not so much apparent as something people said. This led to his commonly being called by the name 'Alexander' when he was young, and since this was something Pompey did not mind at all, people began to call him it to poke fun at him. This is why once, when Lucius Philippus, an ex-consul, was speaking on Pompey's behalf in court, he said that it could hardly be thought strange for a Philip like himself to be fond of an Alexander.*

It is said that even when she was getting on in age Flora, the courtesan, was always talking about her former relationship with Pompey, and used to say that after sex with him she never left his house without the marks of his teeth on her. She also used to tell the story of how when she cited Pompey as her reason for turning down one of his close friends, a man called Geminius, who fancied her and was annoying her with his attentions, Geminius spoke to Pompey, and Pompey passed her on to him. After that, she used to say, he never laid a finger on her again or even met her socially, despite the fact that he was thought still to be in love with her, while she did not take this like a professional courtesan, but was ill for a long time out of grief and longing.* Flora, however, is said to have developed into such a famous beauty that when Caecilius Metellus was embellishing the temple of Castor and Pollux with statues and paintings, he had her portrait painted and put it up in the temple in honour of her beauty. Pompey also treated the wife of his freedman Demetrius—a man who had a very great deal of influence with Pompey, and who left an estate of four thousand talents—with untypical shabbiness and meanness, because he did not want people thinking that he had been overcome by her beauty, which was well known to be irresistible. This shows how extremely cautious and discreet he was in these matters, but even so he did not avoid being criticized by his enemies in this regard: they accused him of frequently neglecting and ignoring public business in order to gratify his wives.*

Here is a story which bears witness to how easily satisfied he was and how unpretentious his tastes were where food was concerned. Once, when he was ill and off his food, a doctor prescribed a thrush for him, but none could be found for sale, because they were not in season. When someone said that they would be able to get them from Lucullus, who kept them all the year round, Pompey said, 'So must Pompey's life depend on Lucullus' extravagant habits?' Then he dismissed the doctor and treated himself instead with something that could easily be found. But this episode happened later in his life.*

[3] While he was still a young adult and was out on campaign with his father, who had been given the job of doing battle against Cinna, Pompey was thrown together with a man called Lucius Terentius, who was his tent-mate. Now, Terentius had been bribed by Cinna, and the plan was that while he was killing Pompey, others were to set

fire to the commander's tent. The plot was betrayed to Pompey while he was at dinner, but so far from showing any signs of discomposure, he drank more freely than usual and behaved in a warm and friendly fashion towards Terentius. As soon as they had gone to bed, however, he slipped out of the tent, set a guard around his father, and then waited quietly. When Terentius judged that the time was right, he got up, drew his sword, approached Pompey's mattress, and stabbed through the blankets many times, assuming that Pompey was lying there. Next, because feelings were running so high against the commander, the whole camp was plunged into turmoil; the soldiers tore down their tents and seized their weapons, committing themselves to mutiny. The commander was too terrified by the uproar to show himself, but Pompey walked to and fro in the midst of it all, imploring the soldiers with tears in his eyes to reconsider. Eventually, he threw himself on the ground in front of the gateway to the camp and lay there weeping and telling those who wanted to leave just to walk all over him. One by one they began to step back out of shame, and all but eight hundred of them were induced in this way to change their minds and resume their allegiance to their commander.*

[4] Immediately after Strabo's death, Pompey was put on trial in his place for stealing public funds. Pompey discovered that most of the thefts had been committed by one of his freedmen, Alexander, and proved it to the court, but he himself was still accused of having in his possession hunting-nets and books from among the booty taken at Asculum. Although he had been given these things by his father after the fall of Asculum, he had lost them again when some of Cinna's personal guards had broken into his house and ransacked it, after Cinna's return to Rome. He had quite a few preliminary skirmishes with his accuser before the trial, in which he proved himself to be quick-witted and unusually stable for his age. This won him a great deal of admiration and popularity, and the upshot was that Antistius, who was a praetor at the time and arbitrator of these disputes,* became so smitten with Pompey that he offered him his daughter in marriage and entered into discussions with Pompey's friends on the matter. Pompey accepted the offer and the arrangements were made in secret, but the high regard Antistius showed for Pompey gave the game away to the masses, and in the end, when Antistius announced that the judges found Pompey not guilty, this

acted like a signal and the people shouted out the ancient, traditional greeting given to newly wedded men, 'For Talasius!'

The origin of this custom is supposed to be as follows. On the occasion when the most eminent Romans abducted the daughters of the Sabines, who had come to Rome to see the athletic competition, some lower-class men—men of client status and ox-herders—seized a tall and beautiful young woman and began to carry her off. In case they met any of their betters and had the woman taken away from them, they called out as they ran, 'For Talasius!', since Talasius was a well-known and popular man. Everyone who heard them applauded and echoed their cry, as a way of showing their pleasure and how they approved of what they were doing. And so, they say, since the marriage turned out to be a fortunate one for Talasius, this acclamation began to be used as a light-hearted way of greeting newly wedded men. This is the most plausible of the stories one hears about Talasius.* Be that as it may, a few days after his acquittal, Pompey married Antistia.

[5] After that, he made his way to Cinna's camp, but before long he became afraid of the possible consequences of some criticisms and complaints that were being brought against him, and he slipped secretly away. On his disappearance, a whispered rumour spread throughout the camp that Cinna had done away with the young man, and as a result of this those who had for a long time resented and hated the man rose up against him. As Cinna fled, he was caught by one of the centurions, who was chasing him with drawn sword. He fell to his knees and held out his signet ring, which was very valuable. But the centurion's response was extremely brusque: 'I haven't come to sign and seal a document, but to punish a tyrant for his evil crimes.' And with these words he killed him. After Cinna's death the reins of government and power passed to an even more capricious man, Carbo. But Sulla was drawing near, and most people longed for him to come. Their circumstances were so grim that even a change of masters seemed highly desirable. The disasters which had overwhelmed the city had reduced it to such a state that, in the absence of any hope of freedom, they looked only for a more bearable form of slavery.*

[6] Pompey was in Italy, in Picenum, at the time, partly because he had estates there,* but mainly because he was happy in the Picenan communities, which had made him feel at home and treated him as a

friend ever since the time of his father. When he saw that the best and most distinguished men of Rome were leaving their homes and flocking from all quarters to the haven of Sulla's camp, he decided to join him not as an empty-handed fugitive begging for help, but after having done him a favour first, and with an army. He therefore set about arousing the people of Picenum to rebellion. He began tentatively, but they were perfectly prepared to follow his advice and refused to listen to Carbo's representatives. In fact, when a man called Vedius said that Pompey had leapt straight from being taught by a pedagogue to doing his own teaching as a demagogue, they were so furious that they immediately fell on Vedius and killed him. After this, the 23-year-old Pompey, who had never been officially appointed to a position of command by anyone, awarded himself the position. He set up a platform in the forum of Auximum, a large city,* and issued an edict ordering the leading men there, two brothers called Ventidius, who had been acting against him on Carbo's behalf, to leave town. He then set about recruiting soldiers, and after duly appointing centurions and commanding officers for them, he set off on a tour of the other communities in the district, where he did the same. Those who sympathized with Carbo left and withdrew at his approach, while all the rest were happy to entrust themselves to his leadership, and so before long he had raised enough men to organize into three complete legions, and had fully equipped them with food, baggage-carts, wagons, and everything else. Then he set out to join Sulla. He was in no hurry, nor did he mind if his journey was no secret; in fact, he found time on the way to damage the enemy's interests, and wherever he went in Italy he tried to stage a revolt against Carbo.

[7] He therefore found himself faced with three enemy commanders at the same time—Carrinas, Coelius, and Brutus. They did not all come up against him head on, or indeed all from any one direction, but surrounded him with their three armies with the intention of overwhelming him. Without the slightest trace of panic, he combined his men into a single force and set out against just Brutus' army, with his cavalry, himself included, forming the first line of attack. When the Gallic cavalry came out against him from the enemy ranks, he rode out in front of the others, struck the first and most formidable of the Gallic horsemen with his spear at close range, and killed him. The rest of the Gauls fell back, but in so doing

they threw their infantry into disarray, and the upshot was that a general rout ensued. After this the three enemy commanders fell out with one another, and each of them withdrew as best he could, while the local towns came over to Pompey's side, since they thought that the enemy forces had scattered out of fear. Next the consul, Scipio, came up to attack him, but before the two armies had come within javelin range, Scipio's troops called out greetings to Pompey's men and changed sides, while Scipio himself fled. Finally, Carbo sent a large number of cavalry squadrons against him at the river Aesis, but he valiantly stood his ground, put the enemy to flight, and pursued them back on to terrain that was awkward and difficult for horses. At this point, since there was no way out for them that they could see, they gave themselves up, and also handed over to him their weapons and horses.*

[8] Sulla had yet to hear of these successes. The initial reports and messages had made him afraid for Pompey's safety, surrounded as he was by all those outstanding enemy commanders, and he was hurrying to his assistance. When Pompey found out that Sulla was near by, he ordered his officers to get the men to arm themselves and form up in lines, so that they would make a dashing and brilliant spectacle for their imperator. He was hoping that Sulla would confer great honours upon him, but the reality exceeded his hopes. When Sulla saw him approaching—when he saw Pompey's army of impressive fighting men standing by, flushed and elated by their victories—he jumped off his horse and, when Pompey addressed him as 'Imperator',* he saluted Pompey in return in exactly the same way. It was beyond all expectations that Sulla would share this title with a young man who was not yet even a senator, when he himself had fought the likes of Scipio and Marius for it.* And everything that followed was in conformity with the warmth of these overtures. For instance, at Pompey's approach Sulla would rise to his feet and draw the toga off his head—things which he was extremely unlikely to be seen doing for anyone else, despite the fact that he was surrounded by plenty of men of quality.

None of this went to Pompey's head, however. Sulla wanted to send him straight away to Gaul, where Metellus was in charge and did not seem to be fulfilling the potential of all the resources at his disposal, but Pompey argued that it would be wrong for him to take the command away from a man who was his senior and was so very eminent, but that he was prepared, with Metellus' permission, to come to his assistance in the war. Metellus accepted this offer and wrote a letter inviting him to come.* Once Pompey arrived in Gaul, he not only accomplished some remarkable achievements on his own, but he also reawoke and rekindled the warlike and bold side of Metellus' character, which was in the process of being extinguished by old age, just as molten, fiery bronze is said to soften anything rigid and cold it is poured over more effectively than fire, and to reduce it too to a molten state. However, just as a champion athlete who has defeated his fellow men and spectacularly won prizes at games all over the world completely discounts the victories of his childhood and even leaves them unrecorded, so it is with Pompey's achievements at this time: although they were extraordinary in themselves, they have been consigned to oblivion by the number and importance of the conflicts and wars he was involved in later, and so I am afraid to bring them up, in case I spend a long time on his first exploits and leave myself little room for those accomplishments and experiences of his which are of major significance and bring out his character particularly well.*

[9] Once Sulla had gained control of Italy and been proclaimed dictator, he repaid the rest of his commanding officers and military leaders by making them rich, promoting them to official posts, and freely granting their various requests with a lavish hand. However, he found Pompey's qualities so impressive, and relied on his help in government so much, that he wanted to find a way to bring him into his family. His wife Metella shared his desire, and they persuaded Pompey to divorce Antistia and marry Aemilia instead. Aemilia was Sulla's stepdaughter, the child of Metella and Scaurus, and she already had a husband at the time, by whom she was pregnant. The whole business with the marriage was therefore a display of tyranny, more in keeping with Sulla's interests than Pompey's character: Aemilia was married to him when she was pregnant with another man's child, and Antistia was humiliated by being driven from his house. This was a heartless act, because Antistia had recently lost her father too, thanks to the fact that she was married to Pompey: he had been murdered in the senate-house, suspected as a result of his relationship to Pompey of being on Sulla's side. Under these circumstances her mother committed suicide—another catastrophe to be added to the tragedy surrounding that marriage. And then, as if this

were not enough, before long Aemilia died in childbirth in Pompey's house.*

[10] Next, news arrived that in Sicily Perperna was in the process of gaining control and was making the island a refuge for the survivors of the opposing party, while Carbo was also hovering off the coast with a fleet, and that in Africa Domitius had launched an attack, while a lot of other important exiles, who had anticipated Sulla's proscriptions and escaped, were gathering there as well. Pompey was dispatched at the head of a sizeable army to deal with these situations.* Perperna immediately abandoned Sicily to him, so Pompey recovered the exhausted communities there for Sulla, and treated all of them with kindness except the Mamertines in Messana. When they asked for exemption from his administration, and cited an ancient Roman law which made it illegal for him to establish jurisdiction over them, he said, 'Stop quoting laws at us! We're the ones wearing swords!'

He was also generally held to have taken unfair advantage of Carbo's downfall and treated him with inhumane cruelty. If he had to be put to death, which was probably inevitable, it should have been done immediately after his capture, and then it would have been the responsibility of whoever gave the order. But Pompey had the man taken to Rome in chains—a man who had three times been consul—and brought before the rostra, where he himself sat as judge and interrogated him closely, to the distress and indignation of those present. Then he ordered him to be taken away and put to death. There is a story that after Carbo had been led away, when he saw the executioner's sword already drawn, he asked to be allowed the space and short amount of time necessary for him to relieve his bowels, which were troubling him.

Gaius Oppius, the companion of Caesar,* adds Quintus Valerius to the list of those Pompey treated cruelly. According to Oppius, Pompey knew that Valerius was an outstandingly erudite scholar, and so, when he was brought before him, he greeted him and took a walk with him. During the walk he asked for and received the answers to some questions he had—and then immediately told his subordinates to take the man away and kill him. But one needs to be very careful about believing anything Oppius says about Caesar's enemies or friends. Pompey had no choice about punishing those of Sulla's enemies who were particularly famous and whose capture was public knowledge, but otherwise he connived at the escape of as many as he could, and in some cases actually helped them on their way. Then again, after he had decided to punish the city of Himera* for having taken the enemy's side, Sthennis, the leader of the popular party there, asked to speak to him and told him that it would be unfair of him to kill people who were completely innocent, while letting the guilty man go. Pompey asked who he was talking about—who the guilty man was—and Sthennis said that he meant himself, because he had got his fellow citizens to act as they had, using persuasion on them if they were his friends and force if they were his enemies. Pompey was so delighted with the man's honesty and dignity that he pardoned first him, and then all the rest. And once, when he heard that his soldiers had been behaving in an unruly fashion as they made their way through the countryside, he put seals on their swords and punished anyone who failed to keep his seal intact.

[11] While he was in Sicily, busy with the affairs of the communities there, he received notification of a decree of the senate, accompanied by a letter from Sulla, ordering him to sail to Africa and make all-out war on Domitius. Domitius had mustered an army many times larger than the one which, not many years previously, Marius had brought over from Africa to Italy and used to apply such pressure on the Roman constitution that he returned from exile and became tyrant.* So Pompey quickly made all his preparations and, leaving Memmius, his sister's husband, in charge of Sicily, he set sail with a fleet of 120 warships and 800 transport vessels laden with food, weaponry, money, and siege-engines. He brought his ships to land partly at Utica and partly at Carthage, and seven thousand of the enemy immediately deserted and joined his forces, which consisted of six legions at full strength. My sources record a ridiculous episode which happened at this point. Some of his troops apparently stumbled upon a hoard of treasure and gained a great deal of money. Once this became public knowledge, all the rest of his men got the idea that the place was full of money which the Carthaginians had hidden away in some time of trouble, and for many days Pompey could do nothing with his men, as they were all out looking for treasure. He just went around laughing at the sight of thousands upon thousands of men digging and turning over the plain, until at last they gave up. They told him that they had been adequately

punished for their foolishness, and would now follow his lead wherever he took them.

[12] Domitius drew up his forces opposite Pompey, with a rugged gully between them that would be awkward to cross, but a heavy rainstorm with driving wind that began in the morning and stayed put deterred Domitius from fighting that day, and he gave the order for retreat. Pompey, however, seized this opportunity to make a rapid advance across the gully and into the attack. He found the enemy in disarray and chaos, disunited and capable of putting up only a patchy resistance, which was not helped when the wind veered round and drove the rain into their faces. However, the storm made things difficult for the Romans too, because they could not clearly see one another, and in fact Pompey himself had a narrow escape from death when he was not recognized and was rather slow in responding to a soldier's demand for the password.

Nevertheless, they succeeded in routing the enemy and inflicting very heavy casualties; it is said that there were only three thousand survivors out of the original twenty thousand. They then acclaimed Pompey as Imperator, but he said that he refused to accept the honour as long as the enemy camp remained intact, and that if they considered him worthy of the title they would first destroy the camp. At this they immediately set out to attack the camp. Pompey fought without his helmet, because he did not want a repeat of the earlier incident.* The camp fell, and Domitius was killed. Some of the rebel cities immediately submitted to him, and others were taken by force. He also captured King Iarbas, who had supported Domitius in the war, and gave his kingdom to Hiempsal. Relying on his run of good fortune and the might of his army, he next invaded Numidia. He penetrated many days' journey into the interior of the country, defeated everyone he met, and made Rome once again an object of fear and terror to the natives, who had been tending to forget it. In fact, he said that he should not leave even the wild animals of Africa without a taste of Roman might and daring, and so he spent quite a few days hunting lions and elephants. They say that it took him just forty days in all to make short work of the enemy, subdue Africa, and settle the affairs of kings, although he was then only 24 years old.*

[13] On his return to Utica, orders arrived by letter from Sulla that he should send the bulk of the army back to Italy, while remaining in Africa with one legion to await his replacement. The letter

distressed and upset him a great deal, but he kept his feelings to himself; his troops, however, made no secret of their indignation, and when Pompey asked them to go on ahead of him, they cursed Sulla, promised that they would never abandon him, and warned him not to trust the tyrant. After his first attempt to calm them down and allay their suspicions met with no success, he got down off the platform and retreated in tears to his tent, but they fetched him from there and put him back on the platform. Much of the day passed with them insisting that he should stay and retain his command, and him begging them to obey orders and not to create trouble. Eventually, as they refused to back down and continued to shout out their demands, he swore that he would kill himself if they persisted, and the clamour then gradually died away.

The first report that reached Sulla was that Pompey was leading a rebellion against him, and he told his friends that it looked as though in his old age he was fated to compete against boys, because Marius was another quite young man who had made life very difficult for him and taken him to the very brink of disaster.* But when he learnt the truth, and realized that the whole population of Rome was intending to welcome Pompey home and escort him into the city as a token of their goodwill, he hastened to outdo them all. He came out of Rome to meet him and gave him the warmest possible welcome, acclaiming him in a loud voice as 'Magnus'—which is to say, 'the Great'—and telling those present to use this title when addressing him. Others, however, say that this title was originally applied to him by the whole army in Africa, and that Sulla merely confirmed it, giving it authority and endurance. But Pompey himself was the last to use the title; it was only many years later, when he was sent to Spain as proconsul to fight Sertorius, that he began to sign his letters and decrees as 'Pompey the Great', since by then the title had become familiar, and had stopped arousing resentment.*

In this context one may admire and respect the ancient Romans for not reserving this kind of title and surname for military successes alone, but also using them to honour political achievements and qualities. Take, for example, the two men to whom the Roman people gave the title 'Maximus', or 'the Greatest': they gave it to Valerius for making peace between them and the senate at a time of discord, and to Fabius Rullus for expelling from the senate some descendants of freedmen who had got themselves enrolled in the senate thanks to their wealth.*

[14] Pompey now asked for a triumph, but Sulla opposed the request on the grounds that by law no one other than a consul or a praetor could be granted this honour. That is why even after defeating the Carthaginians in Spain, which involved fighting greater and more critical battles than Pompey's in Africa, the first Scipio did not ask for a triumph: he was neither a consul nor a praetor. Pompey was still a young man without a full beard on his face, too young to be a senator: if he entered the city in triumphal procession, Sulla argued, his own government and Pompey's prestige would become utterly abhorrent. And he made it clear that as well as refusing him this privilege, he would oppose him and thwart his ambitious plans if he chose to disobey. So far from being cowed by Sulla's words, however, Pompey suggested that Sulla bear in mind the fact that more people worshipped the rising sun than the setting sun, the implication being that his power was increasing, while Sulla's was decreasing and dying away. Sulla did not quite catch what he said, but he could see the expressions and gestures of astonishment from those who did hear him, and he asked someone to tell him what Pompey had said. When he found out, he was taken aback by Pompey's presumption, and cried out twice in succession: 'Let him have his triumph!'

This angered and annoyed a lot of people, but according to my sources Pompey only wanted to irritate them even more, and he planned to ride into the city mounted on a chariot drawn by four of the many elephants he had taken as booty from the kings of Africa and brought back to Rome. But the gate proved too narrow, so he abandoned the idea and changed back to horses. Moreover, when his soldiers, who had not profited as much as they had expected, showed an inclination to kick up a fuss and make a nuisance of themselves, he said that he was completely unconcerned, and would rather forgo his triumph than defer to them. This prompted Servilius, a man of considerable standing in Rome who had previously been the most outspoken critic of Pompey's triumph, to remark that he could now see that Pompey really was 'the Great' and deserved his triumph. There can also be no doubt that if he had wanted to become a senator then, he could have done so. This did not interest him, however, because, they say, he was only after surprising and unusual forms of glory. So, for instance, there would have been nothing particularly amazing in his becoming a senator while still technically too young for it, but it was a dazzling honour for him to be celebrating a triumph before he had become a senator. In fact, this also went quite a long way towards securing his popularity with the masses, since the common people of Rome enjoyed the fact that even after a triumph he was still classified as a knight.*

[15] The rise in Pompey's fame and power worried Sulla, but he thought it would be degrading for him to obstruct it, so he did nothing. There was one occasion, however, when Pompey overrode Sulla's opposition and got Lepidus elected consul by supporting his candidacy and using his own popularity with the Roman people to gain their backing for him. After the election Sulla saw Pompey setting off through the forum with a crowd of friends, and he said, 'I see that you're flushed with victory, young man. And why not? You've done well, and acted most generously: thanks to your influence over the Roman people, Lepidus, the worst of men, has been elected consul with more votes than that paragon of virtue, Catulus. But you'd better not be caught napping; you'd better keep a careful eye on your affairs, now that you've created a stronger rival for yourself.' But the main way in which Sulla showed his hostility towards Pompey was in drawing up his will. He left bequests to others of his friends, and made some of them guardians of his son, but he completely ignored Pompey. However, Pompey accepted this with equanimity and behaved like a true statesman: when Lepidus and some others tried to prevent Sulla's body being buried in the Campus Martius, or even from receiving a funeral at public expense, Pompey came to the rescue and saw that he received a safe and honourable burial.*

[16] Not long after Sulla's death his prophecies began to come true, as Lepidus tried to arrogate Sulla's powers for himself. He did not go about the attempt in a roundabout fashion or make any attempt to disguise it, but went straight to the stage of using armed force, and tried to revive and surround himself with whatever remnants of the opposition, now long enfeebled, had survived Sulla's regime. His colleague, Catulus, had the support of the decent and honourable elements of the senate and people, but although his reputation for morality and justice made him the greatest Roman of his day, he was generally held to be the kind of leader who was more comfortable in the political than the military sphere. The situation

itself, therefore, demanded Pompey, and he did not take long in deciding on his course of action. He attached himself to the aristocratic cause, and was put in command of military operations against Lepidus, who had already fomented rebellion in a great deal of Italy and had Brutus occupying Cisalpine Gaul for him with an army.*

As Pompey advanced he easily defeated everybody, until he reached Mutina in Gaul, where he spent a long time encamped opposite Brutus. Lepidus seized this opportunity to make a dash for Rome. He took up a threatening position outside the city, terrifying the inhabitants with the massive size of his army, and demanded a second consulship. But their fear was dispelled by a letter from Pompey in which he told them he had won the war without fighting a battle. Perhaps Brutus betrayed his men, or perhaps his men changed sides and betrayed him, but at any rate he surrendered to Pompey. He was given a cavalry escort, and he withdrew to a little town on the Po—only to be killed the next day by Geminius, whom Pompey sent to do the job.* Pompey was heavily criticized for this, since at first, when the defection began, Pompey wrote to the senate that Brutus had changed allegiance of his own free will, but later he wrote another letter, after he had had the man killed, bringing various charges against him. (The Brutus who killed Caesar with Cassius' help was the son of this Brutus; as is plain from my Life of the younger Brutus, the military careers and the deaths of the two men were totally dissimilar.*) As for Lepidus, as soon as he had been driven out of Italy, he crossed over to Sardinia, where he fell ill and died of depression caused, we hear, not by his downfall, but by his coming across a note which revealed that his wife was having an affair.

[17] However, Sertorius, a military leader who had nothing in common with Lepidus, was in control of Spain and was threatening Rome with his looming menace.* All the poison of the civil wars met in this man as if he were the disease to end all diseases. He had already killed more than a few inferior commanders and was currently embroiled with Metellus Pius, a man who was an outstanding strategist, but who seemed, now that he was no longer young, to lack the quick reactions needed to seize the opportunities presented in the war and too slow to keep up with things, which were snatched out of his hand by Sertorius' speed and alacrity. Sertorius employed reckless guerrilla tactics against him, and his ambushes and outflank-

ing movements bemused a man who had been trained in conventional warfare and whose troops were immobile and lacked agility. Under these circumstances Pompey retained command of his army and negotiated to get sent out to help Metellus. Even though Catulus gave him a direct order, he refused to disband his army, but remained under arms near the city, constantly finding new excuses, until the senate ratified a motion proposed by Lucius Philippus and gave him the command.* There is a story attached to this episode that a senator asked Philippus, in amazement at the news, whether he thought Pompey should be sent out as proconsul. 'No, I don't,' Philippus said. 'I think he should be sent out pro-consuls!'—the implication being that both the consuls of the time were useless.

[18] Pompey's arrival in Spain had the kind of effect one might have expected on people faced with a new and famous commander: he revived the confidence of the men, and those of the Spanish tribes whose allegiance to Sertorius was somewhat shaky showed signs of restlessness and an inclination to change sides. Sertorius therefore set about disseminating a number of arrogant stories designed to harm Pompey's reputation, and as a joke he used to say that he would need only a cane and a whip to deal with this boy, if he did not have that old woman (meaning Metellus) to worry about. In actual fact, though, he kept a very close watch on Pompey and adopted more cautious tactics. It was Pompey he regarded as a potential threat, since Metellus, contrary to all expectations, had given himself over to a life of luxury and was simply indulging his hedonistic whims. The sudden and extreme transference of Metellus' attention to a life of pretension and extravagance was another factor which dramatically increased the loyalty people felt for Pompey and enhanced his reputation, because he intensified the simplicity of his lifestyle.* This was not particularly hard for him to do, since he was naturally restrained and disciplined where his appetites were concerned.

This was a war which involved many kinds of military activity. The incident that most upset Pompey was the capture of Lauron by Sertorius. He thought he had the enemy surrounded and had started to congratulate himself on the fact, but then he suddenly found that he was the one who was surrounded. This made him afraid to move, and he had to watch the city being burnt to the ground before his very eyes. However, he defeated Herennius and Perperna at Valentia and killed over ten thousand of their troops; and among the Roman exiles who had taken refuge with Sertorius and been given commands by him, these two were particularly expert tacticians.*

[19] Encouraged by this achievement, and with his morale running high, he hastened to attack Sertorius himself, so as to deny Metellus any part in the victory. The two sides met at the river Sucro and battle was joined even though it was already late in the day, because neither of them wanted Metellus to arrive: one of them wanted to fight unaided, the other wanted his opponent to remain unaided. The final outcome of the battle was ambiguous, since on each side one wing was successful. Where the two commanding officers were concerned, Sertorius' accomplishments beat Pompey's, because he overpowered the part of Pompey's army with which he was faced. Pompey, who was on horseback, was attacked by a tall foot soldier. When the two of them clashed and set to, each struck at the other with his sword and hit the other man's hand. The outcome was not the same, however, since Pompey was merely wounded, while he cut off his opponent's hand. More men ran up to attack him, and his men had already turned and fled, but he succeeded in escaping against the odds by abandoning his horse to the enemy. The horse was wearing golden cheek-bosses and very valuable caparisons, and in dividing up these spoils they fell to fighting with one another and lost him.*

Early the next day both sides formed up again for battle with the intention of making victory indisputably theirs, but by now Metellus was near by, so Sertorius retreated and left his men to scatter. The way he used to disband his army like this and then gather them together meant that Sertorius might often travel about on his own—but just as often would take to the field with an army of 150,000 men, like a mountain stream in winter which is suddenly in spate. After the battle Pompey came up to Metellus. When they were near each other he commanded the lictors to lower their fasces* out of deference to Metellus, who outranked him. But Metellus refused to let him do even this, and treated him with nothing but kindness; despite being an ex-consul and the older man, he did not assume any greater privileges, except that when the two armies were encamped together the password was given out to all the men, from both armies, by Metellus. Usually, however, the two armies found themselves in separate camps, because their enemy, with his unpredictable tactics, used to cut them off from each other and keep them apart; he was brilliant at appearing in a number of different places in a short space of time and at drawing them into one battle after another. Eventually, by cutting off their supplies, despoiling the countryside, and gaining control of the sea, he drove both of them out of his part of Spain and they were forced by their lack of provisions to take refuge in other provinces.*

[20] Pompey had already spent and exhausted most of his personal fortune on the war, so he asked the senate for money, with the implied threat that they would see him and his army in Italy if they did not send it.* The consul at the time was Lucullus. Although he was no friend to Pompey, he was anxious to win command of the Mithridatic War for himself, so he quickly arranged for the money to be sent. He did not want to give Pompey any reason to ignore Sertorius and take on Mithridates instead, since Mithridates was expected to be an opponent who would add considerably to one's prestige, while being easy to handle.* Meanwhile, however, Sertorius was treacherously murdered by his friends. Perperna, who had masterminded the plot, attempted to carry on his work, but although he had the same resources and equipment, he lacked the intelligence to put them to the same effect. Pompey therefore lost no time in setting out to attack him. Once he realized that Perperna was out of his depth, he sent out ten cohorts as a decoy, with orders to spread out over the plain. When Perperna turned towards these cohorts and gave chase, Pompey suddenly appeared in force, launched an attack, and won an overwhelming victory. Most of Perperna's senior officers were killed in the course of the battle, but Pompey had Perperna himself put to death when he was brought to him afterwards.* Some people accuse Pompey of callously forgetting events in Sicily, but this is wrong: he was in fact displaying excellent judgement and giving priority to the safety of Rome as a whole. For Perperna had come into possession of Sertorius' papers and was threatening to show letters from some of the most powerful men in Rome, proving that they had been inviting Sertorius to invade Italy because they wanted to overthrow the present constitution and bring about a revolution. Pompey was afraid that this would provoke wars more terrible than the ones that had just finished, and so he killed Perperna and burnt the letters without even reading them.*

[21] After this he stayed in Spain long enough to quell any major

disturbances, and settle and resolve the most inflammable situations, before leading his army back to Italy, where he set out to deal with the Servile War, which was then at its peak.* That is why Crassus, who was in command of the Roman forces, took a risk and precipitated the conflict. The risk paid off, however, and he killed 12,300 of the enemy. But fortune somehow involved Pompey even in this victory, since five thousand of the fugitives from the battle came up against him. He completely annihilated them and then stole a march on Crassus by writing a letter to the senate to the effect that although Crassus had defeated the gladiators in pitched battle, he had eradicated every last trace of war.* The Romans felt so much affection for Pompey that this claim fell on willing ears, and was willingly repeated too. The same went for Spain and Sertorius as well: the entire achievement was credited to Pompey alone, and no one would have denied it even as a joke.

However, all these compliments and high hopes were tinged with a degree of apprehension and fear of the man. People were worried that he would refuse to relinquish his army and would head straight for a Sullan constitution, via armed force and autocracy. So, among the people who ran and greeted him as he approached Rome with expressions of friendship, there were just as many who were motivated by fear as by genuine goodwill. But Pompey put an end to their worries by announcing that he would relinquish the army once he had celebrated a triumph, and after that there remained only one accusation for his critics to bring, which was that he devoted himself more to the common people than he did to the senate, and was determined to restore the authority of the tribunate, which Sulla had demolished, as a favour to the masses. This was true, for there was nothing the Roman people desired more frantically or more intensely longed for than to see that office again, and so Pompey counted himself very lucky to have the opportunity to propose the measure, since he could never have found another way to repay his fellow citizens for their goodwill if someone else had forestalled him in this.*

[22] So he was awarded a second triumph and elected consul,* but it was not these honours that earned him men's admiration and respect. What they counted as evidence of his outstanding qualities was the fact that Crassus, the wealthiest, most eloquent, and most eminent politician of the time, who looked down in haughty disdain

on everyone, including Pompey, did not dare to put himself forward as a candidate for the consulship until he had asked for Pompey's help. Pompey was delighted, because for a long time he had been wanting to find something he could do for him, some act of kindness. He therefore wholeheartedly canvassed and appealed to the people on Crassus' behalf, and told them that gaining Crassus as his colleague would mean just as much to him as gaining the consulship in the first place. As a matter of fact, though, after they had been elected consuls, they quarrelled and disagreed over everything. Crassus had more power in the senate, but Pompey had a great deal of influence with the common people, because he had given them back the tribunate and had let the knights regain the legal right to try cases in court.*

What they enjoyed most of all, however, was the sight of Pompey asking to be discharged from military service. Traditionally, what happened was that at the end of his legal period of military service a Roman knight would lead his horse into the forum before the two men whom they call 'censors', and after enumerating one by one all the leaders and commanders he had served under, and giving an account of his military service, he would receive his discharge. He would also be commended or rebuked, depending on his conduct. Now, at the time in question Gellius and Lentulus were the two censors. So there they were, duly presiding over the proceedings, with the knights passing by them and undergoing their examination, when Pompey was spotted making his way down to the forum, with all the insignia of his office, but leading his horse by hand himself. When he had come close enough for everyone to be able to see him, he told his lictors to make way and brought his horse up to the rostra. Complete silence fell over the astonished crowd, and the sight dazed and delighted the censors too. Then the senior censor asked, 'I require you, Pompey the Great, to tell me whether you have performed your military service according to the law.' And Pompey replied in a loud voice, 'I have served on all the campaigns I was asked to, with the commanding officer in every case being myself.' At these words the people could no longer restrain their cries of joy and broke out into cheers, but the censors stood up and escorted Pompey home, to the delight of the applauding crowd of Romans who accompanied them on their way.*

[23] Pompey's term of office was drawing to a close, but his

differences with Crassus were becoming more serious, when a man called Gaius Aurelius, a member of the equestrian order who had never in his life had any involvement in politics, mounted the rostra during a meeting of the assembly, stepped forward, and said that Jupiter had appeared to him in a dream and had ordered him to tell the consuls that they were not to let their period of office come to an end without first making friends with each other. After this speech, Pompey just stood there without doing anything, leaving Crassus to make the first move: he greeted Pompey warmly by name and said, 'My fellow citizens, I don't think I'm doing anything at all demeaning or humiliating if I concede first to Pompey. After all, this is the man who was still a beardless youth when you chose to call him "the Great", and who had not yet entered the senate by the time you had conferred on him two triumphs.' After this they made up, and then laid down their consulships.

Crassus continued to live the kind of life he had originally taken on, but Pompey began to turn down requests to appear in court to speak on someone's behalf, as he had often used to, and gradually put in fewer and fewer appearances in the forum. In fact, he hardly appeared in public any more, and then only with a considerable retinue. This crowd of attendants made it hard to get to him or even see him, and he particularly enjoyed putting in an appearance surrounded by a huge mass of people, as a way of ensuring that he struck a majestic and imposing figure, since he imagined that the way for him to preserve his dignity was to remain unsullied by any contact or communication with the masses. Life as a private citizen can indeed have a damaging effect on the reputations of people who have made a great name for themselves in war and are therefore at odds with everyday equality. They think they deserve the same prominence in the one domain that they had in the other, or if they failed to make much of a mark in war they find it intolerable that in civilian life, at any rate, they should lack extra privileges. That is why, when the people find in the forum someone famous for his military exploits and triumphs, they try to cut him down to size and get him into their control, but they leave free from their envious assaults the reputation and authority a person gained in warfare if he goes into retirement and withdraws from public life. Events themselves soon showed the relevance of this phenomenon to Pompey's life.*

[24] The pirates' power-base was originally in Cilicia. At first they employed reckless hit-and-run tactics, but their assurance and daring increased during the Mithridatic War, when they put themselves at the king's service. Then, while the Romans were busy fighting one another at the gates of Rome during their civil wars, the sea was left unguarded, and gradually drew them on, like a lure, until they stopped confining their attacks to shipping, and began to ransack islands and coastal settlements as well. By this stage men of wealth and good birth, who would have regarded themselves as having above-average intelligence, were starting to involve themselves in piracy, since the enterprise seemed to bring with it a certain status and cachet. In many places there were also harbours especially for pirates, with fortified signal-stations, where their fleets could put in—fleets that were well equipped for their work with fit and healthy rowers, skilled helmsmen, and ships that were fast and manoeuvrable. But despite all these formidable aspects, it was the hideous brazenness of their fleets that caused the most offence. With their golden stern-flagpoles, purple-dyed awnings, and silver-plated oars, it was as if the pirates relished and prided themselves on their criminal activities. The way that every coastline was familiar with their pipes and lyres and drunken parties, the way they kidnapped prominent people, the way they ransomed whole towns they had captured —all this brought Roman supremacy into utter disrepute. At any rate, there were over one thousand pirate ships, and four hundred towns had been captured by them. They attacked and ransacked holy places which had previously been inviolate and sacrosanct: the sanctuaries at Claros, Didyma, and Samothrace, the temple of Chthonia at Hermione, the temple of Asclepius in Epidaurus, Poseidon's temples at the Isthmus and Taenarum and Calauria, Apollo's at Actium and Leucas, Hera's on Samos and in Argos and Lacinium. The sacrifices they used to offer up with their own hands at Olympus were bizarre, and they used to celebrate a number of secret rites, of which the Mithraic mysteries, which owe their initial introduction to the pirates, have survived up to the present day.*

It was Rome, however, which was the main target of their insolence. They even used to come inland from the coast along the roads to Rome to commit their raids, and ransack the nearby villas. Once they went so far as to grab two praetors, Sextilius and Bellienus, in their purple togas, and abducted not just them, but also their lictors and other attendants. Then there was the daughter of Antonius, a man who had celebrated a triumph: she was captured by them as she was taking a trip into the countryside, and she fetched a very rich ransom. But their greatest outrage was this. If one of their prisoners cried out that he was a Roman and mentioned the word 'Rome', they pretended to be stricken by panic and terror; they would strike their thighs and throw themselves to the ground before him, imploring his forgiveness. They would make such a good show of abasing themselves and begging his pardon that their prisoner would be convinced of their sincerity. Then some of the pirates would put *calcei* on his feet, while others wrapped a toga around him, to make sure, as it were, that no one could ever again make any mistake about his identity. After keeping up the pretence for a long time and extracting all the amusement they could from the man, they would let a ladder down from the ship, right there in the open sea, and tell him he was free to disembark and leave; if he showed any reluctance they would push him off the ship themselves and drown him.*

[25] The pirates' power spread over almost all our sea,* until it became closed and inaccessible to all commercial traffic. This was the chief factor that converted the Romans, who were low on supplies and were expecting a serious shortage, to the idea of sending Pompey out to rid the sea of the pirates. Gabinius, who was one of Pompey's close friends, proposed a bill giving Pompey what was not so much a mere naval command, more a full-blown autocracy, involving unregulated absolute power. According to the terms of the law, Pompey's authority was to extend over the whole sea up to the Pillars of Heracles, and over all land up to four hundred stades from the coast.* Very few countries in the Roman world fell outside this boundary; in fact, all the most important peoples and the most powerful kings were included in Pompey's domain. In addition, he was allowed to choose fifteen legates from the senate for particular positions of command, he was to take from the treasuries and be given by the tax collectors as much money as he wanted, and he was to receive two hundred ships, with the right to draw up the service-lists for both the soldiers and the rowers and to include on them as many men as he thought appropriate.

When these proposals were read out, the people greeted them with extraordinary enthusiasm, but while none of the most important and powerful members of the senate was inclined to envy such unrestricted and unlimited power—it was beyond envy—it still struck them as something to be feared, and so they all, with the exception of Caesar, opposed the law. Caesar endorsed it not because he cared in the slightest about Pompey, but because right from the start of his career he wanted to ingratiate himself with the people and win their support.* All the rest of them, however, laid into Pompey in no uncertain terms, and when one of the consuls told him that if he took Romulus as his model he should expect to meet the same end as Romulus,* he was almost torn to pieces by the masses. When Catulus came forward to speak against the bill, a respectful silence fell over the crowd and they listened to him. He went on for a long time in an appreciative manner, speaking in Pompey's favour without arousing the hostility of the assembled people, but when he advised them to spare such a man and not to keep exposing him to constant dangers and wars, and said, 'If you lose Pompey, who else will you have?', they all shouted back with one voice, 'You!' Catulus stood down, then, having failed to win them over. When Roscius stepped up to speak, no one listened, so he gestured with his hands to get across the idea that they should not send Pompey out alone, but should choose a colleague to go with him.* The story goes that the people, enraged by this suggestion, let loose such a loud cry that a crow which happened to flying over the forum was stunned by it and fell down into the crowd. This makes it look as though when birds slip and fall like that it is not due to the air being ripped and torn apart, and so creating a vacuum, but it seems on the contrary that the sound travels so forcefully and with such strength that it acts like a physical blow and makes a surge or a billow in the air which strikes the birds.*

[26] For the time being the assembly was dissolved, and on the day scheduled for the vote Pompey slipped out of Rome and into the country. When he heard that the law had been passed, however, he returned to the city, but at night, because he thought it would cause offence if a crowd of people flocked to meet him. The next day he appeared in public and offered up a sacrifice of thanks. A special assembly was convened for him, and he managed to add considerably to what had already been voted him; in fact, he almost doubled the men and *matériel* at his disposal. Five hundred ships were manned and equipped for him, and an army was raised consisting of 120,000 legionaries and 5,000 cavalrymen. Twenty-four men who had held

military commands or served as praetors were chosen by him from the senate, and two quaestors were also attached to his staff. The people were so pleased by the fact that the price of goods immediately fell in the market-place that the notion arose among them that the mere name of Pompey had brought the war to an end. Nevertheless, Pompey divided the stretches of open water and the whole extent of the inner sea into thirteen parts and deployed a certain number of ships, and a commanding officer, within each part. With his forces spread simultaneously all over the place, he restricted the movement of entire pirate fleets as he came across them, and then lost no time in hunting them down and bringing them into land. Others hurriedly scattered and escaped, and slunk back from all directions to Cilicia, like bees to a hive. Pompey intended to set out against them himself, with his sixty best ships, but he resisted doing so until he had completely cleared the Tyrrhenian Sea, the Libyan Sea, and the waters around Sardinia, Corsica, and Sicily of their infestations of pirates, which took him forty days in all, with the help of his own tireless energy and the commitment of his commanding officers.*

[27] Back in Rome, however, the consul Piso, a bitter enemy of Pompey's, was impeding his efforts and releasing his crews from active service. Pompey therefore sent his fleet round the coast to Brundisium, while he travelled overland to Rome via Etruria. When news reached Rome of his approach, everyone poured out of the city to meet him, as if they had not seen him off just a few days earlier. What made them so happy was the astonishing speed with which the situation had changed; the market-place, for instance, was now overflowing with goods. Under these circumstances, Piso came very close to losing his consulship. Gabinius had the bill all drawn up and ready for submission, but Pompey stopped him going ahead with it. The same spirit of decency characterized his conduct of all the other matters that required his attention, and then, once he had got what he wanted, he went down to Brundisium and sailed off to continue the war.

Time was pressing, and he bypassed other cities, but he could not resist breaking his journey by visiting Athens, where he sacrificed to the gods and made a speech to the Athenian people. As he was on his way out of the city, he read two one-line epigrams which had been inscribed in his honour. The first one, on the inside of the city gate, ran: 'To the extent that you are aware of your mortality, you are divine.' And the other one, on the outside of the gate, was: 'We awaited you, we paid our respects, we saw you, and now we see you on your way.'*

Some of the pirate flotillas that had remained together and were still roaming the seas away from Cilicia sued for peace and were treated leniently by him, in the sense that after seizing their ships and putting them under arrest he did them no further harm. This encouraged the rest to hope for mercy too, so they avoided the other Roman commanders, made their way to Pompey with their children and wives, and surrendered to him. He spared all their lives, and they proved invaluable in helping him track down, capture, and punish those who remained in hiding, aware of the unpardonable crimes they had committed.

[28] The majority of the pirates, however, and certainly the most powerful ones, had sent their families and their valuables, and all their motley non-combatants, for safe keeping to strongholds and fortresses in the Taurus mountains, while they themselves manned their ships and awaited Pompey's attack at Coracesium in Cilicia. They lost the battle and were blockaded inside the town. In the end they sent tokens of supplication and surrendered themselves and all the towns and islands in their possession—places which they had fortified to make them inaccessible and hard to storm. And so the war was over. Pompey had taken about three months at the most to sweep the sea clear of piracy, and in the process he had captured a large number of ships, including ninety bronze-rammed warships. As for the actual pirates, although he had no intention of putting them to death (there were over twenty thousand of them), at the same time he did not think it would be right for him to let them go and allow them either to disperse or regroup: after all, they were a troublesome and warlike lot. So bearing in mind the fact that man is not and, in the normal course of events, does not become a wild and unsociable creature, but that vicious habits make him into something it is not his nature to be, and reflecting that if a gentler environment can make wild beasts lose their fierce and savage qualities, then even a bad man can be civilized by a change of habits, surroundings, and lifestyle, he decided to make the men live on the land rather than the sea, so that once they had become accustomed to live in towns and work the soil, they would have firsthand experience of a decent life.

Some of them were therefore taken in and accommodated by the small, semi-desolate communities of Cilicia, which were given extra territory, while Pompey restored the city of Soli, which had recently been devastated by King Tigranes of Armenia, and settled a lot of them there. But most of them took up residence, at Pompey's initiative, in Dyme in Achaea, which at the time was short of inhabitants and had a lot of good land.*

[29] Not even his detractors could find anything to criticize in his conduct of this war, but even his friends were unhappy with his treatment of Metellus in Crete. Metellus, a relative of Pompey's colleague in Spain, had been sent with an army to Crete before Pompey had been given the job of dealing with the pirates—Crete being a kind of secondary source of piracy after Cilicia. Now, Metellus had a lot of the pirates trapped and was in the process of eliminating and destroying them, but the ones who still remained under siege sent tokens of supplication to Pompey and begged him to come to the island, which they said was part of his domain, since the whole of it fell within the designated distance from the sea. He welcomed their claim and wrote ordering Metellus to cease hostilities. He also instructed the towns and cities of Crete by letter not to pay any attention to Metellus, and he sent one of his own officers, Lucius Octavius, to act as their commander, and Octavius joined the besieged pirates inside their strongholds and fought alongside them. Leaving aside the anger and loathing this action brought Pompey's way, it also made him look ridiculous: out of envy and the ambitious desire to outshine Metellus he had lent his name to immoral and godless men, and used his own reputation as a kind of talisman to protect them. Even Achilles, people said, was behaving not like a man, but just like a capricious boy who has got overexcited by the prospect of glory, when he signalled to the others and stopped them from striking Hector, 'Lest someone else might gain credit for the blow, and he come second.'* But Pompey actually fought for the state's enemies and saved their lives in order to deny a Roman commander a triumph, after all his efforts. In actual fact, though, Metellus refused to be cowed. He kept the pirates for himself and punished them, and he sent Octavius packing, after abusing and rebuking him in front of the whole army.*

[30] When news reached Rome that the Pirate War was over and that Pompey now had nothing better to do than tour the Greek

cities, one of the tribunes, Manilius, introduced a bill proposing that the war against the kings Mithridates and Tigranes should be turned over to Pompey, along with all the territory and troops under Lucullus' command, and along with Bithynia too, which was currently held by Glabrio, while he retained his naval forces and his mastery of the sea on the same terms as before.* The effect of this was to place the whole Roman empire in the hands of just one man, because the only provinces which were held to be excluded by the provisions of the earlier law—Phrygia, Lycaonia, Galatia, Cappadocia, Cilicia, Upper Colchis, and Armenia—were now added to what he already had, together with the armies and resources with which Lucullus had defeated Mithridates and Tigranes. The aristocrats resented the injustice and ingratitude with which Lucullus was being treated, in that he was being deprived of the glory due to him for his achievements and was handing his triumph rather than the war on to his successor, but this did not seem such an important issue to them; what worried them more was that Pompey's power seemed to form the basis for a tyranny, and they urged and encouraged one another in private to attack the law and not to give up their freedom without a fight. But when the time came, nearly all of them were paralysed by fear of the people and kept silent, except for Catulus, who launched into a lengthy diatribe against the law and the tribune who proposed it. His words had no effect, however, so in a loud voice he repeatedly urged the senate from the rostra to follow the example of their ancestors and find a hill or a crag where they could take refuge and preserve their freedom.* Nevertheless, the law was passed after receiving, we are told, the unanimous vote of all the tribes, and even though Pompey was not in Rome at the time, the powers he was assigned almost equalled those Sulla gained after conquering the city by force of arms. In due course the letters announcing the decisions that had been taken in Rome reached Pompey, but whereas his friends all came up to him and congratulated him, the story goes that Pompey frowned and slapped his thigh, and said, in the tone of one who is already tired of carrying the burden of command, 'Is there to be no end to my labours? It really is better to be born a nobody. Look at me: my military service will never stop, and I'll never shake off the envy that haunts me and live quietly in the country with my wife.' Even his closest friends found the insincerity of these words abhorrent, because they knew that his dislike of Lucullus fuelled his innate ambition and love of power and made him all the more delighted with what had happened.

[31] Of course, his actions soon revealed his true thoughts. Orders poured out in all directions, as he recruited troops and sent for client kings and subject rulers. As he passed through the country he interfered with everything Lucullus had done, often even to the extent of letting people off their punishments or taking back their rewards. In short, he did everything he could to satisfy his ambition and show Lucullus' admirers that their favourite had no authority at all.* When Lucullus protested through the agency of his friends, it was decided that they should meet. The meeting took place in Galatia. As befitted leaders of their stature, with so many important victories to their credit, both men's lictors had their fasces similarly wreathed with laurel for the meeting. However, whereas Lucullus' route had taken him through green and shady parts, Pompey happened to have crossed a parched and treeless stretch of ground. So when Lucullus' lictors saw that Pompey's laurel was all wilting and faded, they gave some of their own laurel, which was still fresh, to be used to decorate and wreathe his fasces. This was widely interpreted as a sign that Pompey had come to steal the glory and rewards that were due to Lucullus for his victories. Both men were of consular rank, but Lucullus was Pompey's senior in this respect, as well as in age; Pompey's two triumphs, however, meant that he took precedence over the other man. Nevertheless, the first meeting was conducted in as diplomatic and friendly a fashion as was possible under the circumstances, with each congratulating and complimenting the other on his achievements and successes. When they met for subsequent discussions, however, the outcome was far from courteous or polite—in fact, they hurled insults at each other. The accusations of Lucullus' avarice and Pompey's hunger for power flew back and forth to such an extent that their friends only just managed to separate the two men.

From his camp in Galatia, Lucullus parcelled out the newly captured land and distributed rewards as he saw fit, while Pompey camped quite close to him and tried to stop anyone listening to Lucullus' orders. Pompey stripped Lucullus of all his troops, apart from sixteen hundred men, whom he considered too insubordinate to be any use to himself, and by the same token were hostile to Lucullus. He also made disparaging remarks about Lucullus' achievements; he used to say in public that Lucullus' opponents had been kings from drama and paintings, whereas, now that Mithridates had resorted to shields, swords, and horses, it was left up to him to take on a real army, and one which had learnt its lessons well. Lucullus retorted that it was Pompey who was going out to fight the mere image and shadow of a war, since as usual he was settling, like a parasitical bird, on the corpses someone else had killed, and was tearing at nothing but the remains of war. This, Lucullus said, was how Pompey had gained the credit for the defeat of Sertorius, Lepidus, and the uprising led by Spartacus, which were actually due to Crassus, Metellus, and Catulus. It was hardly surprising, then, to find him trying to stake a claim in the victories in Armenia and Pontus, when he had somehow contrived to get himself awarded a triumph over runaway slaves.

[32] After Lucullus' departure, Pompey deployed his whole fleet to patrol the sea between Phoenicia and the Bosporus in squadrons, while he himself marched against Mithridates with an army of 30,000 legionaries and 2,000 cavalrymen. He did not think it wise, however, to offer battle. The first thing that happened was that after Mithridates abandoned the hill where he had encamped, on the grounds that, although it was inaccessible and hard to attack, it appeared to lack sources of water, Pompey immediately occupied it himself. Deducing from the kinds of plants and trees growing there and the gullies in the ground that the place did have springs, Pompey ordered his men to dig wells all over the hill, and before long the camp had a generous supply of water. In fact, it was surprising that throughout his time on the hill Mithridates had remained ignorant of how much water there was. The next thing Pompey did was surround Mithridates' camp with fortifications and put him under siege. Forty-five days into the siege, however, Mithridates slipped away with those of his troops who were still fit for battle, after killing those who were ill and unfit for service. Later, Pompey caught up with him near the Euphrates and pitched camp close to his. Since he was worried about the possibility of Mithridates quickly crossing the Euphrates ahead of him, he armed his men in the middle of the night and led them into the attack. At exactly the same time, it is said, Mithridates had a dream in which he saw what was going to happen. In the dream he was sailing on the Pontic Sea; the wind was behind him, the Bosporus was in sight, and he was happily chatting

with the crew, just as someone would who has no reason to fear anything—when suddenly he found himself all alone, tossed about on a small piece of wreckage. Just at this catastrophic point of his dream his friends came up to his bed and woke him up with the news of Pompey's approach.*

Mithridates had no choice but to fight in defence of his camp, and his commanding officers had the troops fall in ready for battle outside the camp. When Pompey saw that they were ready for him, the prospect of fighting in the dark worried him. It seemed to him that all he had to do was surround them to prevent them escaping, and then attack them in the daylight. After all, they did outnumber his own forces. But the advice and recommendations of his most experienced officers convinced him that immediate action was his best plan, since it was not completely dark. In fact, there was still enough light from the setting moon to make people out, and this proved to be the most important factor in the downfall of the king's troops, because the Romans had the moon behind them as they attacked. With the light low in the west, their shadows stretched far ahead of their bodies and reached the enemy, who could not accurately estimate the distance involved and, supposing that the Romans were already upon them, discharged their javelins too early and hit no one. As soon as the Romans saw this they raced forward with a cry and set about killing panic-stricken men who had lost their nerve and turned to flee. In the end, well over ten thousand men were killed, and the camp was captured.*

Mithridates himself, however, cut his way through the Roman lines with a cavalry troop that initially numbered eight hundred, but was soon reduced to three as the troop disintegrated. One of the three was a concubine called Hypsicrateia, who throughout her life had displayed a manly spirit and a readiness to face danger. In fact, the king used to call her Hypsicrates. At the time in question she was dressed like a Persian man and riding a horse. Not only did she prove herself physically capable of enduring the long ride, but she also never gave up looking after the king's person and tending to his horse as well. Eventually they reached a place called Sinora, where the king had stockpiled plenty of money and valuables. From this hoard Mithridates took costly garments and distributed them among those who had regrouped around him after their flight. He also gave each of his friends a lethal poison to carry around with them, in case they were ever in danger of being captured by the enemy and wanted an alternative. He then set out from Sinora with the intention of going to Tigranes in Armenia, but Tigranes refused him entry and put a price of a hundred talents on his head. Mithridates therefore continued his flight past the sources of the Euphrates and through Colchis.*

[33] At the invitation of the younger Tigranes, who was now in open revolt against his father, Pompey invaded Armenia. Tigranes met Pompey by the river Araxes, which rises in the same region as the Euphrates, but then turns towards the east and issues into the Caspian Sea. Pompey and the younger Tigranes then advanced deeper into Armenia, taking joint possession of the various towns and cities they passed on their way. But when King Tigranes, who had recently suffered a crushing defeat at the hands of Lucullus,* found out that Pompey was a lenient and even-tempered kind of person, he first allowed a Roman garrison into his palace, and then gathered together all his friends and relations and set out to surrender to Pompey. He rode up to the Roman camp on horseback, but two of Pompey's lictors came up and advised him to dismount and approach on foot, on the grounds that there was no precedent for anyone ever appearing in a Roman camp on horseback. Tigranes not only did as they suggested in this respect, but he also undid his sword and handed it over to them. To cap it all, when he came into the presence of Pompey himself, he took off his *kitaris* and made as if to place it at Pompey's feet.* He would even have completed his humiliation by dropping to the ground and clasping Pompey's knees in supplication, but before he could go any further Pompey took him by the right hand, drew him forward, and seated him on one side, with his son on the other. He said that as far as the rest of his territory was concerned, he had Lucullus to blame for its loss, since it was Lucullus who had taken Syria, Phoenicia, Cilicia, Galatia, and Sophene away from him, but that he could keep all the territory he had managed to hang on to so far, provided he paid a fine of six thousand talents to Rome to compensate for his crimes. He also said that his son could rule over Sophene. Tigranes was perfectly content with these conditions, and when the Romans saluted him as king he was so happy that he promised to give half a mina of silver to every soldier, ten minas to every centurion, and a talent to every tribune. His son was displeased, however, and responded to an invitation to a

banquet by saying that he did not need Pompey for this kind of honour, since he could find any number of Romans who would do the same for him—a remark which led to his being thrown into prison, where he was kept under guard until Pompey's triumph. Not long afterwards, Phraates of Parthia wrote to Pompey demanding that the young man be handed over to him, on the grounds that he was his son-in-law, and also insisting that the Euphrates be taken as the boundary between the Roman and Parthian empires. In reply Pompey said that Tigranes belonged to his father rather than his father-in-law and that the boundary he would respect would be the one that was fair.*

[34] Leaving Afranius in charge of the Roman troops in Armenia, Pompey set off against Mithridates.* His route inevitably took him through the territory of the peoples who live in and around the Caucasus, the most important of whom are the Albanians and the Iberians. Iberian territory extends up to the Moschian mountains and the Euxine Sea, while the Albanians inhabit the lands to the east, up to the Caspian Sea. At first the Albanians gave Pompey permission to pass through their land, but winter found the Romans still in their territory. Just when it was time for the Romans to celebrate the festival of the Saturnalia, an Albanian force of at least forty thousand men took to the field against them, after crossing the river Cyrnus. (This river rises in the Iberian mountains, is joined by the Araxes as it comes down from Armenia, and ends at twelve mouths which issue into the Caspian. Some writers, however, deny that the Araxes joins the Cyrnus and claim that it is an entirely independent river which runs close to the Cyrnus and issues into the same sea.) Although Pompey could have made a stand against the enemy at the crossing, he let them reach the other side of the river unchallenged, and then attacked them. The Albanians were scattered and took extremely heavy casualties, whereupon their king sent envoys to sue for peace. Pompey overlooked his unwarranted aggression and entered into a peace treaty with him, before marching against the Iberians, who were just as numerous a people as the Albanians, but more warlike. The Iberians were extremely eager to do Mithridates a favour by repelling Pompey, because they had never been part of either the Median or Persian empires, and had even avoided Macedonian rule because Alexander had left Hyrcania in a hurry.* Nevertheless, although the fighting was fierce, Pompey routed them

too. Iberian losses numbered nine thousand, with over ten thousand taken prisoner. Next Pompey invaded Colchis, where he was met at the Phasis river by Servilius, with the fleet which had been patrolling the Euxine Sea.

[35] Mithridates had gone to ground among the peoples on the Bosporus and Lake Maeotis, and it was proving far from easy to pursue him.* Then the infuriating news reached Pompey that the Albanians were up in arms again. Rising to the challenge, he turned back in that direction and recrossed the Cyrnus, which was slow and dangerous work, since the enemy had planted a barrier of stakes along much of its bank. He was faced with an arduous journey through a long stretch of waterless land, so he got his men to fill ten thousand skins with water, and then he marched against the enemy. He caught up with them at the river Abas, where they were drawn up in their battle-lines. Their army, led by Cosis, the king's brother, consisted of 60,000 foot soldiers and 12,000 horsemen, but most of them had inadequate weaponry and were dressed in animal skins. As soon as battle was joined Cosis charged straight at Pompey himself and struck him with a javelin on the flap of his breastplate, but Pompey ran him through at close quarters and killed him. It is said that among the enemy forces in this battle there were Amazons, who had come down from the high country near the Thermodon river. At any rate, after the battle, as they were despoiling the foreigners' corpses, the Romans came across Amazonian shields and boots; but they did not find a single female body. Amazons live in the parts of the Caucasus which come down to the Hyrcanian Sea. The Albanians are not their neighbours, because there are the Gelae and the Leges between them. For two months every year the Amazons meet up with men from these two peoples at the river Thermodon for sex, and then they go away and live by themselves.*

[36] After the battle Pompey set out to march to Hyrcania and the Caspian Sea, but when he was only three days away from his destination he was forced to turn back by the huge numbers of deadly snakes in the region.* He retreated to Lesser Armenia, where he received delegations from the kings of the Elymaeans and the Medes, to whom he wrote friendly letters in reply. However, the Parthian king had invaded Gordyene and was plundering Tigranes' subjects, so Pompey sent an army under Afranius, which successfully

drove him out of the country and pushed him all the way back to Arbelitis.*

A number of Mithridates' concubines were captured and brought to him, but he kept none of them for sexual purposes and returned them all to their parents and families.* Most of them were the daughters and wives of military commanders and rulers, but Stratonice, Mithridates' particular favourite, whom he made responsible for his richest fortress, was apparently the daughter of a harp-player who was not well off, and was old as well. She made such an immediate hit with Mithridates as she played her harp once to entertain him while he was drinking after dinner that he took her off to bed that very night, after dismissing the old man, who was angry at not even getting a kind word from Mithridates. In the morning, however, the old man woke up and found in his house tables laden with gold and silver goblets, a huge crowd of attendants, and eunuchs and slaves bringing him expensive clothing, while outside the house stood a horse, as richly caparisoned as any owned by the king's friends. At first he thought the whole thing a practical joke and he made as if to run outside, until the slaves stopped him and told him that the king had endowed him with the whole of the large estate of a rich man who had recently died, and that the objects here represented just a small proportion of all the property and possessions involved. After a while, when he had finally come to believe them, he put on his purple-dyed cloak, leapt on to the horse, and rode through the town, shouting, 'All this is mine!' If anyone laughed at him he told them not to be surprised at what he was doing; he was so crazy with pleasure, he said, that what was really surprising was that he did not pelt people he met with stones.

This was Stratonice's 'family background and stock'.* She now surrendered her fortress to Pompey and brought him a large number of gifts as well, but he accepted only the things which he thought could be used to adorn temples or which would enhance the splendour of his triumph, and he told Stratonice to keep the rest for herself as a treat. By the same token, when the Iberian king sent him a couch, a table, and a throne, all of gold, and begged him to accept them, he gave them to the quaestors for the public treasury.

[37] In the fortress of Caenum* Pompey also found secret papers belonging to Mithridates, which he read with considerable pleasure, because they afforded plenty of insights into the king's character.

For instance, they included memoranda proving that Mithridates was responsible for having a lot of people poisoned, including his son Ariarathes, and also Alcaeus of Sardis—the latter for having gained more of a reputation for his racehorses than Mithridates. The papers also included interpretations of both his own and his wives' dreams, and lewd letters written by Monime to him, and by him back to her.* Theophanes adds that among these papers there was also found a speech by Rutilius designed to encourage Mithridates to massacre the Romans living in Asia. But it is generally, and rightly, supposed that this is a malicious invention by Theophanes, perhaps because he hated Rutilius, who was certainly a totally different kind of person from himself, or more probably because he wanted to please Pompey, whose father Rutilius had proved in his historical writings to be an utter villain.*

[38] From Caenum Pompey went to Amisus,* where his love of recognition led him into some reprehensible behaviour. He had often taunted Lucullus for acting, while the enemy was still alive, in ways more usually associated with the behaviour of victors after a war has been brought to a successful conclusion—such as issuing edicts and distributing gifts and rewards. But now, with Mithridates firmly in control of the Bosporus and in command of a formidable newly mustered army, Pompey himself was behaving in exactly the same way, and was settling the affairs of the provinces and handing out rewards as if everything were over and done with. Twelve eastern kings paid him a visit here, as well as a large number of princes and potentates, and the upshot of this was that in order to please them he chose, in replying to a letter from the Parthian king, not to address him as 'King of Kings', as everyone else did.

He conceived a passionate longing to annex Syria and to march through Arabia to the Red Sea, so that in every direction his conquests would have brought him into contact with the Ocean which surrounds the inhabited world. For in Africa he had been the first to extend the area of his dominion all the way to the outer sea; then in Spain he had made the Atlantic Sea the boundary of Roman rule; and thirdly his recent pursuit of the Albanians had taken him almost up to the Hyrcanian Sea.* He now wanted, then, to include the Red Sea and therefore to have made a complete circuit in his campaigns, and with this intention he set out. Besides, it had become clear to him that Mithridates was hard to hunt down by military means, and in flight was a more awkward opponent than he was in battle.

[39] Accordingly, declaring that he would bequeath the campaign against Mithridates to a more formidable opponent than himself—namely, starvation—he posted ships to patrol the mouth of the Bosporus and prevent merchant vessels from entering it, with death as the penalty prescribed for anyone attempting to do so. Then he gathered together the bulk of his army and set out. When he came across the still unburied bodies of the men who had died fighting unsuccessfully alongside Triarius against Mithridates, he buried them all with full and magnificent honours. Lucullus' failure to carry out this job was probably one of the main reasons for his unpopularity.* After Afranius had subdued the Arabians living near Amanus for him, he went down into Syria, where he declared the country a province and a possession of the Roman people, since it lacked kings who were truly entitled to their thrones. Then he conquered Judaea and made its king, Aristobulus, his prisoner.* He created a new foundation for some cities in the area, and gave others their freedom by punishing the tyrants who had ruled over them. But his chief occupation was in the judicial sphere, where he settled disputes between cities and kings, or, if he could not personally attend a hearing, he would send some of his friends. So, for instance, when the Armenians and the Parthians asked him to arbitrate a territorial dispute, he sent three men to assess the situation and settle the quarrel.* He was widely known for his effectiveness, but also, and no less, for his integrity and leniency. But he very often used this reputation to cover up crimes committed by his friends and associates, since it was not in his nature to deter or punish bad men. However, people who had dealings with him were glad to put up with their rapacity and arrogance, since they found him personally so congenial.

[40] The person who had the most influence with him was a freedman called Demetrius, a young man of considerable intelligence who had a tendency to abuse the position he was lucky enough to find himself in. Here is one of the stories that are told about him. When Cato the philosopher was still a young man, but already had a considerable reputation and high principles, he visited Antioch. Pompey was not there at the time; Cato just wanted to make a study of the city. As usual, Cato was on foot, while his friends accompanied him on horseback. Outside the city gates, he saw a crowd of men

dressed in white clothes and two groups, one of youths, the other of boys, lining opposite sides of the road. This annoyed him, because he supposed that he was the object of it—that it was a way of honouring and paying respect to him—when that was the last thing he wanted. Nevertheless, he told his friends to dismount and to walk up to the city with him. When he and his party drew near, the man who had organized and arranged the whole thing came to meet them with a garland on his head and a wand in his hand—and asked them where they had left Demetrius, and when he would arrive! Cato's friends burst out laughing, but Cato just said, 'Poor city!', and walked on past the man without making any further response to his questions.*

However, Pompey made Demetrius less offensive to everyone else as well by putting up with his high-handed behaviour with good grace. It is said that at parties, for instance, while Pompey was waiting to receive his other guests, Demetrius would often be found already reclining impudently on a couch, with the hood of his toga pulled down over his head and covering his ears.* Even before returning to Italy, he had bought all the pleasantest precincts and the most beautiful parks in Rome, and there was a lavish garden named 'the Garden of Demetrius' after him, while up until the time of his third triumph Pompey himself lived in a modest and inextravagant fashion. Later, when Pompey was building the magnificent and famous theatre in Rome, he had a house built for himself by it, like a dinghy in the wake of a larger boat, which was more sumptuous than the one he had before, but even this new one was not the kind to cause offence.* In fact, the story goes that when the man who owned it after Pompey first walked into it he asked in surprise where Pompey the Great had held his banquets.

[41] Rome and its affairs had previously not been of the slightest concern to the king of the Arabians who lived around Petra,* but now he became seriously frightened and he wrote to tell of his decision that he was theirs to command in everything. Pompey wanted to make sure that he really meant what he said, so he advanced towards Petra. This expedition was quite heavily criticized in most quarters, because it was seen as an evasion of the pursuit of Mithridates, and people thought that Pompey should concentrate on him, the original enemy, who was once again rekindling the flames of war and, according to reports, was preparing to march through Scythia and Paeonia

and invade Italy.* But Pompey was convinced that it would be easier to put an end to the king's power when he was at war than to capture him when he was in hiding. He was therefore unwilling to waste time and effort in a futile chase, and was finding other things to do which were incidental to the war and would fill in the time.

Chance, however, intervened and resolved the dilemma. One day, when he was quite close to Petra and had already built his camp, he was exercising himself on horseback near the camp when some messengers rode up from Pontus, bringing good news. Bearers of good news are immediately recognizable by the fact that they wreathe the heads of their spears in laurel. As soon as the soldiers saw the messengers approaching they ran and crowded round Pompey. At first he wanted to finish his exercises, but his men clamoured for him to read the letter, so he jumped off his horse, took the letter, and led the way into the camp. There was no speaker's platform, nor had they got around to constructing even the military version of one, which the soldiers make with their own hands by laying large slabs of turf on top of one another, but in the urgency and excitement of the moment they piled up the yoke-animals' saddle-cloths into a raised platform. Pompey mounted this platform and announced that Mithridates was dead—that he had killed himself when his son Pharnaces had risen up in rebellion against him. The reins of government there had devolved entirely on Pharnaces, Pompey explained, and Pharnaces had written to explain the situation to himself and the Romans.*

[42] The troops were of course delighted with the news. Sacrifices and celebrations were the order of the day, since they felt that Mithridates' death was worth the deaths of ten thousand of the enemy. Pompey, who had not expected such an easy conclusion to all his achievements and campaigns, immediately withdrew from Arabia and went to Amisus, passing quickly through the intervening provinces.* At Amisus he found that Pharnaces had left him a great many gifts, and also the bodies of a lot of the royal family, including Mithridates himself. Mithridates was hardly recognizable from his features, because the people who treated his body forgot to dissolve and extract his brain, but his scars identified him for anyone who felt like viewing the body. Pompey himself could not face seeing the body, but sent it off to Sinope in order to avert divine retribution.* He was deeply impressed by the size and magnificence of the clothes and

armour Mithridates had worn, but the sword-belt, which had cost four hundred talents to make, was stolen by Publius and sold to Ariarathes, while Faustus, Sulla's son, asked Gaius, Mithridates' foster-brother, for the *kitaris*, which was a marvellous piece of workmanship, and Gaius surreptitiously got it for him. At the time Pompey knew nothing about all this, but Pharnaces found out later and punished the thieves.

Once he had settled and sorted things out there, he set out again, but this time in a more ostentatious manner. For instance, when he came to Mytilene he gave the city its freedom for the sake of Theophanes,* and he joined the audience for the traditional poetic competition, whose sole theme on this occasion was his exploits. He liked the theatre there so much that he had a sketch made of its form and design, so that he could make the one in Rome like it, only larger and on a grander scale. Then again, in Rhodes he attended lectures by all the sophists and rewarded each of them with a talent. Posidonius even wrote down the lecture he delivered in Pompey's presence, in which he took a position contrary to that of Hermagoras the orator on the subject of the general principles of investigation.* And in Athens Pompey not only treated the philosophers in the same way, but also gave the city fifty talents for its restoration fund.*

He had hoped to set foot on Italian soil in a blaze of glory and with his longing to see his family fully reciprocated, but as it turned out the god whose job it is always to mix a portion of adversity in with the brilliant and important blessings bestowed by fortune had been lurking around for a long time and scheming to make his return less happy than it might have been, since Mucia had lived a promiscuous life during his absence. Pompey had treated the rumours with contempt while he was far away, but as he got close to Italy he seems to have found the time to think the accusations over more carefully, and he sent her a notice of divorce. Neither then nor later did he write down or speak out loud the grounds on which he divorced her, but the charge can be found written in Cicero's letters.*

[43] All kinds of stories about Pompey preceded him to Rome, and the rumour that as soon as he landed he was going to lead his army against the city and establish an impregnable monarchy caused considerable turmoil there. Crassus took his children and his property and slipped out of the city, either because he was genuinely afraid, or, as was more widely believed, because he wanted his

departure to give the rumours plausibility and fan the flames of the hatred people felt for Pompey. So as soon as he had landed in Italy Pompey convened a general meeting of all his troops, and after making an appropriate speech expressing his gratitude, he told them to go back to their various towns and cities and concentrate on domestic matters, while not forgetting to join him again for the triumph. And so the army was disbanded. When this became common knowledge, an incredible thing happened. At the sight of Pompey the Great travelling along unarmed and accompanied by just a few close friends, as if he were returning from an ordinary journey abroad, the inhabitants of the cities he passed felt such affection for him that they poured out of their homes and escorted him on his way. In the end, then, he arrived back at Rome with a larger body of men than the army he had disbanded, which would therefore have been unnecessary for any revolutionary measures he might have been contemplating at the time.*

[44] Since it was illegal for a commander to enter the city before his triumph, he wrote to the senate, asking them to do him the favour of postponing the consular elections, so that he could be there to canvass on behalf of Piso. This request was refused, however, thanks to Cato's opposition to it.* Pompey was so impressed with Cato's candour and the intensity of his unaided public defence of the laws that he wanted to find a way to bring him into his family. To be specific, Cato had two nieces, and Pompey wanted one of them to become his wife and the other his son's wife. Cato was deeply suspicious of Pompey's attentions, which he saw as an attempt to corrupt him—to bribe him, as it were, with a marriage alliance—but his sister and his wife were furious that he was going to turn down the opportunity to have Pompey the Great as a relative. Meanwhile, however, Pompey was spending money on the tribes because he wanted to see Afranius elected consul, and people were making their way to the Garden of Pompey to collect the money. The whole business became a famous scandal, and Pompey came in for some serious criticism, on the grounds that he was now treating the office with which he had been specially rewarded for his victories as something that could be bought by people who were incapable of winning it on their own merits. So Cato said to his womenfolk, 'Some of this criticism is bound to rub off on Pompey's relatives.' At this they agreed that his assessment of right and wrong was better than theirs.

[45] His triumph was on such a generous scale that even the two separate days scheduled for it were not enough and many of the displays that had been planned did not get a showing. In fact, what was left out would have sufficed for another magnificent and gorgeous procession. Banners paraded at the head of the procession showed the countries and peoples over which the triumph was being celebrated. They were as follows: Pontus, Armenia, Paphlagonia, Cappadocia, Media, Colchis, the Iberians, the Albanians, Syria, Cilicia, Mesopotamia, the inhabitants of Phoenicia and Palestine, Judaea, Arabia, and all the pirates who had been defeated on land and at sea. In the course of these campaigns he had captured at least 1,000 strongholds, about 900 towns and cities, and 800 pirate ships, and had founded thirty-nine new colonies. The banners also declared that the extra territories he had acquired for Rome were bringing in 85,000,000 drachmas in taxes, over and above the usual 50,000,000 drachmas of revenue, and that he was making over to the public treasury coined money and gold and silver utensils to the value of 20,000 talents, after deducting the money that had been given to his soldiers, none of whom had received as his share less than fifteen hundred drachmas. As for the prisoners who were displayed in the procession, apart from the pirate leaders, there were the son of Tigranes of Armenia, along with his wife and daughter; Zosime, the wife of King Tigranes himself; Aristobulus, the king of Judaea; Mithridates' sister, five children of his, and some of his Scythian women; and hostages given by the Albanians, the Iberians, and the king of Commagene. Then there was a huge number of trophies, one for every battle in which he had been victorious, either in person or through the agency of his commanding officers. But the major boost to his prestige was provided by the fact that, for the first time in Roman history, not only was this the third triumph he had gained, but he had gained each of them in a different one of the three continents. He was not the first to have celebrated three triumphs, but he brought the first one back from Africa, the second from Europe, and this last one from Asia, so that in a sense it seemed as though the whole world had been subdued by his three triumphs.*

[46] According to those who like to compare and assimilate Pompey with Alexander in every single respect, he was at this time under 34 years old, but in actual fact he was almost 40.* What a boon it would have been for him to have died at this point of his life, since so

far he had enjoyed the luck of Alexander!* In the future his successes would make men hate him and his failures would be beyond redemption. For he used the influential political position he had acquired by legitimate means to bend the rules for the sake of other people, and so decreased his own reputation by the exact same amount that he increased their power. It was the effectiveness and extent of his own power, then, that gradually became his undoing. When an enemy force takes over the strongest parts of a city's defences, it gains the strength of those defences in addition to its own; by the same token, it was thanks to Pompey's power that Caesar found himself in a position to challenge the city and then encompass the downfall and ruin of the very man with whose help he had become more powerful than everyone else.* This is how it happened.

A splendid reception by the senate greeted Lucullus on his return from Asia after being treated with such disrespect by Pompey, and once Pompey was back in Rome the senators increased their efforts to get Lucullus involved in politics, as a way of curbing the high esteem in which Pompey was held.* Although Lucullus was basically now slow to react and his ardour had cooled, so far as action was concerned, since he had given himself over to the pleasures of retirement and a rich man's pastimes, he rushed energetically into the attack, set about defeating Pompey on the issue of administrative measures of his that Pompey had repealed, and with Cato's support gained the upper hand over him in the senate. Repulsed and rejected, Pompey had no choice but to take refuge with the tribunes of the people and link up with young men such as Clodius, who was the most unscrupulous troublemaker of them all. Clodius adopted Pompey and threw him to the people. He humiliated him by having him constantly cavort in the forum, and he took him around everywhere, getting him to put his weight behind decrees and motions that were designed to gratify and flatter the masses. As if he were Pompey's benefactor rather than the cause of his disgrace, he later extracted a reward from him, in that he got him to betray Cicero, who had been Pompey's friend and had helped him enormously in the political sphere. When Cicero was in danger and needed help, Pompey refused even to see him; and when friends of Cicero's came he bolted his front door against them and slipped out of another exit. Cicero secretly fled from Rome, too frightened about what might happen in his trial to stay.*

[47] Caesar had now returned from his campaigns and instituted a policy which earned him effusive gratitude in the short term, and later a great deal of power, but which did Pompey and the city terrible harm. He was a candidate for his first consulship, and it was clear to him that with Crassus and Pompey at odds with each other, if he attached himself to one of them he would make an enemy of the other. He therefore concentrated on reconciling the two of them, an action which in other contexts would have been admirable and worthy of a true statesman, but which was undertaken for base motives and concocted in a cunning and underhand fashion. For once the countervailing powers that used to bring the city, like a boat, back to an even keel were united and unified, they created an irresistible imbalance that overwhelmed the Roman constitution in schism and destroyed it for ever. Cato, at any rate, used to tell people they were falling into the trap of picking on the most recent incident if they claimed that it was the later quarrel between Caesar and Pompey that caused the downfall of the city; it was not their falling out, he would say, but their coming together, not their hostility but their alliance, that was the first and greatest evil for the city.*

Anyway, Caesar was elected consul, but he immediately began to court the favour of the poor and needy by bringing forward proposals for new colonies and grants of land, which demeaned the dignity of his office and in a sense brought the consulship down to the level of the tribunate. When he was opposed by his colleague Bibulus, with Cato standing ready to offer Bibulus his staunchest support, Caesar brought Pompey up on to the rostra in front of the people, and asked him directly whether he approved of the proposed laws. When Pompey said that he did, Caesar went on, 'So if there is any attempt to do violence to the laws,† will you come to the help of the Roman people?' 'Of course,' Pompey replied. 'I'll bring my swords and shield against their threat of swords.'* This was widely held to have been the most meretricious thing Pompey had said or done up until then, and the outcome was that even his friends sprang to his defence and claimed that the words must have slipped out in the heat of the moment. His subsequent actions showed, however, that he had allowed himself to become nothing but a puppet in Caesar's hands. For instance, he married Caesar's daughter, Julia, which stunned everyone because she was betrothed to Caepio and was due to be married to him in a few days; and as a sop to appease

Caepio's anger he promised his own daughter to him, even though she was already betrothed to Faustus, the son of Sulla. Caesar himself married Calpurnia, the daughter of Piso.*

[48] After this Pompey filled the city with soldiers and used force to keep a tight grip on every aspect of political life. For instance, when Bibulus the consul was on his way down to the forum in the company of Lucullus and Cato, they were suddenly set upon by Pompey's men. The lictors' fasces were broken, someone flung a basket of manure over Bibulus' head, and two tribunes who had formed part of his escort were wounded.* Once they had cleared the forum of their opponents in this way, they passed the law about grants of land, and then this became the bait which enabled them to make the people so completely tame and submissive that without interfering at all they just meekly voted for whatever proposals were brought forward. So the administrative measures which Lucullus had disputed were ratified for Pompey; Caesar was assigned both Cisalpine and Transalpine Gaul, along with Illyricum, for a period of five years, and given the command of four full legions; and the consuls chosen for the following year were Piso, Caesar's father-in-law, and Gabinius, who was the most outrageous of Pompey's flatterers.* Bibulus' reaction to these events was to shut himself up in his house for the eight remaining months of his consulship without emerging, although he kept issuing edicts full of insinuations and accusations against Pompey and Caesar. Meanwhile, like a man inspired with the spirit of prophecy, Cato was constantly delivering speeches in the senate which were full of warnings about what the future held for the city and for Pompey, and Lucullus gave up and went into retirement, claiming that he was now too old for politics. This was the occasion of Pompey's comment that if a man was too old for a political life, he was far too old for a life of sensuous luxury.

However, before long Pompey too relaxed, under the influence of the love he felt for his young wife. He started to make her the centre of most of his life, and spent his waking hours with her in the countryside or in public gardens, without worrying about what was going on in the forum. Eventually even Clodius, who was a tribune at the time, came to dismiss him and instituted some particularly scandalous measures. He had already driven Cicero into exile and sent Cato off to Cyprus on a plausible military mission, and Caesar had marched off to Gaul.* As soon as Clodius realized that he was now the people's favourite, because all his political measures were designed to please them, he made it his business to try to repeal some of Pompey's administrative arrangements. He also snatched away Tigranes, Pompey's prisoner, and had him join his circle, and took some of Pompey's friends to court, to use them as a means of testing Pompey's power.* Finally, when Pompey came to attend a court case, Clodius stood in a prominent position and put a series of riddles to the gang of louts he led, who had no respect for anyone or anything: 'What do you call a lewd military commander?' 'What do you call a man in search of another man?' 'What do you call a man who scratches his head with one finger?' And like a chorus which has been well trained in its responses, cued by Clodius giving his toga a shake, they shouted out in answer to each question: 'Pompey!'*

[49] Of course, all this hurt Pompey. He was not accustomed to abuse and had no experience in this kind of battle. But he was hurt even more when he realized that the senate was perfectly happy to see him insulted and condemned to pay a penalty for betraying Cicero. Once things got to the stage where people were getting beaten and even injured in the forum, and a slave belonging to Clodius was apprehended sneaking through a crowd of bystanders towards Pompey with a sword, he made this state of affairs his excuse for staying away from the forum as long as Clodius was in office, though he was also afraid of Clodius' coarse outbursts against him. At any rate, he stayed at home, and with the help of his friends tried to come up with a plan to enable him to appease the anger the senate and the aristocrats felt towards him. Culleo advised him to divorce Julia, as a way of changing allegiance from Caesar to the senate, but Pompey rejected the idea; however, the suggestion that he should engineer the return of Cicero, a man who was bitterly opposed to Clodius and had the senate firmly on his side, met with his approval. With the help of a large body of men he brought Cicero's brother forward to present his petition, and although fighting took place in the forum, with some people wounded and even killed, he managed to get the better of Clodius.* The first thing Cicero did on his return under the new law was reconcile Pompey and the senate. Then by his support of the corn law he made Pompey once again more or less the master of all the land and sea in the Roman empire, since he was given responsibility for harbours, trading-centres, and the distribution of crops; in short, he was responsible for the business side of seafaring

and agriculture. Clodius criticized the law on the grounds that it had not been prompted by the shortage of grain, but rather the shortage of grain had arisen so that the law might be proposed, since Pompey was rekindling his waning power all over again and restoring it to consciousness, so to speak. Others affirm that the law was a trick devised by the consul, Spinther, to keep Pompey confined in a more important role, so that he himself could be sent out to help King Ptolemy. But Canidius, who was tribune at the time, proposed a bill whereby Pompey should go with two lictors, unsupported by an army, and patch up the differences between the king and the people of Alexandria. Pompey was thought to approve of the proposal, but the senate rejected it, arguing with considerable plausibility that they were concerned for his safety. And it was possible to read a pamphlet that had been scattered around the forum and near the senate-house which claimed that Ptolemy had actually asked to get Pompey as his commander instead of Spinther.* Moreover, Timagenes says that there was no real necessity for Ptolemy to leave, and that he abandoned Egypt at the insistence of Theophanes, who was trying to negotiate a pretext for a new and profitable command for Pompey. But although Theophanes' lack of scruples might seem to make the story believable, this is outweighed by the fact that this kind of corrupt and vulgar ambition was not a feature of Pompey's character.*

[50] In his capacity as superintendent responsible for the management and regulation of the trade in grain, Pompey dispatched his agents and friends here and there on jobs, while he sailed to Sicily, Sardinia, and Africa, and stocked up on grain. Just as he was about to put to sea for the voyage home, a strong wind arose out at sea and the helmsmen were hesitant about setting sail. But he led the way aboard and gave the order to weigh anchor, declaring in a loud voice, 'We have to sail; we do not have to live!' This is an example of the kind of daring he displayed, and shows how committed he was to the task. These factors, combined with good luck, enabled him to fill the trading-centres with grain and the sea with merchant ships, and in the end, as a result of his provisions, there was enough left over for grain to be exported abroad, so that everyone profited from the torrent that gushed, as if from a spring, with such abundance.*

[51] Meanwhile, Caesar had become a force to be reckoned with as a result of his wars in Gaul. Although he was apparently far away

from Rome, busy with the Belgae, the Suebi, and the Britons, he was cunningly working behind the scenes among the people, and wherever anything really important was happening, to obstruct Pompey's plans.* For in the first place, just as one might train one's body† by hunting and following the hounds, so Caesar was not only interested in the foreign opponents he was facing, but was using the battles against them as training exercises for his army, to forge and form an irresistible and formidable fighting force. And in the second place he was sending back to Rome all the surplus gold, silver, and other spoils and valuables he gained from all his wars, and as a result of plying aediles, praetors, consuls, and their wives with bribes and offers of financial assistance, he was winning a lot of people over to his cause. As a result, when he crossed the Alps and took up winter quarters at Luca, a large number of ordinary men and women enthusiastically made their way there, and so did two hundred men of senatorial rank, including Pompey and Crassus, and at Caesar's door there could be seen a hundred and twenty fasces belonging to proconsuls and praetors.* He invariably sent these people back home, after filling their minds with hope and their coffers with money, but he negotiated an agreement with Pompey and Crassus whereby they were to seek election as consuls and Caesar was to help them get elected by sending a lot of his soldiers back to Rome to take part in the voting; then, as soon as they had been elected, they were to get themselves appointed governors of provinces, with armies under their command, and confirm Caesar in the provinces he already had for a further period of five years.*

When this deal became public knowledge the leading men of Rome were outraged. Marcellinus even stood up in the popular assembly and asked Pompey and Crassus to their faces whether they were going to seek election as consuls. With the common people insisting on hearing their reply, Pompey went first and said that he might seek election, but then again he might not. Crassus' reply was more statesmanlike: he said that he would follow whichever of the two courses he thought would be in the public interest. Marcellinus kept on at Pompey and was apparently speaking rather forcefully, until Pompey said that he could not think of anything more unfair than Marcellinus' lack of gratitude. After all, he said, it was he who had given Marcellinus something to talk about, whereas previously he had been speechless; he was so full now that he was close to vomiting, whereas previously he had been starving.*

[52] However, although all the other possible candidates now declined to stand for election to the consulship, Cato persuaded Lucius Domitius to announce his candidacy and encouraged him not to give up by arguing that the issue at stake when fighting against tyranny was not the consulship, but freedom. Cato's intensity worried Pompey. Cato already had the whole of the senate on his side, and Pompey did not want to see him detach the more responsible elements among the people and get them to change sides. He therefore sent armed men to stop Domitius coming down to the forum. The torch-bearer who was leading the way was killed, and the rest turned and fled. Cato was the last to fall back, after being wounded in the right forearm while protecting Domitius.*

This was the terrible route Pompey and Crassus took to the consulship, and their subsequent actions showed just as little moderation. First, when the people were in the middle of casting their votes to elect Cato to the praetorship, Pompey dissolved the assembly, citing unfavourable omens as his reason for doing so, and then they bribed the tribes and got Vatinius elected instead of Cato. Second, using one of the tribunes, Trebonius, they introduced bills whereby, as they had agreed, they extended Caesar's command by a further five years, gave Crassus Syria and responsibility for the campaign against the Parthians, and assigned to Pompey the whole of Africa, both Spains, and four legions (though he lent two of them to Caesar, at his request, for the war in Gaul).* Crassus went out to his province as soon as his term as consul was over, but Pompey stayed in Rome for the opening of his theatre. To mark the dedication he held athletic and musical competitions, and also pitted wild beasts against one another. Five hundred lions were killed in the course of these shows, but the main event, and a truly terrifying sight, was a battle between elephants.*

[53] These shows made him a popular and much-admired figure in Rome, but at the same time he was causing just as much offence by making his friends his legates and giving them his armies and his provinces, while he spent his time touring the parks of Italy one after another with his wife. He was so much in love that he was unable to tear himself away from her, but since we hear that she was in love with him too, perhaps that was also a factor. In fact, the love the

young woman felt for her husband, despite the fact that Pompey was rather old to be an object of such passion, was famous. In all likelihood the love she bore her husband was inspired by his self-restraint, since he never had any extra-marital affairs, and his dignity, which was not so stiff that he could not be charming in company. This is something which women seem to have found very attractive, assuming we need not convict even the courtesan, Flora,* of misrepresenting the case. Be that as it may, in a fight that started during the election of the aediles one year quite a few people were murdered near Pompey, and he became so covered with blood that he changed his clothes. The servants who carried the other clothes back to his house ran there in a state of agitation, and when Pompey's young wife, who happened to be pregnant, saw the bloodstained toga, she fell into such a deep faint that she could only just be revived, and the traumatic shock caused her to miscarry. So even the people who were most critical of Pompey's friendship with Caesar could find no fault with his love for his wife. But although she became pregnant again and gave birth to a baby girl, the labour caused her death and the baby too died a few days later.* Pompey made all the arrangements for her body to buried on his Alban estate, but the people insisted on taking her down to the Campus Martius, more because they felt sorry for her than because they wanted to gratify Pompey and Caesar.

Where these two are concerned, it looks as though the Roman people thought more highly of Caesar, even though he was absent, than they did of Pompey, despite the fact that he had the advantage of being right there. For immediately following the end of the marriage alliance, which had previously disguised rather than restrained their ambition, the city was gripped by turmoil, and no public business could be conducted without upheaval and divisive speeches. A short while later the news arrived that Crassus had died in Parthia,* and so this important impediment to the outbreak of civil war was eliminated. As long as the fear which both Caesar and Pompey felt for Crassus had been there, they had somehow continued to treat each other fairly, but as soon as fortune had removed the fresh wrestler from the contest the situation reminded one of the comic poet's description of how, in preparing to meet his opponent, each man 'oils his body and dusts his hands'. This shows how little power fortune has compared with human nature. How could fortune fulfil a person's desires, when all the wide open spaces of such a huge empire could not satisfy two men?† Although they had heard and read that the gods 'divided everything into three parts, and each received his portion of honour', the two of them were not satisfied with the Roman empire.*

[54] However, Pompey once said in the course of a speech that every official position he had ever held had come to him earlier than he had expected, and been laid down sooner than others expected. It is certainly true that he could always support this statement by pointing to how he disbanded his armies. At the time in question, however, he thought that Caesar was not going to dismiss his forces, so he tried to build up his defences against him by securing political appointments, but other than that he did nothing unconstitutional, and rather than giving an impression of mistrusting Caesar, he preferred to have people think that he found him a rather despicable and insignificant figure. But when he realized that public offices were not being awarded as he would have wished, since his fellow citizens were being bribed, he allowed a condition of lawlessness to arise in the city, and before long Rome was filled with talk about the necessity of having a dictator—an idea which the tribune Lucilius* was the first to make explicit in a public speech, when he advised the people to make Pompey dictator. Cato was severely critical of the idea and Lucilius came close to losing his tribunate, but a lot of Pompey's friends came forward and claimed in Pompey's defence that he had never asked for or wanted a dictatorship. Cato congratulated Pompey on this and urged him to support the cause of law and order, and for the time being he did so, out of shame, and Domitius and Messala were created consuls.* Later, however, there was another period of anarchy, and now the calls for there to be a dictator grew more frequent and more blatant, until Cato became worried that his opposition to the idea might be swept aside by force. He therefore decided, as a way of keeping Pompey from the absolute autocratic powers of a dictatorship, to let him have a legal position of some kind.

It was Bibulus, one of Pompey's political opponents, who first voiced the idea in the senate. His suggestion was that Pompey should be made sole consul, on the grounds that the city would then either see an end to the current period of anarchy, or would lose its freedom to the man who would make the best tyrant.* This seemed a strange proposal, coming from Bibulus. Cato then stood up, and everyone fell silent, expecting to hear him speak against the idea. But Cato said that although he personally would not have proposed the motion they were currently considering, yet now that it had been proposed by someone else, he recommended the senate to adopt it, since in his opinion any government was preferable to none, and Pompey would govern better than anyone else in such troubled times. The senate accepted the proposal and voted that once he had been elected consul Pompey should govern alone, but that if, after a minimum period of two months, he felt the need of a colleague he should choose whomever he thought fit. Once his election as consul had been ratified and officially proclaimed by Sulpicius, who was acting as interrex,* Pompey addressed Cato without a trace of hostility. He admitted that he owed him a great deal, and invited him to become a private consultant to the new government. Cato, however, replied that Pompey had no reason to feel indebted to him, since he had said what he had said for the sake of Rome, not for Pompey. And he added that he would take up any offer to act as a private consultant, but that in the absence of any such offer he would speak his mind in public.* This was typical of Cato.

[55] On returning to the city Pompey married Cornelia, the daughter of Metellus Scipio. This was not her first marriage: she had recently been widowed by the death of her first husband, Publius, the son of Crassus, in Parthia. Even apart from her beauty, the young woman had plenty of attractive qualities, in that she was well read, a good player of the lyre, a skilled geometer, and capable of profiting from the philosophical lectures she regularly attended. She also combined these qualities with a character that was free from the unpleasant curiosity which these intellectual interests tend to inflict on young women, and no one could find fault with her father's lineage or reputation.* Nevertheless, some people found the marriage offensive because of Pompey's age, since Cornelia was young enough to have been a more likely bride for one of Pompey's sons, while others, somewhat less crudely, thought that Pompey was ignoring the plight of the city. Rome had chosen him to cure her of the terrible condition in which she found herself and had put herself exclusively into his hands, yet he was donning garlands and offering sacrifices in celebration of his marriage, when his very consulship ought to have reminded him how bad things were, since if his

country had been in a good state the rules would never have been broken like that to allow him to receive it.

One of his jobs was to preside over trials where the charges involved bribery and corruption. He introduced regulations for the conduct of these cases and basically carried out his duties as arbiter in a proper and honest manner, making sure, by his presence with an armed force, that the courts could go about their business in safety, without being disturbed and disrupted. Nevertheless, when his father-in-law, Scipio, was put on trial, he summoned the 360 members of the jury to his house and requested their help, and the prosecutor abandoned the case when he saw Scipio being escorted from the forum to the court by the members of the jury. Once again, then, Pompey found himself being criticized, and this only increased when he stepped up in court to sing the praises of Plancus, despite the fact that he had taken legal steps to put an end to the practice of witnesses being allowed to eulogize the characters of people involved in court cases. Now, Cato happened to be one of the jurors, and he covered his ears with his hands, saying that it was wrong for him to break the law and listen to these words of praise. Cato was therefore thrown off the jury before casting his vote, but in any case Plancus was convicted by a majority of the other votes. Pompey became thoroughly discredited by this, because a few days later an ex-consul called Hypsaeus, who was a defendant in a court case, waylaid Pompey as he was returning home for his evening meal after bathing, clasped him by the knees, and solicited his help. But Pompey walked on past him, only saying in a high-handed manner that apart from spoiling his meal he was achieving nothing. This gained him a reputation for partiality, and he came in for criticism on that score.* In other respects, however, he did a good job of restoring order in every sphere, and he chose his father-in-law as his colleague for the last five months of his period of office. It was also decreed that he should keep his provinces for another four years and be given a thousand talents a year with which to maintain and supply his forces.*

[56] However, Caesar's friends made this an opportunity to demand that Caesar be shown some consideration too, considering all the battles he was fighting in defence of the Roman empire. They said that he deserved either another consulship or an extension of his command, to prevent anyone else coming in and depriving him of the credit for all the things he had worked so hard to accomplish, and

to allow him to retain his position of authority and peacefully enjoy the prestige that might come his way for the successes which were, after all, his achievements. During the debate on this motion, pretending that he regretted all the anger that was being directed towards Caesar and liked the man enough to want to do something about it, Pompey said that there were letters from Caesar in his possession in which Caesar expressed a desire for someone else to take over his command and for him to be relieved of it. He added, however, that Caesar's request for a consulship ought to be granted, even though he was away from Rome. When Cato argued against this and insisted that Caesar could expect to be benefited by his fellow citizens only after disarming and returning to civilian life, Pompey's failure to protest and apparent acceptance of defeat increased people's suspicions about what he really felt about Caesar. He also wrote to Caesar and, with the Parthian War as his excuse, asked him to return the troops he had lent him. Although Caesar knew the real reason why he was asking for them back, he rewarded the men generously and returned them.*

[57] After this, in Naples, when Pompey recovered from a serious illness, the people of the city, following Praxagoras' advice, offered sacrifices of thanks for his preservation. Then their neighbours did the same, and so on, until the practice spread throughout Italy, and every community, whatever its size, was spending day after day celebrating a festival of thanskgiving. People flocked from all directions to line his route, until there was hardly room to move anywhere; roads, villages, and harbours were filled with people feasting and offering up sacrifices. Garlanded crowds welcomed him by torchlight and pelted him with flowers as they saw him on his way, making his journey back to Rome the most wonderful and gorgeous sight imaginable. But at the same time this is said to have been one of the main reasons for the start of the war, in the sense that Pompey's reaction to such overwhelming public joy, as long as it lasted, was a sense of pride which soared beyond rational considerations based on reality. Abandoning the caution which had always enabled him to make safe use of his successes and achievements, he let himself be overtaken by boundless confidence and contempt for Caesar's power, until he felt that to deal with him he would not need military might or have to take any trouble at all, but would bring him down far more easily than he had previously built him up. And then Appius arrived

as well, bringing from Gaul the army which Pompey had lent Caesar. In many ways Appius tended to belittle what had been achieved there, and he spread scandalous stories about Caesar; and at the same time he was busy telling Pompey that this gathering of reinforcements to use against Caesar showed how little he knew of his own power and reputation, when as soon as he turned up he could defeat Caesar with Caesar's own soldiers, given how much they hated Caesar and longed to see Pompey. This gave Pompey's morale an enormous boost, and his confidence filled him with such supreme contempt for Caesar that he actually laughed at those who feared a war, and when people asked where the forces were to keep Caesar away from Rome if he marched against it, he smiled and without showing the slightest trace of concern on his face he told them not to worry. 'All I have to do', he said, 'is stamp my foot on the ground anywhere in Italy, and foot soldiers and horsemen will arise.'*

[58] Caesar too now began to play a more direct and active part in political affairs. He started to stay quite close to Italy's borders, he regularly sent soldiers to the city to take part in the elections, and he used his money to win over and suborn a number of men in official positions. For instance, there was the consul, Paullus, who was induced by a bribe of fifteen hundred talents to change sides; there was the tribune, Curio, whose countless debts were paid off by Caesar; and there was Mark Antony, who had run up debts in tandem with his friend Curio.* And the story circulated of how, on a trip back to Rome from the army, one of Caesar's officers was standing by the senate-house and heard that the senate was refusing to extend the period of Caesar's command. He clapped his hand on his sword and said, 'But this will give Caesar the extension he wants!' And this was not at all untypical of the spirit which guided everything that Caesar was doing and all the plans he was laying.

However, the requests and demands that Curio was making on behalf of Caesar did have a certain popular appeal. He was asking for one of two things to happen. Either the senate should require Pompey to give up his army as well, he said, or should leave Caesar with his too. He argued that as long as they both became private citizens on fair terms or remained equally matched rivals with their current resources there was nothing to fear, but that to weaken either of them was to double the already terrifying power of the other. The consul Marcellus' response to this was to describe Caesar as a brigand, and to call for him to be decreed an enemy of Rome unless he disarmed. But with the help of Antony and Piso, Curio won the argument for the senate's voting on the matter. He asked those who wanted only Caesar to disarm, while Pompey retained his command, to stand to one side, and the majority did move to one side. Then he asked those who wanted both men to disarm and neither of them to retain his command to stand to one side, and only twenty-two remained on Pompey's side, while all the rest supported Curio. Assuming that he had won the day, Curio bounded in a delighted and confident mood from the senate to a meeting of the people, who greeted him with applause and pelted him with garlands and flowers. Pompey had not attended the senate, since it is illegal for army commanders to enter the city, but Marcellus got to his feet and said that he could not sit there listening to speeches; faced with the sight of ten legions already looming over the Alps, he was going in person to send on his way the man who would take the field against them in defence of his country.*

[59] At this everyone changed their clothes as if they were mourning, and then Marcellus, with the senate in his train, made his way through the forum to meet Pompey. He came before him and said, 'I call on you, Pompey, to come to the help of your country. For this you may make use of the forces you already have available, and you may also raise further forces.' Lentulus, who was one of the consuls appointed for the following year, then repeated the same words. But when Pompey began his recruiting drive, some simply refused to obey the summons. The few that joined him did so half-heartedly and with no great enthusiasm, while the majority loudly insisted on a peaceful solution to the problem. For Antony had overridden the senate's protests and had read out in the popular assembly a letter from Caesar which contained proposals designed to be attractive to the masses. That is, he wanted both Pompey and himself to relinquish command of their provinces, disband their armies, entrust themselves to the authority of the people, and submit to an examination of their actions. Lentulus, who was by this time in office as consul, refused to convene the senate, but Cicero, who had just returned from Cilicia, tried to arrange a settlement whereby Caesar should leave Gaul and disband the bulk of his army, but retain Illyricum and two legions while waiting for his second consulship. This was not enough to satisfy Pompey, however, so Caesar's friends conceded that he should give up one of the two legions. But between

Lentulus' opposition and Cato's vociferous insistence that Pompey was making yet another mistake and being duped the settlement came to nothing.*

[60] At this point news arrived that Caesar had seized a large town in Italy called Ariminum and was heading straight for Rome with his whole army. This was not entirely true: he actually had no more than 300 cavalrymen and 5,000 legionaries with him. He chose not to wait for the rest of his army, which was on the far side of the Alps, since he wanted to surprise the enemy with a sudden assault and catch them in disarray, rather than give them time and find them organized and ready for battle. When he reached the river Rubicon, which was where the province assigned to him came to an end, he stood on the bank in silence and held up the crossing, while he apparently contemplated the awesome nature of the enterprise on which he was engaged. Then, like someone who lets himself fall from the edge of a cliff into the depths of a gaping void, he closed his mind against reason and veiled his thoughts against the danger. And calling out only these words in Greek to his immediate companions, 'Let the die be cast!', he led his army across the river.*

As soon as the rumour of his approach reached Rome, the city was in a complete uproar, in the grip of panic and an unprecedented level of fear. The senators and officials hurriedly made their way to Pompey. Tullus asked him what armed forces he had available, and after a short pause Pompey replied hesitantly that the troops who had come from Caesar were all ready, and that he thought the three thousand troops who had been recruited earlier could be organized without too much delay. At this Tullus cried out, 'You have lied to us, Pompey!', and recommended sending a delegation to Caesar to sue for peace. A man called Favonius, who was basically a decent person, but who was under the impression that the insubordination and rudeness with which he often spoke was the same as Cato's candour, asked Pompey why he did not stamp his foot on the ground and call up the forces he had promised.* Pompey put up with these tactless remarks without losing his self-composure, and when Cato reminded him how he had warned him about Caesar right from the start, he replied that while Cato's words had certainly been more prophetic, his own actions had been more friendly.

[61] Cato suggested that Pompey should be made supreme commander, and as an aside he added that the people who cause great

harm are also the people who can put an end to it. He then lost no time in leaving for Sicily, the province he had been assigned, as did everyone else who had a province to go to. But the chaotic situation prevailing throughout almost all Italy made it very difficult to say what exactly was happening. Refugees from outside Rome were flooding into the city from all directions, while the inhabitants of Rome were abandoning the city in droves, because the turbulent and confused situation there weakened the decent members of society and strengthened the unruly elements, until it became hard for the city officials to contain them. It was impossible to put an end to the fear. Moreover, no one gave Pompey the chance to work things out for himself, but everyone went all out to infect him with their own feelings of fear or anguish or doubt, or whatever they happened to be feeling at the time. Contradictory decisions prevailed even within the space of a single day, and it was impossible for him to gain any reliable information about the enemy because so many people were reporting every vague rumour they came across, and then getting annoyed with him if he did not take it for the truth. And so, after formally declaring a state of civil disturbance and ordering the senators to accompany him, with the warning that he would regard anyone who stayed behind as on Caesar's side, he abandoned the city late one evening. The consuls fled without even having carried out the sacrificial rituals which were customary just before a war. But even in this appalling situation Pompey was lucky enough to retain people's affection and loyalty; even though a lot of people were critical of his leadership, no one hated the leader. In fact, one would have found that those who fled Rome because they were unable to abandon Pompey outnumbered those who did so to try to preserve their freedom.*

[62] A few days later Caesar marched into Rome and occupied it. Basically, he treated people fairly and restored calm to the city, but he threatened to kill one of the tribunes, Metellus, for trying to prevent him taking money out of the public treasury, and compounded the savagery of the threat with his next words, when he claimed that it would take less effort for him to kill Metellus than it had done to threaten him with death. Metellus beat a hasty retreat, and after taking what he needed Caesar set out after Pompey. He wanted to drive him out of Italy quickly, before his forces arrived from Spain to reinforce him. But after occupying Brundisium

Pompey had plenty of ships at his disposal, and he immediately got the consuls to board and sent them on ahead to Dyrrhachium with thirty cohorts. Meanwhile, he gave his father-in-law, Scipio, and his son, Gnaeus, the job of sailing to Syria to fit out a fleet. Next he barricaded the city gates, posted his lightest troops on the walls, and told the civilian population to stay quietly at home. He dug up all the ground inside the city, sank trenches, and filled every street in the city with sharpened stakes, except for two, which he used as his route down to the sea. The process of embarkation went without a hitch, and two days later he had the main part of his army on board their ships. He then suddenly gave the signal to the men who were guarding the walls. They ran down to the sea, where Pompey took them on board and transported them all across the sea to Dyrrhachium. The sight of the deserted walls told Caesar that Pompey had fled. He set out in pursuit, and almost fell foul of the stakes and ditches, but the people of Brundisium told him about the trap. So he avoided the city and went round the outside of it—only to find that all the ships had put to sea except two, which had only a few soldiers on board.*

[63] Most people count Pompey's retreat by sea as a piece of inspired leadership, but Caesar himself was puzzled as to why, when he held a strong city and was expecting troops from Spain and had mastery of the sea, he gave all this up and abandoned Italy. Cicero criticizes him as well, for imitating the strategy of Themistocles rather than that of Pericles when his situation resembled the one Pericles had found himself in, rather than the one Themistocles had found himself in.* And Caesar's behaviour showed that he was afraid of a long, drawn-out war. For after capturing a friend of Pompey's called Numerius he sent him to Brundisium to offer Pompey peace with no reparations—whereupon Numerius simply sailed away with Pompey. Caesar had gained control of the whole of Italy in sixty days without bloodshed. Although he wanted to set out after Pompey straight away, he did not have the ships, so he turned back and marched to Spain, to see if he could win the army there over to his cause.

[64] Pompey used this time to put together a huge force. His fleet of five hundred warships and countless Liburnian* and light scouting vessels was absolutely invincible. His seven thousand cavalrymen were the flower of Roman and Italian manhood, all outstanding for their birth and wealth and high hopes. His infantry forces were

drawn from a number of different peoples and needed training, so once he had established himself in Beroea* he put them through their paces, and actually took part in these exercises himself, as if he were still at the height of his powers. It was a great morale-booster for his men to see Pompey the Great, now 58 years old, arming himself as an infantry soldier to take part in some contest, and then, mounted on horseback, easily drawing his sword and smoothly sheathing it again with the horse at full gallop, and in his javelin-throwing displaying not only accuracy, but also strength, in that he could throw further than most of the young men. Kings and princes from foreign countries paid him visits, and there were enough of the leading men of Rome about him to form a complete senate. Two significant arrivals were Labienus, who as Caesar's friend had fought with him in Gaul, but now deserted and came over to Pompey's side, and Brutus, the son of the Brutus who had been killed in Gaul.* Brutus was a man of high principles, and he had never previously spoken to Pompey or even addressed him by name, since he regarded him as his father's murderer; but now he put himself under Pompey's command, believing him to be the liberator of Rome. Cicero too, despite having recommended a different policy in his writing and speeches, felt ashamed not to be one of those who formed the first line in defence of their country.* Sextus Tidius also came to Macedonia. He was very old and had a bad leg, and there was widespread laughter at his expense; but when Pompey caught sight of him he leapt up and ran over to greet him, since he considered it important confirmation that men who were too old and weak for active service should choose to risk their lives with him rather than remain in safety.

[65] The senate met and ratified a proposal of Cato's that no Roman should be killed except in battle and that no city subject to Rome should be plundered, and this made Pompey's party even more popular. Even people to whom the war meant little, because they lived far away or were so weak that nobody took any notice of them, were partisans of Pompey in their minds, at any rate, and in their conversations supported his fight in the cause of justice. They considered it an offence to gods and men alike for anyone not to want Pompey to win. But Caesar also showed himself to be generous in victory, when after defeating and capturing the Pompeian forces in Spain he let the commanding officers go and took the rank and file into his own service.*

After crossing the Alps and racing through Italy, Caesar reached Brundisium shortly after the winter solstice. He crossed over to Greece and landed at Oricum.* He had a friend of Pompey's called Juvius with him as a prisoner,* and he sent him off to Pompey with an invitation to a meeting. At this meeting, he suggested, the two of them should agree to disband all their forces within three days, and then to return to Italy after making up their quarrel and swearing an oath of friendship. Pompey suspected that this offer was just another trap, so he quickly went down to the coast and seized all the places he could find which offered strong defensive positions for his infantry contingents, and all those which offered safe harbours and good places for ships to come into land. The upshot was that, whatever the direction of the wind, it brought Pompey grain or troops or money, while Caesar's situation both on land and at sea was so difficult that he was forced to go in search of battle, and he was constantly attacking Pompey's defences and trying to get him to come out and fight. Caesar won most of these skirmishes, but on one occasion he came close to being crushed and losing his whole army. Pompey fought a brilliant battle which led to a complete rout and the deaths of two thousand men, but fear or something stopped him from utterly overwhelming Caesar's men and chasing them all the way back to their camp. This prompted Caesar to say to his friends, 'Today the enemy would have won, if they had a winner for a commander.'*

[66] Pompey's men were so full of confidence after this victory that they were eager to fight the decisive battle, and Pompey himself wrote to foreign kings and generals and states as if he had already won, but in actual fact he wanted to avoid the risk of battle. He thought his best chance of victory was to prolong the war and take advantage of the enemy's shortage of supplies; otherwise, he could not see how to defeat men who were invincible in battle and had become accustomed to victory through many years of fighting together, but who were too old to have any enthusiasm for everything else that goes with warfare—the time away from home, the constant changes of location, the digging of trenches, the building of walls—and so wanted to join battle and engage his troops as soon as possible. Despite their confidence, Pompey at first somehow convinced his followers that it would be best to do nothing—but then, shortly after the battle, Caesar was forced by shortage of supplies to break camp and march through Athamania to Thessaly. This was too much

for Pompey's men, flushed with pride as they were. Crying out that Caesar was in flight, some were in favour of following him and hunting him down, while others recommended returning to Italy. A number of them sent attendants and friends to Rome to take possession of houses near the forum, since they expected to be standing for office in the near future, and there were plenty who voluntarily made the trip to Lesbos, where Pompey had sent Cornelia for her safety, to give her the good news that the war was over.

The senate met and Afranius proposed that they should attack Italy. He argued that Italy was the ultimate prize in the war, and that whoever won control of it would immediately also gain Sicily, Sardinia, Corsica, Spain, and the whole of Gaul; and he added that it would be disgraceful for Pompey to stand by and watch the land of his birth, the most important thing in the world to him, being abused and enslaved by the slaves and flatterers of tyrants, when it was so close and was reaching out its hands to him in supplication. However, to Pompey's mind, it would do his reputation no good if he fled from Caesar a second time and was hunted when fortune had given him the opportunity to be the hunter, and it would also be quite wrong of him to abandon Scipio and the other ex-consuls who were in Greece and Thessaly, since they would immediately go over to Caesar's side, taking with them a great deal of money and sizeable bodies of soldiers too. It was his opinion that the more a man cared for Rome, the further away he fought for her and the more he saw to it that she never experienced or even heard about the evils of war, but just waited patiently to see who would finally possess her.

[67] Once he had convinced the senate to vote his way, he set out in pursuit of Caesar. He had decided to avoid battle in favour of keeping him hemmed in and starving him into submission, so he stayed close on his heels. Apart from any other reasons he had for thinking it best to avoid battle, he had heard that there was talk in the cavalry contingent of how as soon as they had put Caesar to flight their next job would be to help overthrow Pompey too. Some people say that this is why Pompey failed to make any significant use of Cato, but even while he was marching against Caesar left him on the coast to look after the stores, since he was afraid that as soon as Caesar was out of the way Cato would force him to lay down his command too. And so he followed the enemy without stirring up any trouble, but he was surrounded by criticisms and the accusation,

loudly voiced, that his strategy was not directed against Caesar so much as his country and the senate. People said that he wanted to retain his command for ever, and never to stop having men who thought they deserved to rule the world as his personal attendants and guards, while Domitius Ahenobarbus' habit of calling him 'Agamemnon' and 'King of Kings' brought opprobrium down on Pompey's head as well. And Pompey was just as displeased with Favonius as he was with people who tactlessly spoke their minds when, trying to be funny, Favonius called out at an inappropriate moment, 'So, gentlemen, are there to be no Tusculan figs for us this year either?' Then Lucius Afranius, who had outstanding against him a charge of treachery arising from his loss of the forces in Spain, remarked, when he saw how battle-shy Pompey was, that he could not understand why people who were so quick to accuse *him* did not go out and fight the dealer in provinces themselves.*

This is just a small selection of the criticisms that were levelled against Pompey, and since he was the kind of man who was swayed by what people thought of him and was ashamed to lose face before his friends, he was forced to change his mind and was dragged against his better judgement in the wake of the others' hopes and desires, displaying the sort of behaviour that is inappropriate for the captain of a ship, let alone for a supreme commander with responsibility for so many peoples and armies. He thought it quite right for doctors never to give in to their patients' wishes, and yet he yielded to the unhealthy elements of his army because he was afraid to pay for their safety with his unpopularity. For one can only describe as unhealthy men who were already going around the troops and soliciting their support in their bids for consulships and praetorships, or who were squabbling and competing and canvassing over Caesar's position as pontifex maximus, as Spinther, Domitius, and Scipio were. It was as if they were up against Tigranes of Armenia or the king of the Nabataeans, and not Caesar and the army with which he had taken a thousand cities by storm, subdued more than three hundred peoples, remained undefeated in countless battles against the Germans and Gauls, taken a million prisoners, and killed the same number again in his overwhelming victories on the battlefield.*

[68] Nevertheless, they brought so much pressure to bear on Pompey, and kicked up such a fuss, that by the time he had reached the plain of Pharsalus,* he felt he had no choice but to convene a

council of war. Labienus, the cavalry commander, was the first to stand up and address the meeting. He took a solemn oath that he would not return from the battle unless he had put the enemy to flight, and the others all followed his example. That night Pompey had a dream in which the people applauded as he entered his theatre and embellished the sanctuary of Venus the Bringer of Victory with plenty of spoils.* He found some aspects of the dream encouraging and others disturbing. In particular, he worried that he might become the instrument whereby Caesar's line, which traced its descent back to Venus, would gain in glory and fame, and waves of panic shot through him and kept him restlessly awake. Then during the early-morning watch, when Caesar's camp was perfectly still, a great light blazed out over the camp, and a flaming torch arose out of this light and fell upon Pompey's camp—a sight which Caesar himself says he saw as he was making his rounds of the sentries.

The next day Caesar was intending to decamp to Scotussa,* and his men were in the process of taking down their tents and getting the yoke-animals and their slaves ready to send on ahead, when the scouts returned from a mission to report that the enemy camp was alive with the movement of weaponry and filled with the noise and bustle of men coming out for battle. Then others came with the news that the front ranks were already falling in. So Caesar announced that the day for which they had been waiting had arrived, when they would at last fight men rather than hunger and hardship, and he gave the order for his purple toga to be displayed straight away in front of his tent, since this was the Roman signal for battle. When his men saw the signal they raised a shout of joy, stopped packing up their tents, and went to collect their arms and armour. And as the officers got them to form up in their proper positions, like dancers each man took his place in the line with practised ease and composure.

[69] Pompey kept the right wing for himself, with Antony as his intended opponent, while he posted his father-in-law, Scipio, in the centre to face Lucius Calvinus, and Lucius Domitius held the left wing.* Domitius was supported by most of the cavalry, because nearly all of them had raced there in their eagerness to crush Caesar and annihilate the tenth legion, whose prowess was legendary and in whose ranks Caesar usually fought. When Caesar saw all these horsemen protecting the enemy's left wing, he was worried about the effect such a sensational display of weaponry might have on his men,

so he called up six cohorts from the reserves and posted them behind the tenth legion, with orders to keep quiet and stay out of sight of the enemy. When the enemy cavalry attacked, however, they were to run through the front ranks, and then, whereas normally the best fighting men would quickly throw their javelins and draw their swords, they were to thrust their javelins upwards, trying to wound the enemy in their eyes and faces. Caesar's idea was that these dashing young blades would be too worried about their good looks to stand their ground, and would not be able to face up to weapons aimed straight at their eyes.*

So this is what Caesar was up to. As Pompey surveyed the battle-lines from horseback, he noticed that whereas his adversaries were quietly waiting for the moment of attack in their ranks, most of his own men were far from still, but were showing their inexperience by noisily swirling about. He was afraid that battle would hardly be joined before they would be swept aside, so he ordered the front ranks to stand firm with their spears at the defensive and wait for the enemy attack without breaking formation. Caesar is critical of these tactics. He says that Pompey reduced the force his weaponry would have had if it had been wielded as his men were attacking, and that by preventing his men from making a countercharge—a manoeuvre which is generally better than any other at filling soldiers with enthusiasm and verve as they engage the enemy, and which combines with their yelling and charging to increase their courage—he rooted his men to the spot and cooled their ardour.* And yet Pompey had somewhat more than twice as many men as Caesar's twenty-two thousand.

[70] Now the signal was given on both sides. At the first sound of the trumpet's call to battle, every single man of all the thousands present began to focus on the task at hand, but the imminence of the dreadful moment prompted a few of them—the best of the Romans and some Greeks who were there merely as bystanders—to reflect on how far astray greed and ambition had led the Roman empire. The pick of the manhood and power of a single city was here clashing in internal conflict, with members of the same families bearing arms against one another, brothers arrayed against brothers, all under the same standards. It only proved how insanely blind a thing human nature is when ruled by passion. For had they chosen to rule in peace and enjoy the fruits of their conquests, by this time vast stretches of

land and sea, of unsurpassed quality, would have been theirs to command; and if they were still unsatisfied and wanted to slake their lust for trophies and triumphs, they could have had their fill of wars against the Parthians or Germans. Besides, Scythia and the Indian tribes still represented formidable challenges, and in attacking them they would have been able to cloak their rapacity with the not ignoble pretext of civilizing foreigners. For how could Scythian horsemen, Parthian archers, or Indian wealth have checked the armed onslaught of seventy thousand Romans under the leadership of Pompey and Caesar, whose names had reached their ears long before they had ever heard of Rome, so remote and varied and wild were the tribes these two had attacked and conquered? But now they came together to fight each other, and no sense of regret for what people might think of them led them, men who up until that day had been called invincible, to spare their country. For the alliance between them, Julia's charms, and the famous marriage were at once exposed as the fraudulent and dubious pledges of a partnership based on self-interest and lacking in genuine friendship.*

[71] Soon the Pharsalian plain was filled with men and horses and weaponry, and then on both sides the signals were raised for battle to be joined. The first to charge out from Caesar's lines was Gaius Crassianus, a centurion with a hundred and twenty men under him. In doing so he was fulfilling a firm promise he had made to Caesar. The first person Caesar had seen as he left the camp that day had been Crassianus, and he had spoken to him and asked him how he felt about the battle. Crassianus had raised his right arm and replied in a loud voice, 'You will win a decisive victory, Caesar—and you will have reason to praise me today, whether I live or die!' So, remembering these words of his to Caesar, he rushed forward, drawing large numbers of men after him, and hurled himself into the midst of the enemy. Close fighting with swords began immediately, and losses were heavy. As Crassianus was battling forward, cutting through the front ranks, one of the enemy stood his ground against him and drove his sword in through his mouth with such force that the point went all the way through and emerged out of the back of his neck.*

So Crassianus fell, and at this point on the field the battle was evenly balanced. Meanwhile, rather than leading the right wing straight into the attack, Pompey kept wasting time looking from one wing to the other, and waiting to see how the cavalry got on. The cavalry squadrons now advanced with the intention of outflanking Caesar and driving back into the ranks the few horsemen he had deployed to defend his infantry. But on Caesar's signal his cavalrymen withdrew and the cohorts assigned to prevent the encirclement emerged from the battle-lines at the double and confronted the enemy. There were three thousand men in these cohorts, and as each horse drew close they stood and thrust upwards with their javelins, aiming, as they had been instructed, for the riders' faces. This was the first time Pompey's cavalry had taken part in a battle, and nothing in their training had prepared them to expect anything like this. Lacking the courage and resolve to risk being struck in the eyes and face, they wheeled about with their hands over their eyes and turned to ignominious flight. Caesar's cohorts did not bother to pursue them, but advanced on the infantry lines, choosing to attack at the particular point where the lack of cavalry protection left the wing vulnerable to being outflanked and surrounded. Just as these men fell on their flank, the tenth legion attacked head on as well, and Pompey's lines crumpled and collapsed as the men realized that rather than surrounding the enemy as they had hoped, it was they who were being surrounded themselves.*

[72] It is difficult to say what thoughts went through Pompey's mind when he saw the dust-cloud raised by the fugitives and guessed what had happened to his cavalry, but he behaved like someone who had been driven insane and had taken leave of his senses. It was as if he had no conception that he was Pompey the Great.* Without saying a word to anyone, he walked slowly back to the camp, the very image of the poet's words:

But Zeus the father, throned on high, stirred up fear in Ajax's heart,
And he stood stunned, slung on his back his seven-layered oxhide shield,
And fled, peering to and fro among the throng.*

So Pompey returned to his tent and sat there speechless, until large numbers of Caesar's men burst into the camp, hot on the heels of the fugitives, and then he spoke a single sentence, no more: 'So are even my quarters under attack?' Without another word he got to his feet, gathered together the kind of clothing that would suit his circumstances, and stole away. The rest of his legions also fled. There was considerable slaughter in the camp of attendants and slaves, such as the people whose job it was to look after the tents, but according to

Asinius Pollio, who took part in the battle on Caesar's side, only six thousand soldiers lost their lives.* When Caesar's men took possession of the camp, they could see clear evidence of their adversaries' foolish pretensions. For every tent was wreathed with myrtle branches and embellished with gorgeous couches and tables laden with goblets; large bowls of wine were ready to hand, and the way everything had been prepared and laid out seemed to indicate that these were the quarters of men who were relaxing after a celebratory sacrifice rather than places where men armed themselves for battle, and showed how far their hopes had led them astray, and how thoroughly—but stupidly—confident they had been as they went out to war.*

[73] A short distance from the camp Pompey let the horse have its head. There was no one after him, so he rode on in a leisurely fashion with a very small retinue. The kinds of thoughts going through his head were what one might have expected from a man who for thirty-four years had been accustomed to nothing but victory and supremacy, and was now for the first time, in his old age, experiencing defeat and flight. He reflected on the fact that it had taken just one hour for him to lose the fame and power he had accumulated from so many battles and wars, and that whereas a short while ago he had huge infantry, cavalry, and naval resources to protect him, he had now been reduced to such an insignificant and diminished state that he could retreat without being spotted by those of his enemies who were after him.

He travelled past Larissa to Tempe, where he was so thirsty that he sprawled on the ground and drank from the river.* When he got to his feet again he continued through Tempe until he reached the coast. He rested there for what remained of the night in a hut used by fishermen, and in the morning went on board a river-boat, taking only those of his attendants who were free men, while telling his slaves that they should make their way back to Caesar and need have no fear. Then he sailed along the coast until he saw a good-sized cargo ship which was just about to put to sea. The captain of the ship was a Roman called Peticius, who was not a close friend of Pompey's, but knew him by sight. It so happened that the night before he had dreamt that Pompey—not the Pompey he was familiar with, but a humble and crestfallen man—had spoken to him. In fact, he was in the middle of telling the other men on the ship about the dream, and chatting about grand affairs of state as men do when they have time on their hands, when suddenly one of the sailors drew his attention to a river-boat that was being rowed out from the land, with men in it who were waving their cloaks and reaching out their hands towards them. As soon as Peticius looked in that direction he recognized Pompey and saw that he was just as he had seen him in his dream. He hit his head in amazement and told his men to bring the boat alongside the dinghy. When they had done so, he stretched out his right hand and called to Pompey. He could tell from his appearance that Pompey had fallen on hard times, and so, without waiting for any appeals or explanations, he took on board Pompey and the others, as Pompey requested, and set sail. Pompey was accompanied on to the boat by the two Lentuli and Favonius, and a little later they saw King Deïotarus hurrying in their direction from the shore, so they took him on board as well.* At dinner time Peticius did the best he could for them with what he had available, but when Favonius saw Pompey beginning to take off his own shoes, since he had no slaves, he ran over, undid them himself, and helped him to rub his feet with oil. And after that, for the rest of the journey, Favonius acted as Pompey's attendant and looked after him in all the ways that slaves look after their masters, even including washing his feet and preparing his meals. His service was so generous, straightforward, and sincere, that anyone seeing him might have said: 'Ah, how admirable is everything that noble people do!'*

[74] After sailing round the coast to Amphipolis, he crossed over from there to Mytilene because he wanted to pick up Cornelia and his son.* After beaching his ship on the island, he sent a messenger to the city with news quite different from what Cornelia was expecting. The optimistic news and letters she had received had led her to believe that the war had been decided at Dyrrhachium and that all Pompey still had to do was set out in pursuit of Caesar. When the messenger found her in this frame of mind, he could not bring himself to address her, and it was his tears rather than anything he said that communicated to her the extent and enormity of the misfortune. Then he told her to hurry if she wanted to see Pompey—albeit that she would see him with a single ship, and one that was not his own. When she heard this she threw herself to the ground and lay there for a long time, unable to compose her thoughts or speak a word. But at last she pulled herself together and, once it had dawned

on her that this was not the time for grief and tears, she ran through the city to the coast. Pompey met her and took her in his arms just as her limbs were failing and she was about to collapse. 'Husband,' she said, 'my fortune is to blame for this, not yours! Before your marriage to Cornelia, you sailed this sea with five hundred ships, and now I see you tossed on to a single boat! Why did you come to see me? Why didn't you leave to her cruel destiny the woman who has infected you with her terrible misfortune? If my fortune had been good, I would have died before hearing that my first husband Publius was lying dead among the Parthians. Then it would also have made good sense for me to have seen my original intention through and killed myself after Publius' death.* But now it looks as though I was spared to be the ruin of Pompey the Great as well.'

[75] This is what Cornelia is supposed to have said. And Pompey, we hear, replied, 'Yes, Cornelia, you have known me only when things were good, and it seems that you too were taken in by the unusually long time that good fortune stayed with me. But we are human, and we must endure even this, and continue to put fortune to the test. For it is not beyond the realms of possibility that a man who finds his circumstances altered from one extreme to the other may also find that things change and he recovers what he had lost.' So Cornelia arranged for her valuables and slaves to be brought from the city. The people of Mytilene gave Pompey a warm welcome and invited him to enter the city, but he refused, and repeated what he had already told others—that they should submit to the conqueror without fear, because Caesar was a kind and merciful man. But he turned to Cratippus the philosopher, who had come down from the city to see him, and briefly voiced a few complaints and doubts about Providence. While trying to divert him into a more optimistic frame of mind, Cratippus conceded the validity of what Pompey was saying, because he did not want to upset him or display a lack of tact in arguing against him. After all, through asking Pompey questions about Providence, he could have made it clear that in his opinion† autocracy was just what Rome needed at the moment, as a result of the period of ineffective government it had been through. He could have asked, 'How are we to be convinced, Pompey, that you would have made a better use of fortune than Caesar if it had been you who won? Where is your evidence for this? No, the divine ordering of things must be left as it is.'*

[76] After taking his wife and friends on board, Pompey continued on his way, putting in only at harbours which had the water or food he needed. The first city he came to was Attalia in Pamphylia,* where he was joined by some triremes from Cilicia. Soldiers also began to gather there, and once again he had sixty senators around him. When he heard that his fleet was still intact, and that Cato had taken a lot of the troops on board and was on his way over to Africa,* he expressed regret to his friends and blamed himself for having yielded to pressure and joined battle on land, while failing to make any use at all of the undisputed advantage his naval forces gave him at sea, and he deplored the fact that he had not even brought the fleet round to an anchorage where if things went wrong on land he could immediately have had all that power and might available to even things up at sea. And in fact it was Pompey's worst mistake, and Caesar's best piece of tactics, to have opened up such a large gap between the battle and the possibility of help from the sea.*

But now he had to base his decisions and actions on the reality of his current situation. He sent messengers to some of the towns and cities, while paying a personal visit by ship to others on the coast, to solicit funds and fit out ships. Knowing the speed and swiftness of which Caesar was capable, however, he was afraid that he might launch an attack and overwhelm him before his preparations were complete, so he began to look out for somewhere he could safely withdraw to for the time being. But after due consideration he and his advisers could not find a single province that looked as though it could shelter them, and where the kingdoms were concerned, Pompey himself suggested that their best bet was Parthia. In the short term, he said, the Parthians could take them in and protect them while they were weak, and later they could build up their strength and send them on their way with a very large force. Others inclined towards King Juba in Africa, but Theophanes of Lesbos said that in his opinion it would be crazy for Pompey to abandon Ptolemy in Egypt, which was only three days away by sea.* In the first place, he pointed out, Ptolemy was little more than a child, and in the second place he was indebted to Pompey for the friendship and favour he had shown to his father.* It would be crazy, then, he said, for Pompey to ignore Ptolemy and put himself in the treacherous hands of the Parthians. Since he was refusing to see whether a Roman, and one who was his relative by marriage, would treat him decently, because that would involve taking second place to him, even though he would still have pride of place over everyone else, it made no sense for him to let Arsaces, a man who had failed to protect even Crassus during his lifetime, shelter him.* Moreover, Theophanes went on, he would be taking a young wife, from the house of Scipio, to live among foreigners whose criterion of power was how abusively and violently a man could act, so that she would be faced with the awful prospect, even if she came to no actual harm, of being thought to have come to harm, since she had been subject to those who had the power to inflict it. This consideration alone, it is said, put Pompey off the idea of travelling to the Euphrates—that is, if the route was still being dictated by any rational thought of Pompey's, rather than by his destiny.

[77] Having decided to seek refuge in Egypt, Pompey set sail from Cyprus in a Seleucian trireme accompanied by his wife, along with the rest of his companions, who were on board either warships like his own or in some cases merchantmen. The voyage went safely, and when he found out that Ptolemy was encamped at Pelusium with his army, making war on his sister, he put in there, and sent a messenger on ahead to tell the king of his arrival and ask for his protection. Now, Ptolemy was still quite young, and all administrative business was in the hands of Pothinus, who convened a meeting of the most powerful men in Ptolemy's court—which is to say, the men whom Pothinus wanted to have the most power—and asked each of them to give his views on the matter. It was a terrible thing that the decision about the future of Pompey the Great should be up to Pothinus the eunuch, Theodotus of Chios (a hired teacher of rhetoric), and Achillas of Egypt.* There were other chamberlains and chaperons on the council, but these were the principal members. Pompey had refused to be under obligation to Caesar for his safety, and yet now these were the judges whose verdict he was awaiting as he lay at anchor out at sea, riding the waves.

Most of the people at the meeting fundamentally disagreed with one another, some suggesting that Pompey should be driven away, others that he should be invited in and welcomed. But in a display of eloquence and rhetorical skill, Theodotus argued that neither of these two courses of action was safe; if they took him in, he said, they would have Caesar as their enemy and Pompey as their master, and if they sent him packing they would incur Pompey's anger for expelling him and Caesar's for not holding on to him. Therefore, he said, the best plan was for them to send for Pompey and kill him. That way they would be doing Caesar a favour, and Pompey would be no threat. And then, it is said, he added with a smile, 'Dead men don't bite.'*

[78] Theodotus' plan was approved by the rest, and they entrusted the execution of the deed to Achillas. After enlisting the help of a former officer under Pompey's command called Septimius,* a centurion called Salvius, and three or four assistants, Achillas put to sea and sailed out towards Pompey's ship. Now, all the most eminent of Pompey's companions on this voyage happened at the time to be on board Pompey's ship, which meant that they saw what was going on. And when they saw no signs of a royal or splendid reception, or anything like what Theophanes had led them to expect, but only a few men sailing towards them in a single fishing-boat, they found the implicit lack of respect worrying, and they advised Pompey to have his ship row back far enough into the open sea to be out of range of weapons from the shore. Meanwhile, however, the fishing-boat drew near, and before they could do anything Septimius stood up and saluted Pompey in Latin as Imperator,* and then Achillas greeted him in Greek and invited him to join them on the fishing-boat, because there were extensive shoals, and sandbanks made the sea too shallow for a trireme. At the same time the sight of some ships from the king's fleet being manned, and the shore filling up with heavy-armed infantry, made it look as though there was no escape for them even if they did change their minds. Besides, there was always the possibility that just by acting as if they were suspicious they might give the murderers the excuse they needed for their crime. So Pompey said goodbye to Cornelia, who was already weeping in anticipation of his death, and gathered a small party of people to go on board the boat with him—two centurions, one of his freedmen called Philippus, and a slave called Scythes. And even as Achillas was extending him a welcome from the fishing-boat, Pompey turned back towards his wife and son and quoted the following lines of Sophocles:

> Anyone who goes to traffic with a tyrant
> Is his slave, even if he goes there free.*

[79] With these last words to his family he climbed on board the

boat. It was a long way from the trireme to land, and since none of the men on board had a kind word for him he looked at Septimius and said, 'If I'm not mistaken, you're an old comrade-in-arms of mine.' But Septimius only nodded his head, without saying a thing or making any attempt to be friendly. During the long silence that resumed, Pompey read through the speech in Greek he had prepared to deliver to Ptolemy, which he had written down in a little book he was carrying. As they approached the shore, Cornelia was standing with Pompey's friends on the trireme, watching and trying to guess what was going to happen next. She was beside herself with anxiety, but she began to cheer up when she saw a crowd of men from the king's retinue gathering at the dock, apparently to pay their respects to Pompey and welcome him to Egypt. But Pompey had just taken hold of Philippus' hand for some support as he got to his feet, when Septimius ran him through from behind with his sword, and next Salvius and then Achillas drew their daggers. Pompey used both hands to cover his head with his toga, and endured their blows with nothing more than a gasp, without saying or doing anything to betray his dignity. And so Pompey died aged 59, on the day after his birthday.*

[80] After expressing their horror at the sight of the murder with cries that were loud enough to be heard on land, the people on board the ships weighed anchor with all speed and fled. As they ran for the open sea, a strong wind came to their help and thwarted the Egyptians' plan to pursue them. But they cut off Pompey's head, threw the rest of his body naked off the fishing-boat, and left it exposed as a ghastly spectacle for anyone to see who wanted to. Philippus stayed by the body until people had had their fill of the sight, and then he washed it in the sea and dressed it in one of his own togas. But that was all he had, so he searched along the sea-shore until he found the wreck of a small fishing-boat; the timbers were rotten, but they would do to make a basic funeral pyre for a naked and mutilated corpse.

As he was collecting the wood and building the pyre, a Roman came up to him who was now an old man, but who as a young man had been one of Pompey's comrades-in-arms during his first campaigns. 'Who are you, sir?' he asked Philippus. 'Why should it be up to you to give Pompey the Great his last rites?' When Philippus explained that he was Pompey's freedman, the old man said, 'Well, this noble deed shall not be yours alone. Since I happen to have stumbled upon this pious duty, please let me help you out. I shall not entirely regret my time in a foreign country, and it would cancel out a great many hardships, if by good fortune I found myself in a position to do this, at least—to touch and dress with my own hands the greatest Roman imperator there has ever been.'* And this was how Pompey came to receive his last rites.

The next day Lucius Lentulus, who did not know what had happened, was sailing along the coast on a voyage from Cyprus, when he saw a funeral pyre and someone—he could not yet see who—standing beside it. 'Who is this', he said, 'who rests here at the end of his allotted span of life?' Then after a short pause he groaned and said, 'Could it be you, Pompey the Great?' A little later he went ashore, but he was arrested and put to death.*

This was how Pompey met his end. Not long afterwards Caesar came to Egypt and found traces of the abomination everywhere. One man brought him Pompey's head, but Caesar treated him like a polluted murderer and turned away; another brought him Pompey's signet ring, with its device of a lion armed with a sword, and Caesar burst into tears. He had both Achillas and Pothinus killed, and even the king mysteriously disappeared after losing a battle on the Nile.* As for Theodotus, although the sophist avoided being punished by Caesar by fleeing from Egypt and eking out a miserable existence as a hated vagabond abroad, after Marcus Brutus had killed Caesar and made himself master of Rome, he found Theodotus living in Asia, and he put him to death after subjecting him to every kind of torture.* Pompey's remains were given to Cornelia, who took them to his Alban estate and buried them there.

CAESAR

INTRODUCTION

Caesar is the centre around which the six late republican Lives of its set rotate and a culmination of sorts of all the Roman Lives. For *Caesar* not only is a powerful Life in itself, but it encourages multiple comparisons with other Lives, all exploring the acquisition and use of power, and the response which different natures make to it. Caesar's unparalleled success as a conqueror and his emergence as sole permanent ruler of the Roman state, *dictator perpetuus*, make him the climax and conclusion of the Roman republic, and the forerunner though not the founder of the monarchy to be established by Augustus.

Plutarch's Life suggests how Caesar combined elements of the great men of the last two generations: like Marius he used his wars with northern tribes to compete with the senatorial conservatives; like Sulla he fought a civil war to establish his right to rule and assumed a dictatorship to reshape the republic. Like Pompey, he knew that his successes, his wealth, and his armies set him apart from the senatorial oligarchy. Unlike all these men, however, he developed a clear understanding that radical change was needed, that the flaws in the system could no longer be bandaged over. The ambitions of Pompey, Crassus, and Caesar himself and the self-righteous intransigence of Cato finally brought Caesar to victory over his enemies and domination of the state—and to his assassination.

In sketching the life of this extraordinarily gifted leader, Plutarch suggests a number of themes which create a tangled unity. Caesar's ambition is fundamental, of course, apparent throughout the life, but noted especially in two anecdotes placed just before the formation of the triumvirate in 60 BC (c. 11): in one he asserts, 'I'd rather be first here [a native village in the Alps] than second in Rome', in the other he weeps as he measures himself against Alexander. His ambition points naturally towards monarchy, as king or tyrant. 'King', sometimes a good term in Greek philosophical discourse, when applied to an ideal monarch, in Rome had the hated association of the Tarquins, so that king and tyrant became synonymous. Caesar and his friends may have thought of imitating the Hellenistic kings, successors of Alexander, but Roman experience did not permit this development. When Antony offers a crown to Caesar at the Lupercalia (c. 61), his enemies can unite in a conspiracy to destroy the tyrant, and Brutus, the heir of the Brutus who drove out the Tarquins, can see himself, in such a different situation, as the man chosen to liberate Rome once more.

Fundamental to Plutarch's portrait is Caesar's changing relation to those who help him to power. Early in the Life, Caesar wins the people's favour, and they heap honours upon him (cc. 5, 6, 8, 14).[1] When he returns to Rome as victor, they honour him yet more, then become disenchanted and angry with him (59–61), especially in the Lupercalia episode. Then, after his assassination, they miss him and rage against the liberators, even ripping apart the innocent Cinna (68). The other supporting group, Caesar's soldiers, are equally irrational: their industry and bravery ensure his victory over Pompey, yet they also express their anger and frustration at his continual wars (37) and the lack of their expected reward (51). Caesar must rely on his friends and associates, and on those of his enemies who have returned to Rome and accept his rule. But the friends' behaviour brings his regime into disrepute (51) and their advice falsely flatters (60). Finally the conspiracy is led by those to whom he has extended special favours, in particular Brutus, who 'stood high in Caesar's confidence' and was designated for the consulship (62). Caesar is struck down not so much by his senatorial enemies, but by those who had supported him, or whom he had favoured.

Running through the Life, underlying the rivalry between Pompey and Caesar, is the notion of death as an end, a limit to the most ambitious individuals. The nature of the rivalry suggests that one or the other must die before it is over, but in *Caesar* Plutarch presses beyond this, employing the model of the fight for mastery over Thebes between Oedipus' sons Eteocles and Polynices. In the tragic plot, the two brothers confront and kill each other: such is the madness of civil war.[2] Caesar defeats Pompey, who flees to his death; but Pompey's statue, in Pompey's portico, presides over Caesar's own death (66). The javelins thrust into the faces of his fellow citizens at Pharsalus, which defeated Pompey, become the sword thrusts aimed at Caesar's face and eyes (45, 66). In *Pompey* and *Caesar*, omens foreshadow the defeat of one and the death of the other. Providence guides their destinies, so intrinsic to the fate of Rome. The coda to *Caesar* shows 'his great guardian spirit' presiding over the deaths of his assassins (69). Caesar was not the one who would found the monarchy, but

[1] Cf. C. B. R. Pelling, 'Plutarch and Roman Politics', in I. Moxon, J. D. Smart, and A. J. Woodman (eds.), *Past Perspective: Studies in Greek and Roman Historical Writing* (Cambridge: Cambridge University Press, 1986), 159–87; repr. in B. Scardigli (ed.), *Essays on Plutarch's Lives* (Oxford: Clarendon Press, 1995), 319–56.

[2] The Theban model is alluded to in Plutarch's quotation from Euripides' *Phoenician Women* (*Sull.* 4 and note), but it applies to Pompey and Caesar even better than to Marius and Sulla.

his greatness was awesome, and, as with Romulus, the senate proclaimed him a god (67).

Many of these themes develop and enrich those already apparent in *Alexander*, the first life of the pair. Alexander never dealt directly with a civilian citizen body: his army furnished the brute force which made him king of Asia. They too both adulated him and rejected him, in the mutinies at the Hyphasis and at Opis. As with Caesar, Alexander's associates hurt him on several levels: their greed and dissolute living made his rule look bad, and their flattery corrupted his thinking, while their directness was offensive,[3] and finally, conspiracies were made to kill him. Alexander is already king, and hopes to be called a god, as Dionysus and Heracles were; Caesar thinks to become a king, and is named a god. Greatest of the Greeks, Alexander is set against the greatest man of republican Rome and the precursor of the emperors, Caesar. It was a small leap, then, for Plutarch's contemporaries to think of that other great emulator of Alexander, their own emperor Trajan.

The structure of the Life, as is common, follows a chronological sequence, but an opposition of civil and military affairs is also apparent. Plutarch marks episodes and special moments with special commentary, and introduces the section on the Gallic Wars with three chapters giving an overview of Caesar's conquests, and anecdotes illustrating the bravery and loyalty of his troops and Caesar's own qualities as a general (15–17). The Life begins abruptly, when Caesar is already about 18, and it is probable that a page or two is missing which would have treated Caesar's ancestry (the family traced itself back to Iulus, the son of Aeneas, the Trojan hero who founded Rome, and to Venus, Aeneas' mother) and his appearance and fundamental qualities. The first major anecdote which is preserved, Caesar's capture by pirates, gives a vivid glimpse of Caesar's character in a crisis.

1–11 Caesar's early career, to 61 BC
12–14 Imperator, triumvir, first consulship, 61–59 (anecdotes of ambition: c. 12)
15–27 Campaigns in Gaul, 58–50 (Caesar's generalship, anecdotes of soldiers, cc. 15–17; conference at Luca in 56, c. 21)
28–31 Prelude to the Civil War, 50
32–37 Outbreak of war; campaigns in Italy and Spain, 49
38–47 Campaign in Greece; victory at Pharsalus, 49–48
48–50 Pursuit of Pompey; Egypt, Syria, Pontus, 48–47

[3] Clitus was an example of directness (*Alex.* 50–1), Anaxarchus of flattery (*Alex.* 52); neither was a model of behaviour toward kings.

51	Caesar in Rome; popular discontent, October–December 47
52–4	African campaign; suicide of Cato, 46
55–6	Caesar in Rome, July–October 46
56	Spanish campaign, victory at Munda; animosity, 45
57–61	Caesar a dictator; desire for kingship, Lupercalia episode
62–6	Conspiracy and assassination, 15 March 44
67–9	Aftermath; fate of the tyrannicides

As with *Pompey*, which was prepared at the same time, Plutarch used a number of sources, but the main narrative for the events from the formation of Caesar's pact with Crassus and Pompey down to Caesar's assassination (60 to 44 BC) is based on the account of Asinius Pollio, whom Plutarch respected as a contemporary, a man who was with Caesar at the Rubicon (c. 32) and at Pharsalus (c. 46).[4] Although Plutarch cites Caesar's *Commentaries on the Gallic War* in chapter 22, and his *Civil War* in chapter 44, many of the details he offers in his account do not derive from Caesar. We deduce, therefore, that he found Pollio a more accessible source. He also seems familiar with Caesar's *Anti-Cato* (54), a response to an encomium of Cato by Cicero. Both works were important for his *Cato Minor*. In addition, he cites Livy twice in this Life (47, 63): his very detailed account of these years would have provided a valuable, near contemporary narrative, and Plutarch cites him in other Lives too. Plutarch also cites Tanusius Geminus (22), another contemporary historian about whom little is known: he reported many negative stories about Caesar (cf. Suetonius, *Caesar* 9).[5] Our most important source for this period is Cicero, whom Plutarch used also, though he used works not available to us: Cicero's lost account of his consulship, orginally written in Greek (8, cf. also *Crassus* 13), and two witty remarks (58, 59) which might come from a collection of Cicero's wit. The quotation in chapter 4 seems to refer to one of Cicero's letters. A henchman and biographer of Caesar's, C. Oppius, is cited at chapter 17, and certainly is the source for the two following items, one of which is attributed to Oppius by Suetonius (*Caesar* 53), while in the other Oppius appears as an actor. He may also have supplied much of the biographical information in the early chapters. The historian and philosopher Strabo is cited for a prodigy before the death of Caesar (63).

[4] On Pollio, see p. 220 above.

[5] On Livy, see p. 5 above. Note that the references to Caesar and Tanusius in c. 22 are found also in Appian, *Celtic Wars*, fragment 18 (Tanusius is 'some historian'), which suggests a common source. In c. 44 and *Pomp.* 69, Caesar is cited, as he is also in Appian, *BC* 2. 79. Cf. C. B. R. Pelling, 'Plutarch's Method in the Roman Lives,' *Journal of Hellenic Studies*, 99 (1979) 74–96, at 84–5; repr. in B. Scardigli (ed.), *Essays on Plutarch's Lives* (Oxford: Clarendon Press, 1995), 265–318, at 286–8.

Once more, we can say that Plutarch's narrative is founded upon contemporary or near-contemporary sources. An oral source may lie behind the notice of Caesar's sword captured at Alesia, which the Arverni show, 'hanging in a temple' (26). While many items are preserved in the parallel accounts of Suetonius' Life of Caesar, and the historical narratives of Appian and Cassius Dio, Plutarch assembles his material into a rapid and insightful portrait.

Despite his inability to establish a stable government, Caesar's accomplishments and his overwhelming superiority to his fellow senators, both as general and as political figure, made him a unique figure, a suitable companion to Alexander the Great, and an inspiration and warning to the emperors who would follow him.

Fuller, J. F. C., *Julius Caesar: Man, Soldier, and Tyrant* (London: Eyre and Spottiswoode, 1965). Especially for accounts of battles.

Gelzer, M., *Caesar: Politician and Statesman* (Oxford: Blackwell, 1968). A masterful biography.

Pelling, C. B. R., 'Plutarch on the Gallic War', *Classical Bulletin*, 60 (1984), 88–103.

Rawson, E., *Cicero: A Portrait* (London: Allen Lane, 1975; rev. edn. Ithaca, NY: Cornell, 1983).

Syme, R., *The Roman Revolution* (Oxford: Clarendon Press, 1939). Starting with 60 BC, traces the changes at Rome which led to Augustus' monarchy.

Taylor, L. R., 'Caesar's Early Career', *Classical Philology*, 36 (1941), 113–32.

Weinstock, S., *Divus Iulius* (Oxford: Clarendon Press, 1971).

Yavetz, Z., *Julius Caesar and his Public Image* (London: Thames and Hudson, 1983).

See also the works cited on p. 221–2 above.

CAESAR

[1]< . . . >† Once Sulla was in power he tried to persuade Caesar, using a combination of inducements and threats, to divorce Cornelia, the daughter of the former autocrat, Cinna, and when this attempt failed, he confiscated her dowry and turned it over to the public treasury.* It was Caesar's relationship with Marius that was responsible for his antagonism towards Sulla: the elder Marius had been married to Julia, the sister of Caesar's father, and she had given birth to the younger Marius, who was therefore Caesar's cousin.* Then again, Caesar also felt neglected by Sulla, who was initially busy with all the killings. This annoyed him, and even though he was still barely a young adult he presented himself to the people as a candidate for a priesthood—an attempt which Sulla secretly opposed and made sure was unsuccessful.* Sulla contemplated doing away with Caesar, but others said that it made no sense to kill a mere stripling. To this Sulla replied that they were stupid if they could not see that this boy had the potential to be Marius many times over. This remark was reported to Caesar, and he spent quite a long time in hiding in Sabine territory, moving from place to place. On one occasion, however, illness forced him to move from where he was staying to another house, and even though he travelled under cover of darkness he ran into some of Sulla's soldiers who were searching the area and arresting anyone they found hiding there. Caesar gave Cornelius, the officer in charge of this squad of men, two talents to let him go, and then he made his way straight down to the coast and set sail for King Nicomedes in Bithynia. After only a short stay there he left by boat, but he was captured near the island of Pharmacussa by pirates, who in those days controlled the sea with their huge fleets and innumerable small craft.*

[2] Firstly, when the pirates demanded a ransom of twenty talents for his release, he laughed at them for not knowing whom they had captured and of his own accord undertook to pay fifty. Secondly, after sending members of his retinue here and there around the cities to raise the money, he was left with only one friend and two slaves, surrounded by Cilicians of the most bloodthirsty kind, but he treated them with such disdain that whenever he wanted to sleep he would

send someone out to tell them to be quiet. For the thirty-eight days of his captivity he behaved as if they were his personal guard rather than his captors: he joined in their games and exercises, and tried out on them the poems and occasional prose pieces he wrote. If any of them failed to express their approval of his compositions, he called them to their faces uncultivated barbarians, and to their amusement often threatened to hang them all. This went down well with the pirates, who attributed his bluntness to childish naïvety. But as soon as the ransom money arrived from Miletus and Caesar had used it to buy his freedom, he fitted out some ships and put to sea from the harbour of Miletus to attack the brigands. He found them still at anchor off the island and captured most of them. Taking their money as booty, he lodged the men in the prison in Pergamum, and then paid Iuncus, the governor of Asia, a personal visit, since it was his job, as proconsul, to punish the prisoners. But Iuncus was inclined to cast covetous glances at the money (which was a sizeable sum), and at the same time kept saying that he would consider what to do with the prisoners when he had time, so Caesar ignored him and went to Pergamum. He took the pirates out of prison and crucified them all, just as he had often told them he would on the island, when they thought he was joking.*

[3] Next, with Sulla's power now declining and people in Rome calling him home, Caesar sailed to Rhodes to study under Apollonius the son of Molo, a famous teacher of rhetoric and, by all accounts, a good man too, whose lectures were attended by Cicero as well.* It is said that Caesar had a remarkable gift for political oratory and worked very assiduously to develop this natural talent, until the second rank was indisputably his. However, he allowed the first place to elude him, since he was more involved† in making use of his military abilities to gain prominence, and therefore was too occupied with the campaigns and policies he used to secure his supremacy to attain the degree of eloquence to which his natural talent could have carried him. At any rate, at a later date, in his response to Cicero's *Cato*,* he asked his audience not to compare the speech of a man of war with the eloquence of a naturally gifted orator who had devoted a lot of time to perfecting his art.

[4] After his return to Rome from Greece, he brought an action against Dolabella for maladministration of his province, with evidence supplied by many of the cities involved. Dolabella was

acquitted, but in return for the goodwill of the Greeks Caesar acted as their advocate when they prosecuted Publius Antonius for accepting bribes, the court being presided over by Marcus Lucullus, the praetorian governor of Macedonia. Caesar was so effective that Antonius appealed to the tribunes on the grounds that he could not receive a fair trial in Greece when his opponents were Greeks.*

In Rome his eloquence as an advocate caused a rapid upsurge in his popularity, and the easy friendliness with which he greeted people and chatted with them—he was unusually deferential for someone his age—won him a great deal of loyalty from ordinary people. He also gradually acquired a certain amount of political influence as a result of the banquets and dinners he gave, and in general as a result of the spectacular life he led. The people who wanted to see him fail thought that this influence would last just as long as he kept spending money, and would then quickly vanish, so at first they let it flourish among the common people. It was only later, when it had become too great to dislodge and had its sights set firmly on total constitutional change, that they realized their mistake: however small a thing might appear to be in its early stages, there is nothing that will not soon increase in size if it is left to endure and treated with such contempt that no impediments are put in its way. At any rate, the person who seems to have been the first to mistrust the superficial sparkle of the man and his political programme, and to fear him as one might fear the smiling surface of the sea, and who appreciated the cunning character hidden beneath the warmth and charm of his personality—this was Cicero—used to say that he could glimpse a tyrannical purpose to all his schemes and measures with one exception: 'When I see his hair so perfectly arranged,' he said, 'and when I see him scratching his head with a single finger, I change my mind. It seems inconceivable that anything as terrible as the overthrow of the Roman constitution could ever occur to this man.' But I have got ahead of my story.*

[5] The first demonstration he received of the people's loyalty towards him was when he was elected to a military tribuneship with more votes than the rival candidate, Gaius Popillius.* The second such demonstration was even more obvious, however. When Julia, the wife of Marius, died, as her nephew he delivered a magnificent eulogy of her in the forum, and even went so far as to display pictures of the Marii during her funeral procession, which was the first

time they had been seen in public since Sulla's regime, because they had been pronounced enemies of Rome. Some people loudly condemned this action of Caesar's, but the people shouted them down and resoundingly applauded Caesar on his entry into the assembly, to show how highly they thought of him for having resurrected, so to speak, the honour due to Marius and brought it back into Rome after so long. Now, although it was traditional in Rome for funeral speeches to be delivered over older women, it was not their practice to do so over young women, so that Caesar created a precedent with the speech he delivered on the death of his wife.* Even this helped to make him popular and, in conjunction with his grief, won the support of the masses, who regarded him fondly as a gentle and truly remarkable person.† After his wife's funeral he went out to Spain as quaestor to one of the praetors, Vetus. He never lost the high regard he had for Vetus, and later, when he was a praetor himself, he made Vetus' son his quaestor. At the end of his term of office as quaestor he married Pompeia. This was his third marriage, and he already had by Cornelia a daughter, who was subsequently married to Pompey the Great.*

He spent money copiously, and although people thought that all he was buying with his vast expenditure was ephemeral and short-lived status, he was actually getting the most important things at a bargain price. He is said to have run up a debt of thirteen hundred talents before he held any public office. When he was made supervisor of the Appian Way, he spent huge amounts of his own money in addition to public funds, while as aedile he put on a show involving 320 pairs of gladiators and with his lavish and extravagant disbursements on theatrical productions, processions, and banquets he obliterated all earlier munificence. The effect of all this on the common people was that to a man they tried to find new offices and honours with which to repay his generosity.*

[6] Of the two political groups in Rome, the Sullan party was very powerful, while at the time the Marians were so discouraged and divided that they had no prominence whatsoever.* Caesar wanted to reinvigorate and win the support of the Marian party, and so, just as the extravaganzas he was putting on in his capacity as aedile reached a peak of intensity, he took to the Capitol statues he had secretly commissioned of Marius and of Victory bearing trophies, and set them up there. The next day those who saw the statues, all glittering

with gold and fashioned with consummate skill (and with inscriptions detailing Marius' Cimbrian victories*), were astonished at the boldness of the person who had set them up—whose identity was no secret. Before long the story began to circulate around the city and attracted everyone on to the Capitol to see the sight. Some people in the crowd there began to cry out that in reviving honours which had been buried by legislation and decrees Caesar was trying to make himself tyrant, and claimed that this was a deliberate attempt to see whether the common people had been sufficiently tamed and softened up by his extravaganzas to let him get away with lightly introducing the kind of innovation the statues represented. The Marians, however, encouraged one another, and it was surprising how many of them there suddenly turned out to be: the Capitol was filled with their applause. The sight of Marius also moved a lot of people to tears of joy. They praised Caesar to the skies and said that he was the one man, the only man, who was good enough to be a relative of Marius. The senate met to discuss the situation, and Lutatius Catulus,* the most distinguished man in Rome at the time, stood up and denounced Caesar with the following memorable words: 'In his desire to overthrow the constitution, Caesar is no longer undermining the walls; now he is bringing up his siege-engines.' But Caesar defended himself against this charge and convinced the senate of his innocence, which boosted the morale of his admirers even further. They advised him not to compromise any of his principles, since the people would be glad, they said, to see him overcome all opposition and win supremacy in Rome.

[7] Meanwhile Metellus, the pontifex maximus, had died. The candidates for the highly prized priesthood were Isauricus and Catulus, but although they were both men of great distinction and extremely powerful senators, Caesar refused to give way to them: he went down to the popular assembly and put himself forward as a rival candidate. It was hard to tell which candidate had the most support, so Catulus, who felt he had more to lose from such uncertainty as a result of his greater reputation, wrote to Caesar with an offer of a large amount of money if he would withdraw from the contest—whereupon Caesar borrowed even more money and announced his intention of seeing it through to the finish. On the election day, his mother came to the front door of the house, with tears in her eyes, to see him on his way. As he took his leave of her he

said, 'Today, mother, you'll see your son either pontifex maximus or an exile.' The votes were cast, and it was a close-run thing, but Caesar won.*

The senate and the best men of Rome were alarmed at his victory; they thought he might be a totally disruptive influence on the common people. So Piso and Catulus told Cicero off for sparing Caesar when he was vulnerable during the Catiline affair. It had been Catiline's intention not just to effect a revolution, but to destroy the government and bring about a state of complete anarchy. Before his ultimate plans were discovered, however, he fell foul of some lesser charges and was driven out of Rome, but he left Lentulus and Cethegus behind in the city to continue the work of the conspiracy.* Now, whether or not Caesar secretly gave these men any encouragement or resources is unclear; but after they had been overwhelmingly found guilty in the senate and Cicero, who was consul, had asked each senator present to express his opinion on the matter of their punishment, they all called for the death penalty—until it was Caesar's turn. Caesar got to his feet and delivered a carefully worded speech to the effect that it was both unprecedented and unfair, except in the direst of emergencies, to put to death men of such distinguished rank and lineage without a trial. Instead, he suggested, they should be kept under guard in prison in Italian cities of Cicero's own choosing until after Catiline's defeat, and then later the senate could come to a calm and unhurried decision as to what to do with each of the men individually.*

[8] These views seemed so humane, and the speech in which he expressed them was so powerful, that not only did those who rose to speak after Caesar support him, but even many of those who had gone before him renounced their expressed opinions in favour of his. But then it was the turn of Cato and Catulus to address the issue, and they strenuously objected to Caesar's views; in fact Cato's speech was instrumental in pinning suspicion on Caesar and was a powerful voice of dissent.* The upshot was that the prisoners were handed over for execution, and as Caesar was on his way out of the senate many of the young men who were acting as Cicero's guards at the time flocked to the consul's side wielding drawn swords. But it is said that Curio threw his toga around Caesar and sneaked him away, and that Cicero refused to give the young men the go-ahead when they looked to him for a signal, perhaps because he was afraid of the

common people, or perhaps because the murder would have been, in his view, an entirely criminal and illegal act.*

If this story is true, I cannot understand why Cicero did not mention it in the book he wrote about his consulship.* But anyway, he was later criticized for having failed to take advantage of this perfect opportunity to get rid of Caesar, and for having lost his nerve in the face of the extraordinary support and protection the masses were giving Caesar. A few days later, for example, Caesar entered the senate, and tried to defend himself against the suspicions he had incurred, but met with obstructive outcries; once the meeting had gone on for an unusually long time, a noisy mob of people came and surrounded the senate, demanding Caesar and ordering the senate to release him. Now, there was nothing Cato feared more than a revolution instigated by the poorer members of society, who were setting the whole population alight with the hopes they invested in Caesar, and so he persuaded the senate to give them a monthly ration of grain. This measure increased the state's annual expenditure by 7,500,000 drachmas, but plainly allayed the major fear at the time and served to dismantle and disperse most of Caesar's power—and not a moment too soon, since he was about to become a praetor, and the prospect of his holding this office was even more alarming.

[9] In the event, however, there were no disturbances as a result of his praetorship, but Caesar was affected by a scandal that occurred within his family. Publius Clodius was a man of patrician birth, and was distinguished for his wealth and eloquence, but of all the notorious agitators of the day he was the most insolent and disruptive.* He was in love with Pompeia, Caesar's wife, and she did not discourage him, but the women's quarters were well guarded, and Caesar's mother, Aurelia, who was a person of strict morals, always kept close to the young bride and made it difficult and dangerous for the lovers to meet.

Now, the Romans have a goddess they call Bona, 'the Good Goddess', who is equivalent to the Greek Gynaceia, 'the Women's Goddess'. The Phrygians claim that she originated with them and was the mother of King Midas, while according to the Romans she was one of the nymphs called Dryads and had Faunus as her husband, and the Greeks say that of the mothers of Dionysus, she was the one whose name is not to be spoken.* That is why, when her festival is being celebrated in Greece, the women roof their shelters with slips of vine and, in conformity with the myth, a sacred snake is enthroned alongside the goddess. It is forbidden for any man to attend the rites, or even to be present in the house when they are going on; but the rites the women perform all by themselves during the ceremonies are said to resemble the Orphic rites in a number of respects. So when the time comes for the festival, <which has to be celebrated in the house of>† a man who is currently a consul or a praetor, the house-owner himself leaves, along with any other male members of the household, while his wife takes over the house and arranges things for the celebrations. The most important part of the rites takes place at night, when the celebrations take on a light-hearted tone and are accompanied by a great deal of music.*

[10] This was the festival which Pompeia was celebrating at the time in question. Now, Clodius did not yet have a beard, and this led him to think that he could sneak into the house, so he dressed up and equipped himself as a female harp-player and went there disguised as a young woman. He found the door open, and was brought into the house without encountering any obstacles by the slave-girl on duty, who was in on the secret. She ran on ahead to tell Pompeia, but nothing happened for a while and Clodius was too impatient to wait where he had been left. As he was wandering around the house, which was a large one, trying to stay in the shadows, he bumped into one of Aurelia's ladies-in-waiting, who invited him to come and join in the fun, as one woman would another. When he refused, she began to pull him into the open, and asked him who he was and where he was from. Clodius said that he was waiting for Habra, which was the name of Pompeia's slave, and his voice betrayed him. With a cry, Aurelia's lady-in-waiting immediately leapt away towards the lights and the group of women, calling out that she had caught a man. The women scattered in panic, while Aurelia first called a halt to the goddess's rites and covered up the implements, and then, once she had ordered the doors to be locked, personally went around the house with torches, looking for Clodius. He was found hiding in the room of the slave-girl who had brought him into the house, and after noting who he was the women drove him out of the house.

Even though it was night-time the women left straight away and told their husbands what had happened, and the next day the story spread throughout Rome that Clodius had deliberately committed sacrilege, and that he ought to recompense not only the injured parties, but also the city and the gods. So one of the tribunes arraigned Clodius on the charge of impiety, and the most powerful members of the senate joined forces against him and testified to various other immoral acts of his, including adultery with his sister, who was married to Lucullus.* But the people deployed their resources to combat the efforts of these senators and to keep them from harming Clodius, and offered him invaluable assistance in dealing with the jurors, who were terribly frightened of the masses. Caesar lost no time in divorcing Pompeia, but when he was summoned to testify during the trial, he denied any knowledge of the charges facing Clodius. This statement seemed so implausible that the prosecutor asked him, 'Why then did you divorce your wife?' And Caesar replied: 'Because I insist that my wife should be above suspicion.' Some people say that Caesar's testimony in this trial was sincere, but others claim that he was gratifying the people's desire to get Clodius off. And in fact Clodius was acquitted: most of the jurors handed in verdicts that were written illegibly, because they did not want to run the risk of condemning him, surrounded as they were by a mob of the common people, and at the same time they wanted to avoid the contempt they would earn from the best men of Rome if they acquitted him.*

[11] Immediately after his praetorship Caesar was assigned the province of Spain,* but his creditors were making things difficult for him by raising obstacles and cries of outrage at his proposed departure. He therefore turned for help to Crassus, who was the richest man in Rome, and who needed Caesar's energy and passion for his political campaign against Pompey. Once Crassus had met the demands of the most awkward and insistent of his creditors, and had guaranteed the sum of 850 talents, Caesar left for his province.* There is a story that his route across the Alps took him past a native village, a very run-down place with hardly anyone living there at all, and his companions jokingly asked, for a laugh, 'Even here, do people ambitiously compete for high office and supremacy, do you suppose? Are there envious rivalries between men of power?' But Caesar replied in a serious tone of voice: 'I'd rather be first here than second in Rome.'† Another similar story comes from when he was in Spain: in a moment of leisure he was reading one of the histories of Alexander and became very quiet and withdrawn for a long time, and his eyes eventually filled with tears. In astonishment, his friends

asked him what the matter was. 'Don't you think it's sad,' he said, 'that while Alexander was already ruling over a vast empire at such a young age, I haven't yet achieved anything remarkable?'*

[12] Anyway, as soon as he reached Spain he set to work, and in a few days he had raised ten cohorts in addition to the twenty that were already there. He then marched against the Callaïci and the Lusitani. After conquering them, he carried on to the outer sea, subduing all the tribes which had not previously recognized Roman supremacy. With the war brought to a satisfactory conclusion, he turned to civil administration and settled matters in that sphere too with equal success. Apart from establishing peace between various communities, his most important achievement was to resolve the dispute that was going on between debtors and creditors. He decreed that the creditor should take two-thirds of the debtor's income every year, while the owner of the property kept the remaining third, until the debt had been paid off. With his prestige enormously enhanced by these successes, he left the province: his campaigns there had made him a wealthy man, and he had also enriched his troops, who had proclaimed him 'Imperator'.*

[13] Regulations stated that commanders petitioning for a triumph had to wait outside the city, while candidates for a consulship had to be present in the city to put their names forward. Caesar's return to Rome coincided precisely with the consular elections, so he was caught on the horns of this dilemma. He wrote to the senate asking for permission to announce his candidacy for a consulship through the agency of friends, even while not actually being there himself. Cato's initial ploy to combat Caesar's request was to insist on adherence to the law, but then, when he saw that a lot of the senators were prepared to defer to Caesar, he filibustered and used up the rest of the day with speeches. Caesar therefore decided to forfeit the triumph and go for the consulship.* As soon as he entered the city, he adopted a policy which fooled everyone except Cato. The policy was to effect a reconciliation between Pompey and Crassus, the two most influential men in the city. But by getting them to settle their differences and become friends, he channelled power away from the two of them and on to himself, and so used this apparently altruistic act gradually to bring about a revolution in Rome. For the usual view, that the civil wars were caused by the quarrel between Caesar and Pompey, is wrong: it was their friendship that was

responsible. First they collaborated to overthrow the aristocracy, and only then did they fall out with each other. The upshot as far as Cato was concerned, because he often used to predict the future, was that at the time he acquired the reputation of being an officious merchant of doom, but later people came to see that his advice was sound, even if it was ineffective.*

[14] And so Caesar was escorted to the consulship, protected and surrounded by the friendship of Crassus and Pompey.† He was elected with a clear majority, with Calpurnius Bibulus as his colleague, and as soon as he took up the post he began to introduce the kind of proposals for allotments and grants of land, designed to please the masses, that one might have expected from the most radical of tribunes, but not from a consul. The opposition these measures met with from the aristocrats in the senate gave him the excuse he had wanted for a long time: loudly protesting that he was being driven against his will to the popular assembly and was being forced by the intransigent disrespect of the senate to make overtures to the people, he escaped to the assembly. With Crassus standing on one side of him and Pompey on the other, he asked them if they approved of his proposed legislation. They said they did, and he called on them to help him against the threat of armed opposition. They promised their support, and Pompey even added that he would bring his swords and shield to wield against their swords. This made the aristocrats angry with him—in their view it was a crazy and impulsive thing to say, and they thought he had betrayed the regard in which he was held and the respect due to the senate—but the people were delighted.* Moreover, Caesar tried to avail himself† even more freely of Pompey's influence, by betrothing his daughter, Julia, to him. She was already betrothed to Servilius Caepio, but he told Servilius he would give him Pompey's daughter instead, even though she was not free either, but was promised to Faustus, the son of Sulla. And a little later Caesar married Calpurnia, the daughter of Piso, and got Piso elected consul for the next year. At this point Cato loudly protested that it was intolerable for marriage to be the coin by which leadership of the state was bought and sold, and for women to be the means by which men slotted one another into provincial governorships, military commands, and the control of resources.*

Caesar's colleague, Bibulus, was getting nowhere by trying to obstruct Caesar's legislation, but in fact was often in danger, along with Cato, of being killed in the forum, so he shut himself up in his house for the remainder of his term of office. Pompey, however, as soon as he was married, filled the forum with armed men and helped the people get Caesar's laws passed, and also played his part in gaining Caesar not only Cisalpine and Transalpine Gaul, but Illyricum as well, with four legions for a five-year period.* When Cato tried to object to these measures, Caesar had him taken away to prison, because he expected him to appeal to the tribunes—but Cato went off without saying a word. The best men of Rome of course found Caesar's action highly offensive, but when Caesar also saw that Cato's noble qualities commanded such respect that ordinary people were accompanying him on his way in dejected silence, he quietly asked one of the tribunes to let him go.*

Very few senators joined Caesar in the senate now, while the rest expressed their disgust by staying away. Once Considius, a very old man, told him that they did not come to the meetings because they were afraid of the weaponry and the soldiers. 'So why don't *you* stay at home?' Caesar asked. 'Don't you find these things frightening too?' Considius replied: 'I'm too old to be afraid. I hardly need to worry about the future when I have so little time left to live.' But of all the shocking measures that were being passed at the time, the one which was widely regarded as the worst was the election as tribune, during Caesar's consulship, of Clodius—the man who had violated Caesar's marriage and the secret rites. He was elected for the purpose of getting rid of Cicero, and Caesar did not set out to take up command of his army until with Clodius' help he had come out victorious in his feud with Cicero and had seen him expelled from Italy.*

[15] So much for Caesar's life, as reported by my sources, before Gaul. In the next phase of his life—during the wars he fought and the campaigns with which he subjugated the Gauls—it was as if he had made a fresh start and entered upon a different way of life, one that involved a new kind of achievement.* He proved himself to be at least the equal, as a soldier and a leader of men, of any of the most famous and outstanding commanders there have ever been. In fact, if one were to compare him with men like Fabius and Scipio and Metellus, or with those whose careers coincided with or slightly preceded his, Sulla and Marius and the two Luculli, or even with Pompey himself, whose fame as a commander of consummate skill in

all areas of warfare was then flourishing and spreading over all the world,* one would find that Caesar did better than any of them* either because his wars were fought over more difficult kinds of terrain; or because he annexed a greater quantity of land; or because he defeated more and fiercer enemies; or because the customs he had to deal with in his peace negotiations were more outlandish and incredible; or because he treated his prisoners with greater decency and composure; or because he was more generous in the gifts and rewards he gave his troops. And he surpassed all of them in the number of battles he fought and casualties he inflicted on the enemy. For although he fought in Gaul for somewhat less than ten years, he took over 800 cities and towns by storm, subdued 300 tribes, and in successive pitched battles against a total of 3,000,000 men he killed 1,000,000 and took the same number of prisoners.

[16] He inspired an incredible amount of loyalty and affection in his troops. In order to enhance Caesar's glory, men who on other campaigns had been just average soldiers hurled themselves into battle, however desperate the situation, and proved invincible and irresistible. Consider the case of Acilius, for example: even when his right hand had been severed by a sword after boarding an enemy ship during the sea battle off Massilia, he kept a grip on his shield with his left hand and pummelled his opponents in their faces with it until they gave way and he took control of the ship.* Then there was the behaviour of Cassius Scaeva in the battle of Dyrrhachium: after losing an eye to an arrow, taking javelin thrusts in his shoulder and thigh, and receiving 130 blows on his shield from various weapons, he called out to the enemy as if he was prepared to surrender, but when two of them came over he cut off one man's arm at the shoulder with his sword, and wounded the other man in the face and forced him to retreat, before being surrounded by his kinsmen and saved.*

Once, in Britain, the enemy were attacking the officers in the front rank, who had stumbled into a place that was boggy and full of pools, and because Caesar himself was watching the battle an ordinary soldier thrust his way into the thick of things and fought for a long time with remarkable courage until the natives turned to flight and he had rescued the officers; then he hurled himself into the muddy streams and struggled back across the marsh after all the others, and at last, after swimming some of the way and walking the rest, he succeeded in reaching dry land, without his shield. Caesar was highly impressed, and greeted the man with a cry of joy, but the man hung his head in abject shame and with tears in his eyes begged Caesar's forgiveness for losing his shield.* Then again, off the coast of Africa Scipio once captured a ship of Caesar's which had on board Granius Petro, who had been appointed Caesar's quaestor. Scipio decided to hold the rest of the passengers for ransom, but told the quaestor that he would spare his life. Granius replied, however, that it was not the practice for Caesar's men to accept mercy, but to offer it, and with these words he took his sword and stabbed himself to death.*

[17] It was Caesar himself who nourished and created the conditions for these and other similar acts of valour and resolve. In the first place, he was a generous giver of gifts and rewards, while making it clear that the wealth he accumulated from the wars was not to be used on a luxurious lifestyle for himself or on personal indulgences, but was simply being held in reserve and looked after by him as a common bank from which prizes for courage could be drawn, and that his share in the booty was no more than what he gave his men in reward for merit; and in the second place, he never hesitated to face danger himself nor shirked hard work. His men were not surprised that he was prepared to take risks, because they were aware of his determination to succeed, but they were impressed by his ability to put up with hard work beyond what his body was apparently capable of enduring, since he had a slight build and pale, soft skin, suffered from headaches, and was liable to epileptic fits (an affliction which first occurred when he was in Corduba, we hear*). So far from making his poor health an excuse for taking things easy, campaigning was his way of treating his poor health: he used endless route-marches, meagre rations, and continuous outdoor living and hardship to combat the affliction and keep his body in a fit enough state to resist the attacks. He usually slept in wagons or litters, since he considered rest no more than an investment for future action, and in the daytime he would have himself driven around the outposts and cities and camps, with a single slave sitting by him who had been trained to take dictation while on the move, and a single soldier standing behind him with a sword.

He used to ride at such a furious pace that his first journey from Rome to the Rhône took only eight days.* Riding came easily to him from childhood onwards: he was well versed in the exercise of riding at full gallop with his arms pulled back and his hands joined behind his back. During the Gallic Wars he also trained himself to dictate his dispatches while riding, and he kept two secretaries busy at once —or even more, according to Oppius.* It is also said that Caesar was the first to use letters as a way of communicating with his friends, since the constant pressure of business and the size of the city made it impossible for him to wait for a face-to-face meeting when there was something urgent he wanted to tell them.*

Here is another story that is told as evidence of how easy he was to please where food was concerned. He was once dining in Mediolanum at the house of Valerius Leo, and he was served asparagus dressed in myrrh rather than in olive oil. He ate it without any fuss, and scolded his friends when they complained: 'If there's something you don't like,' he said, 'all you have to do is leave it. But to criticize a *faux pas* of this kind is to commit a *faux pas* oneself.'* Once he was caught out in the open by a storm and driven inside a poor man's cottage. When he found that it consisted of only the one room, which was hardly big enough for a single person, he told his friends that while the strongest had a right to perquisites, the weakest had a right to necessities, and so he told Oppius to rest there, while the rest of them, including himself, slept under the eaves overhanging the doorway.*

[18] Anyway, his first campaign in Gaul was against the Helvetii and the Tigurini, who had burned their own twelve cities and four hundred villages and were advancing through Roman Gaul, just as some years earlier the Cimbri and Teutones had done. This invasion also bore comparison to that earlier one in that the Helvetii and Tigurini were by all accounts just as fearless, and because similar numbers were involved: there were 300,000 of the Helvetii and Tigurini, of whom 190,000 were fighting men. The Tigurini were annihilated at the river Arar by Labienus, whom Caesar had sent to deal with them, rather than by Caesar himself. The Helvetii, however, unexpectedly attacked Caesar and his army as they were *en route* for a friendly city, but he beat a hasty retreat to a natural stronghold, where he regrouped his men and drew them up in battle array. A horse was brought to him, but he said, 'I shall use this horse for the pursuit after the battle is won, but the immediate job is to attack the enemy. Let's go!' And with these words he charged into

the attack on foot. Eventually, after a fierce struggle, he succeeded in forcing the enemy troops back, but was then faced with an even more difficult task at the camp and among the baggage-train. For not only did the men make a stand there and put up a fight, but their children and womenfolk too fought to the death and were cut down alongside them. The upshot was that it was the middle of the night before the battle was really over. Caesar capped this brilliant victory with an action of even greater importance: he combined the survivors of the battle together as a single people and compelled them—there were over 100,000 of them—to return to the land they had abandoned and the cities they had destroyed. The reason he did this was because he was worried about the possibility of the Germans invading and occupying the land if it remained uninhabited.*

[19] His second campaign was fought directly against the Germans in defence of Gaul, even though previously, in Rome, he had entered into an alliance with the German king, Ariovistus. But their conduct towards their neighbours, who were subjects of Caesar's, was intolerable, and it was generally believed that if the opportunity presented itself they would not stay peaceably where they were, but would spread into Gaul and take it over. Now, Caesar detected a certain reluctance to fight among his officers, particularly those young men from noble families who had come out to Gaul with him under the impression that a campaign with Caesar would mean easy living and the chance to make money, so he convened a meeting at which he told them to leave and not to risk battle if they were too feeble and effeminate to face it, and announced his intention of taking just the tenth legion and marching against the foreigners, who, he said, would surely prove no more formidable an enemy than the Cimbri, while he was no worse a general than Marius. At this the tenth legion sent a delegation to him to express their gratitude, while the other legions cursed their commanding officers, and then the whole army, now entirely committed and intent on the task, fell in behind him.* After a journey of many days they finally encamped within two hundred stades of the enemy.

Ariovistus' confidence was considerably shaken just by Caesar's approach. He had not expected the Romans to attack the Germans—in fact, the Germans had thought that Roman resistance would crumble at *their* attack—so he was surprised by Caesar's boldness and he could see that his men's resolve had been weakened too. Then their priestesses' prophecies dismayed them even more. These priestesses used to foretell the future by looking at the eddies of rivers and drawing inferences from the way streams swirled and the noises the water made, and now they told them not to join battle until the new moon had appeared. Caesar heard about this, and he could see that the Germans were not making any aggressive moves, so he decided to attack while their morale was low, rather than stay where he was and wait for the time of their choosing. By making assaults on their fortifications and the hills where they were encamped he goaded and incited them until they were so angry that they came down and fought it out. The Germans were resoundingly defeated, and Caesar pursued them for four hundred stades, all the way up to the Rhine. The whole plain over which he pursued them was covered with corpses and spoils. Ariovistus escaped with a small retinue and crossed the Rhine, but German losses are said to have numbered eighty thousand.*

[20] After this victory Caesar left his army to winter in the territory of the Sequani, but he wanted to attend to matters in Rome, so he went down to the part of Gaul around the river Po, where he was still within his assigned province, because the boundary between Cisalpine Gaul and the rest of Italy is formed by the river known as the Rubicon.* Once he had taken up quarters there, he set about making himself popular. A lot of people came to see him with requests, and they all got what they asked for; in fact, he sent them all back to Rome with something to be going on with for the time being and the promise of more in the future. And what Pompey failed to realize was that for the rest of his Gallic campaigns Caesar was alternately using the armed might of Rome to defeat the enemy, and using the money he gained from the enemy to make the citizens of Rome obedient and subservient to himself.

However, as soon as he heard that the most powerful Gallic tribe, the Belgae, whose lands covered a third of all Gaul, were in revolt and had raised an enormous army, he turned back and advanced on them at great speed. He found them plundering the territory of the Gauls who had remained loyal to Rome, attacked them, and routed their main and largest army, which put up pathetically little resistance. So many men died that the Romans could cross deep lakes and rivers on the bodies clogging them.* All the coastal peoples who had revolted surrendered without a battle, but Caesar marched against the Nervii, the fiercest and most warlike of the tribes in that part of Gaul. The Nervii, who lived in a vast stretch† of woodland, had left their families and belongings in a corner of this forest, as far as possible from the enemy, while they themselves, sixty thousand strong, suddenly attacked Caesar while he was in the middle of building a camp and was unprepared for a battle of this magnitude. They overpowered the Roman cavalry, and then surrounded the twelfth and seventh legions. They had killed all the officers, and it is generally held that the Romans would have been massacred to a man had Caesar not snatched up a shield, pushed his way through the lines of men fighting in front of him, and hurled himself at the Gauls, thus exposing himself to such danger that the tenth legion raced down from the heights and cut their way through the enemy lines to save him. In actual fact, though, Caesar's courage had the effect of making his men fight beyond their normal abilities, as the saying goes. Even so, however, the Nervii did not turn to flight, but were cut down fighting the Romans. And so there are said to have been only 500 survivors out of an army of 60,000, and only three of their 400 councillors remained alive.*

[21] When news of these successes reached Rome, the senate decreed that there should be sacrifices to the gods and celebratory holidays for fifteen days—a longer period of time than for any previous victory. For the fact of the matter was that the number of tribes simultaneously involved in the uprising made the danger seem particularly acute, and because it was Caesar who was the victor, the devotion of the masses for him exaggerated the brilliance of the victory.

Now that Gaul was peaceful, Caesar returned to the area around the Po, took up winter quarters there, and continued to orchestrate affairs in Rome. In the first place, it was as a result of being backed by him and using his money to bribe the masses that candidates for official positions were elected, and the whole point of all their policies was to increase his power. In the second place, most of the men of particular distinction and importance in Rome came to see him in Luca, including Pompey and Crassus, Appius, who was the governor of Sardinia, and Nepos, the proconsul of Spain, until in the end there were a hundred and twenty lictors there, and more than two hundred senators.* They formed themselves into an executive committee and decided that Pompey and Crassus were to be elected consuls, and that Caesar was to be awarded more money and have his command extended for a further period of five years. Anyone with any sense could easily see the paradox involved in this: people who were being given huge amounts of money by Caesar were persuading the senate to give him money as if he had none—although it was not so much a matter of persuasion as of compulsion, and every decree was accompanied by sighs and complaints. Cato was not there, because they had made sure that he was out of the way in Cyprus,* and Cato's devoted follower, Favonius, found that he could get nowhere by raising objections in the senate, so he dashed outside and began voicing his indignation to the masses. His pleas fell on deaf ears, however, and no one was prepared to do anything about the situation, either because they respected Pompey and Crassus or, more commonly, because they wanted to please Caesar and lived in hope of future favours from him.

[22] When Caesar returned to his forces in Gaul, he found the country caught up in a major conflict, since two large German tribes had recently crossed the Rhine with the intention of increasing their territory.* The battle fought against these two tribes—whose names were the Usipes and the Tenteritae—is described in Caesar's *Commentaries*. The invaders were involved in negotiations with Caesar when, despite the truce, they attacked his men while they were on the road. The unexpectedness of this assault enabled them to scatter his 5,000-strong cavalry with their 800 horsemen. They then attempted to repeat the same trick and sent further envoys to him, but he detained the envoys and led his army against the Germans, since he considered it stupid to trust such untrustworthy truce-breakers.* According to Tanusius, Cato's response to the senatorial decree of sacrifices and celebrations in honour of the victory was to say that in his view they should hand Caesar over to the Germans, to avert from the city the evil consequences of his violation of the truce and turn them back on to the guilty party.* Four hundred thousand of the invaders were killed, and the few who managed to cross back over the Rhine were given shelter by a German tribe called the Sugambri.

Caesar used this as an excuse for attacking the Sugambri, and in any case he was anxious to win glory as the first man ever to invade German territory. He threw a bridge across the Rhine, for all its considerable width and even though at that point in its course† it was running particularly high, with rough and turbulent water, and tended to batter and smash the bridge's supports with tree-trunks and bits of wood carried down on the current. But Caesar fixed huge wooden barriers across the river to catch this debris, and once he had curbed the force of the current with this boom, he achieved the absolutely unbelievable feat of completing the bridge in ten days.*

[23] His troops now crossed the river, and met with no opposition. In fact, even the Suebi, the dominant tribe in Germany, marched away into deep and wooded valleys. After putting to the torch the land of any hostile tribes and giving those which remained loyal to Rome grounds for confidence, he returned to Gaul. He had spent eighteen days in Germany.*

It was a particularly bold stroke of his to launch an expedition against the Britons, and he became famous for it. Not only was he the first man ever to take a fleet out into the western part of the Ocean and to attack an enemy by transporting an army across the Atlantic Sea, but he undertook to take possession of an island whose reported size beggared belief, and to do so despite the fact that a great many writers furiously contended that its name and any stories about it were complete fabrications, since it never had existed and did not exist now. With this attempt he advanced the supremacy of Rome beyond the horizons of the known world. He twice sailed to the island from the opposite coast of Gaul, and he fought a large number of battles there which harmed the enemy rather than benefited his own men, because there was nothing worth taking from people who lived such hard and impoverished lives. He did not manage to bring the war to the kind of conclusion he wanted, but before leaving the island he accepted hostages from the king and imposed a tribute.*

Letters from friends in Rome reached him just as he was about to sail across to Gaul, telling him about his daughter's death. She had died in childbirth in Pompey's house. The depth of Pompey's grief was matched by Caesar's, but their friends were desperately worried, because they felt that the bond which had protected the otherwise ailing constitution and preserved a state of peace and concord had come to an end. For before long the baby died too, having survived its mother by only a few days. Despite the protests of the tribunes, the masses carried Julia's body to the Campus Martius and held her funeral rites there, and that is where she still lies buried.*

[24] Caesar's forces were now so large that he had no choice but to divide them between a number of winter quarters, while he as usual made his way to Italy. But all the Gallic tribes rose up in revolt, and huge armies surrounded the various winter quarters and tried to destroy them. The Roman camps too came under attack. The largest and most effective rebel army, under Ambiorix, annihilated the troops led by Cotta and Titurius. Cicero's legion was surrounded and besieged by an army of sixty thousand, and only an extraordinarily heroic resistance, in the course of which every man sustained wounds, prevented them from being overrun.* Caesar was many miles away when the news reached him. He turned back at once and hurried to relieve Cicero, but he was able to raise an army of only seven thousand men in all. When the besiegers became aware of his approach they came to meet him, with the intention of overwhelming what they saw as his pathetically small numbers. But Caesar kept tricking and eluding them, until he reached a suitable place for a small force to defend itself against a numerically superior one, where he built a fortified camp. He refused to let his men engage the enemy at all, but forced them to construct a palisade and wall up† the gates as if they were afraid. The purpose of this strategy was to induce contempt in the enemy, and at last they became so confident that they began to attack in small groups. Then Caesar emerged from the camp, put the enemy to flight, and killed a great many of them.*

[25] After this victory the various uprisings in that part of Gaul died down, and the fact that Caesar spent the winter personally travelling all over the place and keeping a close watch on the trouble spots also helped, because three legions came from Italy to replace the men he had lost. Pompey lent him two of the legions under his command, and the other one was freshly recruited from the part of Gaul around the river Po.* Further afield, however, the first signs of the most serious and perilous war Caesar had to face in Gaul began to appear. Many years previously the seeds had secretly been sown and now the leading men of the region were spreading dissent among the most warlike tribes, whose confidence was increased by several factors: the considerable numbers of fighting men who had assembled there from all quarters, armed and ready; the huge amount of money that had been accumulated; the strength of the cities; and the virtual impregnability of the territory. Moreover, it was winter at the time, which meant that the rivers were frozen and

the forests blanketed in snow, winter streams had turned the plains into bogs, and paths were either undetectable because of the depth of the snow or followed an uncertain and winding course through marshes and across streams. All this seemed to make it completely out of the question for Caesar to do anything about the rebellion. Although many tribes were involved in the uprising, the most conspicuous were the Arverni and the Carnutes, and overall responsibility for the war was given to Vergentorix, whose father had been put to death by the Gauls for his apparently tyrannical plans.*

[26] Vergentorix split his forces up into a number of different divisions and appointed a commander for each division. He then proceeded to win over to his cause the whole region, up to and including the lands near the Arar river. He wanted to use the opportunity created by the existence of an anti-Caesar coalition in Rome to arouse the whole of Gaul to war.* If he had done this a little later, when Caesar was involved in the Civil War, Italy would have been stricken by just as much panic as during the Cimbrian invasion. But as things were the man with the ability to thrive in a state of war and who excelled in emergencies—namely, Caesar—set out as soon as he heard of the rebellion. The speed and energy with which he retraced his route through the depths of winter were a vivid demonstration to the foreigners of the utter invincibility of the army coming against them. There were places they would hardly have expected one of his messengers or dispatch riders to reach, or at least only after a considerable amount of time, yet Caesar appeared there with his whole army and proceeded to devastate their lands, destroy their villages, subdue their cities, and win over those who were inclined to change sides. But then the Aedui declared war on him too. Up until then they had called themselves brothers of the Romans and had received every mark of favour, but now they sided with the rebels. Morale in Caesar's army plummeted at this betrayal, so Caesar broke camp and moved elsewhere. He passed through the territory of the Lingones, with the intention of reaching the Sequani, a friendly tribe whose land lay between Italy and the rest of Gaul, but at this point he was attacked and surrounded by a huge enemy army. Caesar resolved to make this the battle to end the war. He engaged them on all fronts and eventually, after a long time, overpowered and defeated the enemy with considerable loss of life. However, it looks as though he suffered a setback at the beginning of

the battle, because the Arverni show a sword hanging in a temple which they claim is a trophy taken from Caesar. When Caesar himself saw it later, he smiled and rejected his friends' suggestion that he should take it down, since he respected its status as a sacred offering.*

[27] At the time in question, however, most of the Gauls who escaped, including Vergentorix, took refuge in the city of Alesia. Caesar laid siege to the city, but its walls were so high and the number of defenders so great that he was generally expected to fail in his attempt to take it. Then, in the course of the siege, Caesar was threatened by indescribably terrifying danger from outside, when the best warriors from tribes all over Gaul joined forces and marched in force to Alesia. This army consisted of 300,000 men, and there were at least 170,000 fighting men inside the city, so that Caesar was trapped between two enormous forces and came under siege himself. He was forced to build two walls, one facing the city and the other because of the new arrivals, since he felt that his situation would become absolutely hopeless if the two forces joined up.

There were a large number of reasons, of course, why the conflict at Alesia became famous: it was the occasion for deeds of daring and skill the like of which have never been seen in any other battle. But the most impressive thing was the way that Caesar managed to engage and defeat the huge army outside the city without those inside the city having the least idea what was going on—in fact, without even the Romans on guard duty on the wall facing the city knowing what was going on! The first they knew about the victory was when they heard from Alesia the men's cries of horror and the women's wails of grief at the sight, wherever they looked, of Romans carrying into their camp large quantities of shields chased with silver and gold, breastplates stained red with blood, and also cups and tents of Gallic design. This shows how quickly the Gallic army, for all its huge size, vanished and dissolved like a ghost or a dream, once most of its men had died fighting. For a while the people inside Alesia made life difficult for Caesar, and for themselves too, but in the end they surrendered. Their commander-in-chief, Vergentorix, emerged from the city gates on horseback, wearing his most splendid armour and with his horse richly caparisoned. He rode all the way round Caesar, who remained seated, and then dismounted, stripped off his armour, and sat quietly at Caesar's feet, before being taken away to be held in custody until Caesar's triumph.*

[28] It had long been a plan of Caesar's to bring about the downfall of Pompey—just as it had been of Pompey's to do the same to Caesar, of course. For now that Crassus, who had been standing by as a fresh wrestler should either of them need him, had died in Parthia,* the only alternatives were for the one who aspired to supremacy to overthrow the one who already had it, or for the other to avoid this by first removing the one he feared. This fear had come upon Pompey quite suddenly, because he had previously been inclined to despise Caesar and think of him as unlikely to pose any real difficulties; after all, he thought, he had raised Caesar up, so he could bring him down again. But it had been Caesar's plan right from the start, and like an athlete he had put a considerable distance between himself and his rivals and used the Gallic Wars as an exercise ground.* He had trained his troops and enhanced his reputation until as a result of his achievements it had reached a height where it could challenge the fame of Pompey's successes. In the process he had made use of every opportunity that came his way; some of them had been provided by Pompey himself, and others by the times and the dire state of Roman politics. Things had got so bad that candidates for office set up money-tables in public places and shamelessly bribed the masses, and the people went down to the forum as hired mercenaries, to fight with bows and swords and slingshot, rather than with votes,* for whoever had given them money. It was far from unknown for the dignity of the rostra to be demeaned with blood and corpses before the voters went their separate ways, leaving the city in a state of anarchy like a ship adrift without a helmsman. In the end those who kept their heads felt it would be enough if the effect of all this insanity and turmoil on the political life of Rome were nothing worse than an autocracy.*

In fact, a lot of people went so far as to declare in public that the only possible remedy for the state was an autocracy and that when this treatment was being offered by the gentlest of doctors—a subtle reference to Pompey—the state should submit to it. Although Pompey affected to decline the honour, he too was actually putting more effort than anyone else into the project of getting himself made dictator. But Cato realized what was going on and persuaded the senate to make Pompey sole consul, so that the consolation of this more legitimate form of autocracy might divert him from storming his way into a dictatorship. The senate also extended the period of time he could hold his provinces. He had two provinces—Spain and all Africa—which he governed by means of the legates he sent there and the armies he maintained with an annual allowance from the public treasury of a thousand talents.*

[29] Caesar now wrote to solicit a consulship and a similar extension of the time he could hold his provinces. At first Pompey made no response, while the opposition to Caesar's requests came from Marcellus and Lentulus.* This was not the only reason these two had for hating Caesar, and they tended to go beyond what was absolutely necessary in their efforts to discredit and insult him. For instance, they deprived the people of Novum Comum, a colony recently founded in Gaul by Caesar, of Roman citizenship, and when Marcellus was consul he used the lictor's rods to beat one of the councillors of Novum Comum who had come to Rome. He explained that he was giving him these stripes to demonstrate the fact that he was not a Roman citizen, and told him to go back and show them to Caesar.* But Marcellus' consulship came to an end, and by now Caesar had let everyone involved in Roman politics draw freely on the money he had made in Gaul, had paid off the huge debts run up by the tribune, Curio, and had given fifteen hundred talents to the consul, Paullus (which Paullus put towards enhancing the beauty of the forum by replacing the Basilica Fulvia with a wonderful and famous new basilica*). This caucus alarmed Pompey and, making use of his friends as well as his own resources, he now openly began to campaign for Caesar's command to be passed on to someone else. He also wrote to Caesar, asking him to return the troops he had lent him for the Gallic Wars—and Caesar did send them back, after rewarding every single man with 250 drachmas.* But the men who had gone and fetched these troops for Pompey spread scandalous and untrue stories about Caesar, and effectively destroyed Pompey himself by filling him with false hopes. They told him that Caesar's army longed to see him, and that while it was proving difficult for him to control matters in Rome because of the envy inherent in the decaying state, the forces in Gaul were his for the taking and would join him just as soon as they ever appeared in Italy. They explained this by saying that the constant campaigning had made Caesar unpopular with his troops, who were also worried that he might try to set himself up as sole ruler, a prospect which they dreaded. All this went to Pompey's head. On the assumption that he had nothing to fear, he

failed to make adequate provisions for raising troops.* In the speeches he delivered and resolutions he got passed he felt himself to be obstructing Caesar's plans, but the measures he carried against him were of no consequence to Caesar.† In fact, there is a story that on a trip back to Rome from the army one of Caesar's officers was standing in front of the senate-house and heard that the senate was refusing to extend the period of Caesar's command. He clapped his hand on the handle of his sword and said, 'But this will give him it!'*

[30] In actual fact, though, Caesar's demands looked perfectly fair and reasonable. If he laid down his arms, he wanted Pompey to do the same, and he thought that they should both be rewarded in some way by their fellow Romans once they had become private citizens with no official standing. He argued that if they deprived him of his forces and yet authorized Pompey to keep his existing army, they would be setting one of them up in precisely the tyranny for which they were criticizing the other. When Curio raised these proposals before the people on Caesar's behalf he was loudly applauded, and some† people even pelted him with garlands of flowers, as though he were a victorious athlete. Antony, who was one of the tribunes,* brought into the popular assembly a letter of Caesar's he had received which went into these matters and read it out, in defiance of the consuls' wishes. But in the senate Scipio, Pompey's father-in-law, introduced a motion to the effect that if Caesar had not laid down his arms by a certain day, he was to be declared an enemy of Rome. When the consuls asked the assembled senators whether in their opinion Pompey should disband his army, and then again whether in their opinion Caesar should do so, very few indeed expressed their assent to the first idea, but almost all of them expressed their assent to the second. However, when Antony repeated his demand that they should both give up their commands, this met with unanimous approval. But Scipio had Antony expelled from the senate, and Lentulus, who was one of the consuls, cried out that votes were useless—that weapons were the only defence against a brigand—and then the senate broke up and the senators put on mourning clothes to show how they felt about this schism in the state.*

[31] Further letters arrived from Caesar, however, expressing the apparently more moderate demand that, if he gave up everything else, he should be allowed to keep Cisalpine Gaul and Illyricum,

along with two legions, until he registered his candidacy for a second consulship. The orator Cicero, who had just come back from Cilicia and was trying to broker a peaceful solution, set about working on Pompey to make him more flexible. He found Pompey ready to concede every point, but still wanting to deprive Caesar of his troops, so he tried to persuade Caesar's friends in Rome to compromise as well and to agree to a settlement on the basis of the provinces Caesar had stipulated and only six thousand soldiers. Pompey was prepared to relent and grant him these terms, but the consul, Lentulus, refused to let him do so, and expelled Antony and Curio ignominiously from the senate, hurling a volley of abuse after them—and providing Caesar with his most plausible pretext, because his most effective ploy for inciting his forces to action was to show them how men of distinction and high office had fled dressed in slaves' clothes on hired carriages. For this is how they had engineered their escape from Rome, in fear for their lives.*

[32] Caesar had with him no more than 300 cavalrymen and 5,000 legionaries, because the bulk of his army had been left on the other side of the Alps. He had sent men to fetch the rest of his troops, and they were expected, but had not yet arrived. However, since he realized that it would be easier for him to frighten his enemies with an unexpected strike than it would be to overwhelm them with a carefully planned assault, he recognized that the opening phase and initial moves of the enterprise he was engaged on did not immediately need a large force so much as the kind of firm control that could be provided by astonishment at his daring and a rapid use of opportunity. So he convened his senior and junior officers and told them to seize the large town of Ariminum, which lay just across the border from Gaul,† armed with no weapons except their swords and avoiding bloodshed and disruption as much as possible. He put Hortensius in charge of this task-force.*

Caesar himself spent the day in full view of everyone, presiding over and watching gladiatorial training exercises until late in the afternoon, when he tended to his bodily needs and then went in to eat. After briefly chatting with his dinner guests, he got up and went away. Night was beginning to fall. With civil words of farewell to the rest of his guests, he asked them to stay where they were and await his return, but he had given advance notice to a few of his friends to follow him, not all at once but by various different routes. He took a hired carriage and drove for a while along a different route, but then turned off towards Ariminum. When he reached the river which forms the boundary between Cisalpine Gaul and the rest of Italy—the river's name is the Rubicon—the imminent danger made him pensive, and his head reeled with the enormity of the step he was taking. He slowed down, and then came to a halt. Withdrawn and silent, he spent a long time mentally torn between the two alternatives, and even at this late stage his intentions fluctuated wildly to and fro. Then he spent an equally long time voicing his doubts to those of his friends who were with him (who included Asinius Pollio), with a tally of all the troubles that their crossing of the river would initiate for the whole world, and with reflections on how the great tale of it would be their legacy to subsequent generations. Eventually, however, in a burst of intense emotion, as if thrusting aside rational considerations and abandoning himself to whatever the future held, he turned to the river, prefacing the crossing with the usual words spoken by people before embarking on hazardous and uncertain enterprises: 'Let the die be cast!' There were no further delays to his rapid advance; he attacked Ariminum before daybreak and soon occupied it. It is said that on the night before he crossed the Rubicon he had a grotesque dream, in which he was having sex with his own mother—an unspeakable union.*

[33] After the fall of Ariminum it was as if huge gates had opened and let war loose on land and sea alike, all over the world. Law and order in Rome were swept away along with the boundaries of the province, and one would have thought that all the commotion within Italy was caused not by men and women roaming to and fro in terror, as on other occasions, but by whole cities uprooting themselves and fleeing pell-mell through one another. Rome was so inundated, as it were, by refugees and evacuees from nearby villages that it was virtually impossible for any official to win obedience and rational argument made no impression whatsoever; and the city was caught in such heavy seas that it came close to capsizing under its own weight. For nowhere was there any relief from conflicting feelings and violent emotions. Those who were happy with what was going on were out and about on the streets, and given the size of the city were constantly coming across and clashing with people who were too frightened or distressed to tolerate their optimism about the future. Meanwhile, Pompey himself, who was already terrified out of his

mind, was being further confused by all the different remarks that were coming his way. Some people criticized him for having built up Caesar's power to his own and the state's disadvantage, while others accused him of having let Lentulus insult a man who was ready to compromise and was offering a reasonable settlement; and Favonius told him to stamp on the ground with his foot, since he had once boasted to the senate that they did not have to do anything to prepare for the war and need not worry at all, because at the approach of war he would stamp on the ground with his foot and would fill Italy with troops. Actually, Pompey's troops did outnumber Caesar's at this stage of the war, but no one would let him think things through on his own, but bombarded him instead with inaccurate and alarmist reports that Caesar's armed forces were now very close and had carried all before them. Eventually Pompey gave way and allowed himself to be deflected by the prevailing current of opinion. He formally declared a state of civil disturbance and abandoned the city, with orders that the senate was to follow him and that only those who preferred tyranny to their country and freedom should stay behind.*

[34] The consuls fled without even performing the sacrifices customary before leaving the city. Most of the senators fled too, after grabbing as many of their possessions as they could easily lay their hands on—it was as if they were burglars plundering a stranger's house. There were even some people, previously enthusiastic supporters of Caesar, who were now too terrified to think straight and who became needlessly carried away by the force of this exodus. But the saddest thing of all was the sight of the city adrift under the imminent threat of such a ferocious storm, like a ship abandoned by its helmsmen to be wrecked on some chance shore. Still, although the evacuation was tragic, for Pompey's sake people were prepared to make exile their homeland, and they abandoned Rome with the feeling that it was no more than a military camp for Caesar. Even Labienus, a particularly close friend of Caesar's who had acted as his legate and had fought wholeheartedly alongside him throughout the Gallic Wars, now ran away from him and joined Pompey—only to have his money and belongings sent him by Caesar.*

Caesar now set out against Domitius, who was occupying Corfinium with thirty cohorts under his command, and established a camp near the town. The situation looked hopeless to Domitius. He asked his doctor (who was a slave of his) for some poison, and the doctor duly gave him a preparation, which Domitius drank with the intention of dying. A short while later, however, he heard about the incredible kindness with which Caesar treated his prisoners. Appalled at what he had done, he began to regret his hasty decision, but the doctor told him not to worry, since he had drunk a sleeping-draught, not a deadly poison. At this, he leapt to his feet in delight and went to Caesar, who promised him mercy. Domitius escaped, however, and made his way back to Pompey. When news of Caesar's magnanimity reached Rome people began to cheer up, and some of the fugitives turned back.*

[35] Caesar's ranks were swelled not just by Domitius' men, but by all the troops he found mustering in various cities; they had been recruited to serve under Pompey, but Caesar got to them first. Once the size of his army had increased to formidable proportions, he marched against Pompey himself. But rather than awaiting his advance, Pompey retreated to Brundisium. He sent the consuls on ahead with an army to Dyrrhachium, while he himself sailed away from Italy when Caesar attacked a short while later. I will give a detailed account of all this in my *Life of Pompey*. Caesar's desire to go after him straight away was frustrated by his lack of ships, so he turned back to Rome. He had gained control of the whole of Italy in sixty days without bloodshed.*

The city was in a more settled state than he had expected, and he found a lot of senators there too. But although he spoke to them in a reasonable and genial manner, and suggested that they send a delegation to Pompey with very fair terms, they completely ignored him. It may be that they were afraid of Pompey, since they had let him down, but perhaps they thought that Caesar's speech was just a front and that he did not really mean what he said.

When the tribune, Metellus, began citing laws in an attempt to thwart Caesar's intention to withdraw money from public funds, Caesar said that arms and laws had different seasons, and went on: 'And as for you, if you don't approve of what's going on, I suggest you make yourself scarce for the time being. There's no room for free speech in times of war. When a settlement has been reached and I've laid down my arms, then you can come forward and make your addresses to the people. And note that legally I would have been perfectly entitled not to offer this compromise, because just like all the political opponents of mine that I have captured, you belong to me now.' With these words to Metellus, he walked to the door of the treasury. The keys were nowhere to be found, so he sent for some smiths and told them to break the door down. Metellus again tried to object, and he found some support for his attempt, but in a furious tone of voice Caesar threatened to kill him if he did not stop making a nuisance of himself. 'And I'm sure you're aware, young man,' he said, 'that it is harder for me to issue such threats than to carry them out.' These words were enough to frighten even Metellus into leaving, and after that Caesar encountered no further obstacles or impediments to getting everything he needed for the war.*

[36] Spain was his next target, because before marching against Pompey he had decided to drive Afranius and Varro, Pompey's legates, out of the country, and to gain control of the armies which were stationed there, as well as the provinces, in order to leave his rear completely clear of hostile forces. He often risked his life in surprise attacks by the enemy, and shortage of food brought his men terribly close to death too, but he kept up an unremitting campaign of harassment, challenges, and sieges, until by main force he had gained control of their camps and their armies. The commanders fled Spain and went to join Pompey.*

[37] After Caesar had returned to Rome, his father-in-law, Piso, tried to persuade him to send a delegation to Pompey to discuss a settlement, but Isauricus, who wanted to curry favour with Caesar, argued against the proposal. The senate made Caesar dictator, and he proceeded to recall exiles and restore the rights of the sons of those who had suffered under Sulla. He also tried to provide some relief for debtors by a kind of alleviation of the rate of interest, and he undertook a few other similar measures,† but after eleven days he gave up his autocracy and appointed himself and Servilius Isauricus consuls. He then turned to the campaign against Pompey.*

In his haste he soon left all the rest of his forces behind on the road, and put to sea with six hundred picked cavalrymen and five legions, in early January (or Poseideon in the Athenian calendar), at the time of the winter solstice.* After crossing the Ionian Sea he took Oricum and Apollonia, and then sent his ships back to Brundisium again to pick up the troops who had fallen behind. While they were on the march these troops, who were by now past their prime, in terms of physical fitness, and were exhausted by all the hardships they had endured, began to criticize Caesar. 'Where's this man taking us?' they asked. 'Where are we going to end up? He carts us around and treats us like inanimate objects that need no rest. Even swords get worn out by usage, and some consideration is shown to shields and breastplates after such a lengthy period of service. Can he really not tell from our wounds that he has human beings under his command, with the inevitable propensity to suffer as humans do, and to feel pain? Not even a god can hold back wintertime or the windy season at sea, yet Caesar takes risks as though he were running away from his enemies rather than pursuing them.' Muttering these kinds of complaints, they made their way at a leisurely pace to Brundisium; but when they got there and found that Caesar had put to sea, they quickly changed their minds and cursed themselves. They called themselves traitors to their imperator, and cursed their commanding officers too, for having failed to get them to speed up. Then they sat on the cliffs and gazed out to sea towards Epirus, looking out for the ships† which would carry them over the sea to Caesar.*

[38] The army Caesar had with him in Apollonia was no match for the enemy, and the delay in the arrival of the army from Italy put him in a very awkward position. Deeply troubled, he conceived a desperate plan: without anyone else knowing, he would board a boat, equivalent in size to a twelve-oared skiff, and set out for Brundisium, despite the fact that the enemy's huge fleets gave them mastery of the open sea. So one night he disguised himself by dressing as a slave, boarded a boat, and, as if he were a person of no importance, sat down and kept himself to himself. The river Aous began to carry the boat downstream to the sea, but the early morning breeze, which usually kept the waters at the mouth of the river calm at that time of day by repelling the waves from the shore, had been quelled by a strong wind which had been blowing in from the sea all night long. With the sea running high and the resistance of the waves, the river was all churned up and rough, and where it was checked in its course there were roaring breakers and strong currents. There was no way that the helmsman could force his way through, and he told his crew to come about so that he could take the boat back upstream. When Caesar saw what was happening, he revealed who he was. The helmsman was astonished to see him, but Caesar took him by the hand and said, 'Come, my friend. Summon up your courage and

have no fear. You have Caesar as your passenger, and where he sails his good fortune sails with him.' The sailors immediately forgot the storm; they grasped their oars firmly and tried with all their might to force a passage through the river. But it was no good, and after they had taken on a great deal of sea-water at the mouth of the river and come close to being swamped, Caesar very reluctantly gave the helmsman permission to go about. As he made his way back upstream his men flocked to meet him and told him how wrong he was to doubt that he could win the war with them alone, and how much it hurt them to see him worrying and endangering himself over his missing troops, as if he did not trust the ones who were there.*

[39] After this Antony sailed in with the forces from Brundisium,* and with renewed confidence Caesar tried to draw Pompey into battle. Pompey was favourably placed, with both land and sea routes open for him to obtain enough supplies, whereas Caesar never had a great deal and later got into very serious difficulties because of lack of provisions. But there was a particular kind of root that his men ate, chopped up and mixed with milk. Once, in fact, they ran up to the enemy's guard-posts with some loaves they had made out of this root, and threw them inside the palisade or tossed them at the men, with the remark that they would never stop besieging Pompey as long as there were roots like this one to be got from the earth. Pompey, however, took steps to make sure that neither the loaves nor this remark reached the main body of his army, because his men were already unnerved by the ferocity and toughness of their opponents, who seemed more like wild beasts than human beings to them, and this was having a detrimental effect on their morale.*

There was constant skirmishing near Pompey's fortifications, and Caesar always came off best in these minor battles, except once, when he suffered a serious rout and came close to losing his camp. His lines collapsed completely at Pompey's attack; piles of corpses were filling the trenches, and then, as they were driven further back in headlong flight, they began to be cut down at their own palisades and fortifications. Caesar confronted his men and tried to stop the flight, but it was no good: they would not turn back. In fact, when he tried to take hold of the standards, the bearers threw them away, and in the end the enemy captured thirty-two of them. Moreover, Caesar himself almost lost his life in this battle: he put out his hand to check one of the fugitives—a tall, burly man who was running past him—and told him to stop and turn back to face the enemy. The man was so crazed with fright, however, that he raised his sword to strike Caesar, but Caesar's shield-bearer quickly cut off his arm at the shoulder.* As far as Caesar was concerned, his situation was now hopeless. In fact, Pompey's cautious or perhaps unmotivated decision to withdraw after pinning the fugitives inside their camp, rather than following his significant achievement through to its conclusion, prompted Caesar to say to his friends, as he was leaving them, 'Today the enemy would have won, if they had a winner for a commander.' Then he went to his tent and lay down. This was the most harrowing night of his life, and he spent it doing some tough thinking, since he felt that his tactics had been all wrong. The fertile land and prosperous cities of Macedonia and Thessaly lay before him, yet instead of diverting the war there he had established his position where he was on the coast. But since the enemy controlled the sea, he was effectively being besieged by his lack of provisions rather than being the one who was besieging the enemy by military means. After a night spent tossing and turning in anguish at the intractable difficulty of his situation, he decided to lead his army against Scipio in Macedonia, so he broke camp. In this way, he felt, he would either draw Pompey after him to a place where he would have to fight without the advantage of being supplied as he now was by sea, or he would get the better of Scipio, if Pompey did not come to his aid.*

[40] Morale rose throughout Pompey's camp at Caesar's departure. Pompey's staff officers argued that Caesar was retreating after his defeat and excitedly urged him to stay close behind. For Pompey himself was wary of risking a direct confrontation when there was so much at stake. He thought that since he was in a perfect position, whichever way one looked at it, for delaying tactics, he should gradually drain and sap the enemy's strength—which would not take long, he felt, because while it was undoubtedly the case that the best troops in Caesar's army were very experienced and displayed in battle an irresistible courage, they were old enough to have become worn out, in the course of their nomadic military life, by all their shifts on guard-duty and by all the night-watches. They were physically too unwieldy to exert themselves and too weak to retain their commitment, and at the time in question there were also rumours of an epidemic going around Caesar's army, brought on by their

unusual diet. And the most important factor was that Caesar was so low on money and short of provisions that in all probability his army would break up of its own accord before very long.*

[41] These were the reasons that made Pompey reluctant to fight. Cato was the only one who supported him, motivated by consideration for his fellow citizens. (After all, at the sight even of a thousand or so enemy troops fallen in battle Cato covered his head with his toga in grief and left in tears.) But all the rest bitterly criticized Pompey's battle-shy tactics and tried to spur him on to action by calling him 'Agamemnon' and 'King of Kings', with the implication that he was clinging on to his autocratic position and that it flattered his vanity to have so many commanders dependent on him and visiting him in his tent. Favonius, in an absurd imitation of Cato's candour, complained that this year too they would be unable to enjoy Tusculan figs thanks to Pompey's love of power; and Afranius, who had just arrived from Spain, where he had failed miserably in his conduct of the war, and was suspected of having accepted a bribe to betray the army, kept asking why they were not fighting this dealer in provinces, this man who had allegedly paid him for the provinces. Eventually, all this pressure forced Pompey, against his better judgement, to choose direct confrontation, and he set out after Caesar.*

It was a struggle for Caesar to get through most of his journey, since after his recent defeat he met only contempt from all quarters and no one would supply him with provisions. But an unexpected consequence of the capture of the Thessalian town of Gomphi, apart from enabling him to feed his troops, was that he got rid of the disease that had plagued them. There was plenty of wine to be had, and as a result of drinking freely and then turning their route-march into a drunken riot and a kind of Bacchic procession, the men found that their physical constitutions had changed and they had shaken off and overcome the illness.*

[42] Eventually both sides entered the Pharsalian plain and established camps there.* At this point Pompey's mind began to revert to its former channels of thought, and he was also visited by some inauspicious apparitions, such as a dream he had in which he was applauded on entering his theatre in Rome.* But everyone around him was so full of confidence that they had already seized the fruits of victory in their imaginations. For instance, Domitius, Spinther,

and Scipio had set themselves up as rival candidates for Caesar's position as pontifex maximus, and lots of people were sending their subordinates to Rome to buy and take early possession of houses suitable for consuls and praetors, because they assumed that they would be taking up these offices immediately after the war.* The cavalrymen were particularly impatient at the delay in joining battle. With their gleaming armour, well-fed horses, and handsome physical appearance, they made an exceptionally fine display, and the fact that they outnumbered Caesar's 1,000 seven times also filled them with self-assurance. There was a disparity in the numbers of the infantry forces as well, with Pompey's 45,000 drawn up against 22,000 on the other side.*

[43] Caesar gathered his men together, and after telling them that Cornificius was near by with two legions for him, and that there were another fifteen cohorts encamped near Megara and Athens under Calenus, he asked them whether they wanted to wait for these reinforcements or risk battle by themselves.* Their clamorous response was to urge him not to wait, but rather to devise a strategy that would enable them to engage the enemy as soon as possible. As Caesar was undertaking the ritual purification of his forces, he had sacrificed only the first victim when the diviner told him that the decisive battle with the enemy would take place within three days. Caesar asked the diviner whether he could see in the entrails anything indicative of a favourable outcome, and the diviner replied, 'That's really for you to decide rather than me. The message from the gods is that there will be a complete change and alteration from one state of affairs to the opposite. So if you think things are going well for you at present, you should expect to come off worst, and if you think they're going badly, you should expect to come off best.' Then in the middle of the night before the battle, just as Caesar was making the rounds of the sentries, a fiery torch appeared in the sky and seemed to pass over Caesar's camp, blazing brightly, before coming down on Pompey's camp; and during the early-morning watch it was noticeable that the enemy were in a state of panic and confusion. However, so far from expecting battle to be joined that day, Caesar was in the process of breaking camp to march to Scotussa.*

[44] The tents had just been dismantled when scouts rode up to him with the news that the enemy were coming down on to the plain for battle. Caesar was delighted. After praying to the gods for success

he drew his troops up in their battle-lines on a triple formation, with Domitius Calvinus in charge of the centre, Antony on the left wing, and himself on the right.* His original plan was to have the tenth legion around him, but then he saw that the enemy cavalry was being drawn up at this point of the battlefield. Their numbers and the brilliance of their display worried him, so he secretly ordered six cohorts up from the other end of the battle-lines and stationed them behind the right wing, with instructions as to what they had to do when the enemy cavalry attacked. On the other side, Pompey personally took charge of the right wing, while Domitius had the left, and Pompey's father-in-law, Scipio, was in command of the centre. All his mounted troops, however, added their weight to the left wing, with the intention of outflanking their opponents' right wing and causing a decisive rout in precisely the part of the battlefield where the enemy commander was. There was no way, they thought, that any legionary formation, however deep, could stand up to them; they were sure that the enemy would be completely crushed and scattered by the massed charge of so many horsemen at once.

With the signal to advance imminent on both sides, Pompey ordered his legionaries to stand firm with their spears at the defensive and wait for the enemy attack without breaking formation, until they were within javelin range. Caesar says that this was another mistake on Pompey's part, to ignore the fact that blows gain in force when the first clash with the enemy occurs at full tilt, and that fighting spirit is kindled by a charge and blazes up at the point of impact.* He was about to set his troops in motion and was starting out for the battlefield, when the first person he saw was one of his officers, a loyal and battle-hardened veteran, who was trying to inspire his men and was urging them to see if they could match his own prowess. Caesar called out to the man and said, 'So, Gaius Crassinius, what are our prospects? Are we confident about the outcome?' Crassinius raised his right arm and replied in a loud voice, 'We shall win a decisive victory, Caesar—and you will have reason to praise me today, whether I live or die!' True to his words, he was the first to charge the enemy, drawing after him the hundred and twenty men under his command. After cutting through the front ranks, he was pushing and battling his way forward, with both sides taking heavy casualties, when he was cut down by such a fierce sword-thrust through the mouth that the point emerged out of the back of his neck.*

[45] This is how the infantry forces came to clash in the centre. Once battle was joined, Pompey's cavalry rode confidently up from the wing and spread out their squadrons for their intended outflanking of Caesar's right. Before they could attack, however, the cohorts ran out from where Caesar had kept them. They did not use their javelins in the normal way as missiles, or stab at their opponents' thighs or shins, but following Caesar's instructions they aimed for their eyes and tried to wound them in the face. Caesar was aware that Pompey's cavalrymen were new to warfare and still unscarred, and were young men who prided themselves on their good looks and youthful charms, so he hoped they would find this kind of blow particularly disconcerting and would be too frightened—not just at the present danger, but at the prospect of disfigurement as well—to stand their ground. And this is exactly what happened: the upward thrust of the javelins was too much for the young cavalrymen to endure. They could not even bring themselves to face the weapons directly, but turned their heads aside and covered them up, to protect their faces. They got themselves into such a muddle as a result of this that in the end they turned and fled, with Pompey's cause irreparably damaged because of their disgraceful conduct. For as soon as Caesar's men had defeated them, they turned to the infantry. After outflanking them, they attacked them from behind and slaughtered them.*

When Pompey, on the other wing, saw that his cavalry were fleeing and scattered, a change overcame him and he forgot that he was Pompey the Great. Behaving like a man who had been robbed of his wits by some god, he left the battlefield without saying a word and went to his tent, where he sat and waited to see what would happen next. Eventually, after all his forces had been put to flight, the enemy attacked the camp and began to fight the men who were guarding it. At this point he seemed to come to his senses, and they say that he spoke a single sentence, no more: 'So are even my quarters under attack?' Then he took off the clothes he wore for battle that marked him out as the commander-in-chief, changed into something suitable for a fugitive, and stole away. What happened to him later, and how he was murdered after taking refuge in Egypt, I will explain in my *Life of Pompey*.*

[46] When Caesar reached Pompey's camp and saw the enemy dead lying on the ground and others still being killed by his troops, he sighed and said, 'They brought this on themselves. They gradually forced me into a position where if I had given up my forces I would have been condemned in their courts. Was this any way to treat Gaius Caesar after his successes in such critical wars?' Asinius Pollio says that although these words were spoken in Latin at the time, Caesar later wrote them down in Greek.† He also reports that the majority of the casualties were slaves who were killed during the capture of the camp, while no more than six thousand soldiers died.* Most of those who were taken alive were incorporated by Caesar into his own legions, and he granted immunity to a lot of prominent people too, including Brutus, who later murdered him. For a while Brutus could not be found, and it is said that Caesar was racked with anxiety about him, and was overjoyed when he was brought before him safe and sound.*

[47] There were a number of portents surrounding the victory, but the most remarkable was the one said to have happened at Tralles. There was a statue of Caesar in the temple of Victory there, and the ground around it was not only naturally hard in itself, but had a layer of solid stone on top of it—yet apparently a palm-tree sprang up from the ground by the base of the statue. And in Patavium a famous diviner called Gaius Cornelius, who was an acquaintance and a fellow citizen of the writer Livy, happened to be sitting and practising augury on the day of the victory. The first thing he did, according to Livy, was identify the exact time of the battle, and tell others who were there with him, 'The critical moment for this whole business is right now: battle is just being joined.' And later, after watching out for omens and observing the signs, he leapt up in an inspired frenzy and shouted out, 'Victory is yours, Caesar!' The bystanders were amazed, but he took the garland off his head and swore that he would not wear it again until the accuracy of his art had been confirmed by the actual facts. Livy, at any rate, insists on the truth of this story.*

[48] Caesar bestowed freedom on the people of Thessaly to commemorate his victory, and then set out after Pompey. When he reached Asia he gave the Cnidians their freedom as a favour to Theopompus, the compiler of the collection of fables,* and he let all the inhabitants of Asia off a third of their taxes. By the time he put in

at Alexandria Pompey was already dead. Theodotus brought him Pompey's head, but Caesar turned away in abhorrence, and he burst into tears when he was presented with his signet ring.* All of Pompey's companions and friends who had been rounded up by the king as they wandered with nowhere to go in Egypt received his help and support, and he wrote to his friends in Rome that the most important and pleasant result of his victory was that from time to time it allowed him to offer protection to some of the Romans who had fought against him.

As for the war in Egypt, some people claim that he damaged his reputation and risked his life needlessly for no real reason, and it was just that he was so passionately in love with Cleopatra. Others, however, blame the king's advisers, and especially the eunuch Pothinus, who was the most powerful man in the country. He had recently killed Pompey and expelled Cleopatra, and was now secretly plotting to take Caesar's life—which, they say, is why Caesar now started to spend whole nights drinking with friends, as a way of protecting himself.* Pothinus was also openly disagreeable, however, and both his words and behaviour towards Caesar were often rude and offensive. For instance, when Caesar's soldiers were given the worst and oldest grain as their rations Pothinus told them to put up with it without complaining, since it was other people's food they were eating; and at official banquets he would use wooden and earthenware utensils, with the implication that all the gold and silver had gone to Caesar to pay off a debt. The situation was that the father of the present king had owed 17,500,000 drachmas to Caesar, and although Caesar had earlier let his children off the rest of the debt, he was now demanding payment of 10,000,000 to maintain his army. Pothinus advised Caesar to leave Egypt for the time being and get on with things that mattered, and told him that he would be repaid both financially and in terms of gratitude later; but Caesar replied that the last thing he needed was an Egyptian for an adviser, and secretly sent for Cleopatra, who was in the country.*

[49] The only friend Cleopatra took with her was Apollodorus of Sicily. She sailed in a small dinghy to the royal palace, where she landed at dusk, and since she was bound to be spotted otherwise, she got inside one of those bags that are used for holding bedclothes and stretched herself out to her full length, while Apollodorus tied a strap around the bag and carried her inside to Caesar. This ruse is

said to have opened Caesar's eyes to the side of Cleopatra that was far from innocent and to have made him fall for her.* And then, they say, it was after spending more time with her and having succumbed to her charms that he reconciled her with her brother and arranged that she would be co-ruler with him. Subsequently, however, while everybody was feasting to celebrate the reconciliation, a slave of Caesar's, his barber, who was habitually driven by his quite extraordinary cowardice to keep his ears to the ground and poke his nose into everyone's affairs, since he felt he had to know everything that was going on, found out that there was a plot being hatched against Caesar by the general, Achillas, and the eunuch Pothinus. Armed with proof of their guilt, Caesar kept a guard around his quarters, and had Pothinus killed. Achillas escaped to his camp, however, and engaged Caesar in a troublesome war, in which Caesar found himself in the difficult position of fighting with a small force against the resources and army of a huge state. First, he came very close to being cut off from any sources of water when the enemy dammed up the canals. Second, in order to save his fleet from being cut off he had to repel the danger with fire, which then spread from the docks and destroyed the great library.* Third, during a battle off Pharos,* he leapt from the breakwater into a dinghy in order to lend his support to his men in the thick of the fighting, but Egyptian ships bore down on him from all sides, and he had to hurl himself into the sea and swim to safety—a difficult feat which he only just managed. He is also said to have stubbornly held on to a sheaf of papers, even though he was under attack from the boats and was being swamped by the waves, using one arm for swimming and holding the papers above the water with the other. His dinghy had been sunk straight away.* The end came when Caesar brought his forces up against the Egyptian king, who had gone over to the enemy, engaged him in battle, and defeated him. Enemy losses in the battle were heavy, and the king himself disappeared. Caesar then departed for Syria, leaving Cleopatra on the throne of Egypt. Not long afterwards she gave birth to his son, whom the Egyptians called Caesarion.*

[50] From Syria Caesar set out through Asia. In the course of the journey he learnt that Domitius had fled from Pontus with a few survivors after being defeated by Pharnaces, the son of Mithridates, and that Pharnaces was taking full advantage of his victory, in the sense that, with Bithynia and Cappadocia already under his control,

he had set his sights on Lesser Armenia, and was stirring up revolt among all the kings and tetrarchs there.* Caesar therefore immediately marched against Pharnaces with three legions. A great battle took place at the city of Zela, in which Caesar annihilated Pharnaces' army and drove him out of Pontus. In a letter to Matius, one of his friends back in Rome, Caesar used just three words to describe the speed and swiftness of this battle: 'I came, I saw, I conquered.' In Latin the words have an impressive terseness, since they all have the same ending.*

[51] After this he sailed back to Italy and went up from the coast to Rome. It was the end of the year for which he had been elected dictator for the second time, although never before had that office been an annual post, and he was made consul for the following year.* However, people were not entirely happy with him. When his troops mutinied and killed two former praetors, Cosconius and Galba, the only punishment he imposed was to address them as 'civilians' rather than as 'soldiers', and he gave each of them a thousand drachmas and distributed a great deal of the Italian countryside to them in land-grants.* Then there were complaints against him as a result of Dolabella's madness, Matius' avarice, and Antony's drunkenness. Antony also ransacked and rebuilt Pompey's house, as if it were not grand enough as it was. All this aroused resentment in Rome. Caesar was perfectly aware of what was going on, and he did not like it, but for the sake of his political programme he had to make use of men who were prepared to work for him.*

[52] After the battle of Pharsalus Cato and Scipio fled to Africa where, with the help of King Juba, they managed to muster an impressive army.* Having decided to make war on them, Caesar crossed over to Sicily at the time of the winter solstice, and because he wanted it to be clear to his officers right from the start that there was no hope of their staying there for any length of time he pitched his own tent right by the breaking surf. As soon as the wind got up, he boarded his ship and set sail with three thousand foot soldiers and a few cavalrymen.* Once he had disembarked these troops (which he did without the enemy knowing about it), he set sail again, because he was worried about the rest of his army, which constituted the larger part. But they were already at sea by the time he met them, so he brought them all into his camp.

The enemy were confident that they would win, thanks to an

ancient oracle to the effect that victory in Africa was the inalienable right of the Scipios. It is hard to say whether Caesar's response to this, when he found out about it, was a joke designed to belittle Scipio, or was a serious attempt to appropriate the omen for himself. At any rate, there was a man on his side who was basically a person of no distinction or worth, but who did belong to the house of the Africani. His name was Scipio Salvitus, and what Caesar did was put this man in the front rank in every battle as if he were the supreme commander of the army. Caesar was often compelled to harass the enemy and to force the issue until battle was joined, because he was short of both provisions for his men and fodder for his yoke-animals. They had to feed the horses on seaweed, with the salt washed off and mixed with a little grass to make it taste better. The basic trouble was that the country was controlled by the Numidians, who from time to time would suddenly appear in large numbers. Once, for instance, Caesar's cavalrymen were relaxing—in fact, an African was putting on an incredible performance for them, involving him dancing and playing a solo on the flute at the same time; they were seated happily on the ground, with their horses in the care of their slaves, when suddenly the enemy surrounded them and attacked. They killed some of Caesar's men and stayed hard on the heels of the others as they rode in headlong flight back to the camp, and if Caesar, along with Asinius Pollio, had not personally made a sortie out of the camp to help his men and check their flight, the war would have been over then and there.* There was also another encounter in which the enemy gained the upper hand after battle was joined, and it is said that Caesar grabbed a standard-bearer who was running away by the neck, turned him around, and said, 'The enemy are over there!'

[53] Scipio was encouraged by these successes to risk a decisive battle, so he left Afranius and Juba in two separate camps a short distance apart from each other, while he himself set about fortifying a stronghold which overlooked a lake near the city of Thapsus,* with the idea that this would act as base from which they could all set out to battle, and as a place of refuge too. While he was engaged on this work, however, Caesar made his way with unbelievable speed through woods and passes where he could remain unseen, took some of Scipio's men from behind, and attacked the rest head on. Once he had scattered this portion of the enemy forces, he decided to make use of the opportunity and his run of good fortune: he took

Afranius' camp by storm and, with Juba in flight, overran the Numidians' camp equally easily. In considerably less than a full day, then, three camps fell to him and fifty thousand of the enemy were killed, while he lost fewer than fifty of his own men.* However, this is not the only account of the battle. Others say that Caesar himself played no part in the action, since while he was drawing up and deploying his troops he suffered one of his usual fits. As soon as he felt it coming on, with his faculties wavering but not yet fully distracted, he had himself carried to a nearby tower, before the illness took complete possession of him, and stayed there quietly for the duration of the battle. Some of the men of consular or praetorian rank who survived the battle killed themselves as they were on the point of being captured, and Caesar killed a great many more after he had taken them prisoner.*

[54] Cato had not taken part in the battle, but had been left to defend Utica, so since Caesar was anxious to take Cato alive, he hurried to Utica, only to be greeted by the news that Cato had committed suicide. Caesar made no secret of the fact that this irritated him intensely, but why it should have done so was not clear. What he said, though, was: 'Your death makes me feel malice for you, Cato, because you maliciously thwarted me of the chance of saving your life.' However, the speech which Caesar later wrote against Cato, after his death, does not seem to indicate that the author was in a calm or forgiving frame of mind, so we are bound to wonder whether he really would have shown him mercy while he was alive, given that he flung so much anger at him when he was an insensible target. Nevertheless, people look at how decently he treated Cicero and Brutus and countless others who had fought against him and come to the conclusion that the composition of this speech was not motivated by hatred, but by political ambition. The context, they say, is this: Cicero wrote his speech in praise of Cato, which he called *Cato*, and which attracted the attention of a lot of people, as one might expect, since the most eloquent of orators composed it to address the most noble of themes. This annoyed Caesar, who considered that Cicero's praise of the dead man amounted to a denunciation of himself, so he collected together and wrote down a whole lot of criticisms of Cato and gave the work the title *Anti-Cato*. Both works won a great deal of attention, because of people's interest in Caesar and Cato.*

[55] Anyway, the first thing he did on returning to Rome from Africa was deliver a pretentious speech to the popular assembly, claiming that the land he had subdued was large enough to supply the people of Rome every year with 200,000 Attic medimni of grain, and 3,000,000 pounds of olive oil.* Then he celebrated a number of triumphs—one for Gaul, one for Egypt, one for Pontus, and one for Africa.* This last one was ostensibly for conquering King Juba, and no mention was made of Scipio. It was also the occasion when King Juba's son, also called Juba, who was still a mere infant at the time, was carried along in the triumphal procession. He was a captive, but it was a highly fortunate captivity for him, since instead of being an uncultured Numidian, he came to be counted among the most learned writers of Greece.*

Next, after his triumphs, he doled out generous rewards to his troops and won over the common people with feasts and shows. He laid on twenty thousand couches so that he could give a banquet for everybody at once, and he put on shows involving gladiator fights and naval battles to commemorate his daughter Julia, who had died some time previously. Once these shows were over a census was taken, and whereas 320,000 people had been enrolled by the previous census, this time the total was 150,000. This demonstrates how many lives were lost as a result of the civil strife and how severely the population of Rome was depleted, to say nothing of the disasters that gripped the rest of Italy and the provinces.*

[56] Once these civic matters had been taken care of and Caesar had been made consul for the fourth time, he marched to Spain to fight Pompey's sons.* Despite their youth they had assembled a remarkably huge army, and they showed that they had what it takes, in terms of martial spirit, to deserve their position of leadership. In fact, they managed to put Caesar into an extremely dangerous situation. The decisive battle was fought near the city of Munda. When Caesar saw that his men were being driven back and were putting up a feeble resistance, he ran here and there among the ranks and the weapons, calling out and asking his men why they did not just take him and hand him over to the boys, since it clearly would not bother them in the slightest. At last, after a lot of effort, he succeeded in driving the enemy back. Their losses numbered over thirty thousand, but a thousand of his best men had been killed too, and as he was leaving the battlefield he told his friends that although he had

often fought for victory, this was the first time he had fought for his life. This battle was fought and won on the day of the feast of Bacchus, which is exactly the day on which Pompey the Great is said to have gone out to war, four years previously. As for Pompey's sons, the younger one escaped, but Deidius brought in the head of the older one a few days after the battle.*

This was the last war Caesar fought, and the triumph that he celebrated as a result of it tried the Romans' tolerance to the absolute limit. This was not a case of his defeating foreign generals or barbarian kings; he had utterly destroyed the sons and family of a man who had been the greatest of the Romans until he met with misfortune, and it was wrong of him to commemorate the catastrophes that had befallen his country with a triumph and to take pride in actions whose only justification, in the eyes of gods and men, was that he had been left no choice in the matter. Besides, up until then he had never even sent a messenger or a letter back to Rome as public acknowledgement of a victory he had won in the civil wars; he had always scrupulously avoided enhancing his reputation in this way.*

[57] However, the Romans bowed their heads before Caesar's good fortune and accepted the bridle. Since autocracy was, from their point of view, a pleasant change after civil war and turmoil, they proclaimed him dictator for life.* But when permanence is added to the unaccountability of autocracy, tyranny is the result, and this is now what Caesar had, with the acquiescence of the Romans. It was Cicero who first brought up in the senate the idea that Caesar should have extra privileges, but what he was proposing was at least more or less human in scale. But then other senators started to compete with one another to add one superfluous privilege on to another, until they made the man offensive and repellent to even the most mild-mannered of observers because of the pretentiousness and extravagance of the honours that were being voted him. It is thought that Caesar's enemies were just as active in getting these measures passed as his flatterers, because they wanted to have as many grievances against him as possible and to be seen to have entirely plausible grounds for attacking him. Their problem was that in other respects, now that the civil wars were over, Caesar's behaviour was beyond reproach. In fact, it does not seem at all strange that they should have voted to build a sanctuary dedicated to Clemency in gratitude for his even-handed conduct of affairs. Many of those who had fought

against him received pardons, and some, like Brutus and Cassius, were even given offices and honours—they both became praetors.* He even went so far as to do something about the statues of Pompey that had been knocked to the ground, and when he set them back on their feet, Cicero remarked that in the act of raising up Pompey's statues Caesar had created firm foundations for his own.* His friends wanted him to have the protection of a corps of personal guards, and there were plenty of volunteers willing to perform this service, but he would not hear of it, and said that it was better to die once than to spend one's life anticipating death. Instead he wore his popularity, which he regarded as the best and most reliable protective talisman he could have; and so he renewed his efforts to win over the common people with feasts and rations of grain, and the military with new colonies. The most famous of these new colonies were Carthage and Corinth, two cities with the joint destiny of having once fallen at the same time and of now being restored at the same time.*

[58] As for the men of power in Rome, he promised some of them that they would become consuls or praetors some time in the future, and fobbed others off with a variety of honours and privileges. Everyone had their hopes raised by him, since he wanted willing subjects to rule over. When the consul, Maximus, died, for instance, he appointed Caninius Rebilius consul for the single day remaining of the term of office.* The crowd of people walking over to Rebilius' house to greet him and escort him to the forum apparently prompted Cicero to say: 'We'd better hurry, or his consulship will be over before we get there.'

Caesar was innately enterprising and ambitious, and did not change just because he had achieved so much. So far from turning to enjoy the fruits of what he had worked so hard to achieve, his past successes induced and encouraged him to hope for more in the future and engendered in him plans for more grandiose projects and a lust for fresh glory, as though he had exhausted what he already had. What he felt, then, was nothing more or less than self-rivalry—as opposed to having another person as a rival—and a kind of competitive urge to improve in the future on his own past performance.* So he made preparations and plans to make war on the Parthians, and then, after defeating them, to continue on his way beyond the Euxine Sea, through Hyrcania, and past the Caspian Sea and the Caucasus, until he invaded Scythia, and then to overrun the countries on his approach to Germany, and then Germany itself, and to return to Italy through Gaul, so making a complete circuit of his empire which would be bounded on every side only by the Ocean. While this expedition was in progress, he also intended to tackle the digging of a canal across the Corinthian isthmus (in fact, he had already recruited Anienus for the job), and to make a new, deep channel for the Tiber just below the city, altering its course round towards Circeium, so that it issued into the sea at Terracina, which would give commercial travellers to Rome a safe and easy journey. He also dreamed of draining the marshes at Pomentinum and Setia and turning them into a plain which could be cultivated by thousands upon thousands of people; and he wanted to build breakwaters to enclose the stretch of sea nearest to Rome, and then to clear the parts of the coastline around Ostia that were too choked with rocks to offer ships a safe haven, and so to create sufficient harbours and anchorage-points there for the enormous amount of shipping he anticipated. All these projects were at the planning stage.

[59] However, the project to reform the calendar and correct the anomaly that had occurred in reckoning time was brought to a conclusion after careful, scholarly research on his part. This project turned out to be of very definite utility, since the complete muddle in Roman time-keeping, thanks to the disparity between the cycle of the lunar months compared to that of the solar year—a muddle which led to certain sacrificial rituals and other festivals gradually slipping until the seasons in which they took place were exactly opposed to the times when they were supposed to take place—was not restricted to ancient times. Even in Caesar's day most people did not trouble to think about the problem, and only the priests knew the correct time for their rituals, so that they would suddenly and to everyone's surprise insert the intercalary month, which was called Mercedonius. As I have written in my *Life of Numa*, King Numa is said to have been the first to have come up with and made use of this idea of the intercalary month, which offered, however, no more than temporary and limited relief from the error caused by the mismatch between the astronomical cycles involved. However, Caesar set the finest thinkers and mathematicians to work on the problem, and combined already existing approaches into an original and more accurate method of correction. It is still in use by the Romans today, and it does seem to keep them from making as many mistakes as

the mismatch causes for other systems. But even this provoked complaints among those who resented Caesar's power and wanted to see him fail. At any rate when someone happened to mention that Lyra was due to rise tomorrow, the orator Cicero apparently said, 'Yes, by official decree', implying that this was another reform which people had been compelled to accept.*

[60] But the most open and life-threatening outbursts of hatred he met with were a result of his lust for kingship, which first turned the masses against him, and which provided those who had long been secretly working against him with their most plausible pretext for action. And yet the people who were trying to arrange for Caesar to be elevated to this rank spread a rumour throughout the city that the Sibylline books seemed to indicate that the Parthians were vulnerable to a Roman army which was led by a king, but were otherwise unassailable, and once, when Caesar returned to the city from Alba, they went so far as to greet him as 'king', which clearly did not go down at all well with the common people. Caesar therefore angrily said that his name was 'Caesar', not 'King'. This met with no response whatsoever, and he continued on his way looking decidedly unhappy and discontented.*

On another occasion he had just been awarded extraordinary honours by an official decree of the senate, and he happened to be sitting above the rostra. The consuls and praetors approached him, with the whole senate right behind them, to hear what he had to say. Instead of standing up, Caesar acted as if he were giving an audience to mere private citizens, and remained seated to give his response (which was that his honours needed decreasing rather than increasing). This offended not only the senate, but the common people too, because they felt that the city was being insulted by this treatment of the senate, and all those who did not have to stay left at once, filled with foreboding. Caesar then realized his mistake and immediately turned to go home, but as he went he exposed his neck by pulling his toga away from it and called out in a loud voice to his friends that if anyone wanted to slit his throat, he would put up no resistance. Later, however, he used his affliction as an excuse and said that people with his condition tended to lose consciousness if they stood to address a crowd, since their senses quickly became unsteady and whirled around, inducing dizziness and fits. But this was not what had actually happened at the time. Apparently, he had been intending all along to get to his feet at the approach of the senators, but a friend—or rather, a flatterer—called Cornelius Balbus stopped him from doing so by saying, 'You're Caesar, remember? Don't you think you ought to let them treat you as their superior?'*

[61] Another thing that caused offence was the high-handed way he treated some tribunes.* It was the festival of the Lupercalia, which many authors regard as having originated among shepherds, and which also bears some resemblance to the Lycaea in Arcadia. During the Lupercalia large numbers of well-born young men, and many of the city officials too, run naked through the streets of the city and in a light-hearted and humorous manner strike people they meet with hairy pieces of goatskin. A lot of the leading women of the city deliberately get in the way of the runners and hold out their hands to be struck, like children in school, because they believe that this will help them, if pregnant, to have an easy birth, and if barren, to get pregnant.* Caesar was watching the festival from his golden throne above the rostra, arrayed in his triumphal clothing,* and Antony was one of the runners in the sacred race, since he was consul at the time. When Antony entered the forum, he made his way over to Caesar, through the crowd which parted before him, carrying a laurel wreath he had woven around a diadem. He held this diadem out towards Caesar, and there was some applause, but not a great deal, and what little there was had been pre-arranged. But when Caesar rejected the diadem, the assembled people all burst out into applause. Antony offered it again, and again a few people showed their appreciation; Caesar refused it, and again everyone applauded. Since this was the result of his experiment, Caesar got to his feet, giving instructions that the garland was to be taken to the Capitol.* But then it became clear that his statues had been crowned with royal diadems. Two of the tribunes, Flavius and Marullus, went and tore the diadems off, and when they discovered the prime movers among those who had addressed Caesar as 'king', they led them off to prison. A crowd of people followed them, cheering and calling each of the tribunes a new Brutus, after the man who had overthrown the royal dynasty and replaced the monarchy with a system of government that gave power to the senate and the people. Infuriated by their actions, Caesar stripped Marullus and his colleague of their offices, and during a speech denouncing them he not only spoke disrespectfully of the common

people, but repeatedly described the two of them as 'Bruti' and 'Cymaeans'.*

[62] Under these circumstances most people turned to Marcus Brutus. He was generally held to be descended on his father's side from the Brutus of old, and on his mother's side he belonged to the Servilii, another distinguished house; he was also the son-in-law and nephew of Cato. Although essentially he wanted to see the end of the autocracy, this desire had been blunted by the honours and favours he had received from Caesar. Not only had his own life and, thanks to his intercession, the lives of a lot of his friends been spared at Pharsalus after Pompey's flight, but he stood high in Caesar's trust as well. He had been given the most significant of the praetorships for the current year, and was due to become consul three years later, having been preferred to Cassius, the rival candidate, because—so the story goes—Caesar said that although by rights the position should go to Cassius, he could not pass Brutus by.* Once, after the conspiracy was already in motion, Caesar even refused to listen to some people who were telling him to beware of Brutus. He touched his body with his hand and told them, 'Brutus will wait patiently for this hide'—implying that although Brutus had the qualities to make a good ruler, it was precisely because of those good qualities that he would not succumb to ingratitude and let himself be corrupted.*

The revolutionaries saw Brutus as their only or at least their best hope, but they did not dare to talk to him openly. Instead, one night they left messages all over the rostra on which he carried out his duties as praetor, and his seat there, mainly along the lines of: 'You're asleep, Brutus' and 'You're no Brutus'. When Cassius saw that Brutus' ambition was quietly being stirred, he began to put more pressure on him than before and to take more steps to arouse his interest, prompted as much by the personal reasons he had for hating Caesar (which I have explained in my *Life of Brutus*) as by political concerns. Caesar did in fact have his doubts about Cassius, and he once actually said to some friends: 'What do you think Cassius wants? I'm not too keen on him myself: he's too pale.' And on another occasion he is said to have responded to the accusation that Antony and Dolabella were subversives by saying: 'I'm not afraid of these overweight, long-haired men, so much as those pale, lean ones'—that is, Cassius and Brutus.*

[63] But fate, it seems, is unavoidable rather than unexpected.

After all, there were apparently remarkable signs and apparitions to be seen as well. In the case of an event as momentous as this one, it may not be worth mentioning phenomena such as the lights in the sky, the bangs and crashes that travelled around from place to place one night, the flocks of birds which settled every day on the forum. But the philosopher Strabo reports that a lot of people saw fiery men advancing; that the slave of a certain soldier shot a long stream of fire from his hand and seemed to everyone who saw him to be on fire, but was found when it was over to be completely unharmed; and that when Caesar himself was performing a sacrifice, the heart of the victim was nowhere to be found, which was a terrifying omen, since in the ordinary course of nature there is no such thing as a creature without a heart. There is another story too, told by many sources, to the effect that a diviner warned him to beware of great danger on the day in the month of March which the Romans call the Ides, and that when this day arrived Caesar called out to the diviner as he was on his way to the senate and said sarcastically, 'Well, the Ides of March have come!' And the diviner quietly replied: 'Yes, they have come, but they have not yet gone.'*

On the day before, as a dinner guest at Marcus Lepidus' house, he had been lying on the couch and writing letters as usual when the conversation turned to the question of what kind of death was the best, and Caesar quickly raised his voice over everyone else's and said, 'The kind that is unexpected.' Later he was asleep, as usual, beside his wife, when suddenly all the doors and windows of the room flew open at once. Caesar woke up, disturbed by the noise and by the light of the moon that was shining into the room, and noticed that although Calpurnia was deeply asleep, she was muttering and moaning in her sleep, but nothing that made any clear sense. In fact, as it turned out, she was dreaming that he had been murdered and she was holding him in her arms and crying. Some people give a different version of this dream of Calpurnia's. Caesar's house had a cornice which had been added, according to Livy, by an official decree of the senate to make it look beautiful and grand, and in the alternative version of the story, Calpurnia in her dream was upset and crying over the fact that this cornice had fallen and shattered into pieces. At any rate, the next day she asked Caesar to postpone the meeting of the senate and stay at home, if he could, or at least to use sacrifices and other forms of divination to try to find out what the future held, if he regarded her dreams as insignificant. In fact, Caesar too was apparently concerned and somewhat frightened, because he had never previously found Calpurnia to be liable to womanly superstition, and now he could see that she was in a great deal of distress. After plenty of sacrifices, the diviners told him that the omens were unfavourable, so he decided to send Antony to dismiss the senate.*

[64] At this point Decimus Brutus, surnamed Albinus, who was so trusted by Caesar that he was named in his will as his second heir,* but was actually involved in the conspiracy along with Cassius and the other Brutus, stepped in. He was frightened that if Caesar made it through that day the plot would be discovered, so he began to jeer at the diviners and to tell Caesar off for seeming to belittle the importance of the senate and so laying himself open to their accusations and charges. He reminded him that it was he who had requested this meeting of the senate, and told him that all the senators were ready to endorse the proposal that he should be proclaimed king of the provinces outside Italy, and should be allowed to wear a diadem wherever he travelled abroad, by land or sea. The senators, he said, had already taken their seats, and if someone told them to go away for the time being, but to come back again later, when Calpurnia had dreamt more propitious dreams, what sorts of comments would this provoke from his enemies? Who would listen as his friends tried to explain that this was not slavery and tyranny? In any case, he went on, if Caesar was completely committed to writing that day off, it would be better if he went in person and told the senate about the postponement.

Brutus had taken Caesar by the hand as he was talking to him and started to guide him on his way. And Caesar had only just left the house when a slave—not one of his, but someone else's—tried to get to talk to him, but was defeated by the press of the crowd around him. He forced his way into the house, however, and asked Calpurnia if she would let him stay there and would look after him until Caesar returned, since he had very urgent news for him.*

[65] Artemidorus the orator, originally from Cnidos, whose work teaching Greek had made him a close enough friend of Brutus to know most of his affairs, wrote down what he wanted Caesar to know on a petition scroll and brought it to him. After watching Caesar pass on to his attendants every single petition that was handed to him,

he approached him and said, 'Read this one yourself, Caesar, and read it soon. The matters it mentions are urgent and concern you personally.' Caesar took the scroll and although he repeatedly tried to read it there were too many people crowding around for him to have a chance to do so. But it was the only scroll he kept hold of, and he was still holding it when he entered the senate. There is an alternative version of the story, though, according to which this scroll was handed to Caesar by someone else, while Artemidorus was pushed aside by the crowd all the way along the route and failed to get anywhere near him.

[66] There may perhaps have been nothing more than chance at work in all this, but the fact that the place where the senate had assembled that day, the scene of the famous murder and the final struggle, contained a statue of Pompey and was one of the buildings attached by Pompey to his theatre, showed beyond the shadow of a doubt that some higher power was at work, guiding and summoning events there.* In fact, it is said that before the attack Cassius looked over towards the statue of Pompey and silently invoked his aid. Now, Cassius was no stranger to the doctrines of Epicurus, but apparently in the heat of the moment, with danger looming, he was flooded with religious sensibility instead of relying on his rational faculty as usual.*

Antony was a strongly built man, as well as being loyal to Caesar, so he was detained outside by Brutus Albinus, who deliberately engaged him in a lengthy conversation.* As Caesar entered the building the senators stood up out of respect, while Brutus and his fellow conspirators either ranged themselves behind Caesar's seat, or went to meet him, on the pretext that they wanted to support Tillius Cimber in his petition for his exiled brother. And so, arguing the case for recalling Tillius' brother all the way, they followed Caesar over to his seat, where he sat down. He was dismissing their arguments and responding angrily to one or two of them who were presenting their cases more forcefully, when Tillius took hold of his toga with both hands and pulled it down, away from his neck. This was the signal for the attack to begin. The first sword-thrust came from Casca, who struck him in the back of the neck, but was too agitated—not surprisingly, given the enormity of the enterprise he was initiating—to inflict a deep or lethal wound. In fact, Caesar was able to turn around, grab the sword, and hold it fast. Then they both spoke at the same instant. In Latin the wounded man said, 'Damn you, Casca!

What are you doing?', while his assailant said in Greek to his brother, 'Brother, help!'*

This was how it began. Petrified with fear and horror at what was happening, those who knew nothing about the plot found themselves incapable of running away or going to Caesar's help, or even of uttering a word, while those who were primed and ready for the deadly deed each drew a sword. Surrounded on all sides, wherever Caesar turned his gaze he met the thrust of a sword aimed at his face and eyes.* Driven this way and that, like a wild beast he found no escape anywhere from his enemies' blows, because they all had to set to work and be involved in the murder. And so even Brutus struck him once in the groin. Some writers claim that although he fought back against everyone else, and twisted and turned to escape their blows, and cried out for help, yet at the sight of Brutus with his sword drawn he covered his head with his toga and, perhaps by chance or perhaps because he was forced back by his assassins, he fell to the ground by the pedestal on which the statue of Pompey stood. And the pedestal was so drenched with blood from the murder that it seemed as though Pompey himself had presided over the punishment of his enemy, who lay on the ground at his feet, jerking convulsively from his many wounds. For it is said that he was struck twenty-three times, and with all these blows raining down on to the single target of their victim's body many of the conspirators were wounded by one another as well.*

[67] With Caesar lying murdered on the floor, Brutus stepped forward with a view to making a statement about what they had done, but rather than wait to hear him the senators rushed outside and fled. This infected the general populace with so much confusion and mindless panic that some locked up their houses and others abandoned their stalls and places of business. The streets were filled with people running to and from the scene of the crime, either going to see what had happened or leaving afterwards. Antony and Lepidus, Caesar's two closest friends, slipped away and took refuge in friends' houses, but Brutus and his fellow conspirators, without waiting to cool down after the murder, but just as they were, with their swords still drawn, left the senate-house together in a group and set out for the Capitol. So far from looking like people who needed to run away, their faces were flushed with happiness and confidence, and as they went on their way they commended freedom to the

common people and invited the members of the aristocracy they encountered to join them. Some people actually did join their ranks and walked up to the Capitol with them, wanting people to think they had taken part in the deed, and to gain some of the credit for it. Two people who behaved like this were Gaius Octavius and Lentulus Spinther, who later paid the penalty for the deception when they were put to death by Antony and the younger Caesar, without even having enjoyed the benefits of the glory for which they died, since no one was taken in by them. In fact, even Antony and Caesar punished them not for what they had done, but for what they wished they had done.*

The next day Brutus went down to the forum and delivered a speech, and the people listened to him without expressing either approval or disapproval of his actions. It was clear from their total lack of response that although they felt sorry for what had happened to Caesar, they also respected Brutus. In an attempt to promote a general amnesty and keep the peace, the senate decreed divine honours for Caesar and voted to preserve all the measures he had passed while he was in power without changing them in the slightest, and at the same time awarded Brutus and his fellow conspirators provinces and other appropriate honours. This struck everyone as an excellent compromise, and it seemed that things had calmed down.*

[68] However, when Caesar's will was opened, it was discovered that he had left every Roman citizen a substantial legacy, and then, when they saw his mutilated body being carried through the forum, they could no longer restrain or control their feelings. They heaped up benches and railings and stalls from the forum around the body, set light to them, and cremated the body on the spot.* Next, with blazing torches held high, they ran to the houses of the assassins, with the intention of burning them to the ground, while others searched high and low in the city for the men themselves, whom they wanted to capture and tear to shreds. But they did not come across a single one of them: they were all safe behind secure barricades. However, there was a friend of Caesar's called Cinna who happened, according to my sources, to have had a strange dream the previous night, in which he tried to refuse a dinner invitation from Caesar, but Caesar took him by the hand and pulled him along, even though he did not want to go and resisted all the way. Now, when he heard that Caesar's body was being burnt in the forum, he left his house and set

out there as a mark of respect, although he had some misgivings as a result of his dream and was also running a fever. When he came into view, someone in the crowd asked who he was and then, when he had found out, told someone else, and soon the whole crowd was buzzing with the rumour that he was one of Caesar's assassins, since one of the conspirators happened to have the same name as him. The crowd assumed that the man who had just come into the forum was the murderer, and they rushed on him and tore him limb from limb right there in public. More than anything else, this incident made Brutus and Cassius afraid, and a few days later they left the city. I have written in my *Life of Brutus* what they did and what was done to them before they died.*

[69] At his death Caesar was 56 years old. He outlived Pompey by little more than four years,* and the power and dominance he had finally attained, after a lifelong and often life-threatening search, brought him no reward except the name and the fame of it, which served only to arouse resentment in his fellow citizens. However, his great guardian spirit, which he had relied on throughout his life, looked after his interests even after his death by avenging his murder. It harried and hunted his assassins to the ends of the earth, over land and sea, until not one of them remained—until it had punished everyone who had helped at all in the execution of the deed or had even played a part in the planning of it. The most amazing non-supernatural event was what happened to Cassius: after his defeat at the battle of Philippi, he killed himself with the very dagger he had used against Caesar.* The most amazing supernatural events were a huge comet and the faintness of the sunlight. The comet was clearly visible in the sky for seven nights after Caesar's murder before vanishing; and all that year the orb of the sun rose pale and dim, and gave out such a feeble, ineffective warmth that the air loomed murky and heavy due to the weakness of the heat penetrating it, and the crops failed to ripen and mature, but withered and faded thanks to the coolness of the atmosphere.*

But the clearest sign of the gods' displeasure at Caesar's murder was the apparition that appeared to Brutus. Here is what happened. Brutus was on the point of transporting his army across from Abydos to Europe,* and as usual he spent the night resting in his tent, not asleep, but worrying about the future. (No military commander in history ever needed less sleep than him, apparently, or spent more time awake and active.) He thought he heard a noise at the entrance to his tent, so he looked in that direction by the light of his lamp, which was starting to get low, and to his horror saw a man of unnatural height and grim appearance. At first he was terrrified out of his wits, but when he saw that the man just stood in silence by his couch, without saying or doing anything, he asked him who he was. And the apparition replied: 'I am the spirit of your doom, Brutus, and you will see me at Philippi.' Brutus summoned up his courage and said, 'All right. I'll see you there', and the spirit immediately left. So the time came when Brutus found himself up against Antony and Caesar at Philippi. In the first battle he overcame the enemy army which had been deployed against him, put them to flight, and swept through them into Caesar's camp, which he ransacked. As he was about to fight the second battle, however, the same apparition visited him again at night. It did not speak a word, but Brutus realized that the fated hour had come and hurled himself headlong into the danger. He did not die fighting, however: after his army had been scattered he took refuge on a rocky promontory; he placed the tip of his drawn sword on his chest, and with the help of a friend's strong arm, they say, plunged the sword in and died.*

ANTONY

INTRODUCTION

The Lives of Pompey and Caesar delineate the rival ambitions of those extraordinary generals, until Julius Caesar was able to defeat Pompey at Pharsalus. Within four years, however, Caesar's assassination on the Ides of March, 44 BC, opened the way to the ambitions of those who had previously been overshadowed. After the defeat of the 'Liberators' Brutus and Cassius at Philippi in 42, the victors were left to divide the Roman world among themselves. Instead, for the next ten years Antony, one of Caesar's closest associates, and Caesar Octavianus, his great nephew and adopted son, vied for power. Antony controlled the eastern part of the empire, Caesar (as Plutarch calls him) the western. Finally, in 31, they clashed in a naval battle at Actium on the coast of the Adriatic. Antony was defeated and fled to Alexandria; Caesar pursued him to Egypt, where Antony committed suicide rather than surrender. With his death, the civil wars which had tormented Rome since 49 came to an end. Caesar established his autocracy under the cover of a pretended restoration of the republic, and in 28 assumed the title of Augustus. The long years of his rule—he did not die until AD 14—established the monarchy under which Plutarch lived, and which would continue with modifications for centuries.

Plutarch had already written a biography of Augustus in his series of Lives of the Emperors (cf. p. xi in the General Introduction). In *Antony* he focuses rather on how a great leader could lose an empire: what features of his circumstances and his own character could lead Antony to be worsted by a man twenty years his junior? The most obvious cause was his infatuation, growing to an obsession, with Cleopatra: a story which might easily become a standard tale of a man ruined by a bad woman. But Plutarch does not see it so simply. Looking below the surface, he uncovers earlier indications of features of Antony's character which at first appear as virtues, and bring him his success with the troops and his Roman peers, yet gradually reveal themselves as serious flaws, which make him susceptible to flattery, misjudgement, and fatal self-indulgence. Moreover, the relationship between Antony and Cleopatra reveals unexpected depths, and what begins as a dalliance, and the effort of a queen to win privileges for herself and her kingdom, becomes an intimate bonding of souls.

This unusually long life follows a basically chronological format:

1–2 Family and youth
3–13 Antony's early career, to the death of Caesar
14–22 From the Ides of March to Philippi (44–42 BC): the war against the tyrannicides
23–36 From 41 to 37: Antony, Cleopatra, and Octavia
37–52 The Parthian War (36)
53–5 Growing tensions between Antony and Octavian (35–33)
56–69 The Actium campaign
70–87 Alexandria: the deaths first of Antony, then of Cleopatra

In the early chapters Plutarch gives indications of Antony's character: a good soldier, who gets along well with the troops, but is recklessly extravagant. Particularly revealing is the anecdote of his father, who gave away a silver bowl to a friend (because he had spent all his money) but then had to ask pardon from his wife (1). The traits of generosity, desire to please, extravagance, and submission to a woman revealed in the father will reappear in the son. In particular, Fulvia, Antony's wife, trains him to be docile, preparing him for Cleopatra (10). For Antony, despite all his energy, is surprisingly passive in Plutarch's view, easily led by those who know how to flatter him or respond to his needs. With the death of Julius Caesar, the young Octavian steps on to the stage, and with his coldly rational conduct serves as a foil to Antony's variable moods. Conflicts arise which prepare the reader for the great rift later. After the tyrannicides are defeated, Antony is seen triumphantly proceeding through Asia Minor, like a new Dionysus or Heracles (24). The cost to the provincials, however, is terrible, and Plutarch stops to note that Antony seems unaware and too good-natured to see how his henchmen are robbing all they can get.

At this point, Antony, lord of the eastern empire, summoned Cleopatra from Egypt to his court. Cleopatra's arrival—'the barge she sat in, like a burnished throne, burn'd on the water; the poop was beaten gold, purple the sails'[1]—captures Antony, and a new phase of his life begins. From this point he swings back and forth between his obsession with her and with the life of pleasure and self-indulgence which she represents, and the duties of a Roman leader. In lesser hands, this could be a banal story of an unhappy love affair, but Plutarch's narrative searches out in Antony's struggle the complex interplay of weakness and strength, assertion and surrender which reveals his tragic humanity. The qualities which have made him great destroy him, yet the greatness remains.

Shakespeare recognized the drama in this Life, and drew upon Plutarch not only for the plot of *Antony and Cleopatra*, but for some of its best

[1] Shakespeare, *Antony and Cleopatra*, II. ii. 198–201, cf. Plutarch's c. 26.

scenes and dialogue. The description of Cleopatra's barge, the scene with Sextus Pompey at Misenum, Antony sitting with head in hands after Actium, and a number of other impressive moments closely follow Plutarch's visualization, though not his words. Shakespeare recognized the polar worlds of Rome and Alexandria, one serious, the other playful and luxurious, which are already present in Plutarch. Shakespeare, like Plutarch, allows the comments of other participants and bystanders to reveal the implications of the protagonists' actions. Significantly, Plutarch's Cleopatra, changing from temptress to queen and lover, is the model for Shakespeare's Cleopatra, and Plutarch's final tableau where Octavian's guards burst in upon the dying queen and her ladies-in-waiting, becomes, with the slightest of alterations, that fine moment (V. ii.) when Charmian answers to the question, 'Charmian, is this well done?', 'It is well done, and fitting for a princess.'

Plutarch paired Antony with Demetrius Poliorcetes (336–283). Demetrius, an affable, brilliant young commander, had fought alongside his father Antigonus, one of the Successors of Alexander the Great, to win the empire of Alexander, but they were defeated and Antigonus was killed in the battle of Ipsus in 301. Demetrius showed enormous resilience in re-establishing an empire in Greece and Macedonia, but after many vicissitudes surrendered to Seleucus in 285. Despondent, he drank himself to death two years later.

Plutarch explains their similarities in the introduction to *Demetrius* (c. 1):

> They both were lovers, drinkers, soldiers, givers, spenders, outrageous. Their fortunes were similar, since through their lives both experienced great successes and great failures, conquered and lost large territories, unexpectedly lost and unexpectedly recovered. One died as the captive of his enemy, the other almost did.

These parallels do not indicate the richness and subtlety of the portraits, especially in *Antony*, but point the reader where to look: to a kind of energy and excess in all that they do, which leads to both enormous successes and enormous failures. New beginnings seem always possible, and new disasters. Absent, of course, is that sense of moderation, the product of a Hellenic education and the study of philosophy, which Plutarch sees as the ideal. In the same opening chapter of *Demetrius*, Plutarch refers to Plato's dictum (*Republic* 491e), 'If the most gifted minds are subjected to a bad education, they become exceptionally bad.' The context in the *Republic* is the proper education of the guardians: even those fine, carefully selected souls will go sour without the right training.

In the comparatively simple account of *Demetrius*, and the much more subtle narrative of *Antony*, Plutarch examines how these great untrained—or rather, badly trained—natures work out their fortunes. A theme of both Lives is the mutability of fortune: but that mutability is tied directly to the protagonists' own behaviour, and reflects their instability. As Plutarch notes (*Demetr.* 1), even the lives of those who have acted without thinking can be useful to the reader.

As has been seen, Plutarch did his basic source work for *Antony* at the same time as for *Pompey*, *Caesar*, and several other late republican Lives (above, p. xxiv in the General Introduction, and p. 220). For all of these, a major source (probably used directly, though perhaps through an intermediary) seems to have been Asinius Pollio's history of the Civil Wars, which ran from 60 BC down at least to Philippi, and perhaps to Actium. Pollio had been a partisan of Julius Caesar, then of Antony, down to about 40. He probably supplied much of the political detail for this Life. Three other works were especially useful for this Life. Augustus' *Autobiography* narrated in thirteen books his life down to 23 BC, giving the emperor's version of events, some of which could reflect very badly on Antony. Plutarch quotes it (cc. 22 and 68), but it is hard to trace the impact on the Life. Cicero, attacking Antony in his *Second Philippic* (44 BC), refers frequently to events in Antony's early career. Plutarch cites this in his chapter 6 and uses it often for other incidents in chapters 2, 9–14, and 21. He must have known the speech at first hand. Quintus Dellius was another contemporary closely associated with Antony; Plutarch cites his history (c. 59) and seems to use it frequently. It certainly covered the Parthian War, and probably much else, including the description of Cleopatra's visit to Antony (25–7) and his own defection to Caesar (59). Another eyewitness, Olympus, Cleopatra's doctor, whose account Plutarch cites (82), may have provided the details of Antony and Cleopatra's last days in Alexandria.

Plutarch's own family traditions preserved two significant anecdotes: the doctor Philotas' tale to Plutarch's grandfather, Lamprias, of the sumptuous banquets and extravagance in Alexandria (28), and his great-grandfather's story of the hardships involved in supplying Antony's fleet at Actium (68). Antony might have been a favourite of the Greeks, but first his extravagance, then the Civil War, made him a grievous burden. Antony's philhellenism, like so many of his other virtues, was overwhelmed by the dissoluteness of his life.[2]

[2] Antony's surprise at the rapacious exactions of his staff in Asia Minor (24) may be taken as an indication of the imbalance between goodwill and action in dealing with the Greeks which would have afflicted the much poorer mainland Greece as well.

Brenk, F. E., 'Plutarch's Life, "Markos Antonios": A Literary and Cultural Study', in W. Haase and H. Temporini (eds.), *Aufstieg und Niedergang der römischen Welt*, II.33.6 (Berlin and New York, 1992): 4347–469 (with indices 4895–915).

Gowing, A., *The Triumviral Narratives of Appian and Cassius Dio* (Ann Arbor, Mich.: University of Michigan Press, 1993).

Huzar, E. G., *Mark Antony: A Biography* (Minneapolis: University of Minnesota Press, 1978).

Pelling, C. B. R., 'Plutarch's Method of Work in the Roman Lives', *Journal of Hellenic Studies*, 99 (1979), 74–96; repr. in B. Scardigli (ed.), *Essays on Plutarch's Lives* (Oxford: Clarendon Press, 1995), 265–318, with 'Postscript (1994)'.

—— 'Plutarch's Adaptation of his Source Material', *Journal of Hellenic Studies*, 100 (1980), 127–40; repr. in B. Scardigli (ed.), *Essays on Plutarch's Lives* (Oxford: Clarendon Press, 1995), 125–54.

—— *Plutarch: Life of Antony* (Cambridge: Cambridge University Press, 1988). Excellent introduction and historical and literary commentary to the Greek text.

Sherwin-White, A. N., *Roman Foreign Policy in the East, 168 BC to AD 1* (London: Duckworth, 1984).

Swain, S. C. R., 'Cultural Interchange in Plutarch's Antony', *Quaderni Urbinati di Cultura Classica*, NS 34 (1990), 151–7.

Wofford, Susanne L., 'Antony's Egyptian Bacchanals: Heroic and Divine Impersonation in Shakespeare's Plutarch and Antony and Cleopatra', *Poetica*, 48 (1997), 33–67 (special issue, *Shakespeare's Plutarch*, ed. M. A. McGrail).

ANTONY

[1] Antony's grandfather was the orator Antonius, who, as a member of Sulla's faction, was killed by Marius, and his father was Antonius surnamed Creticus, who was not particularly well known or distinguished in the public domain,* but was a fair and honourable man, and above all a generous one, as a single example of his behaviour should demonstrate. He was not well off, and so his wife tended to stop him displaying his kindness, but once, when one of his close friends came and asked him for money, although he did not have any actual money on him, he ordered a young slave to pour some water into a silver bowl and bring it to him. When the slave had done so, Antonius splashed water on to his cheeks, as if he were about to shave, but then, once the boy was out of the way on some other errand, he gave the bowl to his friend and told him it was his to dispose of. Later, when the house-slaves were being subjected to a thorough search, Antonius could see that his wife was angry and was prepared to examine each and every one of them under torture, so he confessed and asked her to forgive him.

[2] Antonius' wife was Julia, from the house of the Caesars, as virtuous and modest a woman as any of her day. Their son, Antony, was brought up by her, and after Antonius' death she was married to Cornelius Lentulus, who was put to death by Cicero as one of Catiline's co-conspirators. She is generally thought to have been the prime mover of the extreme hostility Antony felt for Cicero. At any rate, Antony claims that Cicero refused even to hand Lentulus' corpse over to them until his mother had begged Cicero's wife to intercede for them. But this is generally taken to be false, because none of the men who were put to death by Cicero at the time in question were denied burial.*

Antony had developed into a remarkable young man, they say, when he was smitten, as if by a pestilential disease, by his friendship and intimacy with Curio, an uncultured hedonist who, in order to increase his hold over Antony, introduced him to drinking-sessions, women, and all kinds of extravagant and immoderate expenses, as a result of which Antony got heavily into debt—too heavily for his age—until he owed 250 talents. Curio guaranteed the whole sum, but when Antony's father realized what was going on, he threw Antony out of the house. Next Antony briefly associated himself with the career of Clodius, the most defiant and vile of the popular leaders of the time, who was then throwing the whole constitution into disarray. Before long, however, he had had his fill of Clodius' insane ways and also became afraid of the party that was forming in opposition to Clodius, so he left Italy for Greece, where he spent his time training his body for military contests and learning the art of public speaking. He adopted the so-called Asiatic style of speaking, which was flourishing with particular vigour just then and which bore a considerable resemblance to his life, in that it was a kind of showy whinnying,† filled with vain prancing and capricious ambition.*

[3] When Gabinius, an ex-consul, set sail for Syria and tried to persuade Antony to get involved in the expedition, Antony refused to do so without a commission, but joined his campaign once he had been given command of the cavalry. His first mission was against Aristobulus, the leader of a Jewish revolt. Antony drove Aristobulus out of all his strongholds, the largest of which he was the first to scale. Then he engaged the enemy in battle, put them to flight, even though his small force was vastly outnumbered, and killed all but a few of them. Aristobulus and his son were among the captives.

Next there was an attempt by Ptolemy to persuade Gabinius, with a promise of ten thousand talents, to join him in invading Egypt and restoring him to the throne. Most of his officers were opposed to the plan and, despite being completely captivated by the ten thousand talents, Gabinius was hesitant about the war. Antony, however, had his sights set on great exploits. He also wanted to do Ptolemy a favour and see him get his way, so he helped him win Gabinius over and arouse his enthusiasm about the expedition.* The Romans were more afraid of the journey to Pelusium than they were of the war, since their way lay through deep sand and waterless desert, past the Ecregma and the Serbonian marshes. The Egyptians call these marshes the Outbreaths of Typhon, but they are apparently a remnant of the Red Sea, left behind when it receded, and fed by water percolating through to them at the point where a very narrow isthmus separates the marshes and the inner sea.* However, when Antony was dispatched with his cavalry he not only occupied the narrow pass, but also captured Pelusium, which was a large city, and overcame the garrison there. In this way he simultaneously secured the route for the army and made its commander certain and confident of victory. The enemy too profited from his desire for recognition, in the sense that when Ptolemy reached Pelusium, he was so filled with rage and hatred that he intended to massacre the Egyptians, but Antony intervened and stopped him. And throughout the numerous major battles and fights that followed, Antony frequently displayed great daring and the kind of foresight that marks a leader, most conspicuously on the occasion when he gave victory to the front ranks by encircling the enemy and coming round to take them in the rear. All this gained him battle honours and prizes for valour, but his posthumous kindness to Archelaus was also widely appreciated. Although Archelaus was close to him, and they were guest-friends, he had no choice but to make war on him while he was alive, and then after Archelaus had fallen in battle Antony sought out his body, dressed it up, and gave it a royal burial. As a result he left the people of Alexandria with a very favourable impression, and the Romans involved in the expedition came to regard him as an outstanding soldier.*

[4] On top of these qualities, his appearance was gentlemanly and dignified. His noble beard, broad forehead, and aquiline nose were reminiscent of the virility displayed by Heracles' features in portraits and on statues. There was also an ancient story that the Antonii were descendants of Heracles, originating from Heracles' son Anton, and Antony thought his physical appearance, which I have already mentioned, confirmed the tradition. He also dressed to support the tradition. When he was going to be seen by more than just a few people, he always girded his toga up to his thigh, wore a great sword hanging at his side, and wrapped himself in a rough cloak. Nevertheless, even those aspects of his behaviour which struck other people as vulgar—his boasting and teasing, the habit he had of carousing in full view of everyone, and the way he sat next to someone who was eating and ate standing at the table while out on campaign—aroused an incredible amount of loyalty and longing in his soldiers. He was even somehow charming† where love was concerned, and used it as one of his means for gaining popularity, since he helped people in their love-affairs and did not mind being teased about his own affairs. Then his generosity, and the way he did both his friends and the men under his command favours with no mean or niggardly hand, were not only the cause of the outstanding beginning he made

on the road to power, but also raised his power to even greater heights after he had acquired prominence, despite the countless flaws which held him back. I will give one example of his liberality. He gave orders for one of his friends to be given 250,000 drachmas (or a 'decies', as the Romans call it). His steward was astonished and wanted to show Antony how large a sum it was, so he put all the money out on display. When Antony passed by he said, 'What's this?', and the steward explained that it was the money he had ordered to be given away. Antony was not deceived. He understood the malice of the man's intentions and said, 'I thought a decies was more. This is a paltry sum. Double it.'

[5] But this happened at a later time. When Roman political life was divided into two factions, with the aristocrats attaching themselves to Pompey, who was in Rome, and the popularists summoning Caesar from Gaul where he was on active service, Antony's friend Curio, who had changed sides and was supporting Caesar, brought Antony over to Caesar's cause. Curio, who had a great deal of influence with the common people as a result of his abilities as a public speaker, and also made unstinting use of money supplied by Caesar, got Antony elected tribune and then subsequently one of the priests responsible for divining the flights of birds, whom they call 'augurs'.* No sooner had Antony taken up office than he was of considerable help to those who were Caesar's proxies in government. In the first place, when Marcellus the consul was trying not only to hand over to Pompey all the troops which were already mustered, but also to make it possible for him to raise further troops as well, Antony blocked the proposal by issuing an edict to the effect that the forces already assembled should sail to Syria and help Bibulus in his war against the Parthians, and that the troops Pompey was in the process of raising should not be attached to his command.* In the second place, when the senate refused to allow Caesar's letters to be introduced or read out, Antony drew on the authority vested in his office to read them out himself, and so changed a lot of people's minds, since Caesar's demands, as displayed in his letters, seemed fair and reasonable.* Finally, when two questions had been raised in the senate—one asking whether it was the senators' opinion that Pompey should disband his army, the other asking the same question about Caesar—and only a few senators were in favour of Pompey laying down his arms, while almost all of them were in favour of Caesar doing so,

Antony stood up and asked whether it was the view of the senate that both Pompey and Caesar should lay down their arms and disband their armies together. This proposal was unanimously and enthusiastically accepted, and with cries of congratulation they called on Antony to put the question to the vote. The consuls, however, refused to let this happen, so instead Caesar's supporters put forward a new set of apparently reasonable demands—but Cato spoke out strongly against them, and Lentulus, in his capacity as consul, had Antony expelled from the senate. As he left he fulminated against them, and then, dressed as a slave, he hired a chariot along with Quintus Cassius and set out to join Caesar. As soon as they were shown in to him they loudly declared that the government of Rome was in complete chaos, now that even the tribunes were prevented from saying what they wanted and anyone who spoke out on behalf of justice was harassed and in mortal danger.*

[6] At this Caesar took his army and invaded Italy. This is why in the *Philippics* Cicero wrote that just as Helen was the cause of the Trojan War, so Antony was the cause of the Civil War.* But this is obviously false, because Gaius Caesar was not the kind of malleable or pliant man who would have let anger overwhelm reason; if he had not determined to do so a long time previously, he would not have taken the decision to make war on his country on the spur of the moment, just because he saw that Antony and Cassius had taken to a chariot and fled to him, dressed in poor clothes. All this did was provide him with a plausible excuse and pretext for what he had been wanting to do for a long time. What led him to take on the whole world, as it had led Alexander before him, and Cyrus many years before that,* was an insatiable lust for rule and an insane desire to be first in power and importance—for which the downfall of Pompey was a prerequisite.

So Caesar attacked Rome, conquered it, and drove Pompey out of Italy. He then decided to concentrate first on the Pompeian forces in Spain and afterwards, once he had fitted out a fleet, to make the crossing and attack Pompey. He left Lepidus as military governor of Rome and entrusted Italy and the army to Antony in his capacity as tribune.* Antony immediately won the loyalty of the troops by making it his usual practice to join them in their exercises and at mealtimes, and by rewarding them as much as he could given the circumstances, but everyone else found him highly offensive. He was too lazy to pay attention to the pleas of injured parties, too bad-tempered to listen to petitioners, and he had a poor reputation as regards other men's wives. In short, Caesar's rule, which turned out not even remotely to resemble a tyranny as far as he himself was concerned, was spoiled by his associates, and Antony was the one who was considered the worst offender, since he had the greatest power and so was held to have gone the furthest astray.

[7] Nevertheless, on his return from Spain Caesar ignored the charges against Antony and was perfectly right to do so, since in war he found him energetic, courageous, and a natural leader. So Caesar set sail across the Ionian Sea from Brundisium with a small force and then sent his transport ships back to Gabinius and Antony with orders to board their men and cross over to Macedonia as quickly as possible. While Gabinius shrank from making the difficult crossing in winter and took his army the long way round by land, Antony was worried about how Caesar had been cut off by large numbers of enemy troops. So he repelled Libo, who was blockading the mouth of the harbour, by surrounding his galleys with numerous light boats, embarked 800 horsemen and 20,000 legionaries, and put to sea. The enemy caught sight of him and gave chase, and although he escaped from this threat when a fresh southerly wind engulfed the enemy ships in heavy seas and a deep swell, his fleet was blown off course towards some cliffs and crags jutting out into deep water, and his situation looked hopeless. But suddenly a strong south-westerly wind blew from the direction of the bay and the waves began to run from the land towards the open sea, so that Antony could change direction away from the land. As he sailed confidently along, he saw that the shoreline was covered with disabled ships, because the wind had driven the galleys that were after him there, and quite a few of them were wrecked. Antony took plenty of prisoners and a great deal of booty, captured Lissus, and greatly boosted Caesar's morale by arriving just in time with such a large force.*

[8] Many battles took place, one after another, and Antony distinguished himself in all of them. Twice, when Caesar's men were in headlong flight, he confronted them, turned them around, made them stop and regroup, and so won the battle. There was more talk about him in the camp than anyone else except Caesar. And Caesar made no secret of his opinion of Antony: when the final battle at Pharsalus was imminent, the battle on which the whole issue

depended, he kept the right wing for himself, but he put Antony in charge of the left wing, on the grounds that he was the best tactician apart from himself.* After the victory Caesar was made dictator and went off after Pompey, but he chose Antony as his cavalry commander and sent him to Rome. This post is the second most important when the dictator is in Rome, but when he is away it is the most important and has more or less sole authority. The tribunate remains in place, but all the other offices are dissolved once a dictator has been elected.*

[9] However, one of the tribunes at the time, Dolabella, a young man who wanted to see constitutional changes, was trying to introduce a decree cancelling all debts, and he set about persuading Antony, who was a friend of his and who was always keen to please the masses, to join him and play a part in trying to get the measure passed. But Asinius and Trebellius advised him to have nothing to do with it, and it so happened that Antony strongly suspected that he had been cuckolded by Dolabella. He was furious about it, threw his wife out of his house (she was his cousin, since she was the daughter of Gaius Antonius, who was consul in the same year as Cicero), sided with Asinius, and took up arms against Dolabella, who had occupied the forum in an attempt to carry his bill by force. The senate voted that the situation called for the use of arms against Dolabella, and Antony advanced on him. In the ensuing skirmish there were losses on both sides.*

The upshot of this was that the masses came to loathe him, while at the same time his general way of life meant that he did not find favour with the upright and moral members of society, as Cicero says.* In fact, they intensely disliked him, and were disgusted by his ill-timed bouts of drunkenness, his oppressive extravagance, his cavorting with women, and the way he spent the days asleep or wandering around in a daze with a hangover, and the nights at parties and shows, and amusing himself at the weddings of actors and clowns. At any rate, it is said that he was a guest at the wedding of the actor Hippias, where he drank all night long, and then the next morning, when the people of Rome summoned him to the forum, he presented himself while he was still suffering from over-indulgence and vomited into the cloak one of his friends held out for him. Then there were the actor Sergius, who had a very great deal of influence over him, and Cytheris, a woman from the same school, of whom he was fond; he even used to take her around with him on a litter when he visited various cities, and the litter was accompanied by a retinue as large as his mother's. They were also upset by the sight of his golden goblets being carried around on his excursions out of Rome as if they were part of a ceremonial procession, by the pavilions he set up on his journeys, the extravagant feasts spread out by groves and rivers, the lions yoked to chariots, and the way the houses of upright men and women were used to lodge whores and players of the *sambyke*. They were angered by the thought that Caesar himself was out of Italy, camping out in the open and experiencing great hardship and danger mopping up the remnants of the war, while others were taking advantage of his efforts to revel in luxury and treat their fellow citizens with disrespect.

[10] These habits of Antony's are also generally held to have increased the factional schism and encouraged the troops to turn to acts of terrible violence and rapacity. And so, on his return, Caesar pardoned Dolabella and, once he had been elected to his third consulship, chose Lepidus rather than Antony as his colleague. When Pompey's house was up for sale, Antony bought it, but then became indignant when he was asked to pay up. We have his own words for the fact that this is why he did not accompany Caesar on his African campaign, because he had not been recompensed for his earlier successes. But it looks as though Caesar eradicated most of Antony's inane and dissolute habits, by letting it be known that his offences had not gone unnoticed.*

So Antony gave up that way of life and turned to marriage. He married Fulvia, the former wife of the popular leader Clodius. Now, Fulvia was a woman who cared nothing for spinning or housework, and was not interested in having power over a husband who was just a private citizen, but wanted to rule a ruler and command a commander—and consequently Cleopatra owed Fulvia the fee for teaching Antony to submit to a woman, since she took him over after he had been tamed and trained from the outset to obey women. Not that Antony did not try to get Fulvia too to lighten up, by teasing her and fooling around. For instance, after Caesar's victory in Spain, Antony was one of the large number of people who went out to meet him. Suddenly a rumour reached Italy that Caesar was dead and that his enemies were advancing. Antony turned back to Rome, but dressed himself as a slave, and went to his house after nightfall, saying that he had a letter for Fulvia from Antony. He was shown in to her with his face all covered up. Before taking the letter from him Fulvia asked, in a state of considerable distress, whether Antony was alive. He handed the letter to her without saying a word, and then, as she began to open it, he threw his arms around her and kissed her. Anyway, I have mentioned only this brief tale, but it may serve as an example of many others.*

[11] On Caesar's return from Spain all the leading men of Rome made journeys of many days' duration to meet him, but it was Antony who was conspicuously honoured by him. When journeying through Italy on his chariot he kept Antony with him as his travelling companion, while Brutus Albinus and Octavian (his sister's son, who was later called Caesar and ruled Rome for a very long time) travelled behind him; and when he was made consul for the fifth time, he immediately chose Antony as his colleague.* In fact, however, he planned to resign his consulship in favour of Dolabella, and he went so far as to put this proposal to the senate. Antony spoke out bitterly against the idea; he rained insults down on Dolabella's head and received as good as he gave from the other man, until Caesar was so ashamed at the disruption that he withdrew the motion. Later, when Caesar came forward and proclaimed Dolabella consul, Antony called out that the omens were unfavourable, so Caesar backed down and abandoned Dolabella, who was mightily displeased. As a matter of fact, Caesar seems to have found Dolabella just as loathsome as Antony did, since we are told that once, when someone was criticizing both of them to him, he said that he was not afraid of these overweight, long-haired men, but of those pale, lean ones—by which he meant Brutus and Cassius, who were soon to conspire against him and assassinate him.*

[12] The most plausible pretext for Brutus and Cassius to act was in fact given them accidentally by Antony. It was the time of the festival of the Lycaea at Rome, which the Romans call the Lupercalia, and Caesar, arrayed in his triumphal clothing, was seated on the rostra in the forum watching the runners.* At this festival large numbers of well-born young men, and a lot of the city officials too, thoroughly anoint themselves with oil and run here and there in the forum, playfully touching people they meet with hairy pieces of goatskin. Antony was one of the runners, but he ignored tradition and instead ran over to the rostra with a laurel wreath he had woven

around a diadem. He was lifted up by his fellow runners and put the diadem on Caesar's head, as if to say that he ought to be king. Caesar made a show of turning aside, which so delighted the people that they burst out into applause. Antony urged it on him again, and again Caesar brushed it off. This contest went on for some time, with a few of Antony's friends applauding his attempts to force the diadem on to Caesar, and the whole assembled populace applauding and shouting out their approval of Caesar's refusals. The surprising thing was that although the people behaved as though they tolerated the actual condition of being a king's subjects, they found the mere title offensive, as if it meant the end of their freedom. Be that as it may, Caesar stood up angrily on the rostra, pulled his toga away from his neck, and shouted out that he was baring his throat for anyone who wanted to strike him. Some of the tribunes tore the garland off the statue of Caesar where it had been placed, and the people formed a train behind them, shouting out their approval of what they had done; but Caesar had them removed from office.*

[13] This incident stiffened the resolve of Brutus and Cassius. While they were recruiting into their scheme those of their friends they could trust, Antony's name came up as a possibility. Everyone else was in favour of Antony, but Trebonius spoke out against him and said that Antony had shared his tent and been his travelling companion at the time when they were going out to meet Caesar on his return from Spain; he said that he had broached the subject somewhat delicately and cautiously, and that while Antony had understood what he was getting at, he had not approved of the enterprise. Still, Trebonius pointed out, he had not denounced them to Caesar either, but had faithfully kept the conversation to himself.* The conspirators next began to wonder whether they should murder Antony after killing Caesar, but Brutus put a stop to this plan by arguing that any deed which is undertaken for the sake of law and justice must be pure and untainted by injustice. But they were concerned about Antony's power and the dignity of his official position, so they gave some of their number the job of dealing with him by detaining him outside the senate-house in conversation on some pressing business, once Caesar had gone inside and the deed was about to be done.

[14] This plan was carried out, and Caesar fell in the senate-house. Antony lost no time in changing into slave's clothes and

hiding himself. When he realized that the conspirators were not attacking anyone, but had congregated on the Capitol, he persuaded them to come down by giving them his son as a hostage. Then he took Cassius home and gave him dinner, while Lepidus did the same for Brutus. Antony convened the senate, spoke in favour of an amnesty, and recommended the assignment of a province each to Cassius and Brutus; the senate ratified these proposals and passed a decree to the effect that none of Caesar's measures should be changed. Antony emerged from the senate covered in glory, since he was held to have removed the threat of civil war and to have managed unusually problematic and disturbing events in an extremely sensible and statesmanlike manner.

However, this view of him was soon brought tumbling down by the acclaim of the masses, which led him to think that he could become the undisputed leader of Rome if he could secure Brutus' downfall. Now, it so happened that Antony was due to deliver the customary eulogy in the forum when Caesar's body was brought out for burial. When he saw that the assembled people were extraordinarily moved and beguiled by his words, he tempered his praise with expressions of sorrow and indignation at what had happened, and at the end of his speech he brandished the dead man's bloodstained, sword-slashed clothes, and called the perpetrators of the deed accursed murderers. In this way he whipped the crowd up into such a frenzy of anger that they piled up the benches and tables, cremated Caesar's body there in the forum, and then snatched brands from the pyre and ran to attack the houses of his assassins.*

[15] Brutus therefore left the city, and Caesar's friends united behind Antony. Caesar's wife, Calpurnia, trustingly brought most of the valuables, which altogether were worth four thousand talents, from her house and left them with Antony for safe keeping. Antony was also given Caesar's papers, which contained notes about decisions he had taken and wanted to put into practice. By inserting the names of people of his choosing into these papers Antony managed to get a lot of people elected to offices or to the senate, and he even had some people recalled from exile or freed from prison, making out that this was what Caesar had wanted to do. That is why the Romans scornfully called all these people Charonites, because they were assessed by recourse to the dead man's notebooks.* In general, then, Antony behaved in an autocratic manner, with himself as

consul and his brothers in office along with him—Gaius as praetor and Lucius as tribune.

[16] This was the situation when the young Caesar*—who, as I have already said, was the son of the dead man's sister—came to Rome, as the heir to Caesar's estate. He had been staying in Apollonia at the time of Caesar's murder. He immediately went and greeted Antony as a friend of the family, and reminded him of the property that had been left in his safe keeping, because under the terms of Caesar's will he was obliged to give every Roman citizen seventy-five drachmas. Antony's initial response was to treat him dismissively, thinking that he was hardly more than a boy; he told him he was out of his mind, and warned him of the unbearable burden he was taking on in electing to become Caesar's successor when he was bereft of both good sense and friends. When the young man refused to listen and simply repeated his demand for the money, Antony kept on and on at him with the most insulting language and behaviour. For instance, he opposed him when he was seeking election as a tribune; and when, in accordance with a senatorial decree, he wanted to dedicate his father's golden throne, Antony threatened to haul him off to prison if he did not stop trying to win over the general populace. Eventually, the young man put himself in the hands of Cicero and all the others who hated Antony, and with their help he began to gain the support of the senate, win over the common people, and gather in the troops from the colonies. Now Antony became alarmed and met him on the Capitol for a conference, at which they became reconciled. But then, when he was asleep that night, Antony had a weird dream in which his right hand was struck by a thunderbolt; and a few days later he heard that Caesar was plotting against him. Caesar tried to defend himself, but he could not convince Antony. Their antagonism was renewed at full strength, and both of them rushed around Italy offering enormous financial rewards to the soldiers who had by then settled in the colonies, to try to mobilize them, and each tried to steal a march on the other by being the first to win over to his side the soldiers who were still under arms.*

[17] The most influential man in Rome at the time was Cicero. He kept arousing public opinion against Antony,* until eventually he persuaded the senate to declare him an enemy of the state, to send Caesar the fasces and praetorian insignia, and to dispatch Pansa and

Hirtius, the current consuls, to drive Antony out of Italy. They engaged Antony near the town of Mutina, with Caesar there fighting alongside them, but although they defeated the enemy, they themselves were among the casualties.* Antony's flight was beset with problems, not the least of which was starvation. But it was his nature to excel in difficult situations, and he never got closer to being a good man than when fortune was against him. It is true that it is normal for people to recognize true virtue when difficulties have brought them low, but not everyone is strong enough at these times of reversal to emulate what they admire and avoid what they find distasteful; in fact, some are so weak that they give in to their characteristic flaws all the more readily at such times and cannot keep their rationality intact. On the occasion in question, however, Antony was an incredible example to his men: for all his extravagant and indulgent lifestyle, he did not hesitate to drink stagnant water and eat wild fruits and roots. We even hear that tree-bark was eaten, and that as they crossed the Alps* they resorted to animals which had never before been tasted by human beings.

[18] They were looking forward to linking up with the troops under Lepidus' command on the far side of the Alps, because Lepidus was thought to be friendly towards Antony and thanks to Antony he had derived a great deal of benefit from friendship with Caesar. However, when Antony came and set up camp near by,* he met with a distinct absence of cordiality, and so he decided to take a gamble. His hair was unkempt and ever since his defeat he had allowed his beard to grow long and thick; he put on a dark toga, approached Lepidus' encampment, and began to speak. Many of the men were moved to pity at the sight of him and were stirred by his words—so much so that Lepidus became alarmed and ordered the trumpets to be sounded in order to drown out Antony's voice. But this only made the soldiers feel all the more sorry for him, and they entered into secret talks with him, sending Laelius and Clodius to him disguised as prostitutes.* They told Antony that he could confidently attack the camp, because there were plenty of men there who would welcome him and would kill Lepidus if he wanted. But Antony told them not to lay a finger on Lepidus, and the next day he took his army and tackled the river. He himself was the first to enter the river and make his way towards the far bank, which he could see was already lined with Lepidus' men reaching out their hands to

him and dismantling the fortifications. After entering the camp and making himself master of everything, he treated Lepidus with nothing but kindness: when he greeted him he called him 'father', and although in actual fact he was in total control, he reserved for Lepidus the title and prestige of imperator. This induced Minucius Plancus, who was stationed near by with a sizeable force, to come over to his side as well. And so, having regained power, Antony crossed the Alps into Italy at the head of seventeen infantry legions and ten thousand horsemen. In addition, he left six legions to watch over Gaul under the command of Varius, surnamed Cotylon, a close friend and drinking-companion of his.

[19] Caesar had broken off his alliance with Cicero because he could see he was a partisan of freedom, and through the intermediacy of friends he invited Antony to resolve their difficulties. The three men met on a small island in the middle of a river and held talks for three days.* For the most part they found it fairly easy to reach agreement, and they divided up the whole empire among themselves as if it were an ancestral estate, but the sticking point was the question of who was to be put to death, since each of them wanted to do away with his enemies and protect his relatives. In the end their anger at those they hated led them to betray both the respect due to relatives and the loyalty due to friends: Caesar gave up Cicero to Antony, while Antony yielded to him Lucius Caesar, who was Antony's uncle on his mother's side, and Lepidus was allowed to kill his brother Paullus (though some say that Lepidus gave up Paullus to Caesar and Antony when they demanded his death). I can think of nothing more savage and cold-blooded than this exchange. In the give-and-take of bargaining one murder for another, they were as responsible for the deaths of those they gave as of those they took; but killing their friends was the worst crime, since in these cases they were not even motivated by hatred.

[20] In addition to these deals the soldiers crowded round and demanded that Caesar cement the friendship with a marriage, and so he took for his wife Clodia, the daughter of Antony's wife Fulvia. Once they had agreed to this as well, three hundred men were proscribed and put to death by them. After Cicero had been struck down, Antony gave orders that his head and his right hand were to be cut off—the hand with which he had written his speeches denouncing him. When the head and the hand were brought to him

he gazed at them in joy and broke out into delighted laughter time and again. Then, when he had had enough, he gave orders for them to be fixed over the rostra, as if he were violating the dead man and not merely displaying his own violation of good fortune and abuse of power.* His uncle, Caesar, took refuge from the men who were harrying and hunting him in his sister's house. When the assassins arrived and tried to force their way into her room, she stood in the doorway with her arms spread out and kept repeating in a loud voice: 'You shall not kill Lucius Caesar without first killing me, the mother of your imperator.' By this stratagem she managed to get her brother out of harm's way and save his life.

[21] By and large, the Romans hated the rule of the triumvirate—a feeling for which Antony was chiefly to blame, since he was older than Caesar and more powerful than Lepidus, and because as soon as he had tossed off his troubles he devoted himself once again to his old life of unrestrained hedonism. His general bad reputation was also supplemented by a considerable amount of loathing generated by the house where he chose to live. This had formerly belonged to Pompey the Great,* a man who was admired as much for the self-control, discipline, and openness of his way of life as he was for his three triumphs. So now people found it horrible to see the house closed against leaders, commanders, and official delegates, who were rudely shoved away from the door, while it was packed with actors, stage magicians, and drunken flatterers, on whom Antony squandered the bulk of the money he raised by the most violent and cruel means. For not only did the triumvirs sell the property of those they murdered, as a result of bringing trumped-up charges against their relatives and wives, and not only did they impose every kind of tax they could think of, but once they found out that the Vestal Virgins occasionally acted as bankers for both foreigners and Roman citizens, they charged in and appropriated all these deposits. Since Antony was insatiable, Caesar made sure that the money was shared between them. They also divided up the army for the campaigns the two of them were to fight against Brutus and Cassius in Macedonia, while Lepidus was left in charge of Rome.

[22] So they sailed across, launched their campaign, and took up positions near the enemy, with Antony's forces arrayed opposite Cassius and Caesar's opposite Brutus.* However, Caesar's achievements amounted to little, and it was Antony who achieved all the

victories and successes. In the first battle, at any rate, Caesar was soundly defeated by Brutus: he lost his camp and only just managed to slip out of the grasp of the troops who were pursuing him, although he wrote in his memoirs that he withdrew before the battle in response to a dream one of his friends had dreamt. Antony defeated Cassius—though some writers claim that Antony did not take part in the battle, but arrived afterwards, when his men were already in pursuit. At his own request and orders Cassius was killed by one of his faithful freedmen, Pindar, because he was unaware that Brutus had been victorious. A few days later battle was joined again, and Brutus was defeated and committed suicide. Credit for the victory went largely to Antony, because Caesar was ill at the time. Antony stood over Brutus' corpse and briefly remonstrated with him for the death of his brother Gaius, whom Brutus had killed in Macedonia in retaliation for Cicero's death. To his mind Hortensius was more to blame for his brother's murder than Brutus was, so he gave orders that Hortensius was to be killed over Gaius' tomb, while he draped his extremely valuable purple cloak over Brutus' body and told one of his own freedmen to see to the burial. Later, when he found out that this man had not cremated the cloak along with the body and had stolen a lot of the money which was supposed to be spent on the burial, he had him put to death.

[23] Caesar was so ill that he was not expected to live long, and he now returned to Rome. Antony left Macedonia at the head of a large force and crossed over into Greece in order to raise money from all the eastern provinces.* The triumvirs had promised every soldier five thousand drachmas, and so they needed to tighten up the collection of tribute and their ways of raising funds. At first Antony behaved with exemplary civility towards the Greeks: he diverted the less serious side of his character by listening to discussions, attending athletic competitions, and being initiated into religious mysteries, and his decisions were fair. He enjoyed being described as a lover of Greece, though not as much as he enjoyed being called a lover of Athens, and he showered the city with gifts. When the Megarians wanted to show him that they too had fine things to rival Athens, they insisted on his seeing their council-house. After he had climbed up the hill and seen it, they asked him what he thought of it. 'Small and rotten,' he said. He also took the measurements of the temple of

Pythian Apollo, since he intended to complete it; in fact, in a speech to the senate he undertook to do so.*

[24] Leaving Lucius Censorinus in charge of Greece, Antony crossed over to Asia and took possession of the wealth there. Kings beat a path to his door, while their wives, rivals in generosity and beauty, let themselves be seduced by him. While Caesar in Rome was exhausting himself with feuds and fighting, Antony was enjoying abundant leisure and peace—so much so that he reverted to his usual way of life. Anaxenor and other players of the lyre, pipe-players like Xuthus, a certain dancer named Metrodorus, and a motley band of similar Asiatic players whose lascivious vulgarity surpassed the pests he had brought from Italy, flooded into his residence and made themselves at home, until the altogether intolerable situation was reached where these activities were all he was interested in. The whole of Asia, like Sophocles' famous city, was filled 'both with the smoke of incense, and with hymns of joy and loud laments'.* At any rate, on his entry into Ephesus he was preceded by women arrayed as Bacchants, and men and boys as Satyrs and Pans, and the city was filled with ivy, thyrsi, harps, reed-pipes, and wind-pipes, all hailing him as Dionysus the gracious benefactor. And this is certainly what he was like in a few cases, though generally he was Dionysus the cruel, the devourer.* He used to confiscate property from well-born people and give it as a favour to thugs and flatterers. People often pretended that someone was dead when he was not, asked for his property, and were given it. He gave the estate of a man from Magnesia to a cook who had earned his esteem, we are told, for a single meal. Eventually, when he was imposing a second round of tribute on the cities of Asia, Hybreas summoned up the courage to speak out for all Asia. His rhetorical style was low, and appealed to Antony's taste. 'If you can take tribute twice in a single year,' Hybreas said, 'can you also create two summers for us and two harvests?' Then, in a bold and effective conclusion, because Asia had provided Antony with 200,000 talents, he said, 'If you haven't received this money, you should demand it from those who took it; but if you did get it and you no longer have it, we're in a lot of trouble.'*

These words of his affected Antony deeply because he was unaware of most of what went on, not so much because he was lazy as because he was so straightforward that he trusted the people around him. There was a side to him that was naïve and slow off the mark, although when he did come to realize his mistakes his remorse was profound and he would make a full confession to those he had wronged by his thoughtlessness. He never did things by halves in making compensation or in taking revenge, but he had the reputation of being more likely to go too far when doing a favour than when meting out punishment. Also, his disrespectful jokes and jibes did have the redeeming feature that one could return the jibe with equal disrespect: he enjoyed being laughed at just as much as he enjoyed laughing at others. But this trait of his was invariably his undoing, because he was incapable of imagining that people who were so candid when making a joke were really concerned to flatter him, and so he was easily caught by their compliments. He had no idea that there are people who, so to speak, temper the cloying taste of their flattery with the sharp seasoning of candour; these people use the outspoken remarks they pass over their cups as a means of making their pliancy and submissiveness in affairs of state suggest not sycophancy, but rational submission to superior wisdom.

[25] For a man such as Antony, then, there could be nothing worse than the onset of his love for Cleopatra.* It awoke a number of feelings that had previously been lying quietly buried within him, stirred them up into a frenzy, and obliterated and destroyed the last vestiges of goodness, the final redeeming features that were still holding out in his nature. This is how he was caught. While he was preparing to make war on Parthia,* he wrote to Cleopatra, ordering her to come to meet him in Cilicia, to answer the charge of having helped Cassius with substantial contributions towards his war effort. However, as soon as Dellius,* Antony's messenger, saw what she looked like and observed her eloquence and argumentative cunning, he realized that the idea of harming a woman like her would never occur to Antony, and that she would come to occupy a very important place in his life. He therefore set about ingratiating himself with the Egyptian and encouraging her to come to Cilicia 'dressed up in all her finery', to borrow Homer's words;* and he allayed her worries about Antony, describing him as the most agreeable and kind leader in the world. Since she believed Dellius and also drew on the evidence of her past love-affairs in her youth with Caesar and with Gnaeus the son of Pompey, she readily expected to vanquish Antony.* After all, Caesar and Gnaeus Pompey had known her when she was no more than an unworldly girl, but she would be going to

Antony at the age when the beauty of a woman is at its most dazzling and her intellectual powers are at their height. So she equipped herself with plenty of gifts and money, and the kind of splendid paraphernalia one would expect someone in her exalted position, from a prosperous kingdom, to take. Above all, however, she went there relying on herself and on the magical arts and charms of her person.

[26] Although she received a number of letters from both Antony and his friends demanding her presence, she treated him with such disdain and scorn that she sailed up the river Cydnus on a golden-prowed barge, with sails of purple outspread and rowers pulling on silver oars to the sound of a reed-pipe blended with wind-pipes and lyres. She herself reclined beneath a gold-embroidered canopy, adorned like a painting of Aphrodite, flanked by slave-boys, each made to resemble Eros, who cooled her with their fans. Likewise her most beautiful female slaves, dressed as Nereids and Graces, were stationed at the rudders and the ropes. The wonderful smell of numerous burning spices filled the banks of the river.* Some people formed an escort for her on either side all the way from the river, while others came down from the city to see the spectacle. The crowd filling the city square trickled away, until at last Antony himself was left alone, seated on a dais. The notion spread throughout the city that Aphrodite had come in revelry to Dionysus, for the good of Asia.

Antony sent her an invitation to dinner, but she thought it preferable that he should come to her. Without a moment's hesitation he agreed, because he wanted to show her that he was a good-natured, friendly sort of person. On his arrival he found preparations that beggared description, but he was especially struck by the amazing number of lights. There are said to have been so many lights hanging on display all over the place, and ordered and disposed at such angles to one another and in such arrangements—some forming squares, others circles—that the sight was one of rare and remarkable beauty.

[27] The next day it was his turn to entertain her with a banquet. He desperately wanted to outdo the brilliance and thoroughness of her preparations, but it was in precisely these two respects that he failed and was defeated by her. However, he was the first to make fun of the unappetizing meagreness of what he had to offer. Cleopatra could see from Antony's jokes that there was a wide streak of the

coarse soldier in him, so she adopted this same manner towards him, and now in an unrestrained and brazen fashion. For, according to my sources, in itself her beauty was not absolutely without parallel, not the kind to astonish those who saw her; but her presence exerted an inevitable fascination, and her physical attractions, combined with the persuasive charm of her conversation and the aura she somehow projected around herself in company, did have a certain ability to stimulate others. The sound of her voice was also charming and she had a facility with languages that enabled her to turn her tongue, like a many-stringed instrument, to any language she wanted, with the result that it was extremely rare for her to need a translator in her meetings with foreigners; in most cases she could answer their questions herself, whether they were Ethiopians, Trogodytae, Hebrews, Arabs, Syrians, Medes, or Parthians.* In fact, she was said to have mastered a lot of other languages too, whereas the kings of Egypt before her had not even bothered to learn Egyptian, and some of them even abandoned their Macedonian dialect.

[28] She abducted Antony so successfully that while his wife Fulvia was fighting Caesar in Rome in defence of his affairs,* and while there was a Parthian army hovering near Mesopotamia, with Labienus newly appointed by the Parthian king's generals as commander-in-chief for the planned invasion of Syria,* he was carried off by her to Alexandria where he indulged in the pastimes and pleasures of a young man of leisure, and spent and squandered on luxuries that commodity which Antiphon called the most costly in the world—namely, time. They formed a kind of club called the Society of Inimitable Livers, and every day one of them had to entertain the rest. They spent incredible, disproportionate amounts of money. At any rate, Philotas of Amphissa, the doctor, used to tell my grandfather Lamprias that he was in Alexandria at the time, learning his professional skills, and that he became friendly with one of the royal cooks. Philotas, who was a young man then, was persuaded by his friend the cook to come and see the extravagance involved in the preparations for a feast. So he was surreptitiously brought into the kitchen and when he saw all the food, including eight wild boars roasting on spits, he expressed his surprise at the number of guests who were going to be entertained. The cook laughed and said that there were not going to be many for dinner, only about twelve, but that every dish which was served had to be perfect and it only took a

moment for something to be spoiled. He explained that Antony might call for food immediately and then a short while later might perhaps change tack and ask for a cup of wine, or get interrupted by a discussion. And so, he said, they prepared many meals, not just one, since they could never guess when the exact moment was going to be.

This was the story Philotas used to tell. Some years later, he said, he used to attend Antony's eldest son, whose mother was Fulvia, and often used to join him and his friends for dinner, when the young man was not eating with his father. On one occasion, a certain doctor was becoming rather outspoken and was putting the other guests off their meal, until Philotas shut him up with the following sophism: 'Anyone with a slight fever needs the application of cold; but anyone who has a fever has at least a slight fever; it follows that anyone with a fever needs the application of cold.' The man was so taken aback that he stopped talking, but their young host was delighted. He laughed and said, pointing to a table covered with numerous large goblets, 'Philotas, I'd like you to have all of these.' Philotas acknowledged his goodwill,† but was not at all sure that a mere boy like him had the right to give such a valuable gift; a short while later, however, one of the slaves brought him the goblets sewn into a bag and asked him to put his seal on it. When Philotas refused and expressed a reluctance to take them, the man said, 'Don't be so stupid. There's no need to worry. Don't you realize that this is a present from the son of Antony and that he can give away this much gold if he likes? However, I would suggest that you let us swap you the cups for their worth in money, because it's not impossible that his father might miss some of the cups, which are antiques, valued for their craftsmanship.' These are the stories Philotas used to tell whenever the opportunity arose, according to my grandfather.*

[29] Cleopatra did not restrict her flattery to Plato's four categories,* but employed many more forms of it. She always found some fresh pleasure and delight to apply, whether he was in a serious or a frivolous mood, and so she kept up his training relentlessly, without letting up either by night or by day. She was with him when he was playing dice, drinking, and hunting; she watched him while he exercised with his weapons; at night when he stood at the doors and windows of ordinary folk and mocked the people inside, she wandered aimlessly through the streets by his side. During these

escapades she would dress as a serving-girl, because Antony used to do his best to make himself look like a slave, which would constantly earn him a volley of scorn and not infrequently blows too before he returned home, despite the fact that most people suspected who he was. However, the Alexandrians loved the way he played the fool and joined in his games, though not to a disproportionate or coarse extent. They liked him and said that he adopted the mask of tragedy for the Romans, but the mask of comedy for them.

It would be quite idiotic for me to describe most of the pranks he got up to then, but once, when he was out fishing, he got cross because he was having no luck and Cleopatra was there. So he told the fishermen to swim down and secretly attach one of the fish which had already been caught to his hook. He hauled in two or three fish like this, but the Egyptian queen knew perfectly well what was going on. She pretended to be impressed, but told her friends all about it, and invited them to come and watch the next day. So there were a lot of people on the fishing-boats, and when Antony had cast out she told one of her own slaves to swim over to his hook first and to stick on to it a preserved fish from the Euxine Sea. Antony thought he had caught something and pulled it in, to everyone's great amusement, of course. 'Imperator,' she said, 'hand your rod over to the kings of Pharos and Canobius. It is your job to hunt cities, kingdoms, and continents.'

[30] While Antony was occupied with this kind of childish nonsense, two messages reached him. The first, from Rome, told how his brother Lucius and his wife Fulvia had first fallen out with each other, but had then made war unsuccessfully on Caesar and fled into exile from Italy.* The other message was just as bleak: it told how Labienus and his army of Parthians were conquering all Asia from the Euphrates and Syria up to Lydia and Ionia.* Like a man struggling to wake up on the morning after a drunken night, Antony set out to resist the Parthians and had reached Phoenicia when he received a thoroughly miserable letter from Fulvia, as a result of which he headed for Italy with a fleet of two hundred ships. During the course of the voyage, however, he picked up some exiled friends and learnt that the war had been Fulvia's fault: not only was she a headstrong woman who liked to dabble in politics, but she hoped to draw Antony away from Cleopatra by stirring up trouble in Italy. Coincidentally, however, Fulvia fell ill and died in Sicyon while she

was on her way to him by sea, which created an even better opportunity for reconciliation with Caesar. When he reached Italy, and Caesar made it plain that he did not blame him for anything, while at the same time Antony himself was inclined to hold Fulvia responsible for the crimes with which he was charged, their friends refused to let them look too closely at the whys and wherefores. They arranged a truce between the two of them and divided up the areas of command, with the Ionian Sea forming a boundary such that everything to the east went to Antony and everything to the west to Caesar, while they let Lepidus have Africa and organized matters so that when neither Antony nor Caesar wanted to be consul, the post should go to their friends one by one.*

[31] While this all seemed fine, it needed firmer assurances, and fortune provided them in the person of Octavia, who was Caesar's elder sister, although they did not have the same mother, since hers was Ancharia, while his was Atia.* Caesar was very fond of his sister, who was, we are told, a marvel of womankind. Her husband, Gaius Marcellus, had recently died, so she was a widow; and Antony was generally held to be a widower, now that Fulvia had passed away, since although he made no attempt to deny that he had Cleopatra, he refused to call her his wife. To this extent his rational mind was still resisting his love for the Egyptian. Everyone wanted to see this marriage take place, since they hoped that once Octavia was united with Antony and had won the place in his affections one would expect of a woman like her, with all her dignity and intelligence, as well as her great beauty, she would prove to be the saviour and moderator of all Rome's affairs. So when both men had agreed on this course of action, they went up to Rome and married Octavia to Antony, even though by Roman law a woman was not allowed to remarry within ten months of her husband's death. But in their case the senate passed a decree waiving the time limit.

[32] Now, thanks to Sextus Pompey, who was the master of Sicily and used to raid Italy with his large fleet of pirate vessels under the command of Menas the Pirate and Menecrates, the sea was unsafe for shipping.* But Pompey was generally held to have shown himself to be well disposed towards Antony by taking his mother in when she was banished from Rome with Fulvia, and so they decided to come to terms with him too. The meeting took place on the pier at Cape Misenum,* with Pompey's fleet lying at anchor near by, and Antony's

and Caesar's troops drawn up close at hand. Under their agreement Pompey was to retain Sardinia and Sicily, keep the sea free of pirates, and send a stipulated quantity of grain to Rome. Once this was settled, they invited one another to dinner and after drawing lots it was Pompey's turn to entertain the others first. When Antony asked him where they would have the meal, Pompey pointed to his massive flagship and said, 'There, because that's the only family home Pompey has left'—which was his way of rebuking Antony for occupying the house which had belonged to his father. He stabilized the ship on its anchors, made a kind of gangplank for people to cross from the cape, and welcomed them on board. At the height of the party, when the jokes about Antony and Cleopatra were flying thick and fast, Menas the Pirate came up to Pompey and whispered in an undertone, 'Shall I cut the ship's cables and make you master of Rome, not just Sicily and Sardinia?' Pompey thought in silence for a little while about what he had said and then replied, 'Menas, you should have done it without telling me about it first. For now, let's be content with things as they are. It's not my way to break a promise.' And so, after he had been entertained in his turn by Antony and Caesar, he sailed back to Sicily.

[33] After this settlement Antony sent Ventidius on ahead to Asia, to block the Parthians' advance,* while as a favour to Caesar he let himself be appointed to the priesthood which the elder Caesar had earlier held. In general, they co-operated and behaved civilly towards each other where matters of government and other particularly important issues were concerned. However, Antony was upset by the fact that whenever he and Caesar clashed in some recreational pursuit he always came off worst. Now, among his entourage was a certain diviner from Egypt, who drew up natal horoscopes. Perhaps as a favour to Cleopatra, or perhaps because he wanted to tell the truth, he spoke out bluntly to Antony and told him that for all the great brilliance and importance of his fortune he was being eclipsed by Caesar, and he advised him to put as much distance as possible between himself and the young man. 'Your guardian spirit is afraid of his,' he explained, 'and although it prances with head held high when it is by itself, at the approach of his it is cowed and humbled.' And in fact events did seem to confirm what the Egyptian had said. For instance, it is said that whenever for fun they drew lots or threw dice in any situation, whatever it might be at the time, Antony came

off worst. And again, they often used to pit cocks or fighting quails against one another, and Caesar's would always win.

All this irritated Antony, though he did not show it, and since he was increasingly inclined to listen to the Egyptian, he entrusted his private affairs to Caesar and left Italy. His first stop was Greece, and Octavia, who had given birth to a baby daughter, went there with him. While he was spending the winter in Athens he received news of the first of Ventidius' successes: the report said that Ventidius had won a battle against the Parthians and had killed Labienus and Phranipates, who was the best of King Orodes' military commanders. To mark this victory Antony put on a public feast for the Greeks and acted as gymnasiarch at Athens. Leaving at home the insignia of his military command, he would appear in public wearing a Greek tunic and white shoes, and carrying the gymnasiarch's rods, and would grab the attention of the young men and turn their heads.*

[34] Just before setting out for the war, he took a garland from the sacred olive-tree, and in obedience to a certain oracle filled a jar with water from the Clepsydra* and took it with him. Meanwhile Ventidius was faced with a fresh invasion of Syria by a huge Parthian army under the king's son, Pacorus. When the two sides met in Cyrrhestica, the Parthians were overwhelmed and lost very many men, including, most importantly, Pacorus himself. This was one of the most celebrated achievements in Roman history; the Romans now felt fully repaid for the disasters under Crassus, and the Parthians were confined once more within Media and Mesopotamia, since they had now been soundly defeated in three successive battles.* Ventidius was worried about incurring Antony's jealousy, so he chose not to pursue the Parthians any further and turned instead against those who had rebelled against Rome. He defeated them and also besieged Antiochus of Commagene in the city of Samosata.* When Antiochus asked permission to pay a thousand talents and to make whatever restitution Antony required, Ventidius told him to send a message to that effect to Antony in person, who was now not far away. But Antony refused to allow Ventidius to make a treaty with Antiochus, since he wanted his name attached to at least this one victory, rather than the credit for every success going to Ventidius. However, the siege dragged on, and once the inhabitants of Samosata gave up the idea of compromise, they concentrated on defence. Antony could not achieve anything; he felt stupid and regretted his earlier

intransigence. In the end he had to be content with entering into a treaty with Antiochus by which Antiochus paid him three hundred talents. Then, after settling some minor matters in Syria he returned to Athens and sent Ventidius back to Rome, laden with fitting honours, to celebrate a triumph.

Ventidius is the only man so far to have celebrated a triumph over the Parthians.* He was a man of humble origins, but he took advantage of his friendship with Antony to seize opportunities to achieve great things. In fact, he made such good use of these opportunities that he confirmed what was commonly said about Antony and Caesar—that as military leaders they were more successful through others' efforts than they were through their own. For example, Antony's commander, Sosius, achieved a great deal in Syria, and Canidius, whom Antony left in Armenia, conquered not only the Armenians, but also the kings of the Iberians and Albanians, and advanced as far as the Caucasus.* These successes led to Antony's name and fame spreading far and wide among the peoples of the east.

[35] Antony himself, however, was furious once again with Caesar and his criticisms, so he took a fleet of three hundred ships and sailed for Italy.* The people of Brundisium refused to let his fleet in, so he sailed round the coast and anchored at Tarentum. Here, at her own request, he sent Octavia, who had accompanied him on his voyage from Greece, to her brother. She was pregnant, and had already borne him a second baby daughter.* She met Caesar on the road, and once she had enlisted the support of his friends Agrippa and Maecenas, she spoke with him at length, begging and beseeching him not to connive at her downfall from a state of perfect happiness to one of complete misery. As things were, she said, she was an object of universal admiration, since of the two commanders-in-chief she was the wife of one and the sister of the other. 'But if matters degenerate,' she went on, 'and war breaks out, there is no telling which of you is destined to win and which to lose, but in either case my situation becomes wretched.' Caesar was moved to pity by her appeal and he went to Tarentum with no hostile intentions.* Witnesses saw the wonderful spectacle of a sizeable army lying idle on land and a substantial fleet resting quietly off shore, while the commanders and their associates met on good terms. Antony gave the first dinner, and Caesar let him do so for his sister's sake. They agreed that Caesar

should give Antony two legions for the Parthian War, and that Antony should give Caesar a hundred bronze-rammed warships; but then Octavia made her own separate deal, whereby she requested twenty light ships from her husband for her brother, and a thousand soldiers from her brother for her husband. As soon as they had separated on these terms, Caesar, who wanted to take Sicily, launched his campaign against Pompey, and Antony entrusted Octavia and his children by both her and Fulvia to Caesar's care, and then sailed across to Asia.*

[36] But the awful calamity which had been dormant for a long time, his love for Cleopatra, which seemed to have been lulled and charmed to sleep by better notions, flared up again and regained its confidence the nearer he got to Syria. Eventually, in the manner of the disobedient, intemperate member of the mind's chariot team in Plato's book,* he kicked out of his way everything admirable, everything that might have saved him, and sent Fonteius Capito to bring Cleopatra to Syria. When she arrived he presented her, as a favour, with no slight or trivial addition to her possessions: he gave her Phoenicia, Coele Syria, Cyprus, a great deal of Cilicia, and also the part of the land of the Jews which produces balsam, and that part of the Arabia of the Nabataeans which slopes down towards the outer sea.* These gifts infuriated the Romans, despite the fact that he often used to present even private citizens with tetrarchies and important kingdoms, and that it was far from being the first time that he had deprived someone of his kingdom either. For instance, there was Antigonus of Judaea, whom he had publicly beheaded, even though no other king before him had ever been punished in this way. But what was particularly infuriating about the honours he conferred on Cleopatra was the shame of it all. And he only made things worse by recognizing the twin children she had borne him, whom he called Alexander and Cleopatra, surnamed respectively Sun and Moon. But he was good at glossing over disgraces, and so he used to say that the greatness of the Roman empire showed not in what they took, but in what they gave, and that the more royal blood contributed towards the next generation of a family's children, the more that family enhanced its nobility. At any rate, he used to say that his own ancestor was fathered by Heracles, a man who did not rely on just a single womb for the continuation of his line, and was not cowed by laws like Solon's which tried to regulate conception,* but followed his

natural inclinations and left behind him the origins and foundations of many families.

[37] After Phraates had killed his father, Orodes, and taken over the kingdom,* quite a few Parthians fled the country, including Monaeses, a prominent and influential Parthian, who sought refuge with Antony. Antony was struck by the similarity between Monaeses' misfortunes and those of Themistocles, compared his own prosperity and liberality with those of the Persian kings, and gave Monaeses three cities—Larissa, Arethusa, and Hierapolis, which had once been called Bambyce.* But when the Parthian king made friendly overtures towards Monaeses, Antony was happy to let him go back. His plan was to trick Phraates into thinking there would be peace, and at the same time he demanded the return of the standards which had been captured under Crassus and of any surviving Roman prisoners from the time. Then he sent Cleopatra back to Egypt, before making his way through Arabia and Armenia to the place where his army was to join up with the forces of the allied kings. There were a great many such kings, but the most important of all was Artavasdes of Armenia, who supplied 6,000 horsemen and 7,000 foot soldiers. Antony conducted a review of the army: there were 60,000 Roman foot soldiers and 10,000 Spanish and Gallic horsemen, who were under Roman command; and other tribes and peoples provided 30,000 men, all told, counting both cavalry and infantry. According to our sources, however, this enormous army and all these resources, which terrified even the Indians living beyond Bactria and made the whole of Asia tremble with fear, turned out to do him no good at all, thanks to Cleopatra. He was in such a hurry to spend the winter with her that he launched his attack prematurely and conducted the whole affair in a haphazard fashion. He was not in his right mind, but was constantly gazing in her direction as if he had been drugged or bewitched, and he was more concerned with returning quickly than with defeating the enemy.*

[38] In the first place, then, what he should have done is spend the winter in Armenia, rest his men, who were exhausted after a march of eight thousand stades, and then occupy Media at the beginning of spring, before the Parthians stirred from their winter quarters; but he could not wait and so he set out straight away, leaving Armenia on his left and skirting the territory of Atropatene, which he plundered. In the second place, although there were included in his train, on

three hundred wagons, all the devices required for a siege, including a battering-ram eighty feet long, and although none of these siege-engines could be replaced in time if destroyed, because in the interior no wood grew of sufficient length or hardness, he was in such a hurry that he left them behind, arguing that they were slowing him down. He did leave men to guard the engines, under the command of Statianus, but then he laid siege to Phraata, a large city which held the children and wives of the Median king.* The extent of the mistake he had made in abandoning the siege-engines was immediately exposed by his need for them there; instead he had to come right up close to the city and set about building a mound, which took a long time and a lot of effort. Meanwhile, Phraates came down at the head of a large army, and when he heard that the wagons transporting the siege-engines had been abandoned, he sent a sizeable body of horsemen to attack them. Statianus and his troops were surrounded by these horsemen and ten thousand of them were cut down, including Statianus himself. Once the easterners had possession of the siege-engines, they destroyed them. They also took large numbers of prisoners, among whom was King Polemo.*

[39] Of course, this unexpected blow right at the beginning disheartened all Antony's men, and the Armenian, Artavasdes, gave up on the Roman cause and left, taking his forces with him, even though he was chiefly responsible for the war in the first place.* When the Parthians appeared, flushed with their success and calling out threats and taunts, Antony wanted to avoid perpetuating and increasing the dejection and consternation of his men by leaving them inactive in the face of this, so he took ten legions and three praetorian cohorts of legionaries, and all his cavalry, and led them out in a foraging expedition, the idea being that this would be the best way to draw the enemy into a pitched battle. One day's journey out of the camp, he saw that the Parthians were swarming around him, trying to find a way to attack him on the march. He displayed to his men the signal for attack, but broke camp as if he were intending to withdraw rather than fight, and then marched past the crescent-shaped array of the eastern troops. His orders were that as soon as the front line of the enemy seemed close enough for the heavy infantry to attack, the cavalry should charge at them. The Parthians, drawn up there in battle array, were dumbfounded by the Romans' discipline; they just watched them marching past, keeping the intervals between ranks

and files regular, in perfect control and silence, with their spears at the ready. When the signal was given and the cavalry wheeled and bore down on them yelling and screaming, the Parthians managed to absorb the attack and beat it off, despite the fact that the Romans were too close for them to be able to use their bows and arrows; but when the Roman legionaries engaged them, shouting and clashing their weapons, the Parthians' horses panicked and fell back, and the Parthians themselves turned tail and fled before hand-to-hand combat was joined.

Antony pursued them hard because he had high hopes of ending the whole war, more or less, with that one battle. But after the infantry had given chase for fifty stades, and the cavalry for three times the distance, they counted the enemy dead or captured and found only thirty prisoners and eighty corpses, which made everyone both puzzled and depressed.* On reflection it seemed a grim prospect if in victory they should kill so few of the enemy, but in defeat they should lose as many as they did in the battle over the transport wagons. The next day they packed up and set off for their camp at Phraata, but on the way they met at first a few of the enemy, and then more and more, until eventually they were faced with the whole army which challenged and harassed them from all sides, as if they were a fresh body of men who had never known defeat. It was only with considerable difficulty and effort that they got back safe to the camp. Then the Medes made a sortie from the city against the Romans' mound, and panicked the men defending it into flight. Antony was furious and employed the punishment known as 'decimation' on those who had lost their nerve. What he did was divide the whole lot of them into groups of ten, and then he killed one from each group, who was chosen by lot; the rest, on his orders were given barley rations instead of wheat.*

[40] Both sides were finding the war hard and had reason to fear its next phase. Antony anticipated a famine because it was no longer possible for him to gain provisions without taking considerable losses and casualties;† Phraates knew that the last thing the Parthians were capable of doing was enduring winter outdoors, and he was afraid that if the Romans stuck it out where they were his troops might desert, since the autumn equinox had passed and the air was already beginning to grow heavy. He therefore devised the following cunning scheme. His most notable troops decreased the effort they put into

attacking the Romans when they were out foraging or whenever else they clashed; they allowed them to get hold of some supplies, expressed admiration of their bravery, and said that they were superb fighters and that it was no wonder that their king, Phraates, was impressed by them. Next they began to ride up closer to the Romans and even bring their horses quietly up on a parallel course, and criticized Antony for refusing to allow Phraates the opportunity, which he was eager to take, to make a truce and spare men like them; instead, they said, he just sat there waiting for the assault of those cruel and formidable enemies, famine and winter, who would make it difficult for them to escape with their lives even with the Parthians escorting them on their way. A number of the Romans reported this news to Antony, and although his hopes inclined him to yield to the temptation, he did not send any heralds to Phraates until he had asked these friendly-seeming Parthians whether what they were saying reflected the king's thinking. They assured him that it did and told him he need have no worries or doubts. He sent some of his companions to the king to renew his demand for the return of the standards and the prisoners, because he did not want it thought of him that his sole concern was to get away safe and sound, but when in response the Parthian told him to forget about that, and promised him a safe passage and a cessation of hostilities as soon as he began to leave, he packed up and broke camp in just a few days. But although he was a persuasive public speaker and although no one in those days could rival his ability to move an army by words, in his shame and dejection he chose to forgo boosting the morale of his troops and gave the job to Domitius Ahenobarbus.* While some of his men took this as a sign of his contempt for them and were annoyed, the majority understood the reason and were deeply moved, and so felt all the more inclined to repay his respect for them by respecting his sense of shame and obeying him as their commander.

[41] So Antony was poised to retrace his route. Now, the road led through land which was flat and treeless, and a certain Mardian who was an expert on Parthian practices, and had proved his loyalty to the Romans during the battle over the siege-engines, approached Antony and recommended keeping the mountains close on his right as he retreated, and not exposing an army of heavy-armed men, laden down with baggage, to such a large force of cavalry and archers in bare and open territory. He told him that this was exactly what

Phraates had planned when he beguiled him with a friendly deal to raise the siege, and said that he would show him a short cut which was more plentifully supplied with provisions. On hearing what the man said, Antony paused for thought. Now that he had made a truce with the Parthians, he was reluctant to give them the impression that he did not trust them, but on the other hand he liked the idea of a short cut which would take them past inhabited villages. He asked the Mardian for some assurance of his good faith, and the Mardian offered to let himself be tied up as a prisoner until he had brought the army to Armenia. Bound with chains, then, he proceeded to guide the army, and for two days nothing happened. On the third day, however, by which time Antony had completely forgotten about the Parthians and was marching along in a relaxed and confident mood, the Mardian noticed that a dam blocking a river had recently been demolished and that the water was flooding the road they had to march along. He realized that this was the Parthians' doing, and that they were using the river as an obstacle to make life difficult for them and slow them down, and he warned Antony to watch out and be careful, since the enemy were near by. And just as Antony was deploying his legionaries in line of battle, leaving gaps in their formation for the javelineers and slingers to make their forays against the enemy, the Parthians appeared and rode all around the Romans in an attempt to surround them, and so to confuse them by attacking on all sides at once. The light-armed troops charged out against the Parthians and gave with their slingshot and javelins as good as they got from the enemy's arrows, until they forced them back. But then the Parthians kept returning to the attack, until the Gauls charged with their horses in a tight formation and scattered the Parthians, who were too frightened to renew the battle that day.

[42] Antony learnt his lesson well. He strengthened both his rear and his flanks with large numbers of javelineers and slingers, and had his men adopt a square formation as they continued on their way. He also told his cavalry that after they had repulsed an attack they were not to pursue the enemy for any distance. The outcome of these new tactics was that for four successive days the Parthians suffered at least as many casualties as they inflicted. This took the edge off their enthusiasm, and they began to make winter an excuse for thoughts of leaving.

On the fifth day Flavius Gallus, a skilled and effective officer,* approached Antony and asked for the command of a fair number of light-armed troops from the rear and some horsemen from the van, with whom he intended to achieve a major victory. Antony gave him the men he asked for, and when the Parthians attacked, Gallus beat them back, but instead of employing the normal tactics of withdrawing and enticing them on to the Roman heavy infantry, he took the more risky option of standing his ground and engaging the enemy. The officers in command of the rear saw that he was being cut off and got a message to him calling him back, but he refused to listen. They say that the quaestor, Titius, grabbed hold of the standards and tried to turn them back, while raging against Gallus for causing the deaths of so many brave men. Gallus, however, merely raged back at him and ordered his men to stand firm—while Titius retreated to the Roman lines. As Gallus pushed his way into the Parthians facing him, he failed to notice that large numbers of the enemy were coming round to take him in the rear. With missiles raining down on him from all sides he sent a courier asking for reinforcements. At this point Canidius—a man who wielded a great deal of influence with Antony—and the other officers in charge of the heavy infantry are generally held to have made a serious mistake. Instead of directing the entire body of the heavy infantry *en masse* against the enemy, as they should, they sent only a few men at a time to help Gallus. As one lot were defeated they kept dispatching others until they gradually came close, without even noticing it, to spreading defeat and retreat throughout the whole army. This would have happened if Antony had not personally brought his troops up at the double from the van to confront the fugitives, and if the third legion had not rapidly forced its way through them and stopped the enemy chasing them any further.

[43] At least three thousand men lost their lives, and five thousand more were carried back wounded to their tents. Among the injured was Gallus, who had four arrows sticking into the front of his body. Gallus did not recover from his wounds, but Antony visited the survivors in their tents and tried to cheer them up. He was in tears, deeply moved, and the wounded men grasped his hand, with radiant smiles on their faces, and urged him not to worry about them, but to leave and take care of himself; they addressed him as imperator and said that they were safe as long as he was well. To put it briefly, no other commander of the day seems to have assembled an army which

was more remarkable for its strength, resilience or energy. Their respect for him as their leader, their loyal obedience, the fact that all of them equally, however famous or insignificant they were, and whether they were officers or rank-and-file soldiers, would have sacrificed their lives and safety to win acclaim or rewards from Antony—all this left even the ancient Romans behind. There were a number of reasons for this, as I have already said: his high birth, his eloquence, his straightforward manner, his prodigious generosity, his sense of humour, and his geniality. On the occasion in question, by sympathizing with the pain and distress of the suffering and by giving them whatever they asked for, he made the sick and wounded more wholeheartedly committed to the enterprise than their fit comrades.

[44] However, the victory raised the morale of the enemy so much, cancelling out their earlier reluctance and exhaustion, and made them feel such contempt for the Romans, that they even pitched their tents for the night close to the Romans' camp, since they fully expected at any moment to be plundering deserted tents and valuables whose owners had turned and fled. At dawn they massed in far larger numbers than before; in fact, there are said to have been at least forty thousand horsemen, since the king (who never took part in any battles himself) had sent even his regular bodyguard for what was apparently an assured and easy victory. Antony wanted to address his men and he asked for a dark cloak, to make himself appear more pitiful, but his friends argued him out of it. So he stepped forward in his commander's purple cloak and made a speech in which he praised those of his men who the day before had been victorious and condemned those who had fled the field of battle. The first group then told him not to worry, while the others apologized and said that they would submit to decimation or any other kind of punishment he cared to impose; all they wanted, they said, was for him to stop being so despondent and gloomy. In response he raised his arms and prayed to the gods that if any retribution were due as a result of his previous successes, it should fall on him alone, and that they should grant the rest of the army safety and victory.

[45] The next day they set out with more effective protection, and the Parthians were stunned by what they encountered when they attacked. They rode up under the impression that booty and plunder awaited them, not a battle, but they met with a hail of missiles and could see that the Romans were reinvigorated, refreshed, and

committed. As a result, the Parthians began once again to lose their appetite for battle. At one point the Romans were descending a steep hill with the Parthians attacking them and shooting at them as they slowly extricated themselves from danger. Then the Roman shield-bearers wheeled round and enclosed the light-armed troops within their ranks, dropped down on to one knee, and held their shields out as a defensive barrier. The men behind them held their shields over the heads of the first rank, while the third rank did the same for the second rank. The resulting shape, which is a remarkable sight, looks very like a roof, and is the surest protection against arrows, which just glance off it.* The Parthians, however, mistook the Romans' falling on to one knee as a sign of exhausted weariness, so they put down their bows, grabbed their javelins, and joined battle. But the Romans suddenly leapt to their feet with a shout and lunged forward with their spears. They killed the front ranks of the Parthians and made all the rest fall back. The same thing happened on the following days too, as the Romans made their gradual way along the road.

Famine gripped the Roman army too, since even after a fight they could supply themselves with little grain and were short on implements for grinding it into flour. Such implements had mostly been abandoned because some of the yoke-animals had died and others were being used for transporting the sick and the wounded. It is said that an Attic choenix of wheat sold for fifty drachmas, and that barley loaves cost their weight in silver.* The men turned to vegetables and roots, but they found few with which they were familiar and were forced to experiment also with some they had never tasted before. There was one particular herb they tried which induced madness and ultimately death; anyone who ate it became fixated on the single task of moving and overturning every stone, as if he were achieving something of great importance. The plain was filled with men hunched over close to the ground, digging up and removing stones. Eventually they would vomit bile and die, since they had run out of the only antidote, wine. Many men died in this way, and the Parthians kept on harassing them, until Antony—so the story goes—would often cry out loud, 'Oh, the Ten Thousand!', in awe at Xenophon's men, whose march back from Babylon to the sea had been even longer and who had won their way to safety fighting far greater numbers of enemies.*

[46] Now that the Parthians were incapable of disturbing the army

or disrupting their formation, and had often been defeated and pushed back, they once again began to make peaceful overtures to the Romans who came out after fodder for the animals or grain. Making sure the Romans could see that their bows were unstrung, they told them that they had had enough of resistance and were returning to their homes—except that a few Medes would continue to follow the Romans for a day or two, not to harass them, but to protect their more remote villages. They accompanied these words with so many expressions of goodwill and friendliness that the Romans became hopeful once more, and Antony, when he heard the news, was inclined to take to the plains, since there was rumoured to be no water on the route through the mountains. Just as he was poised to put this plan into effect, however, a man called Mithridates, a cousin of the Monaeses who had been with Antony and had received from him the gift of the three cities,* arrived at the Roman camp from the enemy. Mithridates asked for an audience with someone who could speak Parthian or Syrian, and a close friend of Antony's, Alexander of Antioch, came to see him. After introducing himself and explaining that they had Monaeses to thank for this favour he was doing them, he asked Alexander whether he could see in the distance a range of high hills. When Alexander said he could, Mithridates went on: 'The Parthians are hidden in those hills at full strength, waiting to ambush you. The great plains begin at the foot of those hills and they are expecting you to leave the mountain road and turn in that direction, since you have fallen for their trick. It is true that the mountain road involves thirst and the usual difficulties, but Antony should know that if he takes the route through the plains he will meet the same fate as Crassus.'

[47] Mithridates left after imparting this information. The report thoroughly disturbed Antony, and he called his friends together for a meeting, to which he also summoned his Mardian guide. The Mardian agreed with Mithridates, since he knew that, even if there were no enemy to deal with, they would find no proper road for their journey across the plains and would have to make their way indirectly, using awkward, convoluted routes, and he explained that the mountain road involved nothing more problematic than a single day without sources of water. So Antony chose this route and, once he had given the command that his men were to carry water with them, he led them out under cover of darkness. Most of the men

were hard put to find vessels for the water, however: some had skins they could use, but others had to fill their helmets and bring it like that. However, the Parthians received information about Antony's movements while he was still on the march, and contrary to their usual practice they set out after him in the dark. At sunrise they caught up with the tail-enders. The Romans were exhausted from having missed their sleep and having worked hard, since they had covered 240 stades during the night. They had not expected the enemy to catch up with them so quickly, so the arrival of the Parthians disheartened them. Another problem was that they now had to keep the enemy at bay while advancing, and the fighting increased their thirst. The soldiers in the front reached a river whose water was cold and clear, but brackish and poisonous.* Anyone who drank it was immediately racked by the pain of stomach cramps and an inflamed thirst. The Mardian had warned them about this river, but men still pushed aside those who were trying to stop them getting to it and drank the water. Antony went around begging them to hold on for just a little longer, since there was another river, a drinkable one, not far ahead, and he told them that after that their way lay over terrain which was too rugged for cavalry, so that the enemy would have no choice but to turn back. He also ordered those who were fighting to break off, and gave the signal for pitching camp, so that his men would at least have some shade.

[48] As soon as the Romans began to fix their tents in place, the Parthians, typically, began to pull back. Mithridates came to the camp again and when Alexander joined him he recommended letting the army rest for only a short while before moving out at the double and heading for the river; he told them that the Parthians would chase them only up to the river, but would not cross it. After repeating this information to Antony, Alexander brought back, as a gift from Antony, a great many golden cups and bowls. Mithridates hid as many of these as he could inside his clothing and then rode off. The Romans broke camp while there was still daylight and set out, and although the enemy did not harass them, the Romans needed no help in making that night the most grim and terrifying night of all for themselves. They murdered and robbed anyone who had any gold or silver and plundered the baggage-train of its valuables; they ended up attacking even Antony's own baggage-carriers, cutting up goblets and precious tableware, and distributing the pieces among

themselves. The whole army was seized by confusion and chaos, because they thought they were being routed and dispersed by an enemy onslaught. Antony even summoned one of his bodyguards, a freedman called Rhamnus, and made him swear that, on his command, he would run him through with his sword and cut off his head, to prevent his being captured alive by the enemy or recognized when dead. His friends were in tears, but the Mardian told him not to be disheartened; he knew the river was near by because there was moisture in the air blowing from that direction and the cooler air in their faces was making it easier to breathe; and he added that the time they had been on the road—night was now drawing to a close—confirmed that there was not far to go. At the same time, others brought the news that the disturbance had been caused by criminality and greed from within their own ranks. And so, in order to organize his men and put an end to their confusion and dispersal, he ordered the signal for pitching camp to be sounded.

[49] Day was already dawning and the army was beginning to calm down and regain some kind of order when Parthian arrows started to strike the tail-enders and the signal was given for the light-armed troops to go into action. The heavy-armed troops repeated the manoeuvre whereby they covered one another with their shields, and so stood their ground against the archers, who did not dare to approach them. The front ranks crept forward like this, until the river came into sight. Antony deployed the cavalry on the river bank facing the enemy and sent his disabled men across first. Before long, however, even the Romans who were still at battle had the time and leisure to drink, because when the Parthians saw the river they unstrung their bows, told the Romans that they could cross the river with impunity, and congratulated them effusively on their courage. So the Romans crossed over unmolested, rested, and then resumed their march, still keeping a wary eye out for the Parthians.

On the sixth day after their final battle with the Parthians they reached the river Araxes, which divides Media from Armenia. The river looked formidably deep and fast-flowing, and there was a rumour among the men that the enemy were lying in wait for them there and would attack them as they were crossing. But they made the crossing in safety, and when they stepped on to Armenian soil their reaction resembled that of sailors who have just sighted land from the open sea: they fell to their knees, burst into tears, and threw their arms around one another from sheer joy. However, as they advanced through prosperous land, where after all their hardship there was plenty of everything for them, they began to suffer from diarrhoea and stomach complaints.

[50] In Armenia Antony conducted a review of his troops, and found that 20,000 foot soldiers and 4,000 horsemen had died. They had not all been killed by the enemy: over half had died of illness. They had marched for twenty-seven days away from Phraata, and had defeated the Parthians eighteen times, but these victories had not been decisive or secure, because they had never pursued the enemy far enough to finish things off. This fact made it absolutely undeniable that it was Artavasdes of Armenia who had made it impossible for Antony to bring the war to a close. The sixteen thousand horsemen he had taken home with him from Media had been equipped very like the Parthians and had often fought them before.* If they had been there, the Romans could have engaged the enemy and overpowered them, the Armenians could have taken the fugitives, and then it would not have been possible for the Parthians to recover from their defeats and resume their efforts so often. So everyone was furious with the Armenian and tried to get Antony to punish him. But Antony declined to reproach him for his treachery or alter his usual friendly and respectful attitude towards him, which was sensible, because he was now low on numbers and in need of supplies. Later, however, when he invaded Armenia again, he held out all sorts of promises and proposals to Artavasdes, persuaded him to come within his reach, and then seized him and took him in chains down to Alexandria, where he celebrated a triumph.* This† was something the Romans found particularly offensive, because to please Cleopatra he gratified the Egyptians with the noble and solemn ceremonies proper to his homeland. But I have got ahead of my story.

[51] He now pressed on, despite the fact that it was deep winter and there were incessant snowstorms. Eight thousand men fell by the wayside. He himself came down to the sea, with the few men remaining to him, at a place called White Village, which was situated between Berytus and Sidon.* There he waited for Cleopatra, who took her time in arriving. He missed her terribly, and wandered around aimlessly. Before long he devoted his time to drinking himself into a stupor, although he could not recline at the table for long,

but would often leap to his feet in the middle of drinking and go to look for her. At last she sailed in, with plenty of clothing and money for his soldiers. But some say that although he got the clothing from her, the money he handed out came from his own resources, and he only pretended that it was her gift.

[52] A dispute arose between the Median king* and Phraates of Parthia, apparently over the Roman spoils, and it made the Mede suspicious of Phraates and afraid that he might try to take his kingdom from him. He therefore wrote a letter to Antony, inviting him to come and promising to support him with his own forces in a war against Parthia. Now, the only thing which had stopped Antony defeating the Parthians before was, to his mind, that he had gone there with too few horsemen and archers. He now saw this deficiency being remedied without his having to ask for it, and even in a way which made him the benefactor, and so it was in a very confident frame of mind that he began to make preparations to return inland through Armenia, meet up with the Mede at the Araxes, and then make war.

[53] Back in Rome Octavia wanted to sail to Antony, and Caesar gave her permission to go, though according to most sources this was not meant as a kindly gesture: he wanted her to provide him with a plausible excuse for declaring war if Antony treated her with disrespect and ignored her.* When she reached Athens there were letters waiting there for her from Antony, telling her to stay there and explaining that he was planning an expedition inland. Although she was angry—she was not taken in by his excuses—she wrote asking where he wanted her to send the things she had brought with her for him. She had brought a great deal of clothing for his soldiers, large numbers of yoke-animals, money, and gifts for his officers and friends. Apart from all this, she also had with her two thousand picked troops, equipped as praetorian cohorts, with magnificent armour. Niger, a friend of Antony's, was sent with this message from her, and he added his own praise of her undoubted virtues.

Cleopatra realized that Octavia was coming to take her on in hand-to-hand combat. She was afraid that the combination of Octavia's characteristic dignity with the threat of Caesar's power, as well as the pleasure of her company and her solicitous attentions to Antony, would make Octavia invincible and enable her to gain complete control over her husband. She therefore made a great pretence of passionate love for Antony. She allowed her body to waste away on a meagre diet, looked ecstatic whenever he came near, and when he went away gave just a hint of forlorn sadness. She managed things so that he often saw her weeping, but then she would quickly wipe the tears from her face and conceal them, as if she did not want Antony to notice them. She kept this up throughout the time he was planning his expedition from Syria to join the Median king. Flatterers also worked hard on her behalf. They told Antony off for being so hard-hearted and insensitive that he was destroying the woman who was utterly devoted to him and him alone. They said that although Octavia enjoyed the name of his wife, it was a political marriage, arranged by her brother; Cleopatra, however, a queen with countless subjects, was called Antony's mistress, and yet she did not reject the name or disown it, as long as she could see him and live with him. But if she were driven away, they said, she would not survive the shock. They eventually made him so soft and effeminate that he became afraid of Cleopatra wasting away, so he went back to Alexandria and told the Mede to wait until summer, even though there was a rumour that the Parthians were at one another's throats. Nevertheless, when he did go up to Media,* he won the king over to renew their friendship, and after arranging the marriage between one of the Mede's daughters, who was still a child, and one of Cleopatra's sons, he returned to the coast, with his mind now focused on the civil war.

[54] Octavia did seem to have been treated with disrespect, so when she returned from Athens Caesar told her she should live in her own house. But she refused to leave her husband's house, and she even begged Caesar in person, if it was not too late and he had not already decided on other grounds to go to war with Antony, to make nothing of her situation. After all, she said, it would be a terrible thing if the two greatest commanders in the world were said to have plunged Rome into civil war, one because he loved a woman and the other out of protectiveness. And her actions only showed how much she meant these words. She lived in Antony's house as if he were there, and cared for not only their children, but also his children by Fulvia, in an admirable and even exemplary fashion. She also welcomed any of Antony's friends who were sent to Rome on matters such as taking up some official position, and helped them succeed in getting what they wanted from Caesar. By doing all this, however,

she was hurting Antony without meaning to, because he became hated for wronging a woman of her fine quality.

He also incurred people's hatred for the provisions he made for his children in Alexandria, which seemed to be theatrical, overdone, and anti-Roman. He filled the Gymnasium with a crowd of people, had two golden thrones placed on a silver stage, one for himself and one for Cleopatra, with further thrones, of a more humble design, arranged there for his sons. Then he proclaimed Cleopatra queen of Egypt, Cyprus, Africa, and Coele Syria, with Caesarion as her joint ruler. Caesarion was generally held to be the son of the previous Caesar, who had left Cleopatra pregnant. Next, he proclaimed his sons by Cleopatra 'kings of kings', and assigned Armenia, Media, and Parthia (looking ahead to when he had gained it) to Alexander, and Phoenicia, Syria, and Cilicia to Ptolemy.* While making this announcement, he brought his sons forward for all to see; Alexander was dressed in Median clothes and wore a *tiara* and an upright *kitaris*, while Ptolemy was attired in military boots, a cavalryman's cloak, and a *kausia* supporting a diadem. That is, Ptolemy was dressed in the manner adopted by all the kings since Alexander the Great, and Alexander was fitted out like the Median and Armenian kings.* After the children had greeted their parents, Alexander was given a guard of honour consisting of Armenians, and Ptolemy was given one of Macedonians. On this occasion, and at other times when Cleopatra appeared in public before a large crowd, she appropriated a robe which was sacred to Isis, and assumed the title 'New Isis'.

[55] By disclosing all this to the senate and often denouncing Antony before the Roman people, Caesar tried to incite the masses against Antony. In response, Antony sent counter-accusations against Caesar. The most important charges he brought were, first, that after taking Sicily away from Pompey Caesar had not given him his share of the island; second, that Caesar had never returned the ships he had lent him for the war; third, that after depriving his fellow triumvir, Lepidus, of his office and his rights, Caesar hung on to the army, the territory, and the revenue which had been assigned to Lepidus; finally, and above all, that Caesar had colonized almost all Italy for his own soldiers and left nothing for Antony's men.* Caesar defended himself against these charges by saying that he had removed Lepidus from office because he was abusing his power, and

that he would share with Antony what he had taken in war just as soon as Antony shared Armenia with him. Likewise, Antony's soldiers had no claims on Italy, because they had Media and Parthia, which they had annexed for the Roman empire by their fine efforts in war under their imperator.

[56] Antony received the news of Caesar's reply while he was in Armenia, and he immediately ordered Canidius to take sixteen legions and go down to the coast, while he collected Cleopatra and went to Ephesus, where his fleet was assembling from all quarters.* There were eight hundred ships, including merchantmen; Cleopatra had supplied two hundred of them, as well as twenty thousand talents and provisions for the whole army for the duration of the war. Antony followed the advice of Domitius and some others and told Cleopatra to set sail for Egypt and wait out the war there. But she was afraid that Octavia would again arrange a reconciliation, so she won Canidius over, with the help of a large bribe, to talk to Antony about her and say that, in the first place, it was wrong to exclude from the war a woman who had contributed so much towards his war effort, and, in the second place, that he would regret lowering the morale of the Egyptians, who constituted a substantial proportion of his naval force. And besides, he was to say, he certainly could not see that Cleopatra was the intellectual inferior of any of the allied kings: she had governed a vast kingdom all on her own for many years, and she had also been with him for a long time and had learnt to manage important matters. It was fated that everything should fall into Caesar's hands,* and so these arguments prevailed.

The assembled force sailed to Samos where they relaxed and indulged themselves.* For just as every king, ruler, tetrarch, tribe, and community from the lands between Syria, Lake Maeotis, Armenia, and Illyricum had been ordered to send or bring men and *matériel* for the war, so every craftsman in the arts sacred to Dionysus had been compelled to congregate on Samos; and while, all around, almost the whole inhabited world was filled with sighs and groans, a single island resounded, day after day, with the music of pipes and lyres, as the theatres were packed and choruses competed with one another. Every city also sent an ox for a communal sacrifice, and kings entered into rivalry over the parties they held and gifts they gave. The upshot of all this was that the question began to circulate: 'If their preparations for war are treated as an occasion for such extravagant festivities, what kind of victory celebrations will they put on when they win?'

[57] Once these festivities were over, Antony gave the artists of Dionysus Priene to live in, and then sailed to Athens, where he again amused himself with diversions and theatrical performances. Now, Octavia was particularly loved by the Athenians and had been awarded a number of privileges there; this made Cleopatra jealous, and she set about winning the people over by putting on a number of extravaganzas. So the Athenians decreed privileges for her and sent a delegation to her house with a copy of the decree. The delegation included Antony, who was, after all, an Athenian citizen; he stood before her and delivered a speech on behalf of the city. Meanwhile, he sent men to Rome to throw Octavia out of his house.* She left with all Antony's children, except for the eldest of Fulvia's sons, who was with his father, and they say that she was in tears, upset by the idea that people might take her to be one of the causes of the war. The Romans felt sorry for Antony rather than her, especially those of them who had seen Cleopatra and knew that she was no more beautiful or attractive than Octavia.

[58] Caesar was deeply concerned when he heard about the speed and size of Antony's preparations; he did not want to have to fight out the war that summer, since he was nowhere near ready. Moreover, the taxes he had imposed were proving unpopular: people in general were required to give up a quarter of their income, and freedmen an eighth of their capital. They felt this was outrageous of him, and it led to turmoil throughout Italy. Antony's tardiness in starting the war is therefore held to be one of his greatest mistakes. He allowed Caesar time to get ready and let the turmoil die down, since people were angry only while the money was being exacted, but once it had been exacted and they had handed it over, they calmed down. Then again, Titius and Plancus, two ex-consuls who were on Antony's side and had spoken out very strongly against Cleopatra's staying during the campaign, were treated with such insolence by her that they fled over to Caesar and revealed to him the content of Antony's will, with which they were familiar. The will was lodged with the Vestal Virgins,* who refused to give it up when Caesar asked for it, and told him that if he really wanted it he should come and get it himself. So he did just that. First he read it through by himself, marking various discreditable sections, and then he

convened the senate and read it out to them. This did not go down well with most of the senators, who considered it weird and awful to call a man to account while he was still alive for what he wanted to happen after his death. Caesar particularly latched on to the will's provisions regarding Antony's burial. Antony had given instructions that, even if he died in Rome, his body should be ceremonially escorted through the forum and then sent to Cleopatra in Egypt. Calvisius, a companion of Caesar's,* also brought forward further charges regarding Antony's relationship with Cleopatra. He said that to please her Antony had given her the contents of the library of Pergamum, which consisted of 200,000 individual book-rolls; that at a banquet, in front of all the guests, he had got up and massaged her feet to fulfil some wager or compact; that he had let her get away with having the Ephesians greet her as their mistress, while he was right there beside her; that often, in the middle of hearing the pleas of tetrarchs and kings from his seat on a dais, he had received from her billets-doux written on tablets of onyx and crystal, and read them there and then; and that once, in the middle of a speech by Furnius, one of the most eloquent and highly regarded men in Rome, Antony saw Cleopatra being carried through the forum on a litter, and he leapt to his feet, left the court in mid-session, and accompanied Cleopatra on her way, with his hand resting on the litter.

[59] In fact, though, it was generally believed that most of the charges Calvisius brought up were false. But Antony's friends in Rome did their best to intercede with the people on his behalf, and sent one of their number, Geminius, to beg Antony not to stand by while his authority was officially removed and he was declared an enemy of Rome. Geminius sailed to Greece, but Cleopatra suspected he was acting in Octavia's interests, so at dinners he became the constant butt of jokes, and was insulted by being allocated the least prestigious couches. He put up with everything, however, and waited for a chance to have a meeting with Antony. Eventually he was told to deliver his message in the middle of a meal. He said that most of the discussions he had come for required a clear head, but that, drunk or sober, there was one thing he was sure of, and that was that all would be well if Cleopatra were sent back to Egypt. Antony lost his temper at his, and Cleopatra said, 'Geminius, you have done well to confess the truth without having it tortured out of you.' A few days later, then, Geminius fled back to Rome. He was far from being

the only one of Antony's friends who was driven away by the intolerable drunkenness and coarse humour of Cleopatra's flatterers. The same thing happened to Marcus Silanus, for instance, and to Dellius the historian. Dellius adds that he was also afraid that Cleopatra was hatching a plot against him, which Glaucus, the doctor, told him about. What happened was that Dellius got on the bad side of Cleopatra by remarking once at dinner that while they were being served sour wine, in Rome Sarmentus was drinking Falernian. Sarmentus was one of Caesar's little boyfriends, for whom the Roman word is *deliciae*.

[60] Once Caesar had got far enough with his preparations, a decree was passed declaring war on Cleopatra and depriving Antony of the authority which he had surrendered to a woman.* In his speech Caesar added that Antony was under the influence of drugs and had no authority over even himself, and that their opponents in the war would be Mardion the eunuch, Pothinus, Iras (Cleopatra's hairdresser), and Charmion, who were in charge of the most important aspects of Antony's administration.*

It is said that certain portents occurred before the war. Pisaurum, a colony established by Antony on the Adriatic, was swallowed up by chasms which opened up in the earth. Sweat oozed from a stone statue of Antony in Alba for a number of days and wiping it away did not make it stop. While he was in Patrae the Heracleum was struck by thunderbolts and burnt to the ground. The figure of Dionysus in the Gigantomachy in Athens was shaken loose by high winds and crashed down into the theatre. Now, Antony linked himself to Heracles by birth and, as I have already said, to Dionysus by his lifestyle, and was called a new Dionysus. The same storm also struck the huge statues of Eumenes and Attalus, which had been inscribed with Antony's name, and knocked them over, while leaving all the other statues safe. Cleopatra's flagship, which was called the *Antonias*, was also the object of a terrifying portent: some swallows made their nest under the stern, but others attacked them, drove them away, and killed the baby birds.*

[61] So the two sides assembled their forces for the war. Antony had at least 500 warships, quite a few of which were octaremes and decaremes,* fitted out in a splendid and ostentatious fashion, while his army consisted of 100,000 foot soldiers and 12,000 horsemen. The subject kings who fought alongside him were Bogus of Africa,

Tarcandemus of upper Cilicia, Archelaus of Cappadocia, Philadelphus of Paphlagonia, Mithridates of Commagene, and Sadalas of Thrace. These kings were actually there in person, while Polemo sent an army from Pontus, as did Malchas from Arabia and Herod of Judaea, as well as Amyntas, the king of the Lycaonians and Galatians. The king of the Medes also sent a force of auxiliaries. Caesar had 250 warships, 80,000 foot soldiers, and almost the same size cavalry contingent as the enemy. Antony's domain extended from the Euphrates and Armenia to the Ionian Sea and Illyricum, while Caesar's stretched from Illyricum to the Western Ocean and from there back down again to the Tyrrhenian and Sicilian Sea. Africa was divided: the parts opposite Italy, Gaul and Spain, all the way to the Pillars of Heracles, were under Caesar's control, while Antony held the parts from Cyrene to Ethiopia.*

[62] However, Antony was more or less entirely an appendage of Cleopatra by now—so much so that, although he had a definite advantage on land, for her sake he wanted victory to go to the fleet, despite being able to see that, in order to supplement his inadequate crews, the trierarchs were seizing and carrying off from 'long-suffering' Greece* travellers, muleteers, harvest labourers, and youths just out of childhood, and that even then the ships lacked their full complements, and were undermanned and incompetently handled. Caesar's ships, however, had not been built as showpieces for their height or mass; they were manoeuvrable, fast, and fully manned. With his fleet gathered at a perfect state of readiness in Tarentum and Brundisium, he sent a message to Antony calling on him to stop wasting time, but to come and bring his forces with him. He said that he would personally guarantee Antony's fleet unhindered access to havens and harbours, and would pull his army back a day's ride from the coast, until he had safely disembarked his troops and established a camp. Antony responded in kind to this boastful talk by challenging Caesar to single combat, despite the fact that he was an older man, and by insisting, if Caesar declined to take up this offer, that the armies should fight it out at Pharsalus, as Caesar and Pompey once had many years before.* However, Caesar made the first move, and while Antony was lying at anchor off Actium, in the place where Nicopolis now stands, he crossed the Ionian Sea and landed at a village in Epirus called Toryne, or 'stirring-spoon'. Antony was worried, because his land forces had not yet arrived, but Cleopatra made

a joke out of it and said, 'What's so terrible about Caesar sitting on the stirring-spoon?'*

[63] When the enemy sailed against him early the next day, Antony was afraid that his ships would prove easy prey because they still had no marines on board, so he armed the oarsmen and lined them up on the decks where they could be plainly seen, and then he had the ships raise their oars in the air like wings on both sides and he deployed them in a tight formation in the mouth of the strait near Actium with their prows pointing out to sea, as if they were fully manned and ready to resist any attack. Defeated by Antony's superior tactics, Caesar withdrew. Another scheme of Antony's which is generally held to have been ingenious was his depriving the enemy of fresh water by enclosing the sources within certain barricades, since the villages thereabouts had little water, and it was not of a good quality. He also treated Domitius* with generosity, contrary to Cleopatra's wishes. Domitius, despite suffering from a fever, had taken a small boat and gone over to Caesar, which upset Antony a great deal, but he still sent him all his gear, along with his friends and attendants. But no sooner had Domitius changed sides than he died, apparently at the shame of his disloyalty and treachery being exposed.

Domitius' was not the only defection: among the kings, Amyntas and Deïotarus went over to Caesar's side.* Since his fleet never enjoyed any success and was always too late to offer any real assistance, Antony had no choice but to turn his attention back to his land forces. But Canidius, the commander of the land forces, changed his mind in the light of the riskiness of their situation; he recommended sending Cleopatra home and pulling back to Thrace or Macedonia, where they could let a land battle decide the issue. Dicomes, the king of the Getae, was promising to come to their help with substantial reinforcements, and Canidius added the argument that there was no disgrace in their yielding control of the sea to Caesar now that the Sicilian War* had given him all the practice he might have needed at naval warfare, whereas it would be shocking if Antony, who was far more experienced in land battles, did not make use of the strength and preparedness of his vast force of legionaries, but squandered this great resource by dividing it up among the ships. However, Cleopatra prevailed with the view that the war should be decided at sea, although her mind was already turning to thoughts of flight, and she was deploying her forces in positions from which they could most easily extricate themselves in the event of defeat, rather than where they would contribute towards victory.

There were long walls stretching down to the docks from the camp, and Antony often made his way between these walls without a care in the world. But a slave alerted Caesar to the possibility of capturing Antony as he walked down towards the sea there, and Caesar sent men to lie in wait for him. These men came very close to fulfilling their mission, but in fact they succeeded only in abducting the man who had been walking in front of Antony, since they emerged from their hiding-place too soon. Antony himself only just managed to escape by running away.

[64] Once he had decided to fight at sea, Antony burnt all but sixty of the Egyptian ships and manned the best and largest of the Roman ships, which ranged from triremes to decaremes, with a complement of 20,000 legionaries and 2,000 archers. It was at this point, as the story goes, that an infantry officer, a scarred veteran of very many battles fought for Antony, burst into tears as Antony was passing by and said, 'Imperator, why do you despise these wounds and this sword of mine, and pin your hopes on wretched planks of wood? Leave sea battles to Egyptians and Phoenicians, but give us land: that is where we are accustomed to stand; that is where we either die or defeat the enemy.' Antony made no reply, but merely gestured with his hand and composed his features as if to tell the man not to be disheartened, and walked on by. In fact, though, he was not particularly confident himself, since he insisted on the ships' captains taking their sails on board with them, when they were intending to leave them behind. The reason he gave was that not a single one of the enemy should be allowed to make good his escape.*

[65] No fighting could take place that day, or for the next three days, because a strong wind whipped up the sea, but on the fifth day, with the weather fine and the sea calm, battle was joined.* Antony and Publicola were in command of the right wing, with Coelius on the left and Marcus Octavius and Marcus Insteius in the centre. Caesar put Agrippa in command of his left wing and reserved the right wing for himself. The land forces—that of Antony under Canidius and that of Caesar under Taurus—lined the shore in silence. Of the two commanders, Antony made the rounds of all his ships in a rowing-boat. His advice to his men was to trust in the weight of the ships and

so to stand firm and fight exactly as if they were on land, while he ordered the captains to maintain their positions when the enemy launched ramming attacks without moving, as if their ships were lying at anchor, and to guard the narrows at the mouth of the strait. As for Caesar, there is a story that he left his tent while it was still dark and was walking towards the ships when he met a man driving a donkey. He asked the man's name, and the man, who recognized Caesar, said, 'My name is Lucky and my donkey's name is Victor.' And that is why when Caesar later erected a display of ships' prows on the spot, he also set up a bronze statue of a donkey and a man.* After undertaking a general survey of his array of ships, he was taken to the right wing in a boat. He was astonished to see how still the enemy ships were keeping in the strait. It was as if they were riding at anchor, and for a long time that is what he believed they were doing, and so he kept his own ships about eight stades away from the enemy. But at midday a sea wind began to blow, and Antony's men became impatient at the delay. They were sure that ships as tall and large as theirs would be invincible, and so they started the left wing forward. Caesar was delighted to see this happen. He had his right wing back water, because he wanted to draw the enemy even further out of the bay and away from the strait, until he could surround them with his own manoeuvrable ships and then join battle with ships which were too bulky and undermanned to have much agility or speed.

[66] Even when the battle was getting to the stage of close engagement, no ramming or crushing took place. Antony's ships were too slow to generate the momentum necessary to make the impact of ramming effective, and Caesar's ships were not just wary of a head-on collision with hard and cruel bronze-armoured prows, but were also not so foolhardy as to attempt to ram the enemy ships in the side, because their beaks were easily broken off wherever they crashed into the ships, which were made of large squared-off beams joined together with iron and lashed to one another. So the fight resembled a land battle or, to use a more precise image, an assault on a walled town. For three or four of Caesar's ships would cluster around one of Antony's, while the marines wielded mantlets, spears, javelins, and flaming missiles; the troops on Antony's ships even shot at the enemy with catapults mounted on wooden towers.*

Agrippa began to extend the left wing in order to come round behind the enemy, and so Publicola was forced to respond by moving against him, but in doing so he became separated from the centre. The ships in the centre were thrown into confusion and were engaged by the enemy ships under Arruntius. Although the battle was still undecided and could have gone either way, suddenly Cleopatra's sixty ships were seen hoisting their sails for flight and breaking away through the mass of fighting ships; they had been deployed behind the large warships and caused chaos as they forced their way through. The enemy looked on in amazement as the ships took advantage of the wind to head for the Peloponnese. This was the point at which Antony showed beyond the shadow of a doubt that he was not governed by the considerations proper to a ruler or to a true man—in fact that he was not governed by his own mind at all. Someone once said as a joke that a lover's mind lives in someone else's body, and by the same token Antony was pulled away by Cleopatra as if he were grafted on to her and had to go wherever she went. As soon as he spotted her ship sailing away, he forgot everything else. In an act of treachery, he ran away from the men who were fighting and dying for him, transferred over to a quinquereme, allowing only Alexas of Syria and Scellius to board with him, and set out after the woman who had already destroyed him and would merely add to his ruin.

[67] Once she recognized him, she had a signal of acknowledgement raised on her ship, and so Antony drew up alongside and was taken on board. But he did not see her, nor was he seen by her: he went forward alone to the prow and sat in silent self-absorption, holding his head in his hands. Just then, however, Liburnian ships from Caesar's fleet were sighted in hot pursuit. Antony gave orders that the ship was to be turned around to face them prow on, and this checked all their pursuers except for Eurycles of Laconia, who bore confidently down on him, brandishing a spear from the deck of his ship as if he intended to hurl it at Antony. Standing in the prow, Antony asked, 'Who is it who pursues Antony?' 'I am Eurycles the son of Lachares,' he replied, 'and thanks to Caesar's good fortune I have the chance to avenge my father's death.' (Lachares had been beheaded by Antony after being caught up in a charge of piracy.) However, Eurycles did not ram Antony's ship, but the other of the two flagships, which spun around when he struck it with his bronze beak and fell foul of his, broadside on. So he captured this ship, and

one other, which was carrying valuable household equipment. As soon as Eurycles was out of the way, Antony resumed his position, sitting silently in the prow. He spent three days there on his own, perhaps because he was angry with Cleopatra, or perhaps because he was ashamed to face her, but then, when they landed at Taenarum, Cleopatra's ladies-in-waiting managed to get them to talk to each other, and then persuaded them to share a meal and go to bed together.

Soon quite a few of their transport ships and some of their friends who had survived the rout began to rally around them. The news they brought was that the fleet was lost, but that the land forces still held together, as far as they knew. So Antony sent messengers to Canidius with orders that he was to pull back with the army through Macedonia and into Asia as quickly as possible, while he planned to cross over to Africa from Taenarum. First, however, he selected a single transport ship, with its rich cargo of coined money and valuable royal paraphernalia in gold and silver, and presented it publicly to his friends, for them to share and use to keep themselves safe. They refused his gift with tears in their eyes, but he spoke to them in a kind and friendly tone of voice, telling them to cheer up and begging them to accept the gift. Then he sent them on their way, with a letter from him to Theophilus, his procurator in Corinth, instructing him to ensure that the men stayed safe and in hiding until they had negotiated a reconciliation with Caesar. This Theophilus was the father of Hipparchus, who had a very great deal of influence with Antony, but was the first of his freedmen to go over to Caesar's side, and later settled in Corinth.

[68] This was how things stood with Antony. At Actium the fleet held out against Caesar for a long time, and it was only after it had sustained serious damage from the high seas that arose and battered it head on that they gave up, after nine hours of fighting. At the most, about five thousand men lost their lives, but, as Caesar himself has recorded, three hundred ships were captured. Antony's flight was not common knowledge, and at first, when people found out, they found the story incredible. They could not understand how he could have gone off and left nineteen legions of undefeated infantry soldiers and twelve thousand cavalrymen too. After all, he had often experienced both good and bad fortune, and had been trained by the vicissitudes of countless battles and wars. His men missed him and

expected him suddenly to appear from somewhere, and the extent of their trust and courage is shown by the fact that even after his flight had become undeniable they held together for seven days, ignoring the messages Caesar's heralds delivered to them. But in the end, once their commander, Canidius, had sneaked away under cover of darkness and abandoned the camp,* they found that they were leaderless and had been betrayed by all their senior officers, so they surrendered to the victor.

Caesar next sailed to Athens. After coming to terms with the Greeks he distributed the grain he had left from the war among the cities, which were in a bad way because their money, slaves, and yoke-animals had been stolen. At any rate, my great-grandfather Nicarchus used to tell how he and all his fellow citizens were forced to carry a stipulated measure of wheat on their shoulders down to the sea at Anticyra, and how whips were used to keep them moving at a brisk pace. They had taken one such load, and the second was already measured out and ready for transporting, when news arrived of Antony's defeat. This saved the city, because Antony's procurators and soldiers fled straight away, and the citizens divided the grain among themselves.*

[69] Antony landed at Paraetonium in Africa and sent Cleopatra on ahead to Egypt. That left him with nothing but solitude to enjoy, and he wandered around aimlessly here and there with two friends—a Greek, the orator Aristocrates, and a Roman, Lucilius. Elsewhere I have described how at Philippi Lucilius helped Brutus escape from his pursuers by convincing them that he was Brutus and surrendering to them, and how Antony spared his life. Lucilius was so grateful to Antony for sparing him that he became a loyal and trustworthy friend, and stayed with him right up to the bitter end.*

When the man to whom he had entrusted his forces in Africa defected with them to the enemy, Antony determined to kill himself, but his friends stopped him and he went to Alexandria, where he found Cleopatra engaged in a major and extraordinary enterprise. The isthmus separating the Red Sea from the sea off Egypt, which is regarded as the border between Asia and Africa, is three hundred stades wide at its narrowest point, where the two seas squeeze it most. Cleopatra had undertaken to lift her fleet on to dry land and drag it across the isthmus at this point, with the intention of launching it in the Arabian Gulf, taking a great deal of money and a substantial army, and finding somewhere away from Egypt to settle and live, far from the dangers of slavery and war. But the first ships were burnt by the Arabs living around Petra as they were being dragged along, and Antony was still under the impression that his army at Actium was holding together, so she gave up this attempt and guarded the approaches to Egypt instead.

Antony left the city and the company of his friends and moved to Pharos, where he ran a jetty out into the water and built himself a house by the sea. He spent his time there, an exile from the world of men, claiming to find Timon's way of life both satisfying and admirable. After all, he said, his experiences had been similar to Timon's: he too had been wronged and treated with ingratitude by his friends, and so had come to mistrust and hate the whole human race.

[70] Timon was an Athenian who lived round about the time of the Peloponnesian War, as we can infer from the plays of Aristophanes and Plato, where he is made fun of as a bad-tempered misanthrope.* He avoided and actively resisted all social intercourse, but he enjoyed the company of Alcibiades, who was then a brash young man, and used to shower him with kisses. When Apemantus expressed his surprise and asked him the reason for this, Timon replied that he liked the young man because he knew that he would cause the Athenians no end of trouble. Apemantus was the only one who was occasionally allowed to join him, on the grounds that he felt much the same way as him and admired his way of life. Once, during the Festival of the Pitchers, the two of them were having their own feast off by themselves, and Apemantus said, 'Timon, what an excellent party we're having!' 'It would be,' Timon replied, 'if you weren't here.' There is a story that once he ascended the speaker's platform in the Athenian Assembly. This was so unusual that the crowd fell silent with intense anticipation. Then Timon said, 'Men of Athens, I own a small plot of land, which has a fig-tree growing on it, and in the past many of my fellow citizens have hanged themselves from this tree. Now, I'm intending to build a house there, and I wanted to give you advance notice of this, so that any of you who feel so inclined can hang themselves before the fig is cut down.'

After Timon's death, he was buried by the sea at Halae, but the part of the shore in front of the grave collapsed, and the sea washed around the tomb so that nobody could get near or approach it. The inscription on the tomb was as follows:

Here I lie, having brought to its final end an ill-starred life of misery.
My name is no business of yours. I wish for you vile people nothing but a vile death.

They say that he composed this inscription himself while he was alive, but there is another one, which has achieved wide circulation, by Callimachus:

> This tomb houses Timon. I loathed mankind, so walk on by.
> Curse me all you like, just so long as you walk on by.

These are a few of the many stories about Timon.

[71] Canidius brought Antony the news of the loss of his forces at Actium in person, rather than entrusting it to anyone else, and at the same time Antony heard that Herod of Judaea had gone over to Caesar, taking with him a number of legions and cohorts. Reports also began to arrive that the defection to Caesar by the client kings was becoming general, and that his forces outside Egypt were all falling apart. None of this news upset him, however: it was as if he was pleased to have relinquished his hopes, since that meant he could also relinquish his cares. He left his beach-house, which he called the Timoneum, found accommodation in Cleopatra's palace, and then set the city on a course of eating, drinking, and displays of generosity. For instance, he had the son of Cleopatra and Caesar enrolled among the young men who had come of age and conferred the *toga virilis* on Antyllus, his son by Fulvia, and to mark the occasion Alexandria was filled for many days with symposia and revelry and celebrations.* Antony and Cleopatra dissolved their club, the Society of Inimitable Livers, and formed another one instead. This new club was just as devoted to sensuality, self-indulgence, and extravagance as the other one, but they called it the Society of Partners in Death. Their friends registered themselves as those who would die together, and they all spent their time in a hedonistic round of banquets. Cleopatra was putting together a collection of various types of lethal poisons, and she tested each of them to see which of them was painless, by giving them to prisoners who had been sentenced to death. When she saw that the fast-acting ones brought a swift but painful death, whereas the gentler ones were slow to take effect, she started experimenting with wild animals, and watched as her men set various creatures on one prisoner after another. This became her

daily routine, and she found that in almost every case only the bite of the asp induced a sleepy lethargy without any convulsions or groans; their faces covered with a sheen of light sweat and their senses dulled, the men painlessly lost the use of their limbs and resisted all attempts to stir them and wake them up, just like people who are fast asleep.

[72] They also sent a delegation to Caesar in Asia to ask, on Cleopatra's behalf, that her children might be allowed to inherit the rulership of Egypt, and, on Antony's behalf, that he might live as a private citizen in Athens, if Caesar did not want him to do so in Egypt.* Because they had so few friends left, and were in any case mistrustful of them because so many others had defected, they sent the children's tutor, Euphronius, as their spokesman. Alexas of Laodicea, who had been introduced into Roman society by Timagenes, had formerly been the most influential Greek in Antony's entourage—and had also been the most violent of the tools Cleopatra had set to work against Antony, to eradicate any thoughts he might entertain in Octavia's favour. But after he had been sent to King Herod to curb his impulse to defect, he had stayed there and betrayed Antony. Later, he had the effrontery to seek an audience with Caesar, relying on Herod's influence to keep him safe. But Herod was no help to him at all, and he was immediately thrown into prison and taken in chains to his homeland, where he was put to death on Caesar's orders. And so Antony was repaid while he was still alive for Alexas' treachery.

[73] Caesar rejected Antony's request, and told Cleopatra that she would meet with decent treatment provided she either put Antony to death or threw him out of Egypt. He also sent, as a personal messenger from himself to Cleopatra, a freedman called Thyrsus, who was a man of considerable intelligence, with the ability to speak persuasively on a young commander's behalf to a haughty woman with an astonishingly high opinion of her own beauty. Thyrsus had longer meetings with her than any of the other delegates, and was treated with remarkable respect, which made Antony wonder what was going on. In the end he seized Thyrsus and had him flogged, before letting him return to Caesar with a letter from him, saying that Thyrsus' arrogant and supercilious ways had infuriated him at a time when his temper was short because of all his troubles. 'If you find what I've done intolerable,' he said, 'you've got my freedman,

Hipparchus. You can string him up and flog him, and then we'll be quits.'* Cleopatra next tried to redeem herself in Antony's eyes and allay his suspicions by paying him an excessive amount of solicitous attention. She celebrated her own birthday in an unpretentious way that suited their unfortunate circumstances, but she marked his with extremely flashy and costly festivities. In fact, a lot of the guests arrived at the banquet poor, but left rich. Meanwhile, however, Caesar was receiving a stream of letters from Agrippa in Rome urging him to return, since affairs there demanded his presence.

[74] This meant that war was postponed for the time being, but at the end of the winter Caesar again made his way through Syria while his commanders advanced through Africa.* Pelusium fell, and despite a rumour that Seleucus had surrendered the city with Cleopatra's connivance, she let Antony put Seleucus' wife and children to death. By now Cleopatra had built for herself, near the temple of Isis,* a wonderfully imposing and beautiful tomb and monument, and she collected there the most valuable of the royal treasures—gold, silver, emeralds, pearls, ebony, ivory, cinnamon—and also a great deal of firewood and tow. This made Caesar worried about the possibility of the woman getting desperate and burning up all the treasure, so he was constantly sending her friendly messages designed to keep her hopes up, even while he was advancing on the city with his army. Finally, he took up a position near the Hippodrome,* but Antony came out against him and fought a brilliant battle, in which Caesar's cavalry was routed and had to retreat back to their camp with Antony in pursuit. Antony felt good after this victory. He marched into the palace, went up to Cleopatra with his armour still on, kissed her, and introduced to her the man from his army who had fought with the greatest distinction. As the prize for valour, Cleopatra gave the man a golden breastplate and helmet—which he took with him when he deserted over to Caesar's camp in the night.

[75] Antony repeated to Caesar his earlier challenge to single combat, but Caesar replied that there were all sorts of routes for Antony to take to death. Antony realized that there was no better way for him to die than in battle, so he decided to launch a combined land and sea attack on Caesar. At dinner, we hear, he told his house-slaves to serve him food and wine with a more lavish hand than usual, since there was no way of knowing whether they would be able to do so tomorrow, or whether they would be serving other masters,

while he lay a lifeless, non-existent husk. When he saw that these words of his had brought tears to the eyes of his friends, he told them that he would not be leading them into the battle, since what he wanted from it was a glorious death rather than life and victory. Round about the middle of that night, the story goes, with fearful anticipation of the future keeping the city quiet and subdued, there were suddenly heard the harmonious sounds of all kinds of musical instruments, and the loud voices of a crowd of people making their way with Bacchic cries and prancing feet; it was as if a troop of Dionysian revellers were noisily making their way out of the city. Their course seemed to lie more or less through the centre of the city and towards the outer gate which faced the enemy forces, where the noise climaxed and then died down. The general interpretation of this portent was that Antony was being deserted by the god with whom he had always felt a strong similarity and affinity.*

[76] At daybreak Antony posted his land forces on the high ground in front of the city and watched as his ships put to sea and bore down on the enemy fleet. Since he expected to see his fleet win, he kept the land forces inactive. When his crews got close to the enemy, however, they raised their oars to salute Caesar's men, who returned their greeting. At this signal Antony's men changed sides, and all the ships combined to form a single fleet and sailed directly for the city. No sooner had Antony been confronted with this spectacle than his cavalry abandoned him and went over to the enemy. Following the defeat of his infantry, Antony retreated back to the city, crying out that Cleopatra had betrayed him to his enemies, when he had made war on them in the first place only for her sake. Cleopatra was afraid of what he might do in his anger and desperation, so she took refuge in her tomb, released the portcullises, which were reinforced by bolts and bars, and sent men to Antony with instructions to tell him that she was dead. Antony believed this report and said to himself, 'Antony, why wait? Fortune has robbed you of the only remaining reason for life to be dear to you.' He went into his room, where undid his breastplate and took it off. 'Cleopatra!' he cried. 'It is not the loss of you that hurts, because I shall be joining you very soon. What hurts is that for all my great stature as a commander I have been shown to have less courage than a woman.'

Now, Antony had a faithful slave called Eros, to whom he had long ago entrusted the job of killing him in an emergency. He now asked him to keep his word. Eros drew his sword and held it out as though to strike Antony, but then averted his face and killed himself. Seeing Eros on the ground at his feet, Antony said, 'You have done well, Eros. Although you were not able to do it yourself, you have taught me what I must do.' He stabbed himself in his belly and fell back on the couch. But the blow was not immediately fatal, and his position on his back on the couch stopped the blood pouring from the wound. When he recovered consciousness, then, he asked the people there to finish him off, but they ran out of the room, leaving him crying out and writhing in pain, until the scribe Diomedes came from Cleopatra. She wanted him brought to her in the tomb.

[77] At the news that she was still alive, Antony eagerly ordered his slaves to lift him up, and he was carried in their arms to the door of her burial chamber. Cleopatra refused to open the door, but she appeared at a window and let down ropes and lines, with which the slaves made Antony secure. Then Cleopatra and two ladies-in-waiting, the only people she had allowed into the tomb with her, hauled him up. Witnesses say that this was the most pitiful sight imaginable. Up he went, covered with blood and in the throes of death, stretching his arms out towards her as he dangled in the air beside the wall of the tomb. It was not an easy job for a woman: clinging to the rope, with the strain showing on her face, Cleopatra struggled to bring the line up, while on the ground below people called out their encouragement and shared her anguish. At last she got him inside and laid him down. She tore her clothes in grief over him, beat her breast with her hands, and raked it with her nails. She smeared some of his blood on her face, and called him her master, husband, and imperator. For a while her pity for him almost made her forget her own troubles. But Antony asked her to calm down and give him a drink of wine: perhaps he was thirsty, or perhaps he was hoping for a speedier release. After drinking, he advised her to look to her own safety, if she could do so without disgrace, and of all Caesar's companions to trust Proculeius most; and he begged her not to mourn his recent misfortune, but to think of all the good luck he had enjoyed and count him happy. After all, supreme fame and power had been his, and now he had been honourably defeated by a fellow Roman.

[78] He had just breathed his last when Proculeius arrived on a mission from Caesar. After Antony had stabbed himself and been

taken off to Cleopatra, one of his bodyguards, Dercetaeus, had picked up the sword, hidden it under his clothing, and made his way stealthily out of the building. He ran to Caesar and, with the bloody sword as evidence, was the first to bring the news of Antony's death. When Caesar heard the news, he withdrew further into his tent and wept for a man who had been his brother-in-law, his colleague in office, and his partner in numerous military and political enterprises. Then he took their correspondence, called in his friends, and read the letters out to them, to show that while he had written politely and fairly, Antony had always been rude and arrogant in his replies. After this he dispatched Proculeius on his mission, which was to take Cleopatra alive, if possible, not only because he was worried about her treasure, but also because he thought it would add significantly to the glory of his triumph if he were to bring her back with him. She refused to give herself up to Proculeius, but she did talk to him, after he had approached the burial chamber and was standing outside one of the doors at ground level, through which their voices could carry, for all that they remained securely bolted and barred. The gist of their conversation was that she asked for her children to be allowed to inherit the kingdom, and he told her that she could trust Caesar absolutely, with no need to worry about a thing.

[79] Proculeius looked the place over and returned to deliver his report to Caesar. Then Gallus was sent to engage Cleopatra in conversation again. He went up to the door and deliberately prolonged the discussion. Meanwhile, Proculeius put a ladder up against the wall and climbed in through the window which the women had used to bring Antony in by. He lost no time in going down, accompanied by two slaves he had brought with him, to the door where Cleopatra was standing listening to Gallus. One of the two women who had been locked inside the burial chamber with Cleopatra shouted out, 'Oh no, Cleopatra, they're going to get you alive!' Cleopatra turned around, saw Proculeius, and made an attempt to stab herself with the little dagger—the kind robbers use—that she happened to have tucked into her belt. But Proculeius ran up, wrapped his arms around her, and said, 'No, Cleopatra, that would be wrong. It would be a crime against you, and it would be a crime against Caesar, since you would deprive him of an excellent opportunity to display his kindness, and you would be implicitly accusing the most even-tempered of leaders of dishonesty and intransigence.' While saying

this he took her dagger away from her and shook out her clothes to see if she had any poison hidden there. Another person Caesar sent was a freedman, Epaphroditus, with instructions to keep a very close watch on her to make sure she stayed alive, but otherwise to do everything to keep her comfortable and happy.

[80] Now Caesar himself rode into the city, conversing with the philosopher Arius, whom he had riding on his right: this was a way of immediately raising Arius' profile in Alexandria and of making people admire him, as someone who was held in such conspicuously high regard by Caesar. He entered the Gymnasium and ascended a dais that had been built for him. The people there were terrified out of their wits and were prostrating themselves before him, but he told them to get up and said that he gave the city of Alexandria an absolute pardon, for three reasons: first, in memory of its founder, Alexander; second, because he admired the beauty and grandeur of the city; and, third, as a favour to his friend Arius.* In addition to receiving this signal honour from Caesar, Arius also successfully interceded for the lives of a large number of people, including Philostratus, whose skill at impromptu speaking was unrivalled by any other sophist of the time, and who illegitimately claimed affiliation with the Academy. This led Caesar to loathe the man's character and to refuse to listen to his pleas, so with his long white beard and draped in a dark cloak he used to traipse along behind Arius, constantly reciting the line, 'If the wise are wise they save the wise.' When Caesar found out what he was doing, he gave him his pardon, but not so much because he wanted to relieve Philostratus' fear, as because he did not want people to think badly of Arius.

[81] Among Antony's children, his son by Fulvia, Antyllus, was betrayed by his tutor, Theodorus, and beheaded. During the execution Theodorus stole a very valuable gem which the boy used to wear around his neck and sewed it into his belt; he denied the theft, but was found out and crucified. Cleopatra's children were kept under lock and key along with their servants, but otherwise had a relaxed regime. Caesarion, however, who was rumoured to be Caesar's son, had been sent abroad by his mother, plentifully supplied with money, to travel to India via Ethiopia. But Rhodon—another tutor from the same mould as Theodorus—persuaded him to return, on the grounds that Caesar had invited him back to take up his kingdom. The story goes that when Caesar was wondering what to do with

him, Arius remarked, 'A plurality of Caesars is not a good thing.'* And so Caesarion was put to death by Caesar, but this happened later, after Cleopatra's death.

[82] Permission to bury Antony was sought by a number of kings and commanders, but Caesar would not deprive Cleopatra of the body, and she gave it a sumptuous, royal burial with her own hands. Caesar allowed her every facility she wanted for the occasion. But as a result of all the mental and physical suffering she had endured—her breast was inflamed and ulcerated where she had beaten it in her grief—she contracted a fever, and she welcomed this as a chance to stop eating and to release herself from life without anyone interfering. One of her close friends, Olympus, was a doctor, and she confided the truth to him. He became her confidant and helped her waste her body, as he himself has recorded in the account he published of these events.* But Caesar became suspicious, and used threats and her fears for her children as a weapon against her. These threats and fears undermined her resolution as if they were siege-engines, until she put her body in the hands of those who wanted to tend it and care for it.

[83] A few days later Caesar made a personal visit to talk to her and put her mind at ease. She was lying dejectedly on a straw mattress, but as soon as he came in she leapt up, despite wearing only a tunic, and prostrated herself on the ground before him. Her hair and face were unkempt and wild, her voice trembled, and her eyes were puffy and swollen; there was even plenty of visible evidence of the way she had lacerated her breast. In short, her body seemed to be in just as bad a state as her mind. Nevertheless, her famous charisma and the power of her beauty had not been completely extinguished, but shone through her wretchedness from somewhere inside and showed in the play of her features. Caesar told her to recline on her mattress, while he sat down beside her. She began to try to justify her actions, blaming them on necessity and saying that she was afraid of Antony, but Caesar raised objections and disproved every point, so soon she adopted the pitiful, pleading tone of a woman who wanted nothing more than to go on living. In the end, however, she gave him an inventory she had taken of all her valuable possessions—but one of her stewards, a man called Seleucus, proved that she was making away with some of her things and hiding them. At this, she leapt to her feet, grabbed Seleucus by the hair, and pummelled his

face with her fists, until Caesar stopped her with a smile. 'But Caesar,' she said, 'it just isn't right, is it? You don't mind coming to talk to me even when I'm in such a terrible state, and yet my slaves denounce me for keeping aside a little of my jewellery. And I'm not even doing it for myself, of course—I'm too wretched for that. It's so that I can give a few things to Octavia and your Livia, and ask them to make you more compassionate and kind towards me.' Caesar liked this speech of hers and was completely convinced that life was still dear to her. Before going away, he told her that he left it up to her to look after her valuables and that he would treat her more gloriously than she could ever have expected. He was sure he had taken her in, when actually it was she who had taken him in.*

[84] One of Caesar's companions was a young man of distinction called Cornelius Dolabella. He was quite attracted to Cleopatra and so, when she asked him to let her know what was going on, as a favour to her, he got a message secretly to her with information that Caesar was planning to break camp and march by land through Syria, and had decided to send her and her children away in two days' time. As soon as she heard this news, she asked Caesar for permission to pour libations for Antony. He said she could, and so, accompanied by her ladies-in-waiting, she was carried to his tomb. She fell on his coffin and said, 'Antony, my darling, just recently I buried you with hands that were still free, but now I pour libations as a prisoner of war. As a captive, I cannot disfigure this body of mine with the rites of mourning and lamentation; my body is a slave, closely watched and preserved for the triumph to be celebrated over your defeat. So expect no further honours or libations: you will receive no more from Cleopatra now that she is a slave. In life nothing could come between us, but now in death it seems that we will change places: you, the Roman, will lie here, and I—ah, poor me, I will lie in Italian soil, and never possess more of your land than that. I do not appeal to the gods here, because they have let us down, but I implore you, by any of the gods of the underworld with the power and potency to grant my prayer, not to abandon your wife* while she is alive, and not to let me be the centrepiece of a triumph celebrated over you. No, bury me here in this tomb beside you, knowing that the worst and most terrible of all the countless miseries I have borne has been this brief period of life without you.'

[85] After this lament she garlanded and embraced the coffin, and

then ordered her slaves to prepare a bath for her. Once she had finished bathing, she reclined on her couch and proceeded to eat a spectacular midday meal, in the middle of which a man arrived from the countryside with a basket. The guards asked what he had brought, so he opened the lid and showed that under the leaves the basket was filled with figs. He smiled when the guards expressed astonishment at the size and beauty of the fruit, and asked them to help themselves. They were not at all suspicious of him, and they told him he could go in. After her meal Cleopatra took a writing-tablet which she had already written on and sealed, and sent it to Caesar. Then she ordered everyone out of the room except her two ladies-in-waiting, and shut the door behind them.

Once Caesar had unsealed the writing-tablet, he found inside a passionate and emotional plea that she should be buried with Antony. It did not take him long to guess what she had done. His first thought was to go there in person and see if he could help, but then he ordered some of his men to go as quickly as possible and investigate the situation. But the tragedy had unfolded rapidly. His men ran there and found the guards unaware that anything had happened. They opened the door, and saw Cleopatra lying dead on a golden couch, dressed like a queen, with one of her two ladies-in-waiting, Iras, dying at her feet. The other, Charmion, was so weak that she could hardly stay upright or stop her head from slumping forward, but she was trying to arrange the diadem which adorned Cleopatra's brow. One of the men hissed in anger, 'A fine day's work, Charmion!', and she replied: 'Yes, nothing could be finer. It is no more than this lady, the descendant of so many kings, deserves.' These were her last words, and she fell where she was, beside the couch.

[86] The asp is said to have been smuggled in with the basket of figs and leaves, hidden underneath them, exactly as Cleopatra had commanded; and the story goes that the creature struck at her body without her being aware of it. Then, after removing some of the figs, she spotted the snake and said, 'Here it is, then,' and made sure that the snake could bite her naked arm. However, others say that the asp was kept shut inside a water jar, and that as Cleopatra was trying to get it to come out by provoking it with a golden distaff, it lunged at her and fastened on to her arm. But no one knows the true story: after all, it was also said that she carried poison around inside a

hollow hairpin, which was hidden in her hair, despite the fact that there were no marks on her body, and there were no other indications that she had taken poison either. However, there were also no sightings of the snake inside the room, although people said they saw its trail on the part of the shore overlooked by the windows of the room. Some people do in fact say that two faint puncture marks were seen, though they were barely visible, on Cleopatra's arm. This is the version Caesar seems to have believed, because he had a picture of Cleopatra carried along in his triumphal procession, with the snake clinging on to her. Anyway, these are the various versions of what happened.

Caesar was annoyed that the woman was dead, but, impressed by her nobility, he gave orders that her body was to be buried alongside Antony's with the kind of splendid ceremony suitable for a queen. He also arranged for her attendants to receive an honourable burial. Cleopatra was 39 years old when she died, and she had been queen for twenty-two of these years, with Antony as her co-ruler for fourteen of them.* Some writers have Antony aged 56, others 53, at the time of his death.* Antony's statues were pulled down, but Cleopatra's stayed in place, because one of her friends, a man called Archibius, paid Caesar a thousand talents to keep them from sharing the fate of Antony's statues.

[87] Antony left seven children by three wives. Only the oldest, Antyllus, was put to death by Caesar, while Octavia took in the rest and brought them up along with his children by her. She arranged for Cleopatra, his daughter by Cleopatra, to be married to Juba, one of the most cultured kings ever, and thanks to her Antonius, the son of Antony and Fulvia, became so important that while Caesar's particular favourites were Agrippa and then Livia's sons, the third place was held to be, and genuinely was, occupied by Antonius.

Now, Octavia had had two daughters by Marcellus, and one son, also called Marcellus. Caesar adopted this Marcellus as his son, and had him marry his daughter as well, while he arranged for Agrippa to marry one of the two daughters. But Marcellus died tragically soon after his marriage, and Caesar was finding it difficult to choose another trustworthy son-in-law from among his friends. Under these circumstances, Octavia proposed that Agrippa should divorce his present wife and marry Caesar's daughter instead. Caesar thought this was a good idea, and then she won Agrippa round to it too, so she took back her daughter and married her to Antonius, while Agrippa married Caesar's daughter.

Of the two surviving daughters from Antony's marriage to Octavia, one was married to Domitius Ahenobarbus, and the other—Antonia, famous for her virtue and her beauty—was married to Drusus, who was the son of Livia and therefore Caesar's stepson. The sons of Drusus and Antonia were Germanicus and Claudius: Claudius later became emperor, and of Germanicus' children, Gaius reigned for a few brief and demented years before being put to death along with his children and wife, while Agrippina had a son, Lucius Domitius, by Ahenobarbus, before marrying Claudius Caesar. Claudius adopted her son and changed his name to Nero Germanicus; and Nero Germanicus became emperor in my lifetime. He killed his mother and came very close to destroying the Roman empire with his capricious and insane ways. He was the fifth in descent from Antony.*

ROMAN MONEY AND MEASURES

Money

10 asses or 4 sesterces = 1 denarius

1,000,000 sesterces or 250,000 denarii = 1 decies

Plutarch considers 1 denarius = 1 drachma; 6,000 denarii or 24,000 sesterces = 1 talent

Capacity, dry

1 medimnus = 51.8 l. (91.2 pt., 11.4 gal., 1.5 bushels)

Length/Distance/Area

1 Greek stade = 600 Greek feet or 177.6 m. (582.7 ft.)

1 Roman foot = 296 mm. (11.65 in.)

1 Roman mile (5,000 Roman feet) = 1,480 m., 1,618.5 yds. (= 4,855.5 ft.)

1 iugerum = 28,800 square feet (Roman)

Plutarch considers 1 Roman mile = 8 stades

Plutarch speaks of the Greek plethron as equivalent to the Roman iugerum, although the plethron is usually only 10,000 square feet.

SPECIAL TERMS

augur one of the Roman priesthoods, which among other duties observed the flight of birds to learn whether a particular public action was approved by the gods

clientela the total of those 'clients' who were obligated to a prominent Roman who had assumed the role of patron towards them. Originally, the patron–client relationship existed within Rome between persons of unequal social status. Later, the great military victors and provincial governors included conquered peoples and kings, or those who owed them favours, among their *clientela*

equites or **knights** the social order below senators, defined by the size of their financial holdings. Not being senators, they could not hold offices in the *cursus honorum* (see below)

fasces the bundle of rods, the emblem of office, borne by the lictors. An axe was included when the official had the power of capital punishment

imperator the title given to victors in the field by their troops; sometimes the senate granted or confirmed the title. Later it was used as a title by Augustus and his successors, coming to mean 'emperor'

knights see *equites*

lictors special attendants who accompanied the consuls and certain other magistrates

optimates those defending the traditional senatorial oligarchy

plebs originally, all Roman citizens who were not privileged patricians. In the second and first century BC, usually all Roman citizens not senators or *equites*

pontifex maximus head of the college of pontiffs, the priests who presided over the state cult

popular assembly any one of the several types of formal assemblies (*comitia*) of the Roman people, but more frequently simply a public meeting called by a magistrate (*contio*)

populares those senators and their followers challenging the senatorial oligarchy, especially through the tribunes of the people or by appealing to the popular assembly

princeps senatus the senator placed first on the senatorial list by the senators, a great dignity, conferring the privilege of speaking first on any motion in the senate

procurator under the republic, an agent of a provincial governor or other official

rostra the speakers' platform in the assembly place (*comitium*) at Rome, so called from the beaks (*rostra*) of the captured ships mounted on it

senatus consultum ultimum a decree of the senate ordering the consuls to take all measures necessary to safeguard the state

triumvir one of a committee of three, in particular the committee (the so-called 'second triumvirate') of Antony, Lepidus, and Octavian in 43 BC, established to organize the state. The unofficial 'first triumvirate' was the political compact between Pompey, Caesar, and Crassus, made in 60 BC

Units of the Roman Army

The army as reformed by Marius contained the elements listed below; units were frequently considerably below book strength. Cf. L. Keppie, *The Making of the Roman Army* (Totowa, NJ: Barnes and Noble, 1984). Note that Caesar (*Civil War* 3. 89. 2) says that at Pharsalus in 48 BC he had 22,000 men in 80 cohorts, giving an average strength of 275 men per cohort instead of 480.

1 century = 80 men, under a centurion
1 cohort = 6 centuries
10 cohorts = 1 legion (4,800 men)

The Roman Cursus Honorum

The standard offices of a senatorial career (the *cursus honorum* or 'path of offices') were quaestor, aedile, praetor, consul, censor. One could be tribune of the people after being quaestor. The aedileship was optional in the sequence. The consulship was normally the highest office, held at the age of 40 by the most distinguished. Only two consuls were chosen per year, and after their term in office held the rank of *consulares*. Few senators became censors. Praetors and consuls were vested with *imperium*, that is command in war and in law: the power to give orders and exact obedience. After their term of office, they were regularly sent to the provinces or frontier areas as propraetors or proconsuls. Dictator was a special office created to tide the state over a particularly difficult crisis, and had an *imperium* superior to all others.

NOTE ON ROMAN NAMES

Roman names normally have three elements, a praenomen or first name, a nomen or family name, and a cognomen or added name, as in Marcus Tullius Cicero, although some, like Gaius Marius, have no cognomen, as Plutarch remarks at *Marius* 1. There were very few male praenomens, and these were regularly abbreviated as indicated in the table below. Cognomens were often inherited, as Cicero's was. They could be doubled, or honorific ones added, as with P. Cornelius Scipio Africanus. When a man was adopted, he changed his name, but kept an adjectival form of his family name as an additional cognomen: thus when L. Aemilius Paullus' son was adopted by a Scipio he became P. Cornelius Scipio Aemilianus. Women were regularly called by the feminine form of their father's family name, e.g. Cornelia. Plutarch, like the Romans themselves, used the nomen or cognomen, and occasionally the praenomen, in various combinations. In the index, names will be found under the form used by Plutarch, but giving the additional names when known. The normal Latin form writes Iu- (Iulius, Iunius) where English uses Ju- (Julia, Julius, Juncus).

Abbreviations of Common Praenomens

A.	Aulus	P.	Publius
Ap.	Appius	Q.	Quintus
C.	Gaius	Ser.	Servius
Cn.	Gnaeus	Sp.	Spurius
D.	Decimus	Sex.	Sextus
L.	Lucius	T.	Titus
M.	Marcus	Ti.	Tiberius
M'.	Manius		

EXPLANATORY NOTES

THE PARALLEL LIVES

Given in the order of the tripartite edition, with abbreviations.

Theseus–Romulus	Thes.–Rom.
Solon–Publicola	Sol.–Pub.
Themistocles–Camillus	Them.–Cam.
Aristides–Cato the Elder	Arist.–CMaj.
Cimon–Lucullus	Cim.–Luc.
Pericles–Fabius Maximus	Per.–Fab.
Nicias–Crassus	Nic.–Cras.
Coriolanus–Alcibiades	Cor.–Alc.
Demosthenes–Cicero	Dem.–Cic.
Phocion–Cato the Younger	Phoc.–CMin.
Dion–Brutus	Dion–Brut.
Aemilius Paullus–Timoleon	Aem.–Tim.
Sertorius–Eumenes	Sert.–Eum.
Philopoemen–Flamininus	Phil.–Flam.
Pelopidas–Marcellus	Pel.–Marc.
Alexander–Caesar	Alex.–Caes.
Demetrius–Antony	Demetr.–Ant.
Pyrrhus–Marius	Pyr.–Mar.
Agis and Cleomenes–Tiberius and Gaius Gracchus	Ag.Cl.–Grac.
Lycurgus–Numa	Lyc.–Num.
Lysander–Sulla	Lys.–Sull.
Agesilaus–Pompey	Ages.–Pomp.
Imperial Lives	
Galba, Otho	Galb., Oth.
Independent Lives	
Aratus, Artaxerxes	Arat., Artax.

PLUTARCH'S SOURCES

Although Plutarch did not have the easy familiarity with Roman historians that he had with Greek writers, the fact that he regularly wrote several Lives dealing with the same period gave him the opportunity to become acquainted with the major sources, to which he would add specific sources related to each Life. The lives of Cato and Aemilius Paullus overlapped with those of Scipio Africanus, Flamininus, Philopoemen, and Scipio Aemilianus. For all of these Polybius' *Histories* were a major source, supplemented by Livy. Posidonius, who continued Polybius' work, was probably an important source for *Tiberius and Gaius Gracchus*, *Marius*, *Sulla*, and *Pompey*; Cornelius Nepos for *Gracchi*.

For the last generation of the republic, which Plutarch treated not only in *Pompey*, *Caesar*, and *Antony*, but also in *Sertorius*, *Crassus*, *Lucullus*, *Cicero*, *Brutus*, and *Cato Minor*, Plutarch used Sallust's *Histories*, Asinius Pollio, and Livy. Where possible he employed contemporary sources, especially the writings of his protagonists, such as the speeches of Cato the Elder and the Gracchi and the *Memoirs* of Sulla. Other contemporary sources include the letters of Nasica in *Aemilius* and of Cornelia in *Tiberius and Gaius Gracchus*, and the histories or memoirs of Catulus and Rutilius Rufus in *Marius*, Theophanes of Mytilene in *Pompey*, Oppius in *Caesar*, and Dellius, Cicero, and Octavian in *Antony*. Cicero's letters and speeches are referred to often, as well as special works such as *Cato, or On Old Age* for *Cato the Elder*. Occasionally Plutarch has the opportunity to use his own personal knowledge or autopsy, most strikingly in *Sulla*, where he gives specific information on the campaigns in Boeotia and Athens, and in *Antony*, where he recalls traditions passed down in his own family. More detailed information appears in the Introductions to the individual Lives.

Our major narrative sources are Polybius and Livy for the periods where they survive and the histories of Dio Cassius and Appian. Polybius' history went down to 146 BC, but for the second century survives only in extensive fragments. Livy's history went down to Augustus, but survives only to book 45, 167 BC, after which we must make do with very brief summaries, called *Periochae* (*Per.*). Appian's *Civil War* (*Bellum civile*, *BC*) treats the internal wars of the Romans, beginning with the Gracchi. He also wrote a *Mithridatic War* (*Mith.*), *Spanish Wars*, and *Celtic Wars*, which are occasionally relevant. Cicero's correspondence and speeches provide us with details of political manoeuvring (often we can follow events day by day), names, and the major issues of his day. Our information is supplemented by the accounts of Diodorus Siculus (Diod.), who wrote in the years 60–30 BC, and Velleius Paterculus (Vell.), who probably finished his work in AD 30. For the African campaigns of Marius and Sulla, Sallust's *Jugurthine War* (*Bellum Jugurthinum*, *Jug.*) is important, as are Caesar's *Commentaries on the Gallic War* (*Bellum Gallicum*, *BG*) and on the *Civil War* (*Bellum Civile*, *BC*) for his Life. Modern scholars also make use of the preserved fragments of the lost historians who preceded Livy, on which see E. Badian, 'The Early Historians', in T. A. Dorey (ed.), *Latin Historians* (London: Routledge and Kegan Paul 1966), 1–38.

An essential reference tool for Roman republican history is T. R. S. B. Broughton, *Magistrates of the Roman Republic*, vols. 1 and 2 (New York: American Philological Association, 1951–2) and 3 (Atlanta: Scholars Press, 1986), which has been cited as *MRR*. This provides a list of all magistrates and their legislation and chief actions, with source references, and is complemented by a list of the careers of all who held magistracies. *The Oxford Classical Dictionary*, 3rd edn., ed. S. Hornblower and A. Spawforth (Oxford: Oxford University Press, 1996), here cited as *OCD*[3], is a rich and up-to-date repository of information on persons, places, and institutions mentioned by Plutarch. A short but useful account of late republican history may be found in H. H. Scullard, *From the Gracchi to Nero: A History of Rome from 133 BC to 68 AD*, 5th edn.

(London: Methuen, 1982). M. Beard and M. Crawford, *Rome in the Late Republic* (Ithaca, NY: Cornell University Press, 1985) provide an overview of the issues and problems of the period, with an excellent bibliography. Two works which give a broad overview of major problems in this period are E. Badian, *Foreign Clientelae (264–70 BC)* (Oxford: Clarendon Press, 1958), pp. 226–51, and P. A. Brunt, *Social Conflicts in the Roman Republic* (London: Norton, 1971). Finally, one should note the three recent volumes of the *Cambridge Ancient History*, 2nd edn. (Cambridge: Cambridge University Press): viii, *Rome and the Mediterranean to 133 BC*, ed. A. E. Astin *et al.* (1989); ix, *The Last Age of the Roman Republic, 146–43 BC*, ed. J. A. Crook *et al.* (1994); and x, *The Augustan Empire, 43 BC–AD 69*, ed. A. K. Bowman, E. Champlin, and A. W. Lintott (1996).

Collections of inscriptions and historical fragments in Latin or Greek are occasionally cited in the notes by the following abbreviations: *CIL*: *Corpus Inscriptionum Latinarum* (1863–); *FGrHist*: F. Jacoby, *Die Fragmente der griechischen Historiker* (1923–); *IG*: *Inscriptiones Graecae* (1873–); *ILS*: H. Dessau, *Inscriptiones Latinae Selectae* (1892–1916).

Note. Except where otherwise indicated, all dates throughout the following notes are BC.

CATO THE ELDER

8 *territory of the Sabines*: Tusculum, south-east of Rome, was in Latium; the Sabine country, where the people were considered hardier and independent, lay east and northeast of Rome. Cato's full name was M. Porcius Cato.

in honour of his courage: nothing is known of this ancestor.

'new men': The Romans could use the term *novus homo* for one who was the first member of his family to enter the senate, or, more restrictedly, for the first to hold the consulship. To do both, as Cato did, was extraordinary. Others who rose in this fashion include C. Marius and Cicero.

word for someone astute: this sentence seems to refer to Cato's great-grandfather, since he already had that name, as Cato's statement shows. Priscus is not otherwise attested in the gens Porcia.

Persephone: a goddess, daughter of Demeter and queen of the underworld.

9 *ablaze with his success*: Hannibal, the Carthaginian leader in the Second Punic War (218–201), led an army in Italy from 217 to 203. Cato would have been 17 in 217.

call for vinegar: that is, the lowest grade of wine.

Manius Curius: Curius Dentatus, four times consul, defeated Pyrrhus of Epirus, who was invading Italy, in 275. He triumphed twice in 290, and again in 275.

9 *Fabius Maximus*: Fabius Maximus, who had earlier controlled Hannibal by his delaying tactics, took Tarentum in 209, during the Second Punic War.

10 *Nearchus*: this meeting is reported by Cicero, *On Old Age* 39–41, from which Plutarch's account may derive. Modern historians consider it invented.

Valerius Flaccus: L. Valerius Flaccus, consul in 195, censor in 184. Cato's rise to influence and office in Rome would not have been possible without the patronage of this member of an old aristocratic family at the beginning of his career.

11 *Scipio the Great*: i.e. P. Cornelius Scipio Africanus Major, whose policy of carrying the war against the Carthaginians into Africa was strongly opposed by Fabius Maximus. Cato was his quaestor in 204 as he prepared for the invasion of Africa; Scipio's policy led to Hannibal's return to Africa, his defeat at Zama in 202, and Carthaginian surrender.

12 *his rowers*: Pliny (*Natural History* 14. 91) explains the reference: Cato drank the wine of the rowers he sailed with when going to and returning from Spain during his consulship.

rather than support them: cf. Cato's *On Farming* 2. 7, where he recommends selling old slaves. A. E. Astin (*Cato the Censor* (Oxford: Clarendon Press, 1978), 349–50) argues, however, that both passages are rhetorical statements of the need for austerity, and not good evidence for 'regular and systematic practice'.

13 *called Houndsgrave even today*: in Greek, *Kynos sēma*. Xanthippus was the victor of Mycale in 479 and the father of Pericles. The story is found also in *Them.* 10.

year of his consulship: 195.

province of Sardinia: in 198.

14 *Plato says*: *Symposium* 215a–e.

that of Lysias: Lysias was famous as a representative of the plain style, which did not aim at arousing strong emotions.

more than an ox: fish were considered a delicacy, and could be extremely expensive; an ox would be used for working, not eating. The saying, in slightly different form, is found in Polybius 31. 25. 5–6.

15 *not abuse this position*: cf. the similar anecdote at *Them.* 18.

needed lictors: lictors were the official attendants who accompanied Roman magistrates.

'what the sea hardly lapped at,' he said: the point was that the man had sold his ancestral farm to support his extravagant lifestyle.

King Eumenes: Eumenes II of Pergamum (197–158) was Rome's major ally in the war against Antiochus III. He visited Rome in 172 to denounce the actions of Perseus of Macedon. A delegation from Rhodes came at the same time, fearing that Eumenes was hostile to them (cf. Livy 42. 11–

14). Since Cato was sympathetic with Rhodes, this may explain his hostility here. Of the generals to whom Cato contrasts him, Epaminondas, a Theban, had won the battle of Leuctra (371), Themistocles the battle of Salamis (480), Pericles led the Athenians in the Peloponnesian War, and Hamilcar was the Carthaginian leader in the First Punic War.

16 *lacked feet, head, and heart*: this delegation was sent in 149 to avoid a war between Nicomedes of Bithynia and Attalus of Pergamum. In early Rome, the heart was regularly associated with intelligence. The same story appears in Polybius 36. 14. 1–5.

left his cap and belt there: after the defeat of King Perseus of Macedon in 168, Rome took a thousand Achaeans to Rome and detained them, including the historian Polybius, who while in Rome became a friend of the younger Scipio Africanus. Rome finally released the detainees in 150. Cato refers to Odysseus' adventure escaping from the cave of the man-eating Cyclops, *Odyssey* 9.

his feet in battle: i.e. to steal on the journey and flee in the battle: rather he should march on the journey and fight in battle.

17 *'Nearer Spain'*: in 195. The province was Hispania Citerior, the part to the north.

Polybius says: book 19. 1.

18 *Scipio the Great*: Plutarch (like Nepos, *Cato* 2. 2) is mistaken. The Scipio who campaigned in Spain in 194 was not Africanus, who, although he did hold his second consulship in 194, only campaigned against the Boii and Ligurians in north Italy. This is the praetor, P. Cornelius Scipio Nasica, who was awarded Spain and won a victory south of the Ebro (Livy 35. 1. 3–4).

whom he executed: for the Lacetani, just south of the Pyrenees, cf. Livy 34. 20. The execution of the six hundred deserters probably refers to the *praedones* or outlaws whom Cato captured and executed at Bergium (Livy 34. 21), since execution of deserters was not common.

When Scipio complained: Cato should have yielded command to Scipio Nasica at the end of his year, but apparently did not.

Tiberius Sempronius: consul of 194, who fought against the Boii, a Celtic tribe in northern Italy. The reference to Thrace and the Danube that follows is unclear: perhaps Plutarch's source referred to the earlier movements of the Boii from the Danube basin into Italy.

Antiochus the Great: Antiochus III Epiphanes (king 223–187) attempted to restore the power of the Seleucid kingdom and especially to oppose the influence of Rome in the eastern Mediterranean. Cato, serving in the low rank of military tribune, played an important part, under the consul Manius Acilius Glabrio, in his defeat at Thermopylae in 191 (c. 13).

19 *independence from Philip and the Macedonians*: by the victory of T. Quinctius Flamininus over Philip V at Cynoscephalae in 197. Cf. Plutarch's *Flamininus*.

19 *in my account of his life*: *Flam.* 15.

Amphictyonic decree: the Amphictyonic league was a religious and political association of Greek states connected with the sanctuary at Delphi.

Persian outflanking and encircling manoeuvre: at the battle of Thermopylae in 480, during the Persian Wars.

20 *Firmans*: a cohort of troops from Firmum (mod. Fermo) in Italy.

22 *Petillius against Scipio*: in 187, two tribunes of the people, both named Q. Petillius, brought charges against P. Scipio Africanus (according to Valerius Antias cited in Livy 38. 50–3). When Africanus faced down the charges, at the encouragement of Cato they charged L. Scipio Asiaticus, his brother the consul for 190, who had defeated Antiochus (Livy 38. 54–5). Livy's account is rather confused, but he refers to a speech of Cato, 'On the Money of Antiochus', delivered on the question.

just under fifty cases: more precisely, forty-four.

Servius Galba: Livy (39. 40) also says that Cato was 90, but Cicero more correctly says (at *Brutus* 20. 80) that he prosecuted Galba when he was 86, in the year of his death. Ser. Sulpicius Galba as praetor in Spain in 151 had killed and enslaved a large number of Lusitanians.

Paullus, the conqueror of Perseus and the Macedonians: L. Aemilius Paullus, the subject of the Life in this volume. Nestor was the wise old commander in Homer's *Iliad*.

candidacy for the censorship: in 185, for the year 184. For Cato's unusually severe censorship, see also *Flam.* 18. 3–19. 4; Livy 39. 42. 5–44. 9; Astin, *Cato the Censor*, 78–103; and H. H. Scullard, *Roman Politics, 220–150 BC*, 2nd edn. (Oxford: Oxford University Press, 1973), 153–65. Cato and Valerius had already campaigned for the censorship in 189 (when one of their rivals was M'. Acilius Glabrio, Cato's commander at Thermopylae in 191) and lost.

23 *confiscate a man's horse*: the censors could name or remove a man from the prestigious position of being a cavalryman with a state-supplied horse (*eques equo publico*). Cf. Livy 39. 42 and 44; *Aem.* 38; Astin, *Cato the Censor*, 81–2; and Scullard, *Roman Politics*, 159–60.

Hydra-like diseases of luxury and effeminancy: the Hydra of Lerna, a mythical many-headed beast which sprouted two heads every time one was cut off, was finally conquered by Heracles. Valerius would take the role of Heracles' companion Iolaus, who cauterized each wound as a head was cut off to prevent regrowth.

24 *Lucius Quinctius*: L. Quinctius Flamininus, consul in 192.

into Cato's mouth: Cicero, *On Old Age* 12. 42.

source of the story: Livy 39. 42.

25 *Manilius*: the man's name is found only here, and seems incorrect; it may be Manlius: cf. Astin, *Cato the Censor*, 80.

celebrated a triumph: 6 November 189, over Antiochus.

prosperity and wealth: the two referred to are Ariston of Chios, a third-century Stoic philosopher (more likely than Ariston of Ceos, a peripatetic philosopher), and the sixth-century tyrant Scopas of Thessaly, who was famous for his wealth and patronage of the poet Simonides (cf. Plutarch *Cim.* 10 and Plato, *Protagoras* 339a–c).

26 *Titus*: T. Quinctius Flamininus.

Basilica Porcia: one of the earliest basilicas, it stood in the Roman forum, and was destroyed in 52 BC when the senate-house, which stood next to it, was burnt down in the riots following the funeral of Clodius. It takes its name from Cato's family name, Porcius.

27 *especially rich family*: we know of her only from Plutarch's account, though her name must be Licinia, since her son was called M. Porcius Cato Licinianus.

she breastfed the baby herself: unusual in a wealthy family, but Plutarch approved of the idea, and was pleased that his own wife, Timoxena, had breastfed their child (*Consolation to his Wife* 609e).

rough parts of the river: i.e. of the Tiber.

28 *the battle against Perseus*: the Roman victory at Pydna in 168, cf. also *Aem.* 21.

the sister of Scipio: Aemilia Tertia was blood sister of the son of Aemilius Paullus who was adopted by the son of Scipio Africanus the Elder and became Scipio Aemilianus, the younger Africanus.

a lot of slaves: on his treatment of slaves, see cc. 4 and 10, and Astin, *Cato the Censor*, 261–6 and 349–50.

29 *for a stipulated amount of money*: D. Sansone (*Plutarch: The Lives of Aristides and Cato* (Warminster: Aris and Phillips, 1989), 225), suggests that this was 'to ensure monogamy', reasonably understanding the passage to mean that there was a single fixed payment to establish a relationship with a single woman, not, as has appeared to some, that a male slave would pay a fee for each visit to any female slave.

massive profits: the innovation seems not to be in sharing the investment, but in spreading fifty units over fifty ships, so that the loss of a ship only represented a small loss. Cato's share was held by his freedman Quintio because a law prohibited senators or their sons from owning cargo ships.

30 *Diogenes the Stoic philosopher*: this embassy of the heads of the three major philosophical schools (Plutarch omits the Peripatetic philosopher Critolaus) to Rome in 155 marks a watershed in Roman intellectual history. Carneades was a representative of the sceptical Academy, and displayed his dialectical and rhetorical skills by, among other presentations, arguing for and against justice on consecutive days.

Gaius Acilius: this Acilius also wrote in Greek a history of Rome down to his own day.

31 *Isocrates' teaching*: the orator and teacher Isocrates died in 338 at the age of 98, and was famous for the slowness with which he composed.

32 *whose brother, then, was Scipio*: cf. note to p. 28, *the sister of Scipio*.

Pisistratus, the Athenian tyrant: in the sixth century BC. In c. 6 of the Comparison which follows Cato's Life Plutarch denies the truth of Cato's comment: 'If he wanted to have noble children, he should have married a noble woman in the beginning, not have been content with sleeping with a common, unmarried woman, so long as it was not noticed, and when he was discovered, taking a father-in-law who was the easiest to persuade, rather than the one who was the best relation.'

33 *whom he named Salonius*: M. Porcius Cato Salonianus, born about 154 when Cato was 80. Cf. also c. 27. The other son died about 152, when praetor designate, before he actually held office (thus Cicero, *Tusculan Disputations* 3. 70 and Aulus Gellius, *Attic Nights* 13. 20. 9, against Plutarch and Livy, *Per.* 48, who say he was praetor). Plutarch in the Comparison finds the marriage completely inappropriate: 'Cato's marriage, out of his class and out of season, spread a serious reproach against this [self-control]. For it was not well done for a man of such an age to present his full-grown son and his young wife with a girl, daughter of a paid public clerk. Whether he did it for his own pleasure or from anger with his son over the prostitute, the fact and the excuse are shameful.'

books of history: his *Origins*, which began with the origins of Rome and the Italic peoples, written in Latin in seven books, and now lost.

book on farming: the *De Agricultura*, which still survives.

34 *Masinissa of Numidia*: Masinissa (238–148) and his Numidians had aided Rome against Carthage at the end of the Second Punic War, and over the years was favoured by Rome in any dispute with Carthage. Now some fifty years later, Carthage was at the point of war. Cato went on his mission in 153, four years before he died.

'It seems . . . Carthage should cease to exist': Plutarch gives a Greek version of Cato's famous saying, 'Carthago delenda est' (cf. Pliny, *Natural History* 15. 74). It is frequently referred to, but never given verbatim in Latin.

Publius Scipio, surnamed Nasica: P. Cornelius Scipio Nasica Corculum, consul in 162, censor in 159, consul for the second time in 155. He worked earnestly for peace with Carthage.

35 *the rest are flitting shades*: a quotation from Homer, *Odyssey* 10. 495.

the correctness of this pronouncement: the reference is to Scipio Aemilianus, who, like his adopted grandfather, was awarded the title of Africanus for his victory over Carthage in 146, at the age of 39.

Cato the philosopher: M. Porcius Cato Uticensis (the subject of another Plutarchan biography, *Cato Minor*), rather than surrender to Caesar committed suicide at Utica in Africa, 46 BC (cf. *Caes.* 54). The family tree is confusing, and Plutarch is not reliable. Fortunately Aulus Gellius (*Attic Nights* 13. 20) noted the difficulty and gives us a full account. Cato's elder son Licinianus had a son M. Porcius Cato (consul 118); the younger son Salonianus had two sons, Marcus and Lucius. Lucius was consul in 89, but Marcus, who never was consul, was father of Cato Uticensis. Plutarch has not distinguished the two grandsons named Marcus. Salonianus' praetorship and death is not otherwise mentioned: Plutarch has confused it with Licinianus' death as praetor designate (cf. note to p. 33, *whom he named Salonius*), which is well attested. The problem may be that the text needs emendation: cf. Milolaj Szymánski, 'Who is Who in Cato's Progeny? (Plut. Cat. Mai. 27, 7)', *Hermes*, 125 (1997), 384–6.

AEMILIUS PAULLUS

42 *'his stature and qualities'*: from Homer, *Iliad* 24. 630, the passage in which Priam and Achilles, the father and the killer of Hector, sit and wonder at each other, and try to understand what sort of person each is.

'could one find than this?': from a lost play of Sophocles (fragment 579 Radt).

pernicious, disagreeable ones: Democritus was a fifth-century atomist philosopher, who argued that all bodies gave off a constant stream of atoms, which in daytime created the images we see, and at night those we dream.

to luck or to intelligence: this introductory paragraph, addressed particularly to Plutarch's friend Sosius Senecio (note the 'you' singular at the end of the paragraph) is a major statement on Plutarch's purpose in writing the Life: see p. xiv above. The two figures are united not only by their noble principles but also by the good fortune which they shared.

charm of his speech: Plutarch reports King Numa's possible contact with Pythagoras, the Greek philosopher who migrated to Croton in Italy about 530 BC, where he founded a philosophic sect whose tenets influenced Plato and other later philosophers: cf. *Num.* 1 (where Plutarch notes the chronological difficulties) and 8. *Num.* 8 also offers the different tradition that Mamercus was one of the sons of Numa, who named him after Pythagoras' son Mamercus, and then gave him the nickname Aemilius.

43 *Lucius Paullus*: L. Aemilius Paullus, consul in 219 and 216, was forced by his colleague, Terentius Varro, to fight Hannibal at Cannae in 216. The Romans suffered a disastrous loss, and Paullus was killed. Cf. *Fab.* 14–16.

the aedileship: Paullus was aedile in 193, and made augur probably in 192. The aediles were responsible for the administration of Rome, for the food supply, and for the festival games. Augurs were members of one of the four major Roman colleges of priests, and, as Plutarch says, were responsible for making rulings on bird omens and other matters. The position was considered important politically.

how to serve the gods: Cf. e.g Plato, *Euthyphro* 14c–d, and Pseudo-Plato, *Definitions*, 413a.

44 *equivalent in dignity to that of a consul*: Aemilius was praetor in Further

Spain in 191, and continued as propraetor in 190 and 189. Praetors in Spain were regularly given proconsular authority (*imperium*) in this period. At this time, the Romans were fighting against Antiochus in Greece under T. Flamininus: cf. his Life, and *CMaj.* 12–14. Contrary to Plutarch, Livy 37. 46. 7–8 and 37. 57. 5–6 records a major defeat and a victory. Livy (58. 5) says Aemilius was awarded a *supplicatio* (a special ritual of thanks to the gods) by the senate, but in an inscribed list of his honours (*elogium*) a triumph is recorded (cf. *MRR* i. 362). The former seems more probable.

44 *dowry owed to his wife*: cf. Polybius 18. 35. 6. At the husband's death, the dowry reverted to the wife.

was an ex-consul: Papiria, daughter of C. Papirius Maso, consul in 231. On her two children, see below in this chapter.

45 *go unnoticed by everyone else*: Plutarch tells the same story in his *Advice on Marriage* 141a.

gave him the surname Scipio: the elder son was adopted by Q. Fabius Maximus, called Cunctator, who fought against Hannibal, and was given the name Q. Fabius Maximus Aemilianus. He fought at Pydna under his father (cf. c. 15) and became consul in 145. The younger son was adopted by P. Cornelius Scipio, son of Africanus, and became P. Cornelius Scipio Aemilianus, then later won the surname Africanus, like his adopted grandfather, for his victory over Carthage. He too fought at Pydna (cf. c. 22). Later he conquered Numantia in Spain and opposed the reforms of Tiberius Gracchus (cf. *Grac.* 21).

the other of Aelius Tubero: i.e. M. Porcius Cato Licinianus (cf. *CMaj.* 20, where the woman is called Tertia) and Q. Aelius Tubero. Both fought at Pydna (cf. cc. 21, 27, 28).

being elected consul: in 182. H. H. Scullard, *Roman Politics, 220–150 BC*, 2nd edn. (Oxford: Oxford University Press, 1973), 170, notes that he reached consul rather later than he might have wished. He ran more than once before this and was defeated: cf. Livy 39. 32. 6.

46 *announce his candidacy*: we do not know the occasion: Plutarch may be thinking of the occasions on which he ran before winning the consulship in 181.

no fonder parent in Rome: it is possible that this Greek education only began after Aemilius defeated Perseus in 168, when his younger son from Papiria would have been about 17. Polybius (31. 29) suggests that Scipio Aemilianus learned to hunt only after he had access to Perseus' dogs and huntsmen.

47 *explanation of the whole affair*: Antiochus the Great had been defeated at Thermopylae in 191 (cf. *CMaj.* 12–14) and at Magnesia in 190; Philip V of Macedon in 196 at Cynoscephelae (near Scotussa, see c. 8 below and cf. *Flam.* 7–8); and Hannibal and the Carthaginians in 204 at Zama.

failed to carry them out: Plutarch gives a brief history of the Macedonian kings who succeeded Alexander the Great, from Antigonus and his son Demetrius Poliorcetes, through Antigonus Gonatas, Demetrius II, Antigonus Doson, and Philip V (238–179). Doson means 'about to give'.

48 *lies told by his other son, the inferior one*: The story is told at great length in Livy 40. 5–24, cf. Polybius 23. 7

too scared to meet him: these are Perseus' campaigns of 171 and 170 against the successive consuls P. Licinius and A. Hostilius.

49 *invade Italy*: Perseus' moves were designed to strengthen his position in the Balkan peninsula. The Dardanians lived in Illyria; the Basternae lived along the Danube. The Illyrians were on the Adriatic coast. By 'lower Gaul' Plutarch means the Po valley.

Campus Martius: the area in Rome, near the Pantheon, where the elections took place. This was the election for 168. The year at this time began on 15 March.

50 *work on divination*: Cicero, *On Divination* 1. 103, 2. 83. In Cicero, however, the dog's name is Persa.

dominion over the rest of the world: Aemilius' outspoken speech also appears in Polybius 29. 1 and in Livy 44. 22. 2–15.

51 *began to mingle with Perseus' troops*: these special infantrymen, according to Livy 44. 26. 3, would follow the cavalry and when any riders were wounded, leap up on their horses and take their place, as well as fight on the ground as needed. The camp at Maedica was in the north-east of Macedonia.

52 *all the wealth he had guarded for them*: Livy (44. 26–7) also describes Perseus' refusal to pay the Gauls and Genthius' Illyrians (c. 13): both he and Plutarch undoubtedly draw on Polybius.

53 *resist sleep better*: the same story is found in Livy 44. 33. 8–10.

the impetus of its downward motion: cf. Livy 44. 33. 1–3. In what follows, Plutarch criticizes the notion that underground water condensed from earth only at the moment a well was opened, arguing instead for streams or springs running through the earth.

54 *as these two were*: the following chapters, 15–21, describe the preliminaries and the battle of Pydna (near mod. Katerini), 22 June 168. See Livy 44. 33–46 and Map 3. The first step was to cross over the west side of Olympus to come down into the Macedonian plain. For a discussion of the topography and action, see N. G. L. Hammond, 'The Battle of Pydna', *Journal of Hellenic Studies*, 104 (1984), 31-47.

son-in-law of Scipio Africanus: P. Cornelius Scipio Nasica Corculum, consul in 162 and again in 155, censor in 159, and *princeps senatus* in 147 and 142. Immediately below, Plutarch will use a letter of his as a source.

Polybius got wrong: F. Walbank, *A Historical Commentary on Polybius*, iii: *Commentary on Books XIX–XL* (Oxford: Clarendon Press, 1979), 378–9, offers a succinct account of the fragments of Polybius' account of the battle. This passage in Plutarch is listed as 29. 14.

54 *a note about this business to one of the kings*: this letter (*FGrHist* 233) is cited only by Plutarch. Cf. also cc. 16, 18, and 21. Walbank, *Historical Commentary*, p. 380, notes, 'Nasica's version diverged from P[olybius]'s at several points, usually to its author's greater glory.' Plutarch gives Nasica's march as taking one day; Livy, more probably, says that it took two (44. 35. 15). See the table and map in Walbank, pp. 381–2. Pythium, the site of a sanctuary of Apollo, as Plutarch says, was high up on the mountain, near modern Hagioi Apostoli.

55 *systematically, using instruments*: Xenagoras is not otherwise known. His measurement came to about 2000 m. (6,560 ft.); to this should be added the altitude at the Pythium, about 900 m. (2,950 ft.). Olympus' height is today calculated as 2,985 m. (9,793 ft.).

56 *it finally vanished*: this eclipse is dated to 21 June 168. Livy (44. 37. 8) states that this was the night of 3 September, indicating that at this time the Roman calendar was out of phase with the sun. According to Livy (44. 37. 5–8), C. Sulpicius Gallus (consul in 166 and author of a book on astronomy), explained the coming eclipse to the troops beforehand; some other authors say the explanation was given afterwards.

57 *Bronze Shields*: a corps of heavily armed soldiers in the Macedonian phalanx. Cf. also *Sull.* 16 and 19.

58 *feelings it aroused in him*: the Macedonian phalanx at this time consisted of close ranks of men armed with long pikes which stuck out well ahead of the line. As the phalanx advanced, the enemy was pushed back, without having an opportunity to strike their opponent. The ranks behind would angle up their pikes, but be ready to drop them if a gap appeared in the line. Plutarch follows Polybius (29. 17–18), here and immediately below.

sacrifice to Heracles: the Macedonian kings considered Heracles an ancestor, and so a special source of help. For this reason, perhaps, Aemilius had also sacrificed to him (c. 17).

a man called Posidonius: this is not the better known Stoic philosopher and historian, Posidonius of Apamea, who lived *c.*135–51, but an otherwise unknown contemporary of Perseus, cited only by Plutarch (*FGrHist* 169), here and in cc. 20 and 21.

59 *the Pelignians*: like the Marrucinians (see text below), a people of central Italy, who fought in the Roman army.

60 *fighting with unrivalled heroism*: for the following incident, cf. also *CMaj.* 20, which specifies that the younger Cato married Aemilia only sometime after this battle.

according to Nasica: Livy (44. 42. 7–8) gives the Macedonian losses as twenty thousand dead and eleven thousand captured. The fine appearance of the Macedonians' élite three thousand was mentioned in c. 18.

before the tenth: that is, between *c.*3 and 4 p.m.

61 *pleasure in his victory*: this story of the 17-year-old Scipio Aemilianus is mentioned in Livy 44. 44. 1–3, and may be from Polybius, who in

another passage (31. 29. 7) uses the same phrase as Plutarch, 'like a young pedigree hound'. He destroyed Carthage in 146, and Numantia (in Spain) in 133 (cf. *Grac.* 7). Fortune's retribution will come later, at the time of Aemilius' triumph (c. 35).

62 *Pella*: the royal capital, some 56 km. (35 mi.) west of present Thessalonike. Extensive remains have been excavated.

went to Galepsus: Amphipolis was east of Thessalonike, on the Strymon river, and Galepsus a seaport somewhat further east.

lying like a Cretan to the Cretans: Plutarch plays on the proverb, 'All Cretans are liars'.

Cabiri: divinities associated with certain mystery sanctuaries, including Thebes, Lemnos, and Samothrace. The name, while probable, replaces a lacuna in our manuscripts.

63 *there was truth in the lie*: the same story is found also in Livy 45. 1. 1–6, Cicero, *On the Nature of the Gods* 2. 6, and Valerius Maximus 1. 8. 1.

the actual day of the battle: the first story concerns the victory of the Locrians over Croton in the south of Italy in the sixth century, when the news reached Olympia (Strabo 6. 261; Cicero, *On the Nature of the Gods* 2. 6); the second refers to the simultaneous victories of the Greeks over the Persians at Plataea and Mycale in 479. Herodotus (9. 100) reports that it was those at Mycale who learned of the victory at Plataea: either Plutarch's memory has erred, or he knew another tradition for this story.

eyewitness report straight from the army: the battle of Lake Regillus in 499: cf. *Cor.* 3, and Cicero, *On the Nature of the Gods* 2. 6, 3. 11 and 13.

rebellion against Domitian: in AD 88 L. Antonius Saturninus, legate of Upper Germany, rebelled, but was defeated by the legate of Lower Germany: cf. Suetonius (*Domitian* 6), who mentions the advance news of victory.

64 *twenty thousand stades*: from Mainz, the site of the battle, to Rome by modern highway is about 1,300 km. (810 mi.), or 7,300 stades.

in true Cretan fashion: cf. the proverb cited in the note to p. 62, *Lying like a Cretan . . .*

65 *even if the coward prospers*: Livy (45. 7–8) describes the meeting and a similar speech on fortune delivered to Aemilius' own staff (cf. c. 27).

entrusted him to Tubero: Q. Aelius Tubero, his son-in-law (cf. 5).

66 *make way for the conquerors*: this pillar has been found and is in the museum at Delphi, with the inscription, 'L. Aemilius L. f. imperator de rege Perse Macedonibusque cepet', that is, 'L. Aemilius, son of Lucius, commander, took [this booty] from Perseus and the Macedonians'. Plutarch, long a priest at Delphi, would have known the monument well.

Phidias had sculpted Homer's Zeus: the saying is also recorded by Polybius (30. 10. 6) and Livy (45. 28. 5).

ten commissioners arrived from Rome: those sent by the senate in 167 to assist Aemilius in organizing Macedonia: cf. Livy 45. 17. 2–3 and 45. 29–31.

67 *attention even to trivial details*: Plutarch himself paid attention to trivial duties in his home town of Chaeronea: cf. *Rules for Politicians* 811b–c.

as much pleasure as possible to the guests: the saying is found in Polybius 30. 14, Livy 45. 32. 11, and Plutarch's *Table Talk* 615e–f.

Tubero, who, as I have said: cf. 5.

68 *so little profit and gain for each man*: this operation of calculated mass terrorism crippled an area which had caused frequent trouble for Rome, while warning others not to think of opposing Rome. Plutarch's figure of eleven drachmas (= 11 denarii) is considerably lower than Livy's, who says (45. 34. 5) that the operation was very profitable, netting a total of 400 denarii for each Roman cavalryman and 200 for each infantryman. Perhaps Plutarch refers only to the looting, not the organized theft of the gold and silver and sale of the captives.

planned to hold the assembly: for this opposition, cf. the similar passage in Livy 45. 36. 1–6.

69 *killed twenty-three opponents in single combat*: M. Servilius Pulex Geminus, consul in 202, would now be quite old, a living reminder of the Hannibalic Wars. He is given a long speech by Livy (45. 37–9), ending with the same challenge as found in Plutarch.

Illyrians and Africans: referring to the triumphs over King Genthius and the Illyrians by L. Anicius Gallus in 167 and over Syphax of Numidia by Scipio Africanus in 201, as Livy (45. 39) makes clear. In both cases, the kings were led in the triumph, as Aemilius wished to do with Perseus.

70 *a description of the procession, taken from my sources*: Aemilius triumphed for three days in early September 167. Plutarch unfortunately does not specify his source(s), using only the generic 'they say' (*legousin*). The description in Livy 45. 40 suffers from a large lacuna. The account in Diod. 31. 8. 10–12 is rather different.

71 *Thericlean goblets*: a type of cup named after the famous Corinthian craftsman Thericles.

72 *from one side of the scales to the other*: cf. Achilles' words at *Iliad* 24. 525–33: Zeus has two jars at his door, one of evil and one of good. To some men he gives from both jars, to some only from the evil one. No one receives all good.

adopted by other families: cf. 5.

73 *the conqueror, has lost his*: cf. the similar speech in Livy 45. 41.

74 *between Antony and Caesar*: that is, in 43, when Mark Antony was fighting Caesar Octavianus (Octavian).

candidates for the office of censor: Appius Claudius Pulcher, consul in 143, opposed the election of Scipio Aemilianus as censor in 143. Appius was elected censor himself for 136.

75 *most sacred of all the offices at Rome*: Aemilius was censor in 164, with Q. Marcius Philippus as colleague. On this office, see *CMaj.* 16 and accompanying notes. The property valuation mentioned below determined voting rights and liability to military service and taxation.

along with his fellow priests: as augur: cf. c. 3. A magistrate could summon one or more augurs to conduct the auspices at the dedication of a temple or for another occasion. See J. Linderski, 'The Augural Law', *ANRW* II.16.3 (1986), 2146–312 at 2225.

two days later he died: in 160. At the funeral games given by his sons among the entertainments were the comedies *Brothers* (*Adelphoe*) and *Mother-in-Law* (*Hecyra*) by the poet Terence.

76 *Spaniards, Ligurians, and Macedonians in town*: i.e. the three peoples over whom he had triumphed: cf. cc. 4, 6, and 10–34.

have the whole estate: cf. Polybius (31. 28. 1–3), who values the estate at 'over sixty talents', i.e. 360,000 drachmas.

TIBERIUS AND GAIUS GRACCHUS

83 *first part of this narrative*: Plutarch refers to the Lives of the Spartan kings Agis and Cleomenes which are paired with and preceded those of the Gracchi: see p. 78 above.

two triumphs: Ti. Sempronius Gracchus senior, consul in 177, censor 169, consul for the second time in 163, married Cornelia, the second daughter of P. Cornelius Scipio Africanus.

death to Cornelia: the portent is mentioned, among others, by Cicero (*On Divination* 1. 18. 36), who says that Gaius Gracchus had written about it.

King Ptolemy: if the story is true (Plutarch is our only source), this may be Ptolemy VIII Psychon (*c.*182–116). Since he was engaged off and on in conflict with his brother Ptolemy VI, a powerful marriage alliance with Rome would have been valuable. See E. Gruen, *The Hellenistic World and the Coming of Rome* (Berkeley, Los Angeles, and London: University of California Press, 1984), ii. 708–9.

the younger Scipio: P. Cornelius Scipio Aemilianus Africanus Minor, the son of Aemilius Paullus who was adopted by the son of the elder Scipio Africanus (Cornelia's brother). Scipio married his cousin *c.*152.

84 *that of a runner*: the Dioscuri, Castor and Pollux, were sons of Zeus and brothers of Helen of Troy. Castor was the runner, Pollux the boxer. Plutarch in this chapter sets his two protagonists side by side, to show their differences.

slap his thigh: for this behaviour by Cleon, a successor to Pericles, cf. *Nic.* 8.

persuasive and flamboyant: Cicero (*Brutus* 125–6) especially praises Gaius' oratory, which he thought should be read by every aspiring orator.

84 *Drusus*: M. Livius Drusus, a political opponent, cf. c. 29 below. This extravagance is also recorded in Pliny, *Natural History* 33. 53. 147.

85 *older than Gaius*: Tiberius was born *c.*163–162, and died in 133; Gaius was born in 154, and died in 121.

noble birth: for the augurate, cf. note to p. 43, *the aedileship*. Plutarch is ingenuous here: Tiberius' family connections would have played the major part, and the fact that his father had been augur.

man of his day: Appius Claudius Pulcher, consul in 143, censor in 136.

for her marriage: we have no other account of this, but another fragment of Polybius mentions the dowry of Scipio's daughters after his death in 183 (Polybius 31. 27). Plutarch likes the story, and is glad to see that Polybius seems to support its use here. Livy (38. 57. 4) is one of those reporting the alternative story, though he also is aware of the difficulty.

the younger Scipio: this would have been during the Third Punic War, against Carthage, in 147, before the marriage, which has already been mentioned out of order (c. 1). Older officers often took younger relatives or family friends with them as *contubernales*, in this case more aides than 'tent-mates', Plutarch's literal translation.

according to Fannius: cf. pp. 79–80 above.

86 *elected quaestor*: in 137, under C. Hostilius Mancinus. Numantia finally fell to Scipio Aemilianus in 133.

scrupulous fairness: Tiberius senior had been praetor in Spain in 180, and continued serving there till 178.

anxious to recover: the quaestor was the financial officer for the army.

87 *stripped of their weapons*: the famous episode of the Caudine Forks, in 321, when a Roman army surrendered to the Samnites: cf. Livy 9. 1–11.

most . . . powerful man in Rome: Scipio Aemilianus, who had triumphed over Carthage, was also, of course, Tiberius' brother-in-law: cf. c. 1. What must be explained in the following sentences, therefore, is why Scipio did not do more than he did for Tiberius. Aemilianus waged war at Numantia in 134 and 133.

88 *small rent to the public treasury*: Plutarch here begins a brief sketch of the development of the problem of the public land (*ager publicus*), a problem which our few sources do not clarify greatly, though Appian gives a longer résumé (*BC* 1. 7–8). From the earliest times, public land came to Rome when it conquered the territory of enemies. This was distributed in various ways, but a part was made available to private individuals, who over the years often came to pay little or no rent. In 367, under extremely strong popular pressure and after a ten-year struggle, a law was passed to limit the right of possession of public land to 500 iugera (about 125 hectares or 326 acres): see Livy 6. 35.4–10, 42. 9–14, Plutarch, *Cam.* 39, and other sources. Two and a half centuries later, this system had completely broken down. Plutarch uses the Greek word plethron to translate

iugerum, as do Appian and other authors, although the standard Greek plethron was much smaller.

Gaius Laelius: C. Laelius Sapiens, consul in 140, perhaps the year he made his proposal, although we have no other source for this.

appointed tribune: he was elected tribune of the people in 134, taking office for 133 on 10 December 134.

89 *address . . . philosophical writings to him*: Cicero says that Diophanes was the most eloquent Greek of his day. Blossius' studies with the Stoic philosopher Antipater identify him as a philosopher as well. After Tiberius' death he joined Aristonicus, who led a revolt in Asia Minor (cf. note to p. 99, *came to nothing*). He committed suicide after Aristonicus was captured in 130.

more famous than him: this is probably S. Postumius Albinus, who became consul in 110, though only Plutarch reports this rivalry.

written by Tiberius' brother Gaius: cf. p. 80 above.

walls and monuments: we have vivid testimony of this kind of activity from the graffiti and electioneering slogans written on the walls of Pompeii.

Tiberius' father-in-law: the men were, respectively, P. Licinius Crassus Dives Mucianus, who would become pontifex maximus in 132 and consul in 131; P. Mucius Scaevola, consul this year (133) and pontifex maximus in 130, after Crassus' death; and Appius Claudius Pulcher, consul and censor, and currently *princeps senatus*. The collaboration of these three extremely prominent men, all related to each other (Crassus was a blood brother of Scaevola, and had married Pulcher's sister) and through Pulcher to Tiberius, indicates the existence of a powerful faction in the senate in favour of some reform, or at least of winning the support of an important segment of the people: see D. C. Earl, *Tiberius Gracchus: A Study in Politics* (Brussels: Latomus, 1963). Plutarch plays down the differences among the great families.

mildly worded: we do not have the exact terms of the first law: the principal thrust seems to have been to reinstate the 500-iugera maximum, thus freeing up land for poorer farmers. According to Appian (*BC* 1. 9), it also permitted allotments of 250 iugera for children of possessors, and specified that the extra land was to be distributed by a three-man committee.

90 *call their own*: this passage seems to be taken directly from one or more speeches of Tiberius.

one of the tribunes: M. Octavius is known only for his opposition to Tiberius: cf. e.g. Appian, *BC* 1. 12; Cicero, *Brutus* 25. 95. There are numerous small differences between Appian and Plutarch: most notably, Appian mentions neither the harsher law nor the politeness of the disputants.

91 *regulates the mind*: Plutarch adds a gratuitous comment on the role of

sound nature and training, both in politics and in the undisciplined rites of Dionysus. Plutarch alludes to Euripides' *Bacchae* 315–18: 'Restraint is always present in one's nature. Consider: even in Bacchic dances the woman who is self-controlled will not be corrupted.'

91 *would be fined*: this interdiction of all business was used only in the severest crisis, and usually involved an external enemy against whom troops had to be levied. The temple of Saturn was the site of the *aerarium* or public treasury. Only Plutarch reports these measures.

called a dolon: this heightening of tension and move towards violence is not mentioned by Appian. The *dolon* appeared to be a staff, but concealed a blade.

the wealthy members of society there: again, Plutarch portrays the conflict as between the wealthy and populace, ignoring the strong backing Tiberius had in the senate from some leading families. A major problem in understanding these events is how they shifted from a fairly normal jockeying for position among the senatorial oligarchy to radical polarization, within a very short period.

removed Octavius from his office: Roman practice had not to this point had a procedure for removing a magistrate from office, especially a tribune, who was protected by strong sanctions. Plutarch has Tiberius explain his reasoning in c. 15: the tribunes should speak for the people, and when they do not, they can be removed. In fact, for many years tribunes had often functioned as agents of the major senatorial families.

93 *what was going on*: this struggle is not described in Appian, *BC* 1. 12.

committee of three: in Latin, *triumviri agris iudicandis adsignandisque*: that is, 'for adjudging and assigning lands'.

one of his clients: the name is uncertain: Appian (*BC* 1. 13) gives Q. Mummius; Orosius (5. 8. 3), Minucius; only Plutarch identifies him as a client. If he were a Mucius, he would probably have been a relative of Mucius Scaevola, one of Tiberius' supporters: cf. c. 9.

nine obols: in Latin, nine asses, a pittance. Even the elder Cato spent thirty asses on dinner, and thought he was being thrifty (*CMaj.* 4).

Publius Nasica: P. Cornelius Scipio Nasica Serapio, consul for 138 and pontifex maximus until his death in 132, was a cousin both of Scipio Aemilianus and of Tiberius, since his mother was the elder sister of Tiberius' mother, Cornelia. He reappears in cc. 19–21.

94 *the king's heirs*: Attalus III, king of Pergamum, died in 133, and willed his kingdom to the Roman people. Eudemus is otherwise unknown. Cf. also Livy, *Per.* 58; Pliny, *Natural History* 33. 11. 148. Plutarch presents Tiberius' response as a proposal to the people, although Livy (*Per.* 58) suggests it was just an idea to be voted on later.

king of Rome: Q. Pompeius was consul in 141, censor in 131. The accusation of wanting to become king, the worst possible in an oligarchy where no one man should have permanent power over others, was still repeated by Cicero, *On Friendship* 12. 41. It was a charge which led to the death of Julius Caesar (cf. *Caes.* 60–1, 64).

common people: presumably in Tiberius' father's time citizens preferred to sneak home quietly in the dark, rather than be recognized as late drinkers. On the other hand, Tiberius had reason to fear assassination.

inviolable under the law: T. Annius Luscus, consul in 153, raises directly the question of the sacrosanctity of the tribunes, which had been granted at the establishment of the magistracy in 494, to protect the tribunes from violence.

95 *persuasiveness and skill*: what follows is a most unusual example in Plutarch of an extended verbatim quotation from a preserved speech, although elsewhere he reports contemporary texts, such as the poems of Solon and the indictment of Alcibiades. Tiberius argues eloquently, even sophistically, for a limitation on the tribune's inviolability, and will himself then suffer violence at the hands of his enemies.

96 *further laws*: Plutarch is our only source for these laws, and some scholars doubt their ascription to Tiberius. The attempt at re-election was unusual, if not illegal.

safety of the basket: one form of public augury at Rome used special chickens. When they were fed by their keeper, the *pullularius*, it was a bad omen if they ignored their food, but good if they ate eagerly.

97 *fickle tyrant*: the charge of tyranny recalls that of kingship, as well as Julius Caesar's fear of seeming whimsical by staying at home when omens warned him before his assassination (*Caes.* 64).

Fulvius Flaccus, a senator: M. Fulvius Flaccus, consul in 125, and also a supporter of Gaius Gracchus. From 130 on he was one of the land committee set up by Tiberius' law; in 122, a tribune along with Gaius.

have Tiberius killed: this consul was Mucius Scaevola, one of the drafters of Tiberius' original law (cf. c. 9 and note, *Tiberius' father-in-law*). After Tiberius' death, however, he defended the murderers: see Cicero *On his House* 91, and other references in *MRR* i. 492.

98 *asking for a diadem*: another sign of royalty and, for Plutarch, a suggestion of Caesar (cf. the scene at the Lupercalia, *Caes.* 61). Appian (*BC* 1. 15) gives a version of this scene less favourable to Tiberius.

the end of his toga: this action has been much discussed. The best suggestion is that it indicates that he will perform a religious action (Nasica was pontifex maximus).

killed by a sword: the two killers of Tiberius are otherwise unknown. The battle was outside the temple of Fides (Good Faith) on the south-west corner of the Capitoline hill.

99 *snakes in there with him*: Villius is otherwise unknown. He received the punishment given to parricides.

came to nothing: Aristonicus, a bastard half-brother of Attalus III, did not accept Attalus' testament and tried to claim the kingdom of Pergamum, ruling under the name of Eumenes III. He was captured by the Romans in 130.

99 *chose Publius Crassus*: this is P. Licinius Crassus Mucianus, who had advised Tiberius (c. 9 and note, *Tiberius' father-in-law*).

Cornelius Nepos: the Roman biographer and historian of the time of Cicero, occasionally cited by Plutarch. Here he probably refers to a Life of Gaius Gracchus. The Brutus that Nepos mentions was D. Iunius Brutus Callaecus, consul in 138.

100 *died in Pergamum*: probably in 132.

'do such deeds as he': Homer, *Odyssey* 1. 47.

Gaius and Fulvius: for Fulvius cf. c. 18 and note, *Fulvius Flaccus, a senator*. Gaius, of course, is Gaius Gracchus. Plutarch thus prepares the transition to Gaius' Life, which begins in the next chapter.

Life of Scipio: this life, probably paired with *Epaminondas* as the first of the series, is now lost.

101 *consul Orestes*: L. Aurelius Orestes, consul in 126. Plutarch does not mention that, before leaving in 126, Gaius opposed the attempt of the tribune Iunius Pennus to prevent non-citizens from settling in Rome: cf. *MRR* i. 508.

champions of the people: Cicero, *On Divination* 1. 26. 56, quoting the historian Coelius Antipater, who reported that he had heard the story told before Gaius' tribunate. By introducing it here, Plutarch closely connects the fates of Tiberius and Gaius, and gives a sense of inevitability and tragedy to the whole.

102 *popular leadership*: Gaius' appeal showed both his interest in the welfare of the soldiers, whom Plutarch equates with the people, and his influence with provincials.

receive the delegates: Micipsa's gift again shows the dangerous power of Gaius' family connections. Micipsa's kingdom had been established many years ago by Gaius' grandfather, Scipio Africanus.

before the proconsul: as chief financial officer, the quaestor would be expected to stay in the province. Gaius returned to Rome in 124, in his third year of service. He had to return if he wished to run for election as tribune for 123.

silver and gold: the vivid image is translated directly from Gaius' speech, which is quoted, along with other passages from this speech, by Aulus Gellius, *Attic Nights* 15. 12: 'cum Romam profectus sum, zonas, quas plenas argenti extuli, eas ex provincia inanes retuli; alii vini amphoras quas plenas tulerunt, eas argento repletas domum reportaverunt.' This speech before the censors was well known in antiquity.

conspiracy at Fregellae: Fulvius Flaccus as consul in 125 had proposed a law to give Roman citizenship to the Italians, which was rejected. This prompted Fregellae, a city in Latium near modern Ceprano with the status of Latin colony, to rise in arms: it was destroyed in 124 (Livy, *Per.* 60).

vast crowd of Italians: an indication of the strong support that Gaius (and earlier Tiberius) had throughout Italy, and not just among the urban plebs, although in general Plutarch makes little of this compared to Appian. Cf. C. B. R. Pelling, 'Plutarch and Roman Politics', in B. Scardigli (ed.), *Essays on Plutarch's Lives* (Oxford: Clarendon Press, 1995), 319–56, esp. 333–7. Italians could not have voted in the election, though they had a deep interest in the outcome. Plutarch may include Roman citizens living outside Rome in the category of Italians.

103 *a disappointing fourth*: ten tribunes were elected annually during the summer and took office on 10 December. This election was in July 124.

the tribune Genucius: apparently an incident in 241, the time of the war with Falerii. The following incident is not otherwise known.

citizen without trial: Cicero (*In Defence of Rabirius* 12), makes it slightly more general—that no capital judgement be made concerning a Roman citizen without the people's authorization. For full ancient references to Gaius' legislation, see *MRR* i. 513–14; for a rapid overview, E. Badian, *OCD*[3] s.v. 'Sempronius Gracchus, Gaius'. Plutarch does not mention two important laws: one to establish farming of the tithe in Asia through contracts leased by the censors in Rome, and another that consular provinces should be determined before the election of the consuls who would be sent there.

banished Tiberius' friends: P. Popillius Laenas, as consul of 132, together with his colleague P. Rupilius, had charge of the senatorial inquisition into supporters of Tiberius: cf. c. 20, and Cicero, *On Friendship* 37.

mother of the Gracchi: Pliny (*Natural History* 34. 31) describes her seated statue, which was in the portico of Metellus. A statue base inscribed 'Cornelia f. Africani Gracchorum', 'Cornelia, daugher of Africanus, [mother] of the Gracchi', found in 1878 in the portico of Octavia, may be the one referred to (*CIL* vi. 2, 10043).

104 *distributed the common land among the poor*: this was probably a re-enactment of the agrarian law of Tiberius.

those of Roman citizens: this proposal, perhaps moved in two phases, was not passed. Cf. *MRR* i. 518. Appian (*BC* 1. 23) places this, and the law changing the lawcourts, after Gaius' re-election in July, and perhaps in the following year, 122.

deciding court cases: this change applied only to courts handling charges of extortion by magistrates in the provinces (*de repetundis*), which since their establishment in 149 had had juries limited to senators. Since the knights, or equestrian class, were not senators, they had no direct role in politics, and thus provided some check on the senatorial class. The exact nature of this major reform is uncertain, since Appian, *BC* 1. 22

(contrary to Plutarch and Livy *Per.* 60, who has six hundred knights added to three hundred senators), says Gaius completely replaced the senators in the juries with knights. In the same year, another tribune, M'. Acilius Glabrio, also carried a law dealing with such cases.

104 *democratic basis*: Cicero (*On Friendship* 96), however, ascribes this change to C. Licinius Crassus, tribune in 145. Plutarch makes a similar comment on the relation between speaker's position and democracy in *Them.* 19, when the seating of the Athenian Assembly was changed so that it faced the sea.

105 *oppressive to the people*: Plutarch is our only source for this action against Q. Fabius Maximus.

from the rostra: a notable judgement by Plutarch, asserting both the fundamental integrity of Gaius and the superiority of actions to words in winning popular support.

needing a leg-up: although Appius Claudius had already built the first stretch of the via Appia in 312, and Roman milestones date back to 250, Gaius' roads were distinctive for their straightness and the regular use of milestones. Cf. R. Chevallier, *Roman Roads* (Berkeley and Los Angeles: University of California Press, 1976). The Roman mile was about 1,479 m. or 1,618.5 yds.

106 *the people's insistence*: these were the elections for 122. C. Fannius, however, later opposed Gaius' policy, c. 33. He is probably the same as Tiberius' companion at Carthage, c. 4.

Tarentum and Capua: the colony at Tarentum is well attested, but only [Aurelius Victor,] *On Distinguished Men* 65. 3, mentions Capua, and the sending of a colony there is problematic.

Livius Drusus: M. Livius Drusus, consul in 112 and censor in 109. This tribune should be distinguished from his son Marcus, tribune in 91, whose assassination led to the Social War.

rival demagogues in comedy: Plutarch seems to be thinking of Paphlagon and the Sausage Seller in Aristophanes' *Knights*, who compete in trying to win over the people with favours.

107 *the country's poor*: nothing seems to have come of this proposal, however.

destroyed by Scipio: Carthage had been taken by Scipio (cf. c. 4) and razed to the ground in 146, ending the Third Punic War. The site nevertheless remained attractive. Gaius' colony failed, but Augustus, pursuing a plan of Julius Caesar's (cf. *Caes.* 57), established a colony which became the capital of the province of Africa.

108 *distribution of land*: this is M. Fulvius Flaccus, consul in 125, last mentioned at c. 18, who was a tribune this year. The committee mentioned is a new one established for the colony at Carthage, not the triumviral committee set up in 133, of which Fulvius had been a member since 130.

blows and violence: Scipio had died at the age of 56 in 129, seven years before, most likely of natural causes. For Plutarch's lost biography, cf. the note to p. 100, *Life of Scipio*.

or 'Heraea' in Greek: Juno as patroness of Carthage plays a prominent role in Virgil's *Aeneid*. Tanith, the Phoenician goddess of the Punic city, was identified with Hera and Juno.

his favoured candidate: L. Opimius, consul in 121, had, as praetor, taken and destroyed Fregellae in 125 (cf. c. 24 and note, *conspiracy at Fregellae*).

109 *relevant period of time*: the senate wished to counter the influence on the elections of non-voting but very interested Italian allies, who were in large part pro-Gracchan (cf. c. 24 and note, *vast crowd of Italians*). According to Appian (*BC* 1. 23), those without a right to vote were to stay at least forty stades, five Roman miles (7.4 km.), from the city.

Fannius' lictors: lictors were special attendants who accompanied the consuls and certain other magistrates.

conflict and confrontation: Plutarch stresses that Gaius wished to avoid physical confrontation.

hiring them out: the show was public entertainment, and remained free, but the magistrates charged for the seats, which apparently occupied much of the audience space. This incident, and the magistrates' reaction, is not mentioned elsewhere.

110 *Sardinian laughter*: the expression is used variously, but here seems to refer to those who laugh while not realizing their own defeat. From the Greek word comes our own 'sardonic', which has a different meaning.

for this purpose: Appian (*BC* 1. 25) gives a slightly different report: a citizen named Antyllus (*sic*), who had tried to dissuade Gaius from his course, was murdered by an associate of Gaius' with a dagger. Plutarch's bias for Gaius is clear in this and the following chapter. Gaius' measured behaviour is brought out by the contrast with the vulgarity of Fulvius and the hypocrisy of Opimius.

111 *the common people*: here Plutarch seems to use the voice of the crowd to express his own judgement, or at least to raise a question in his readers' minds.

to . . . put down the tyrants: this is the *senatus consultum ultimum*, ordering the consul to take all measures to safeguard the state (*ne quid res publica detrimenti caperet*), which Cicero famously recalled in the first of his speeches *Against Catiline* (1. 2. 4). Fulvius and Gaius were called tyrants, presumably, because they were accused of wanting to take control of the city.

when he was consul: both during and after his consulship in 125, Fulvius fought in southern Gaul; he celebrated a triumph in 123.

112 *trust the laws and the gods*: Licinia's unusually long speech again allows Plutarch to present an extremely favourable view of Gaius' efforts. Cf. also the slightly longer speech of Cleopatra at the tomb of Antony, *Ant.* 84.

112 *her brother, Crassus*: M. Licinius Crassus, who did not enter into politics. Licinia was the daughter of Licinius Crassus Mucianus: cf. c. 21.

113 *sanctuary of Diana*: perhaps the small temple which was once on the site of the theatre of Marcellus.

there with him: M. Pomponius was the friend to whom Gaius addressed his book (cf. p. 80 above); Licinius would have been his brother-in-law or one of his family. [Aurelius Victor,] *On Distinguished Men* 65, identifies this person as P. Laetorius.

the wooden bridge: that is, the Pons Sublicius, which crossed the Tiber at the Forum Boarium. Gaius' friends imitate the legendary Horatius Cocles, who also defended this bridge to protect his fleeing friends, as in Macaulay's famous poem.

Philocrates: this slave is named Euporus by Velleius Paterculus (2. 6. 5); Valerius Maximus (6. 8. 3) knows of both names.

grove of the Furies: the grove of Furrina (a Roman goddess, once of major importance, whom Cicero, like Plutarch, connected with the Furies at Athens (cf. Cicero, *On the Nature of the Gods*, 3. 18. 46)) was located outside the walls on the Janiculum hill, roughly where the Villa Sciarra is today.

114 *melted lead instead*: Valerius Maximus (9. 4. 3) includes the lead as a variant, but it is not mentioned by Cicero, *On the Orator* 2. 269. Valerius also reports that Septimuleius was a friend of Gaius, not Opimius.

thrown into the river: although one version says that Gaius' body was sent to his mother, Cornelia, Plutarch prefers to have him end like his brother (cf. c. 22), in the river, and thus also fulfil Licinia's prophecy (c. 36).

keep her dowry: as was usually the case: cf. *Aem.* 4 and note, *dowry owed to his wife*.

'an act of insanity': there would have been a word-play in Latin between *concordia*, 'concord', and *vecordia*, 'madness', which Plutarch imitates in Greek with *homonoia/aponoia*. The temple of Opimius was a rebuilding of the earlier temple originally constructed in 367, after the strife leading to the Licinio-Sextian legislation, and was rebuilt again by the future emperor Tiberius in AD 10. The ruins of this last are visible today on the slopes of the Capitoline hill, overlooking the forum.

king, Jugurtha: Opimius went as head of a commission of ten legates to divide the kingdom of Numidia between two claimants, Jugurtha and Adherbal, both sons of Micipsa—probably in 116. He and his associates were accused of taking bribes to favour Jugurtha (Sallust, *Jug.* 16. 2–5, 20). Finally, in 109 a court was set up to deal with the charges, and Opimius was condemned along with other consulars (Cicero, *Brutus* 128)—a judgement which Cicero's speaker finds unfair. Opimius went into exile at Dyrrhachium (mod. Durrës or Durazzo), and died there. According to Cicero, he had a monument in the forum (*In Defence of Sestius* 67. 140).

115 *house at Misenum*: Cape Misenum and its neighbour Baiae on the Bay of Naples became favourite resorts of the Roman upper class: Cornelia's house is the first known to us in that vicinity, though in 187 her father, Africanus, had retired to a villa at Liternum, a few miles up the coast.

MARIUS

123 *Metellus 'Macedonicus'*: it was a regular practice for a victorious commander to be honoured with an epithet recalling the people defeated. Plutarch wrote a treatise, now lost, entitled *Which of the Three Names Is the Main One?*

Posidonius: see p. 121 above. Plutarch also quotes him on the meaning of Marcellus' name (*Marc.* 1), and on his and Fabius' nicknames (*Marc.* 9; *Fab.* 19).

first names: Roman women in the classical period used only the feminine form of the family name of their father (thus Cornelia, Julia), though sisters could also be distinguished by order of birth (e.g. Cornelia major, secunda).

Pelopidae: in Greek practice, a family could be designated by a famous ancestor: thus the Heraclidae from Heracles, the Pelopidae from Pelops, though this was not a legal part of the name.

Callinicus: the names mean, respectively: 'thin', 'wearing a neck-collar', and 'short-leg' (but cf. *Sull.* 2 and note, *gained him his name*); 'rememberer', 'hook-nosed', and 'beautiful victory'.

harsh and bitter character: Plutarch occasionally refers to statues of his protagonists, e.g. *Sull.* 2; *Per.* 3; *Alex.* 4. Gaul here refers to Cisalpine Gaul, that is, Italy north of the Apennines. On this statue, cf. also the note to p. 145, *the plain by Vercellae*.

other men's slaves: on the importance of a proper education to Plutarch, see pp. 118–19.

124 *methods of upbringing*: this picture of rustic poverty is misleading, since Marius' family would have been of equestrian status and therefore possessed of substantial wealth, though hardly a sum comparable to a major senatorial fortune. They certainly did not till the land themselves, though Marius no doubt emphasized his country origin in speaking to his soldiers and the people. Marius was born *c.*157.

besieging Numantia: Scipio Africanus Aemilianus besieged and took the Celtiberian capital of Numantia in Spain in 134 and 133: Marius would have been there with Gaius Gracchus (cf. *Grac.* 13). The patronage of this powerful aristocrat would have been extremely helpful to Marius.

elected tribune: in 119. Plutarch does not distinguish clearly the many Caecilii Metelli active at this time. Marius' supporter is probably L. Caecilius Metellus Delmaticus, consul in 119. The patronage of the Metelli, as one of the most powerful families in the city in this period, guaranteed Marius' career. His public confrontation with Metellus (see below) is thus all the more impressive. Plutarch does not mention his quaestorship, to be dated to 123–121.

124 *against the proposal*: the motion was to narrow the passages along which the voters filed to vote, making it harder for others to influence them. The consul, Metellus' colleague, was L. Aurelius Cotta.

125 *which they call 'plebeian'*: the aediles were generally responsible for the administration of the city, grain distribution, and public games. The two kinds, curule and plebeian, had historically different origins, the curule, as Plutarch says, being more prestigious. The magistracy would have been important for Marius, because it conferred full senatorial dignity.

prosecuted for bribery: he was elected praetor for 115.

126 *all their lives*: the patron–client relationship, in which someone of lesser rank looked to his superior in wealth, power, and status for support, was fundamental to Roman society at all levels, and had recognized public obligations. Nevertheless, the term 'client' could be offensive, especially to a senator.

curule seat: the curule seat was a special folding chair, used only by curule aediles, praetors, consuls, and censors. Since Marius had just been elected praetor, he considered himself independent of his patron. Plutarch, however, understood that Marius had spoken of office in general, not of the office of praetor, and so gives a more precise statement. It seems unlikely that Plutarch did not know that the praetorship was a curule office. This passage is important for our knowledge of the legal status of clients: see M. Gelzer, *The Roman Nobility* (New York: Barnes and Noble, 1969), 65.

Further Spain: this was in 114. Further Spain or Baetica included most of Andalusia.

in his Life: *Caes.* 1. Though an ancient patrician family, the Iulii at this time were not politically prominent.

127 *with him as his legate*: the consul was Q. Caecilius Metellus Numidicus (brother of Delmaticus), the year 109. Both continued in the province in 108, Metellus as proconsul. After the division of Micipsa's kingdom of Numidia between Adherbal and Jugurtha made by the Romans (cf. *Grac.* 39 and note, *king, Jugurtha*), Jugurtha had attacked Adherbal, thus bringing a succession of Roman armies against him, which he had bribed or defeated up to this point. The war was difficult because of the large tracts of sparsely inhabited terrain, with only a few scattered cities. The war is brilliantly described by the Roman historian Sallust in a monograph, *The Jugurthine War* (*Jug.*), which is one of Plutarch's sources.

128 *killing a guest-friend*: the story of T. Turpilius Silanus and the revolt of Vaga, in which all the Roman officers were killed except Turpilius, is given by Sallust (*Jug.* 66–9). Without mentioning Marius' role, he considers the execution justified. Cf. also Appian, *Numidian War* 3.

young adult: the minimum age for the consulship at this time was probably 42. Marius was already 48. Metellus' remark brutally reminded Marius of the difference in their social status. Plutarch's probable source, Sallust, gives Metellus' son's age as about 20 (*Jug.* 64).

consular elections: that is, in midsummer 108. Cf. Sallust, *Jug.* 73.

129 *raise an army*: he would take office as consul on 1 January 108, but as consul designate he could begin enrolling an army.

token of his commitment: Marius' decision to abandon the property qualification for service in the army, although he probably did not realize it, completely changed the nature of the Roman army. Henceforth, soldiers would be dependent on the political clout of their commanders to receive land and monetary awards for their service, and they could be used in Rome to support the commander's political objectives. However, the change also created a more efficient class of professional soldier.

portraits of other people: the Roman nobility kept busts of their distinguished ancestors in their homes, and paraded them at funerals.

Bestia and Albinus: L. Calpurnius Bestia, consul in 111, and Sp. Postumius Albinus, consul in 110, both of whom had fought in Numidia.

to be popular: cf. the long speech attributed to Marius in Sallust, *Jug.* 85.

130 *Life of Sulla*: *Sull.* 3. The following account draws heavily on Sallust's account of the negotiations (*Jug.* 102–13). L. Cornelius Sulla, Marius' quaestor, was to become the mortal enemy of Marius, from the time of this incident. Plutarch has passed over Marius' three difficult years of campaigning as consul and proconsul, 107–105.

131 *impending deluge of war*: Plutarch picks up the water image he has used in *Pyrrhus*. See p. 117 above.

elected Marius in his absence: for 104, his second consulship. Plutarch resumes with the same notice in c. 12, after his digression.

outnumbered the fighting men: the Cimbri came from northern Denmark (Jutland), and, joining with their neighbours the Teutones and Ambrones, migrated down into the Rhône valley about 110. The Cimbri defeated a Roman army at Arausio (mod. Orange) in 105, having already defeated two other armies. Their progress can be traced through archaeological evidence as well as the scanty literary sources. The following ethnographical digression seems to be based on Posidonius, who is quoted on this subject by the geographer Strabo (7. 293 = *FGrHist* 87 F 31).

from the Etruscans: from the sixth to the fourth century the Gauls or Celts (the Greek word) had infiltrated or invaded Italy, and eventually taken possession of the Po valley, which had been under Etruscan control.

northern part of the Ocean: i.e. to the Baltic Sea.

the Bear . . . Pontic Scythia: i.e. from the British Isles to the Sea of Azov and the Ukraine.

132 *as far as Hercynia*: the Cimmerians are mentioned in *Odyssey* 11 as a

people living in darkness, but in the seventh century a people with this name invaded Asia Minor from the steppe via the Caucasus and attacked the cities of the Aegean coast. The connection with the Cimbri is quite speculative. Hercynia was a rather vague area in north central Europe, which by Plutarch's day (though perhaps not in his mind) was stabilized in the forested mountains extending around Bohemia and through Moravia to Hungary.

132 *ghosts of the dead*: Homer, *Odyssey* 11. 13–18. On the way to visit the dead, Odysseus passed the Cimmerians, who lived in perpetual darkness. The passage explains that in northern latitudes the celestial pole is much closer to overhead than in the Mediterranean region, a fact which is responsible for the extraordinarily long winter nights and summer days in that region.

the city of the Carthaginians: Scipio Aemilianus was elected consul in 147, contrary to the law setting the steps and ages of the senatorial career, so that he could lead the Romans against Carthage.

133 *his sacrilegious crimes*: this apparently gratuitous vignette reminds the reader, though not Marius, of the mutability of fortune, already seen often in *Pyrrhus*.

triumphal robes: the triumphing general wore a robe modelled on that traditionally worn by Jupiter and the ancient Roman kings; to wear it when transacting business showed an incredible arrogance, which Plutarch neatly juxtaposes to Jugurtha's end. One of the extravagant honours voted for Caesar was the right to wear triumphal clothing in public, as he did at the Lupercalia: see *Caes*. 61 and note, *his triumphal clothing*.

Numantia: cf. c. 3.

134 *against Spain*: after their victory at Arausio (cf. c. 11 and note to p. 131, *outnumbered the fighting men*), the Cimbri attempted to enter Spain, but were repelled by the Celtiberians.

how to behave: the anecdote is mentioned by Cicero, *In Defence of Milo* 9, and Valerius Maximus 6. 1. 12 (who say Lusius was a military tribune; according to Valerius, the name of the soldier was C. Plotius, not Trebonius).

135 *in the face of that threat*: Marius was re-elected as consul for the third time, for 103.

such critical danger: L. Appuleius Saturninus, as tribune this year, also carried a law to give Marius' veterans each 100 iugera of land in Africa. Later the censors tried to expel him from the senate, but he was re-elected as tribune for 100, when he embarked on a radical programme of legislation (cf. cc. 29–30).

not disliked by the masses: Q. Lutatius Catulus joined Marius in his fourth consulship, in 102.

banks of the Rhône: according to Orosius (5. 16. 9), at the confluence with the Isère.

named after him: the canal ran from Arelate (mod. Arles) to the sea at modern Fos-sur-Mer, north-west of Marseilles. This canal, freeing the Rhône river traffic, would have been immensely valuable to the city of Massalia (mod. Marseilles) and Arelate. It is mentioned in Strabo 4. 1. 8, p. 183, and Pliny, *Natural History* 3. 34, but no remains of it are securely identified.

to force a passage there: that is, they returned north and east around the Alps, to take another pass, probably the Brenner. Noricum is roughly modern Austria.

137 *as Carbo and Caepio did*: Cn. Papirius Carbo, as consul, had been badly defeated in 113 at Noreia, in Noricum; the proconsul Q. Servilius Caepio and the consul Cn. Mallius Maximus had been disastrously defeated at Arausio in 105, losing some eighty thousand men, cf. note to p. 131, *outnumbered the fighting men*.

playing a role along with her: Plutarch, using the same word (*sunhupokrinomenos*) as in the scene with Saturninus (cf. 14), suggests that it probably was an act; Frontinus (*Stratagems* 1. 11. 12) states clearly that it was a show. Q. Sertorius in Spain similarly used a white deer to awe his troops (*Sert.* 11).

quite remarkable: Alexander of Myndus wrote books on animals and marvels, in the first century AD.

138 *Ameria and Tuder*: today, Ameli and Todi in Umbria.

would win the war: Cybele, or Magna Mater, the Great Mother, was an Anatolian goddess, with her major shrine at Pessinous in Asia Minor, but she had been honoured at Rome since her worship was brought there during the Second Punic War.

got to hear about it: Diod. 36. 13 gives a similar story. Plutarch seems disposed to believe it, or at least find it impressive, as he does the vulture story.

139 *Aquae Sextiae*: modern Aix-en-Provence.

Romans under Mallius and Caepio: at Arausio in 105 (cf. note to p. 137, *as Carbo and Caepio did*).

140 *'Ambrones' by descent*: only Plutarch reports that the Ligurians were also called Ambrones. It looks like a misunderstanding of the event in his source, or pure invention.

by Marius' design: by accident, because it had been started by the slaves getting water, rather than as a planned attack.

142 *over a hundred thousand of the enemy*: Plutarch is restrained: Velleius Paterculus (2. 1. 2) says 150,000 dead; Orosius (5. 16. 12) 200,000 dead and 80,000 prisoners; and Livy (*Per.* 68) 200,000 dead and 90,000 prisoners.

denied by some writers: the notice is indeed suspect, because booty did not belong to the soldiers (although they often took it), but to the state.

There was also a story that Marius sold off booty to the soldiers at a low price (Cassius Dio 27. 94).

142 *how fields are fattened*: Archilochus of Paros, the seventh-century Greek poet, wrote of his own participation in a civil war.

for his triumph: in his triumphal procession, a victor paraded the booty and prisoners he had won in his victory: note the parade of L. Aemilius Paullus described in his Life, *Aem.* 32–4.

traditional for such occasions: that is, with the edge of the toga veiling the head, the practice of magistrates performing religious acts, called *cinctus Gabinus*. The pyre represented a dedication to the gods of part of the booty.

consul for the fifth time: for 101.

143 *attacked the fortresses*: Catulus took up a fortified position on the river Adige (Atiso), which runs down from the Brenner pass, past Trent and Verona. The exact route of the Cimbri and the place of Catulus' defence are disputed; some also suggest that the Cimbri came down further east, along the river Natisone (reading 'Natiso' in Plutarch), which flows past Cividale del Friuli, on the road to ancient Aquileia.

144 *the now defenceless land*: Catulus apparently retreated south of the Po.

their share in the honour: that is, because they were still in the north.

central Italy: the movements of the armies in the Po valley are quite uncertain.

145 *while fleeing through the Alps*: the Sequani were a Celtic tribe. Other sources mention one captured Teuton king, Teutobod.

by the bent point: thus the javelin impeded the enemy, and being bent could not be immediately reused.

the plain by Vercellae: this was traditionally taken to be the city now known as Vercelli, in the Piedmont region between Turin and Milan, but now is largely agreed to be near the city of Rovigo, close to the mouth of the Po. The Latin sources speak of the Campi Raudii or Campus Raudius (Vell. 2. 12. 5, Florus 1. 38. 14, [Aurelius Victor,] *On Distinguished Men* 67. 2). The Celtic term *vercelli* is a general word for a place where one can mine alluvial deposits. See E. Badian, 'From the Gracchi to Sulla', *Historia*, 11 (1962), 197–245, at 217 (repr. in R. Seager (ed.), *The Crisis of the Roman Republic*, Cambridge and New York: Cambridge University Press, 1969), with reference to the original Italian article of J. Zennari. Badian notes that Marius' statue at Ravenna, seen by Plutarch (c. 2), is probably connected with this battle.

as Sulla . . . reports: Sulla's account of the battle in his *Memoirs* appears to have been strongly biased against Marius, as one might expect. Marius himself may not have trusted Catulus and his troops, as they had retreated before the Cimbri before.

extreme malice towards him: Catulus wrote a memoir 'On his Consulate and Deeds' (cf. Cicero, *Brutus* 35, 132), which here Plutarch may cite indirectly. Catulus also had a strong anti-Marian bias.

146 *the fortune of that day*: Catulus later erected a temple in the Campus Martius to 'Fortune of this day' (*Fortuna huiusce diei*). Vows before battle were not uncommon. Marius himself built a temple to Honour and Courage (*Honos et Virtus*) when he returned to Rome.

as I have said: in c. 11.

147 *now known as August*: the battle of Vercellae took place, then, on 30 July 101. The Calends was the first day of the Roman month. The Roman calendar, before the reform of Caesar (cf. *Caes.* 59), was often out of phase with the solar year. The month Sextilis was changed to August in 8 BC, in honor of the emperor Augustus. For other ancient references to this battle, see *MRR* i. 570.

148 *dignity of his rank*: at the time, he was consul, and Catulus proconsul.

the time of the Gallic invasion: that is, in 390, when the Gauls captured Rome, before being driven off by Camillus, who was considered the second founder of the city, after Romulus.

from hearing the law: since Camerinum, in Umbria, was an allied city with supposedly equal rights, it was illegal for Marius to make its citizens Romans. This is the first instance of a consul awarding citizenship to an individual or group for valour, a practice which was to become common. Once more, Marius raises the question of the treatment of the Italian allies who fought in the Roman army alongside the Romans.

concern to him: this should be Metellus Numidicus, who had been Marius' commander in Africa: cf. cc. 7–10 and note to p. 127, though some doubt whether it was this Metellus who opposed Marius for the consulship.

149 *Glaucia and Saturninus*: C. (?) Servilius Glaucia, tribune of the plebs for 101, presided over the tribunician elections for 100, during which a successful candidate, Nonius, was murdered (by Saturninus, Plutarch says below (c. 29), cf. also Appian, *BC* 1. 28) and L. Appuleius Saturninus (already mentioned in c. 14) took his place. Glaucia was elected praetor for 100.

Rutilius . . . an honest and reliable source: cf. p. 120 above.

rather than a colleague: L. Valerius Flaccus: a deputy because he had so little political influence compared to Marius.

through the other five: M. Valerius Corvus or Corvinus, consul six times between 348 and 299, and twice dictator in 342 and 301, was politically active into his nineties.

his agrarian legislation: Plutarch, focusing on the conflict with Metellus, does not explain that this legislation included both a law to distribute land in the Po valley won from the Cimbri as a result of the victory at Vercellae, and another to establish a number of new colonies. These bills would have greatly increased the prestige of Marius among the rural populace both allied and Roman, who, according to Appian (*BC* 1. 29), strongly supported the measure.

149 *in an inescapable trap*: this Metellus is certainly Numidicus.

150 *as Pindar puts it*: the fifth-century Greek lyric poet. This is from a lost poem, fragment 205 (Maehler).

if it was a law: Marius adds a condition which keeps the matter open, for there was doubt whether Saturninus' proposal was in fact legal, since it was carried by violence and against the auspices (cf. Appian, *BC* 1. 29).

151 *studying philosophy in Rhodes*: Plutarch has constructed a short portrait of an honest man, who puts virtue before ambition, to serve as a foil to Marius. The trick of Saturninus and Marius, as well as the violence used by Saturninus to get the law approved, is also described at length by Appian (*BC* 1. 29–31). It should be noted that Metellus as censor in 102 had tried to expel Saturninus and Glaucia from the senate (Appian, *BC* 1. 28). Plutarch's *Life of Metellus* is lost, if he ever wrote it: it is not in the ancient Lamprias catalogue of his works.

cutting off their water supply: Plutarch condenses here, almost to the point of incomprehensibility. At the time of the elections in December 100, riots and the murder of Memmius, Glaucia's opponent for the consulship (which Glaucia sought illegally while holding the praetorship), led the senate to pass the *senatus consultum ultimum* (as they had against Gaius Gracchus in 122: cf. *Grac.* 35 and note, *to put down the tyrants*). Then Marius, as consul, used force to pen up Glaucia and Saturninus and their supporters, who barricaded themselves on the Capitol. Marius forced them into submission, and giving them a guarantee, put them in custody in the senate-house. For references see *MRR* i. 574–6, and especially Appian, *BC* 1. 32–3.

public faith: in Latin, *fides publica*, an official guarantee in the name of the people. Cicero notes, however, that *fides publica* could not be given without the senate's approval (*In Defence of Rabirius on a Charge of Treason* 10. 28).

came down into the forum: an angry mob lynched them on 10 December 100. Saturninus' property was confiscated, his house razed, and his laws annulled.

investigation of people's lives and habits: such as the censors performed: cf. *CMaj.* 16.

152 *Cappadocia and Galatia*: Metellus Numidicus was recalled late in 99, after the new tribunes took office (the tribune of the previous year who had opposed his recall, Furius, was lynched by the assembly called to try him), and Marius left for Asia Minor soon after. Cappadocia and Galatia were in eastern and central Anatolia respectively. On his trip there, see T. J. Luce, 'Marius and the Mithridatic Command', *Historia*, 19 (1970), 161–94, esp. 161–8.

Mother of the Gods: note that the priest of Cybele had predicted his victory at Aquae Sextiae, c. 17.

addressed so bluntly: Mithridates VI Eupator, of Pontus (120–63), the most powerful king in the Mediterranean world at this time, was rapidly expanding his kingdom from its base on the south shore of the Black Sea, and had just fallen out with Nicomedes III of Bithynia over a combined attempt to gain control of Cappadocia.

surrender of Jugurtha to Sulla: cf. c. 10. Plutarch regularly speaks of Bocchus as Numidian, though he was king of Mauretania. For his friendship with Sulla, cf. *Sull.* 5. Although Bocchus' monument is commonly dated to 91, Plutarch (our only evidence) is a poor guide, since he may be using a flashback to reintroduce the major theme of his life, Marius' rivalry with Sulla (cf. also *Sull.* 6). The Social War will delay the confrontation. At whatever time, Bocchus would have been trying to advance Sulla's interests, to his own advantage. The Victory group was shown on a coin of Sulla's son Faustus (see M. H. Crawford, *Roman Republican Coinage* (Cambridge: Cambridge University Press, 1974), 426/1).

153 *a match for the Romans*: Plutarch treats the Social War of Rome with its Italian allies (*socii*) very summarily, since Marius took little part in it. M. Livius Drusus, tribune for 91 (and son of the Drusus who had opposed Gaius Gracchus, cf. *Grac.* 29–31), attempted a programme of reform aimed at gaining support for extending Roman citizenship to the allies, but was unsuccessful and finally murdered. Soon after, there followed a series of uprisings by the Italian allies, which coalesced into what was basically a civil war, with all the violence that implies. In late 90 the consul C. Iulius Caesar carried a law granting Roman citizenship to Latin and Italian communities, which checked the spread of the revolt and encouraged loyal allies. The fighting continued in 89, but the war was effectively over by 88, by which time full citizenship had been potentially extended to all peoples south of the river Po. For Sulla in the Social War, cf. *Sull.* 6.

slightest chance of success: Marius fought this battle against the Marsi in 90, after taking the command of the consul Rutilius Lupus, who was killed in battle (cf. Livy, *Per.* 73). However, his command was not continued into 89. Appian (*BC* 1. 46) gives the credit for the victory to Sulla.

gave up his command: in the light of his future behaviour, this seems a weak explanation by Plutarch for his non-reappointment. But he may have had some health problem, or found fighting old allies unsatisfying.

against Mithridates: more precisely, P. Sulpicius Rufus, tribune in 88, introduced a bill to replace Sulla, who was consul and had already been given the command by the senate, with Marius, as is described below. Sulpicius provided the catalyst to provoke the vicious events of 88. Cf. also *Sull.* 8–10.

154 *a hold on Roman life*: Cornelia, mother of the Gracchi, a generation before had had a villa at Misenum, on the bay of Naples (cf. *Grac.* 40 and

note, *house at Misenum*). Marius' house was subsequently bought by Cornelia, the daughter of Sulla, and then by the fabulously wealthy L. Licinius Lucullus, subject of a Plutarchan life. Later, it became imperial property, and the emperor Tiberius died there.

155 *murdered him*: the son of Sulla's colleague Q. Pompeius Rufus, and Sulla's son-in-law.

forced into exile: Sulla returned to Rome with his army, occupied it, annulled Sulpicius' laws, and decreed exile and death to Marius and his partisans. After passing a number of laws, he left the consuls-elect, Cinna and Octavius, in Rome and departed for his province and the war against Mithridates.

called Solonium: the villa was on the road to Ostia. The following account of Marius' flight reads like a novel, with many detailed episodes. The major points, such as the capture in Minturnae, however, are confirmed in other sources.

father-in-law Mucius: more precisely, Q. Mucius Scaevola 'Augur', the famous expert in law, was the maternal grandfather of young Marius' wife, Licinia.

156 *steer clear of Terracina*: in modern terms, Marius' route south-east along the coast from Ostia takes him first to the promontory of Circeo, then to Minturno, where the river Gargano (ancient Liris) enters the sea. Granius was able to sail to Ischia (Aenaria), 60 km. (37 mi.) south, but Marius is abandoned on the shore at the entrance to the river. It seems likely that Plutarch has confused the promontories of Circeo and Gaeta. From Circeo it would be a walk of some 65 km. (40 mi.) to Minturnae, going through the centre of Terracina, which Marius wished to avoid. Instead, from Gaeta, it is about 17 km. ($10\frac{1}{2}$ mi.).

157 *most powerful office seven times*: the same story is found in Appian, *BC* 1. 61.

Musaeus was wrong: Musaeus was a mythical pre-Homeric poet, to whom various poems were later ascribed.

twenty stades: 3.6 km. (2.3 mi.).

which was called Aenaria: that is, modern Ischia.

159 *leave him alone to rest*: the story of Fannia and her husband is found also in Valerius Maximus 8. 2. 3.

a Gaul or a Cimbrian: in fact, Appian (*BC* 1. 61) and Livy (*Per.* 77) say a Gaul; Valerius Maximus (2. 10. 6) and Velleius Paterculus (2. 19), a Cimbrian.

'I cannot kill Gaius Marius': there is a similar story in Appian (*BC* 1. 61), where, however, it precedes the story of the search party and the fisherman.

160 *once it had been taken in*: Marica was an Italic deity, named also by Virgil, *Aeneid* 7. 47.

put to sea: the sanctuary would be that of Marica. Appian (*BC* 1. 61) gives a different story of Marius escaping covered with leaves and leaping upon a fishing-boat.

set sail for Africa: Marius had settled many of his veterans in Africa, and could expect support from them. From Minturno, Marius sailed to Ischia; then to Erice, near Trapani in Sicily; then to the island of Djerba (Meninx), just off the coast of southern Tunisia; and from there north to Carthage; and then again south to Qerqena (Cercina), off the coast from Sfax.

on the lookout for Marius: one of the two Sicilian quaestors was based in Lilybaeum, not far south of Eryx.

to ask for help: Marius' son had been separated from him while they fled from Rome (c. 35); P. Cornelius Cethegus was one of those proscribed by Sulla (cf. Appian, *BC* 1. 60). The king is Hiempsal II of Numidia.

161 *as Marius ever experienced*: Cercina was the site of a colony of Marian veterans, where he could be safe.

Mithridates' forces in Boeotia: for these events of late 88 and early 87, see *Sull.* 11. Sulla penned Mithridates' general Archelaus in Athens, which he then besieged during 87.

war against them: in the absence of Sulla, L. Cornelius Cinna and Cn. Octavius, the consuls for 87, fell out at once. When Cinna tried to enrol new citizens and recall Marius, there was open fighting in the forum. Octavius' forces won, and he expelled Cinna, replacing him with L. Cornelius Merula, but Cinna won the support of an army, joined with Marius, and, as Plutarch says, occupied Rome (cf. Appian, *BC* 1. 64–70).

162 *Telamon in Etruria*: on the Tuscan coast, just north of Orbitello. Appian (*BC* 1. 67) says he arrived with only five hundred soldiers.

obey all his commands: Plutarch is tendentious: only Cinna was interested in recalling him.

betrayed to him: Ostia was Rome's port city, at the mouth of the Tiber.

the Janiculum: the modern Gianicolo, on the north bank of the Tiber.

163 *to him*: Q. Caecilius Metellus Pius, son of the Numidicus whom Marius had forced into exile (cf. cc. 28–9 and notes).

eventual success: Plutarch gives three categories of diviners: soothsayers, perhaps astrologers, from Babylon; haruspices, who interpreted the liver of sacrificed animals; and unofficial (apparently) interpreters of the Sibylline books. The senate had a set of prophecies, which were kept on the Capitol, but other collections circulated.

butchered him: Appian (*BC* 1. 71) gives a fine description of Octavius sitting on his curule chair, waiting to be killed by Censorinus. According to him, the meeting with the senators (see c. 43) preceded the consul's death.

163 *folds of his toga*: in place of pockets, Romans used the deep folds of the toga.

164 *the Bardyaei*: a troop of slaves selected by Marius from among the many who had joined his army in Etruria. Cinna and Q. Sertorius finally killed them (c. 44, end). The meaning of the name is uncertain. Cf. *Sert.* 5; Appian, *BC* 1. 74.

unfortunate consequences: M. Antonius, consul in 99, censor in 97, and especially famous as an orator; he was the grandfather of the triumvir Mark Antony. His murderer, P. Annius, was a military tribune.

165 *triumph over the Cimbri*: cf. cc. 24–7.

volleys of javelins: at *Sert.* 5, Plutarch says the Bardyaei numbered some four thousand.

with a substantial army: Sulla did not in fact return to Italy until 83. He was occupied with the siege of Athens until it fell on 1 March 86 (*Sull.* 14).

166 *the new year*: 86 BC. Cinna was Marius' colleague.

'Fearsome . . . when the lion is gone': Marius sees Rome as the abandoned lair of Sulla. The author of the verse is not known.

Posidonius says: cf. p. 121 above.

167 *from his home to Athens*: Antipater was a famous Stoic philosopher of the second century BC.

his seventh consulship: according to Livy (*Per.* 80), he died on 13 January, not 17.

168 *committed suicide*: the young C. Marius, who had been in exile with his father (cf. cc. 35, 40), held the consulship in 82, at the age of 26, with Cn. Papirius Carbo; he attempted to defend the city from Sulla, but was besieged in Praeneste (mod. Palestrina), where he committed suicide after unsuccessfully trying to escape. Cf. *Sull.* 28–9, 32; Appian, *BC* 1. 94; Livy, *Per.* 88. In speaking of the slaughter of 'the best and most distinguished', Plutarch probably alludes to his order, given as Sulla was about to take Rome, to have the leading men of the opposition killed, including Q. Mucius Scaevola, the pontifex maximus (Appian, *BC* 1. 88).

SULLA

175 *expelled from the senate for this*: P. Cornelius Rufinus, consul in 290 and 277 and successful general against Pyrrhus, was expelled in 275 for this immoderate display of wealth. Cf. also Aulus Gellius, *Attic Nights* 4. 8, and Valerius Maximus 2. 9. 4. A Roman pound was about 327 g. ($11\frac{1}{2}$ oz.). Later generations marvelled that this was considered a large amount, but noted that political considerations motivated the move.

original circumstances: these stories suggest that for a period Sulla had considerably less income than a person of his class thought adequate, until he received the bequests mentioned in c. 2. A. Keaveney, *Sulla, the Last Republican* (London and Canberra: Croom Helm 1982), 8–9, suggests that Sulla was snubbed by other aristocrats at this time, leading both to his association with actors and his later pride in his accomplishments.

gained him his name: implying that Sulla meant 'red', or 'covered with red', an etymology not otherwise known. The name was already borne by his great-grandfather. The usual derivation is from *surula*, 'little leg' (diminitive of *sura*), and thus one of those derived from a physical peculiarity.

176 *actor called Metrobius*: Metrobius was still with him in 79: see c. 36.

make war on Jugurtha: in 107. Cf. *Mar.* 10 and accompanying notes. Jugurtha had for some years been opposing Roman dispositions regarding his kingdom.

177 *kept his anger to himself*: Sulla brought back Jugurtha to Marius in 105, ending the war. Marius celebrated his triumph on 1 January 104: cf. *Mar.* 12.

alliance with Rome: he was legate in 104, when Marius was in Gaul preparing to meet the Germanic tribes (cf. *Mar.* 12–14). The Tectosages were a Gallic tribe. In 103 he was military tribune, and Marius was still in Gaul. The Marsi may be the Germanic tribe of that name known later. Only Plutarch reports these missions (see *MRR* i. 566 n. 10 and iii. 73).

great military commander: Q. Lutatius Catulus, as consul for 102, had retreated before the Cimbri south of the river Po. Cf. *Mar.* 23. This brief note is apparently meant to include as well Sulla's role in the battle of Vercellae (101 BC, *Mar.* 24–7). Although the report in *Marius* tends to denigrate Marius' role, using the accounts of Catulus and Sulla, it appears in fact that even Sulla did not have much to say of his own part.

178 *as Sulla himself says*: A reference to Sulla's *Memoirs*: see p. 172 above.

lethal deity for its devotees: an allusion to a passage from Euripides' *Phoenician Women*, 531–4: 'Why do you pursue the most vicious of divinities, Ambition, son? Don't. The goddess is not just. She has come into many homes and many prosperous cities, and left destruction for those who used her.' Jocasta is trying to prevent the conflict of her sons Polynices and Eteocles over Thebes, but they will kill each other in their fury. The citation underscores the tragic irrationality of Marius and Sulla's rivalry. Plutarch frequently uses tragic quotations and tragic imagery in his *Lives*: see especially *Antony*.

he failed to secure: the dates of this unsuccessful attempt at the praetorship and of his subsequent tenure of the offices of praetor and of propraetor in Cilicia are disputed. *MRR* ii. 14 puts the praetorship in 93, while others argue for 97 or 95 (with an intervening unattested aedileship): see the references at *MRR* iii. 73–4. In the first case, this electoral defeat would have been in 95, in the latter two, in 99. Recently, T. C.

Brennan, 'Sulla's Career in the 90's: Some Reconsiderations', *Chiron*, 22 (1992), 103–58, has argued that Sulla held the praetorship in 97, but remained in Cilicia for several years (96 until 93 or 92), which seems to deal with most problems. In each case, the propraetorship follows immediately on the praetorship.

178 *become an aedile*: the aediles were responsible for the public games, and were expected to put on a good show from their own resources. Sulla's connection with Bocchus would ensure the best of wild animals. In fact, when Sulla did become urban praetor, one of whose duties was to put on the Ludi Apollinares, he put on display a hundred unchained lions, along with Numidian hunters, sent by Bocchus (cf. Seneca, *On the Brevity of Life* 13. 6).

'You're right . . . because you bought it': the speaker is more likely C. Iulius Caesar Vopiscus, aedile of 90, than Sex. Iulius Caesar, consul of 91.

mission to Cappadocia: his official province was Cilicia, variously dated (see above) to 96, 94, or 92, but the senate saw that the situation in Cappadocia needed attention.

made Ariobarzanes king: for the ambitions of Mithridates, cf. note to p. 152, *addressed so bluntly*. Mithridates, a few years before, had installed his son on the throne, with Gordius as regent. The Romans intervened, and allowed the Cappadocians to choose their own king, Ariobarzanes. Mithridates acceded, withdrew Gordius, then allowed him to expel Ariobarzanes and reclaim the throne. Sulla was dispatched to handle the situation, and did.

179 *friendship and alliance*: the Parthians had succeeded the Seleucids as rulers of the territory from the Euphrates to the Indus, with Ctesiphon, near modern Baghdad, as their capital. They were naturally interested in the expansion of Roman interests in Asia Minor, and in Armenia, where they had a client king. This first official contact was friendly, but relations hereafter frequently led to war, including the invasions of Crassus in 54–53 (cf. *Cras.* 16–33), Mark Antony in 36 (cf. *Ant.* 37–52), and Trajan in AD 114–16. This meeting fixed the Euphrates as a boundary between the two spheres of influence.

a Chaldean: that is, someone practised in divination in the Babylonian tradition. Sulla listened to them frequently.

withdrew the accusation: the accusation was politically motivated, as frequently. This is the C. Marcius Censorinus who later killed the consul Octavius and brought his head to Cinna in 87 (cf. *Mar.* 42 and note, *butchered him*).

surrender of Jugurtha to Sulla: cf. c. 3, and *Mar.* 32. The date usually given is 91, but Plutarch does not date it firmly.

utmost danger to Rome: the continuing tension over citizen and other rights for the Italian allies erupted into war, 90–88. Cf. *Mar.* 33. Note however, that Plutarch gives no details of Sulla's military actions during the Social War, but presents Sulla's attitude towards his own fortune. He knew, of course, that there would be many battles later. For Sulla's campaigns in 90 and 89 against the Marsi, Pompeii and Stabiae, and the Samnites, see Keaveney, *Sulla*, 48–52.

Timotheus the son of Conon: an Athenian naval commander of the second quarter of the fourth century.

180 *a more amenable colleague*: Q. Caecilius Metellus Pius was Sulla's colleague in his second consulship, in 80, and became a relative when Sulla married his cousin Caecilia, daughter of L. Caecilius Metellus Delmaticus, consul of 119, and pontifex maximus from before 114 to his death in 104 (see below).

Memoirs to Lucullus: the mother of L. Licinius Lucullus, consul of 74 and an outstanding general, was Caecilia Metella, sister of Q. Caecilius Metellus Numidicus, the father of Metellus Pius. According to Plutarch, *Luc.* 1, Sulla dedicated the *Memoirs* to him, 'as someone who could have written them better himself'.

near Laverna: Laverna is an Italian goddess of gain and thieves: here Plutarch apparently refers to a shrine of that goddess, though some have emended to a more obvious place-name, Aesernia. A scholion to Horace, *Epistles* 1. 16. 60 records a grove of Laverna along the via Salaria, by which Sulla may have passed. (Cf. also the Lavernal Gate, named from a nearby altar of Laverna, Varro, *On the Latin Language* 5. 164.)

181 *called Albinus*: A. Postumius Albinus, consul in 99, was a legate under Sulla, aiding the siege of Pompeii in 89. There are other versions in Valerius Maximus 9. 8. 3 and Orosius 5. 18. 22.

the war against Mithridates: Mithridates, whose expansionism had caused Sulla to go to Cappadocia (c. 5), had continued to annoy the Romans, and a command against him seemed necessary, as well as politically desirable for both Marius and Sulla.

the pontifex maximus: the year is 88. For Caecilia, see above.

as Titus says: that is, Livy, in his lost book 77. For Livy, see p. 5 above.

inability to have children: the name Ilia is probably corrupt: some have suggested Julia. Her daughter, Cornelia, purchased the house of Marius at Baiae (cf. *Mar.* 34). Neither Aelia nor Cloelia is otherwise known.

182 *this happened later*: Sulla passed a death sentence on Marius later in 88 (c. 10); he captured Athens in 86 (c. 14).

abroad and over the seas: Cf. *Mar.* 34.

unfinished business: Sulla, as consul for 88, had received the province of Asia and the command against Mithridates, but was still needed to finish the Social War. He left Rome to press the siege of the rebel city of Nola in Campania. Plutarch passes over the complex political situation, revolving around the tribune P. Sulpicius Rufus' attempt to improve the Italians' position as citizens. Sulla opposed this, but Sulpicius used Marius' support to oppose him, in return for helping Marius get the Mithridatic command.

183 *reputation for exceptional knowledge*: the Etruscans had a long tradition of divinatory lore, including augury (interpretation from flights of birds), which was an important part of Roman state religion, and other less offical practices. The great year, when the celestial bodies returned to their starting-point, was variously calculated, but was always more than 10,000 solar years. Plutarch treats the problem of the reliability of divine signs in different periods in his works *Why are Delphic Oracles No Longer Given in Verse?* and *Oracles in Decline*. As both a priest of Delphi and a philosopher, he was directly interested in this problem, as well as in keeping a right attitude towards the gods while avoiding superstition.

temple of Bellona: the Roman warrior-goddess had her temple in the Campus Martius, just west of the Capitoline hill.

second to none: cf. *Mar.* 35.

suspending all public business: the exact nature of the halt is disputed. Sulla had returned to Rome in haste because of days of rioting in the city, and declared either a *iustitium* (temporary suspension of jurisdiction and judicial operations) or *feriae* (a public festival, which closed the courts and limited public life).

184 *chased to Marius' house*: cf. *Mar.* 35. Pompeius' son had married Sulla's daughter, Cornelia. Their child, Pompeia, became the second wife of Julius Caesar.

take it to Marius: here and in what follows, Plutarch's narrative moves rapidly between what was happening in Rome and Sulla on the march, so that some events are reported out of chronological order. The sequence here is that Sulla, temporarily defeated, fled Rome to the army at Nola. In Sulla's absence, Sulpicius carried a law to give Marius the Mithridatic command, and dispatched the military tribunes to Nola. Q. Pompeius Rufus, the other consul, who had also escaped Rome and fled to Nola, likewise was removed from his assigned command (*provincia*).

war was inevitable: the confrontation with the praetors took place as Sulla was *en route* to Rome with his army.

too dangerous an option: he may also have been disturbed by the desperateness of this move: no Roman army before had marched against the city. The soldiers were forced to choose between following their legally appointed commander, the consul, or the vote of the public assembly. But they had just been used against rebel Italians, who previously had fought by their side. The march on Rome and the taking of the city are described by Appian (*BC* 1. 57–8).

Minerva or Bellona: the Cappadocian goddess Ma, identified with the Roman warrior-goddess Bellona (cf. c. 7) or Minerva (as a warrior-goddess) or Semele (the mother of Dionysus).

185 *At Pictae*: this name of a post some thirteen Roman miles (19 km.) from Rome is an emendation for 'Picenae' of the manuscripts.

Esquiline hill: in modern Rome, roughly the area between the Colosseum and the main railway station, with S. Maria Maggiore at the high point.

temple of the goddess Earth: the temple of Tellus was near the modern S. Pietro in Vincoli.

driven out of the city: for his flight, cf. *Mar.* 35–40.

186 *elected consul*: L. Cornelius Cinna was elected with a more conservative colleague, Cn. Octavius, for 87.

to fight Mithridates: Vergilius was tribune for 87. Plutarch does not mention the legislation carried by Sulla, among which were laws requiring that all measures be approved by the senate before being brought before the assembly, limiting the action of tribunes in other ways, and adding three hundred members to the senate. See *MRR* ii. 40, with references, and Keaveney, *Sulla*, 67–9. Sulla left Italy in spring 87.

kingdoms to his friends: in 91 Mithridates had expelled Nicomedes IV from Bithynia and Ariobarzanes from Cappadocia. Rebuked by Rome, he had withdrawn from Nicomedia, but when Nicomedes at Roman instigation then attacked Pontus, he occupied (in 89) the greater part of the Roman province of Asia and ordered the massacre of all Italians in the province: perhaps 80,000 (Plutarch, c. 24, says 150,000). Bithynia was put in the charge of Mithridates' son Pharnaces. In 88 he gained control of the Aegean as well and sent part of his fleet to invade Greece.

187 *Braetius' career*: Plutarch took special interest in the fighting at his home town of Chaeronea: see also below, cc. 16–19. L. Licinius Lucullus was Sulla's quaestor. Plutarch honoured him with a biography because he saved Chaeronea when a Roman centurion billeted there in the winter of 88–87 was killed: see *Cim.* 1–2.

force to bear against it: Aristion had taken power in 87, with the help of Archelaus, whose troops held Piraeus.

188 *and the Lyceum*: amidst the general waste, and the destruction of Athens, Plutarch singles out the violation of the groves where Plato and Aristotle had established their schools.

at least the same value: Plutarch as a long-time priest for the sanctuary had a special interest in its history. The Amphictyons were a body of delegates from neighbouring states who administered the sanctuary. Epidaurus was a sanctuary of Asclepius, Olympia of Zeus.

the royal gifts: Croesus had dedicated four large silver jars (*pithoi*, cf. Herodotus 1. 51), of which this was the sole remaining. The others had probably been melted down by the Phocians in the fourth century, during the Sacred War.

driven Antiochus out of Greece: Flamininus had defeated Philip V at Cynoscephalae in 197 (*Flam.* 8), and Aemilius Paullus his son Perseus at

Pydna in 168 (*Aem.* 22). Acilius Glabrio had driven Antiochus III out of Greece by his victory at Thermopylae in 191.

188 *dignity of the shrines*: Plutarch lists the gifts of the first two at *Flam.* 12 and *Aem.* 28

189 *made . . . Fimbria kill Flaccus*: for Marius, cf. *Mar.* 41–4; for Octavius' murder, *Mar.* 42; for Flaccus' murder, c. 23 below.

that much pepper instead: the goddess is Athena. The insult is that pepper, as a spice imported from the orient, was much more expensive. In addition, Aristion's behaviour of dancing and partying during the daytime violated Greek norms of propriety.

190 *the Persian Wars*: Athenian orators regularly spoke of the greatness of their past and of predecessors such as the legendary King Theseus (of whom Plutarch wrote a Life), Eumolpus, a legendary poet, and their victories against Persia at Marathon and Salamis.

began at that point: Cerameicus was a district of the city, extending from within the walls, past the Dipylon or Double Gate, out along the road to Eleusis. The Heptachalchum, only mentioned here, must have been near by. At *On Talkativeness* 505a–b, Plutarch says the men were in a barber's shop.

Piraeus and the Sacred Gates: these two gates were on the north-west section of the wall. The Sacred Gate adjoined the Dipylon Gate.

191 *the Deluge occurred*: Athens fell on 1 March 86. On 1 Anthesterion the Athenians recalled the ancient deluge which only Deucalion and Pyrrha survived.

an architectural masterpiece: the arsenal, built in the fourth century near the Zea harbour, and praised by Vitruvius (book 17, preface), is fully described in the plans for the building, preserved on an inscription (*IG* ii^2. 1668). Several bronze statues, buried to protect them from destruction, perhaps at this time, were found in Piraeus in 1959 and are on display in the Piraeus museum.

off Munychia: Munychia was one of the harbours of Piraeus.

reinforcements from Thessaly: L. Hortensius, a legate of Sulla's. Taxiles' men were protecting the pass of Thermopylae against his arrival from the north.

192 *meet him with his army*: that is, he went up high on the east slope of Parnassus and then down to Tithora. This Caphis is from Chaeronea, like Plutarch, although it has been suggested that the text be emended to read 'of Tithora', making him the same person as Caphis the Phocian (c. 12). See Herodotus 8. 32 for the Persian War incident.

plains of Elateia: on the road to Thermopylae, and west of Archelaus' army. For the ensuing movements and the battle of Chaeronea (cc. 16–20) Plutarch offers us a native's familiarity with the terrain.

193 *order to do so*: Lebadea and its shrine to Trophonius were south of Elateia, Panopeus to the west, and both near Chaeronea.

the town had been destroyed: by the Persians in 480, cf. Herodotus 8. 33–4, and again by Philip II.

escapes from danger: A. Gabinius and Erucius are both identified as military tribunes of Sulla. Erucius is named as the commander of the special Chaeronean force at c. 18, and their two different roles may have caused confusion. On Juba II of Mauretania, see p. 172 above.

194 *he would also win*: the first battle is that of Chaeronea, the second that of Orchomenus (cc. 20–1).

leaving Murena: L. Licinius Murena, another legate of Sulla's.

named after this cow: for the story of Cadmus, the Phoenician who came to Greece and founded Thebes, and the cow, cf. Euripides, *Phoenician Women* 638–42; Ovid, *Metamorphoses* 3. 10 ff. *Thor* is the Aramaic word for 'bull'; the Phoenician is *shor*: see F. Altheim and R. Stiel, *Die Aramäische Sprache unter den Achaimeniden* (Frankfurt a. M.: Klostermann, 1963) i. 228.

195 *outflank the Romans*: cf. Keaveney, *Sulla*, 94, for a map of the battle.

196 *during the Saturnalia*: a Roman festival in December in which the social rules were loosened and slaves were allowed to speak freely.

197 *escape to Chalcis*: Chalcis, on Euboea, had a harbour where Mithridates' fleet could meet them.

heroes of this manoeuvre: the inscription of this trophy on Thurium has been found, with the text that Plutarch describes: see John Camps *et al.*, 'A Trophy from the Battle of Chaironeia of 86 BC', *American Journal of Archaeology*, 96 (1992), 443–55.

hatred for the Thebans: the Thebans had supported Mithridates.

what he had taken from them: cf. c. 12.

used against him: L. Valerius Flaccus, after Marius died in January 86, was elected consul for 86 in his place and given Marius' command against Mithridates. Plutarch reports his death in c. 23.

he reached Meliteia: a village in Achaea Phthiotis, between Thermopylae and Thessaly.

198 *at Tilphossium*: in Boeotia, near Haliartus, not far from Orchomenus.

supposed to grow: the Melas (mod. Mavropotamos) crossed navigable marshes and ran into the Cephisus, which flowed into Lake Copais (now drained).

199 *sticking out of the marshes*: this gives an approximate date for the composition of the Life: two hundred years from 86 BC would be AD 115. The Life may have been written five or ten years earlier, which fits our other information. See General Introduction, p. x. Plutarch rounds out his account with a last reference to his own personal knowledge.

haven of Sulla's camp: in 85 Cinna was consul with Cn. Papirius Carbo.

temple of Apollo is situated: according to Appian (*Mith.* 54), Mithridates himself proposed the settlement. Delium is on the border of Attica and Boeotia, near the sea.

200 *Cappadocian that you are*: Archelaus was a Cappadocian, but Sulla also notes that Cappadocia is not Rome, and further that Cappadocians had traditionally served as slaves—as Archelaus was to Mithridates. The notion is the old one, found already in Herodotus, that all subjects of an oriental king are slaves.

abandon Asia: as usual in this Life, Asia means the Roman province of Asia.

201 *great deal of damage*: the Maedians were a Thracian people, who had been incorporated into Macedonia, but had re-established their independence. The next year the new governor of Macedonia, L. Scipio, had to repeat the action: see Appian, *Illyrian Wars* 5.

good terms with Sulla: Fimbria, an officer of Flaccus (cf. c. 20), murdered his commander and took over his army. He then crossed over into Asia Minor and began harassing Mithridates, driving him out of Pergamum and penning him up for a time in Pitane. Fimbria's exact rank is disputed: see *MRR* iii. 92.

in the Troad: that is, on the Asian side of the Hellespont.

four cohorts: a standard cohort had 600 men, so 2,400 men.

202 *150,000 Romans in Asia on a single day*: most historians find the figure of 80,000, given by Valerius Maximus (9. 2. 3 ext.) for the Italians massacred when Mithridates took over the province of Asia, more reasonable.

near Thyateira: in Lydia, on the route between Pergamum and Sardis.

commited suicide in his camp: according to Appian (*Mith.* 59–60), in Pergamum, in the sanctuary of Asclepius.

initiated into the mysteries: the mysteries of Eleusis, at the sanctuary of Demeter and Persephone.

still largely unknown: Apellicon of Teos, a Peripatetic philosopher, had supported Aristion the tyrant (also a philosopher) at Athens. Aristotle was the founder of the Peripatetic school, and Theophrastus his first successor. Aristotle wrote both philosophical dialogues and treatises for the general public (exoteric works) and lectures and other private material (esoteric works). Apparently the esoteric works (which paradoxically are what have come down to us) were kept in his library and were not generally available, even within the school.

203 *now in circulation*: Tyrannion, a scholar and friend of Cicero, was responsible for organizing Aristotle's works as we have them, and Andronicus, a Peripatetic philosopher at Rome, for publishing them by having them copied.

careless and uneducated: Aristotle's library was left by him to Theophrastus, and by Theophrastus to his student Neleus of Scepsis (in the Troad), who left them to his descendants, who had no interest in their content and allowed them to suffer damage. The Peripatetic philosophers between Theophrastus and Apellicon had not had access to these texts, or only to bad copies of them. Strabo (on whom see p. 172 above) gives a slightly fuller account, 13. 1. 54. The transfer of books is listed in the text of the will of Theophrastus found in Diogenes Laertius 5. 52. For a thorough and sceptical review of this story, concluding that there was little effect on Aristotelian studies, and that Tyrannion's work was minor, see. J. Barnes, 'Roman Aristotle', in J. Barnes and M. Griffin (eds.), *Philosophia Togata II: Plato and Aristotle at Rome* (Oxford: Clarendon Press, 1997), 1–70. Plutarch's own philosophical studies would have used these new texts. Again, in Sulla there is a contradiction: he destroys the Lyceum of Aristotle (c. 12), but he saves his books.

arts sacred to Dionysus: Aedepsus was a popular spa, with hot springs, on Euboea. Actors and musicians formed themselves into guilds as 'craftsmen of Dionysus'. For Sulla's pleasure in their company, see cc. 2 and 36. The notice on gout is not in Strabo's extant *Geography*, but must be from his lost *Historical Notes*. See p. 172 above.

repopulate their town: this story of Halae, which so neatly catches Sulla's charm and viciousness, seems to be local Boeotian lore.

fleet of twelve hundred ships: Sulla crossed north Greece to Dyrrhachium (mod. Durrës or Durazzo, in Albania). Appian (*BC* 1. 79) says Sulla sailed from Piraeus, with sixteen hundred ships. Sulla undoubtedly marched with the army to Dyrrhachium, sending the ships separately.

away out of his sight: satyrs had a human form with goatish and equine features, including pointed ears, hoofs, and tail. Strabo describes the extraordinary Nymphaeum at Apollonia in similar terms, 7. 5. 8. The episode, just before Sulla's invasion of Italy, with the green dell, fire, and satyr, recalls the eruption of flame at Laverna as well as the anomalies Plutarch associates with Sulla (c. 6).

204 *four hundred and fifty cohorts*: the equivalent of forty-five legions, 270,000 men. Appian (*BC* 1. 82) says the two consuls had only two hundred cohorts of 500 men each, 100,000 men, and that Sulla had 40,000 men (*BC* 1. 79). Sulla landed at Brundisium (mod. Brindisi) in spring 83, when the consuls were L. Cornelius Scipio Asiaticus and C. Norbanus. The fifteen commanders included the consuls and C. Marius the younger, son of the great general. In the following paragraphs, Plutarch gives a very impressionistic account of Sulla's advance through Italy to Rome against all the forces the consuls could muster, not attempting to follow army movements or provide a clear chronology. Thus, he uses Sulla's mention of divine signs to introduce the victory at Mount Tifata which follows. From Brundisium, Sulla went up the via Appia to Tarentum and Silvium (in Apulia), then into Campania, where he was met by Norbanus and Marius. Appian gives a somewhat more coherent narrative, *BC* 1. 84–8.

204 *ribbons hanging off it*: study of the livers of sacrificed victims was a common form of divination.

the city of Capua: the battle of Mount Tifata, near Capua, where Norbanus and Marius had tried to stop Sulla from continuing towards Rome. Appian (*BC* 1. 84) gives the enemy losses as six thousand.

as it is now known: the burning of the temple of Jupiter on the Capitol, 6 July 83, could be interpreted as the end of an era. Though built by the Tarquins, it was thought to have been dedicated immediately after their expulsion, in 509.

205 *Mithridates and Tigranes*: the battle took place near Fidentia and Placentia (mod. Fidenza and Piacenza) in the Po valley in 82, when M. Terentius Varro Lucullus was trapped by the forces of Cn. Papirius Carbo (consul for 82) but broke out, forced a battle, and won. As has been noted, Plutarch's method collects, out of their chronological order, various prodigies listed by Sulla. This Lucullus brother was the great general, already mentioned as a relative and officer of Sulla's (cc. 6, 11). He defeated Mithridates (74–72) and Tigranes of Armenia (69).

took all sixty back to his camp: this took place at Teanum Sidicinum (mod. Teano) in Campania in 83, when Scipio attempted to relieve Norbanus, who had retreated to Capua after his defeat (cf. c. 27).

found the fox more troublesome: these words recall those of Lysander in the parallel biography (*Lys.* 7): 'Where the lion-skin doesn't work, you have to use that of the fox.'

battle at Signia: Marius had just become consul for 82, at the age of 26 or 27; his colleague was Carbo, consul for the third time. Marius tried to block Sulla at Signia (mod. Segni) in Latium, as he advanced up the via Latina. The battle is placed at a spot called Sacriportus by Appian (*BC* 1. 87) and other sources. Sulla's legate Cn. Cornelius Dolabella was also present.

206 *including Fenestella*: cf. p. 172 above.

sailed off to Africa: Marius was besieged by Sulla in Praeneste. Keeping the focus sharply on Sulla, Plutarch skips the rest of the fighting, except for the battle in c. 29. He not only omits all the fighting in northern Italy, but also completely suppresses Sulla's march to Rome after his victory over Marius. After taking control of the city (though as a proconsul he could not enter it), and slaying various enemies, Sulla marched into Etruria to fight against Carbo at Clusium, then rushed back to defend the siege of Praeneste against efforts to liberate Marius. Cn. Pompeius Magnus, the future opponent of Caesar, had raised his own personal army to support Sulla, then, together with M. Licinius Crassus Dives, the future triumvir, brought Etruria into the Sullan camp (see *Pomp.* 6–8). Q. Caecilius Metellus won the Po valley for Sulla; Servilius won a victory near Clusium.

207 *facing the future with confidence*: after Sulla had returned to Praeneste,

Pontius Telesinus and M. Lamponius, leading armies of Samnites and Italians whom Sulla had reduced in the Social War, made a lightning move to Rome, to force Sulla to abandon his siege, and pitched camp about a mile from the city. Both Pompey, from Etruria, and Sulla, from Praeneste, marched against them. The battle of the Colline Gate was fought on 1 November 82. The ancient accounts of the battle (Appian, *BC* 1. 93; Livy, *Per.* 88; Velleius Paterculus 2. 27, Orosius 5. 20. 9) are difficult to interpret: for a reconstruction, cf. Keaveney, *Sulla*, 143–5 and his n. 28.

Dolabella and Torquatus: for Dolabella, cf. note to p. 205, *battle at Signia*. L. Manlius Torquatus was Sulla's proquaestor.

Crassus was posted: M. Licinius Crassus (cf. note to p. 206, *sailed off to Africa*, and Plut. *Cras.* 6).

208 *Rome had fallen to the enemy*: after the collapse of the left wing, and Sulla's retreat, Sullan survivors had fled to Praeneste to Ofella, Sulla's commander there, asking that he lift the siege and bring the army to help the remnants of Sulla's army at Rome.

was now encamped there: Antemnae, at the confluence of the Anio and the Tiber, is hardly more than 3 km. (2 mi.) from Rome.

sanctuary of Bellona: the Circus Flaminius was near the temple of Bellona, in the area west of the Capitoline hill near the Tiber. Livy (*Per.* 88) and Florus (2. 9. 24) say the prisoners were assembled in the Villa Publica, an open area used by the censors when enumerating citizens, located just to the north of the temple. Both were suitable for large assemblies.

209 *interests of the general populace*: Plutarch states his own ideal of a leader: one who combined aristocratic values with concern for the people. He saw some of these qualities, for example, in Pericles: cf. *Per.* 9, 15, 39.

capricious, vain, and cruel instead: Plutarch is clearly thinking of the emperors of his own lifetime, who also held 'positions of great power'. He also comments on the corruption of power at *Rom.* 26.

Gaius Metellus: his precise identity is uncertain.

proscribed eighty men: thus Sulla invented the grisly practice of proscription, which was to continue through the civil wars of the next generation. Sulla published (Latin *proscribere*) a list of men declared to be outlaws—in theory, of the state, but, in practice, members of the opposing faction—and as Plutarch explains, anyone could kill them with impunity. Keaveney, *Sulla*, 148–68, offers an overview of Sulla's proscriptions.

210 *arms of their mothers*: the pathos of this list recalls Plutarch's earlier denunciation of civil bloodshed (c. 4).

about to be captured: Praeneste was surrendered in mid-November, after the first proscription list was proclaimed, since Marius' name was on it. Marius killed himself when an attempt to escape through a tunnel failed, cf. *Mar.* 46.

211 *rinsed his hands*: the brother whom L. Sergius Catilina killed first was perhaps a brother-in-law, Q. Caecilius. For Sulla, he brutally killed his sister's husband, M. Marius Gratidianus, a nephew of the senior Marius (cf. Livy, *Per.* 88, Valerius Maximus 9. 2. 1, and others). This Catiline later organized the treasonous conspiracy put down by Cicero in 63.

proclaimed himself dictator: in 82, after the deaths of the consuls, Marius and Carbo (who had been followed and killed by Pompey in Sicily), Sulla, at his own imperious suggestion, was officially chosen dictator by the Roman voters, with the broad mandate of 'writing laws and re-establishing the state', *dictator legibus faciendis et reipublicae constituendae*. Any decree of his became law: all Rome and its empire were in his control. The last dictator had been appointed in 202, for the sole purpose of holding consular elections in the necessary absence of the consuls. Plutarch's comments on his powers are extremely general, and do not give the major legislative reforms by which Sulla hoped to re-establish the senatorial government of Rome on a firm footing. See the list in *MRR* ii. 74–5, and p. 173 above.

in Pompey's house: cf. *Pomp.* 9.

siege of Praeneste: cf. c. 29.

release the centurion: Ofella's candidacy would have violated Sulla's new law on the requirements for and intervals between offices. Ofella had held no previous senatorial post. Appian (*BC* 1. 101) has Sulla tell a fine story of a farmer trying to rid his cloak of lice: only fire would work.

striking spectacle by the exiles: that is, those who had fled Rome during the years 87–83.

212 *right to elect consuls*: the date of Sulla's abdication is disputed, and depends partially on the amount of time necessary to complete his reforms: until recently it was placed in 79, just after the consular elections for 78 (e.g. *MRR* ii. 82). E. Badian, 'Additional Notes on Roman Magistrates', *Athenaeum*, 48 (1970), 1–14, at 8–14, argued that he abdicated when he assumed the consulship for 80 (he is never termed both consul and dictator); others have argued for later dates in 80. See the summary of arguments in *MRR* iii. 74–5, with the conclusion, 'a date after 80 seems quite improbable'. Sulla held the consulship in 80, with Q. Caecilius Metellus Pius.

made war on Pompey: M. Aemilius Lepidus was elected consul for 78. When Sulla died, he tried to oppose his funeral. He soon started an uprising, but was defeated (with Pompey playing a major role) and died in 78. Cf. *Pomp.* 15–16.

as an offering to Heracles: Sulla revived an old custom. At *Roman Questions* 267e–f Plutarch suggests that wealthy Romans gave these feasts (called *pollucta*) to avoid the ill will of the populace and limit their own luxury, since Heracles also avoided excess. Another approach would say that it was an example of conspicuous consumption which won the favour of the people and helped to maintain an aristocrat's status. Crassus did the same (*Cras.* 2 and 12), as did Lucullus (Diod. 4. 21. 4).

polluted by a funeral: Sulla, as a priest (he was an augur), had to avoid the ritual pollution of a death in his house.

213 *the cost of funerals*: his own *lex Cornelia sumptuaria*, which limited expenses not only at funerals but at banquets too: cf. Aulus Gellius, *Attic Nights* 2. 24. 11.

segregated into different areas: segregation was introduced by Augustus, according to Suetonius, *Augustus* 44.

'Don't worry, Imperator': Imperator, 'Commander', in Greek *autokrator*, was the title given to victors in the field by their troops; sometimes the senate gave or confirmed the title. Sulla's extended command had given it special importance, and it became a symbol of military authority, later co-opted by Augustus and his successors (since all commanders were subordinate to them). Thus *imperator* came to mean 'emperor'. Here the title of respect contrasts with the playful context.

shameless kinds of feelings: Plutarch had little use for lecherous old men, who he felt violated nature. Cf. *CMaj.* 24 and 33; *Cic.* 41; *Pyr.* 26.

transvestite roles: Roscius was much admired by Cicero, who studied his technique and defended him in his *Defence of the Comic Actor Roscius*. Nothing is known of the others. Sorex, as *archimimos*, may have led his own troop. Metrobius was a *lysiodos*, or lysis-singer, of whom Plutarch clearly disapproved. See C. Garton, *Personal Aspects of the Roman Theatre* (Toronto: Hakkert, 1972), 147–67.

214 *any amount of washing*: A. Keaveney and J. A. Madden, 'Phthiriasis and its Victims', *Symbolae Osloenses*, 57 (1982), 87–99, identify this not as an infestation of lice but as a bad case of scabies caused by itch mite, *Sarcoptes scabei*. He would have died not of this, but of liver failure, whose symptoms are found in the attack mentioned in c. 37. The argument is rejected by J. Schamp, 'La Mort en fleurs: Considération sur la maladie "pédiculaire" de Sylla', *Antiquité classique*, 60 (1991), 139–70, who argues, with many earlier scholars, that phthiriasis is a purely literary or propagandistic death visited on the wicked. There is no doubt that Plutarch finds it disgustingly appropriate, even though the description conflicts with the other partying in this same chapter. But, Plutarch might say, Sulla combined contradictions.

died there of phthiriasis: Acastus, king of Iolcus, was one of the legendary Argonauts; Alcman, a lyric poet in seventh-century Sparta; Pherecydes of Syros, a sixth-century mythographer; Callisthenes, a philosopher and historian of Alexander the Great; and Mucius Scaevola would be the jurist and consul of 133. Eunus' slave revolt was in 134.

new constitution for them: Dicaearchia is the original Greek name for Puteoli (mod. Pozzuoli), the port city on the Bay of Naples. Sulla, in retirement near by, was perhaps considered a patron. Cf. Valerius

Maximus 9. 3. 8. Granius would have been one of the chief magistrates of the city, a *duumvir iure dicundo*.

215 *funeral arrangements*: see c. 34 and note, *made war on Pompey*.

another of a lictor: that is, the statues of Sulla as magistrate, no doubt dictator, with his official attendant.

a part in the funeral: in a detailed description of the funeral, Appian (*BC* 1. 105–6) mentions neither the rain nor the wind. Plutarch wishes to bring out the divine fortune which followed him his whole life.

more harm to his enemies: Sulla's is a traditional wish, expressed also in the fifth century by Cyrus the Younger (Xenophon, *Anabasis* 1. 9. 11). Cyrus did not live to accomplish his wish; Sulla did. He may have imitated the verse of Ennius for Scipio Africanus the Elder: 'Here lies one whom no citizen or enemy was able to repay for what he did.' The pair of Lives continues with the Comparison of Lysander and Sulla.

POMPEY

223 *'I . . . love this son of his'*: from Aeschylus' lost *Prometheus Unbound*: Heracles' father, Zeus, had fastened Prometheus to a rock, but Heracles freed him.

and abused it: Cn. Pompeius Strabo, consul in 89, captured the rebel town of Asculum in Picenum (mod. Ascoli Piceno), thus helping end the Social War (on which, cf. *Sull.* 6). He made enemies by keeping the spoils, and by not defending Rome against Cinna and Marius in 87 (cf. c. 3).

fond of an Alexander: Plutarch notes a resemblance to the representations of Alexander the Great (cf. *Alex.* 4), with the same 'mobility . . . about the eyes', which was often remarked upon. L. Marcius Philippus, consul in 91 and censor in 86, was a supporter (cf. c. 17). Alexander's father was also named Philip. From the beginning, Plutarch establishes Pompey as a kingly figure.

224 *grief and longing*: Pompey's relation with Flora (cf. c. 53, but otherwise unknown) is indicative of a weakness in his character, yielding too easily to his friends, against his own best interests.

his wives: Pompey married five times (Antistia, Aemilia, Mucia, Julia, and Cornelia), but Plutarch thinks especially of the last two, and the influence of their fathers Caesar and Metellus Scipio, cf. cc. 47, 55. On Demetrius, cf. c. 40.

later in his life: Lucullus and Pompey fought over the Mithridatic command, cf. cc. 20, 30.

225 *allegiance to their commander*: in 87, Strabo was cautiously opposing Cinna. The story is doubtful, but both Pompey and L. Terentius were on Strabo's council of advisers, as we learn from an inscription set up after

the siege of Asculum in 89 (*ILS* 8888, text in Latin and English in J. Leach, *Pompey the Great* (London: Croom Helm, 1978), 218–20).

arbitrator of these disputes: Pompey was defended by L. Philippus (cf. c. 2 and note, *fond of an Alexander*), the great orator Hortensius, and Cn. Papirius Carbo, who would be consul for 85. P. Antistius was not a praetor, but presided over the court.

226 *about Talasius*: Plutarch knows other explanations too: cf. *Rom.* 15, *Roman Questions* 271f–272a, and Livy 1. 9. The legendary rape (more correctly, snatching) of the Sabine women occurred soon after the foundation of Rome in 754, and was engineered by Romulus to get women for the exclusively male settlers.

form of slavery: Plutarch passes quickly over the years after L. Cornelius Cinna along with Marius captured the city in 87 (cf. *Mar.* 41–4), then ruled along with Carbo until his death early in 84, while Sulla was in the East. Sulla's rule was to prove no better, cf. *Sull.* 30.

he had estates there: these large estates in Picenum (covering parts of modern Marche and Abruzzo) provided a source both of money and of men.

227 *Auximum, a large city*: modern Osimo. This recruitment by a private citizen rather than an authorized magistrate is extraordinary. Sulla had invaded Italy in early 83: for the civil war which followed in 83 and 82, cf. *Sull.* 27–30. The decision to gather the army and ally himself early with Sulla was the foundation of his future career.

228 *weapons and horses*: the chapter gives a whirlwind account of Pompey's first battles in north and central Italy, which established his fame as a general, and deserved the accolade of Sulla in the following chapter. Cf. also Appian, *BC* 1. 87–8, 90, 92. It is difficult to reconstruct the movements of the armies in this area in 83 and 82: Carbo seems based in the north, at Ariminum (mod. Rimini). C. Carrinas was praetor in 82; Coelius is probably C. Coelius Antipater (cf. C. Tuplin, 'Coelius or Cloelius', *Chiron*, 9 (1979), 137–45); Brutus may be M. Iunius Brutus (praetor in 88) or more likely L. Iunius Brutus Damasippus (praetor in 82). L. Cornelius Scipio Asiaticus also lost an army to Sulla at Teanum through fraternization (*Sull.* 28): this could be the same occasion, ascribed to Pompey, but more likely Scipio lost a second army. Pompey fought Carbo at the Aesis (just north of Ancona). Some have suggested that this refers to a battle where he supported Metellus (cf. c. 8 and Appian, *BC* 1. 87) and that Plutarch displaced events from after the meeting with Sulla (c. 8) to this chapter, but our knowledge is insufficient to prove this.

addressed him as 'Imperator': on this salutation to victorious commanders—but only those holding legal *imperium*—see note on p. 213, '*Don't worry, Imperator*'. We do not know exactly when or where Pompey met Sulla. Expecting much, and getting more, is the leitmotif for

Pompey's treatment by the Romans in the first half of the Life. Diod. 38–39. 10 give another example of Sulla's praise.

228 *had fought . . . Scipio and Marius for it*: Sulla seduced Scipio's army at Teanum, and defeated the younger Marius at Sacriportus in early 82. But Sulla was already Imperator because of his victories in the East.

229 *inviting him to come*: Q. Caecilius Metellus Pius (praetor in 89, and proconsul 88–82) was sent to Cisalpine Gaul by Sulla in 83.

his character particularly well: the comparison with Metellus, and the athletic imagery, highlight Pompey's youth and brilliance. Plutarch apologizes, but he regularly uses early events (childhood or first campaigns) to establish basic traits of his protagonist. In fact, chapters 10–15, the Sullan years 82–79, continue the detailed account of how Pompey built up his position, enjoying Sulla's patronage but maintaining a certain independence.

230 *in Pompey's house*: the short-lived marriage put Pompey in an élite circle: a son-in-law of Sulla and of M. Aemilius Scaurus (consul for 115, censor in 109, and *princeps senatus* from 115 until his death in 89 or 88) and with connections to the Metelli. Antistius had been murdered with others in the senate-house on the orders of young Marius in 82, before Sulla could enter the city.

to deal with these situations: Pompey was sent as propraetor with six legions against M. Perperna Veiento, the Marian governor of Sicily, who fled to Sertorius in Spain, and Carbo, who was captured, and then later (c. 11) against Cn. Domitius Ahenobarbus.

companion of Caesar: cf. p. 300 above.

231 *the city of Himera*: on the north coast of Sicily.

and became tyrant: cf. *Mar.* 41–3.

232 *the earlier incident*: i.e. when he was not recognized and almost killed.

only 24 years old: Pompey restored the Numidian throne to Hiempsal, who had opposed Marius when he was in Africa (*Mar.* 40). Pompey was born in 106.

233 *very brink of disaster*: referring to the young Marius.

stopped arousing resentment: Plutarch carefully orchestrates the appreciation of Pompey's achievement (as Pompey himself had), noting his ability to seem to yield, but still get his way. Sulla's decision to greet him as 'Magnus' is a sign of Pompey's imposing victories and potential political influence.

234 *thanks to their wealth*: the digression on M'. Valerius Maximus, who ended the secession of the plebs in 494, and Q. Fabius Maximus Rullus, who as censor in 304 ruled that freedmen should be enrolled only in the four urban tribes, makes an implicit comparison between their action in resolving tension in the state and Pompey's behaviour, both now and in the future. Livy (9. 46. 14–15) mentions Fabius' limitation of

freedmen to the urban tribes, but not the freedmen's expulsion from the senate.

235 *classified as a knight*: Pompey triumphed on 12 March, though the year is uncertain: 81 or 80. Cf. R. Seager, *Pompey: A Political Biography* (Oxford: Blackwell 1979), 12. Plutarch notes that he could have been made a senator if he chose.

honourable burial: the consuls elected for 78 were M. Aemilius Lepidus, an opponent of much of Sulla's legislation, and Q. Lutatius Catulus, a solid supporter of the senate. Sulla died in January 78.

236 *with an army*: Lepidus began his rebellion while still consul. M. Iunius Brutus was his legate in Cisalpine Gaul in 77. Some scholars accuse Pompey of supporting Lepidus' election, so that he would then be able to step in and save the day.

sent to do the job: Pompey besieged Brutus at Mutina (mod. Modena). Geminius is the friend to whom Pompey gave up Flora (c. 2). Catulus, meanwhile, defeated Lepidus outside Rome (Appian, *BC* 1. 107).

totally dissimilar: Plutarch refers to his *Brutus*, which presents the younger Brutus as acting from philosophic motives, up to his suicide after his defeat at Philippi.

his looming menace: Q. Sertorius, an associate of Marius and Cinna, fled Sulla in 83 and established himself in Spain as governor. He was expelled in 81, but returned at the invitation of Lusitanians and anti-Sullan exiles in 80. Q. Caecilius Metellus Pius, after serving as consul for 80, was named proconsul of Further Spain, and tried to expel him. Cf. the full-scale treatment in Plutarch's *Sertorius*, our chief source, with C. F. Konrad, *Plutarch's Sertorius: A Historical Commentary* (Chapel Hill, NC: University of North Carolina Press, 1994), and P. O. Spann, *Quintus Sertorius and the Legacy of Sulla* (Fayetteville, Ark.: University of Arkansas Press, 1987).

237 *gave him the command*: again Pompey manages to circumvent those who would block him from command. He was given Nearer Spain, where he arrived in spring 76. For L. Philippus, cf. c. 2 and note, *fond of an Alexander*.

the simplicity of his lifestyle: the portrayal of Metellus as weak and hedonistic does not reflect the difficulties of the guerrilla warfare Sertorius conducted or the successes Metellus had. Nevertheless, by 77 Sertorius had control of most of Roman Spain. Again, Plutarch's comparison shows Pompey's greater energy (or his better propaganda).

238 *expert tacticians*: Lauron (mod. Lauro) is on the coast south of Saguntum (cf. *Sert.* 18). Perperna had joined Sertorius after being driven out of Sicily by Pompey (c. 10).

and lost him: Appian (*BC* 1. 110) has Metellus and Pompey fight the battle of the Sucro (mod. Jucar, south of Valencia) together, but this seems mistaken. Cf. *Sert.* 19 and Konrad, *Sertorius*, 167–8.

238 *lower their fasces*: lictors were the official attendants of magistrates with *imperium*; they each carried a bundle of rods with an axe in the centre (fasces) as a sign of the power to punish.

239 *in other provinces*: Metellus spent the winter in Gaul.

if they did not send it: Sallust's version of the letter Pompey sent to the senate is preserved (*Histories* 2. 98). There, the threat seems quite clear that if supplies were not sent, he would bring his army to Italy, and the war would come with him.

easy to handle: L. Licinius Lucullus, consul for 74, in fact received the command he wanted. Mithridates had made a treaty with Sulla (cf. *Sull.* 24), but after Nicomedes IV willed his kingdom to the Romans in 76 or 75, Mithridates prepared to oppose the Roman takeover, and even asked Sertorius for an alliance.

brought to him afterwards: Sertorius was killed in autumn 73; Pompey captured and executed Perperna probably early in 72. Cf. Konrad, *Sertorius*, 217.

without even reading them: some suggested that Pompey should be easy on Perperna because he had not fought him in Sicily (cf. c. 10). Plutarch admires instead Pompey's statesmanlike act in not publicizing Sertorius' correspondence, which might have led to more civil war: cf. the similar situation when Agesilaus did not publish the conspiracy that Lysander had been planning (*Ages.* 20). Pompey set up a trophy in the Pyrenees, listing 876 towns that he had captured.

240 *at its peak*: Pompey made a significant reorganization of Spain, granting Roman citizenship to many, thus building a strong *clientela* there. The Thracian slave Spartacus escaped from a gladiatorial camp at Capua and raised a Servile War in 73. In 72 he defeated two consular armies, and command was given to M. Licinius Crassus, who had almost completed the war by early 71 (Appian, *BC* 1. 121): 'at its peak' is Plutarch's exaggeration.

every last trace of war: the senate summoned Pompey to help. Hearing of Pompey's arrival (cf. *Cras.* 11), Crassus forced the last battle, but Pompey was still able to share the glory. Moreover, the senate's summons gave Pompey an excuse for keeping his army intact in Italy. Thereafter Crassus never trusted Pompey, though they made alliances.

forestalled him in this: more than expressing gratitude, Pompey wished to win the support of the people (here including the knights) by restoring the full force of the tribunate, and giving them a means of controlling in some way the senate. In 75 the consul Cotta had removed the Sullan restriction on ex-tribunes holding other offices in the *cursus honorum*; Pompey and Crassus intended to restore the tribune's right to present legislation to the people. This was done without difficulty once they were elected.

elected consul: Pompey was elected consul for 70, together with Crassus, after the senate exempted him from the Sullan law regulating accession to the consulship (he had still held no other regular magistracy, and was only 36). Pompey celebrated his second triumph on the last day of 71, and entered office the next day.

241 *try cases in court*: besides restoring the tribunes' legislative powers, the consuls supported a tribunician proposal to change the composition of juries for extortion (*repetundae*) trials from senators only to equal groups of senators, knights, and a group called *tribuni aerarii* (apparently a special class of knights). This ended the senate monopoly established by Sulla, which had caused scandal, both earlier and in the trial of Verres, which Cicero successfully prosecuted this year.

accompanied them on their way: the censors for 70, the first since 86, held the standard review of the knights with a public horse (cf. *CMaj.* 16 and *Aem.* 38), but the scene described looks specially staged for Pompey. Plutarch uses every opportunity to show how unusual Pompey's career was, and the effect it had on the populace. Pompey moved directly from knight to consul. However, his military career meant that Pompey had not built up the experience in working within the structures of government and the senate which other senators had earned, and this was to hamper him in political life in Rome.

242 *Pompey's life*: retirement gave him a chance to work on political relationships quietly, meeting with senators and building up his *clientela*. It was to pay off in his appointment against the pirates, and then against Mithridates.

243 *to the present day*: an important notice on the introduction of the ancient Iranian god Mithras into the Roman empire. Mithraic rites flourished in Plutarch's day.

244 *and drown him*: this long digression, fascinating in itself, serves also to augment the significance of Pompey's suppression of piracy, which brought peace to the provinces, temples, and Rome itself. Cf. also Appian, *Mith.* 92–3. *Mith.* 63 gives a slightly different list of temples sacked. The capture of the praetors is mentioned by Cicero, *For the Manilian Law* 32. M. Antonius, consul in 99, whose daughter was captured, had held a three-year command in Cilicia against the pirates, and had celebrated a triumph in 100. *Calcei* were the boots worn by upper-class Romans: Plutarch elsewhere associates them with senatorial governors (*Rules for Politicians* 813e). Caesar also was captured by pirates, but was of different mettle: see *Caes.* 2.

all our sea: that is, the whole Mediterranean. The most dangerous shortage, one at its height in winter 68/67, was that of grain from Sicily and Africa to feed the Roman populace.

four hundred stades from the coast: A. Gabinius was tribune of the people for 67. Four hundred stades is about 75 km. (47 mi.).

245 *win their support*: C. Iulius Caesar, the future dictator, at this time was at

the beginning of his career: he was quaestor in Spain in 69 and 68, but had also been seized by pirates. Cf. *Caes.* 2, 5.

245 *same end as Romulus*: that is, in one version, torn to pieces by the senators: *Rom.* 27; Livy 1. 16. The consul is C. Calpurnius Piso.

to go with him: Catulus was the consul for 78 (c. 15); L. Roscius Othos was a tribune, not the famous actor. Cf. also Cassius Dio 36. 24–36.

strikes the birds: Plutarch likes this sort of scientific digression (cf. *Flam.* 10), but it also confirms the strength of the crowd's support for Pompey.

246 *commanding officers*: historians note the excess of forces, but Pompey did not do things by halves. His first effort was to clear the waters off Italy, to protect the grain supply. Cf. also Appian, *Mith.* 95–6.

247 *on your way*: the Athenians both honour him and remind him of his mortality.

248 *a lot of good land*: this is an unusually far-sighted measure, perhaps related to the social status of some of the pirates (cf. c. 24). Contrast Caesar's crucifixion of his captors, *Caes.* 2. Plutarch, continuing the philosophic note, suggests that his own ideas on man's natural bent towards a civilized life were also Pompey's. The settlements in eastern Cilicia were not in fact in Roman territory, suggesting Pompey had decided that Rome must annex this area.

he come second: cf. Homer, *Iliad* 22. 205–7.

the whole army: Pompey had command over land up to 75 km. (47 mi.) inland; the proconsul Q. Caecilius Metellus Creticus had command over Crete, with a similar responsibility to deal with pirates. Octavius apparently fought against Metellus' troops. It is not clear whether Pompey had a superior *imperium*, but in any case Metellus did not recognize it. Cassius Dio (36. 18–19) gives more details. Pompey's thirst for glory causes him to deny others their own glory (cf. c. 19, with Metellus Pius, and 21, with Crassus), a dangerous situation in an oligarchic government.

249 *same terms as before*: C. Manilius, a tribune for 66, proposed the law, which was supported in a major speech to the people by Cicero (*For the Manilian Law*). In 70 Lucullus had driven Mithridates west into Armenia, and then fought the Armenian king, Tigranes, but since then he had had trouble with his troops and with Roman business interests in Asia. Cf. *Luc.* 5–35. In 67 Pontus and Bithynia had been assigned to M'. Acilius Glabrio.

preserve their freedom: the reference seems to be to the various secessions of the plebs, when they were oppressed by the senate—such as to the Mons Sacer (cf. *Cor.* 6).

250 *no authority at all*: Pompey wished to establish his own authority, and keep the patronage of these rulers and cities for himself. Plutarch also wishes to draw the parallel with Agesilaus' harsh treatment of Lysander, who had been commander on the coast of Asia Minor before him: *Ages.* 7.

252 *Pompey's approach*: on dreams in Plutarch, cf. F. E. Brenk, 'The Religious Spirit of Plutarch', *ANRW* II. 36.1 (1987), 248–349, at 322–7.

and the camp was captured: it is difficult to follow movements in Pompey's campaign from our sources: Pompey pushed Mithridates back to the river Euphrates, but the king kept escaping. Our accounts of this decisive battle are conflicting: cf. Appian, *Mith.* 100; Cassius Dio 36. 49.

253 *and through Colchis*: Tigranes was his son-in-law and king of Armenia. Mithridates came down to the Black Sea and to Colchis, a territory at its eastern end.

at the hands of Lucullus: cf. *Luc.* 25–9.

at Pompey's feet: the *kitaris* was the traditional Iranian head-dress. In the Comparison of Cimon and Lucullus c. 3, Plutarch credits this humility to the drubbing Lucullus had given him.

254 *one that was fair*: for the Parthian empire, cf. note to p. 179, *friendship and alliance*. Pompey had already negotiated with Phraates III, the current king, before attacking Mithridates: cf. Livy, *Per.* 100; Cassius Dio 36. 45. 3.

set off against Mithridates: chapters 34–7 follow Pompey's course on the edges of the Black Sea and the Caucasus mountains. Plutarch creates an exotic narrative of strange names and battles, recalling the adventures of Alexander the Great, Pompey's model. Leaving behind Armenia (extending from the Euphrates to the Caspian), Pompey went into Iberia (mod. Georgia) and Albania (Azerbaijan), fighting the Albanians on the river Cyrnus (Kura), then down to Colchis on the Black Sea. The inhabitants were (and are) fiercely independent mountain tribes.

left Hyrcania in a hurry: Alexander had not come into this area, although he came to Hyrcania on the south shore of the Caspian.

255 *far from easy to pursue him*: Mithridates had fled to the Bosporan kingdom in Crimea, near the Sea of Azov, which was a part of his empire. Later, his son Phraates revolted against him, and he committed suicide (cf. c. 41).

live by themselves: this territory was the legendary home of the Amazons, whose queen was said to have met Alexander (*Alex.* 46).

snakes in the region: arrival at the Caspian Sea would have been a fine feather in Pompey's cap.

256 *back to Arbelitis*: after returning west of the Euphrates into Lesser Armenia, Pompey received delegations from Darius, king of Media Atropatene, to the south of Armenia, and the Elymaeans, from south-west Iran (though some have suggested a small kingdom of that name in the north). Phraates hoped to profit from the Roman attack on Tigranes to annex Gordyene, a vassal state. Afranius repulsed him.

parents and families: Alexander, too, had refused to touch the captured wife and family of Darius (*Alex.* 21).

256 *'family background and stock'*: Plutarch ends this folk-tale with an ironic quote from the speech of the hero Glaucus on his genealogy, Homer, *Iliad* 6. 211. Perhaps we are meant to think of the new riches Pompey is acquiring so rapidly.

fortress of Caenum: at an uncertain spot in the Lycus (mod. Kelkit) valley.

257 *back to her*: Alcaeus is known from inscriptions as one of the leaders of his home city of Sardis. Monime was a Milesian woman, Mithridates' wife, and fiercely independent: see *Luc.* 18.

an utter villain: on Theophanes of Mytilene, see p. 220 above. Rutilius Rufus was renowned for his integrity, while Plutarch considered Theophanes a scoundrel (cf. c. 49). On Rutilius' history, see p. 120 above. For Mithridates' massacre, cf. note to p. 186, *kingdoms to his friends*.

went to Amisus: Pompey came to Amisus (mod. Samsun), on the Black Sea coast and one of Mithridates' residences, in spring 64, and reorganized Pontus as a Roman province.

the Hyrcanian Sea: the once great Seleucid empire had by now been reduced to roughly modern Syria, Lebanon, and Palestine, with weak kings supported by the Romans. Arabia here means especially the Nabataean kingdom centred in Petra; the Red Sea is the Indian Ocean. For Pompey in Africa, cf. c. 12 (though with no mention of getting to the Atlantic); in Spain, cc. 18–20; near the Caspian Sea, c. 36. The weakness of Syria both created a power vacuum and made it attractive for conquest.

258 *reasons for his unpopularity*: Lucullus had failed to bury the seven thousand soldiers, including 150 centurions and 24 military tribunes, of his legate C. Valerius Triarius who had fallen at Zela in 67 in a battle with Mithridates. Cf. *Luc.* 35.

Aristobulus, his prisoner: Judaea had been set up as a separate state by the Maccabees. At this time (autumn 63) Aristobulus was fighting for the throne against his brother Hyrcanus, who was supported by the Nabataean leader Aretas. Pompey installed Hyrcanus.

settle the quarrel: Phraates had reinvaded Gordyene and Tigranes had asked for help. The judges awarded the territory to Tigranes.

259 *response to his questions*: Demetrius was from Gadara, in the Decapolis, south of the Sea of Galilee. M. Porcius Cato was known for his uncompromising Stoic ideals, and became a leading optimate, as we shall see. Here Plutarch again wishes to make a point about the use and display of wealth, which will later be applied to Pompey. Cf. *CMin.* 13.

covering his ears: this way of wearing the toga was considered careless and rude.

to cause offence: Pompey celebrated his third triumph in 61 (cf. c. 45), bringing back all his wealth from the East, and completed his theatre in 55.

lived around Petra: Plutarch treats as separate Pompey's march against

Petra, capital of Aretas and the Nabataeans, although it was closely tied to the conquest of Judaea.

260 *and invade Italy*: that is, coming around the Black Sea and through the Balkans.

and the Romans: Pharnaces took control of the Bosporan kingdom in the Crimea, under Roman supervision, in 63. Josephus (*Jewish Antiquities* 14. 53–4) reports that Pompey heard the news at Jericho, not Petra, and therefore did not leave at once.

the intervening provinces: for Amisus, cf. note to p. 257, *went to Amisus*. Plutarch passes over the enormous number of administrative measures taken by Pompey during his command, which reshaped the face of Asia Minor and the Levant from this time on.

to avert divine retribution: Pompey wishes to respect the body, sending it to the city where others of the family were interred. Plutarch reminds his readers of powers greater than men, even as Pompey looks at Mithridates' corpse.

261 *for the sake of Theophanes*: for Theophanes of Mytilene, cf. p. 220 above. Mytilene had been severely punished by Lucullus for aiding Mithridates (*Luc*. 4).

principles of investigation: the talk of Posidonius, the philosopher and historian (cf. p. 219 above) may have responded to the arguments of Hermagoras of Temnos, active in the mid-second century, the famous author of a book on rhetoric which focused on the question of 'invention', the search for suitable arguments for a case. Some authors report that Pompey also met Posidonius during the Pirate War. Pompey probably invited him to write a history of his deeds, as Cicero did (cf. *Letters to Atticus* 2. 1. 2). According to Strabo (11. 1. 6), Posidonius undertook a history of Pompey, of which we have no trace.

its restoration fund: restoration was needed after Sulla's siege (cf. *Sull*. 12–14).

Cicero's letters: Pompey had married Mucia, the daughter of Q. Mucius Scaevola and sister of Q. Metellus Celer and Q. Metellus Nepos, and had by her three children, Gnaeus, Sextus, and Pompeia. Caesar was said to have seduced her (Suetonius, *Caesar* 50. 1). Cicero's extant letters mention the divorce (*Letters to Atticus* 1. 12. 3), but do not give a reason for it.

262 *contemplating at the time*: the welcome by large crowds and fears that he would march on Rome are similar to the occasions when he returned from Africa and Spain (cc. 13, 21). Plutarch is silent on events in Rome during Pompey's absence, which included various attacks on his supporters and the conspiracy of Catiline, put down by Cicero in 63. Pompey found himself disconnected from events in Rome. Cf. Seager, *Pompey*, 56–71.

Cato's opposition to it: Pompey wished to support his long-time legate, L.

Afranius, for the consulship of 60. This is the first of Cato's opposition tactics which Plutarch records. In the name of tradition and the independence of the senate (the optimate ideal), Cato drove the great men into each other's arms. His decision not to let Pompey marry his niece was incredibly short-sighted, though principled (cf. *CMin.* 30).

263 *subdued by his three triumphs*: the triumphal procession took place on 28–9 September 61, coinciding with Pompey's forty-fifth birthday. Cf. also the account in Appian, *BC* 1. 116–17. The amount of wealth brought into the city was incredible: the treasury received some 480,000,000 sesterces, plus the enormously increased revenue from the new provinces. Pompey had also gained immense private wealth. He was at the high point of his career.

he was almost 40: actually, he was born in 106 and was now 45.

264 *the luck of Alexander!*: some even said that he triumphed wearing Alexander's cloak (Appian, *BC* 1. 117).

more powerful than everyone else: Plutarch diagnoses Pompey's chief weakness as yielding what properly should be his to his friends, as he had done for Geminius (c. 2), and as he was to do for Caesar. Agesilaus had been fatally hurt when, out of friendship, he defended Sphodrias after he attacked Athens; Pompey repeats the mistake on a much larger stage.

esteem in which Pompey was held: there was a strong movement in the senate to limit Pompey's overwhelming influence as much as possible. Lucullus, though reluctant, was pressed into service (cf. *Luc.* 38, 42).

too frightened . . . to stay: pursuing Pompey's need for support, Plutarch moves to his friendship with P. Clodius, culminating in Clodius' infamous tribunate in 58, during which Clodius, pursuing a personal vendetta, had Cicero exiled.

265 *greatest evil for the city*: Caesar returned from his province of Spain in 60, before the consular elections, but was blocked by Cato from standing for office until he had disbanded his army. Forgoing his triumph, Caesar ran for, and was elected to, the consulship for 59 along with M. Calpurnius Bibulus; then he arranged his compact with Crassus and Pompey (cf. *Caes.* 13), called the first triumvirate, although it had no official standing. The historian of the Civil Wars, Asinius Pollio, began his history at this point. At this time Caesar was by far the weakest of the three.

'against their threat of swords': Caesar's agrarian bill had been blocked in the senate, and again when he brought it before the people. According to their agreement, Pompey expressed his willingness to use his veterans to make sure that the legislation passed.

266 *daughter of Piso*: Pompey's acceptance of the pact and his marriage to Julia (April 59) is for Plutarch evidence of his passivity in relationships. Q. Servilius Caepio, who had intended to marry Julia, married Pompeia instead; Caesar married the daughter of L. Calpurnius Piso, who would be consul for 58.

were wounded: this was on the day of voting for the agrarian law (cf. *CMin*. 32, Cassius Dio 38. 6. 1–3).

Pompey's flatterers: Pompey's numerous measures in the East had never been ratified by the senate: now they were ratified by a single law. Caesar was given the provinces he wanted for an extended period and a large army. Crassus' business interests were satisfied by remitting one-third of the contracts which tax farmers had undertaken in Asia. Gabinius was the tribune who had proposed giving Pompey the pirate command. Cf. *Caes*. 14.

off to Gaul: Clodius, as tribune for 58, exiled Cicero (cf. c. 46) and had Cato appointed by a special tribunician law to be quaestor *pro praetore* in Cyprus.

267 *testing Pompey's power*: after relying on Pompey's support in 59 and 58, Clodius made a number of moves which hurt Pompey. Cato's mission to Cyprus interfered with Pompey's eastern settlement; Tigranes was taken by force from house arrest; Clodius killed a friend of Pompey's who tried to retrieve him; and his band of ruffians attacked Gabinius (not mentioned by Plutarch).

shouted out . . . 'Pompey!': Plutarch cites an example of Clodius' impudence, from his prosecution in 56 of T. Annius Milo, who as tribune in 57 had proposed Cicero's recall. Scratching the head with one finger was a sign of effeminacy: cf. Plutarch's *How to Profit from Your Enemies* 89e, citing none other than Pompey.

get the better of Clodius: the assassination attempt by Clodius' slave was on 11 August 58. Cicero, with the help of his brother Quintus, was recalled in June 57; he returned to Rome on 4 September (cf. *Cic*. 33). Pompey's adviser is a tribune for 58, Q. Terentius Culleo.

268 *instead of Spinther*: the question of who was to restore Ptolemy XII Auletes to the throne in Egypt involved much political wrangling in 56, detailed in Cicero's correspondence. The consul for 57, P. Cornelius Lentulus Spinther, wanted the assignment, in connection with his proconsulship in Cyprus, but Pompey thought to take the job. Others became involved, including Clodius and a tribune, C. Caninius (not Canidius) Gallus. Pompey lost interest, and Ptolemy was finally restored in 55 by Gabinius, who was governor of Syria. See Seager, *Pompey*, 115–20, 132.

Pompey's character: Timagenes of Alexandria, a rhetorician and historian—and later a friend of Antony (*Ant*. 72), Augustus, and Asinius Pollio—was brought to Rome from Egypt as a prisoner by Gabinius in 55. For Theophanes, see p. 220 above. Plutarch criticizes the story on the basis of his own estimate of Pompey's character.

with such abundance: Plutarch rhetorically embellishes his report of Pompey's last major external command.

269 *to obstruct Pompey's plans*: for Caesar's actions in Gaul, see *Caes*. 18–20.

269 *proconsuls and praetors*: the consuls and proconsuls each had twelve lictors carrying fasces, praetors six.

period of five years: at the 'conference of Luca' (mod. Lucca in Tuscany, which was in Cisalpine Gaul) in April 56 Pompey, Crassus, and Caesar patched up their pact, which had almost broken down, and they again decided which provinces each would be assigned, depending on the joint consulship of Crassus and Pompey in 55 and on Pompey's troops to enact their measures. Cf. *Caes.* 21; *Cras.* 14. The meeting showed the emptiness of the idea of senatorial government. Crassus had met Caesar earlier at Ravenna (Cicero, *Letters to Friends* 1. 9. 9), and some scholars doubt whether he was present at Luca, since Cicero does not mention it, and Crassus and Pompey were not on speaking terms. Cf. Seager, *Pompey*, 122–4.

270 *had been starving*: Cn. Cornelius Lentulus Marcellinus was consul for 56; earlier he had been one of Pompey's legates against the pirates. In *Cras.* 15, he speaks in the senate, not the popular assembly.

protecting Domitius: this consular election was quite irregular: see Seager, *Pompey*, 127–8. Cato, now back in Rome, encouraged his brother-in-law, L. Domitius Ahenobarbus, to run for consul, as if it were the old days. Pompey's men disabused him. Plutarch uses Cato to indicate how far Pompey had moved from the old senatorial system. The dynasts could not control elections without violence, but control them they did.

for the war in Gaul: Pompey and Crassus were first elected consuls for 55, then conducted the elections for the other offices, which allowed them to exclude Cato, using violence and bribery. C. Trebonius' law gave Crassus and Pompey five-year terms as proconsuls in Syria and the two Spains respectively. Caesar's commands were continued for another five years. Pompey apparently did not receive Africa, although the error appears also in *Caes.* 28, *CMin.* 43, and Appian *BC* 2. 18. Pompey lent Caesar only one legion: Caesar, *Gallic War* 8. 54; the error also appears at *Caes.* 25.

a battle between elephants: Pompey's theatre, the first stone theatre in Rome, also had a temple of Venus Victrix at the top of the auditorium and a magnificent portico adorned with statues. The battle of the elephants (although Cassius Dio 39. 38. 2 says there were eighteen, not two as might be thought) suggests to the reader the upcoming conflict between Caesar and Pompey: 'a truly terrifying sight'.

271 *the courtesan, Flora*: cf. c. 2.

a few days later: Julia died in August or early September 54.

Crassus had died in Parthia: at Carrhae, on 9 June 53. Cf. *Cras.* 31.

272 *the Roman empire*: Plutarch's commentary removes the reader from the events of the moment, giving a more distant perspective of the approaching contest, in particular the relation of fortune to human nature. Excess of ambition was already a major factor in Marius and Sulla: see especially

Mar. 45–6. The quotations from an unknown comedy and from Homer (*Iliad* 15. 189) heighten the style and distance the perspective. In the Homeric passage, Poseidon laments that Zeus does not recognize his right under their agreement to intervene in the fighting at Troy.

the tribune Lucilius: C. Lucilius Hirrus, tribune in 53, a cousin of Pompey.

created consuls: the elections for 53 were delayed, and Cn. Domitius Calvinus and M. Valerius Messala took office only in July 53.

the best tyrant: the elections for 52 were again delayed, by rioting and the murder of Clodius. Bibulus, Caesar's colleague as consul in 59, proposed the sole consulship to avoid a dictatorship.

273 *acting as interrex*: Pompey was elected sole consul for 52. Sex. Sulpicius Rufus served as interrex, the officer who conducted elections if the consuls had died or left office before new ones were appointed.

speak his mind in public: this meeting was held at Pompey's home outside the city: *CMin.* 48.

lineage or reputation: Cornelia, the daughter of Q. Caecilius Metellus Pius Scipio Nasica (whom Pompey was to take as his consular colleague in August 52), appears a paragon. She reappears, significantly, in c. 74 and thereafter.

274 *on that score*: T. Munatius Plancus Byrsa, tribune for 52, was successfully prosecuted by Cicero under Pompey's law against violence. Pompey probably sent a letter rather than speaking: see *CMin.* 48. P. Plautius Hypsaeus was not an ex-consul, but an unsuccessful candidate for the consulship in 53.

maintain and supply his forces: this continuation meant that Pompey would legally keep his army after Caesar's command had expired, a major cause of the coming conflict. It was probably for five years (Cassius Dio 40. 56. 2).

275 *returned them*: Plutarch skims over the various manoeuvres of 51 between Caesar, Pompey, and the *optimates*. Pompey asked for these troops (cf. note to p. 270, *for the war in Gaul*) in 50.

276 *horsemen will arise*: Plutarch finds Pompey's 'boundless confidence' in his own prestige involves a serious underestimation of the difficulties of the imminent confrontation. An important factor would be the loyalty of Caesar's troops to him. Plutarch's accounts in *Pomp.* 57–9, *Caes.* 29–31, and *Ant.* 5 are among our most important sources for the events immediately preceding Caesar's invasion of Italy (others are Cicero, *Letters to Atticus* 7. 3–9; Caesar, *BC* 1. 1–7; Appian, *BC* 2. 30–3; Cassius Dio 40. 64–6, 41. 13; [Caesar,] *BG* 8. 55; and Suetonius, *Julius Caesar* 29–33). His accounts use the same sources, but differ significantly (see C. B. R. Pelling, 'Plutarch's Adaptation of his Source-Material', *Journal of Hellenic Studies*, 100 (1980), 127–40, at 139–40 (repr. in B. Scardigli (ed.), *Essays on Plutarch's Lives* (Oxford: Clarendon Press, 1995), 125–54, at 151–4)). *Pomp.* 57–9 selects as important the mental states and

preparation of Pompey (confident, unprepared) and Caesar (actively engaged, at the gates of Italy), the apparently fair and reasonable proposals of Caesar, the actions of Marcellus and Lentulus to support Pompey, and the breakdown of Cicero's attempt at compromise. Curio and Antony appear as means for Caesar to make his proposals and win the support of the people, weakening Pompey's ability to recruit an army. Cf. notes to p. 326, *new basilica*, and to p. 368, *whom they call 'augurs'*.

276 *his friend Curio*: the individuals listed here are L. Aemilius Paullus, consul for 50, C. Scribonius Curio, a tribune for 50, and Mark Antony (M. Antonius), a tribune for 49. For Curio and Antony, see *Ant.* 2 and 5.

277 *in defence of his country*: C. Claudius Marcellus was the other consul for 50; L. Calpurnius Piso Caesoninus was a censor in this year. Marcellus dismissed the senate before it could vote on Curio's second motion.

278 *came to nothing*: according to Caesar himself, his letter was read in the senate on 1 January 49, as well as in the popular assembly. Cicero returned from Cilicia, where he had been governor, on 4 January. Caesar under his proposal was also to have Cisalpine Gaul. L. Cornelius Lentulus was consul for 49. For Plutarch's compression, which causes some distortion, see note to p. 327, *schism in the state*. Plutarch combines the two senate meetings of 1 December 50 and 1 January 49 into one. Caesar's own account is in his *Civil War* (*BC*), 1. 1–6.

across the river: the small river Rubicon, near Ariminum (mod. Rimini), marked the border of Cisalpine Gaul and Italy at that time; crossing it with an army was an invasion of Italy. Cf. *Caes.* 32; Caesar, *BC* 1. 7–13 (with no mention of the Rubicon).

he had promised: the speakers here are L. Volcacius Tullus, consul in 66, and M. Favonius, praetor in 49.

279 *preserve their freedom*: Cato's suggestion was rejected, and Pompey was given no greater power than he already had, so that he had no legal power over the consuls and the other provincial governors until he was named commander-in-chief at the end of the year. He declared a *tumultus*, or 'civil disturbance' (cf. *Caes.* 33).

280 *a few soldiers on board*: on 19 February Pompey left Rome for Brundisium (mod. Brindisi). Caesar pursued him there first (before going to Rome, not after, as Plutarch says). Caesar arrived at Brundisium on 9 March, but could not get at Pompey, who sailed on 17 March to Dyrrhachium (mod. Durrës or Durazzo) on the other side of the Adriatic. Caesar then returned to Rome (arriving probably on 31 March), confronted the tribune L. Caecilius Metellus, and then headed for Spain. For these events, see *Caes.* 34–5; Caesar, *BC* 1. 15–33.

found himself in: Cicero in a letter (*Letters to Atticus* 7. 11. 3) laments Pompey's decision, and compares Themistocles' strategy in 480 of abandoning Athens to the Persians with Pericles' in 432 of confining the Athenians in the city until the Spartans left. But Pompey had control of the sea, and Caesar had no ships to follow him.

countless Liburnian: Liburnian ships were lighter, faster-sailing ships than the standard warship.

281 *in Beroea*: in Macedonia, modern Veria. Appian (*BC* 2. 49) gives a list of the various contingents.

killed in Gaul: T. Labienus, one of Caesar's best commanders, had joined Pompey in Italy. For M. Iunius Brutus and his father, cf. c. 16 and accompanying notes.

defence of their country: Cicero joined Pompey after an anguished decision, apparent in his letters (cf. *Cic*. 37–8).

his own service: the senate met in Greece, as a kind of government in exile. Cato had abandoned Sicily to Caesar's legates when he heard Pompey had left Italy (*CMin*. 53). Caesar, in Spain, defeated Pompey's two legates, L. Afranius and M. Petreius, but allowed them to join Pompey in Greece.

282 *landed at Oricum*: Caesar stopped at Rome long enough to be proclaimed dictator and hold the consular elections for 48, in which he was chosen consul along with P. Servilius Isauricus (*Caes*. 37). Crossing the Adriatic, he landed at Oricum and Apollonia, south of Dyrrhachium.

as a prisoner: Juvius is Plutarch's or a copyist's error for (Q.) Vibullius (Rufus): cf. Caesar, *BC* 3. 9. 8.

'if they had a winner for a commander': Pompey established himself at Dyrrhachium, placing Caesar in a difficult position until Antony was able to break Pompey's blockade and bring across the rest of Caesar's army, after which Caesar pressed a siege. But when Pompey broke the line, he did not press his gains. Cf. Caesar, *BC* 3. 59–71.

284 *in provinces themselves*: Favonius laments not eating figs from Tusculum near Rome; Afranius (cf. note to p. 281, *his own service*) reproaches Pompey for not attacking Caesar.

on the battlefield: Plutarch laments the lack of backbone in Pompey (contrast e.g. Pericles' resistance to Athenian pressure, *Per*. 33), comparing his duty with that of a doctor, but also criticizes the thoughtlessness of the senators. Years before, Pompey had defeated both Tigranes and Aretas, the Nabataean king (cc. 33, 41).

plain of Pharsalus: in Thessaly, modern Farsala.

285 *plenty of spoils*: Pompey dreams of his theatre at Rome, in which the tiers of seats served as steps to a temple of Venus Victrix (cf. note to p. 270, *a battle between elephants*). According to Appian (*BC* 2. 76), the Caesarian password at Pharsalus was Venus Victrix.

Scotussa: north of Pharsalus, in Thessaly.

held the left wing: Cn. (not Lucius) Domitius Calvinus had Caesar's centre; and L. Domitius Ahenobarbus Pompey's left wing. Pompey's father-in-law was Metellus Scipio (cf. note to p. 273, *lineage or reputation*).

286 *straight at their eyes*: cf. *Caes*. 45; Appian, *BC* 2. 76. This tactic is not mentioned by Caesar in his account.

cooled their ardour: Caesar, *BC* 3. 92.4–5, cf. *Caes*. 44.

287 *lacking in genuine friendship*: once again, Plutarch uses the device of the thoughtful bystander to distance the reader from the action and reflect on the implications of the battle. Scythia (that is, the Ukrainian steppe) had been a goal of King Darius of Persia; India of Alexander the Great. There are similar reflections in Appian, *BC* 2. 77; they may already have been in Asinius Pollio's account.

back of his neck: Crassianus' loyalty and bravery, coming straight at the opposing weapons, so that he is gruesomely struck in the mouth, contrasts with Pompey's cavalry's fear of being hit in the face. See *Caes*. 44 and note, *the back of his neck*.

288 *being surrounded themselves*: as usual in Plutarch, the battle itself is described only briefly.

Pompey the Great: Plutarch plays on the name, which before had seemed so appropriate: see chapter 13. Pompey, however, unlike his predecessors called 'Maximus', did not resolve civic disputes, but fought a civil war.

among the throng: Homer, *Iliad* 11. 544–6: the great warrior Ajax, beset by the Trojan troops, feels fear, and retreats, much against his will. Cf. Appian, *BC* 2. 81.

289 *lost their lives*: on Pollio, see p. 220 above.

went out to war: cf. the same scene in Caesar, *BC* 3. 96. 1.

drank from the river: the river Peneius, which runs through Tempe. The narrative takes a novelistic turn as it follows Pompey's escape.

290 *on board as well*: the two Lentuli were the consuls for 57 (Lentulus Spinther) and for 49 (Lentulus Crus): cf. cc. 49 and 59. King Deïotarus of Galatia had been with Pompey's army at Pharsalus.

'Ah . . . everything that noble people do!': a tragic verse, probably from Euripides.

Cornelia and his son: Amphipolis was at the mouth of the river Strymon on the north coast of the Aegean. His wife, Cornelia, was at Mytilene on the island of Lesbos, probably with Sextus, his younger son, by Mucia. Caesar was in hot pursuit: cf. Caesar, *BC* 3. 102.

291 *Publius' death*: her first husband, P. Crassus, died with his father in Parthia: cf. c. 55.

'must be left as it is': Pompey is aware of the mutability of fortune, but laments to Cratippus of Pergamum, a leading Peripatetic philosopher of his day. Imagining Cratippus' possible response, Plutarch gives his own thoughts on divine Providence and especially on Rome's need for autocracy at this time. Pompey's defeat did much to ensure the establishment of monarchy at Rome.

292 *Attalia in Pamphylia*: on the south coast of Asia Minor.

over to Africa: Cato would resist in Africa until, besieged by Caesar in 46, he chose to commit suicide rather than surrender to him.

help from the sea: Pompey had made this mistake by allowing himself to be pressured by the other senators: cf. cc. 66–7.

three days away by sea: given Plutarch's low opinion of Theophanes (cf. cc. 37, 49) it is probable that he found his advice sophistic and poorly thought out. Once more, Pompey is seen yielding his own opinion to a friend's. The same reasoning is found in Appian, *BC* 2. 83. Other cities and provinces refused to receive the fugitives.

shown to his father: through the agency of Gabinius, Pompey had helped to restore Ptolemy Auletes, the father of the present 15-year-old king. Young Ptolemy was the brother of Cleopatra, with whom he was presently at war at Pelusium, a port on the easternmost mouth of the Nile.

293 *shelter him*: this may refer to the empty promise by Surena, Arsaces' general, to let Crassus and his men go away safely, *Cras.* 30.

Achillas of Egypt: Achillas was the commander of Ptolemy's army. The narration of this debate and Pompey's death is very similar in Appian (*BC* 2. 84–5), including the verse in c. 78. Cf. also Caesar, *BC* 3. 104.

294 *'Dead men don't bite'*: again, a rhetorician delivers bad advice eloquently argued: at *Brut.* 33 Plutarch explicitly castigates Theodotus' desire to show his wit by proving both sides wrong.

Septimius: he had been a military tribune under Gabinius in Syria. Appian (*BC* 2. 84) calls him Sempronius.

saluted Pompey . . . as Imperator: a sad reminder of Sulla's salutation of the young Pompey (c. 8), not mentioned by Appian.

even if he goes there free: from an unknown play of Sophocles.

295 *his birthday*: his actual age was 58, and he died exactly thirteen years after his third triumph—also on his birthday—in 61.

296 *'there has ever been'*: in death, Pompey receives from an anonymous Roman the title he craved: he is 'the greatest', *maximus*.

put to death: this Lentulus is the consul of 49, who had fled Pharsalus with Pompey, c. 73. Note the refrain-like repetition, 'Pompey the Great'.

on the Nile: for Caesar and Ptolemy's murderers, cf. *Caes.* 48 and Appian, *BC* 2. 90. Caesar (*BC* 3. 106–12) relates that he also was attacked by Pothinus and Achillas.

every kind of torture: Cf. *Brut.* 33, though Appian says it was Cassius (*BC* 2. 90). The Agesilaus–Pompey pair continues with the Comparison of the two men.

CAESAR

302 *public treasury*: the first chapter or two of *Caesar*, which might have spoken of his family, appearance, and character, is missing. He was born on 12 July 100, into a patrician family. Sulla captured Rome in 82 from Carbo and the young Marius (son of the great Marius), the political heirs of Cinna, his bitter enemy. See *Sull.* 27–32. In 82 Caesar was 18.

Caesar's cousin: Caesar's father had the same name as he, C. Iulius Caesar. The elder Marius was a bitter enemy of Sulla and an ally of Cinna: see *Mar.* 35, 41–4, *Sull.* 8–10.

was unsuccessful: according to Velleius Paterculus (2. 43. 1.) and Suetonius (*Caesar* 1), the priesthood was that of the *flamen dialis*, or priest of Jupiter, and Caesar was nominated by Marius and Cinna before Marius' death (13 Jan. 86). How Sulla blocked it is not clear. (Hereafter Suetonius' *Caesar* will be cited as Suet.)

small craft: Plutarch simplifies the narrative by combining a trip to the East in 81, in service with the propraetor of Macedonia M. Minucius Thermus—during which he visited the court of Nicomedes IV of Bithynia—with a later trip in winter 75–74 to study in Rhodes (cf. c. 3)—during which he was captured by pirates (Suet. 4). He is silent on the allegations that Caesar became Nicomedes' passive homosexual partner; contrast e.g. Suet. 2. Pharmacussa is a small island near Miletus.

303 *they thought he was joking*: on the extent of piracy at this period, see *Pomp.* 24. The proconsul of Asia in 75–74, M. Iunius Iuncus (cf. *MRR* iii. 113), was busy settling Bithynia, which had just been left to the Roman people (cf. note to p. 239, *easy to handle*). This early anecdote shows Caesar's self-confidence, humour, charm, decision, dynamism, ruthlessness, and not least, his ability to seem less dangerous than he was.

Cicero as well: the date is not under Sulla (see note to p. 302, *small craft*), but winter 75–74. For Cicero's studies, cf. *Cic.* 4. Though it has been questioned, the name is correct: Apollonius Molo was the son of Molo.

to Cicero's Cato: his *Anti-Cato*: cf. c. 54.

304 *opponents were Greeks*: the prosecution of Cn. Cornelius Dolabella, consul for 81 and proconsul of Macedonia 80–77, belongs in 77, after Caesar's first trip to the East and the death of Sulla. The second case was in 76, against C. (not Publius) Antonius Hybrida, with M. Terentius Varro Lucullus presiding not as governor of Macedonia (which he was in 72–71), but as *praetor peregrinus* in Rome, the official who arbitrated disputes involving foreign plaintiffs.

ahead of my story: on Caesar's gesture, which was considered effeminate, cf. *Pomp.* 48. Cf. Suet. 45. 2–3 on his careful dress. The witticism of Cicero is not preserved among his works: cf. p. 300 above. As in the pirate anecdote, Plutarch notes that Caesar's appearance was deceptive, like a calm sea. The reference may be to one of Cicero's letters; it is not found in his extant works.

Gaius Popillius: he was military tribune in 72 or 71, cf. Suet. 5 and *MRR* iii. 105, 168. Caesar may also have been a legate under M. Antonius Creticus in 73.

305 *the death of his wife*: both the elder Marius and his son, the younger, had been outlawed by Sulla; but both, as consuls (the elder Marius seven times), would deserve to have their images carried in the traditional manner in a funeral procession of one of their family. Julia died in 69, after Caesar had become quaestor. His own wife, Cornelia, must have died soon after. Her funeral would have had political importance too, since Cornelia was the daughter of Cinna.

Pompey the Great: Caesar was quaestor in Further Spain in 69–68 for C. Antistius Vetus, whose son of the same name was quaestor for Caesar in Further Spain in 61. Pompeia was the daughter of Q. Pompeius Rufus (consul in 88) and of Sulla's daughter Cornelia: Caesar divorced her in 61, cf. c. 10. Julia was married to Pompey in 59, cf. c. 14.

repay his generosity: thirteen hundred talents would be 31,200,000 sesterces, an enormous sum. He was *curator viae Appiae* before or at the same time as being curule aedile, in 65. In each case, adding his own money, he spent considerably more than the public budget.

no prominence whatsoever: there were no political parties as such at Rome, but there were general sentiments which individuals tended to follow, described under the terms *optimates* and *populares* (see p. 77 above), which in this case would be the Sullans and Marians respectively.

306 *Cimbrian victories*: in particular those of Aquae Sextiae and Vercellae: cf. *Mar.* 11–27.

Lutatius Catulus: Q. Lutatius Catulus, consul of 78, a leader of the *optimates*. Caesar had earlier shown his opposition to them by supporting Gabinius' proposal to give Pompey the pirate command: cf. *Pomp*. 25.

307 *but Caesar won*: the two other claimants in early 63, after Q. Caecilius Metellus Pius' death, were P. Servilius Vatia Isauricus, consul for 79, and Catulus. Caesar had been a pontiff since 73, but both the others had more seniority in the priesthood, cf. *MRR* ii. 113–14. The pontiffs, one of the four major colleges of priests, oversaw the state cult and advised magistrates and individuals on sacred law. The pontifex maximus was the leader of the college and its spokesman before the senate. Caesar needed more loans to bribe the voters more heavily.

the work of the conspiracy: the conspiracy of L. Sergius Catilina to overthrow the government, long maturing, finally came to a head in November and December 63, and was put down by Cicero, who was consul. It was at this time he delivered his four Catilinarian orations. Catiline portrayed himself as being in the Marian tradition, and Caesar, as well as Crassus, was accused of supporting him (cf. *Cras.* 13; *Cic.* 20). C. Calpurnius Piso had been consul in 67, P. Cornelius Lentulus Sura consul in 71, and C. Cornelius Cethegus was a senator. Cf. also the account of the conspiracy in Sallust's *Catilinarian Conspiracy*, where at c. 49 the author expressly states that Piso and Catulus wanted Cicero to invent an accusation against Caesar. Sallust himself was a Caesarian. For Plutarch's different treatment of the conspiracy in *Caesar*, *Cicero*, *Cato Minor*, and *Crassus*, see C. Pelling, 'Plutarch and Catiline', *Hermes*, 113 (1985), 311–29.

307 *men individually*: cf. the two speeches of Caesar for clemency and of Cato for execution in Sallust, *Catilinarian Conspiracy* 51–2. According to Sallust, Caesar recommended imprisonment in Italian cities, without the possibility of new discussion in the senate—a somewhat different proposal from what Plutarch says here. Cf. also Cicero, *Against Catiline* 4. 7–8.

voice of dissent: cf. *CMin*. 23; *Cic*. 21. Cato, being only tribune designate, spoke after Caesar, who was praetor-elect, and others with more seniority.

308 *criminal and illegal act*: Caesar had called on the tribunes for help without success, and was threatened by the Roman knights assembled to protect Cicero: cf. Sallust, *Catilinarian Conspiracy* 49. 4; Suet. 14. He was protected by C. Scribonius Curio, consul in 76 and father of Caesar's later supporter and friend of Antony (cc. 29–31, *Ant*. 2, 5).

about his consulship: clearly Plutarch has read this book: see p. 300 above.

insolent and disruptive: Caesar's praetorship in 62 in fact began with major disturbances: Caesar tried to give Pompey, rather than his enemy Catulus, the credit for restoring the temple of Jupiter on the Capitol and to give Pompey the command against Catiline. The resulting turmoil led to a *senatus consultum ultimum* and Caesar's suspension from office, but he was able to make peace and return to office. Cf. M. Gelzer, *Caesar: Politician and Statesman* (Oxford: Blackwell, 1968), 55–8. Plutarch is either ignorant of or suppresses this incident. P. Clodius (born one of the patrician Claudii, he changed his name in 59 when he transferred to plebeian status so he could become tribune) was quaestor designate in December 62, at the time the Bona Dea affair erupted (see below).

not to be spoken: many stories circulated about Dionysus' birth, infancy, and upbringing. The unnameable mother may be Persephone, queen of the dead. *Bona*, 'good', is a title, not a name.

309 *a great deal of music*: cf. *Cic*. 19. On the cult, see H. H. J. Brouwer, *The Bona Dea: Sources and a Description of the Cult* (Leiden and New York: Brill, 1989).

310 *sister . . . married to Lucullus*: Clodia was married to L. Licinius Lucullus, consul of 74 and victor over Mithridates, who himself accused her (cf. *Luc*. 38; *Cic*. 29; Cicero, *In Defence of Milo* 73). She was a sister of the Clodia attacked by Cicero in his *Defence of Caelius* and thought to be the Lesbia of Catullus' poems.

if they acquitted him: cf. *Cic*. 28–9. The Clodius case became a major incident, involving many important political figures. Caesar, who seems directly involved, sidesteps the issue.

province of Spain: he was proconsul of Further Spain in 61 and 60, but because of the Clodius affair he could leave only in March.

left for his province: M. Licinius Crassus, subject of a Life by Plutarch, had grown wealthy during the proscriptions of Sulla. For his rivalry with Pompey, who had now come back from the East, see *Pomp.* 21–3, 47, 51–2 and the *Life of Crassus*. Plutarch introduces the members of the triumvirate which will be formed (although Pompey has been mentioned casually earlier, in c. 5).

311 *'anything remarkable?'*: Plutarch inserts here, before the formation of the triumvirate, two statements on Caesar's ambition, one making an explicit comparison with Alexander, who had conquered the world by the time of his death at 32. Suetonius (*Caesar* 7) and Cassius Dio (37. 52. 2) place a variant story—of Caesar's looking at a statue of Alexander in the temple of Heracles in Gades (mod. Cadiz) and weeping—during his quaestorship eight years before. Plutarch has transposed a Spanish story to what he considers a suitable moment.

'Imperator': Caesar needed military glory and money: his campaigns won him both. He drove tribes out of the hills of the Herminus range, south of the Duero on the Portuguese–Spanish border: cf. Cassius Dio 37. 52–3. For the title imperator, see note to p. 213, *'Don't worry, Imperator'*. He left in June 60 so that he could be in Rome for the elections.

go for the consulship: his triumph had been voted by the senate, and Caesar had made splendid preparations.

312 *it was ineffective*: the three men made an unofficial pact to work together, often called the first triumvirate. Cf. *Pomp.* 47. Cato, who emerged as a kind of prophet for the *optimates*, by his intransigence (as in refusing Caesar a triumph) forced the three to combine their efforts to achieve their individual aims. It is at this point that Asinius Pollio began his history (see p. 220 above). Only Plutarch and Appian (*BC* 2. 8–9) place this pact before the elections; Cicero (*Letters to Atticus* 2. 3. 3) places it after, perhaps in December.

the people were delighted: Caesar's first project was the passing of two agrarian laws, which would benefit Pompey's veterans and landless urban citizens. See R. Seager, *Pompey: A Political Biography* (Oxford: Blackwell, 1979), 86–7; Gelzer, *Caesar*, 72–4. Pompey's support, with its threat of bringing his veterans into the city, was essential (cf. *Pomp.* 47).

control of resources: for these marriages, cf. *Pomp.* 47 and note, *daughter of Piso.*

313 *five-year period*: cf. also *Pomp.* 48 and note to p. 266, *Pompey's flatterers.*

let him go: Caesar had hoped to scare Cato into appealing to the tribunes, but Cato allowed himself to be arrested and Caesar himself had to intervene. In *CMin.* 31, this incident is connected with the first agrarian law.

313 *expelled from Italy*: Pompey and Caesar helped arrange Clodius' transition to plebeian status (cf. note to p. 308, *insolent and disruptive*), which Pompey soon regretted (*Pomp*. 48–9). Clodius, as tribune for 58, immediately carried a proposal to exile Cicero because of his execution of the Catilinarian conspirators. Caesar kept his army outside Rome, and only left in March 58 (cf. Cicero, *On his Return, in the Senate* 32; Cassius Dio 38. 17). Cicero left Rome on 20 March. Here Plutarch gives Caesar all the blame: in *Pomp*. 48 Clodius is the moving force, whereas in *CMin*. 33 he is working for the triumvirs. The emphasis changes to put each man's concerns and decisions centre stage. Plutarch passes over other legislation, especially the ratification of Pompey's eastern arrangements, a law on provincial government, and a rebate to the tax farmers (cf. *Pomp*. 48 and note, *Pompey's flatterers*).

new kind of achievement: at the beginning of Caesar's Gallic campaigns (58–50 BC), Plutarch stops for an estimate of him as conqueror and general (cc. 15–17). The encomium, using comparisons with the greatest Roman generals, sets him above all Romans, even Pompey, as a commander. It is followed by two chapters of anecdotes drawn from his campaigns.

314 *over all the world*: there are Homeric reminiscences in the phrase: cf. *Iliad* 22. 268, Achilles challenging Hector, and *Odyssey* 9. 20, Odysseus identifying himself.

better than any of them: Fabius and Scipio Africanus were the great generals against Hannibal, Scipio Aemilianus defeated Carthage and Numantia, L. Licinius Lucullus brought down Mithridates, M. Terentius Varro Lucullus fought in Thrace. For Marius, Sulla, and Pompey, see their Lives in the present collection. Metellus is probably Numidicus, who did much to defeat Jugurtha (cf. *Mar*. 7–8), and of whom Plutarch planned a Life (cf. *Mar*. 29).

control of the ship: at the siege of Massalia, in summer 49: cf. Valerius Maximus 3. 2. 22 and Suet. 68.

surrounded by his kinsmen and saved: cf. Caesar, *Civil War* (hereafter *BC*) 3. 53. 3–5 (who reports 120 holes in the man's shield), Valerius Maximus 3. 2. 23, Suet. 68, and many other writers. For Dyrrhachium, in 48 BC, cf. c. 39.

315 *losing his shield*: Caesar campaigned in Britain in 55 and 54, cf. c. 23. For this story, cf. Valerius Maximus 3. 2. 23 and Cassius Dio 37. 53. 2–3.

stabbed himself to death: Granius is not otherwise known. For Scipio in Africa in 47, cf. cc. 52–3. All four anecdotes probably derive from Pollio.

Corduba, we hear: for his occasional epileptic fits, cf. cc. 53 and 60, Suet. 45, and Appian, *BC* 2. 110. He was in Corduba (mod. Córdoba) in September 49 (Caesar, *BC* 2. 19), but no doubt on other occasions as well, as quaestor and proconsul.

only eight days: at the end of March 58: cf. Caesar, *Gallic War* (*BG*) 1. 7.

1. This was after he had tarried in Rome, cf. note to p. 313, *expelled from Italy*.

316 *according to Oppius*: C. Oppius was a henchman of Caesar's. Cf. p. 300 above.

wanted to tell them: cf. Suet. 56, where it is noted that for secret matters he used a cipher, substituting D for A, and so on.

'commit a faux pas oneself': according to Suet. 53, this was flavoured oil, so perhaps we should understand in Plutarch myrrh-flavoured oil.

overhanging the doorway: cf. Suet. 72: Oppius had fallen sick in a forest, and this hut was the only place that could be found.

317 *remained uninhabited*: this chapter summarizes the events of Caesar, *BG* 1. 1–29, for 58 BC, when the Helvetii, a Gallic people, attempted to march through Gallia Narbonensis, though the numbers are somewhat different. For an analysis of Plutarch's account of the Gallic Wars, see C. B. R. Pelling, 'Plutarch on the Gallic Wars', *Classical Bulletin*, 60 (1984), 88–103. In speaking of the battle of the Arar (Saône, *BG* 1. 12), Caesar does not mention Labienus. Caesar was attacked *en route* to Bibracte, the Aeduan capital. He mentions the removal of his and others' horses (*BG* 1. 25. 1), but compares the invasion of the Cimbri and Teutones not to that of the Helvetii, but of the Germans of Ariovistus (*BG* 1. 33. 4, cf. c. 19).

fell in behind him: this campaign (Caesar, *BG* 1. 30–53) was fought in 58, at the request of the Gauls (*BG* 1. 31–33). Caesar rebuked his men at Vesontio (Besançon): cf. *BG* 1. 39–41. The tenth was his favourite legion.

318 *numbered eighty thousand*: Caesar mentions the women diviners at *BG* 1. 50. 4–5, and the battle and flight at 1. 52–3.

known as the Rubicon: the Sequani inhabited the territory around modern Besançon. The Rubicon (cf. c. 32) was a small river north of Ariminum (mod. Rimini), not securely identified, and formed the border between Cisalpine Gaul and Italy. Though based in Cisalpine Gaul, Caesar still influences—and corrupts—Roman politics.

bodies clogging them: for the war in 57 with the Belgae, who lived north of the Seine and Marne, cf. Caesar, *BG* 2. 1–34. For the bodies in the rivers, *BG* 2. 10. 2–3.

319 *remained alive*: for the battle with the Nervii, the fiercest of the Belgae, see Caesar, *BG* 2. 25–6; for Caesar with the shield, *BG* 2. 25. 2.

more than two hundred senators: the meeting at Luca was in April 56. Cf. *Pomp*. 51 and note, *period of five years*. Appius Claudius Pulcher (the brother of Clodius), praetor for 57, was governor of Sardinia for 56. Q. Caecilius Metellus Nepos, consul in 57, was proconsul in Nearer Spain for 56–55.

320 *in Cyprus*: he had been assigned the province of Cyprus by Clodius in 58: cf. *Pomp*. 48. He returned later in 56.

320 *increasing their territory*: Plutarch skips the minor campaigns of 56 and the election of Pompey and Crassus as consuls for 55, and their legislation (cf. *Pomp.* 52), and moves on to the campaigns of 55.

untrustworthy truce-breakers: Caesar describes the campaign against the Usipites and Tencteri (thus Caesar's text) in *BG* 4. 1–19, the attack on the cavalry at 4.12, and his retaliation on the unprepared Germans at 4. 14–15. He estimates there were 430,000, of whom few escaped.

the guilty party: Cato argued that Caesar had broken the treaty, not the Germans. For Tanusius, see p. 300 above.

321 *in ten days*: the Rhine bridge, described in *BG* 4. 17, was a remarkable engineering feat, clearly intended to awe the Germans, as Caesar suggests. To cross with boats was not appropriate 'to his honour or that of the Roman people'.

eighteen days in Germany: cf. Caesar, *BG* 4. 19. He broke up the bridge on his return.

imposed a tribute: Caesar made a preliminary expedition in late 55 (*BG* 4. 20–38), then a second in 54 (*BG* 5. 2–23). Plutarch exalts the enterprise, which extended the boundaries of the known world into the outer ocean (as Alexander had done in reaching the Indian Ocean), although the inhabitants had little wealth, as some had dreamed. In Plutarch's day, Britain, like Gaul, was a Roman province.

lies buried: Pompey had married Julia to seal his compact with Caesar and Crassus (c. 14); she died in late August or early September. On Pompey's affection for her, cf. *Pomp.* 53. On the games Caesar later held for her, cf. c. 55. After his assassination, Caesar's funeral pyre was made near her tomb (Suet. 84).

322 *being overrun*: this is the orator Cicero's brother, Quintus Tullius Cicero, who was a legate of Caesar's.

a great many of them: the revolt occurred in winter 54/53, and is described in Caesar, *BG* 5. 24–52 (his stratagem, 5. 50–1).

around the river Po: Pompey loaned one legion, not two: cf. *Pomp.* 52 and note, *for the war in Gaul*.

323 *tyrannical plans*: the revolt was calmed but not crushed. Plutarch passes over the campaigning season of 53. The Gauls led by Vercingetorix (Plutarch's Vergentorix), the head of the Arverni, began an organized and united attack on the Romans in early 52, beginning with the massacre of Roman traders at Cenabum (mod. Orléans).

Gaul to war: on the troubles at Rome following the murder of Clodius, cf. *Pomp.* 54 and notes.

324 *a sacred offering*: the battle with Vercingetorix' cavalry is found in Caesar, *BG* 7. 66–7, but the sword is not mentioned.

until Caesar's triumph: Plutarch's summary is rapid and encomiastic, but does not exaggerate the difficulty of the operation, running from July to

September 52, and described by Caesar in *BG* 7. 68–90. Caesar gives the men outside as 240,000, those inside as 80,000 (7. 76. 3, 7. 71. 3). Vercingetorix was led in Caesar's triumph in 46 (cf. c. 55), then executed. After this outstanding success, Plutarch omits the campaigns of 51, which are described by Hirtius in his continuation of Caesar's *Commentaries* (*BG* 8), and moves directly to Caesar's confrontation with Pompey.

325 *died in Parthia*: in June 53: cf. *Pomp.* 53 and note, *Crassus had died in Parthia.*

an exercise ground: Plutarch sees Caesar as having a consistent plan for making himself sole ruler (similar to Alexander's aim of conquering all Asia) and using the Gallic campaigns as an exercise to prepare himself for the decisive match. This seems to attribute to Caesar aims only clear from hindsight, but the problem of Caesar's goals at various stages of his career continues to trouble scholars. Plutarch's view is adopted e.g. by Gelzer, *Caesar*, 169: 'His political position in Rome was far too precarious, and the most serious battle was yet to be fought. With this in view he forged his Gallic army into an instrument the like of which no Roman statesman had ever possessed, and his ability to finance his policies was likewise without precedent.'

rather than with votes: Plutarch refers to the violent gangs which dominated Roman politics in the 50s.

nothing worse than an autocracy: some kind of monarchy looked like the solution to Rome's problems. The city needed a doctor and helmsman to cure and guide it. The images are similar to those used of Pericles (*Per.* 9, 33) and by Plato in the *Republic* and elsewhere, but point to the founding of the principate by Augustus.

326 *a thousand talents*: Pompey was made sole consul for 52, but only well into the year, because of the violence which accompanied the consular elections. Cf. *Pomp.* 54. His two Spanish provinces were continued (he did not have Africa: cf. *Pomp.* 52 and note to p. 270, *for the war in Gaul*). Unlike Caesar, he stayed at Rome and governed them through legates.

Marcellus and Lentulus: while Caesar was asking for an extension of his command so that he would not have to give up his *imperium* and army (and thus become vulnerable to prosecution, which was being threatened by Cato, cf. c. 22) until he became consul, M. Claudius Marcellus, consul for 51, was working to have Caesar lose his consulship on 1 March 50, with the idea that the victory at Alesia had ended the Gallic War. Lentulus would be L. Cornelius Lentulus Crus, who would be consul in 49.

show them to Caesar: on the proposal of the tribune Vatinius, Caesar had, as consul in 59, founded a colony at Novum Comum (mod. Como) in Cisalpine Gaul, with its citizens considered Roman citizens. Marcellus treated this action as illegal and void.

new basilica: Curio was Caesar's henchman, cf. c. 8. L. Aemilius Paullus, consul of 50, extensively restored the earlier Basilica Fulvia, or Aemilia et Fulvia, built in 179: its remains are still visible in the Roman forum.

In *Caes.* 29–31, Plutarch uses flashbacks to tie past action to the crisis of the moment. He begins with Caesar's request to renew his commands and to hold a consulship, then follows briefly the opposition of Marcellus up to the end of his consulship (31 December 49). He then uses a flashback to recall Pompey's opposition to Caesar's continuing in a command, his request for two of Caesar's legions, and the false confidence inspired by the reports of the men who brought the legions back to Italy. Turning to Caesar's proposals, he supports the statement that they seemed fair and reasonable by recalling in a second flashback the popular approval when Curio read a letter of Caesar to the people. The following reference to Antony reading a letter seems at first to continue the flashback, but probably picks up the action from the end of Marcellus' consulship, and describes an event of 1 January, when Caesar's letter was also read in the senate. Scipio's proposal certainly belongs to the senate meeting of 1 January. Antony's proposal to poll the senators on both generals' laying down their arms seems a doublet of Curio's proposal in *Pomp.* 58. Both serve to confirm that Caesar's proposals were reasonable and supported by the majority of the senate, as later events reveal the hostility of the senatorial leadership, especially the consuls. See notes to p. 276, *horsemen will arise*, and to p. 368, *whom they call 'augurs'*.

326 *250 drachmas*: cf. c. 25, and *Pomp.* 56.

327 *for raising troops*: on Pompey's false confidence, see *Pomp.* 57.

'But this will give him it!': cf. the similar story in *Pomp.* 58.

one of the tribunes: Marcus Antonius, or Mark Antony, a man close to Caesar, who came to power after his assassination, as told in Plutarch's *Antony*.

schism in the state: this meeting took place on 1 January 49, but Antony's division of the senators seems a doublet of that of Curio in *Pomp.* 58. The proposals to disarm and the angry words of the presiding consul also seem similar. Caesar's own account is given in his *BC* 1. 1–6.

328 *in fear for their lives*: Cicero returned from Cilicia, where he had been governor, on 4 January. On 7 January the senate passed the *senatus consultum ultimum*, a decree requiring the consuls to take all steps to preserve the republic, and Antony and Curio were expelled from the senate and fled to Caesar in Cisalpine Gaul (cf. also *Ant.* 5).

this task-force: Ariminum (mod. Rimini) was in Italy. It was seized on the morning of 11 January 49.

329 *an unspeakable union*: according to Suet. 31, which gives a very similar account of this day, he inspected plans for a gladiatorial school he was building, and got the mules for his carriage from a bakery. (Surprise would allow him to win Ariminum easily.) Also, there appeared a vision of a piper, presumably Pan, who sounded a trumpet to rouse the soldiers to war. The account is probably from Asinius Pollio, whom Plutarch mentions: see p. 300 above. A dream of intercourse with one's mother

meant that one was to take possession of one's country: cf. e.g. Herodotus 6. 107. Plutarch, however, calls it 'unspeakable', a violation of what is right, just as the invasion was.

330 *stay behind*: Plutarch captures the confusion in Rome and Italy. The senate had not expected Caesar to act, or at least not without his other legions. Pompey left Rome on 17 January, declaring that he would consider as enemies those who stayed behind (cf. Caesar, *BC* 1. 33. 2). He may not have had as many troops as Caesar, and many he had had just come from Caesar's service (cf. *Pomp*. 60).

sent him by Caesar: T. Labienus, one of Caesar's best commanders, joined Pompey on 22 January.

331 *fugitives turned back*: L. Domitius Ahenobarbus withdrew to his stronghold of Corfinium with his army, rejecting Pompey's request to join him, and soon surrendered (21 Feb.). Cf. Caesar, *BC* 1. 19–23. In the mean time, Caesar had seized most of northern Italy. Domitius later fought at Massalia and at Pharsalus.

without bloodshed: cf. *Pomp*. 62–3, with the misleading displacement of Caesar's stay in Rome before his march to Brundisium.

332 *everything he needed for the war*: the tribune L. Caecilius Metellus attempted to block Caesar's access to the state treasury. Cf. Caesar, *BC* 1. 33. 3. Cicero found this threat scandalous: *Letters to Atticus* 10. 4. 8 and 10. 8. 6.

went to join Pompey: Caesar defeated L. Afranius and M. Petreius in Spain, after rescuing himself from a difficult position near Ilerda: Caesar, *BC* 1. 34–87. Gelzer, *Caesar*, 217, writes, 'In a campaign of forty days the best army controlled by the enemy had been put out of action.' M. Terentius Varro surrendered soon after. Caesar acquired seven legions. Afranius fled to Pompey and fought at Dyrrhachium and Pharsalus (cf. *Pomp*. 66, 67).

campaign against Pompey: Caesar was named dictator while still at Massalia (mod. Marseilles), which had resisted him under the leadership of Domitius Ahenobarbus, the fugitive from Corfinium. He was in Rome in December 49. Caesar's father-in-law was L. Calpurnius Piso Caesoninus (consul for 58). Besides passing his legislation, Caesar held elections, and he and P. Servilius Isauricus were chosen consuls for 48.

the winter solstice: the Roman calendar was ahead of the solar year at this time. Caesar later reformed it: cf. c. 59.

333 *over the sea to Caesar*: Caesar was able to transfer seven legions to Oricum and Apollonia, south of Dyrrhachium (mod. Durrës or Durazzo), where Pompey was based (cf. *Pomp*. 65). The complaints of the soldiers call the reader's attention to their long marches and difficult battles, their loyalty, and especially to Caesar's separation from a major portion of his troops, which was to cause him great difficulty. Antony was not able to reach Caesar with these troops until the end of March.

334 *the ones who were there*: this story, not found in Caesar but reported in Suet. 58. 2, Appian, *BC* 2. 57, and Cassius Dio 41. 46, sounds apocryphal, but conveys the pressure of the moment, Caesar's daring, and his self-confidence. The use of the third person by Caesar recalls the same practice in his *Commentaries*. Caesar did get a strong letter to Antony through.

forces from Brundisium: they had to escape the blockade: cf. *Ant*. 7; Caesar, *BC* 3. 26–9.

effect on their morale: on this episode, cf. Caesar, *BG* 3. 48. The comparison with beasts also appears in Suet. 68 and Appian, *BC* 2. 61.

335 *arm at the shoulder*: this Pompeian success is found at Caesar, *BC*. 3. 67–9, and Appian, *BC* 2. 61–2. The episode of Scaevus (c. 16 above) immediately precedes it in both narratives. Note that by displacing the Scaevus episode away from the success, Plutarch makes this sequence more negative for Caesar.

did not come to his aid: Q. Caecilius Metellus Scipio Nasica had been proconsul in Syria in 49, and had brought his troops into Macedonia. Caesar's decision, as Plutarch notes, was a major change in strategy, which Caesar explains at *BC* 3. 78.

336 *before very long*: for the confidence of the Pompeians, cf. also *Pomp*. 66.

he set out after Caesar: cf. *Pomp*. 67 and notes.

overcome the illness: Gomphi in Thessaly, having learned of Caesar's defeat, did not admit him, so he stormed the town and plundered it as an example. Caesar, *BC* 3. 80, does not mention the drinking, but Suet. 67 notes that he sometimes allowed this. Plutarch records it as a weak parallel to Alexander's Carmanian bacchanal, *Alex*. 67.

established camps there: the Pharsalian plain lay in the centre of Thessaly, near the city of Pharsalus.

entering his theatre in Rome: for the explanation of the dream, see *Pomp*. 68, which adds a second part that indicates he is giving honour to Caesar. Lucan (*Civil War* 7. 7–24) interprets even this first part as a sign of the end of Pompey's good fortune, as he recalls happy days in the past.

337 *after the war*: Domitius Ahenobarbus (cf. c. 34), P. Cornelius Lentulus Spinther, consul for 57, and Caecilius Metellus Scipio Nasica (cf. c. 39). Cf. *Pomp*. 67.

on the other side: Plutarch gives the figures for soldiers as found in Caesar, *BC* 3. 88–9; many scholars consider them exaggerated.

risk battle by themselves: Q. Cornificius was Caesar's quaestor in Illyricum; Q. Fufius Calenus was a legate with the authority of a praetor (*legatus pro praetore*) who had been sent earlier to southern Greece.

march to Scotussa: Scotussa was north of Pharsalus. Caesar had offered battle for three days. The fire in the sky, often mentioned, was associated with Caesar's success: cf. *Pomp.* 68; Appian, *BC* 2. 68; Lucan, *Civil War* 7. 153–60.

338 *on the right*: in the centre was Cn. Domitius Calvinus (to be distinguished from the Pompeian Domitius Ahenobarbus). Caesar (*BC* 3. 89. 3) says that he put P. Cornelius Sulla on the right, and he himself stayed on the left, opposite Pompey. Cf. *Pomp.* 69.

the point of impact: see Caesar, *BC* 3. 92. 2–5; cf. *Pomp.* 69.

339 *the back of his neck*: the centurion showed not only the loyalty and courage of Caesar's troops, but their fearlessness of enemy weapons, even in their faces. Contrast Pompey's gentleman cavalry, below (c. 45). Caesar gives his name as C. Crastinus (*B.C.* 3. 91. 1), the usual form in other accounts, and reports the wound at 3. 99. 1–2. Cf. *Pomp.* 71.

and slaughtered them: Caesar's successful use of his reserve cohorts against the cavalry turned the whole battle: cf. *Pomp.* 71; Caesar, *BC* 3. 93–4. However, Caesar does not mention aiming at the faces of the cavalry, which would not win him praise at Rome. In *Pomp.* 69, Plutarch says the soldiers were specifically instructed to do this, and the orders are alluded to at *Caes.* 44.

Life of Pompey: cf. on Pompey's reaction, *Pomp.* 72; on his flight and death, 73–80.

340 *six thousand soldiers died*: Caesar refers to the threat of prosecution if he had laid down his office: cf. note to p. 326, *Marcellus and Lentulus*, and Suet. 30. Casualty figures for the battle vary widely. These are from Pollio (cf. *Pomp.* 72); Caesar (*BC* 3. 99. 3) gives fifteen thousand total for the Pompeian side. This passage has puzzled scholars, since it is not clear why Caesar would write in Greek afterwards. Some emend to have Pollio write in Greek, or to say that Caesar spoke first in Greek, then in Latin. On Pollio, see p. 300 above.

safe and sound: Caesar's general policy was clemency, since he hoped to avoid the divisions of the Sullan period and reconcile his enemies to his position. The reference to M. Iunius Brutus points towards Caesar's own end (cf. cc. 62, 64, 66).

the truth of this story: Tralles was a city in Caria in Asia Minor. Patavium is modern Padua, the home town of Livy. On Livy as a source for Plutarch, see p. 300 above. His books for this period are lost.

collection of fables: C. Iulius Theopompus was important locally and honoured by a number of statues, but we know nothing of his collection of myths (*FGrHist* 21).

341 *signet ring*: for Pompey's murder, cf. *Pomp.* 77–80. Caesar arrived three days after Pompey, with 3,200 men and 800 horse (Caesar, *BC* 3. 106). Theodotus was a rhetorician and adviser at the Egyptian court, who convinced the Egyptians to kill Pompey (cf. *Pomp.* 77).

a way of protecting himself: this mention of the usually restrained Caesar's drinking parties suggests a weak parallel with Alexander's parties.

341 *was in the country*: the 15-year-old King Ptolemy XIII was the son of Ptolemy XII Auletes, who had run up large debts at Rome while trying to regain his throne, which he finally did in 55. After the death of his father, Pothinus and the army commander, Achillas, ran the country and drove out Cleopatra VII, the king's sister. Suet. 54 says Auletes owed 6,000 talents, almost twice Plutarch's figure, but he includes Pompey as debtor. Caesar's account of his stay in Alexandria and the brief war are found in *BC* 3. 106–12.

342 *made him fall for her*: Cassius Dio (42. 34) puts even more emphasis on Cleopatra's charms, and their devastating effect on Caesar.

the great library: the library at Alexandria was already a major cultural centre under Ptolemy II Philadephus in the third century. According to Seneca, *Dialogues* 9. 9. 5, 400,000 volumes were lost (a probable emendation from 40,000, based on Orosius 6. 15. 31; the number is derived from Livy); Aulus Gellius (*Attic Nights* 7. 17. 3) says the library held 700,000 volumes and all were lost. See P. M. Fraser, *Ptolemaic Alexandria* (Oxford: Clarendon Press, 1972), 334–5. We do not hear of this library again. The allegation that Antony gave the large library of the kings of Pergamum to Cleopatra (as a kind of replacement) is probably false (*Ant.* 58–9).

battle off Pharos: the island held the tall lighthouse which was considered one of the Seven Wonders of the world.

sunk straight away: for this episode, cf. Suet. 64.

Caesarion: Ptolemy XV Caesar, killed by Octavian in 30. Oppius (cf. p. 300 above, and Suet. 52) denied that the child was Caesar's, as did later official tradition. But Antony found it useful to assert Caesar's paternity. He was made co-ruler with Cleopatra. Cf. *Ant.* 54, 81.

343 *tetrarchs there*: Caesar left Egypt in June 47. Pharnaces, the son of Mithridates VI (whom Pompey after Mithridates' death had allowed to keep his Bosporan kingdom in the Crimea, cf. *Pomp.* 41 and note, *and the Romans*) hoped to profit by Pompey's defeat to regain his father's territory. Domitius Calvinus, sent after Pharsalus to stop him, had been defeated at Nicopolis in Lesser Armenia. The tetrarchs were rulers in Galatia, of whom the most powerful was Deïotarus, who had fought on Pompey's side at Pharsalus (cf. *Pomp.* 73).

the same ending: in Latin 'veni, vidi, vici'; in Greek also three words, *ēlthon*, *eidon*, *enikēsa*, but without the same endings. Zela was in Pontus. Caesar's friend C. Matius appears below, c. 51.

consul for the following year: Caesar arrived in Rome at the beginning of October 47. He had met with Cicero soon after landing in Italy: *Cic.* 39. He had been named dictator for the second time in 48, after Pharsalus, for an entire year (for problems connected with dating, cf. *MRR* ii. 272, 284–5 and iii. 106–7). Antony was his cavalry commander (*magister equitum*) and second in command (cf. *Ant.* 8). Caesar and M. Aemilius Lepidus were chosen consuls for 46.

in land-grants: the soldiers mustered in Campania for the planned African war had mutinied, and had driven off Caesar's representative, C. Sallustius Crispus (the future historian), killed the two men of praetorian rank, and marched towards Rome. Caesar spoke to them on the Campus Martius, calling them 'Quirites', the normal form of address to citizens who were not soldiers, and promised them rewards after the fighting, though they were penalized one-third of their pay. Plutarch does not develop this as he might have, as a parallel to the mutiny of Alexander's soldiers at Opis, *Alex*. 71.

prepared to work for him: P. Cornelius Dolabella, as tribune, introduced popular bills to abolish all debts and was only stopped by Antony after the senate passed a *senatus consultum ultimum*. The case against C. Matius is not known. Dolabella and Antony are treated more fully in *Ant*. 8–10.

an impressive army: Juba I of Mauretania, son of the Hiempsal who had opposed Marius (cf. *Mar*. 40 and note, *to ask for help*) had defeated Caesar's propraetor, Curio (cf. c. 29), in 49. Other Pompeians had arrived in Africa as well, including L. Afranius, who had been defeated in Spain (cf. cc. 36 and 53). Caesar's campaign is described in [Caesar,] *African War*, written by a follower of his.

a few cavalrymen: Caesar landed at Hadrumetum on 28 December 47.

344 *then and there*: the incident is not found in [Caesar,] *African War*, but the presence of Pollio suggests that it was taken from his account.

Thapsus: Thapsus was on the east coast of modern Tunisia.

345 *fifty of his own men*: the battle of Thapsus took place on 6 April 46. [Caesar,] *African War* 86. 1, gives ten thousand enemy killed.

taken them prisoner: for Caesar's epilepsy, cf. c. 17 and note, *Corduba, we hear*. Juba and Petreius committed suicide together, Faustus Sulla and Afranius were executed ([Caesar,] *African War* 94, 95). Caesar's usual policy was to kill those he had once pardoned but who still fought against him.

Caesar and Cato: Cato's suicide at Utica, near modern Tunis, was instantly famous: he appeared the stern Stoic statesman and last champion of republican liberty, refusing to yield to the tyrant. Caesar's annoyance stemmed from his desire to show his generosity in not punishing his enemy. But when Cato became a hero of the opposition, glorified in Cicero's *Cato*, he tried to puncture the balloon, without success. Neither work survives. For the death of Cato, cf. *CMin*. 66–70.

346 *olive oil*: Caesar returned to Rome on 25 July. For his honours, including the dictatorship for ten years (to be assumed one year at a time), and his whirlwind of legislation, cf. Gelzer, *Caesar*, 278–92. The Julian calendar was introduced at this time (cf. c. 59). The words reported by Plutarch refer only to his subjugation of Africa. The amount of oil mentioned equals the indemnity assigned to Lepcis Magna (a major city on the coast) alone.

346 *one for Africa*: the four triumphs were held between 20 September and 1 October. Cf. also Suet. 37.

writers of Greece: Juba II, whom Plutarch cites in *Sull.* 16 and elsewhere. Cf. p. 172 above.

Italy and the provinces: although Caesar did make a census of Rome, the figures given represent an arbitrary reduction in the number of those eligible for distributions of grain, not the new head-count. Cf. Suet. 41, Cassius Dio 43. 21, and Gelzer, *Caesar*, 287.

Pompey's sons: Caesar left Rome at the beginning of November and arrived in Spain a month later. He was named sole consul for 45 after he left. Pompey's sons, Cn. Pompeius Magnus and Sextus (Sextus was 29, Gnaeus somewhat older), had combined old legions and new recruits to create a sizeable force, which Caesar's legates had not been able to defeat.

347 *after the battle*: Caesar was pressed for troops, since many had been released after the African campaign. He met Gnaeus at Munda, south of Corduba (Córdoba) in modern Andalusia. Sextus escaped and later reappeared as the independent commander of a large fleet in the struggles of Octavius and Antony: see *Ant.* 32. The Liberalia, the festival mentioned by Plutarch, was held on 17 March, the day Pompey left Italy.

reputation in this way: the fifth triumph was celebrated in October 45.

dictator for life: the senate declared him *dictator perpetuus* shortly before 15 February 44, the date of the Lupercalia. Cf. *MRR* iii. 107. But Plutarch thinks also of honours granted before this. Cf. the list in Suet. 76.

348 *became praetors*: both future assassins, Brutus and C. Cassius Longinus, were named praetors for 44.

for his own: the statues had been removed after the battle of Pharsalus.

at the same time: they had both been destroyed by Rome in 146.

term of office: C. Caninius Rebilus (*sic*) replaced Q. Fabius Maximus for the last day of 45.

his own past performance: here Plutarch thinks of Alexander, who was also his own chief competitor, trying to outdo himself, cf. *Alex.* 40. The following passage sounds like Alexander's last plans, which are not found in Plutarch (the ending of *Alex.* may be missing) but are in other writers. On Caesar's plans, see Z. Yavetz, *Julius Caesar and his Public Image* (London: Thames and Hudson, 1983), 159–60. He certainly intended a campaign against Parthia in the near future. Some projects were executed by later emperors.

350 *compelled to accept*: the Julian calendar, with regular leap years, replaced the old one on 1 January 45, and is still the one we use—with refinements proclaimed in 1582 by Pope Gregory XIII. For Numa's contribution, cf. *Num.* 18.

unhappy and discontented: here and in the chapters which follow, the masses, who had supported Caesar so eagerly before, turn against him. The Sibylline books were official books of prophecy and the recommendation was actually presented to the senate, cf. Suet. 79. Rex, 'king', was also a Roman cognomen, as Caesar was. Suet. 78–87 give an account of the events leading up to the assassination and the deed itself which overlaps Plutarch's at many points.

351 *'treat you as their superior?'*: Caesar's efforts to reduce his honours were opposed by flatterers, who wanted to make him feel superior: cf. Anaxarchus' words to Alexander, *Alex.* 52. L. Cornelius Balbus was one of Caesar's principal agents in Rome.

way he treated some tribunes: the mistreatment of the tribunes is connected in other sources with the use of 'king' by the crowd, not with the Lupercalia: cf. Appian, *BC* 2. 108; Cassius Dio 44. 10.

to get pregnant: the ritual took place on 15 February. Cf. *Ant.* 12, and the account of the ritual in *Rom.* 21.

his triumphal clothing: one of the extravagant honours voted for Caesar was the right to wear the clothing of a triumphing general, traditionally the regular garb of Jupiter or of the early kings of Rome (cf. Cassius Dio 43. 14).

taken to the Capitol: that is, to be dedicated to Jupiter.

352 *'Bruti' and 'Cymaeans'*: L. Caesetius Flavius and C. Epidius Marullus were deprived of their tribunician power by vote of the senate. The tribunes were thought particularly to represent the people. The consul L. Iunius Brutus drove out the Tarquin kings in 509: cf. *Pub.* 1; *Brut.* 1. Brutus, however, also means 'stupid', and Cymaeans were famous for lack of wit. Plutarch brings this incident in to make the transition to Brutus the assassin.

pass Brutus by: see in general Plutarch's *Brutus*. Plutarch develops the idea that friends can be dangerous to the ruler, as in the conspiracies against Alexander.

let himself be corrupted: the suggestion, more clear in *Brut.* 8, is that Brutus will be Caesar's successor, but is content to wait for a natural death.

Cassius and Brutus: Cassius hated Caesar for having taken some lions he was training for his games as aedile: cf. *Brut.* 8. Caesar's statement, in the form 'Yon Cassius has a lean and hungry look', was made famous by Shakespeare in his *Julius Caesar*, which draws heavily on Plutarch's *Caesar* and *Brutus*.

353 *'Yes . . . but they have not yet gone'*: Plutarch prepares for Caesar's death, as he did for Alexander's, by a series of omens and prodigies: cf. also Suet. 81; Appian, *BC* 2. 115. Strabo was a historian and geographer: cf. p. 172 above. The Ides of March fell on the fifteenth day of the month.

354 *dismiss the senate*: Calpurnia's dreams clearly foreshadow Caesar's death. For Livy, cited also at c. 47, see p. 300 above.

354 *his second heir*: D. Iunius Brutus Albinus had been an associate of Caesar's since the Gallic Wars. He was named as a secondary heir, if the primary heirs did not inherit: Suet. 83. Caesar's principal primary heir was his grand-nephew, C. Octavius, adopted posthumously as C. Iulius Caesar Octavianus (Octavian). See note to p. 357, *wished they had done*, and note to p. 373, *chose Antony as his colleague*.

very urgent news for him: this slave is also mentioned by Appian (*BC* 2. 116), in similar words, and with the same lack of further information.

355 *summoning events there*: the senate met on this day in a room off the portico attached to the theatre which Pompey had dedicated in 55 (cf. *Pomp*. 52).

rational faculty as usual: the Epicureans held that the gods were not directly involved in human affairs and that when a man died, his atoms dispersed and he was no more. Cassius expounds this to Brutus at *Brut*. 37.

lengthy conversation: Antony's loyalty to Caesar was questioned: cf. c. 62 and *Ant*. 13. Albinus seems an error: in *Brut*. 17, as in our other sources, it is C. Trebonius who stops Antony.

356 *'Brother, help!'*: L. Tillius Cimber had been appointed governor of Bithynia and Pontus, but had not yet left to take up his post. The first blow was struck by C. Servilius Casca Longus, who then called to his brother Publius.

his face and eyes: the expression recalls the soldiers' javelins thrust in the faces of Pompey's cavalry at Pharsalus, c. 45.

one another as well: Caesar's words to Brutus, 'You too, Brutus?' (in Greek, *kai su, teknon*?, 'You too, son?', not Latin 'et tu, Brute?'), are recorded in Suet. 82. Here Plutarch focuses on the revenge of Pompey.

357 *wished they had done*: Antony and C. Iulius Caesar Octavianus (Octavian), the future Augustus, once they had gained power in Rome in 43, proscribed many senators, including C. Octavius Balbus and P. Cornelius Lentulus Spinther: cf. *Ant*. 19–20. For the events immediately after the assassination, see *Ant*. 14–15; *Brut*. 18–20; *Cic*. 42. The exact sequence of events is disputed.

things had calmed down: more likely Brutus spoke on the same day. By the next day, Lepidus' troops had occupied Rome. The senate met on 17 March, ratified Caesar's acts, gave an amnesty to the conspirators, and allowed a public funeral for Caesar and his will to be read, but they did not vote to honour Caesar as a god or assign new provinces until later. Plutarch has compressed his narrative.

on the spot: the will included 75 denarii per person, according to *Brut*. 20. Plutarch now shows how the people shift again, and turn against the assassins. The funeral was on 20 March. For Antony's speech then, cf. *Brut*. 20 and Suet. 84.

358 *before they died*: C. Helvius Cinna, a tribune, was mistaken for L.

Cornelius Cinna, a praetor and conspirator. Brutus and Cassius left Rome in early April: cf. *Brut.* 21 ff.

little more than four years: actually rather less: Pompey died on 28 September 48; Caesar on 15 March 44.

used against Caesar: Antony and Octavian defeated Cassius and Brutus at the battle of Philippi (in Macedonia) in 42 (cf. *Ant.* 22; *Brut.* 41–52); for Cassius' suicide, cf. *Brut.* 43.

coolness of the atmosphere: the comet, the 'Julian star', was celebrated by Virgil, Horace, and other poets. Cf. Suet. 88, which says it appeared in the period 20–30 June while Octavian was celebrating games for Caesar.

from Abydos to Europe: that is, across the Hellespont.

359 *plunged the sword in and died*: Cf. *Brut.* 36, 48, 52. No Comparison between Alexander and Caesar is preserved, though it probably was written.

ANTONY

365 *the public domain*: M. Antonius, consul for 99 and a leading orator, was killed in 87: cf. *Mar.* 44. His son, M. Antonius Creticus, received his honorific epithet even though he was defeated by Cretan pirates in 72 or 71 and died soon after. Plutarch's anecdote about him introduces early the themes of generosity and loyalty to friends important to this Life.

denied burial: Julia was daughter of L. Iulius Caesar, consul for 90; for P. Cornelius Lentulus Sura, see *Cic.* 17–22.

366 *capricious ambition*: Plutarch knew very little of Antony's early life. For his relations with C. Scribonius Curio and P. Clodius, Plutarch rewrites Cicero, *Philippic* 2. 44–8. In Greek terms, one Roman denarius equals one drachma, and so 24,000 sesterces or 6,000 denarii equals 1 talent. Two hundred and fifty talents equals Cicero's figure of six million sesterces, a very large sum. According to Cicero, Antony was associated with Clodius in 58. As Plutarch's metaphors indicate, the Asian style was rather florid.

about the expedition: A. Gabinius was the consul of 58; Ptolemy XII Auletes, king of Egypt and father of Cleopatra, had been dethroned in 58.

the inner sea: Pelusium was the easternmost coastal city of Egypt. The Serbonian marshes (mod. Sabkhat el-Bardawil) are fed by sulphurous springs (Typho was a monster associated with volcanoes) and infiltration from the Mediterranean.

367 *an outstanding soldier*: Archelaus had married Ptolemy XII's daughter Berenice, and ruled briefly as king of Egypt.

368 *whom they call 'augurs'*: Antony was elected tribune (for 49) and augur (a priesthood which Cicero held as well) in 50, as the conflict between Caesar and Pompey was coming to a head. But he had already served

with Caesar in Gaul in 54 and was quaestor in Gaul under Caesar in 51 (see *MRR* iii. 19–20). For Curio's lavish spending at this time, cf. *Pomp.* 58 and *Caes.* 29.

This chapter emphasizes the role of Antony in the outbreak of the Civil War. Plutarch reports first his election and opposition to Marcellus over the troops for Parthia, then his reading of Caesar's letter, the opposition of the consuls, and finally his expulsion from the senate and flight to Caesar. Nothing is said of the attitude of Pompey, or even of the senatorial leaders, apart from their actions against Antony, or his against them. As in *Caes.* 30, Antony is made to call for a poll of the senators, as Curio had in *Pomp.* 58. See notes to p. 276, *horsemen will arise* and to p. 326, *new basilica*.

368 *attached to his command*: Antony took office on 10 December 50, when C. Claudius Marcellus and L. Aemilius Lepidus Paullus were consuls. How Antony could block Marcellus' action with an edict is not clear. The troops already gathered had been Caesar's in Gaul (cf. *Pomp.* 57; *Caes.* 29). M. Calpurnius Bibulus, proconsul in Syria, was to use them to defend Syria against the Parthians. In the event they stayed in Italy and Pompey used them against Caesar.

fair and reasonable: on these letters, cf. *Pomp.* 59 and *Caes.* 30.

369 *in mortal danger*: Antony and Cassius were expelled on 7 January. Cf. *Caes.* 31.

the cause of the Civil War: Caesar crossed the Rubicon into Italy probably on the night of 10 January 49, and met the tribunes in Ariminum (mod. Rimini): cf. *Caes.* 32; Caesar *BC* 1. 8; Cicero, *Philippic* 2. 55.

many years before that: Cyrus the Great founded the Persian empire in the sixth century; Alexander the Great conquered it in the years 334–323, cf. Plutarch's *Alexander*.

in his capacity as tribune: Caesar conquered Italy, then Spain, returning to Rome in December 49: cf. *Caes.* 33–6; *Pomp.* 60–3; Caesar, *BC* 1. 1–3. 6. M. Aemilius Lepidus, the future triumvir, was left as praetor, Antony as both tribune and propraetor.

370 *with such a large force*: Caesar sailed from Brundisium (mod. Brindisi) on 4 January 48. The Pompeian commander L. Scribonius Libo then blockaded Brundisium, but Antony broke the blockade. After crossing the Adriatic, he took Lissus (mod. Lezhë or Alessio), north of Dyrrhachium (mod. Durrës or Durazzo).

371 *apart from himself*: for these battles, see *Caes.* 39–46, *Pomp.* 65–72, and Caesar, *BC* 3. 41–99; for Antony's two confrontations with the troops, see Caesar *BC* 3. 46, 65. At Pharsalus Pompey was decisively defeated (9 August 48).

a dictator has been elected: the second in command to the dictator had the ancient title of 'cavalry commander' (*magister equitum*).

losses on both sides: P. Cornelius Dolabella, a tribune for 47, pushed for radical reforms, and was opposed by his fellow tribunes C. Asinius Pollio, the historian, and L. Trebellius Fides. The story of Dolabella and Antony's wife, Antonia, is probably taken from Cicero, *Philippic* 2. 99, who gives no date for the affair.

as Cicero says: the rest of this paragraph is an elaborate catalogue of extravagances put together from various passages of Cicero, *Philippic* 2, some referring to the year before, some to later: see C. B. R. Pelling, *Plutarch: Life of Antony* (Cambridge: Cambridge University Press, 1988), 137–40. Cytheris was a notorious mistress of Antony. Apparently Antony was the first at Rome to harness lions to chariots: Cicero, *Philippic* 2. 58; Pliny, *Natural History* 8. 55. The *sambyke* was a stringed instrument associated with carousing.

372 *had not gone unnoticed*: Caesar was consul for the third time in 46, then later dictator, with Lepidus, not Antony, as cavalry commander. The reference to Antony's words is probably not from Antony's speech, but Cicero *Philippic* 2. 72, where Antony is quoted.

373 *an example of many others*: Fulvia, through her marriages to P. Clodius (killed near Rome in 52) and Scribonius Curio (killed in 49, fighting for Caesar in Africa), took an extremely active role in Roman politics. After marrying Antony, she profited financially from the proscriptions after Caesar's death, and when Antony was in the East, joined with L. Antonius to fight Octavian in the war which culminated with the siege of Perugia (cf. cc. 28, 30). See D. Delia, 'Fulvia Reconsidered', in S. Pomeroy (ed.), *Women's History and Ancient History* (Chapel Hill, NC: University of North Carolina Press, 1991), 197–217. The story of the letter is reworked from Cicero, *Philippic* 2. 76–8, but Plutarch misdates Antony's aborted journey to Spain in early March 45 (at a time when Caesar was having great difficulties) to after Caesar's victory at Munda (17 Mar.).

chose Antony as his colleague: Caesar favoured Antony even ahead of C. Octavius, the grandson (not son) of his sister Julia, who at this time was only 18 but at Caesar's death was adopted as his son, with the name C. Iulius Caesar Octavianus, and first joined with, then fought, Antony for control of the empire, as the Life will narrate. Octavian triumphed, and ruled Rome as Augustus Caesar until AD 14. Plutarch will subsequently call him 'Caesar'. D. Iunius Brutus Albinus should be distinguished from the leader of the assassins, M. Iunius Brutus.

assassinate him: in 44 BC, Caesar became consul for the fifth time, with Antony, while continuing as dictator. Caesar's intention to appoint Dolabella in his own place was thwarted by Antony, but after Caesar's assassination Dolabella was appointed consul by the Liberators, with the consent of Antony. C. Cassius Longinus and M. Brutus were the two leading conspirators. Shakespeare elaborates Plutarch's phrase: 'Let me have men about me that are fat; | Sleek-headed men and such as sleep o' nights. | Yon Cassius has a lean and hungry look; | He thinks too much; such men are dangerous' (*Jul. Caes.* I. ii).

373 *watching the runners*: cf. also *Caes.* 61 and Cicero, *Philippic* 2. 84–5. The diadem, a simple headband, had become a symbol of royalty. Since the expulsion of King Tarquin in 509, Rome had had an abhorrence of kings, although Caesar was already receiving almost regal honours.

374 *removed from office*: this incident probably occurred earlier, when Caesar's statue was decorated with a wreath and diadem, but is put together with the Lupercalia incident by Plutarch (or his source).

kept the conversation to himself: Cicero mentions Trebonius' testing of Antony (*Philippic* 2. 34), but Plutarch consciously elaborates it and inserts it in this much later context, after the Lupercalia incident, when Antony's position should have been clear. For the conspiracy, cf. *Caes.* 62–6 and *Brut.* 10–17.

375 *the houses of his assassins*: cf. for these events *Caes.* 67–8 and *Brut.* 18–20, with different perspectives. Shakespeare re-created Antony's speech in the famous scene in *Julius Caesar* III. ii.

the dead man's notebooks: Charon was the ferryman of the dead: Plutarch translates the Latin *Orcini* (Orcus was the Roman lord of the dead), used of slaves freed in their masters' wills.

376 *young Caesar*: this is Octavius, now called Caesar Octavianus (in English regularly Octavian), the future Augustus Caesar: see note to p. 373, *chose Antony as his colleague*. He arrived at Rome in early May 44. Plutarch regularly calls him Caesar; in these notes he is called Octavian.

still under arms: the disagreements of May–November 44 are selectively presented, ignoring Brutus and Cassius, who were still in Italy. Plutarch sets up a contrast between Octavian's calculation and Antony's bluster. Plutarch is the sole source for Antony's dream.

against Antony: most famously in his speeches called *Philippics*, the most impressive of which, the second, was written in November 44.

377 *among the casualties*: Mutina (mod. Modena) was the site of two battles in April 43, in which both Pansa and Hirtius were killed.

crossed the Alps: actually, they crossed the Apennines and marched along the coast into Provence, but Antony himself spoke of the Alps.

set up camp near by: Antony met up with Lepidus' army in mid May 43. Lepidus had been appointed proconsul of Narbonese Gaul and Nearer Spain in 44 by Julius Caesar, and had been cautiously watching events.

disguised as prostitutes: Laelius and Clodius are not otherwise known.

378 *talks for three days*: this meeting, on an island in the river Reno near Bononia (mod. Bologna), at the end of October 43, established the (second) triumvirate, by which the triumvirs, Antony, Lepidus, and Octavian, ostensibly as a committee to reform the constitution (*tresviri rei publicae constituendae*), assumed control of the state. Octavian had forced his own election as consul in August; Cicero had served his usefulness. The increased power of and support for Brutus and Cassius

encouraged the three leaders to unite. For the traffic in death which follows, cf. also Shakespeare, *Julius Caesar* IV. 1.

379 *abuse of power*: Cicero was killed on 7 December 43. Some versions, including Plutarch, *Cic.* 47, say that both hands were cut off.

Pompey the Great: the opponent of Julius Caesar: cf. his Life in this collection.

Caesar's opposite Brutus: Plutarch, presuming the reader familiar with the general history of the Civil Wars, leaps to the confrontation of Octavian and Antony with Brutus and Cassius at Philippi in October 42. There is a much more detailed account in *Brut.* 24–37, which is used by Shakespeare in *Julius Caesar* act V. For an account of Philippi, see J. F. C. Fuller, *The Decisive Battles of the Western World*, i (London: Eyre and Spottiswoode, 1954), 207–16. The victory of Antony and Octavian meant the end of the republican cause, for which Julius Caesar had been assassinated.

380 *money from all the eastern provinces*: the defeat of Brutus and Cassius meant that the triumvirs now controlled the eastern and wealthier half of the empire. From this point on, Antony will make this his power base.

381 *undertook to do so*: Megara was a small city between Athens and Corinth. The temple of Pythian Apollo was at Delphi.

'both . . . joy and loud laments': Sophocles, *Oedipus the King* 4–5.

Dionysus the cruel, the devourer: only Plutarch places the close association of Antony with Dionysus so early. Later it will become more significant: cf. cc. 25, 60, 75. Plutarch plays on the cult-names of Dionysus, Gracious Benefactor, and Devourer: the alternate faces of the god indicate the different facets of the man.

'we're in a lot of trouble': the orator Hybreas, who became ruler of Mylasa in south-west Anatolia, was a prominent Roman supporter. The anecdote is suspect, but the amount levied from Asia was vast: in 41, Antony demanded that nine years' tribute be paid in two years.

382 *love for Cleopatra*: Cleopatra, queen of Egypt, the last of the Macedonian dynasty of kings and queens who had ruled Egypt since Alexander's conquest, was at this time (41 BC) about 28. Previously she had furnished troops to Antony's opponents, and now she would have to make amends.

make war on Parthia: Parthia, the empire controlling Mesopotamia and areas further east, was considered a serious threat to Rome's eastern frontier. A Roman army led by Crassus had been totally defeated by the Parthians at Carrhae in 53 (cf. *Cras.* 17–33; *Pomp.* 53; *Caes.* 28). Antony will lead several expeditions against the Parthians: cf. cc. 28, 37 ff.

Dellius: an associate of Antony's, who wrote a history of this period which Plutarch knew and used (see p. 363 above).

Homer's words: quoting *Iliad* 14. 162, where Hera is trying to seduce Zeus so that she can have her own way.

382 *expected to vanquish Antony*: Julius Caesar had been in Egypt after Pompey's death, in 48–47, when Cleopatra was 21, cf. *Caes.* 49. Their encounter is the subject of G. B. Shaw's *Caesar and Cleopatra*. Gnaeus Pompey had been sent to Egypt in 49; only Plutarch suggests an amorous relation.

383 *filled the banks of the river*: the meeting took place at Tarsus in Cilicia. Compare Enobarbus' report in *Antony and Cleopatra* II. ii. 195–223. The description, while splendid, is probably not far from the truth: the Egyptian kings voyaged in sumptuous ships, and the queens had long identified themselves with Isis.

384 *Medes, or Parthians*: Plutarch lists peoples neighbouring or near to Egypt, from Ethiopia in the south, to the Trogodytae, who lived along the Red Sea, to Hebrews and Arabs, and the Medes and Parthians of Mesopotamia and further east.

in defence of his affairs: referring to the Perusine War: cf. c. 30.

the planned invasion of Syria: this Q. Labienus is the son of Julius Caesar's general T. Labienus, who had sided with Pompey; for the attack, cf. c. 30.

385 *according to my grandfather*: an unusual family reminiscence, valuable for its immediacy and vividness of detail. Lamprias is portrayed in conversation several times in Plutarch's *Table Talk*. Philotas the doctor is known from an inscription at Delphi, where he lived for some time. Both Amphissa and Chaeronea were extremely close to Delphi.

Plato's four categories: cf. Plato, *Gorgias* 464c, and generally 462c–466a, where Plato contrasts the spurious, flattering arts of sophistry, rhetoric, pastry-cooking, and cosmetics with the genuine arts of law-giving, justice, medicine, and gymnastics.

386 *exile from Italy*: Lucius Antonius and Antony's wife Fulvia attempted to oppose Caesar in Italy with arms, raising eight legions and occupying Rome, but were besieged in Perusia (mod. Perugia) by him in the winter of 41/40 and starved into surrender (the Perusine War). Caesar spared the two leaders, but not the city. Antony would have known more of this than Plutarch suggests.

Lydia and Ionia: Labienus' campaign as leader of the Parthians began in spring 40, went through Syria, and through Cilicia to the shores of the Aegean, including Ionia and probably Lydia: many Romans joined him. He met no effective resistance until early 39 (cf. c. 33).

387 *their friends one by one*: Plutarch describes the conference of Caesar and Antony at Brundisium (mod. Brindisi) in September 40. The new division gave Caesar more power in the West than he had had before; it also marks the beginnings of the division in the empire which was to be confirmed by Diocletian at the end of the third century AD, and become the basis of the separation of the western and eastern halves of the empire. Lepidus retained Africa, his original portion, but without Egypt.

his was Atia: Octavia was born about 70, and was in fact Octavian's full sister (Plutarch confuses her with an older sister, Octavia major).

unsafe for shipping: this younger son of Pompey the Great had caused a great deal of trouble for Octavian in the preceding years, and now had a fleet of some 200–250 ships. He was finally defeated by Octavian in 36, in the campaign mentioned at the end of c. 35. Menas had been the slave of Pompey the Great, and was now a freedman.

Cape Misenum: the northernmost promontory of the Bay of Naples. For the scene which follows, cf. *Antony and Cleopatra* II. vi–vii. They probably met in August 39.

388 *the Parthians' advance*: P. Ventidius had a distinguished career as one of Antony's generals. He had probably been sent earlier, after the Brundisium conference, as Appian says (*BC* 5. 65).

389 *turn their heads*: winter 39–38 BC. The gymnasiarch, or magistrate in charge of athletic displays, fulfilled a major function in Greek cities. The Athenians renamed the Panathenaic Games the Panathenaia Antonieia on this occasion, and Antony received other honours too. As gymnasiarch, he supervised the contests. Plutarch puns with wrestling terminology: Antony grabs and twists heads as a wrestler might (cf. Plutarch's *Curiosity* 521b: an attractive woman 'twisted' an athlete's head, using the same verb).

water from the Clepsydra: a famous well below the north-west corner of the Acropolis.

three successive battles: Ventidius defeated Pacorus in spring 38, in the Cyrrhestica region of Syria, north of Antioch. For Crassus' defeat, cf. note to p. 382, *make war on Parthia*.

city of Samosata: modern Samsat in Turkey, on the right bank of the Euphrates, the capital of the small kingdom of Commagene.

390 *triumph over the Parthians*: the emperor Trajan invaded Parthia successfully in AD 114. Although he died before returning to Rome, his triumph was celebrated posthumously in 117 or 118. Trajan may have been thinking of the invasion when Plutarch was writing.

as far as the Caucasus: Pompey had earlier extended Roman influence into this area. See *Pomp.* 34–6 with note to p. 254, *set off against Mithridates*.

sailed for Italy: in spring 37. The agreement with Octavian and Sextus Pompey had broken down, and negotiations were needed.

second baby daughter: this may be incorrect: Antonia minor was born in January 36. However, another daughter may have been born and died in infancy.

no hostile intentions: Plutarch's use of direct speech for Octavia's words here emphasizes her role as go-between, a positive harmonizing influence in contrast to Cleopatra's divisive behaviour.

391 *sailed across to Asia*: autumn 37. The agreement of Tarentum (mod.

Taranto) also renewed the triumvirate for five years, and other matters were arranged. Antony never received the troops promised by Octavian.

391 *Plato's book*: Plato, *Phaedrus* 254a, the famous passage in which the unruly part of the tripartite soul, excited by love, tries to break loose from the control of the intellect and drag the whole soul heedlessly off course.

towards the outer sea: it was usual for loyal and able client kings to have their realm increased, but this territorial reorganization was extraordinary. The exact time when some of these territories were allotted is disputed; some apparently were made over prior to 37. Coele Syria, or 'Hollow Syria', is the inland country behind the Lebanese coastal plain, that is, the territory around Damascus.

regulate conception: cf. *Sol.* 22. Solon made a law 'exempting sons born out of wedlock from supporting their fathers'. Plutarch's understanding is that he thus punishes those who have intercourse only for pleasure, not children.

392 *taken over the kingdom*: after Pacorus' death (c. 34), the Parthian kingdom was unstable. Phraates attempted to eliminate opposition by killing his father and all his brothers, thus provoking a revolt of the Parthian nobles. This gave the occasion for Antony to invade in 36 BC, as described at length in the following chapters (37–52). Plutarch probably drew most of his material from the history of Antony's officer Dellius, an eyewitness. For the geography of the campaign, see Map 7.

called Bambyce: the gift of cities as feudal territory was common in the eastern empires. Themistocles, after his victory over Persia, had had to flee Greece and take refuge in Persia, where King Artaxerxes gave him three cities. Cf. *Them.* 29.

defeating the enemy: other ancient sources also criticize Antony's timing, but it would have been unwise to wait till the following year and give Phraates more time to organize his resistance.

393 *wives of the Median king*: to avoid confusion, Plutarch does not name this king, who was also called Artavasdes. He reappears at cc. 52 and 53.

King Polemo: this defeat of Statianus was a major loss. The Parthians used the same tactics which had destroyed Crassus in 53, heavy attacks with mounted archers, who could quickly retreat and attack again. The cavalry of the Armenian king, Artavasdes, would have been an important defensive force, but he deserted Statianus' convoy (see c. 39). Polemo, king of Pontus, was a Roman client.

war in the first place: Plutarch has not mentioned what Cassius Dio tells us (49. 25. 1), that Artavasdes had incited Antony to attack through Media because of his hostility to the Median king, the other Artavasdes (cf. c. 38).

394 *puzzled and depressed*: again the Parthians have fought with light-armed troops and mounted archers, which allowed them to retreat rapidly.

instead of wheat: the vicious practice of decimation had become common in this period, and was ordered by Julius Caesar in 49, Domitius Calvinus in 39, and Octavian in 34.

395 *Domitius Ahenobarbus*: after fighting for Brutus, Cn. Domitius Ahenobarbus joined Antony, and played a significant role until he deserted him shortly before Actium. See cc. 56 and 63. Shakespeare assigns him (as Enobarbus) a major role.

396 *a skilled and effective officer*: Flavius Gallus is otherwise unknown.

399 *which just glance off it*: the Roman special formation, called *testudo*, or 'tortoise', looked like a slanted tiled roof.

cost their weight in silver: the choenix was about a litre, and this price hundreds of times higher than usual.

far greater numbers of enemies: the march of these Greek mercenaries from deep in Mesopotamia, near Baghdad, to the Black Sea was made famous in Xenophon's *Anabasis*.

400 *gift of three cities*: cf. c. 37. Mithridates is not otherwise known, nor is Alexander of Antioch, below.

401 *brackish and poisonous*: the rivers in this area are saline because of gypsum and salt deposits: this was perhaps the Talkheh. The following river (c. 49) would then be the Shiāh Chāi.

403 *fought them before*: cf. cc. 37, 39. Here Plutarch speaks of sixteen thousand horsemen rather than six thousand as before. It is possible that Artavasdes started with six thousand but promised more, as he had earlier, at the time of Crassus' invasion of Parthia: cf. *Cras.* 19.

celebrated a triumph: in 34 BC. This was not the standard Roman triumph, but a Dionysiac procession, also called a triumph in Greek. Artavasdes was put to death by Cleopatra.

Berytus and Sidon: modern Beirut and Saïda.

404 *the Median king*: Artavasdes of Media, cf. c. 38 and note, *wives of the Median king*.

treated her with disrespect and ignored her: the time is summer 35. After the Parthian War (during which Octavian had succeeded in defeating Sextus Pompey, and sent Lepidus into exile), Plutarch focuses on Antony's choice between Octavia (and an agreement with Octavian) and Cleopatra. Much of the account of Cleopatra's wiles seems to be Plutarch's imaginative reconstruction.

405 *go up to Media*: either in 34 or, more likely, 33.

406 *Cilicia to Ptolemy*: this is the occasion sometimes called the 'donations of Alexandria'. Both Plutarch and Cassius Dio (49. 41) consider it an important moment, when Antony turns away from Rome, although Antony probably wanted to create some blend of Roman and oriental ceremonial. Caesarion was said to be the son of Julius Caesar. The gifts were gestures, since the territories remained under normal proconsuls and client kings. Africa in this list means the territory of Cyrene. After

the twins, Alexander the Sun (Helios) and Cleopatra the Moon (Selene), cf. c. 36, Cleopatra had borne Antony another son, Ptolemy Philadelphus, in 36 BC.

406 *Median and Armenian kings*: Alexander wore the erect turban (called both *tiara* and *kitaris*) of the Median kings (recalling Alexander the Great, who also adopted this head-dress); Ptolemy wears traditional Macedonian dress, including the *kausia*, a kind of woollen shepherd's cap.

nothing for Antony's men: Plutarch refers back to the actions of Octavian in 36 during Antony's Parthian campaign.

407 *assembling from all quarters*: Octavian and Antony move towards war. The following chapters (56–69) lead up to the great clash, and Antony's débâcle, at Actium. Canidius Crassus was to be commander of the land forces at Actium, cf. c. 63.

fall into Caesar's hands: an unusual statement, indicating Plutarch's understanding that the emergence of a single ruler, Octavian, was somehow destined. Cf. S. Swain, 'Plutarch: Chance, Providence, and History', *American Journal of Philology*, 110 (1989), 272–302.

indulged themselves: spring 32. Only Plutarch mentions this interlude.

408 *throw Octavia out of his house*: this was an act of divorce (May–June 32).

lodged with the Vestal Virgins: a common practice for safe keeping of important documents.

409 *a companion of Caesar's*: Calvisius Sabinus had been consul in 39.

410 *surrendered to a woman*: Octavian's preparations occupied 32; Cleopatra (but not Antony) was declared an enemy of Rome. The second five-year term of the triumvirate had presumably expired in 33, but both men used offers to resign as propaganda against the other. The legal positions of both were extraordinary, but Antony was also removed as consul designate for 31, although he used the title on his coinage.

Antony's administration: only Plutarch names these Egyptians in this connection; Cleopatra's female associates, Iras and Charmion, figure in her death scene (c. 85). Some think Pothinus is listed by confusion with the powerful Egyptian who killed Pompey in 48 BC, and then was killed himself (*Pomp*. 77, 80), but this seems unlikely.

killed the baby birds: Plutarch uses lists of prodigies at important moments in certain Lives (cf. e.g. *Caes*. 43, 47, 63, and F. Brenk, *In Mist Apparelled* (Leiden: Brill, 1977), 28–38, 184–213). Here he focuses on Antony's coming defeat. Eumenes and Attalus were two kings of Pergamum; apparently the Athenians had simply changed the names on the statues to Antony, to honour him: a common practice at this time.

octaremes and decaremes: these were names for two classes of large ships, literally 'eight-oar' and 'ten-oar', but the exact meaning is uncertain (e.g. eight men to an oar, or four banks of oars on each side?).

411 *from Cyrene to Ethiopia*: Plutarch heightens the coming battle by the epic and historiographic technique of the catalogue before the encounter. The

effect is also to make the battle a grand confrontation of the eastern and western halves of the Roman empire, from Gibraltar to the Euphrates. The time is late summer 31.

'long-suffering' Greece: the quotation is from Euripides, *Heracles* 1250.

many years before: a reference to the battle of Pharsalus, 48 BC, in which Pompey was finally defeated: cf. c. 8.

412 *'Caesar sitting on the stirring-spoon?'*: Cleopatra's allusion is vulgar: it should be an uncomfortable position for Octavian. Some take *torynē* as being also a slang word for penis, in which case the joke is more obscene.

Domitius: Cn. Domitius Ahenobarbus, already mentioned at cc. 40 and 56. Cf. note to p. 395.

went over to Caesar's side: Amyntas, king of the Galatians (Gauls who had settled in central Asia Minor), and Deïotarus Philadelphus, king of Paphlagonia.

the Sicilian War: the war in which he had defeated Sextus Pompey's fleet.

413 *to make good his escape*: in battle, ships normally used oars alone. Plutarch implies that the real reason was to permit an escape if necessary.

battle was joined: 2 September 31. The actual course of the battle of Actium is difficult to ascertain, despite (or because of) various accounts. In particular, the role of Cleopatra is debated. Many think that Antony and Cleopatra were actively trying to break out of a blockade, rather than fight for a victory.

414 *a donkey and a man*: this statue was much later brought to Constantinople and erected in the hippodrome (Niketas Choniates, *History* 650).

from wooden towers: the techniques used are those of siege warfare; in particular, we do not hear elsewhere of using mantlets (protective covers) in sea battles.

417 *abandoned the camp*: Canidius went to join Antony (see c. 71), perhaps because he did think he could hold the troops loyal.

divided the grain among themselves: important personal testimony on the effect that the wars of the dynasts had on the provinces. All their wealth and supplies were drained, and even landowners like Nicarchus were treated as slaves. The Chaeroneans were carrying grain from Boeotia to Anticyra, a port on the Corinthian Gulf.

the bitter end: Plutarch tells the full story at *Brut*. 50. Plutarch might have mentioned it also in this Life when speaking of Philippi at c. 22, but holds it for here.

418 *a bad-tempered misanthrope*: cf. Aristophanes, *Lysistrata* 809–15, and *Birds* 1549. The plays of Plato the comic poet (not the philosopher) are lost. The story of Alcibiades is told differently at *Alc*. 16. Shakespeare's play *Timon of Athens* is based on this figure, but his source is chiefly Lucian's *Timon, or The Misanthrope*.

419 *revelry and celebrations*: both boys mark the standard beginning of

adulthood, Caesarion in the Greek way by enrolling in the military training programme, Antyllus in the Roman by putting on the toga of an adult citizen.

420 *to do so in Egypt*: Octavian in late 31 was in Samos and Ephesus: various embassies are reported in our sources, some more likely than others. Octavian desperately wanted to keep negotiations open, until he could reach Alexandria, so that he could capture the treasury and army of Antony, and perhaps be able to capture Cleopatra alive, to lead in his triumph: cf. c. 78.

421 *then we'll be quits*: Shakespeare develops the relationship between Thidias (i.e. Thyrsus) and Cleopatra in an even more enigmatic manner than Plutarch (*Antony and Cleopatra* III. xiii).

advanced through Africa: Octavian returned to Rome in late 31, but immediately returned to the East. The early part of the year was spent moving his army from Asia Minor to Egypt; he arrived at Alexandria in late July 30. Pelusium, near modern Port Saïd, guarded the approach to Egypt.

near the temple of Isis: Cleopatra, the 'New Isis' (c. 54), in preparing for death associates herself with her patron goddess.

near the Hippodrome: just east of the city of Alexandria.

422 *similarity and affinity*: Antony had presented himself as a new Dionysus (cf. cc. 24, 60), and now Dionysus and his band of revellers had left the city to join the enemy.

425 *his friend Arius*: this entrance into the captured city would have been a carefully staged event, with the procession and public speech of clemency for the city. Arius Didymus, a Stoic philosopher, was perhaps being groomed for an important role in the city, though none is known, and later he was made procurator in Sicily. Afterwards, he declined an important administrative post in Egypt.

426 *'A plurality . . . not a good thing'*: a play on a famous passage in the *Iliad*, where Odysseus says that a plurality of leaders is not a good thing (2. 204).

the account he published of these events: Olympus' account may be an important source for this portion of Plutarch's narrative.

427 *had taken him in*: Plutarch subtly plays with his reader, as Cleopatra does with Octavian: it is not quite clear how much is deception, how much real. Was the scene with Seleucus staged? *Antony and Cleopatra* V. ii closely follows Plutarch's final chapters.

abandon your wife: Cleopatra speaks of herself as wife. The following scene, with the ritual bath and meal, combines wedding and funeral imagery.

429 *fourteen of them*: this number may be corrupt, since she had only met Antony at Tarsus in 41 (c. 26), so eleven would be correct. It is most unusual that Plutarch makes a joint obituary notice for Antony and

Cleopatra rather than just for his hero: the biography has become a joint biography.

the time of his death: it is more likely that he was born in 83 BC, and died at the age of 52 (53 by the inclusive Roman count).

430 *descent from Antony*: this genealogical account demonstrates that Antony's line was closely mingled with that of Augustus, and in fact produced the emperors Claudius, Gaius (Caligula), and Nero before dying out. Being the ancestor of Nero, however, was a mixed honour. See the stemma below, Antony's Descendants by his Last Three Wives.

Antony's Descendants by his Last Three Wives

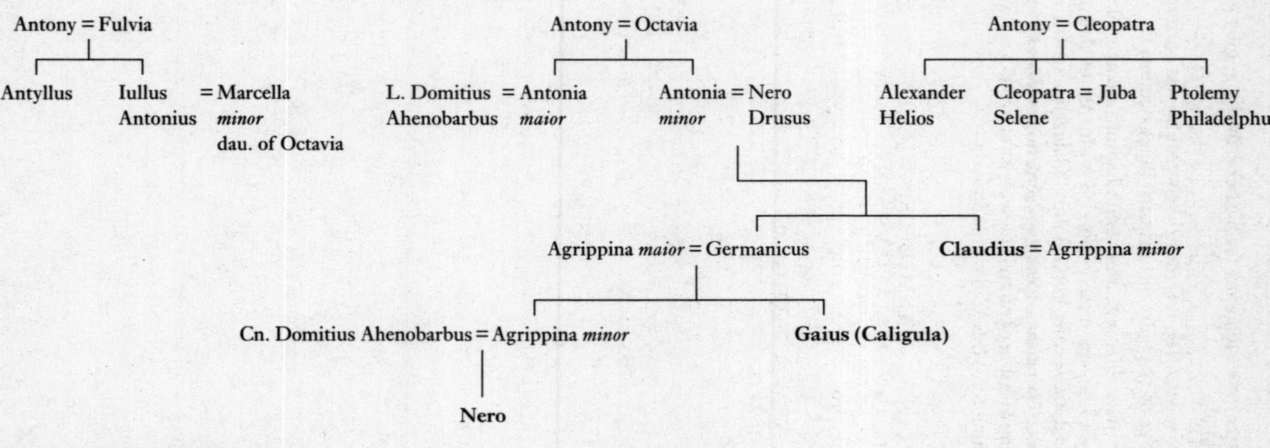

Emperors are shown in bold type

TEXTUAL NOTES

CATO THE ELDER

4.4: Reading ἐρέταις with MS S.
15.1: Reading τό τε περὶ τὰς κατηγορίας with Sansone.
21.5: Reading ἀνεργάστην χώραν.
22.1: Retaining the MSS reading φιλόσοφον.

AEMILIUS PAULLUS

5.4: Reading ⟨οὐ⟩ πολλὰς ἀπήλλαξαν with Ziegler.
9.3: The text from 'sank' to the end of sentence is highly uncertain and conjectural: there are irredeemable lacunae in the Greek.
12.7 Reading the Teubner text, but without a lacuna after εἶχεν, and then παρασκευῆς ⟨στρατιω⟩τῶν δέκα μυριαδές with Reiske and Sintenis.
14.11: Reading ὁρῶμεν δὲ καὶ ὅτι πέτρας with Reiske.
15.10: Reading πρὸς κάθετον δ' ἐμέτρει with Coraes.
16.8: Filling the lacuna with Latte's conjecture.
18.6: Translating, with some hesitation, as if there were no lacuna.
30.2: Reading, with Ziegler, πορφύραις ⟨σοβαρῶς οὕτ⟩ως καὶ πανηγυρ⟨ικῶς⟩ ἔξωθεν.
31.5: Retaining Λιβύων with the MSS.

TIBERIUS AND GAIUS GRACCHUS

4.3: Reading εἰ μή with Stephanus.
14.4: Retaining παραφαίνουσι with the MSS.
22(1).6: Retaining λαμπρότερον with the MSS.
23(2).10: Reading εἰσενηνοχώς . . . ἐξενηνοξέναι with the MSS.
27(6).3: Reading μόνον ⟨ὄν⟩ with Blass.
33(12).5: Reading ἀρχόντων with the MSS.
35(14).4: Reading τὸν τοῦ πατρός with Gärtner.

MARIUS

2.4: Some such word has clearly dropped out of the text.
15.5: Reading ἐκείνη with Wuhrmann.
15.7: Reading μέγα ⟨μέρος⟩ with Reiske.
23.2: Retaining the MSS reading Ἀτισῶνα here and later in the chapter.

SULLA

2.6–7: Something appears to have dropped out from the text, perhaps mentioning other early lovers of Sulla's.
7.8: Omitting ⟨ἀνθρώπων⟩.
10.8: Reading Οὐεργίλιον with Flacelière.
21.2: Reading φυγόντος with recent editors.
26.3: Reading ἀκριβῶς ⟨γεγραμμένοις⟩ with Reiske.
27.8: Reading ⟨πλείονας⟩ ἡμέρας with Ziegler.
29.7: The Teubner (and Loeb) εἴτ' is surely a misprint for εἶτ'.

POMPEY

41.7: Reading καὶ ⟨λόγον⟩ . . . ποιούμενος.
47.7: There is no compelling reason to mark a lacuna at this point in the text.
51.2: Deleting περικείμενος with van Herwerden.
53.10: Reading ἀπέχρησεν with Coraes.
75.5: Reading τὸ δ' ἀποφαίνεσθαι with Solanus.

CAESAR

1.1: Several paragraphs appear to have been lost from the beginning of this Life, presumably on Caesar's family and early career.
3.3: Reading μᾶλλον ἀπασχοληθείς with Bowie.
5.5: Reading ὑπερθαύμαστον ἦθος.
9.7: Filling the probable lacuna according to Ziegler's suggestion.
11.4: I follow Pelling in reading the MSS text here, but without μᾶλλον.
14.1: Retaining the readings of the majority of MSS, without ὥσπερ, and with κατήχθη instead of προήχθη.
14.7: Retaining ὑποδραττόμενος with the MSS.
20.7: Reading συνεχεῖς with Madvig.
22.6: Retaining πόρου with the MSS.
24.6: Retaining ἀνοικοδομεῖν with the MSS.
29.6: Omitting the lacuna and punctuating as, for instance, the Loeb does.
30.2: Reading ⟨ἔνι⟩οι with Ziegler.
32.3: Reading Ἀρίμινον ⟨ὅμορον⟩ τῆς Κελτικῆς with Ziegler.
37.2: The lacuna marked in the Teubner text is probably not necessary.
37.9: Reading τάς ⟨τε⟩ ναῦς with Reiske.
46.2: Retaining the MSS reading ὑπ' αὐτοῦ.

ANTONY

2.8: Reading κομπώδη τινα φρυαγματίαν.
4.5: Reading ἀναφρόδιτος with Sansone.
28.10: Reading τὴν μὲν προθυμίαν, Stadter.
40.1: Reading τραυματιῶν with Campe.
50.7: Reading ὃ μάλιστα with Sansone.

INDEX OF LITERARY AND HISTORICAL SOURCES CITED BY PLUTARCH

(* identifies authors of whom works are preserved; the rest are known only through fragments, such as are cited in Plutarch. Most have a fuller entry in the *Oxford Classical Dictionary*, 3rd edn. (1996). Cat = *Cato*, Aem = *Aemilius Paullus*, G = *Tiberius and Gaius Gracchus*, M = *Marius*, S = *Sulla*, P = *Pompey*, C = Caesar, A = *Antony*, and the reference is to chapter number.)

*Aeschylus, fifth-century Athenian tragedian: P1
Alexander of Myndus, first-century AD author: M17
anonymous comic poet: P53
anonymous epigram: Cat1
Antipater of Tarsus, second-century Stoic philosopher: M46
*Antiphon (the fifth-century sophist?): A28
Antony, Mark, triumvir: A2, 10
*Archilochus of Paros, seventh-century Greek poet: M21
Ariston of Chios, third-century Stoic philosopher: Cat18
Asinius Pollio, C., Caesarian and historian of the Roman Civil War: P72, C46
*Cato, M. Porcius, the censor and subject of a Life: Cat *passim*; A66
*Cicero, M. Tullius, first-century orator: Cat17, Aem10, G22, P42, 63, C4, 8, 58, 59, A6
*Cornelius Nepos, first-century biographer: G21
Cornelius Sulla, P., the famous general and dictator, author of *Memoirs*, cited at: M25, 26, 35, S4, 5, 6, 14, 16, 17, 19, 23, 24–5, 27, 28, 37
Dellius, Q., friend of Antony and historian: A59
Democritus, fifth-century Greek philosopher: Aem1
*Euripides, fifth-century Athenian tragedian: S4, P73, A62
Fenestella, first-century Roman historian: S28
*Homer, poet of *Iliad* and *Odyssey*: Aem34, G21, M11, P29, 36, 53, 72, A25
*Iulius Caesar, C., the dictator, author of *Commentaries* on his Gallic War and the Civil War, and of *Anti-Cato*, a polemic against Cato: P69, C22, 44, 54
Iulius Caesar Octavianus, C., the emperor Augustus, author of an autobiography: A22, 68
Juba II of Mauretania, historian: S16
*Livy (T. Livius), first-century historian: Cat17, S6, C47, 63

Lutatius Catulus, Q., consul 102, author of memoirs: M25, 26, 27
Musaeus, mythical poet: M36
Olympus, Cleopatra's doctor: A82
Oppius, C., contemporary biographer of Caesar: P10, C17
*Pindar, fifth-century Greek poet: M29
Piso, C., Roman historian: M45
*Plato, fourth-century Greek philosopher: Cat7, G4, M2, 46, A29, 36
*Polybius, second-century Greek historian: Cat10, Aem15, 16, 19
Posidonius, second-century Macedonian (?) historian: Aem19–21
Posidonius of Apamea, first-century Greek historian and philosopher: M1, 45
Rutilius Rufus, P., first-century Roman historian: M28
Scipio Nasica Corculum, P. Cornelius, second-century Roman senator: Aem15–18, 21, 26
*Sophocles, fifth-century Athenian tragedian: P78 (spoken by Pompey), A24
*Strabo of Amaseia, first-century historian and geographer: S26, C63
Tanusius Geminus, first-century historian: C22
Theophanes of Mytilene, friend and historian of Pompey: P37, 42, 49, 76, 78
Timagenes, first-century rhetorician and historian: P49

INDEX OF PROPER NAMES

(Authors are collected and more fully identified in the Index of Sources. Cat = *Cato*, Aem = *Aemilius Paullus*, G = *Tiberius and Gaius Gracchus*, M = *Marius*, S = *Sulla*, P = *Pompey*, C = *Caesar*, A = *Antony*. Roman names are usually placed under those used by Plutarch, whether nomen or cognomen. Offices, i.e. the consulship (cos.), praetorship (pr.), or tribuneship of the people (tr. pl.) are given to distinguish similar names.)

Abas, river: P35
Abydos: C69
Academy, at Athens: S12
Acastus, son of Pelias: S36
Achaea, Achaeans, region of Greece: Cat9, P28
Achillas of Egypt: P77–80, C49
Achilles: P29
Acilius, C., historian: Cat22
Acilius, Caesarian soldier: C16
Acilius Glabrio, M'., cos. 191: Cat12, 14, S12
Acilius Glabrio, M'., cos. 67: S33, P30
Acontium: S17, 19
Acropolis (Athenian): Cat5
Actium: P24, A62, 63, 68, 69, 71
Adige, river: M23
Adriatic Sea: Aem9, A60
Aedepsus: S26
Aedui: C26
Aegium, port on the Gulf of Corinth: Cat12
Aelia, wife of Sulla: S6
Aelius Tubero, Q.: Aem5, 27, 28
Aemilia, daughter of Scaurus: S33
Aemilia, wife of Pompey: P9
Aemilia, wife of the elder Scipio Africanus: Aem2
Aemilia Tertia, daughter of Aemilius Paullus: Cat20, Aem10
Aemilius, town-crier: Aem38
Aemilius Lepidus, M., cos. 187, 175: Aem38
Aemilius Paullus, L., cos. 182, 168: Cat15, 20, Aem *passim*, S12
Aemilius Paullus, L., cos. 50: A19
Aenaria (Ischia): M37, 40
Aeschylus: P1
Aesis, river: P7
Aeson, river, at Pydna: Aem6
Aetol/ia, -ians, region of Greece: Cat13
Afranius, L., cos. 60: P34, 36, 39, 44, 67, C36, 41, 53
Africa: Cat3, 27, Aem6, 31, G4, 23, 31, 32, M7, 9, 10, 12, 35, 40–2, S1, 3, 5, 28, P10–14, 38, 45, 50, 52, 66, 76, C16, 28, 52, 55, A10, 30, 54, 61, 67, 69, 74
Africanus: *see* Scipio
Agamemnon, Greek hero: P67, C41
Agis IV of Sparta: G1
Agrippa, M.: A35, 65, 66, 73, 87
Agrippina minor, mother of Nero: A87
Ahenobarbus: Aem25; *see also* Domitius Ahenobarbus
Ajax, Greek hero: P72
Alba: C60, A60
Albanians: P34, 35, 38, 45, A34
Albinus, A. Postumius, cos. 99: S6
Albinus, Sp. Postumius, cos. 110: M9
Alcaeus of Sardis: P38
Alcibiades: A70
Alcman, Greek poet: S36
Alesia: C27
Alexander (Helios), son of Antony and Cleopatra: A36, 54
Alexander, freedman: P4
Alexander, Macedonian officer: Aem18
Alexander, son of Perseus: Aem37
Alexander of Antioch: A46, 48
Alexander of Myndus: M17
Alexander the Great: Aem8, 12, 23, 31, P2, 34, 46, C11, A6, 54, 80
Alexandr/ia, -ians, Egyptian city: P49, C48, A3, 28, 29, 50, 53, 54, 69, 71, 80
Alexas of Syria (Laodicea): A66, 72
Alps: Aem6, M15, 18, 23, 24, P51, 58, 60, 65, C11, 32, A17, 18
Amanus: P39
Amazons: P35

Ambiorix: C24
Ambrones: M15, 19, 20
Ameria (Ameli): M17
Amisus: P38, 42
Amphictyons: S12
Amphipolis: Aem23, 24, P74
Amphissa: A28
Amyntas, king of the Lycaonians and Galatians: A61, 63
Anaxenor: A24
Anaxidamus of Chaeronea: S17, 19
Ancharia, mother of Octavia: A31
Ancharius, Roman senator: M43
Andronicus of Rhodes: S26
Anicius, L., cos. 160: Aem13
Anienus: C58
Annius, P.: M44
Annius Luscus, T., cos. 153: G14
Antemnae: S30
Anthedon: S26
Anticyra: A68
Antigonus I Monophthalmus (the Great): Aem8
Antigonus II Gonatas: Aem8
Antigonus III Doson: Aem8
Antigonus of Judaea: A36
Antioch: P40
Antiochus of Commagene: A34
Antiochus the Great: Cat12–14, Aem4, 7, S12
Antipater of Tarsus, Stoic philosopher: G8, M46
Antiphon the sophist: A28
Antistia, wife of Ap. Claudius: G4
Antistia, wife of Pompey: P4, 9
Antistius, P.: P4
Anton, son of Heracles: A4
Antonia major, wife of L. Domitius Ahenobarbus: A87
Antonia minor, wife of Nero Drusus: A87
Antonias, ship of Cleopatra: A60
Antonius, C., praetor 44: A15, 22
Antonius, L., cos. 41: A15, 30
Antonius, M., cos. 99: M44, P24, A1
Antonius, M., triumvir: *see* Antony, Mark
Antonius Creticus, M., father of Mark Antony: A1
Antonius Hybrida, P. (actually C.), cos. 63: C4, A9
Antonius Iullus, son of Antony and Fulvia: A87
Antonius Saturninus, L.: Aem25
Antony, Mark (Antonius, M.): Aem38, P58, 59, 69, C30, 31, 39, 44, 51, 61–3, 66, 67, 69, A *passim*
Antyllius, Q., lictor: G34
Antyllus, M. Antonius, son of Antony and Fulvia: A28, 71, 81, 87
Aous: C38
Apellicon of Teos: S26
Apemantus: A70
Aphrodite, goddess: S34, A26
Apollo, god: Aem15, S17, 19, 22, 29, 32, P24, A23
Apollodorus of Sicily: C49
Apollonia: S27, C37, 38
Apollonius, son of Molo: C3
Appian Way: C5
Appius Claudius: *see* Claudius Pulcher, Ap.
Aquae Sextiae (Aix-en-Provence): M18
Aquillius, M'., cos. 101: M14
Arab/ia, -ians (Nabataeans): P38, 39, 41, 42, 45, A27, 36, 37, 61
Arabian Gulf: A69
Arar, river (Saône): C18, 26
Araxes, river: P33, 34, A49, 52
Arbelitis: P36
Arcadia: C61
Archedamus of Aetolia: Aem23
Archelaus, commander of Mithridates: S11, 15, 16, 17, 19–24
Archelaus, Delian merchant: S22
Archelaus, king of Cappadocia: A61
Archelaus, king of Egypt: A3
Archelaus, satrap: M34
Archibius: A86
Archilochus: M21
Arethusa: A37
Argos: P24
Ariarathes: P42
Ariarathes, son of Mithridates: S11, P37
Ariminum (Rimini): P60, C32, 33
Ariobarzanes: S5, 22, 24
Ariovistus: C19
Aristion, tyrant of Athens: S12, 13, 23
Aristobulus, Jewish leader: P39, 45, A3
Aristocrates: A69
Ariston, philosopher: Cat18
Aristonicus of Pergamum: G20
Aristophanes: A70
Aristotle: S26
Arius: A80

Armen/ia, -ians: S5, P28, 30–4, 39, 45, 67, A34, 37–9, 41, 49, 50, 52, 54–6, 61
Armenia, Lesser: P36, C50
Arpinum: M3
Arruntius, L., cos. 22: A66
Arsaces, king of Parthia: S5, P76
Artavasdes of Armenia: A37, 39, 50
Artemidorus: C65
Arverni: C25, 26
Asclepius, Greek god: P24
Asculum: P4
Asia (western Anatolia or continent): Cat12, Aem7, G20, 21, M11, 31, S11, 22–5, P37, 45, 46, 80, C2, 48, 50, A24, 26, 30, 33, 35, 37, 67, 69, 72
Asinius Pollio, C., cos. 40: P72, C32, 46, 52, A9, 69
Assus, river: S16, 17
Ateius, M.: S14
Athamania: P66
Athens, Athenians: Cat5, 8, 12, 22, M46, S6, 11, 12, 13, 14, 26, P27, 42, C43, A23, 33, 53, 54, 57, 60, 68, 72
Atia, mother of Caesar Octavianus: A31
Atlantic Sea: P38, C23
Atropatene: A38
Attalia: P76
Attalus I of Pergamum: A60
Attalus Philometor of Pergamum: G14
Attica: S15
Aurelia: C9, 10
Aurelius, C.: P23
Aurelius, Q.: S31
Auximum: P6
Aventine, hill in Rome: G36

Babylon: A45
Bacchus: C41, 56; *see also* Dionysus
Bactria: A37
Baetis, river (Guadalquivir): Cat10
Baiae: M34
Balbus, commander under Sulla: S29
Bambyce: *see* Hierapolis
Bardyaei: M43, 44
Basilica Fulvia: C29
Basilus, L. Minucius: S9
Basternae, a Celtic tribe: Aem9, 12
Bataces: M17
Belaeus: M40
Belgae: P51, C20
Bellienus, praetor: P24
Bellona: S7, 9, 27, 30
Beroea: P64
Berytus: A51
Bestia, L. Calpurnius, cos. 111: M9
Bibulus, M. Calpurnius, cos. 59: P47, 48, 54, A5
Bithynia: Cat9, S11, 22, P30, C1, 50
Blossius of Cumae: G8, 17, 20
Bocchus, king of Mauretania: M10, 32, S3, 5, 6
Boeorix: M25
Boeotia: M41, S11, 15, 20, 22, 26
Bogus, king of Libya: A61
Bona: C9
Bosporus: S11, P32, 35, 38, 39
Braetius Sura: S11
Britain, Britons: P51, C16, 23
Brundisium (Brindisi): Cat14, Aem36, S27, P27, 62, 63, 65, C35, 37–9, A7, 35, 62
Bruti: C61
Brutus, L. Iunius, cos. 509: C61, 62
Brutus, M. Iunius (assassin of Caesar): P16, 64, 80, C46, 54, 57, 62, 64–9, A11–15, 21, 22, 69
Brutus, M. Iunius, father of assassin: P16
Brutus, M. Iunius, pr. 88: S9
Brutus Albinus, D. Iunius: C64, 66, A11
Brutus Callaecus, D. Iunius, cos. 138: G21
Brutus Damasippus, L. Iunius(?): P7

Cabiri, gods of Samothrace: Aem23
Cadmus: S17
Caecilia Metella, wife of Sulla: S6, 13, 22, 33–5, 37
Caecilius Metellus (unidentified): P2
Caecilius Metellus, C.: S31
Caecilius Metellus, L., tr. pl. 49: P62, C35
Caecilius Metellus Creticus, Q.: P29
Caecillus Metellus Delmaticus, L., cos. 119: M4, S6
Caecilius Metellus Macedonicus, Q., cos. 143: G14, M1
Caecilius Metellus Nepos, cos. 57: C21
Caecilius Metellus Numidicus, Q., cos. 109: M7, 8, 10, 28, 29, 31, 42, C15(?)
Caecilius Metellus Pius, Q., cos. 80: Cat24, M42, S6, 28, P8, 17–19, 31, C7
Caecilius Metellus Pius Scipio, Q., cos. 52: P55, 62, 66, 67, 69, 76, C30, 44
Caecilius Metellus Scipio Nasica, Q.: C16, 39, 42, 52, 53, 55
Caenum: P37, 38

Caepio, Q. Servilius: P47
Caepio, Q. Servilius, cos. 106: M16, 19
Caesar, C. Iulius (dictator): M6, P10, 16, 25, 46–9, 51–4, 56–77, 80, C *passim*, A5–8, 10–16, 18, 25, 33, 54, 71, 81
Caesar, L. Iulius, cos. 64: A19, 20
Caesar, Vopiscus, C. Iulius(?): S5
Caesar Octavianus (Octavian, later Augustus), C. Iulius: Aem38, C67, 69, A11, 16, 17, 19–24, 28, 30–5, 53–6, 58, 60–3, 65, 66–8, 71–87
Caesarion, son of C. Iulius Caesar and Cleopatra: C49, A54, 81
Calauria: P24
Calenus: C43
Callaïci: C12
Callidromum, Greek town: Cat13
Callimachus: A70
Calliphon of Athens: S14
Callisthenes of Olynthus, historian: S36
Calpurnia, wife of Caesar: P47, C14, 63, 64, A15
Calpurnius Bibulus, M., cos. 59: C14
Calvinus, Cn. Domitius, cos. 53, 40: P54, 69
Calvisius Sabinus, C.: A58, 59
Camerinum: M28
Campania: S27
Campus Martius: G24, 29, M34, S38, P15, 53, C23
Canidius: *see* Caninius
Canidius Crassus, P., lieutenant of Antony: A34, 42, 56, 63, 65, 67, 68, 71
Caninius Gallus, C.: P49
Caninius Revilius (Rebilus), C., cos. suff. 45: C58
Cannae: Aem2
Canobus, in Egypt: A29
Caphis of Chaeronea: S15
Caphis of Phocis: S12
Capitol, at Rome: Aem 30, G15, 17, 19, 20, 24, 34, 35, M12, 30, 32, S6, 10, 27, C6, 61, 67
Cappadoc/ia, -ians: M31, 34, S5, 9, 11, 22, 23, P30, 45, C50, A61
Capua: G29, S27
Carbo, Cn. Papirius, cos. 113: M16
Carbo, Cn. Papirius, cos. 85, 84, 82: S22, 28, 29, P5–7, 10
Carneades, Academic philosopher: Cat22, 23
Carnutes: C25
Carrinas, C., pr. 82: P7
Carth/age, -aginians: Cat26, 27, Aem22, G31, 32, 34, M12, 40, P11, 14, C57
Casca Longus, C. Servilius: C66
Caspian Sea: P33, 34, 36, C58
Cassius Longinus, C. (assassin of Caesar): P16, C57, 62, 64, 66, 68, 69, A11–14, 21, 22, 25
Cassius Longinus, Q., tr. pl. 49: A5, 6
Cassius Sabaco, Roman senator: M5
Cassius Scaeva, Caesarian soldier: C16
Castor: S8, 33, P2
Catiline (L. Sergius Catilina): S32, C7
Cato, M. Porcius, father of the censor: Cat1
Cato, M. Porcius, the censor: Cat *passim*, Aem5, 21
Cato Licinianus, M. Porcius, son of the censor: Cat20, 24, Aem5, 21
Cato Priscus, (M.) Porcius, great-grandfather of the censor: Cat1
Cato Salonius, M. Porcius, son of the censor: Cat24, 27
Cato Uticensis, M. Porcius: Cat27, P40, 44, 46–8, 52, 54–6, 59–61, 65, 67, 76, C8, 13, 14, 21, 22, 28, 41, 52, 54, 62, A5
Catulus, Q. Lutatius, cos. 102: M14, 15, 23–7, 44, S4, 34
Catulus, Q. Lutatius, cos. 78: S34, P15–17, 25, 30, 31, C6, 7, 8
Caucasus: P34, 35, C58, A34
Celtiberi, people of Spain: Cat10, M3
Celtoscythians: M11
Celts, Celtic: M11
Censorinus, C. Marcius: S5
Censorinus, L.: A24
Cephisus, river: S16, 17, 20
Ceraetae: M3
Cerameicus at Athens: S14
Cercina (Qerqena): M40
Cethegus, C. Cornelius: C7
Cethegus, P. Cornelius: M40
Chaeron, founder of Chaeronea: S17
Chaeron/ea, -eans: S11, 16–18, 21–3
Chalcis (on Euboea): S19, 20
Chaldeans: M42, S5, 37
Charmion, attendant of Cleopatra: A60, 85
Chilo, slave of Cato: Cat20
Chthonia: P24
Cicero, M. Tullius, orator: Cat17, Aem10, G22, P42, 46, 48, 49, 59, 63, 64, C3, 4,

7, 8, 14, 31, 54, 57–9, A2, 6, 9, 16, 17, 19, 20, 22
Cicero, Q. Tullius: C24
Cilic/ia, -ians: P24, 26–30, 33, 45, 59, 76, C2, 31, A25, 36, 54, 61
Cimbri: M11, 15, 23, 24, 25, 26, 39, 44, C18, 19, 26
Cimmerians: M11
Cimon, Athenian statesman: Cat5
Cinna, C. Helvius, friend of Caesar: C68
Cinna, L. Cornelius, cos. 87–4: M41–4, S10, 12, 22, P3–5, C1
Circeium: M36, C58
Circus Maximus: S30
Cisalpine Gaul: P16, 48, C14, 20, 31, 32
Claros: P24
Claudia: G4
Claudius, Ap., killed in 82: S29
Claudius Caesar, Tib., emperor: A87
Claudius Marcellus: M20, 21
Claudius Pulcher, Ap., cos. 143: Aem38, G4, 9, 13
Claudius Pulcher, Ap., cos. 54: P57, C21
Clemency, sanctuary of: C57
Cleomenes, king of Sparta: G1
Cleon of Athens: G2
Cleopatra: C48, 49, A10, 25–33, 36, 37, 50, 51, 53, 54, 56–60, 62, 63, 66, 67, 69, 71–4, 76–9, 81, 82, 84–7
Cleopatra (Selene), daughter of Antony and Cleopatra: A36, 87
Clodia, wife of Caesar Octavianus: A20
Clodius Pulcher, P.: P46, 48, 49, C9, 10, 14, A2, 10
Cloelia: S6
Cnid/os, -ians: C48, 65
Coelius, commander at Actium(?): A65
Coelius Antipater, C.(?): P7
Colchis: P32, 34, 45
Colchis, Upper: P30
Commagene: P45, A34, 61
Concord, temple of: G38
Considius, senator: C14
Copillus, leader of Tectosages: S4
Coracesium: P28
Corduba (Córdoba): C17
Corfinium: C34
Corinth: Cat12, M1, C57, 58, A67
Cornelia, daughter of Sulla: M34
Cornelia, mother of the Gracchi: G1, 4, 8, 25, 34, 40
Cornelia, wife of Caesar: C1, 5
Cornelia, wife of Pompey: P55, 66, 74, 75, 78–80
Cornelia Postuma, daughter of Sulla: S37
Cornelius: C1
Cornelius, C., seer: C47
Cornelius Balbus, L.: C60
Cornelius Merula, L.: M41
Cornelius Nepos: G21
Cornelius Scipio: *see* Scipio
Cornelius Sulla: *see* Sulla
Cornificius, Q.: C43
Cornutus: M43
Corsica: Aem36, P26, 66
Cosconius: C51
Cosis of Albania: P35
Cotta, L. Aurelius, cos. 119: M4
Cotta Aurunculeius, L.: C24
Crassianus, C., centurion: P71
Crassinius, C.: C44
Crassus, M. Licinius, cos. 70, 55: S28–30, P21–3, 31, 43, 47, 51–3, 55, 76, C11, 13, 14, 21, 28, A34, 37, 46
Crassus, P. Licinius, son of cos. 70, 55: P55, 74
Crassus Dives Mucianus, P. Licinius, cos. 131: G9, 21
Cratippus, philosopher: P75
Cret/e, -ans: Aem15, 16, 23, 26, 32, G37, P29
Culleo, Q. Terentius: P49
Cumae: G8, 17, 20
Curio, C. Scribonius, cos. 76: S14, C8, A2, 5
Curio, C. Scribonius, tr. pl. 50: P58, C29–31
Curius Dentatus, M'.: Cat2, 8
Cyclades: S11
Cyclops: Cat10
Cydnus, river in Cilicia: A26
Cymaeans: C61
Cyprus: P48, 77, 80, C21, A36, 54
Cyrene: A61
Cyrnus: P34, 35
Cyrrhestica, region of Syria: A34
Cyrus the Great of Persia: A6
Cytheris, actress: A9

Danube, river: Cat12, Aem9
Dardanians, people living north of Macedonia: Aem9

Dardanus: S24
Darymna: S26
Deidius: C56
Deïotarus, Galatian king: P73
Deïotarus Philadelphus, king of Paphlagonia: A61, 63
Delium: S22
Dellius, Q.: A25, 59
Delos: S22
Delphi: Aem28, 36, S12, 29
Demeter, Greek goddess: Aem26
Demetrius, son of Philip: Aem8
Demetrius I Poliorcetes, son of Antigonus I Monophthalmus: Aem8
Demetrius II, son of Antigonus II Gonatas: Aem8
Demetrius of Gadara, freedman of Pompey: P2, 40
Democritus, Greek philosopher: Aem1
Demosthenes, Athenian orator: Cat2
Dercetaeus: A78
Diana, sanctuary of: G37
Dicaearchia (Pozzuoli): S37
Dicomes, king of the Getae: A63
Didyma: P24
Diogenes, stepson of Archelaus: S21
Diogenes, Stoic philosopher: Cat22
Diomedes: A76
Dionysius I, tyrant of Syracuse: Cat24
Dionysus (*see also* Bacchus), god: S26, C9, A24, 26, 56, 57, 60, 75
Diophanes of Mytilene: G8, 20
Dioscuri (*see also* Castor, Pollux): Aem25, G2
Dolabella, Cn. Cornelius, cos. 81: S28, 29, C4
Dolabella, P. Cornelius, cos. suff. 44: C51, 62, A9–11, 84
Domitian, Roman emperor: Aem25
Domitius Ahenobarbus: *see also* Ahenobarbus
Domitius Ahenobarbus, Cn.: P10–12
Domitius Ahenobarbus, Cn., cos. 32: A40, 56, 63, 87
Domitius Ahenobarbus, L.: A87
Domitius Ahenobarbus, L., cos. 54: P52, 67, 69, C34, 35, 42, 44, 50
Dorylaeus, commander of Mithridates: S20
Drusus, M. Livius, cos. 112: G2, 29–32
Drusus, Nero Claudius: A87
Dryads: C9
Dyme: P28
Dyrrhachium (Durrës or Durazzo): S27, P62, 74, C16, 35

Earth (as a deity): S9
Ecregma marshes: A3
Egypt/, -ians: P49, 76, 77, 79, 80, C45, 48, 49, 55, A3, 27, 37, 50, 54, 56, 58, 59, 64, 69, 71–3
Elateia: S16
Elimiae, region of Macedonia: Aem9
Elymaeans: P36
Epaminondas, Theban statesman: Cat8
Epaphroditus: A79
Ephes/us, -ians: S26, A24, 56, 58
Epicurus: C66
Epidaurus: S12, P24
Epirus:Aem29, C37, A62
Eros, slave of Antony: A76
Eros, god: A26
Erucius, legate of Sulla: S16, 18
Eryx, in Sicily: M40
Esquiline, hill in Rome: S9
Ethiop/ia, -ians: A27, 61, 81
Etruria, Etruscans: M11, 41, S7, P27
Euboea: S11, 23
Euctus, a Macedonian: Aem23
Eudemus of Pergamum: G14
Eulaeus, a Macedonian: Aem23
Eumenes II of Pergamum: Cat8, A60
Eumolpus, legendary poet: S13
Eunus, slave leader: S36
Euphrates, river: S5, P32, 33, 76, A30, 61
Euphronius: A72
Euripides, tragic poet: S4
Europe: P45
Eurycles of Laconia: A67
Euxine (Black) Sea: M34, 45, P34, C58
Evander of Crete: Aem23

Fabius Maximus, Q., cos 121: G27
Fabius Maximus, Q., cos. 45: C58
Fabius Maximus Aemilianus, Q., cos. 145: Aem5, 15, 35
Fabius Maximus Rullus, Q., censor 304: P13
Fabius Maximus Verrucosus, Q., Cunctator: Cat2, 3, Aem5, C15
Falerii: G24
Fannia, woman of Minturnae: M38
Fannius, C., cos. 122: G4, 29, 32, 33

Faunus: C9
Fausta, Cornelia, daughter of Sulla: S34
Faustus, L. Cornelius, son of Sulla: S34, P42, 47, C14
Favonius, M.: P60, 67, 73, C21, 33, 41
Fenestella, Roman historian: S28
Fidentia: S27
Fimbria, C. Flavius: S12, 23–5
Firmans: Cat13
Flaccus, L. Valerius, cos. 86: S12, 20, 23
Flamininus, L. Quinctius, cos. 192: Cat17
Flamininus, T. Quinctius, cos. 198: Cat12, 17, 19, Aem 8, S12
Flavius, L. Caesetius: C61
Flavius Gallus: A42, 43
Flora: P2, 53
Fonteius Capito, C.: A36
Fregellae: G24
Fufidius: S31
Fulcinia, mother of Marius: M3
Fulvia, wife of Antony: A10, 20, 28, 30–2, 35, 54, 57, 71, 81
Fulvius, an ex-consul: G11
Fulvius Flaccus, M., cos. 125: G18, 21, 32, 34–9
Furies, grove of at Rome: G38
Furnius, C.: A58

Gabinius, A., cos. 58: P25, 27, 48, A3, 7
Gabinius, A., legate of Sulla: S16, 17
Gaius, foster-brother of Mithridates: P42
Gaius Iulius Caesar, emperor (Caligula): A87
Galat/ia, -ians: M31, P30, 31, 33, A61
Galba, ex-praetor: C51
Galba, Ser. Sulpicius, cos. 144: Cat15, Aem 30, 31
Galba, Ser. Sulpicius, legate of Sulla: S17
Galepsus, an Aegean seaport: Aem23
Gallus, C. Cornelius: A79
Gaul, Gallic, Gauls: Cat17, Aem6, 9, 13, G36, M2, 11, 24, 27, 39, 43, P7, 8, 16, 48, 51, 52, 57, 59, 64, 66, 67, C15, 18–27, 29, 32, 55, 58, A5, 37, 41
Gelae: P35
Gellius Publicola, L.: A65, 66
Gellius Publicola, L., cos. 72: P22
Geminius: P2, 16
Geminius, C.: A59
Geminius, enemy of Marius: M36, 38
Genthius, Illyrian king: Aem9, 13
Genucius, tr. pl. 241: G24
Germanicus: A87
Germany, Germans: Aem25, M11, P67, 70, C18, 19, 22, 23, 58
Getae: A63
Glabrio: *see* Acilius Glabrio, M'.
Glaucia, Servilius: M28
Glaucus, doctor: A59
Gnathaenius, an Argive woman: Aem8
Gomphi: C41
Gordius of Cappadocia: S5
Gordyene: P36
Gracchus, C. Sempronius: G *passim*
Gracchus, Ti. Sempronius: G *passim*
Gracchus, Ti. Sempronius, the elder: Cat12, G1, 4, 17
Graces, the: M2
Granius, stepson of Marius: M35, 37, 40
Granius of Dicaearchia: S37
Granius Petro: C16
Great Mother (Cybele): M17, 31
Greece, Greeks: Cat8, 9, 12, 13, 20, 22, 23, Aem6, 7, 12, 25, 28, 29, M11, 46, S11, 12, 17, 18, 19, 20, 34, P30, 65, 66, 70, C49, 55, A2, 23, 24, 33, 59, 62, 68, 69, 72
Gynaceia: C9

Habra: C10
Halae: S26, A70
Hamilcar Barca, Carthaginian general: Cat8
Hannibal, Carthaginian general: Cat1, 12, Aem7, G1
Harpalus, minister of Alexander: Aem15
Hebrews: A27
Hector, Trojan hero: P29
Hedylium: S16, 17
Hellespont S23
Helvetii: C18
Heptachalcum, at Athens: S14
Hera, Greek goddess: P24
Heracles, Greek hero: Aem17, 19, S35, P1, A4, 36, 60, 61
Heracleum at Patrae: A60
Hercynia: M11
Herennius, C.: M5, P18
Hermagoras, Greek philosopher: P42
Hermione: P24
Herod, king of Judaea: A61, 71, 72
Hiempsal II of Numidia: M40, 12
Hierapolis (Bambyce): A37

Himera: P10
Hipparchus: A67, 73
Hippias, actor: A9
Hippocrates, the doctor: Cat23
Hirtius, A., cos. 43: Aem38, A17
Homer: Aem28, 34, G21, M11
Homoloïchus of Chaeronea: S17, 19
Hortensius, L.: S15, 17, 19, 35
Hortensius Hortalus, Q., son of orator: C32, A22
Hostilius Mancinus, A. cos. 170: Aem9
Hybreas of Mylasa: A24
Hypsaeus: P55
Hypsicrateia: P32
Hyrcan/ia, -ians: P34, C58
Hyrcanian Sea: P35, 36, 38

Iarbas: P12
Iberians: P34, 36, 45, A34
Ilia(?), wife of Sulla: S6
Illyr/icum, -ians: Aem9, 31, P48, C14, 31, A56, 61
Ind/ia, -ians: Aem12, P70, A37, 81
Insteius, M.: A65
Ion, a Macedonian: Aem26
Ionia: A30
Ionian Sea: Aem36, S20, C37, A7, 30, 61, 62
Iophon, son of Pisistratus: Cat 24
Iras: A60, 85
Isauricus, P. Servilius Vatia, cos. 79: C7
Isauricus, P. Servilius Vatia, cos. 48: C37
Isis: A54, 74
Isocrates, Greek orator: Cat23
Isthmus: P24
Ital/y, -ians: Cat1, 2, 14, Aem6, 9, 15, 20, 30, 39, G8, 9, 21, 24, 25, 33, M11, 16, 23, 24, 32, 34, 36, 39, 41, 45, S11, 17, 27, 31, P6, 9, 11, 13, 15, 20, 21, 40–3, 53, 57, 58, 60–6, A2, 6, 18, 30, 33, 35, 55, 58, 61, 84
Iulii: *see* Caesar *and* Julia
Iuncus: C2

Janiculum, hill in Rome: M42
Jews, Jewish: A3, 36
Juba I of Numidia: P76, C52, 53, 55
Juba II of Mauretania: S16, C55, A87
Judaea: P39, 45, A36, 61, 71
Jugurtha, king of Numidia: G39, M7, 8, 10–12, 32, S3, 6
Julia, daughter of Caesar: C14, 23, 55
Julia, daughter of Caesar Octavianus: A87
Julia, mother of Mark Antony: A1–2
Julia, wife of Marius: M6, C1, 5
Julia, wife of Pompey: P47, 49, 70
Julius Caesar: *see* Caesar, C. Iulius
Junonia (Carthage): G32
Jupiter, Roman god: Cat21, P23
Juvius: P65

Labienus, Q.: A28, 30, 33
Labienus, T.: P64, 68, C18, 34
Lacetani, Iberian people: Cat11
Lachares: A67
Lacinium: P24
Laconia, Laconians: A67
Laelius Sapiens, C., cos. 140: G8
Lamponius the Lucanian: S29
Lamprias, grandfather of Plutarch: A28
Laodicea: A72
Larissa, in Thessaly: S23, P73
Larissa, in Syria: A37
Lat/ium, -ins: Aem25, G29, 30
Lauron: P18
Laverna: S6
Lebadea: S16, 17
Leges (Caucasian people): P35
Lentulus Clodianus, Cn., censor 70: P22
Lentulus Crus, L. Cornelius, cos. 49: P59, 73, 80, C29–31, 33, A5
Lentulus Spinther, P. Cornelius, assassin?: C67
Lentulus Spinther, P. Cornelius, cos. 57: P49, 67, 73, C42
Lentulus Sura, P. Cornelius, cos. 71: C7, A2
Lepidus, M. Aemilius, cos. 78: S34, 38, P15–17, 31
Lepidus, M. Aemilius, triumvir: C63, 67, A6, 10, 14, 18, 21, 30, 55
Lesbos: P66, 76
Leucas: P24
Leucus river, at Pydna: Aem16, 21
Libo, L. Scribonius: A7
Liburnians: P64
Libyan Sea: P26
Licinia, wife of C. Gracchus: G21, 36, 38
Licinius: *see also* Crassus
Licinius, friend of C. Gracchus: G37
Licinius, S.: M45

Licinius, slave of C. Gracchus: G2
Licinius Crassus, P., cos. 171: Aem9
Licinius Philonicus: Aem38
Ligurians: Aem6, 18, 39, M15, 19
Lingones: C26
Liris, river (Gargano): M41
Lissus, city on the Adriatic: A7
Livia, wife of Octavian: A83, 87
Livy (T. Livius): Cat17, S6, C47, 63
Luca (Lucca): P51, C21
Lucanians: S29
Lucilius, friend of Brutus: A69
Lucilius Hirrus, C.: P54
Lucretius Ofella, Q.: S29, 33
Lucullus, L. Licinius, cos. 74: Cat24, M34, S6, 11, 27, P2, 20, 30–3, 38, 39, 46, 48, C10, 15
Lucullus, M. Terentius Varro, cos. 73: S27, C4, 15
Lupercalia: C61, A12
Lusitani: G21, C12
Lusius, C.: M14
Lutatius Catulus: *see* Catulus, Q. Lutatius
Lycaea: C61
Lycaon/ia, -ians: P30, A61
Lyceum, at Athens: S12
Lyd/ia, -ians: A30
Lygdamis, Cimmerian king: M11
Lyra: C59
Lysias: Cat7

Macedon/ia, -ians: Cat12, 15, Aem7–10, 12, 16–20, 24, 28, 29, 31, 32, 34, 36, 38, 39, S11, 12, 15, 23, 27, P34, 64, A7, 21, 22, 23, 54, 63, 67, C4, 39
Maecenas, C.: A35
Maedica, in Macedonia: Aem12, S23
Maeotis, Lake (Sea of Azov): M11, S11, P35, A56
Magnesia: A24
Malchas, king of Arabia: A61
Malea, Cape: S11
Mallius: G11
Mallius, L., Roman soldier: Cat13
Mamercus Aemilius: Aem2
Mamertines: P10
Mancinus, C. Hostilius, cos. 137: G5, 7
Manilius, C.: P30
Manilius, Roman senator: Cat17
Manlius (Mallius), Maximus, Cn., cos. 105: M19
Marcella major, daughter of Octavia: A87
Marcellinus, Cn. Cornelius Lentulus, cos. 56: P51
Marcellus, C. Claudius, cos. 50: P58, 59, A5, 31, 87
Marcellus, M. Claudius, cos. 51: C29
Marcellus, son of Octavia: A87
Marcius Philippus, Q., cos. 186, 169: Aem38
Mardian: A41, 47, 48
Mardion, eunuch: A60
Marians: C6
Marica, grove: M39
Marius, C., seven times consul: M *passim*, S3, 4, 6–10, 12, 28, P8, 11, C1, 5, 6, 15, A1,
Marius, C., father of the famous Marius: M3
Marius, C., son of the famous Marius: M35, 40, 46, S27–30, 32, 33, P13, C1, 19
Marius, M. Gratidianus: S32
Marrucinians: Aem20
Mars, Roman god: M46, S19
Marsi: S4
Martha, prophetess: M17
Marullus, C. Epidius: C61
Masinissa, king of Numidia: Cat26
Maso, L. Papirius, cos. 231: Aem5
Massalia (Marseilles): M21, C16
Matius, C.: C50, 51
Maximus: *see* Fabius Maximus
Med/ia, -es: S16, P34, 36, 45, A27, 34, 38, 39, 46, 49, 50, 52–5, 61
Mediolanum (Milan): C17
Megar/a, -ians: C43, A23
Melas, river: S20
Meliteia: S20
Memmius: P11
Menas the Pirate: A32
Menecrates: A32
Meninx (Djerba): M40
Mercedonius: C59
Merula, L. Cornelius: M45
Mesopotamia: P45, A28, 34
Messala, M. Valerius, cos. 53: P54
Messala, Valerius: S35
Messana: P10
Metella: *see* Caecilia Metella
Metella, wife of Sulla: P9
Metellus: *see* Caecilius Metellus
Metellus (another): C15
Metellus (yet another?): C35

Metrobius: S2, 36
Metrodorus: A24
Micipsa, king of Numidia: G23
Midas: C9
Midias of Athens: S14
Miletus: C2
Milo, Macedonian commander: Aem16
Minerva, Roman goddess: S9
Minos, legendary king of Crete and underworld judge: Cat23
Minturnae: M37–9
Misenum, Cape: G40, M34, A32
Mithraic mysteries: P24
Mithridates, king of Commagene: A61
Mithridates VI of Pontus: M31, 34, 35, 41, 45, S5, 6, 8, 10–13, 15, 18, 20, 22–4, 27, 34, P20, 30–2, 34–9, 41, 42, 45, C50
Mithridates the Parthian: A46–8
Mithridatic War: M34, 45, S7, 8, 22, P20, 24
Molo: C3
Molus, river: S19
Monaeses: A37, 46
Monime: P37
Moors, Moorish: M41
Morius, river: S17
Moschian mountains: P34
Mucia, wife of Pompey: P42
Mucius(?), tr. pl. 133: G13, 18
Mucius Scaevola: G9
Mucius Scaevola, P., cos. 133: S36
Mucius Scaevola, Q., the augur: M35
Mummius, C.: S9
Mummius, L., cos. 146: M1
Munda: C56
Munychia: S15
Murena, L. Licinius: S17, 18, 19
Musaeus, mythical poet: M36
Muses, the: M2, S17
Mutina (Modena): P16, A17
Mycale: Aem25
Mytilene: G8, P42, 74, 75

Nabataeans (see also Arabia): P67
Naples: P57
Nasica: *see* Scipio Nasica
Nearchus of Tarentum: Cat2
Neleus of Scepsis: S26
Neon of Boeotia: Aem23
Neoptolemus, satrap: M34
Nepos: *see* Caecilius Metellus Nepos *and* Cornelius Nepos
Nero Claudius Caesar Germanicus (L. Domitius Ahenobarbus), emperor: A87
Nervii: C20
Nestor, Homeric hero: Cat15
Nicarchus: A68
Nicomedes IV of Bithynia: S22, 24, C1
Nicopolis (Actium): A62
Nicopolis, mistress of Sulla: S2
Niger: A53
Nile, river: S20, P80
Nola: S8, 9
Nonius, nephew of Sulla: S10
Nonius, Roman senator: M29
Norbanus, C., cos. 83: S27
Noricum: M15
Novum Comum: C29
Numa, King: Aem2, C59
Numant/ia (city in Spain), -ians: Aem 22, G5–7, 13, 21, 36, M3, 13
Numerius, friend of Marius: M35
Numerius, friend of Pompey: P63
Numid/ia, -ians: Cat26, G39, M32, 40, S3, P12, C52, 53, 55
Nymphaeum: S27

Ocean, the: M11, P38, C23, 58
Ocean, Western: A61
Octavia, sister of Caesar Octavianus: A31, 33, 35, 53, 54, 56, 57, 59, 72, 83, 87
Octavian: *see* Caesar Octavianus
Octavius, Cn., cos. 165: Aem26
Octavius, Cn., cos. 87: M41, 42, 45, S12
Octavius, L.: P29
Octavius, M., tr. pl. 133: G10–12, 15, 25
Octavius, M., commander at Actium: A65
Octavius Balbus, C.: C67
Odysseus, Homeric hero: Cat9, M11
Oedipus, spring of: S19
Olocrus, Mt.: Aem20
Olympia: Aem28, S12
Olympus, city of Lycia: P24
Olympus, doctor of Cleopatra: A82
Olympus, Mt.: Aem13, 14, 15, 17
Opimius, L., cos. 121: G32, 34, 35, 37–9
Oppius, C.: P10, C17
Orchomenus: S20, 21, 22, 26
Orestes, L. Aurelius, cos. 126: G22, 23
Oreus, in Euboea: Aem9
Oricum, port in Epirus: Aem30, P65, C37
Oroandes, a Cretan: Aem26
Orobazus: S5

Orodes: A37
Oropians: Cat22
Orphic rites: C9
Orthopagus, hill at Chaeronea: S17
Ostia: M35, 42, C58

Paccius, Roman soldier: Cat10
Pacorus, Parthian prince: A34
Paeon/ia, -ians: Aem18, P41
Palatine, hill in Rome: G33
Palestine: P45
Pamphylia: P76
Panopeus: S16
Pansa Caetronianus, C. Vibius, cos. 43: Aem38, A17
Paphlagonia: S22, 23, P45, A61
Papiria, wife of Aemilius Paullus: Aem5
Paraetonium: A69
Parapotamii: S16
Parma: M27
Parnassus: S15
Parthenon, temple in Athens: Cat5
Parth/ia, -ians: S5, P33, 36, 38, 39, 52, 53, 55, 70, 74, 76, C28, 58, 60, A5, 25, 27, 28, 30, 33–5, 37–42, 45–50, 52–5
Parthian War: P56, A35
Patavium (Padua): C47
Patrae: *see* Heracleum
Patrae, Greek city: Cat12
Patronis: S15
Paullus: *see* Aemilius Paullus
Paullus, L. Aemilius, cos. 219, 216: Aem2
Paullus, L. Aemilius, cos. 50: P58, C29
Pelignians: Aem20
Pella, city of Macedonia: Aem23
Peloponnese: Aem25, A66
Peloponnesian War: A70
Pelusium, Egyptian city: P77, A3, 74
Pergamum: G14, 21, S11, 23, C2, A58
Pericles, Greek statesman: Cat8, P63
Peripatetics: S26
Perperna Veiento, M.: P10, 18, 20
Perrhaebia, region of Macedonia: Aem15
Persephone, Greek goddess: Cat1
Perseus, king of Macedon: Cat15, 20, Aem7–10, 12, 13, 16, 19, 23, 24, 26–9, 33, 34, 36, 37
Pers/ia, -ians: Cat13, 23, Aem12, 25, A6, 37
Persian empire: P34
Persian Wars: S13
Pessinous: M17
Peticius: P73
Petillius, Q., Roman tribune: Cat15
Petra (by Mt. Olympus): Aem15
Petra (Nabatea): P41, A69
Petrachus, at Chaeronea: S17
Pharmacussa: C1
Pharnaces, son of Mithridates VI: P41, 42, C50
Pharos, island at Alexandria: C49, A29, 69
Pharsalus, in Thessaly: P68, 71, C42, 52, 62, A8, 62
Phasis, river: P34
Pherecydes, mythographer: S36
Phidias, Greek sculptor: Aem28
Philip V of Macedon: Cat12, 17, Aem7, 8, 12, 31
Philippi, in Macedonia: S23, C69, A69
Philippus, freedman of Pompey: P78–80
Philippus, L. Marcius, cos. 91: P2, 17
Philo, arsenal of: S14
Philoboeotus: S16
Philocrates, slave of C. Gracchus: G38
Philostratus: A80
Philotas of Amphissa: A28
Phoc/is, -ians: S12, 15
Phoenic/ia, -ians: P32, 33, 45, A30, 36, 54, 64
Phraata: A38, 39, 50
Phraates III of Parthia: P33
Phraates IV of Parthia: A37, 38, 40, 41, 52
Phranipates, Parthian commander: A33
Phryg/ia, -ians: P30, C9
Picenum: P6
Pictae: S9
Pillars of Heracles: Aem6, P25, A61
Pindar, freedman of Cassius: A22
Pindar, Greek poet: M29
Piraeus: S12, 14, 26
Pirate War: P30
Pisaurum: A60
Pisistratus, tyrant of Athens: Cat24
Piso, C., historian: M45
Piso, C. Calpurnius, cos. 67: P27, C7
Piso, M. Pupius, cos. 61: P44
Piso Caesoninus, L. Calpurnius, cos. 58: P47, 48, 58, C14, 37
Plancus, L. Munatius, cos. 42: A18, 58
Plancus Byrsa, T. Munatius: P55
Plataeans: Aem25
Plato, philosopher: Cat2, 7, M2, 46, A29, 36, 70

Po, river : M24, P16, C20, 21, 25
Polemo, king of Pontus: A38, 61
Pollux: S8, P2
Polybius, Greek historian: Cat9, 10, Aem15, 16, 19, G4
Pomentinum: C58
Pompaedius Silo: M33
Pompeia, wife of Caesar: C5, 9, 10
Pompeius, A.: M17
Pompeius, Cn., son of Pompey the Great: P62, A25
Pompeius, Q., cos. 141: G14
Pompeius Rufus, Q., cos. 88: S6, 8
Pompey, Garden of: P44
Pompey (Sex. Pompeius), son of Pompey the Great: A32, 35, 55, 62
Pompey the Great (C. Pompeius Magnus): S28, 29, 33, 34, 38, P *passim*, C5, 11, 13–15, 20, 21, 23, 25, 28–31, 33–7, 39–46, 48, 51, 56, 57, 62, 66, 69, A5, 6, 8, 10, 21
Pomponius, M.: G37
Pontic Sea (Black Sea), *see* Euxine: P32
Pontius: S27
Pontus (region in Anatolia): M31, S11, 22, 24, P31, 41, 45, C50, 55, A61
Popillius, C.: C5
Popillius Laenas, P., cos. 132: G25
Poseidon: P24
Posidonius, Greek historian and philosopher: M1, 45, P42
Posidonius, Macedonian(?) historian: Aem19–21
Postuma: *see* Cornelia Postuma
Postumius, seer: S9
Postumius Albinus, A., Roman historian: Cat12
Postumius, Sp.: G8
Pothinus: P77, 80, C48, 49
Pothinus, associate of Antony: A60
Praeneste: M46, S28, 29, 32, 33
Praxagoras: P57
Priene: A57
Proculeius, C.: A77–9
Prometheus: P1
Ptolemy (VIII of Egypt?): G1
Ptolemy XII Auletes: P49, A3
Ptolemy XIII of Egypt: P76, 77, 79
Ptolemy Philadelphus, son of Antony and Cleopatra: A54
Publicola: *see* Gellius Publicola
Publius: P42
Pydna: Aem16, 19, 23, 24
Pyrrhus, king of Epirus: Cat2
Pythagoras, Greek philosopher: Aem2
Pythium, on Mt. Olympus: Aem15

Quinctius: *see* Flamininus, L. Quinctius
Quintio, freedman of Cato: Cat21
Quintus Antyllius: *see* Antyllius
Quintus Metellus: *see* Metellus, Q. Caecilius

Ravenna: M2
Red Sea: P38, A3, 69
Rhamnus: A48
Rhine, river: C19, 22
Rhodes: P42, M29, C3
Rhodon: A81
Rhône, river: M15, C17
Romulus: P25
Roscius Gallus, Q., actor: S36
Roscius Otho, L.: P25
Rubicon, river: P60, C20, 32
Rubrius, tr. pl.: G31
Rufinus, P. Cornelius, cos. 290, 277: S1
Rufus, L: G19
Rutilius Rufus, P., cos. 105: M10, 28, P37

Sabines: Cat1, P4, C1
Sadalas, king of Thrace: A61
Sagra, river, in southern Italy: Aem25
Salamis, island near Athens: Cat5
Salonius, client of Cato: Cat24
Salvenius, soldier: S17
Salvius, centurion: P78, 79
Salvius, Pelignian commander: Aem20
Samnites, Italic people: Cat2, G7, S29
Samos: P24, A56
Samosata: A34
Samothrace, Aegean island: Aem23, 26, P24
Sardinia: Cat6, G22, 23, P16, 26, 50, 66, C21, A32
Sarmentus: A59
Saturn, temple of: G10
Saturnalia: S18, P34
Saturninus, L. Appuleius: M14, 28, 29, 30, 35
Satyreius, P., tr. pl. 133: G19
Scaurus, M. Aemilius, cos. 115: S33, P9
Scellius: A66

Scipio, father of Cornelia: *see* Caecilius Metellus Pius Scipio Nasica
Scipio, Q. Caecilius Metellus Pius: *see* Caecilius Metellus Pius Scipio
Scipio Aemilianus Africanus (the Younger), P. Cornelius: Cat9, 15, 20, 24, 26, 27, Aem5, 22, 35, 39, G1, 4, 7, 8, 13, 21, 31, M3, 4, 12, 13
Scipio Africanus (the Elder), P. Cornelius: Cat3, 11, 15, 18, 24, 26, Aem2, 5, 15, 38, 39, G1, 4, 17, M1, P14, C15
Scipio Asiaticus, L. Cornelius, cos. 190: Cat15, 18
Scipio Asiaticus, L. Cornelius, cos. 83: S28, P7, 8
Scipio Nasica: *see* Caecilius Metellus Scipio Nasica
Scipio Nasica Corculum, P. Cornelius, cos. 162, 155: Cat27, Aem15–18, 21, 26
Scipio Nasica Serapio, cos. 138: G13, 19–21
Scipio Salvitus: C52
Scopas of Thessaly: Cat18
Scotussa (Cynoscephalae): Aem8, P68, C43
Scribonius Curio: *see* Curio, Scribonius
Scythes, freedman of Pompey: P78
Scyth/ia, -ians: M11, S16, P41, 45, 70, C58
Seleucus, commander: A74
Seleucus, steward: A83
Seleucus Nicator: Cat12
Semele: S9
Sempronius Gracchus: *see* Gracchus
Sentius, C., pr. 94: S11
Septimius: P78, 79
Septimuleius, friend of L. Opimius: G38
Sequani: M24, C20, 26
Serbonian Lake: A3
Sergius, actor: A9
Sertorius, Q.: M1, 44, P13, 17–21, 31
Servile War: S36, P21
Servilii: C62
Servilius, naval prefect of Pompey: P34
Servilius, pr. 88: S9
Servilius, senator: P14
Servilius, Sullan legate in 82: S28
Servilius, Sullan supporter in 82: S10
Servilius Caepio: C14
Servilius Pulex, M., cos. 202: Aem31
Servius Galba: *see* Galba, Ser. Sulpicius
Setia: C58
Sextilius, P.: M40
Sextilius, praetor: P24
Sibylline books: C60
Sicilian Sea: A61
Sicilian War: A63
Sicily: Cat3, M40, S36, P10, 11, 20, 26, 50, 61, 66, C52, A35, 55, 63
Sicyon/, -ians: Cat22, A30
Sidon: A51
Signia: S28
Silanus, M. Iunius: A59
Silvium: S10
Sinope: P42
Sinora: P32
Social War: M32, 33, S6
Socrates: Cat7, 19, 23, M46
Soli: P28
Solon: A36
Solonium, villa of Marius: M35
Sophene, territory of south-western Armenia: P33
Sophocles, tragedian: P78, A24
Sorex, actor: S36
Sosius, C., lieutenant of Antony: A34
Spain, Spanish: Cat5, 10, 11, Aem4, 6, 39, G5, 27, M1, 6, 14, P13, 14, 17, 18, 21, 29, 38, 52, 62, 63, 65–7, C5, 11, 12, 21, 28, 36, 41, 56, A37, 61
Spartacus: P31
Spinther: *see* Lentulus Spinther
Spurius Postumius: *see* Postumius, Sp.
Statianus: A38
Statilius Taurus, T.: A65
Sthennis of Himera: P10
Strabo, Cn. Pompeius, cos. 89: P1, 4
Strabo, historian: S26, C63
Stratonice: P36
Sucro, river: P19
Suebi: P51, C23
Sugambri: C22
Sulla, L. Cornelius, dictator: M10, 25, 26, 32–5, 41, 45, 46, S *passim*, P5, 6, 8–11, 13–16, 21, 30, 42, 47, C1, 3, 5, 14, 15, 37, A1
Sullans: C6
Sulpicius Rufus, P., tr. pl. 88: M34, 35, S8–10
Sulpicius Rufus, Ser., cos. 51: P54
Syr/ia, -ians: Aem7, P33, 38, 39, 45, 52, 62, C49, 50, A3, 5, 27, 28, 30, 34, 36, 46, 53, 54, 56, 66, 74, 84

Taenarum: P24, A67
Talasius: P4
Tanusius: C22
Tarcandemus, king of upper Cilicia: A61
Tarentum (Taranto): Cat2, 14, G28, S27, A35, 62
Tarpeian Rock: M45, S1, 10
Tarquin, Tarquins: Aem25, G15
Taurus mountains: Aem7, P28
Taxiles, commander of Mithridates: S15, 19
Tectosages: S4
Telamon: M41
Telesinus the Samnite: S29
Tempe: P73
Tenteritae: C22
Terentius, L.: P3
Terracina: M36, 38, C58
Tertia: *see* Aemilia Tertia
Teutones: M11, 15, 18, 20, 24, C18
Thapsus: C53
Thebes: S19
Themistocles, Athenian statesman: Cat8, P63, A37
Theodorus: A81
Theodotus of Chios: P77, 78, 80, C48
Theophanes of Mytilene: P37, 42, 49, 76, 78
Theophilus: A67
Theophrastus of Eresus, philosopher: S26
Theopompus, fabulist C48
Thermodon, river: P35
Thermopylae: Cat13
Theseus, legendary Athenian hero: S13
Thessalus, son of Pisistratus: Cat24
Thessaly: Aem7, 9, S11, 15, 20, 23, 27, P66, C39, 41, 48
Thrac/e, -ians: Cat12, Aem15, 16, 18, 32, S11, 15, A61, 63
Thucydides, Athenian historian: Cat2
Thurium, hill at Chaeronea: S17–19
Thuro, mother of Chaeron: S17
Thyateira: S25
Thyrsus: A73
Tiber, river: Aem30, C58
Tidius, S.: P64
Tifata, Mt.: S27
Tigranes, son of Tigranes II: P33, 45
Tigranes II of Armenia: S27, P28, 30, 32, 33, 36, 45, 48, 67
Tigurini: C18
Tillius Cimber, L.: C66
Tilphossium: S20
Timagenes: P49, A72
Timoleon, Greek commander: Aem1
Timon of Athens: A69, 70
Timonassa, wife of Pisistratus: Cat24
Timotheus, son of Conon: S6
Tithora: S15
Titinnius of Minturnae: M38
Titius, M., quaestor: A42, 58
Titius, Q., businessman: S17
Titurius: C24
Titus: *see* Livy
Titus Annius: *see* Annius Luscus, T.
Titus Flamininus: see Flamininus, T. Quinctius
Torquatus, L. Manlius, cos. 65: S29
Toryne, village in Epirus: A62
Tralles: C45, 47
Transalpine Gaul: M11, P48, C14
Trebellius Fides, L.: A9
Trebonius, C., cos. 45: P52, A13
Trebonius, soldier: M14
Triarius, C. Valerius: P38
Troad: S24, 25
Trogodytae, people on the Red Sea: A27
Trophonius, Greek hero: S17
Tuder (Todi): M17
Tullus, L. Volcacius, cos. 66: P60
Turpillius: M8
Tusculum, town near Rome: Cat1
Tyrannion, Aristotelian scholar: S26
Tyrrhenia: G8
Tyrrhenian Sea: Aem6, P26, A61

Usipes: C22
Utica: M8, P11, 13, C54

Vaga: M8
Valentia (Valencia): P18
Valeria, wife of Sulla: S35, 37
Valerius, Q.: P10
Valerius Corvinus: M28
Valerius Flaccus, L.: M28
Valerius Flaccus, L., cos. 195: Cat3, 10, 16, 17
Valerius Leo: C17
Valerius Maximus, M'.: P13
Varius Cotyla, L.: A18
Varro: C36
Vatinius, P.: P52
Vedius: P6
Velia, city of Italy: Aem39

Ventidii, brothers: P6
Ventidius, P., lieutenant of Antony: A33, 34
Venus, Roman goddess: M46, S19, P68
Vercellae: M25
Vergentorix: C25–7
Vergilius, M., tr. pl. 87: S10
Vestal Virgins: Cat20, A21, 58
Vettius, friend of C. Gracchus: G22
Veturius, C.: G24
Vetus: C5
Victory (as deity): M32, S6, 11, 19, C6, 47
Villius, C.: G20
White Village (Leuke Kome): A51

Xanthippus, Athenian naval commander: Cat5
Xenagoras, scientist: Aem15
Xenocrates, Greek philosopher: M2
Xenophon of Athens: A45
Xerxes: S15
Xuthus: A24

Zela: C50
Zeus, Greek god: Aem28, S17, 19, P72
Zosime: P45

A SELECTION OF OXFORD WORLD'S CLASSICS

	Classical Literary Criticism
	The First Philosophers: The Presocratics and the Sophists
	Greek Lyric Poetry
	Myths from Mesopotamia
APOLLODORUS	The Library of Greek Mythology
APOLLONIUS OF RHODES	Jason and the Golden Fleece
APULEIUS	The Golden Ass
ARISTOPHANES	Birds and Other Plays
ARISTOTLE	The Nicomachean Ethics Physics Politics
BOETHIUS	The Consolation of Philosophy
CAESAR	The Civil War The Gallic War
CATULLUS	The Poems of Catullus
CICERO	Defence Speeches The Nature of the Gods On Obligations The Republic and The Laws
EURIPIDES	Bacchae and Other Plays Medea and Other Plays Orestes and Other Plays The Trojan Women and Other Plays
GALEN	Selected Works
HERODOTUS	The Histories
HOMER	The Iliad The Odyssey

A SELECTION OF OXFORD WORLD'S CLASSICS

HORACE	The Complete Odes and Epodes
JUVENAL	The Satires
LIVY	The Dawn of the Roman Empire The Rise of Rome
MARCUS AURELIUS	The Meditations
OVID	The Love Poems Metamorphoses Sorrows of an Exile
PETRONIUS	The Satyricon
PLATO	Defence of Socrates, Euthyphro, and Crito Gorgias Phaedo Republic Symposium
PLAUTUS	Four Comedies
PLUTARCH	Greek Lives Roman Lives Selected Essays and Dialogues
PROPERTIUS	The Poems
SOPHOCLES	Antigone, Oedipus the King, and Electra
STATIUS	Thebaid
SUETONIUS	Lives of the Ceasars
TACITUS	Agricola and Germany The Histories
VIRGIL	The Aeneid The Eclogues and Georgics

A SELECTION OF **OXFORD WORLD'S CLASSICS**

THOMAS AQUINAS	**Selected Philosophical Writings**
FRANCIS BACON	**The Essays**
WALTER BAGEHOT	**The English Constitution**
GEORGE BERKELEY	**Principles of Human Knowledge** and **Three Dialogues**
EDMUND BURKE	**A Philosophical Enquiry into the Origin of Our Ideas of the Sublime and Beautiful** **Reflections on the Revolution in France**
CONFUCIUS	**The Analects**
ÉMILE DURKHEIM	**The Elementary Forms of Religious Life**
FRIEDRICH ENGELS	**The Condition of the Working Class in England**
JAMES GEORGE FRAZER	**The Golden Bough**
SIGMUND FREUD	**The Interpretation of Dreams**
THOMAS HOBBES	**Human Nature** and **De Corpore Politico** **Leviathan**
JOHN HUME	**Selected Essays**
NICCOLO MACHIAVELLI	**The Prince**
THOMAS MALTHUS	**An Essay on the Principle of Population**
KARL MARX	**Capital** **The Communist Manifesto**
J. S. MILL	**On Liberty and Other Essays** **Principles of Political Economy** and **Chapters on Socialism**
FRIEDRICH NIETZSCHE	**Beyond Good and Evil** **The Birth of Tragedy** **On the Genealogy of Morals** **Twilight of the Idols**

A SELECTION OF **OXFORD WORLD'S CLASSICS**

THOMAS PAINE	**Rights of Man, Common Sense, and Other Political Writings**
JEAN-JACQUES ROUSSEAU	**The Social Contract** **Discourse on the Origin of Inequality**
ADAM SMITH	**An Inquiry into the Nature and Causes of the Wealth of Nations**
MARY WOLLSTONECRAFT	**A Vindication of the Rights of Woman**

A SELECTION OF **OXFORD WORLD'S CLASSICS**

	Bhagavad Gita
	The Bible Authorized King James Version *With Apocrypha*
	Dhammapada
	Dharmasūtras
	The Koran
	The Pañcatantra
	The Sauptikaparvan (from the Mahabharata)
	The Tale of Sinuhe and Other Ancient Egyptian Poems
	Upaniṣads
ANSELM OF CANTERBURY	**The Major Works**
THOMAS AQUINAS	**Selected Philosophical Writings**
AUGUSTINE	**The Confessions** **On Christian Teaching**
BEDE	**The Ecclesiastical History**
HEMACANDRA	**The Lives of the Jain Elders**
KĀLIDĀSA	**The Recognition of Śakuntalā**
MANJHAN	**Madhumalati**
ŚĀNTIDEVA	**The Bodhicaryāvatāra**

A SELECTION OF **OXFORD WORLD'S CLASSICS**

	The Anglo-Saxon World
	Beowulf
	Lancelot of the Lake
	The Paston Letters
	Sir Gawain and the Green Knight
	Tales of the Elders of Ireland
	York Mystery Plays
GEOFFREY CHAUCER	**The Canterbury Tales** **Troilus and Criseyde**
HENRY OF HUNTINGDON	**The History of the English People 1000–1154**
JOCELIN OF BRAKELOND	**Chronicle of the Abbey of Bury St Edmunds**
GUILLAUME DE LORRIS and JEAN DE MEUN	**The Romance of the Rose**
WILLIAM LANGLAND	**Piers Plowman**
SIR THOMAS MALORY	**Le Morte Darthur**

A SELECTION OF **OXFORD WORLD'S CLASSICS**

	An Anthology of Elizabethan Prose Fiction
	An Anthology of Seventeenth-Century Fiction
	Early Modern Women's Writing
	Three Early Modern Utopias (Utopia; New Atlantis; The Isle of Pines)
FRANCIS BACON	Essays
APHRA BEHN	Oroonoko and Other Writings The Rover and Other Plays
JOHN BUNYAN	Grace Abounding The Pilgrim's Progress
JOHN DONNE	The Major Works Selected Poetry
BEN JONSON	The Alchemist and Other Plays The Devil is an Ass and Other Plays Five Plays
JOHN MILTON	Selected Poetry
SIR PHILIP SIDNEY	The Old Arcadia
IZAAK WALTON	The Compleat Angler

The Oxford World's Classics Website

www.worldsclassics.co.uk

- Information about new titles
- Explore the full range of Oxford World's Classics
- Links to other literary sites and the main OUP webpage
- Imaginative competitions, with bookish prizes
- Peruse the Oxford World's Classics Magazine
- Articles by editors
- Extracts from Introductions
- A forum for discussion and feedback on the series
- Special information for teachers and lecturers

www.worldsclassics.co.uk

MORE ABOUT OXFORD WORLD'S CLASSICS

American Literature

British and Irish Literature

Children's Literature

Classics and Ancient Literature

Colonial Literature

Eastern Literature

European Literature

History

Medieval Literature

Oxford English Drama

Poetry

Philosophy

Politics

Religion

The Oxford Shakespeare